AN EVENING WHEN ALONE

Four Journals of Single Women in the South, 1827–67

THE PUBLICATIONS OF THE
SOUTHERN TEXTS SOCIETY

Michael O'Brien, Chair of the Editorial Board

AN EVENING WHEN ALONE

Four Journals of Single Women in the South, 1827–67

EDITED BY MICHAEL O'BRIEN

Published for the Southern Texts Society
by the University Press of Virginia
Charlottesville and London

THE UNIVERSITY PRESS OF VIRGINIA
Copyright © 1993 by the Southern Texts Society

First published 1993
First paperback edition 1997

Library of Congress Cataloging-in-Publication Data

An Evening when alone : four journals of single women in the South,
1827–67 / edited by Michael O'Brien.
    p.   cm. — (The Publications of the Southern Texts Society)
Includes index.
  ISBN 0-8139-1440-x (cloth)
  ISBN 0-8139-1732-8 (paper)
  1. Single women—Southern States—Diaries.   2. Single women—
Southern States—History—19th century.   3. Single women—Southern
States—Social conditions.   4. Southern States—History—19th
century.   I. O'Brien, Michael, 1948–   .   II. Southern Texts
Society.   III. Series.
HQ800.2E94   1993
305.48'9652—dc20   92-39514
                                                               CIP

Printed in the United States of America

For Owen

"They . . . may serve to while away a rainy evening when alone."

Ann Lewis Hardeman on her journals
April 28, 1862

Contents

Illustrations

Preface

This is the first volume in the publications of the Southern Texts Society.
Since it is hoped that the society will continue for many years and volumes,
it will help to say a word about its provenance and purpose, before going
on to matters relevant to this volume alone.

In 1988 a group of scholars met at Miami University to discuss aspects
of the intellectual history and culture of the American South. During the
meeting it was observed that the study of (let alone the teaching about)
that culture was hampered by a shortage of accessible texts, especially by
figures who wrote before the twentieth century. Many important Southern
intellectuals—about whom the scholars present had written—can only be
read in rare editions, in periodicals on microfilm, or in manuscript. It was
thought that this situation cried out for remedy. But what remedy? The
founding group, which subsequently evolved into the Southern Intellectual
History Circle, decided to sponsor the Southern Texts Society, to which
the circle stands as a sort of godparent. It was also decided that the society
was to be a permanent and independent institution, whose administrative
headquarters might safely be entrusted to another permanent institution,
the Southern Historical Collection of the University of North Carolina at
Chapel Hill. The formal purpose of the society is "the identification, editing,
and publication of a series of book-length collections of manuscript or rare
printed materials important to understanding the culture of the American
South and its expressive life."

What impelled this creation? Writing about Southern history and literature has been fundamentally transformed in the last two generations. Our
understanding of the region's race relations, social structure, economic development, religion, and education is vastly different from the perceptions
of 1945, changing pari passu with the social experience of the region. Literary scholars have become newly sensitive to the problem of canons, the
issue of what texts are conventionally read, why, and by whom. Scholars
of intellectual life—placed at the intersection of social and literary history—have begun to identify a richer and more complex body of thought in

the history of Southern culture than previously had been suspected. These three impulses have converged upon the problem of texts: social history has broadened the range of problems to which texts are relevant; the scrutiny of canon formation has reinforced a disposition to reconsider the conventional patterns; intellectual history has begun to indicate where unsuspected strengths may lie.

But it is one thing to read about a culture and another to read the culture itself, that is, to read the primary sources that show the subtleties of a culture's self-awareness. Without such sources being placed in the public domain of cultural life, scholarship can become sterile and private and lose one of its central purposes, the restoration and preservation of cultural memory. For the history of scholarship, both in the United States and Europe, shows texts and critical understanding to be mutually dependent. The establishment of institutions designed to preserve the record has marked a culture's commitment to history and permanence. In Germany the first volume of the *Monumenta Germaniae Historica* was published in 1826. François Guizot began the *Collection des mémoires relatif à l'histoire de France* in the same decade and founded the Societé de l'histoire de France in 1834, which has since published some five hundred volumes of source materials. In England the Camden Society was founded in 1838 in honor of William Camden with the intention of publishing documents relating to the early history and literature of the British Empire. Victorian England was profligate of such societies: the Hakluyt Society for exploration, the Selden Society for law, the Parker Society for Anglicans, and the Early English Text Society, whose efforts led eventually to the *Oxford English Dictionary*. In the South, history combined to stunt such parallel developments. The peculiar dynamics of a slave society, the Civil War, the poverty of the postbellum economy, all served to prevent or make undesirable the systematic restoration of the textual foundations of cultural memory. The task since has been accomplished only piecemeal, by state historical societies and the university presses. For the plausibility of the venture was complicated by the fact that the South's culture has been ground contested by classes, genders, races, subregions and states, and disciplines. Historically these groups have not always conversed, though they often (but not always) have shared a sense that there is or was a place where—if they so chose—a conversation could be held.

These contests have been a hindrance to the formation of an eclectic canon. But they offer also an opportunity, for they made Southern culture and hence created the agenda of the Southern Texts Society. Our volumes, cumulatively gathering over the years, are intended to suggest that these varying elements may usefully be held together in the mind, that there is a value to such a collective discourse. This will be marked by the small but significant aesthetic detail that the society's books will be issued in volumes uniformly printed and bound. Though what is said by the words in the books must and will differ, the print will be the same, the binding identical. A reader can place them on the library shelves adjacently: now a volume of a proslavery writer's essays, then a volume of women's diaries, now a doctor's memoirs, then a slave narrative. This is what cultural memory and tradition can mean: not unity of memory or purpose but a connected recognition of legitimacy founded upon a shared body of texts that evolves as the society changes.

It may seem odd to feel such a restoration of memory to be necessary. Is not the South routinely held to be the part of American culture where memory matters? But, in fact, whereas the South's political and racial memory has been vivid (though often vague), its cultural memory is uneven and ill informed. It is familiar and sound doctrine to observe that Southern blacks and women have been denied access to their own past. But it is even true that Southern men, even conservative Southerners, have been often ignorant of their intellectual tradition. American and Southern conservatives celebrate and write about John Randolph, but there is no modern edition of Randolph's writings. The number of figures—black and white, male and female, liberal and conservative—who figure as important names in monographic discussion but who can be read only in rare book rooms, is legion. These are people who labored long to think about their culture. They deserve to be read and to sit familiarly on modern Southern shelves.

I have been pronouncing these doctrines for several years in several places. When I ended up as chair of the Editorial Board of the Southern Texts Society, it was suggested that I might be expected to offer a text and not just a sermon, and sooner rather than later. My first impulse was to provide a full and corrected edition of the memoirs of Frederick Adolphus Porcher, the antebellum South Carolinian intellectual, which are now available only in a mangled periodical form but whose manuscript sits, waiting for a conscientious editor, in the archives of Charleston. Certainly this would have been work in my usual line. But my mind turned instead to the 1827 journals of Elizabeth Ruffin, which I had recently read in the Southern Historical Collection. I remembered the pleasure of the experience, the rare sense of having touched a fresh and distinctive mind. I had made a note to myself that someone should publish them, probably someone else. But I was conscious that they were an awkward length, too long for a periodical, too short for a book. As I went on to other archives, for the more general purposes of researching the intellectual culture of the antebellum South, I began to notice other women's diaries, also interesting, also not quite a convenient length. The idea of this book formed in my mind, though it took time and accident for the focus to rest upon the voices of single women.

Now that the task is done, I need to record my obligations. My main one is to David Moltke-Hansen, who turned my vague ambition of publishing texts into an institution, provided the Southern Historical Collection as its home, and over the years has offered more shrewdness, help, and advice than I have deserved. I once edited a book with him, which usually kills a friendship rather than creates one. It is a testimony to his civility that I seem to have undertaken to edit many more. He is one of an increasingly rare breed, the archivist who is a practicing historian, the organizer who thinks. Fortunately he is a young dinosaur; it will be long before we can no longer look upon his like again.

I need also to thank all the members of the Southern Intellectual History Circle, especially those who agreed to serve on the board of the Southern Texts Society: Anne Jones, Thadious Davis, and Elizabeth Fox-Genovese. Likewise, I am grateful to the other members of the board, who have brought to bear upon the early deliberations of the society their various expertise: Fred Hobson, David Shields, and Clyde Wilson. John McGuigan helped immeasurably in bringing the Society and the University Press of Virginia together; Nancy Essig, the Press's director, has been unfailingly helpful.

As for the creation of the book itself, I am first under an obligation to the staff of the archives where the original manuscripts of the journals reside: the Southern Historical Collection (David Moltke-Hansen, Richard Shrader, and John White), the Louisiana and Lower Mississippi Valley Collections in Hill Library at Louisiana State University (Faye Phillips, Judy Bolton, Anne Edwards, and Sally Proshek), and the Mississippi Department of Archives and History (Michael Hennen). But I also had occasion to use the Special Collections at the Perkins Library of Duke University, the Tennessee State Library and Archives, the Family History Library of the Genealogical Society of Utah, the South Caroliniana Library, the South Carolina Historical Society, and the Virginia Historical Society (where Frances Pollard was graciously punctilious). Second, the project was greatly helped by a research grant from Miami University, which enabled me to use the talented energies of Sarah Gardner in making a first rough transcription of the journals. And the staff of the King Library at Miami—Jenny Presnell, William Wortman, and Scott Van Dam—contrived to resolve a number of problems. Third, I need to thank the National Endowment for the Humanities, which gave me an Interpretive Research grant between 1987 and 1989 which, though intended for wider purposes than this book, nonetheless made it possible.

Near Washington in Mississippi, Nancy and John Williams were kind enough to show me around Selma plantation, which with a few additions and rearrangements of walls is substantially unchanged from the diarist's day. Mrs. Williams in turn introduced me to Mrs. Pat Dale of Vidalia, who shared her careful reconstruction of the Brandon family genealogy, as well as various courthouse records. Mrs. Alma Carpenter of Natchez was also helpful. In my initially vain pursuit of the original of the Selma journal, Martha Swain of Texas Women's University foraged around for me in the kinship networks of Mississippi with her usual kindness and knowledge. Jane and William Pease read the North journals, caught various errors, and provided valuable information about the Petigrus. The historian of the Hardeman family, Nicholas Perkins Hardeman of Garden Grove in California, though he was then ill, read through the transcription of Ann Hardeman's journal and assisted me in grasping various nuances of his family's genealogy. Since his death, his widow Ada Mae Hardeman has continued his kindness in providing me with a photograph of Ann Neely. For other illustrations, I am obliged to Mrs. John H. Daniels, David Allmendinger, Nancy Williams, and to several of the archives above mentioned.

Lastly, I should acknowledge that this book has profited from a number of readings by other historians and critics. Since this is my first venture into women's history and no wise man enters that battlefield without guides, I took especial care to consult veterans. At Miami University, Mary Frederickson and Mary Cayton read the entire manuscript, helped me to gain confidence that I had not entirely blundered, and pointed out where I had; Andrew Cayton, Carl Pletsch, and Jack Kirby read the introduction and improved it. From elsewhere, I had readings from Anne Jones, Steven Stowe, Lisa Tyree, and Richard Lounsbury. As usual, Patricia O'Brien preserved me from many follies of exuberance and indiscretion (I speak only of prose). The society was wise enough to select Elisabeth Muhlenfeld as a reader for the manuscript, and I am especially under an obligation to her for a detailed scrutiny, a thing to expect from one of the editors of Mary Chesnut, whose work has set a standard which the Southern Texts Society would do well to emulate. I also need to thank Peter Darlow of Chichester in Sussex, who offered a first translation of the French passages in the Selma plantation journals.

It would have been simpler to have edited Frederick Porcher, I suppose, but perhaps less rewarding. I think that intellectual historians like myself are well advised, now and again, to step beyond their customary discipline, to struggle with genealogy, to scan census records, to be concerned with cousinage, to exchange privately printed books with horn-rimmed ladies in search rooms. We are reminded that thoughts exist in more than books, that there are more thinkers than those who claim the title, that much of value can be caught in fragments of diaries, letters, and bits of fugitive paper. A certain skepticism is lost, a certain directness gained. In that spirit, perhaps I can end this preface by saying, simply, that I came to like these diarists, to sympathize with their lives, and to feel their predicaments. I do not know that any act in my scholarly life has given me greater pleasure than editing these pages. Elizabeth Ruffin, also an ironist who sometimes stumbled upon directness and the woman who started this book on a Virginian plantation in 1827, once observed: "Don't be alarmed my delicate readers, am sorry to shock any one of your senses by such an . . . ungenteel confession."

AN EVENING WHEN ALONE

Four Journals of Single Women in the South, 1827–67

Introduction

THE CONTEXT

This volume prints journals from the Old South. They were written by four single women who encompassed a diversity of condition, time, and place within the planter class. The journals take the reader from Virginia in 1827 to Mississippi in 1867, with pauses in northern and Virginian spas, in the Delta, and in South Carolina. They move through the various forms of singlehood, from gregarious belle to lonely spinster. There are two young women, barely twenty, poised upon marriage, one reluctantly, the other with calculation. There is a governess in her early thirties, beginning an independent career. There is an old woman, struggling in the midst of an extended family.

It has been natural that the study of antebellum Southern women has concentrated upon the married. In this, Southern scholarship has not distinguished itself from the main currents of women's history. At the center of our understanding has grown to be the plantation mistress. We have been offered varying versions of her—as victim, as heroine, as exploiter, as quasi abolitionist, as proslavery ideologue—but her centrality has been assumed.[1] Yet the unmarried woman was not a rare phenomenon. Indeed there is evidence that her numbers grew in the nineteenth century and the condition of singlehood came to seem less reprehensible, less a failure to marry and more a desirable option, than in earlier centuries. The social historians and demographers have not measured the situation for the whole South. But it is known, for example, that in 1848 "exactly half of all adult white female

Charlestonians were married, almost a third were single, and a fifth were widowed."[2] Put another way, half of the adult women in that city were unmarried. This is no small marginality.

Of course, to put it this way is to distort. At some point all women were single, if only because they had yet to marry. But it might be a fair guess that before 1860 about a fifth to a quarter of all adult white Southern women were unmarried for life.[3] So, while it has been customary to see the natural trajectory of the Southern woman as that from belle to matron, it was as natural for her to move from belle to spinster. What these women, those temporarily and permanently single, made of their world has been little studied and understood, and it seems worthwhile to offer them an occasion to speak. It is relevant to this volume, however, that the filter of those voices is a particular genre, the journal.[4]

The homes and archives of the South are full of such journals, carefully preserved by nieces or nephews in memory of a vanished and regretted order. Within the family, each is kept like an old bedstead riddled with Sherman's bullets, to point a moral; someone, someday, plans to publish it, so that the lady in the journal shall not be forgotten. In the manuscript collections, for generations they have been plundered as evidence, first to tell us about slavery or the Civil War, later to inform the textures of social history. Very seldom have these journals been considered for what they were, fashioned things, crafted in and by a particular life, a kind of literature habitually made even by the unliterary.

Journals answered varying needs. Many married women wrote them, though to keep one required time, a moment of quiet, a thing hard to find in a household with children to be born and nurtured, with husbands to be watched, with slaves to be commanded, with sickness to be tended. Single women had more time, more rainy evenings alone. And younger women had the most time. Moreover, it was conventional that a young lady keep a journal. This had been so at least since the mid-eighteenth century. For, in its earlier forms, the journal was recommended for education. It was a literary exercise, by means of which sensibility might be enriched, records kept for future amusement, pleasures and understandings shared. This was especially true of the travel journal, which the itinerant was expected to bring home to her family, in the way many now bring back photographs from their vacations.[5]

By the late eighteenth century, the journal had become a literary genre, whose prominence encouraged young ladies to keep still more journals. In Jane Austen's *Northanger Abbey*, finished in 1803 and published in 1818, Henry Tilney expostulates mockingly to Catherine Morland on the value of keeping a journal, after she has confessed to negligence in the matter. "Not keep a journal! How are your absent cousins to understand the tenour of your life in Bath without one? How are the civilities and compliments of every day to be related as they ought to be, unless noted down every evening in a journal?" More, and significantly, he stresses its literary benefits: "It is this delightful habit of journalizing which largely contributes to form the easy style of writing for which ladies are so generally celebrated." Nowhere does he say that it might help the diarist to engage in what the French call "l'invention du moi." [6] Only gradually, as Romanticism transmuted the confessional into the psychological, did journals grow intimate, presupposing a veil between the self and the world, attempting to define and express a "self." [7] These four journals might be said to have been composed in the mid passage of this transformation. Most were written in the expectation that others would read them, usually other members of the family, usually soon after their composition. In this sense they mingle the individual voice of the diarist with the context of circumambient sisters and brothers and parents, and hence the journals can usefully be considered as family records, a discursive variant on the flyleaf of the family Bible. Nonetheless the journals often express something idiosyncratic, disjunctive, unwelcome to the family. For the convention did grow that the diarist might use the journal less for education, more as a private occasion where matters unsayable in open parlor were licensed to be set down, where the woman might write her truths alone. By degrees, the diarist might come to forget an audience other than herself. Thus the first journal included here, from 1827, is dominated by an awareness of a reader. The last, by 1867. almost completely lacks that expectation. [8]

This tension between community and privacy was the sharper because a single woman was almost never at the center of a community, at least in its form as a family. As a girl, she was tributary to parents. As a young lady, drifting past the usual age of marriage, she became problematical. Parents and friends grew doubtful of her. In middle and old age, she was either alone in her own household (sometimes shared with other single women), or more usually she stayed in the household of her family, of the brothers or sisters who had married. No matter her ubiquity, the spinster was seen as an oddity in a culture very concerned with defining and celebrating the normalities of domesticity. Above all, she was not a mother, even though she might be surrounded by children. So she stood a little aside, acquiring thereby the advantages of a double vision, of being in but not of the domestic world.

For such a person a journal is a natural genre, being flexible in all but its obligation to chronology. Indeed it has been argued that this very vagueness made it peculiarly useful for all nineteenth-century women. Other imaginative avenues available to them, especially fiction and poetry, had strict prescriptions, conformities, that expressed even as they limited the range of a woman's imagination.[9] But the journal did not require a beginning, a middle, or an end. No one had to get married on the last page; the sun did not have to set over the Parthenon in the last stanza. The journal might be self-scrutinizing, but did not have to be. It might express gifts of narration, even of plot, but it might not. A journal was simultaneously autobiography and memoir, and diarists decided for themselves where the emphasis should lie.

The most gifted women have used the freedom of the genre to produce remarkable works; one need only mention the diaries of Virginia Woolf, Alice James, Anais Nin, to make the point. Among Southern women's writings, the work of Mary Chesnut stands unrivaled. But Chesnut's achievement was a logical outcome of the great mass of women's journals composed in her culture, and it is fitting she herself should appear in one of the antebellum journals in this volume. Chesnut's accomplishment was to infuse the commonplace with her special insight, grace, and artifice. Though each of these four diaries has moments that pass exacting standards of critical scrutiny, none stands on Chesnut's literary level. The justification of their publication rests less in their felicity, more in their miscellany of standpoints, experiences, and techniques. Placed in the public domain, they will aid our understandings. They would all be surprised to find themselves thus exposed. None were grooming themselves for posterity's interest. None would echo Cecily on her diary in *The Importance of Being Earnest:* "You see, it is simply a very young girl's record of her own thoughts and impressions, and consequently meant for publication. When it appears in volume form I hope you will order a copy." [10]

Being miscellaneous, these journals are various in content and theme. Some deal with travel, seeing the exotic, remembering people, denoting the contrast with home. "The Virginians are unusually scarce here this season nothing but Yankees scarcely who have almost taught me to speak like them, they are vastly agreeable for all that," wrote one diarist from Saratoga Springs in New York. "I feel now as if really in old Virginny the engine that puffed us here was the Pocahantas, & the hotel at which we stay bears the name of the famous old Indian chief! Everything has looked so like home . . . that I did not realize the distance that seperated me from home," wrote another from Richmond.

Most chronicle family life, its incidents and anniversaries. "I have spent the Christmas holidays with Mrs P—— and family—on Christmas eve they had an oyster supper at which Dr L—— was invited accidentally." And, "The anniversary of my lamented bros death 14 years ago he was taken from us." Being domestic, few deal with public affairs, except when the context grew inescapable. "There seems to be great excitement throughout the entire Country—Companies are organizing & wearing badges—&c. besides many other demonstrations of Antagonism—War! War!! War!! is the cry through North & South!"

Only one diarist expressed even a small qualm about slavery, and that not in her journal proper. But all denoted its presence, and most gave their slaves a name beyond the generic title of "servants." "In the afternoon while I was paying a visit at the Coles cabin Betsey brought me a card." "I think I hear Hector's voice now speaking to Miss Maria." "Succeeded very well with the Machine had Florence & Eliza to sew yesterday must finish a pair to-day if possible." Yet none had words for slavery as a social system, as an abstraction, only words for individual moments of contact between mistress and slave. Though all wrote from within the planting class, it is striking how borrowed and insecure were the prerogatives that a single woman, whether young or old, possessed as a member of that class. Though she might live in a large house and be tended by slaves, a daughter was a dependency of parents, a governess was a servant to employers, an old spinster was reliant upon relatives. These were ambivalences of which most were aware, but not feelings that created marked sympathy for slaves.

All observed and characterized marriage, though no diarist was married. "The trials of matrimony the married are welcome to for me." "Dr D——married at last he apologized for the long delay by stating the difficulty of meeting with a person of comparatively equal intelligence and talents, and now we may all hope that he has found his match." "On this day also my dear Bethenia was bereft of a kind husband Dr Vizer they had been married nearly one year."

None discussed sexuality, though all were aware of gender, in the terms that predated the modern characterization of the category. " 'Tis bad to be a woman in some things, but preferable in others." "Am I not right to say, that woman is the most singular of all the created things we know of?" Most were skeptical of men. "There were but 2 ladies at the table, men enough however." Several explicitly condemned the nature of male power, and a few expressed pity for the price men pay for their worldly ambition. "For men's most golden dreams of pride and power, / Are vain as any woman's dream of love."

Nearly all were sharply aware of their dependency upon others, not always men. "I can soon put an end to these petty vexations for vexations they must be called which rob us of independance, let them be clothed in what garb they may." "My dear Eva gave me a dollar to give to Edward as she had heard me say I was out of money—I however borrowed some from sister Mary."

All touched on religion, and it seems a pattern that religious belief grew with years and suffering. Youth permitted lightness, experience brought an almost frantic piety. The oldest diarist made her journal a virtual prayer book, a book of hours, a conversation with God. "May God help me by his grace to discharge my duty towards them with an eye single to his glory." "May they be protected guided & governed by the wisdom & Grace of Almighty God—& may this bereavement be sanctified to us all." "O that God may help me for I feel as if I needed his assistance."

Some had a sharp self-awareness, where the diarist was both subject and object. "I will remember the remark for I took it as a lesson—though in justice to myself I must say I only a little ridiculed his egregious nonsense." A few stepped into dialogue with themselves, usually in admonition. "Nothing gives me pleasure, and almost every thing annoys me, even kind attentions, what an ungrateful being I am." At least one set up a conversation between herself as reflective diarist, herself as the object of the diary, and an imagined reader. "I forbear to dwell on the after circumstances of the days unpleasant and painful in the extreme; suffice it to say a detail of them would create little interest, and produce less reciprocity of feeling and sentiment from an unsympathetic reader—you don't understand me, therefore will cease this mysterious and unintelligible jargon."

All expressed fears about the future: of marriage, of children, of age, of death. "She said that she had thought it a pity that I had no children. . . . I consider this a compliment of the most flattering kind—but I do not know whether or not I should join in the regret." "If he looks old what must I seem?" "A disease of the heart it is said occasioned her awfully sudden end. I felt inexpressibly shocked when I heard it . . . to have closed her eyes in apparent perfect health, & awake in Eternity!" "O help me I pray as I enter the dark Valley of the Shadow of death—& sustain me until I reach it."

Though the desire for independence deserves consideration as among the journals' more consistent topics, perhaps their predominant theme—for all but one diarist—is loneliness, its presence and looming persistence. "My companion left after breakfast, quite sorry to part with him because loneliness makes the time hang heavily." "Having no one to whom I may breathe one word about my loneliness and cheerless situation it is still something to be able to come to this book and transfer however feebly and imperfectly some of the feelings that I fear will one day make me commit some act of rashness of which I may repent afterwards." "I took my evening walk as usual *alone*." "Lonely I have been, lonely I am, and lonely I am likely to be."

In general, the movement of the journals—as they appear to the reader— is from youth to age, from innocent irony to embittered sadness, from an old social order to its destruction. But the pleasure and usefulness of journals lie not in what generalizations they may support but the particularities they embody. As such, it is better to be specific.

THE DIARISTS

Elizabeth Ruffin

No young lady of the Old South would have fitted better in a Jane Austen novel than Elizabeth Ruffin. She had the Austen tone: dry, intelligent, skeptical, conservative. She had the social standing of an Austen heroine, being the daughter of middling rural gentry. She had the experience of the summer season at a fashionable watering place, the custom of reading and acquiring genteel accomplishments, the problem of a brother. She thought much on marriage, not always with enthusiasm. She kept two journals, which survive in separate small volumes. The first begins on February 4, 1827, when she was one day short of being twenty years old and was living on Evergreen plantation in Prince George County, Virginia; it continues for five weeks in a chronicle of her daily life. The second is a travel journal detailing her trip between July and September 1827 to northern resorts and back home. Nothing unusual happened in these months, as she was fond of pointing out. The journals justify themselves less by their incidents, more by their tone of voice, which is one of the most unusual in the record of Southern writing. And, since vagueness about people and time is one of the strongest characteristics of that voice, it is necessary to situate a scrutiny of Elizabeth Ruffin within a few facts.

Though you would not know it from her journal, Elizabeth Ruffin lived in a complicated family. Her mother had been twice married, and first to a widower. In 1799 Rebecca Cocke had married George Ruffin, a planter who had had in 1794 by his first wife, Jane Lucas Ruffin, a son called Edmund. He grew into the brother who inhabits Elizabeth's journal, but whom the world better knows as the Old South's foremost agricultural reformer, firer of the first shot at Fort Sumter.[11] After her marriage Rebecca Ruffin had six children, of whom two died as infants and four survived: Jane Skipwith (b. 1800), Juliana (b. 1806), Elizabeth (b. 1807), and George Henry (b. 1810). In 1810 George Ruffin himself died, leaving a will that somewhat favored his son Edmund against the interests of his widow. In 1812 Rebecca Ruffin successfully sued to gain guardianship of her own children, to acquire possession of the slaves she had brought to the marriage, and to ensure that Evergreen plantation should pass on her death to her children and not to Edmund. Her stepson was left with a secondary and smaller farm, called

Elizabeth Ruffin Cocke.
(Courtesy of the Virginia Historical Society, Richmond)

Coggin's Point, which he had inherited from his grandfather and to which he moved in 1813. In that same year he married Susan Hutchings Travis, by whom he was to have eleven children. There seem to have been no irrevocably hard feelings between Rebecca and Edmund. After the latter's study at the College of William and Mary in 1810 and before his removal to his own farm, he lived with his stepmother, and in the early 1820s she named him guardian of her unmarried children, including Elizabeth. Just to complicate matters further, Rebecca later married again, to Peter Woodlief.[12] Hence Elizabeth Ruffin in 1827 was living between two households: Evergreen, the home of her mother and stepfather, the ancestral home of the Ruffins; and Coggin's Point, the lesser farm of her guardian and half brother.

Very few of these names appear in her journal, because Elizabeth Ruffin denoted people as categories—beaux, clergymen, bachelors—and she wrote as though she were alone. A young lady who spent her twentieth birthday with "no company," all hands being from home, dining solitaire on a slice of broiled bacon, had reason to believe in her solitude. Her impulse to keep a journal had much to do with her loneliness. Elizabeth wanted someone to talk to, so she began a journal and found company in the form of readers. That she imagined readers—that is, she imagined us—and sustained a running dialogue with them is one of the journal's pleasures, for the illusion of dialogue was a device she handled with great skill and much wit. When, for example, she peeped into an improper novel, she implicated her readers in the escapade: "Don't be alarmed my delicate readers, am sorry to shock any one of your senses by such an *unlady-like* and ungenteel confession, but entreat not the disclosure." When she went from Evergreen on an excursion, she congratulated her "already heartily tired" readers upon their escape from the tedium of the plantation. When speaking invidiously of short people, she politely exempted from her characterization "all my small readers." In part, this voice was the natural literary device of a young woman who read Henry Fielding and Tobias Smollett and whose diction had an easy conversational eighteenth-century air. To read Elizabeth Ruffin is to be taken on a walk through rooms and gardens, as an intelligent and ironic young woman talks, now of herself, now of her situation, now of others, and looks often toward us, with an ear cocked to anticipate our reaction.

But the device of the reader and the voice of irony had roots other than in rhetoric or the usages of the novel. Elizabeth Ruffin liked to keep a certain distance, to be above or beside the foolish human fray. Indeed, one suspects, she exaggerated her solitude the better to keep her distance. The merit of inventing a reader, for Elizabeth, was that we are obliged to react as she wished, at least in the moment of her invention.

She was very conscious of being a woman, whom society expected to want and feel certain things. She knew young women were supposed to be ignorant of public affairs, agreeable, gossipy and curious, obsessed with love and marriage, genteel and vain. She played off her reader's expectations, by effecting a distance from these traits even when she knew she embodied them. Thus, it was typical of her to write: "While reading, was surprised by B———'s stepping in on a pretence of a little business, but in reality only a plea to see us; (see our vanity; woman-like) that urgent matter negotiated, set out again." And, likewise: "My own share of that article curiosity (woman like) got me in to a little difficulty to-day." Elizabeth liked to sport in the gaps between expectation, perception, and reality. This was partly for amusement, partly in earnest. She knew a woman's traits were supposed to be inferior. But did the self-aware woman establish her legitimacy by denying the inferiority or denying her possession of the traits? Elizabeth used irony to do both, because she was unsure about the whole business. If women were thought to be curious, she would express curiosity but transcend it by self-awareness of the trait.

By the same token she did not want to be a man, even when she recognized that men had worldly advantages, the chief of these being independence. Thus she was irked that though she wanted to go to church, her dislike of going unescorted prevented her. This sensation prompted an ambivalent outburst: "Oh! the disadvantages we labor under, in not possessing the agreeable independence with the men; 'tis shameful, that all the superiority, authority and freedom in all things should by partial nature all be thrown in their scale; 'tis bad to be a woman in some things, but preferable in others, 'tho you may crow over me, and glory in the unlimited sphere of your actions and operations, I envy you not and would not change with you to-day." More scathingly, she would mock the pretensions of her male readers. One day, observing that she had done little work, she wrote: "All things neglected and [I] give place to the strange infatuation of novel-reading so popular with us *silly, weak* women whose mental capacities neither desire nor aspire to a higher grade, satisfied with momentary amusement without substantial emolument, and a piece of *weakness rarely indulged* (laying aside all enjoyment) by the more *noble, exalted* and *exemplary* part of society the men of course who seek alone after *fame, honor, solid benefit* and *perpetual profit:* construe the compliment as you please, exacting not from me an explanation which might be unwelcome to your superior ears."

By way of emphasizing her intellectual and moral independence of the category of gender, she said that she would refuse marriage and children. She would choose celibacy and the fate of the old maid. She told her friends of this plan and jocularly argued her case with beaux and old gentlemen alike, much to their befuddlement. And it was not entirely a joke. She was little enchanted with the young men who came her way. She was uneasy at the thought of "squalling children," she was unsure that either husband or offspring were indispensable to happiness. She much prized "the sweets of independence," which were "greatly preferable to . . . *charming servitude* under a lord and master." She thought spinsterhood might be more peaceful, for "the trials of matrimony the married are welcome to for me, take my advice and be content with the negative enjoyment attendant on undisturbed *celibacy.*" Still, it was partly banter with her. When during her travels she visited the Shakers and looked upon the face of genuine celibacy, she recoiled. True, she admired the Shakers' neatness, honesty, dancing. But she also felt they were denying human nature. "Oh! how deluded and misguided in their religious principles, they're scarcely a whit behind the Pharisees in my opinion they are setting up and establishing their own righteousness by the sacrifice of every thing that flesh and blood are capable of, they are striving and struggling to secure eternal life (not as other Christians do by faith in Christ) but by self-denial, mortification and forbearance in every imaginable shape."

In fact, evidence other than her journal indicates that Elizabeth was reluctant even to embrace the limited independence that Virginian society allowed her. A year after her journal ends, she turned twenty-one and emerged from Edmund's guardianship. She seems to have had some money of her own and some slaves. She requested, with urgency, that Edmund continue to order her affairs. "*This legal independence*—what a mistaken notion is entertained of it: what an undesirable possession it is in my opinion," she wrote to him a bare few weeks after reaching her majority. "I am heartily tired of the pleasure already, but what is to be done?" She felt no more competent, no more wise, because a clock had moved a little forward. "If you would just only forget what age and law have entitled me—and act precisely as *my guardian still* in the management of all my business I should deem it a peculiar favor." Edmund seems to have agreed, in both informal and legal matters. She was to write to him for advice when perplexed over whether to marry her cousin Harrison Henry Cocke, being unsure whether marrying cousins was wise "on the score of blood" and being worried that he was not enough of a Christian.[13] She consulted him over the sale of slaves, he counseling the brute economic sense of selling all of them, even though it might mean the separation of families on the auction block. She struggled, in opposition, to find a more humane way and even contemplated the heresy of asking her slaves' opinion in the matter. "Poor creatures!" she wrote. "I really think they ought to have a voice in the matter, in as much as their individual happiness is concerned: if they are willing to endure present hardships in preference to being sold, or vice versa—either I am all acquiescence—to their choice or desire." [14]

Her relationship with Edmund merits a brief mention. History knows best the grim Edmund Ruffin, the serious scientist, the earnest secessionist, the disappointed Confederate who was to put a musket to his mouth in 1865. Elizabeth's Edmund cut a different figure. In her fond eyes "brother," as she always called him, appeared as a bumbling eccentric. While she respected her "*undefatigable brother's search* after knowledge," it often amused her. Even his marl pits, whose fertilizer he felt would preserve and reform his world, she regarded with dry skepticism: "By B's solicitation went to see his newly discovered Marl-banks, and whilst his interested tongue spared not words of commendation, his ears open to every thing like a foretelling future beneficial results, and his very eyes appeared *charmed* and *dazzled* with the *transcendant beauty* and *lustre* of the sight; I for want of science, and experience could form not the least conception of its *invaluable nature,* and saw nothing at all but a mixture of pulverized shell and sand, which would never have attracted notice or attention from me." Instead, she showed her reader Edmund Ruffin lugged into a milliner's shop in Philadelphia, where he did his best to be polite. She commended him for being "so attentive, so accommodating and even now . . . groaning under sacrifice and self-denial for my convenience," waiting on mantua-makers, "all too without murmuring or scolding in the least." "Who will believe me?" she asked. "Certainly no soul at home." We see him preferring a Roman Catholic service to her Presbyterian one, and being thought a connoisseur of church music. We see him bored by the society of a watering place, fleeing to the circulating library, talking too much, being stiff in his Virginia pride. We are told he was so marked by "solidity and venerableness" that he was sometimes mistaken for her father, so socially awkward that he was sometimes presumed to be a bachelor. We see him doing serious party tricks with gas and candles in a rock spring and marching resolutely ahead on a country walk while others scrambled after him. We see him very fond of an argument, a man whom the unwary might think "the rudest and most uncivilized of overbearing combatants," a man who would engross "two-thirds of the conversation." She was, by her own confession, not comfortable in sharing intimacies with him: "I have ever felt a backwardness in or delicacy in telling you any thing that particularly concerned myself. . . . To *talk* with you freely and unreservedly—I could not—for any possible freedom of speech, would be overpowered by the foolish but natural feeling of embarrassment." But constraint did not diminish fondness, which lasted the years. Her last letter of those that survive was to him, "my dear Brother." [15]

Despite her trepidations and jests, Elizabeth did, in fact, marry her cousin. As she feared, matrimony proved full of trials, though her natural pleasure in the vagaries of human behavior survived her wedding day. She had children, who doubtless squalled but who gave her immense satisfaction. When some had nearly reached the age at which she had kept her own journal, she wrote with the same ironic amusement of their experiences as she had of her own. In 1848, corresponding with her daughter Tariffa, she sketched the beaux coming to call on her other daughter Rebecca and her Dorsey cousins. "The bouquets are coming in daily, nicely enveloped notes, for attending concerts, moonlight walks, and all such 'signs of promise' of which you shall here after hear." One young man "compliments the girls to their faces which they well understand," just as Elizabeth had understood in 1827.[16] Many pleasures survived marriage, including her love of food, a topic often dwelled upon in her journal, which has loving descriptions of peaches, corn bread, and perch, and a complaint about gaining weight.

But she had married a sailor, a commodore, who was frequently absent on naval cruises in the Mediterranean or around Latin America. They went temporarily to live in Pensacola in Florida. They had six children, Horatio, Elizabeth, Tariffa, Eliza, Juliana, and Rebecca. Judged from the scraps of evidence that survive, they seem to have been happy together, when they had the chance.

One July day in Pensacola—Elizabeth's undated letter to Mary C. Ruffin was to explain—answering to her old temptations, Elizabeth bought the family four dozen peaches, "the first we had seen . . . a great rarity." It was "impossible to resist their importunities." The twins, Horatio and Elizabeth, begged their share. An hour before dawn that night, the slave who slept in the nursery heard Horatio make a faint noise. "She got up felt and found him speechless, in a cold sweat, perfectly limber." She carried him to Elizabeth and Harrison's bedroom, "where we were aroused believing him to be dying." They could feel no pulse, saw dry froth at his mouth, rubbed him with camphor, and set him in a warm bath, so that he revived, only to experience a convulsion. The doctors came and bled him "in the temple artery, which revived him very much," enough even to speak a little. He clung to his mother but soon became insensible again, having more fits, growing weaker through the day and toward midnight. "The physician came in at that moment and took H one side to tell him he was dying, this satisfied me all was over but . . . at that agonizing moment when I was leaving the bed side of a dying child (to save me the pain of looking on) to indulge my grief, I was attracted by a faint noise on the other bed and there was our darling Betty who had been asleep seized with just such a fit as we had first seen Horatio in; can you imagine the agony of that moment for words can't express it? one dying—the other to survive only a few hours." The parents never knew why this had happened. Autopsies proved nothing. Perhaps the peaches caused it, being unripe, harvested too soon, and brought a distance in a ship's hold. They did not know.[17]

The experience deepened her commitment to religion. In 1827 she had gone to church often, she had written of reading the Bible (though only once) and of perusing religious periodicals. But she had worn her religion lightly. Later, in the moment of agony after she buried her two children next to one another, she wore her religion like a pall. God, she felt, "knows what is best both for us and them, of their happiness we can't have the shadow of a doubt and their early escape from this world of sin, sorrow and suffering ought and does afford me great consolation." It was hard to lose them, especially Betty "the most engaging little creature . . . and devoted to me, couldn't turn around but 'twas 'my mother.' "[18] Elizabeth hoped to learn acquiescence.

And perhaps she did. She was to have need of it, not in grief for others but for herself. By 1849 she had the symptoms of tuberculosis: shortness of breath, debility, emaciation, ulcerations in her right lung, then in her left. She went from Virginia to the Gulf Coast, to Mobile and her sister Juliana's house, in the hope of recovery or alleviation. She slept long nights, dressed with her sister's help, was brought down to sit on the couch. She was constantly in pain, the more so because her husband was on a Latin American cruise, unaware of the seriousness of her condition. Realizing that her illness was terminal, she regretted the decision to leave Virginia and her surviving children and family. She wanted to die at home, at Evergreen.[19] But she was too ill to travel; the doctor said she might not make it to the dock at Mobile. So she lay still, enduring stoically, holding in her grief, looking to her God. She wrote several times to "Brother," wanting to say something before she died. "[I] am now struggling for breath to sit up at all and it is a great effort to exercise my mind on any one subject. In all this prostration I'm sustained by a strong Hope that I would not exchange for ten thousand worlds and I want you also when your flesh and spirit are wasting to have even a more solid ground of consolation than I always feel." She wanted him to turn his secular talents "in a religious channel," to repent. " 'Tis true," she said, "the world has crowned you with much flattering honor and compliment, your worldly friends will abide by you but when that last hour arrives they may watch around your dying bed till the moment you most need them and then when you reach the Jordan of death you will find all, all gone and not a kind hand extended to your aid." At that moment—which was her moment now—she hoped he would at least have Christ. She felt she did. And her sister Juliana, describing the death, endorsed the impression of Elizabeth's last "confidence and unwavering trust in God and her Savior."[20]

The Selma Plantation Diarist

Before the diarist, there is the matter of the journal, about which there is a certain mystery. It is to be found in two forms. The original manuscript is at Louisiana State University; it bears no identifying marks. In the same place, there is also a typescript of the journal, at the head of which is written "Owner: Miss Pearl Guyton." Miss Guyton, it seems, presided for decades over the history classes of Natchez High School, wrote textbooks of Mississippi history, composed pageants, and left her mark on many students. She liked to collect old things. She had corresponded for some four years with the LSU archivist, Edwin Adams Davis, had gone antique-hunting with him in Natchez, and entertained vain hopes that the *Journal of Southern History* might publish the journal, when she sold it to him in 1939. As part of the deal, the archive agreed to make a typescript and gave Miss Guyton two copies. She, in turn, gave a carbon copy to the Mississippi Department of Archives and History, though without informing them of the location of the original, perhaps from embarrassment at having sold it away from her native state.[21]

This second, carbon copy in Jackson was bound in black and on its cover was stamped in gold "Anonymous Diary, Adams County. 1835–1837." Above it someone has added in white ink, "Wilson (Margaret) Diary." Midway within the journal is the partial transcription of a letter, ascribed to Nellie Wailes Brandon and dated January 9, 1942, which begins, "francois tells me that you all got the little old Diary of Miss Wilson from Jackson, Miss." (the recipient of the letter is unnamed). It goes on to explain that Margaret Wilson was from Pittsburgh and was governess to the Margaret Brandon Smith family of Selma plantation near Washington, Mississippi, from 1834 to 1848. It adds that, "the children having all grown up," she went on to found a school, the Wilson Academy, in Washington with her sister Mary. It makes a few suggestions about the veiled figures that drift through the journal, before concluding: "This old Diary was said to have been found in the ruins of the old Wilson Academy which was pulled down (in the 1920's) when that new road (No.61) went through Washington, Miss." Mrs. Brandon, aside from being a descendant of many of the diarist's subjects, was a historian and an editor, with especial knowledge of the village of Washington.[22]

But is this the journal of Margaret Wilson? Mrs. Brandon and Miss Guyton are not authorities to take lightly but people who might be expected to have known. Yet we need to note a significant fissure in our evidence. Miss Guyton first owned the journal and had given Edwin Davis no reason to label it other than an "Anonymous Diary." It was Mrs. Brandon who named the diarist. We have no evidence whether Mrs. Brandon consulted Miss Guyton or even saw the original manuscript: indeed the phrasing of her 1942 letter suggests only a look at the "Diary . . . from Jackson," that is, the typescript in the Mississippi Department of Archives and History.

But perhaps Mrs. Brandon knew more than Miss Guyton. Certainly the former showed some knowledge by successfully identifying several of the journal's dramatis personae. She was vague on provenance—the journal "was said to have been found"—but very decisive in her identification of Margaret Wilson. She may have reliably known both the find in the rubble and the name of the governess. If Brandon family memories spoke of Margaret Wilson, that is evidence of a sort. But it is only a claim, made more than a century after the diarist put down her pen to listen to the singing of her pet bird, Billy. We need evidence closer to the 1830s.

What is the internal evidence of the journal? The diarist declined to label her notebook and nowhere gave herself a name within it. She did, however, record the training of her successor as governess. "If this day were the 9th of February 1837—I would most probably resign my post to Margaret and wish her success and fortitude." And three days later, "Spent most part of yesterday in reading—Margaret W—— sat with me doing the same." And later still, "I would not let Margaret commence coming into the school on friday for good luck sake, but I have been writing for her a system of regulation for the different studies and exercises of every day, I hope it may be of some service to her." And immediately afterwards, "Margaret stays in the school with me all day, I wonder if she is not both frightened and disgusted at the task before her." And this Margaret seems also to wait for letters from Pittsburgh. So it is, at least, possible that the diarist was the predecessor of Margaret Wilson, the memory in the Brandon family.

In fact, there is no contemporary evidence to confirm the name of the diarist, no letter from Mrs. Smith that speaks of her employee, no reference in some other Natchez journal of the 1830s. There is later evidence of a Margaret Wilson and a Mary B. Wilson, who bought $1,000 worth of land in Washington from Wiley M. Wood on September 26, 1850. This may well be the land of the Wilson Academy.[23] Moreover, the name Margaret Wilson occurs twice in the antebellum federal census for Adams County.[24] In the 1850 census a Margaret Wilson is given as the governess for the family of James A. Gillespie, a planter; regrettably, her age is not given, but she is identified as having been born in Pennsylvania. In the 1860 census a Margaret Wilson, aged thirty-five, born in Pennsylvania, is given in the household of Samuel Burns, a merchant; in the same household is Alexander G. Wilson, aged thirty-three, also from Pennsylvania; both Wilsons are described as "common school teachers," but there is no indication whether they are man and wife or brother and sister. The Margaret Wilson of the 1860 census is too young to be the diarist, for she would have been ten years old in 1835.

In the absence of an age for the Margaret Wilson of the 1850 census, it is impossible to know whether she is the diarist removed to being governess to the Gillespie family or the 1860 Margaret Wilson just starting her career as a teacher.[25]

But, leaving aside problems of identification, two things require attention, the context of the diarist and her nature. It is best to begin with the world she observed, before turning to the quality of her observation.

Her setting was Selma plantation, situated a mile or so to the north of Washington, Mississippi, the first stop on the Natchez Trace as it proceeded northeast from the Mississippi River toward Nashville. Between 1802 and 1820 Washington was the capital of the Territory of Mississippi, and as such predicted greatness for itself. For some years population and wealth accrued, but Natchez resented a competitor so close and so inferior, and Jackson was to displace it as the state capital. Robbed of a raison d'être, Washington dwindled to just four hundred citizens in 1835. By 1842 the free black William Johnson, the chronicler of Natchez, could ride out into the countryside and note of the village: "Tis the first time that I have seen the Town for several years, and how bad it looks Diserted Completely." But, in truth, its citizens lived as much in Natchez and the country as in the village itself. And, even dwindled, the village boasted unusual resources. Jefferson College, the oldest institution of higher education in the Old Southwest, had been very slow to justify its foundation in 1802 and never was a great success, but it did briefly show signs of life in the 1830s. The faculty in that decade included one of the South's more indefatigable romantic novelists, Joseph Holt Ingraham. There was also the Elizabeth Academy for Girls, created in 1819. And the town, which stood trustee to these colleges, had the scientist Benjamin L. C. Wailes and the historian John Wesley Monette.[26]

Selma plantation itself dated from the 1780s, having been founded by Gerard Brandon, an Irishman and veteran of the Revolution in South Carolina.[27] Brandon prospered, had nine children with his wife, Dorothy Nugent Brandon, and died in 1823. Most famous of the children was Gerard Chittoque Brandon, who became governor of Mississippi in 1828. The others did nicely, marrying and intermarrying with the wealthy of one of the world's richest plantation regions, owned by families growing, spreading, building, enslaving: the Dunbars, the Surgets, the Stantons, the Postlethwaites. Upon Gerard Brandon's death, his estates were divided and Selma fell to his daughter, Margaret Lindsay, who had married a young Captain James Smith from nearby Fort Dearborn in 1818. The Smiths thus came by substantial land and the house itself, a simple wooden structure with a porch, a modest reception room, about six or seven bedrooms, constructed on the small scale characteristic of plantation homes built before wealth made possible ambition and munificence. They also came by slaves, who by the time of Margaret Smith's death in 1856 had multiplied to forty-two.[28] The Smiths had three children: Sarah, born in 1821, who lived for only two years; James who died in 1836 when twelve; and Mary, the only child to survive long and the only Smith child to inhabit the journal.[29] The captain died in 1830.

Thus the diarist entered a plantation household owned and administered by a woman. Indeed Selma was peculiarly a woman's world, quite without a resident patriarch. Next to Mrs. Smith, the plantation's dominant figure was Miss Maria Chambers, the sister of Governor Brandon's first wife, Margaret Chambers Brandon. Wife and sister had come to Mississippi from Bardstown, Kentucky, in 1816, but the wife had died in 1820. Miss Maria had stayed on and migrated into the Smith household, probably because she would have been an awkward inheritance for the governor's second wife. Miss Maria is the villain of the journal, alternately caressing, catty, bullying. The diarist came to loathe her, and that reaction may not have been singular. In the Brandon family cemetery, Margaret Smith (whom the diarist so admired) is affectionately memorialized in eighteenth-century cadences: "Her life was spent in doing good, and in performing charitable acts. So she lived beloved & died lamented by all who knew her." By contrast, Miss Maria has a headstone that notes her relationship to Governor Brandon, gives neither birth nor death dates, and observes as her only characteristic, her single quality, that she was "Never Married." [30]

This is the local context of the journal. Evidently Margaret Smith decided that her daughter Mary needed a governess and turned to Pittsburgh as a source. We do not know how the diarist came to be employed, but the source was logical. There were powerful trade routes from western Pennsylvania down the Ohio and Mississippi rivers to Natchez. People had been migrating downriver, and sometimes returning, for more than a generation. Many of the names and people in the journal had been born in Pennsylvania or came of families with Pennsylvanian roots the Postlethwaites, the Lambdins, the Cochrans. Out of this rich connection, the diarist came.

We do not know if the diarist's time in the South was a sojourn or the beginning of a lifetime's domicile. We do know that she missed Pittsburgh like "a poor desolate Exile" and counted the days since she had left and the days until she should revisit.[31] Our ignorance of her long-term plans stems partly from the diarist's ambivalence about the future. She described life as like the moment before a concert, as "this entertainment of shifting scenes, the instruments still getting tuned, our spirits still getting ready for enjoyment, but the concert will never commence and the happiness anticipated never be realized! not here at any rate." Not thinking she would ever hear the music, she seldom bothered to describe or anticipate it. Partly this was because marriage, the usual vision in a young woman's future, was not a happy topic for her. When she did think of it, it was with misgiving, with so little enthusiasm that her mind ran to Mrs. Malaprop's advice in *The Rivals* that it was best to found a marriage upon aversion.

She thought more about the past than the future, but even there was selective. For all her reader can know, she had no family: the journal mentions no mother, father, brother, sister. It may be that she was an orphan; at one point she speaks of "beings deprived of parents." Soon after she rages that mothers can be destructive, rending, cruel to those not their "paramount object of praise and indulgence," which suggests she may have been adopted into a family and neglected. Only three figures from her life in Pennsylvania recur: Mrs. Bonnet, Sabina (the one older, the other contemporary, but both friends), and a nameless man. Or rather, a man named with mingled sadness and irony, "the Shadow." He seems to have been the reason she left Pennsylvania. She had fallen in love with him, thought herself encouraged, confessed her infatuation, and been rejected. She thought that the experience had touched her reason and health, that the derangement required a convalescent absence from Pittsburgh, and she was not sure the absence had entirely healed her. But what she had endured was very often on her mind and once drove her to compose a sad and defiant poem.

So she was youngish and single, perhaps thirty or so. But she felt time slipping away. She looked at a friend in her early twenties and already possessed of two children, and felt a twinge of aging. She noted a few gray hairs, some rheumatism in her shoulder, and a little myopia. She had no children, though she was told she had a gift for them, a gift she was unsure she wanted to exploit. When she heard a child cry in the night, she puzzled that "I don't know how any body can wish for children." Hence, though her profession as a teacher placed her much in their company, they do not loom large in her imagination; she refers to her school with irritation as a chore from which the weekend and vacation would mercifully deliver her. It seems to have worn her down, given her little pleasure. But then she was often irritated. She characteristically described herself as angry, depressed, ill. The first words of the journal are, "I have been very angry this day." Even the pleasantries of country life could occasion unhappiness: a night's rain might cool the air, "the country is full of flowers, but all that does not cheer me up, I am not well, and not happy."

Sometimes she could manage something better. Playing the sad music of Bellini cheered her, as did reading, writing in her journal, and visiting her friend Eliza Cochran. She took great pleasure in playing with and training her pet birds, so much so that pupils brought her birds as a gift. She liked nature, a "lovely garden, flower beds, shady arbors, retired seats[,] dark avenues." "Thank God," she wrote, "I have a heart for the enjoyments of nature, and a spirit of hope that is almost happiness at times." But the "almost" was characteristic.

For she was determined upon sadness and misanthropy. She had known unhappiness as a sustained condition and found happiness to be only fleeting. "What is happiness?" she asked herself. "Surely not a continued state, I am convinced that it is merely the exaltation of a few moments either of the imagination or of the senses . . . [this] is the only kind of happiness I have ever experienced." Like happiness, the emotions of regret and anger flicker through the journal. But loneliness is its persistent tone. This stemmed from her age and condition, but also from her circumstances: the often-dull routine of a plantation, where the days were spent in repetitive gossip, where the weather and state of the garden were the staples of conversation. And she felt the loneliness of exile from home, her "guiding star": "lonely I have been, lonely I am, and lonely I am likely to be for five months to come." But there was more to it than exile. She felt an incapacity for love, felt herself to have loved too few people and to have been too little loved. Her poem speaks of "withered feelings, ruined health, / Crush'd hopes, and rifled heart."

But she took pleasure in her accomplishments, the necessary accomplishments of a governess. She played the piano and the guitar, she read the latest literature, she wrote songs and poetry, she knew French (she claimed to be French), she was pleasant in society. Indeed she mingled in the best of Natchez and Adams County society in the company of her employer, whose family (with the cunning exception of Miss Maria) treated her with respect and equality, more as a member of the family than the first of servants.

Service in Adams County, of course, was not that found in *Jane Eyre* but the servitude of slaves. They appear in her journal episodically, carelessly, for a document written on a plantation with dozens of slaves. They bring her drinks, drive the carriage, wake her up too early by the blowing of the horn. Not often are they named, just characterized as "the servants" or "the negroes." Perry is an exception, because he died in an accident. And Cora, a child who seems to have waited on her. And Hector, because she was always waiting anxiously for letters from Pittsburgh, and Hector fetched the mail from Natchez. It was his slowness that excited one of her few general remarks on the subject, as she listened for his return: "Perhaps the waggon is coming—no it is only some negro chopping wood, how long that old fellow takes to go to Natchez: a whole day, he went this morning before sun rise, and it is almost 7 O'Clock, but every body has easy time here, children, negroes, cats, dogs, all do just as they please—I suppose it is as well, and certainly it will make no difference fifty years hence—but still I wish the old man would hurry a little more." Elsewhere, she wrote with kindred impatience: "Mrs Smith's new overseer was here too to consult on the management of the people what trouble the wretches do give her."

Her world was mostly secular. Though she did not reject religion and would sometimes offer up a prayer, she was inclined to talk of God only in conventional phrases ("God forbid") and would invoke that God of the skeptical, Providence. She did not read the Bible, she did not go to church, she prayed only for health. One day she joked about having sung three hymns, as though unused to the experience, perhaps because she may have been Roman Catholic. Her reading was resolutely secular and very contemporary. She seems to have fallen upon the latest literature—Dumas, Dickens, Marryat, Soulié—immediately upon its publication and took care to form and render very firm opinions. Her reading was fashionable; her criticism was not. French literature she liked; the English she abominated. "What a sprightly, and graphic way the french have, or at least their writings," she observed. "When I read those books of the modern french litterature I am always seized with [the] violent desire of setting off for France." Her fondness for France was so profound that when France was opposed to the United States, the diarist rallied to Paris in verses composed in French. By contrast, England was unattractive. She hated Dickens's *Pickwick Papers,* thought Marryat's *Diary of a Blasé* ordinary, was displeased by Disraeli's *Henrietta Temple,* and was driven to issue the firm advice, "I think English novelists should write one book and quit."

An exception to this derogation was Fanny Kemble. her favorite writer, probably her heroine. The English actress had published, just a few months before the Selma journal begins, the journal of her tour of the United States from 1832 to 1834. A reading of the two volumes may have instigated the Selma journal. Certainly it bears many marks of such an inspiration: the habit of referring to people by their initials. the fierce pride in home, the interspersing of the diarist's own verse, the insistence on a woman's prerogative of critical judgment, the mingling of introspection and blunt observation, the sense of a dialogue that the diarist is aware will be overheard. To confess an admiration for Fanny Kemble was to say something about being a woman, something modern, something bold, something independent of men.

Not that the diarist always avoided men. Wounded in spirit though she thought herself, she was not so deadened that her eye for men was quite averted. She rather fancied a younger member of the Brandon family, "a very interesting youth who has won my very affectionate regard." A visiting doctor was "certainly very handsome." Still, men were a problem, pressing their unwanted attentions, being tedious and long-winded, peddling their "usual palaver." She had, after all, been made deeply unhappy and even ill by a man. And she felt this was no "strange adventure, but a common tale, /

of woman's wretchedness." She took a dry satisfaction in the thought that while women might be made wretched by love or marriage, men had a comparable doom. Men were led on by "golden dreams of pride and power," and these, like love, were in vain. "Both end in weary brow, and withered heart." The company of women seems to have given her more satisfaction, partly because a single woman in a household of women had more occasion to derive such satisfaction. The only two figures unambiguously admired and celebrated in the journal are her friend Eliza Cochran and her employer Margaret Smith, the latter saintly and unreal, the former bright and warming. Men are episodic, women constant. Evidently, this was the diarist's verdict on her experience, probably her decision about the shape of her life to come.

Jane Caroline North

She was known as "Carey" to her family. She was pretty, wore clothes well, flirted, gossiped vivaciously. Men were attracted to her and she to them. That is, Carey North was a belle. She knew—sometimes she knew—it was a role, to be played to the hilt. As a country cousin once remarked, in vain hope of her unworldliness, "You know well how to estimate those things, called by the world pleasures." [32] And so she did. She liked them. This can be discerned from the unusually full records she left, in the form of letters to her mother, her aunts, her sisters, eventually her husband. And, now and again, she kept a journal.

She was the daughter of Jane Gibert Petigru North of South Carolina, who had married Dr. John Gough North in 1827 and become his widow in 1836. The Norths had three surviving children: Jane Caroline, Mary Charlotte, and Louisa Gibert, the last two known as Minnie and Lou. At the death of her husband, Mrs. North and her infants returned to live at her "family homestead" Badwell, in Abbeville County.[33] It had once held a large family: William and Louise Gibert Pettigrew's surviving children numbered five daughters and four sons. These had fared variously. Of the sons, Jack went west, Thomas became a naval captain, Charles a soldier, and James Louis (who changed the surname from Pettigrew to Petigru, something more resonantly Huguenot) became Charleston's greatest lawyer, most obdurate Unionist, and sharpest wit. For the sisters, good matches into prosperous low-country families had been made: Harriette was married to Henry Deas Lesesne, Adèle to Robert F. W. Allston, Louise to Philip Johnston Porcher. Only Mary Petigru never married; she evolved into Carey's "Aunt May." At Badwell the Norths lived out Carey's childhood and adolescence, partly with

Jane Caroline North Pettigrew, painting attributed to Thomas Sully. (Courtesy of Mrs. John H. Daniels)

their own money, partly with the assistance of James Louis, who became the family patriarch and who looked upon Badwell as his country estate. He much liked to embellish it, with additions like an avenue of white oaks, a fountain, a springhouse, a sundial, an adorned family burialplace.[34]

Because her father was dead, she had so many aunts and uncles, and she liked to venture beyond the quiet up-country world of Badwell, Carey North lived among various households. During the Charleston season she stayed with Uncle Tom and Aunt Anne or Uncle Henry and Aunt Harriette. In the early summer, near Georgetown, she would visit Aunt Adèle and Uncle Allston. Although her mother seems to have had little interest in society, she knew that her daughter needed it, if only to secure an adequate husband. Society might be amusing, but for a young lady and her mother it was also a serious business, demanding hard work.

The journals of Carey North were written when she had had at least two Charleston seasons, and one trip to secondary mountain resorts in the Carolinas. The journals record two trips in 1851 and 1852, when she was about twenty-three and twenty-four. In the former year she was hazarded in one of the prime markets for an eligible daughter, the resorts of western Virginia. A year later, she was taken farther afield, to Saratoga Springs in New York, to New England, and to Canada. In the former case, she traveled with her Uncle Henry and Aunt Harriette Lesesne, who brought along their young sons Hal and James. In the latter, she went with her Uncle Thomas and Aunt Anne Petigru, accompanied by their daughter Mattie. The journals are the record of a mature—even cynical—belle, though one somewhat relaxing from the rigors of a Charleston season. Understanding requires some preliminary grasp of that phenomenon, the belle.

To be a successful belle was not easy. The obligations and vexations were many. There was the matter of dress, for example, what to wear and when. Visiting Mrs. Grant in Charleston, Carey reported to her concerned and vigilant mother that "I wore my blue cashmere, nice light gloves, and new pink bonnet, so that my dress was very *neat, not* remarkable for the want of my silk." That is, she was telling her mother that she understood a visit of a few minutes to an older lady required decorum, not extravagance. A "small tea drinking" visit, on the other hand, to Mrs. Giles and her son, merited the silk. When evening visitors came, she wore "the green & lilac with short sleeves, high necked plain body *fitting* exquisitely, and a pink neck ribbon." To her satisfaction, there were "many compliments paid me on the handsome dress and beautiful fit." In Charleston in the season, variety was essential. In one week Carey had four balls to attend, "the St Cecilia tomorrow Tuesday—Wednesdays the Alstons—Thursday the Blacklocks give a party, next Tuesday an other St Cecilia."[35] Then there was a fancy dress ball.

Her cousin Mattie went as a shepherdess, with "a double skirt white dress," trimmed in blue with rosettes, with a bodice of blue silk laced with a silver cord, "low in the neck, but with a chemisette of null muslin," a straw hat worn to one side, her hair plaited, and a shepherdess's crook "twined with ribbon & some jasmin vines." Carey herself went as Titania, the dress copied from an engraving from Shakespeare. "The dress was a double skirt of illusion body to match, the upper skirt looped on each side with a pink wreath ending in a bouquet composed of the water lilies I wore last year and pink flowers, around my waist was a pink wreath *terminating* in a large rose at the peak, down to the front of my dress was a wreath to match those looping the side, my hair curled down my back à la Undine, a wreath of beetles wings (very becoming) with a small bouquet on one side I wore around my head, a pretty pair of silver wings." To this were added a butterfly of silver paper on each arm, a bouquet on each shoulder, and a wand. It went well enough, though Carey was disappointed, for she had a dress, "my Undine," to which her Titania costume was as nothing. But she had recently worn it, and being "so decided a *hit*," it would be remembered and her want of variety would be reproached.[36]

The belle had to keep a record of compliments, by way of a scorecard. Joe Pyatt, for example, at the fancy dress ball "turned to me as I stood near & said 'Miss Caroline I always thought your hair handsome. but never knew before that it was so long, it is really beautiful.'" This was pleasant. But a belle needed a navigational instinct to enjoy the amiabilities of flirtation while evading its dangers. A line had to be observed between pleasantry and courtship. For flirtation could take various forms, being sometimes an exploration. With Mr. Coles of Virginia, for instance, Carey was disposed to grant some latitude, being unsure what might develop and interested enough to promise him a stroll in the Lovers Walk at White Sulphur Springs. After all, he was "the most romantic, Byronic, sentimental personage." If exploration failed, the belle and the beau might come to a mutual understanding that nothing more need develop, that flirtation could hover at mere pleasantry. But too often the belle—certainly this belle—had to enforce this understanding. Stricker Coles, for example, at whose "nonsense" (her usual word for flirtatious banter) she laughed, went too far. "On one occasion he said, 'you know I love you Miss Carey you know your power' I thought it time to stop." And flirtation had its rules of status. Older men who were married might flirt, by way of compliment to youth and beauty. But single older men did so at their peril. Mr. Barney at the springs preoccupied Carey for a whole evening, and she disapproved: "Poor old gentleman! it is painful to hear how foolish he is talking love & nonsense to the young ladies—and really an intelligent agreeable man when conversing sensibly." A belle also had to guard herself against aberrations. Poor Lieutenant Riall, for example, his brain addled by a fever contracted in Africa (or so she said) would not take no for an answer and followed her around like a puppy. What was a girl to do, except try and palm him off on another belle? Even then, he ended up proposing, and she had to be stern.

The belle, of course, had to judge other belles, not just as competition but as models. At the fancy ball, Carey chronicled, one "young lady might have passed as the inmate of some Eastern Harem," with pantalettes "quite scant" that stopped "short of her ankles by two inches," setting off her "very small foot." Such immodesty was scarcely fair. But, fortunately, "she is to be married next Tuesday." Others, still more fortunately, blundered. Miss Horry wore a dress in the style of Mary, Queen of Scots. The dress was fine, "but ah! she looked so ugly" and "somebody asked me if I had seen the 'lady who went as an *owl.*' "[37] In Virginia she was to observe of a young lady: "Miss Chapman is beautiful as a statue in the face, perfectly colorless & faultless features—figure indifferent & manners boisterous. The sister is not pretty but very pleasant & talkative." Of another she noted: "She is an uncommon nice girl tall, fair, & with magnificent auburn hair. withal not pretty, eyebrows too light freckled & teeth dark, but one of the most affable agreeable girls I have ever met." For the competition was also, potentially, the source of female friendship, and stricture had to be balanced against the need for companionship. Still, it was soothing to be able to write that another belle was "not pretty."

The belle had to know families, the crossweaving of intermarriage, the better to locate her present and possible place. She had to estimate fortunes and probabilities, know whether this family had a record of madness or insolvency, or that family was reliable but dull. In this judgment mothers and aunts and even uncles were indispensable. They policed the boundaries of the belle, who was never a free agent. When Mr. Vanderhorst paid undue attention to Carey at the springs, Uncle Henry was displeased at his devotions. "It is stupid but I dont encourage him, & cant help it, both Uncle & Aunt are so particular that I think they attribute more to the foolish man than they [should]. He has identified himself with our party but I have nothing to do with it."

The belle usually had to understand rank and status, an understanding she inherited and confirmed. At church in Richmond a "portly old gentleman" offered the Lesesnes and Carey a share of his family pew. They accepted, though "Aunt Harriette had whispered to me that she thought our friend a dry goods merchant & so he proved to be. She is very correct in her conjectures about people generally, amusingly so sometimes." To be approached by someone of inferior rank, who claimed parity, could be "too dreadful."

Hotels were a special problem, especially those in lesser resorts. The one in Charlottesville was "a most distracted place ill furnished poorly kept," where the landlord advised that ladies take their seats for dinner early before "rough looking men," "desperate specimens," "queer, hard visaged people" rushed to gobble their food. Strangers had to be treated with polite reserve, at least until they could be placed, a connection established. Carey once met a talkative woman at a hotel, then again on the train, who would not let her alone. Eventually "just before she left the Cars she came to me & said 'dont you want to know who I am? you must think it funny a stranger should be as sociable' 'I would be happy to know who you are,' I answered. 'I am Miss Barnwell sister of Mrs Pinckney, I knew you were a Miss North, I knew your Grandfather & Uncle' &c I was really glad to find out who she was, for her *talk* was so peculiar that I was certain she was distracted & think so a little still." The peculiar who belonged to proper society required a different demeanor from those beyond its boundary.

A belle did not need to be well read, although some acquaintance with the latest novels helped. The Norths at Badwell liked to read books out loud to one another, and Carey did her share. In fact her reading was respectable: the poetry of Thomas Moore and Longfellow, the history of Voltaire and Macaulay, the fiction of Dickens and Thackeray. She took the *Mémoires d'un père* of Jean-François Marmontel and William Robertson's *Charles V* to the beach with her, though we do not know if she read them.[38] More certain is that while there, she took upon herself the tutoring of her cousin Adèle Allston. As Adèle's mother reported, Carey "gives Adele 2 lessons in music of an hour each day, then she practices 2 hours herself, then she gives 2 hours to reading history, and 2 hours to reading and writing french." We do know she liked *David Copperfield* better than most of Dickens' novels, for its intermingling of the pathetic and the ludicrous. And we know that she disliked Thackeray's *Pendennis* for its confusing plot and cynical demeanor.[39] But her journals show only modest attention to the printed word, just the odd reference to Hawthorne and—when in Quebec in 1852—reading Casimir Delavigne's play about Don Juan. Literacy was less important than some command of music, the ability to sing, to play the piano, to decorate a salon.

In truth, Carey was uncertain about intellectual women. In her 1851 journal she described a meeting with Louisa McCord, the essayist, the antifeminist, the bold analyst.[40] "She is a masculine clever person, with the most mannish attitudes & gestures, but interesting & very entertaining" was Carey's reaction. (That intellectuality denoted the unfeminine was not an opinion confined to men.) Mary Chesnut, whom she met in 1852 at Saratoga Springs, Carey came to like better, though her first reaction was cool: "Mrs James Chesnut is here, she is friendly & agreeable, mais je ne l'aime pas!"

Her later judgment was more considered: "She [Chesnut] is certainly clever, & sometimes very amusing, but she impresses me as a person who having gained a reputation rather beyond her merit, makes a constant effort to not fall short. I like her better however than I did last winter—yesterday we were walking for sometime together talking very pleasantly, after a while (speaking of some one else having led to it) she said 'I always prefered shining in conversation to attracting by dress, or paying much attention to any thing of that sort.' It was not said at all in a manner that was either vain or unpleasant—but it finished off completely the opinion I had formed of her." It is an interesting anecdote, not least because Chesnut was less than candid about herself. The future Civil War diarist had been a belle herself and never quite shed the role.

Among a belle's sundry obligations, the development of a political ideology did not loom large. Carey had a politics of sorts, because political affiliation was a factor in the judgment of a family's standing, and because the daughter of a Petigru was obliged to be a Unionist. Hence Carey was disapproving when, at the Virginia springs, her fellow South Carolinians shunned the visiting Millard Fillmore. She differed from those who suggested South Carolina should separately secede in 1850. When Louisa McCord spoke unflatteringly to her of "submissionists," Carey defended a staunch Unionism, though perhaps not in a loud voice.[41] Later, in 1861, married, mistress of a large plantation, secession seemed a different matter to her. In 1851 slavery was a straightforward part of the fabric of her life. Leaving South Carolina for Virginia, she was struck by the greater number of mulattoes, whom she found a "most sturdy saucy looking set"; they made her pine to see "the true ebony" of her familiar servants. In her family the slaves were casually known as "the nigs."[42]

A belle was, quintessentially, a wife-in-the-making, granted the right of playfulness in the knowledge that marriage would abrogate or curtail the right. As such, she had to balance the short-term pleasures of flirtation and society against the long-term importance of betrothal. Beaux and husbands were clean different things. This insight can be seen in Carey's decision to marry, which portrayed the cool skeptical intelligence that informs all her journals and letters.

The Petigrus of South Carolina had cousins in North Carolina, who still bore the old name of Pettigrew. The branches had once lost touch but, by Carey's time, had resumed a relationship. The Pettigrews had very substantial plantations in northeastern North Carolina, in Washington County, at the mouth of the Roanoke River and to the south of Albemarle Sound. In 1851 the family possessed three eligible brothers, Charles Lockhart, William

Shepard, and James Johnston, who were aged respectively thirty-five, thirty-three, and twenty-three.[43] Charles was the dullest, William the richest, Johnston the cleverest. William she seems to have disdained; he was shy about women, devoted to his sister Ann, tremulous.[44] But Carey had a protracted flirtation with Johnston, which was the easier because in 1849 he had come to Charleston to work in the law office of James Louis Petigru. They were of an age, which helped, and he found her fascinating, which helped still more. His sister Mary discerned as early as 1849 that he was "head and ears in love with . . . fair cousin Carie." They talked of books, he gave her a copy of Thomas Moore's poetry, they looked at the stars together. "Last night," she wrote to Johnston in 1849, "I kissed my hand to Orion and his beautiful belt for the twentieth time since you have been away—he inspires my dreams sometimes."[45] There was a certain expectation about them, though nothing fixed, and in their own letters they bantered about having only the love of brother and sister, a sure sign that something more was at stake.

But there was also Charles, who was much older and much plainer, but who—as Mary Pettigrew observed even in her 1849 letter to Johnston—seemed "also to entertain high notions of her character." Carey kept up a correspondence with him. They talked about the family and discussed music, for they shared a taste for opera and she could tell him about divas—Lind, Parodi—who came to Charleston. He would tell her about agricultural matters, uncertainly: "I hope you take an interest in corn growing as well as cotton and rice plantations. We, engaged in the grain interest, are about commencing to plant and the impression is, that the season will prove propitious." But was she interested? The Pettigrews knew that the Petigrus and Norths were fashionable people and that Carey was a shrewder judge of mull muslin than of grain. William, at least, knew it; soon after Johnston moved to Charleston, he issued a caveat to his younger brother: "Our relatives, in Charleston, appear to be more fashionable than our branch of the family, if I may judge from your letter: But, I hope you will endeavour to endure their peculiarities with what fortitude you can, remembering that there are but few persons whose minds are correctly balanced."[46]

Johnston she decided against. He was brilliant, everyone including James Louis Petigru agreed, but he did not have much money, his trajectory was uncertain, and he was solitary.[47] Late in 1851 Carey told an anecdote of him in Europe, which shows her awareness of this last characteristic. A young member of the Rutledge family had been crossing Lake Geneva on a steamer, recognized Johnston, and entered into conversation: "When they arrived at the town, Rutledge told Johnston the hotel where he was going, Johnston named a different one as his destination—they parted, exchanged cards, & never met again—Had Mr Rutledge not been with a party of ladies, I dare say James would have joined him, but it shows the old aversion to society."[48] And then again, Johnston was probably cleverer than Carey, which—for a woman who prized being in control—may have been no advantage.

Charles, richer, duller, less agile in mind, she decided would do. They were married in St. Michael's Church, in Charleston, on April 20, 1853, and had their honeymoon in Europe. The decision speaks volumes, for Charles was a quiet planter in an obscure corner of the South. He was no more fond of society than Johnston, perhaps less so. He was less prosperous than William, as Charles had but one plantation, Bonarva, and William had two, Magnolia and Belgrade. But Charles was family, he was kind, he loved her unambiguously, he would make a devoted father. In short, he was safe. And Carey understood the value of safety, she being the daughter of a widowed mother, a belle who grew up adjacent to prosperity rather than possessed of it. Carey knew the value of a dollar; she noticed when ice cream in Richmond was better and cheaper than its counterpart in Charleston.

As it turned out, safety proved elusive. Carey and Charles had eight children,[49] a difficult war, and a worse Reconstruction. Northeastern North Carolina was a battleground between Confederacy and Union, slaves were rebellious, and in 1862 the whole household, black and white, was obliged to evacuate to Cherry Hill, their plantation near Badwell in South Carolina.[50] Carey, who had become a stern and vigilant plantation mistress, did not take kindly to this dislocation, to emancipation, or to straitened circumstances. Her postbellum letters have an iron grimness about holding on, managing the freedmen, finding food, doing the washing, dining on rusks, selling an ax for a dollar. In February 1866 she had just $15 in cash to her name.[51] The Pettigrews had land at Bonarva, and they tried to prosper. But, in truth, Charles had not been very good at managing a plantation even in the 1850s and the agriculture of Reconstruction offered little margin for error. Things grew worse, debts mounted, Carey grew more religious. William gave up planting altogether to become an Episcopal minister, Charles's sister Mary and her new husband took over Bonarva, and Charles and Carey moved in 1872 to William's old plantation Belgrade. But Charles fell ill, worsened, grew better, and then died in late 1873. Carey struggled on, with the help of her son Charles, but the debts remained unsettled. In 1882 Mary sold Bonarva. In 1885 the creditors foreclosed on the rest of the Pettigrew land.[52] Carey herself died in 1887, of a short and painful illness, and was laid in the family vault at Bonarva next to her husband.

Ann Lewis Hardeman

One needs to begin with family, for it dominated the life and imagination of Ann Hardeman.

The founder of the Hardemans in the western South was Thomas Hardeman, who came from Virginia to Tennessee in the late eighteenth century. He was a merchant and the father of thirteen children by two successive wives, who were sisters. His eldest son, Nicholas Perkins Hardeman, was born in 1772 and shared his father's migration westward; in time he founded a general store in Franklin, Tennessee, and married Ann Neely, who bore him seven children: Thomas in 1799, William P. in 1801, Ann Lewis in 1803, Lavenia Caroline in 1804, Mary Neely in 1805. D. (oddly, always just called D.) in 1806, and, belatedly, Sarah Jane Eleanor in 1816. Only two of these, Thomas and Mary, stayed in Tennessee, for migration was a marked characteristic of the Hardemans. The founding patriarch is said to have observed of his children that he would "rather hear about them doing well a great distance away than to see them daily doing nothing."[53] And they took his advice, for the family fanned out over generations through Mississippi, Arkansas, Missouri, Texas, Oregon, and California. D. Hardeman went to Texas, where other Hardemans had gone before him, and became a very rich planter in Matagorda County. Sarah married Oscar J. E. Stuart in 1837 and moved to Mississippi. William married Mary Moore Murfree Hilliard of Tennessee in 1824 and seems to have lived there until about 1835, when they bought for $9,120 a plantation of 760 acres just a few miles to the south of Jackson, Mississippi.[54] Perhaps then, though more probably in 1847, his mother and two unmarried sisters joined them, for William and Mary had no children and acquired relatives by way of compensation.

Thus by 1849 there was a small family group living in central Mississippi that interconnected with other Hardemans, Hilliards, Murfrees (and many other families) spread from Virginia to California but focused on the region from central Tennessee to eastern Texas. These families visited and revisited one another with remarkable facility and frequency, the easier for the coming of the railroad and the proximity of the Mississippi River. The Mississippi family group had three separate households. In one lived William and Mary, Ann and Caroline, and mother Ann Neely Hardeman, a household ranging in age from forty-eight to seventy-three. In another lived Oscar and Sarah Stuart and their six children: these were, in order of their births between 1838 and 1849, James Hardeman, Oscar Ewing, Adelaide, Annie Elizabeth, Edward, and Sarah Jane. In a third lived Anna and James Sessions, with their new baby, Anna. Anna Sessions was the daughter of "Clerk Tom" Hardeman of Williamson County, the brother who had stayed in Tennessee and died in 1836; she had married into a family that was prominent in Adams County, Mississippi.

Then everything changed. In early 1849, giving birth to her last child, Sarah Stuart fell ill. After a struggle of some months, she died. Being a woman of wisdom, she understood that Oscar Stuart was not the man to care for six children. So she requested that her reliable sister Ann assume the burden. She entailed upon her children some means that would help, though not enough.[55] Suddenly, the spinster aunt of forty-six had become a sort of mother. She had no money of her own, was never to have money of her own. She lived upon the charity of her brother and sister-in-law, and they generously agreed to take in the six children. The father, Colonel Stuart, spun off into a bachelor limbo. The three households shrank into two.

This is the locus of the journal: William Hardeman's household, as seen through the strained eyes of Ann Lewis Hardeman, struggling to meet and understand the responsibilities of motherhood, without either the title of mother or the means to exercise motherhood's prerogatives. It begins in 1850, thirteen months after her world changed. It continues until 1867, a year before her death. In between was written one of the more remarkable human documents that the nineteenth-century South has to offer.

It would be easy to miss the document's force. Ann Hardeman was a simple woman. She had none of Elizabeth Ruffin's dry wit, experienced none of Carey North's brilliant society, did not read French periodicals like the Selma diarist. Ann Hardeman read hardly anything beyond the Bible, had almost no sense of humor, traveled little in fact or imagination, was repetitive, and had few gifts of narrative or observation. The journal begins slowly, as just a series of dull family routines and rounds. But it gathers pace, as her life changed and was changed, especially by war. She was a faithful chronicler of the immediate world she inhabited, faithful to both its familiarities and its disruptions. But this can be said of many antebellum journals. What makes her journal distinctive was that she was a frighteningly candid chronicler of her own emotions, whose integrity and force are the essential subject matter of the journal. They are not varied emotions, nothing quicksilver or engaging like Mary Chesnut's, but slow, intense, and vulnerable.

She was surrounded by people whom it is necessary to know, for they were her world. They are the more important because Ann Hardeman—Aunt Ann as she was always known—did not control her world but was trapped in it.

William and Mary Hardeman were, it seems, a close couple. In 1848, during his wife's absence, William wrote to his sister Ann of his loneliness and observed: "I feel now most sensibly how necessary Mary is to my happiness. I have lived so long with her, and so happily—for however the truth may be—I feel that never was man more blest in a wife than I have been." By the same token Mary Hardeman would write anxiously about his welfare when he was absent and, after his death, found her world bereft.[56] Whether out of sisterly affection or simple insight, Ann Hardeman always spoke of her brother with warmth, chronicled with care his movements as a plantation owner, noted his generosities, eulogized him in death as someone cheerful, loyal, generous. What we have of his letters does little to challenge this characterization. He appears as sanguine, once expressing the hope that "we may float on the stream of time in happy, contented, ignorance of each others faults, and verify, that 'if ignorance is bliss, 'twere folly to be wise.'"[57] Childless, he gave his home and money to his nephews and nieces, sisters and mother, not grudgingly but gladly.[58] The last words of the journal are a tribute to him.

Mary Hardeman was a different matter. Hardeman family members did not always like William's wife. Her letters show a stern authoritative woman, jealous of her prerogatives, watchful of her status, clumsy about the expression of her affections, and so sometimes chilly in her formality. She was, one infers, the strongest figure in the household, a person around whom circumspection was advisable because reproof might be sharply forthcoming. In 1859 James Stuart advised his sister Bettie to use caution in writing to the family, to abjure levity, for "Aunt Mary always takes the letters and reads them and at the table makes it a point to comment upon anything she pleases." In 1863 Edward Stuart wrote from the Virginia front to patch up "past dissentions," and to say, "I hope dear Aunt, that though the interest of my Fathers Family, and yours may be different, that though we who for so long a time have lived together are seperate now, that our affections may remain the same, that I especially who have in a measure had my love for you alienated by disagreements, and wrongs fancied or real, may now that we are seperated part in love."[59] Such hopes seem to have gone awry. After the war letters to Aunt Ann from her nephews and nieces would fail to convey good wishes to Aunt Mary, and Aunt Ann would reprove them for it: "I know this is disagreeable & may be treated with silent contempt but I trust when you get older you will see the wrong of not having done so." Bettie, at least, tried a letter, but evidently without conviction. As Aunt Ann reported, "I was in yr aunt Marys room one night not long since & she spoke of you with much feeling & regretted your alienation—your letter she said was not what it should have been & only a few lines."[60]

To be sure, Mary Hardeman's position was not enviable. She ran a household not of her own making, inhabited by sisters-in-law, mother-in-law, nephews, nieces, all with their complicated demands and emotions. She necessarily shared with Ann Hardeman the disciplining of the children, and they did not always like it. As even Edward was forced to admit to her, "I know that I have often given you much trouble perhaps pain."[61] She was the outsider, the in-law. Perhaps even more unforgivably, she was a patron empowered by her own property, which may have exceeded her husband's. Their property seems, in the main, to have been jointly owned. But in the Hinds County real and personal tax roll of 1849, she is credited with thirty-two slaves under the age of sixty, and her husband with none; she had a pleasure carriage, a $75 watch, a $50 clock, fifty head of cattle, gold and silver worth $200, and a $250 piano. He had one horse worth $50. With the authority of her own money, she extracted the deference that money conferred. She was generous, but everyone knew the price of her generosity. Ann Hardeman, in particular, was her dependent. The entry in the journal for February 13, 1860, states the scale of the dependence: "I have all my life wished to have a certain sum allotted me—but it has never been convenient to do so—I could not make a proper or correct estimate myself & consequently it was neglected or not spoken of any more—but to-night I had occasion to borrow a little money & the subject was again agitated—I mentioned five dollars per month—sister Mary generously sd she thought one hundred dollars for Ma & myself would do for the balance of the yr. I wished to borrow $5.00 & she brought me 15 I wld not accept it as a gift but took it as an allowance."

William and Mary underwrote the household. The father of the children, Oscar Stuart, seems for such purposes to have been of little use. "The Colonel," as he was called, was related to the Stuart family that produced J. E. B. Stuart, the Confederate general, but Oscar's branch was less splendid and had become disconnected from its Virginia roots. Indeed, as a Virginia relative was obliged to explain to him in 1866, "Your father (James) was a man of fine appearance & talent, but eccentric & high tempered, & ultimately became insane & died in the Asylum in Williamsburg. I saw him there in 1824. Your mother removed southward, & intercourse between the families ceased."[62] The Colonel drifted in and out of the Hardeman household, offering and receiving intermittent affection from his children, traveling in search of an elusive fortune. He moved to St. Louis and failed, he moved to Kentucky and failed, he moved around Mississippi and failed. He tried being a lawyer; he sold "Double Cotton Scrapers and Double Ploughs" for the salvation of vexed planters; he was an agent for the Confederacy. He grew inordinately fat, such that the competence of tailors was severely tested. And, to be fair, he had bad luck. In 1866 his office burned down.

A letter written by the Colonel after the Civil War, to Captain James Eads of St. Louis, sums up the former's problems and his character. "Sir," he wrote. "In the summer of 1852, you inflicted upon me a personal injury, which subjected me to many months of excruciating suffering, heavy expences, a partial lameness, which increases with increasing years, a deranged action of my nervous system, and an occasional attack of bone rheumatism." As a result, he was forced to abandon a promising business in St. Louis. For this, "the loss I sustained by your assault upon me aided and abetted as you know you were by some very rough men," who came upon him "when I was off my guard drinking a mint julep," he demanded some just compensation. Even then, in 1852, he could have sued Eads, was urged to do so, but "my reply uniformly was Southern gentlemen were not in the habit of asking compensation in money for bodily injuries." Moreover, he knew that he would secure such damages as would ruin Eads and his family, one distinguished by a mother who was a "christian lady" and by children. Stuart, who "had left little sons and daughters in Mississippi," knew the value of such "sacred ties," knew and forebore. But now he was old, ruined by time and the war, preparing to "appear before a tribunal—where we will both be judged by an Omniscient God." Should not justice be done? For "how convenient it would be to have the money I spent necessarily while in the hospital for nursing stimulants, board & surgical aid, amounting to several hundred dollars and the gold you won of me, when your four queens first beat my four jacks, and your four kings, afterwards, beat my four queens— and subsequently your four aces beat my four kings—all with the mechanical certainty and specific gravity of your subtle volition, the predestined power reserved to yourself in the several deals in which you dealt to me." After all, Stuart had entered the poker game not for vulgar gain, but because "I was anxious by reason of the boats deficient larder to participate in the egg supper which it was suggested we should play for (price $5)." So how about it? "Respectfully, Oscar J. E. Stuart." [63]

He was not always so low. In fact, after the war, he looked back on his antebellum life with some nostalgia. In 1860, he remembered, he had "about $10,000 of property in possession, and had several thousand dollars due to me. I usually had a few hundred dollars on hand and if I suddenly needed money I had a plenty of friends among monied men, who were ever ready to advance me whatever sum I needed in cash, or to furnish a sight draft, or check on New Orleans, and by getting on the cars I could realize the money upon it in 24 hours." After the war was another matter, what with the robberies of "strong armed political banditti," the enervations of aches and pains. [64]

No doubt such a man could offer many amusements, and his children seem to have been fond of him. But, seen from the standpoint of Ann Hardeman, obliged to care for his children, matters would have seemed less uproarious. Indeed, it is in letters to and about the Colonel that Aunt Ann came closest to irony. In 1866, when he received a commission as a major-general (though in what army is unclear), she observed: "He will no doubt *reflect honour* upon his *Eppaulets*—hope too that it may brace him sufficiently to keep his *chair* instead of the horizontal position he likes *so much.*" [65]

Within the Hardeman household two other adult figures need mention, Caroline Hardeman and Ann Neely Hardeman, Ann's sister and mother. Like Ann, Caroline was a single woman and had "lived through much affliction." They were born only one year apart, and they seem to have been close. When Caroline was absent, even nearby, Ann would note, "We are lonely without her." She helped with the children, they worked together. "Sister C & myself made a good many experiments—succeeded tolerably," an entry for 1854 reads. But in June of that year Caroline died of "congestion of the heart & lungs." The loss came so unexpectedly that it dazed Ann. "I cannot realize that she is gone—& often find myself almost talking to her—I depended so much upon her for every thing." The loss ran deeper than she knew, although she knew much of it. "O how dreary is my life with out thee my dear lamented sister," she reflected upon the third anniversary of the death. For the loss was of the only woman in the household who was her contemporary and friend.

There remained her mother, which became part of the problem. Instead of Ann and Caroline and "Ma," there was now just Ann and "Ma." Ann Neely Hardeman and her daughter became bracketed together as the odd single women of the house. When visitors came to the house as guests of the mistress, Mary, they did not always visit the aging women, somewhat shut away. And "Ma" was very old, having been born in 1776 and having survived her husband by forty-four years at her death in 1862. She appears in the journal silently, moving about the house, going out, staying in, working at odd chores. Ann Hardeman, almost until the moment of her mother's death, took her for granted; it is probable that she had never known a household without her mother in it. Her death at eighty-six occasioned no surprise, pain, but only a little regret. Mother was "not in her accustomed place."

And then there were the six children: James, Oscar, Adelaide, Bettie, Edward, and Sarah Jane.

Of these, the youngest did not survive long, only until May 1853 and her fourth year. Next to, perhaps more than, the death of her sister, the loss of Sarah Jane made a deep and scarring impression upon Aunt Ann. It dramatized the central pathos of her life, the helplessness of her dependence and the ambivalence of being aunt and mother. The description of the death is one of the few retrospective and considered narratives in a journal that was usually written quickly, spontaneously, with no emotion recollected in tranquillity. In Aunt Ann's account, the beloved playful child falls suddenly ill, endures pain stoically, and sees a vision of Heaven before death. At the narrative's focal point is this passage: "Some months previous to her illness she awoke in the night & asked me if I would let her call me Ma saying 'my own Ma is in Heaven—will you let me call you Ma?' I told her yes—she never called me by any other name—after that." It is a narrative, compounded of a conventional Victorian death-bed scene and wrenching honesty. Where fiction and a wish end, and verisimilitude begins, is hard to see.

Of the other children, James was the eldest and dearest to Aunt Ann, a clever child who graduated first in his class at the University of Mississippi. Oscar was slower, more earnest, more religious. Edward was slowest, least noticed, the one who never got to college, the one of whom it was observed he was "always a reader . . . never a student."[56] Of the two surviving sisters, Adelaide was the smart one, mischievous yet responsible, the one who would look to her duties but smile as she did them. Bettie was the simple one, lazy, often confused, well-meaning, the sort of child who would lose a satchel. As brothers and sisters go, they were close enough to one another, though the boys did boyish things, fishing, hunting, breaking legs; and the girls did girlish things, playing with dolls, sewing for the slaves, having parties at which they might be crowned queen. Aunt Ann worried sometimes about the consequences of such a division—"I fear that the boys do not feel such an identity with their sisters as they ought"—but not much.

This was her family world at the mid passage of her surviving journal, if to it one adds a steady procession of cousins, nieces, nephews, aunts, uncles, and in-laws who came briefly—and sometimes for several years—to visit on their way to and from Texas, New Orleans, North Carolina, or Tennessee. Her broader social world was Jackson, Mississippi, the state capital since 1822, a city situated at the nexus of a broadening system of communications. By 1840 it had a railroad to Vicksburg, where travelers could secure steamboats down to New Orleans or up the River as far as one might wish to go. In 1858 a direct rail link to New Orleans was finished, onto which the Colonel might hop to go to town and cash in his credit; in fact, the Hardeman home stood very close to its tracks and Ann Hardeman could lie awake and listen for "the carrs."[67] To the east, a track ran to Meridian, and to the north, one might travel into Tennessee and on eastward. Being a capital, Jackson had an intermittent population of politicians and a permanent one of state officials, lawyers and judges, to tend to the state's business: many of these and their families inhabit the journal. It had the leading churches of several denominations, notably of the Episcopal diocese of Mississippi. Mary Hardeman was an Episcopalian, and so the bishop, William Mercer Green, and his family feature in the journal, as do accounts of and names from Ann Hardeman's own Methodist church. The city had assorted amenities: an occasional theater, balls at the Governor's Mansion, Masonic lodges, a state Lunatic Asylum (of which William Hardeman was a commissioner in 1852),[68] and a penitentiary. It had the state fair, which the family would attend, and once even a tournament. There were merchants in abundance, no colleges that survived, but a large population of private schoolteachers, some of whom instructed the Stuart children when Aunt Ann herself did not do so. The city was well stocked with doctors, many of whom treated the family, and some of whom were friends. Indeed the Hardemans mixed mostly with Jackson's professional classes and the Hinds County planters they served; between them, these people ran the city and the county. It was a small world they tried to order. The 1860 census lists a population for Jackson of 4,388, of whom 1,601 were slaves and nineteen were free blacks.[69]

Slaves feature extensively in the journal. There was Jinny (sometimes called Jenny), who made the fires and was a nurse, who was sometimes careless with the children's clothes, whose child Daniel fell ill of the yellow fever. There was Eliza, who had a little girl called Belle. There was Isbel the cook, who had a "very religious" daughter prone to fits that led her to fall in the fire. There was Julia, who had a son called Nelson and a daughter called Phillis. Aunt Ann, in her care for children, took especial note of the health of the slaves and their offspring. A typical entry reads, "No school yesterday all well except the servants Jenny, Green, Angeline & Hester." But her concern was not always dispassionate; a slave's ill-health might oblige her to supply a place: hence, "since Eliza has been sick (16th July '59) I have had a good deal more to do than usual." And she had to control them, not always successfully: "Some trouble on Sun. morning with Eliza & Mary" reads an entry. Another has: "I lost control of my temper to-night Eliza provoked me very much—was insolent—& behaved very badly. I will try & regain my balance—anger is majestic—but makes *slaves* of weak minds." Not being one of nature's authoritarians, Ann Hardeman usually found the effort of enforcing discipline upsetting: "Servant woman did not do well— feel badly this morning nervous & excitable yet making an effort to retain my balance." But Aunt Ann was not the commander of slavery in her world. Her domain was too narrow, on the margins of the household which Mary Hardeman dominated. In some ways she shared their tasks, for the spinster had responsibilities in sewing, which she shared with slaves like Eliza and Florence, all of them eventually obliged to struggle with the newfangled sewing machine.

Slavery was not a social order that Aunt Ann challenged, and it was one whose passing she regretted. When she and Mary Hardeman in late 1866 tried to restore La Vega plantation, she wrote elegaically to Adelaide of its fall from grace: "Well we went over to dear old La Vega to-day & the tears wld come & they afford so much releif. . . . every thing is in a dilapidated condition—& really if any one had undertaken to ruin the place as a job of work for which they expected a rich reward—it could have been done no better—as nothing has been neglected in the effort of destruction—Your garden in which you took so much pleasure shews no vestige of its former beauty—the honey suckles are around the trees about the cistern yet—& I plucked the leaves from one of them to send you." Many of the old slaves returned as hired servants, which she found a comfort. But on the whole she viewed the transition to free black labor as a symptom of decline. The ex-slaves who fixed up the house at La Vega, she complained, "charge the most exhorbitant prices & in many instances do their work very indifferently." To use the labor of "the freed people" was "a real annoyance." [70]

None of this need surprise, for Ann Hardeman was a deeply conservative woman who, though she suffered in and from the world she inhabited, did not question its legitimacy. Family, religion, discipline, social order were her presumptions. Indeed family and religion were almost indistinguishable for her, God being the God not just of Abraham and Isaac, but of James, Oscar, Adelaide, Bettie, and Edward, a God charged with caring for them. Aunt Ann was a Methodist who knew Wesley's sermons and sang his hymns. Her Bible, which she often quoted (usually from memory), was preeminently the Old Testament of the Psalms and the New Testament of the epistles of St. Paul, texts which offered a God stern but merciful, who would answer mortal appeals but also dispensed griefs whose purpose was the learning of submission. Submission was a mantra that Aunt Ann chanted to herself when her world would break. Her God valued meekness, for "the servant of the Lord must not strive; but be gentle unto all men, apt to teach, patient, in meekness instructing those that oppose themselves." She prayed constantly—and her journal is as much a prayer book as it is a chronicle—that God would be as "the shadow of a great rock in a weary land" to herself and her family, that his arms would hold up her falling children. She believed in charity, without which one became "as sounding brass, or a tinkling cymbal." She valued "goodness and forbearance and longsuffering." She looked forward to a world where no one would be sick, where the dead would live in familial amity, where "the wicked cease from troubling" and "the weary be at rest." Her relations with God were not always easy, as his sternness seemed so often to outrun his mercy, and she struggled to keep her temper with him. She told herself, "May I be more resigned to His righteous Providence toward me & submit to them all without *murmuring* or *complaint*." Yet she did complain and she did murmur.

Religion was of a piece with good habits. Aunt Ann had rules, which she set down in her journal. She wanted to have a good temper, "to please those with whom we are connected," to be industrious, to act promptly and regularly, to anticipate needs and manage affairs wisely. Each day would have its allotted task. On Monday, Tuesday, and Wednesday she would repair clothing and "be patient diligent & industrious." On Thursday she would "attend to the *wash particularly* & have every article noted & required to be returned in due time." On Friday she would be "diligent." On Saturday morning she would gain "time for a little rest," and on Saturday evening she would "prepare work for the ensuing week" but "save time enough to get the mind off the world a little." But every day, she promised herself, she would write for two hours, both letters and her journal.

The physical evidence suggests that usually she kept her promise of regular entries. Most were written immediately after the event; very few are retrospective; some are entries that were cumulative, with a little more added each day. We do not know if journals before the first entry here of June 24, 1850, ever existed. That entries or even volumes after 1850 have disappeared is a safe inference.[71] She seems sometimes to have written on odd scraps of paper that were later transferred into the bound volumes, but could have easily been mislaid. The entries are censored, usually at moments when she was breaking her own rules of mildness and submission, when her anger outran her discipline. Whole pages, or parts of pages, have been neatly excised by razor or scissors. We do not know the identity of the censor. It may have been Aunt Ann herself, reviewing her words and repenting of intemperance. Possibly it was Robert B. Mayes, the son of Bettie Stuart's husband, into whose hands most of the journal passed. In a 1911 letter to Dunbar Rowland, the Mississippi historian, Mayes announced his intention to edit the Civil War letters of the Stuarts and "the diary by their aunt-mother, Miss Ann L. Hardeman. This last has in it so much of a private nature that it will require much editing."[72]

It is not clear why she decided to keep a journal. Unlike most diarists, unlike Elizabeth Ruffin, Ann Hardeman almost never personified her relationship with the text. Only once did she write, when retiring for the night, "so good bye journal." Only once did she reflect on the journal's possible readers. When finishing the last page of a bound volume in April 1862, she wrote: "This closes my fifth book of journallising—dear James desired to have them but I think the best disposition I can make of them would be to burn them—but I must comply with the requisitions of the 15th Psalm—'Though I promise to my loss I must make my promise good'— they are perfect nondescripts & may serve to while away a rainy evening when alone—if sufficiently legible—I trust dear James—they may remind you of your Aunt Ann—who loves you." On the whole she wrote without a sense of any reader but herself and God. What she intended for her journal is obscure; what she did in it is less so. She prayed, she talked to herself, she marked the anniversaries of family life. Above all, she denoted and eased her loneliness. Her journal is a history of how and why that loneliness increased almost beyond her endurance.

Through the 1850s the journal records an even rhythm of life, regarded by Aunt Ann with some calmness, except when (as with Sarah Jane and Caroline) death intervened. Things went well enough with the surviving children, the odd illness, the odd scrape, little more. James went off to the University of Mississippi in 1855 and after graduation settled to reading law and became engaged to a neighbor's daughter. Oscar went to the same college in 1859, in the year that Adelaide and Bettie, at their uncle's expense, were sent off to a girls' school in Burlington, New Jersey. At the end of 1859, Aunt Ann's duties as "maternal aunt" had all but ceased, save for Edward and the now-adult James. Life grew simpler, less engaged. An entry for December of that year has: "I have done nothing this week but look over & arrange old letters & papers have sewed a little to-night."

In the spring of 1860 she began to suffer odd pains. On March 23 she felt weak, "very badly every way," spoke of "an attack" and began to think about death. On April 7 her head felt painful, and on the sixteenth she was "sick all day." In late April she had a bout of vomiting, took to her bed, and a doctor came. On May 13 "a sudden but severe pain struck me at the edge of my right shoulder," and she could scarcely take a deep breath. Early in June she complained of fatigue. After July 30 the journal falls silent for more than two months, resuming on October 7 with: "I have been suffering for some time with my head & ear—the last two months seem to have been entirely lost to me." The next day she elaborated: "My head & ear still on the sick list—but seem to be improving—not so painful except occasionally the most acute pains run through my neck, head, & ears, fear I shall lose the use of my left ear—but I am truly thankful that I am able to sit up & work a little—& have no *constant pain*—my appetite is good—but my entire system seems paralysed—slightly." She could not discharge her duties, could not even manage a letter to her nieces, spoke of herself as "an invalid." In early November she confusedly noted: "My neck—Ear & Head—are sick with—with Carbuncle—or Tumour of some kind which makes me very nervous indeed." Late in the same month, she wrote: "My neck & eye improving slowly feel greatly depressed in spirits." On December 3, "I feel the want of energy—my poor ear & jaw & neck are improving *very slowly*—my mouth all to one side—if I should recover I shall not I fear have a human appearance." Summing up on New Year's Eve, she called herself "a wreck."

Nearly a year later, there is the chilling entry: "My head still feels very bad. Dr Cabiness brought out the Electrical Machine."

It seems likely that she had acute mastoiditis, an infection of the mastoid bone. The bone, located behind the ear, is honeycombed with air cells and "connected to a cavity in the upper part of the bone called the mastoid antrum." To it, infections of the middle ear can spread. There can then occur "severe pain, swelling, and tenderness behind the ear, as well as pain within the ear . . . fever, a creamy discharge from the ear, progressive hearing loss, and some displacement of the outer ear." In its most severe form, the infection can spread inward beneath the skull (the mastoid bone is, in fact, not a separate bone but part of the skull) and cause meningitis, brain abscesses, or blood clotting. If it spreads outward, it can occasion facial palsy.[73] Today treatment is simply by antibiotics. In the 1860s doctors could only try to deal with the symptoms.

Coping with this illness was strain enough. But the world of public affairs, to which she had paid no attention, began to add cruelly to her burdens. Through the end of 1860, absorbed by her own troubles, the emergency of secession eluded her interest. But on January 5, 1861, she noticed: "There seems to be great excitement throughout the entire Country—Companies are organizing & wearing badges—&c. besides many other demonstrations of Antagonism—War! War!! War!! is the cry through North & South! O that God may allay the impending Storm." Politics began to intrude, as Mississippi seceded, a Confederacy was formed, regiments were mustered, James went to fetch Adelaide and Bettie from their school in New Jersey, and James and Oscar went off to war in Virginia.

It drove her frantic. She had always been religious, but now her journal became a litany of desperate prayers, repeated and repeated, that God would protect her children. She ransacked the newspapers for news, she began to echo Confederate ideology, she studied battle lines and military history. Her nerves were raw with worry and vigilance. Did Oscar and James have enough to eat? Did they have warm blankets? The good news of a battle won lifted her, the spiraling bad news of danger and death left her weeping and exhausted. "Perhaps," she explained to herself, "I have let Satan get the advantage—by thinking too much about my dear absent ones & the Army." "I am too sensitive," she knew.

On top of this, partly because of it, she felt her position in the family deteriorate. No doubt they were busy, Mary and William Hardeman, Anna and James Sessions. Aunt Ann was ill and talked too much and worried too much. No doubt she was tedious and they shied from seeking her out. (The infection of mastoiditis would have made her stench.) Her temper seems to have grown unwontedly short, and they chastised her for it. "I am continually being chided by some one," she complained in July 1861. "I talk too much & it seems to annoy every one as my memory is not sufficiently restored to make myself agreeable," she wrote later. Sometimes she thought that "all are kind & forbearing toward me." Sometimes she found that "I am rather a bore to the entire family—never knowing when it suits their pleasure or convenience to have any intercourse with me." Sometimes she was angry and puzzled: "I cannot realize the depreciation of my family—if it be from physical causes it should call forth their *sympathies*—if *mental*—their *sympathy* & *kindness*—& forbearance but it is difficult to bear with persons who are cut off from society by ill health—& have of course become splenetic & disagreeable generally."

She sat in her room, aging and alone, nursing her health and trying by force of prayer and will to preserve the children she loved, worrying that her "petitions do not reach the the the throne of grace." She felt alone and irrelevant, just "a burden to every body." "*I do value their happiness,*" she wrote of her family, "but do not think my life valuable (*to any one now*) but God knows best & into His hands do I in humble confidence commend myself & all those in whom I have an interest by right—& whether that right is recognised by them or not." She sat and wept: "I have felt some little bitterness in my soul—tears flowed more freely than usual." And her present misery cast a bleak light back on her past, made her feel the emptiness of having served a function that was now past, of having borrowed a maternity. "I have felt in all its bitterness the position which I have occupied for some years—but have been by affliction released from it—the fact of having some one to rest my starved affections upon has hitherto filled a vacuum in my life—but I am now set aside—and those whom I have fondly cherished—& loved are consigned to another—& I am trying to bear the alienation of the dear ones who were consigned to me by their dear Mother on her death bed." She sat and drifted into despair.

Reality proved as bad as fear. James was killed in September 1862 at the battle of Second Manassas, serving with his cousin J. E. B. Stuart. The general had sent him on a raid beyond enemy lines; James had returned to find the battle engaged, lost his horse, seized a musket, and charged. An old school friend recognized the body, stripped by the enemy.[74] The entry in her journal reads: "God help me. 'would to God I had died for thee' my James my dear James." In that anguished phrase, she reached for her claim to maternity. It is King David's lament for his son: "'Would God I had died for thee, O Absalom, my son, my son!"

Then William died on March 27, 1863, after a short sharp illness. Six weeks later Oscar was killed. His commanding officer, John Barksdale, wrote to Colonel Stuart in explanation: "Your son . . . was killed in the engagement at Mary's Hill. Some of the men belonging to his Regt. report that he and several others were shot after they had been compelled to surrender. This was I think, done in the excitement and heat of battle when men's passions set all restraint at defiance and was not the result of a deliberate determination to give no quarter." [75] News of the deaths of her nephews reached Aunt Ann in watered versions, written for her woman's weakness by men who did not understand her acquaintance with suffering.

Soon after, Colonel Stuart moved the family to Haynesville in Alabama, away from Federal raids. There Aunt Ann awaited the ruin of her country, as a lesser postscript to the ruin of her family. Her journal scarcely exists for this period. It may be that she stopped keeping it, that she lost heart. More likely, paper being short, she kept it on scraps that were easily lost. Only Edward was left to soldier on, sometimes ill and hospitalized, sometimes on campaign. Though just seventeen in 1864, he was to see enough to distinguish between youth and experience. To Adelaide he wrote in 1864 of "the fickleness of fortune, the uncertainty of fate, the vicissitudes of life, [which] combine to render thorny the pathway I would tread. I feel tired sometimes and like exclaiming 'Day by day old sorrows leave us, and new ones come fleeting in.' In my earlier youth I expected to force my way by vigour and storm, the realities of life, were forgotten, and neglected in dazzling dreams of the future. Now I am oppressed by anxiety, troubled with a knowledge of incapacity." [76] Adelaide went off to Columbia, South Carolina, to become one of the young ladies who signed the bank notes which so confidently predicted redemption upon the signing of a peace treaty between the Confederacy and the United States. Bettie stayed with Aunt Ann until forced to become a school teacher.

After the war Ann Hardeman had no fixed home. The household of William and Mary, her old refuge, was gone. With so many men dead, her world came very close to being a world of women, which had its companionships but also uncertainty. Edward became a carpenter and strayed about for work, to be seldom seen or heard from, while the Colonel went about his usual feckless business. The women huddled together for support. For a while Ann lived in lodgings with Bettie and another niece, Annie Sessions, in Franklin City, Mississippi, while Adelaide made a living as a schoolteacher. Then Bettie had to seek work as a governess, tried to find a place for her aunt, but could not. [77] "I grieve to think that you are all wanderers & exiled," Mary Hardeman commiserated, while herself being obliged to stay with her family in Tennessee, her brother in Arkansas, or the Sessions until affairs could be sorted.

The branch of Ann's family in Texas, some of whom had stayed for long periods in Jackson in the 1850s, offered to take her and sent her money, though they too were reduced in circumstances. While Ann brooded unhappily on the thought of a migration, she lived by makeshift hospitality. "God only knows what is to become of *me* for I know not upon what coast I may be stranded or into whose hands I may fall as I am yet afloat," she wrote in May 1866. In fact, everyone wanted to help, though not all could. Eventually Mary Hardeman returned to restore her plantation at La Vega, fix up the house, and give Ann back a home. But Aunt Ann was angry at the prospect of the old hospitality, renewed without the ameliorating bonds of her brother's affection or the presence of her nephews and nieces. To Adelaide she confessed, "I do not think it just or right that I should be thrown upon the hospitality of this family." But Texas seemed a worse option: "It really makes me feel nervous & hysterical to think of it—but I see no other alternative—no place that I can lay my weary old grey head & call it *home!!* but if I can get there perhaps I may be associated with a *part at least* of *my family*—my heart sickens at the thought of never seeing any of you again until the morning of the resurrection!!" As she hesitated, nearer relatives cautioned against going, and Mary spruced up La Vega and moved in along with the Sessions. Bowing to necessity, Aunt Ann returned to a corner room, to sit "thinking thinking until her thoughts are turned into a definite channel by some surrounding which claims her attention & so her life glides on—*wearily enough* I do assure you."[78] By now, she was sixty-four.

She seldom saw Adelaide, Bettie, or Edward, though Adelaide was good about writing and the children all cared deeply for her in their own way. Bettie married Judge Robert B. Mayes, a widower with several children who, at the end of 1867, volunteered to provide a home for both Ann and Adelaide. Aunt Ann received the invitation with kindly skepticism, since it was a promise of a home that the judge and Bettie, who lived in lodgings, did not yet own. She wrote to Adelaide, then alone and a schoolmistress, a few words of advice about the wisdom of a single woman living with relatives. "If you continue teaching you will be *beyond a doubt* be an 'old Maid'! (*hope you may be a good one*) & a room will be waiting for an occupant—Judge Mayes said when he was here some time ago—that he wanted *you* to live with them." This was not a good idea. "I do hope . . . you may find comfortable quarters in your *own domicil*—there is no state of life exempt from cares & trials of every kind & it behooves us to select the one which combines the greatest amount of facilities to render us *happy* & *useful* both to ourselves & to our fellow creatures—& when the marriage *vows* are *regarded* by *each*—they have nothing to fear—life moves on with 'a ripple on the stream'—but if trouble comes—two can bear it better than one." That is, the married couple will have the consolation of each other in moments of stress, the "old maid" no comfort but herself. And so Aunt Ann counseled the wisdom of a single woman living alone. She further counseled a little indulgence, a limit to self-sacrifice: "It is your christian duty to do *justice* to *your self*. . . . you know we are to love our neighbour as ourself but how is this possible unless we love ourself? be a good *Bible christian* my dear child & do *your duty* to *Miss A. L. Stuart*—who needs some leniency extended to her." But, still more urgently, she counseled Adelaide that an aging spinster was wise to marry: "I don't want you to be an invalid old maid—or wife—I wish you to enjoy life while it is granted to you—but I want you & Edward to get married *before you get old*—take warning by me—here I am left without any resource—& feel that I am a dreg to everybody & do not know what to do with my self." [79] It was her last piece of advice, in the last letter of hers we have. She died on January 22, 1868.

Editorial Note

THE MANUSCRIPTS

The two journals of Elizabeth Ruffin are contained in the Harrison Henry Cocke Papers at the Southern Historical Collection of the University of North Carolina at Chapel Hill. The first volume is bound in brown leather, with only the back cover surviving; it measures 4¼ by 8 inches and its spine runs along the short end, which means she wrote in it broadside. All its leaves are loose, resting within the detached binding. On the back cover, on the outside leather, is written "Elizabeth Ruffin," in her own hand. Someone else, presumably an archivist, has put page numbers in pencil on each page. Ruffin evidently used an old book once commenced for accounts. On the front flyleaf is written, in a different hand: "to p Woodlief 6 / By Sundries to amt of debit £11.0.5. / All balanced to this date Febry 13th 1797—"

The second volume is also bound in brown leather and measures 4¼ by 6¼ inches. It has one loop in the middle of the front binding, on the edge where it is opened, and two on the back: this was evidently for locking it, by sliding a ribbon through all three loops. After the flyleaf, there are seven blank pages before Ruffin began her entries. The journal ends abruptly with the word "Saturday," after which twelve pages are blank. Again, someone has numbered the pages in pencil. On the flyleaf Ruffin wrote her name. "Miss Julia R. Cocke," in another hand, is written in ink on a slip of paper pasted inside the front cover of the diary. Beneath Ruffin's name, in a third hand and in pencil, is: "Miss Elizabeth Ruffin, Prince George Cty, Virginia.

1827. A diary kept by a young lady when she and her Brother Mr Edmund Ruffin made a trip North, a great journey at that time. Rebecca Henley her daughter 1899 Williamsburg, Va."

The Selma plantation journals are to be found in the Louisiana and Lower Mississippi Valley Collections, Hill Library at Louisiana State University in Baton Rouge. They are contained within a single notebook measuring 6 by 7 inches, with a brown marbled cover; on the front is pasted, "*ANONYMOUS DIARY* / 1836–1837 / M-19d #533." Between the first and second journals there is a blank page. After the final entry, there are seven blank pages, then at least four that have been cut out almost entirely. It is not possible to see whether they originally contained writing, although it looks as though they did not. On the inside of the back cover, at the bottom, someone has written in pencil: "—/? n/x."

The journals of Jane Caroline North are in the Pettigrew Family Papers at the Southern Historical Collection. The 1851 journal is in three small note-books, that each measure 3 ¾ by 5 ⅞ inches. The covers are of brown leather. On the first is written in ink (though not perhaps by North): "*J. C. N. 1851, Journal of an Excursion to the Virginia Springs*"; on the second, "*J. C. N. 1851, Journal of an Excursion to the Virginia Springs, No 2*"; on the third, "*J. C. N. Sept 1851, Journal of an Excursion to the Virginia Springs, No 3*." In each, as with the Ruffin journals, someone later has marked the page numbers. Pages 34 and 35 of the second notebook are blank; North evidently jumped over these pages, but whoever paginated the diary numbered them. The 1852 journal is in a single notebook, with a light brown cover, that measures 4¾ by 7⅛ inches; on the cover is written, "Journal—1852," and on the flyleaf, "J. Caroline North—August 1852."

The Hardeman diaries are mainly to be found in the Oscar J. E. Stuart Papers at the Mississippi Department of Archives and History in Jackson. They consist of four small cheap volumes with marbled covers and a num-ber of fragmentary leaves. The volumes all measure 6 by 7¼ inches and are marked in white ink, in the following manner, by someone other than Ann Hardeman.

1. "Diary of Ann L. Hardeman 1850–1852": this volume has a green cover and contains the entries for 1850, 1851, and 1852.

2. "Diary of Ann L. Hardeman, 1853–1855": this, too, has a green cover, and it contains the entries for 1853 to 1855.

3. "Fragments of Diaries of Ann L. Hardeman 1857–1865": this has a black cover. This volume is less straightforward. It is, in fact, a notebook out of which all the pages (the pages are blue, different from the fragments within) have been cut, except for two leaves, on which there are some penciled mathematics and pasted newspaper clippings. On the back flyleaf is the

name Delia E. Brown (a daughter of the family with whom the Hardemans took refuge in Alabama during the Civil War). Tucked inside are two journals. The first, beginning April 1857 and ending September 1857, is from a volume much like those of the others, except that it is 6¼ by 7½ inches and the cover is missing. The second, beginning August 1863, is smaller, being only 5¼ by 7 inches: it also has its cover missing though clinging to the spine are the remnants, which indicate that the cover was originally gray.

4. "Diary of Ann L. Hardeman 1858–1863": this has a black cover. Contrary to its labeling, however, this runs from 1858 to 1862; also within it are five fragmentary leaves, which run from June 1862 to August 7, 1865.

There are a few entries to be found outside the Stuart Papers. Those for October to December 1866 are in the John Bull Smith Dimitry Papers at Duke University; they are contained in a very small notebook, about 2½ by 4½ inches, bound in cheap yellow paper. The entry for March 28, 1867, is a fragment in the Mayes-Dimitry-Stuart Papers, Mississippi Department of Archives and History.

EDITORIAL PRINCIPLES

In editing I have tried to produce a clear readable text, which omits nothing from the original manuscripts and is faithful to the diarists' original spelling, capitalization, and punctuation. However, as is inevitable, there are exceptions which need explanation.

I have standardized the form of dating for each journal entry. Thus "Teusday 9th" (Ann Hardeman habitually misspelled Tuesday) has become "Tuesday, July 9." Sometimes this has meant reconstructing the date from internal evidence and context. On the occasions when the original text is too confused to make this possible, I have defined the range of options. Hence, for example, in the Hardeman diary a late entry in 1866 begins "June 15th Sat." In fact, June 15 fell on a Friday in 1866, and June 16 was a Saturday. The entry itself does not help to clear up Hardeman's confusion. So the dating reads, "Friday, June 15, or Saturday, June 16." Because of this regularization, I have begun the first word of each entry with a capital letter, even when it was not so in the original.

I have denoted in the text illegible words and torn or censored passages. Hence [. . .] means a single word is illegible and [. . . .] means more than a single word; { . . .} means a short torn passage and { . . . .} means a long one. The passages, censored by excision, are almost exclusively in the Hardeman journal. I have used ⟨ . . . ⟩ to mean a short censored passage and ⟨ . . . . ⟩ a long one. Sometimes, when an excision is very extensive, I have used a formulation like 〈*seven pages*〉 to indicate the length of material that has been cut out. I have placed the material that follows such long excisions in a separate entry, when there is no way of knowing whether such material was written on a different day.

I have added periods when a diarist has omitted them at the end of a sentence, or at the end of entries where she does not have a dash. When a sentence ends well before the end of a line, and the next begins at the beginning of the next line, I have added a paragraph indentation.

I have standarized the lengths of dashes, though they vary wildly in the original manuscripts. I have resisted the temptation to replace dashes with periods, since the former are of the essence of nineteenth-century punctuation. However, very occasionally, where a diarist in a moment of exuberance wrote both a dash and a period, which tends to confusion, I have deleted the dash. Likewise, I have standardized the abbreviations of names. I have lowered raised letters, so that "M^r" is transcribed as "Mr." All words rendered in italics can be assumed to have been underlined in the original.

Occasionally a diarist would put quotation marks at the beginning of a quotation but forget to do so at the end, or vice-versa. In these cases, I have silently remedied the deficiency. I have also inserted missing parentheses.

I have corrected misspellings that seem to result from a slip of the pen, invariably words that the diarist has elsewhere correctly spelled. Very rarely, I have inserted a word, when a diarist has forgotten to do so but clearly intended it. These are denoted by square brackets and set in italics. I have deleted inadvertent repetitions of a word or phrase.

I gave much thought to providing a table of emendations, which would indicate the corrections I have made to the original manuscript. There is much dispute among professional editors as to the scope of such a table. Some believe that it should represent the original manuscript by noting when a word is interlined after another, when another is deleted, when a writer has corrected her spelling, where there is an ink blot etc. I doubt the usefulness of this kind of list for a reader, though (for the aficionado) I have placed a full version of such a table on deposit in the Southern Historical Collection. It is enough to note here that the Ruffin, Selma, and North manuscripts are very clean, with very few corrections made by the diarists. The Hardeman journal, on the other hand, is very untidy, full of corrections and interlineations. Evidently Ann Hardeman policed her journal with care, which is to be expected in a woman who tutored her nephews and nieces in grammar. Even during the Civil War, after getting an orthographically inadequate letter from him at the front, she enjoined Edward to be watchful in these matters: "You have forgotten dear Edward a part of yr school exercises at five years old. . . . you must *learn* it *over again*—remember it is a duty you owe to yrself & to those who *love you* & feel solicitous for your improvement. I know you write under many disadvantages—& I do not regard the *writing* . . . as much as the *spelling* & *placing* yr *capitals properly*—I found the old spelling book just now in the book-case & I cut the *directions* for placing the capitals out—which I send a part of it for yr *instruction* & a part for yr amusement."[1]

These are considerations common to all the journals. Some, however, have posed idiosyncratic problems. The North journal has a peculiarity to do with dates. Beginning on September 3, 1851, North placed dittos on each line in the margin under her dated entry, "Sunday 3 d," to indicate that the text to the right continued to chronicle that same day; if the day's entry ran over to a subsequent page, she put in the margin an abbreviated date, e.g. "Aug 3 d," on the top line and continued with dittos at the right margin of each line until a new day's entry began. I have only transcribed a date at the beginning of each entry. I have also silently corrected an error in her dating. In setting down her record of each day, she gave correct dates until Sunday, August 10, 1851. But then, in switching from her first notebook to her second, she jumped to Monday, August 12, which is incorrect. On August 16 she herself noticed the error and corrected it for subsequent entries. I have given the correct dates for the five misdated entries.

In the Hardeman journal there are some similar problems of dating. Ann Hardeman was, on the whole, a scrupulous timekeeper. But her illness made her tired and perhaps affected her memory and as the journal moved into the 1860s, she was sometimes confused about days and dates. When possible I have cleared up the confusion; when not possible I have defined the range of the confusion. More troubling is that she did not always write entries confined to a single day or, it seems, written on a single day. That is, she wrote what I have come to denominate in my own mind as "rolling entries." They begin by referring to a particular day but go on to a second day, sometimes with warning, sometimes not. When the sense has made it possible, I have split these rolling entries into discrete entries, applicable to particular days. When the sense is too entangled, I have left well alone, merely indicating the range of dates which the entry encompasses. There is especial confusion about dates and entries around May 1860, doubtless due to the onset of her illness.

ANNOTATION

Annotation is an inexact business, to say the least. I have done my best to identify people, books, and quotations. I have not burdened the notes with my sources for this information, since that would be to annotate the annotations. However, a few sources require and deserve comment.

By far the largest category of annotation is the naming of people. I have by no means managed to run down everyone, but enough I think to establish patterns and networks of families, friends, and acquaintances. I have been obliged to become a genealogist, which is a chastening experience for someone who mistakenly thought he knew something about the complexity of the past. For such information, I have relied on the large number of (usually privately printed) works on families that can be found in various archives, especially those in the Mississippi Department of Archives of History and the Tennessee State Archives. The South Caroliniana Library at the University of South Carolina has a biographical file, and generations of South Carolinians have been interested in genealogy, some of it published in the early volumes of the *South Carolina Historical and Genealogical Magazine.* The archives in Jackson have a much larger and more thorough biographical file, which refers names to newspapers and tax records, as well as offering an index to the otherwise inaccessible but indispensable volumes of Goodspeed's *Biographical and Historical Memoirs of Mississippi* (Chicago, 1891). It also has many cemetery records, a few of them published but most in manuscript, as well as the assorted notations of genealogists. Especially useful was the *Profile & Business Directory of the City of Jackson, Ms* (Jackson, Miss., 1860) and the two volumes of William D. McCain's *The Story of Jackson* (Jackson, Miss., 1853), which has a wealth of random information. For the Hardeman journal, I went through the federal census for Hinds County, Mississippi, for both 1850 and 1860.[2] Many names were identified by this method. These can be discerned by the fact that the census has enabled me to estimate an age for persons at the time Ann Hardeman mentioned them. But the ages are approximate, since I have merely taken the ages given in the census and correlated them with the dates of the entries. An age therefore could be off by a year or so, and of course relies upon the unreliable accuracy of the census taker. But it is better than nothing. I also looked through the deed records for Hinds County, gathered conveniently on microfilm at the Family History Library of the Genealogical Society of Utah in Salt Lake City.

The Selma plantation journals posed a greater problem of identification because of the diarist's habit of using initials. Here, too, I used the resources of the Jackson archives, but also the greater knowledge of local students of Natchez. (In the hope of finding the name of the diarist, if other than Margaret Wilson, I went—fruitlessly—through such official records of Adams County as were contemporary with the journal while at the Family History Library in Utah.) Mostly I built on clues, usually the name of a plantation, which led to families and names. A few names being established, the mention of family relationships provided other names. For a while, I considered replacing the initials with the full names of the dramatis personae. But, knowing some names firmly, others probably, some not at all, I would have produced an inconsistent text. Moreover, I grew convinced that the diarist's use of initials was a conscious imitation of Fanny Kemble, and so to alter them would be to sacrifice an essential element of the journal.

THE JOURNALS

The Journals of Elizabeth Ruffin

1827

FIRST JOURNAL

Sunday, February 4, 1827 Church today, sadly disappointed; no preacher in consequence of bad weather; chatted a while with the belles and beau transacted a little money business, a thing unusual with me on preaching occasions; but 'necessity has no law', nor was I solo either, others equally concerned with myself in similar matters—returned over the *middling muddy* roads attended by two *youths* (pardon the *disrespect*) gentlemen rather, tho' I'm sure one has not the advantage of age over me, spent the remaining few hours quite agreeably, considering I was the only entertainer, no easy task to one not gifted with the conversational powers; took leave at twilight, run mad notion to go eight miles but could not by any means be persuaded to stay raining in the bargain; *boys* wont have prudence till taught the necessity from sad experience; this the birth day of a particular friend at present far away; may the many returns be ushered in with joyful anticipations to be eventually realized, with a prosperous and profitable termination—

Monday, February 5 Averaged six words to-day, not more I'm sure, dark, gloomy, and dismal in the extreme, no company all hands from home; dined on a slice of broiled bacon; beguiled away the time enjoying Don-Quixote, wish no greater momentary amusement could it always come anew, hope to spend no more of my birth-days so gloomily and lonely; not an unfavorable omen of future prospects I hope, for I should not be willing to have future joys and expectations partake of the nature and appearance of this doleful day; to-gether with strumming on the piano, sewing, and reading have gotten through the day eat heartily of my supper; doing no violence to my inclination or appetite heaping also twice act as an exhilerative, but of its effects shall see nothing to-night in as much as I voluntarily yield myself to the all powerful Somnus,[1] with whom I'm on very good terms, and to whose influence and sway make no resistance or opposition, but yield ready submission to his welcome calls—Good-night you'ill hear from me again tomorrow—

Tuesday, February 6 To-day equally unpromising with the preceding, notwithstanding its unlikeliness was unexpectedly visited by a *young beau,* Mr ———, must have been very anxious to see to induce him to turn out but; '*Amor vincit omnia,*'[2] (excuse pedantry on the occasion) however appropriate the quotation may be this not for *you* to judge but *myself,* discoursed largely on many subjects, religion, *masonry* on which last theme of the extent of my knowledge you can form some opinion as I'm a woman; if understood; not forgetting a wide expatiation on that *theme* of *themes, Love,* that *exhaustless fund* including its numberless ramifications tho' after all to no purpose in as much as no mutual edification was imparted; but why expect any from an every-day topic rendered almost insipid from a universal resort when all others fail to entertain? why look for amusement or entertainment from repeated recitals of *Cupid*'s machinations; even *he* the god of gods who traverses the world and carries all before him, becomes at times an unwelcome guest from his identical and reiterated contrivances and experiments; after the departure of my visitor, searched in the New-Monthly Magazine, a London periodical work,[3] met with much instructive and amusing matter, the residue of time engrossed with the childish amusement of writing on the damp walls in the drawing-room, hard pushed for employment don't you think? tho' you pronounce me extremely communicative I'm not enough so to initiate *you* into one little circumstance that transpired, and thereby afford you diversion at my own expence; *woman-like,* if I stop not 'twill leak out. Good-bye for the present—

Wednesday, February 7 Amused myself the forenoon painting; completed in the afternoon three letters; little work done you may guess; bothered over the Chinese-puzzles till my patience (which is little at any time) was tried and threadbare, all to no purpose as I succeeded in the accomplishment of very few; eat supper and resorted to sleeping at which business lost no time—

Evergreen plantation as it is today. (Courtesy of David F. Almendinger, Jr.)

Thursday, February 8 Lounged about the house lonesome indeed an acknowledgement never made by me before; ten days now and know not how many shall enjoy this *charming, enviable* solitude; *poor batchelors* hard must their lot be, some excuse to be made for their *many* matrimonial essays hoping thereby to step into a more agreeable situation, notwithstanding they may pronounce the horrors of batchelorship insupportable the change may possibly remove them from the *frying pan* to the *fire;* the trials of matrimony the married are welcome to for me, take my advice and be content with the negative enjoyment attendant on undisturbed *celibacy,* but you say if my experience will testify to and corroborate the truth of my observation you don't know but you might lend an ear to your counsellor, but discouragement can not succeed effectually from merely an *anticipated experimentalist;* but every one to his mind and each enjoy without murmur the consequences—took a walk up the road, in the evening, my usual practice when time and circumstances permit, at which time give free scope to my never-to-be realized imaginations, consequently so much thought indulged to no purpose; tonight Mr Harrison's wedding; unsuccessfulness is no insuperable barrier as we see in this instance patience and indefatigable pursuit oftentimes accomplish our aim; take encouragement *ye professed* and *incorrigible candidates—*

The Ruffin journals: " 'tis bad to be a woman in some things, but preferable in others." (Courtesy of the Southern Historical Collection, Wilson Library of the University of North Carolina at Chapel Hill)

Friday, February 9 Bridal morning not as unclouded as could be wished; portentous I hope of no ill—completed a job commenced five years ago of which sample you may judge of my *industrious habits;* had an ironical compliment paid me recently by —— on my *extreme industry,* would not have him know this fact to confirm his opinion; took a small peep in Tom-Jones,[4] don't be alarmed my delicate readers, am sorry to shock any one of your senses by such an *unlady-like* and ungenteel confession, but entreat not the disclosure—

Saturday, February 10 Spent the whole day lolling and reading; finished the first volume of—shall not say what, but leave you to guess having given you a previous hint; no work done, all things neglected and give place to the strange infatuation of novel-reading so popular with us *silly, weak* women whose mental capacities neither desire nor aspire to a higher grade, satisfied with momentary amusement without substantial emolument, and a piece of *weakness rarely indulged* (laying aside all enjoyment) by the more *noble, exalted* and *exemplary* part of society the men of course who seek alone after *fame, honor, solid benefit* and *perpetual profit:* construe the compliment as you please, exacting not from me an explanation which might be unwelcome to your superior ears—

Sunday, February 11 Would have rode some distance to Church, but disliked going alone—oh! the disadvantages we labor under, in not possessing the

agreeable independence with the men; 'tis shameful, that all the superiority,
authority and freedom in all things should by partial nature all be thrown
in their scale; 'tis bad to be a woman in some things, but preferable in
others, 'tho you may crow over me, and glory in the unlimited sphere of
your actions and operations, I envy you not and would not change with you
to-day—you are now chuckling at my protested and decided *preference* and
request permission to indulge your own opinion of the matter; which privilege I grant you—spent the day (in spite of the non-accomplishment of my
desired and intended project), much to my mind among, other things, read
a cursory account of the religious reformation with all the obstacles and
difficulties to be encountered and surmounted previous to its establishment,
commenced during the reign of Henry the 8th, who supported and encouraged it with all his power and supremacy; sanctioned and assisted by his
successor, but undergoing a complete decline and apparent abolition after
the succession of Mary, whom I left exercising her authority *woman-like,* and
the results and consequences of whose power shall pry into at my leisure.
(Excuse digression)—had a visitor late in the evening, after the discussion
of many stale topics retired: with him came three letters from friends which
of course ensured him a double welcome—don't tell my *confession* if you
please—

Monday, February 12 Was unexpectedly and agreeably surprized at receiving
a box of *oranges not quite as large* as *Calves-heads;* from an absent relative; many
thanks to him for his kind remembrance; dined on another present, a nice
dish of perch, plyed a pretty good knife and fork, being my favorite fish—
did other petty matters not worth mentioning much less being adapted to
the *amusement, attention* and *necessarily consequent edification* of my *literary* and
liberal perusers—

Tuesday, February 13 Completed the volume on the reformation and reflect
with wonder and astonishment on the almost incredible proceedings of that
'bloody-Queen' a most suitable appellation indeed; to what extreme cruelty,
persecution, and martyrdom were carried and that not merely with her
approbation but in absolute compliance with her peremptory commands;
notwithstanding her indefatigable exertions to exterminate the reforming
spirit which then partially prevailed, and to which she was so declared
and bitter an enemy and tho' her influence and authority was powerful as
the reigning sovereign of all England; yet all her endeavors were incom-
petent to the effectuating her most desirable aim; the fury of persecution
did rage universally and violently and her inhuman spirit gloried, delighted,
and sanctioned the spectacle of barbarity and bloodshed; instead of perse-

cution having the wished-for-end, namely the extirpation and destruction of all heretics it had the contrary effect of making them more positive and persevering in the cause of truth and served not totally to extinguish but rapidly increase the light of the reformation and advocates for it; it was confirmed and purified by the ordeal through which the ever-memorable martyrs passed, and the light of their burnings have shed an imperishable and unextinguishable lustre and glory to be handed down to the latest generation, the ashes of martyrdom ought to awaken from stupor and stimulate to effort and industry all professors of Christianity at the present day— The Inquisition in a short time with all its enormities and horrors was established as an effectual method of preserving the Romish faith among the Spaniards; this of course was a most agreeable thing to the Pope, who would have had the establishment of them throughout all Christendom, in order to prevent the circulation and inculcation of any doctrine prejudicial to his interest or derogatory to his dignity. The desire of Queen Mary's ambition appears not to manifest itself in the pleasure of swaying the sceptre of royalty and dominion over the whole English nation, but merely to exercise her influence in the re-establishment of papacy and the utter abolition of all Protestantism—but another of the *faculty* of *Batchelors* has come, so you'ill be reasonable enough (after hearing so much of my tongue) to dispense with my company for the entertainment of my guest of whom you shall hear tomorrow—

Wednesday, February 14 In compliance with the promise of an introduction to my visitor, will proceed to gain your favor (for I know he is a friend universally and if you whoever you may be, are capable of estimating worth must like and receive him as such) by giving him his due, so I'm not backward to express my opinion of his being truly estimable and exemplary, in all things that is as far as my knowledge goes; we talked no *slander* last night or this morning; something unusual isn't it for two to get out of hearing and not to indulge a little in that popular thing particularly in the ladies circle? I shall not say what my disposition was that way; so it was; I met with no encouragement to prosecute a slanderous suit from him, and the consequence was a resort to some other theme for conversation—you may laugh and imagine we had no time to slanderize or discourse on any thing that savored not of a *particular nature;* but you mistake; that *enduring hobby* was rode less than common, 'tis possible you know for people to have presentiments in some things at certain times, and for fear of the inevitable consequence choose to direct the general streams into another channel: this hypothesis is rather unintelligible and would prefer your remaining in ignorance in the matter, so shall not come out explicitly. My companion left after breakfast, quite

sorry to part with him because loneliness makes the time hang heavily—
received some novels by a servant,—from a distant gentleman; thank him
much for his accommodating disposition which all the rest of the sex is
greater under *certain circumstanses* some of which I could name if prudence
dictated—Copied with the best of my *illegible* powers some poetry for a
young Lady, who had once the original but has now to content herself with
a transcript of my intolerable writing; and for her I'm sure the unenvi-
able decypherer of *this* feels a sincere sympathy; I will not fail to tell you
(but promise no explanation) some fearful anticipations were suddenly and
agreeably relieved, by a little accidental circumstance which shall remain
concealed where it is—

Thursday, February 15 Rained incessantly all day; finished a novel and fearing
to offend your delicacy; regarding (among the *refined* of society) my future
standing and *reputation,* and dreading the frown of *overstrained modesty:* I say I
hope, (after the statement of so many *good reasons*), you will excuse me for
not naming it; and pardon and pity my depraved and ungenteel taste for
liking and feeling much interest in it—picked up a number of the American-
Farmer, looked in the 'Ladie's-department', to supply the deficiency in the
'poet's corner'; pored over a long letter from a father to his newly married
daughter;[5] admirable advice it was. with the exception of the part where
she is particularly cautioned against all *endeavors* of getting the upper-hand;
I do not like *that,* she is perfectly excusable in my opinion if she can do
so creditably; *hen-pecked* is a most *charming sound* in my *ears* and wish no
greater evidence of a good, indulgent husband; so you see I've disclosed my
matrimonial aim, and thereby warn my *youthful readers* in case of *possibilities;*
don't admonish me 'not to kick before spurred' which conclusion you must
draw from my unnecessary and timely admonition—A walk in the evening
twilight—hour engaged on the Piano: had almost forgotten to tell you the
present of a fine wild Turkey killed by —— done all I shall do to it; dried
and prepared the wings for summer resign my share to any epicure that will
come for it; eat plentifully of the oranges which are fast decaying, sorry for
the circumstance, but glad of the excuse to *stow away*—

Friday, February 16 Cannot with truth say I've done any thing all day; the
fine, lovely morning drove me out the house to enjoy recreation; met with
a thesis on Hypochondria, perused it to satisfy myself about its causes and
effects; curiosity and interest excited because some cases of it are among my
acquaintance, if they would read that (for I'm sure it must be a burlesque)
they would be ashamed afterwards to feel and acknowledge themselves so
completely the dupes of imagination; he makes it to originate altogether in

fancy and have not the least shadow of reality—Took a *perpendicular* game with the battle-dores, had no one to join me; went in the garden in the evening and conversed awhile with the most audible and distinct Echo I ever heard, owing I imagine to the peculiar state of the atmosphere; the result of the *conversation* between *us* was a general alarm among the servants, who all ran to inquire who was wanting, and what's the matter; think I'll debar myself the satisfaction and *edification* of such *dialogues* if the consequences are so terrifying—

Saturday, February 17 Saturday being usually a day of *jobbing* have done nothing of any importance; repaired a book which was pretty much dilapidated and worsted from use, covered it neatly and value it highly because a present from brother; quarrelled and scolded one hour in the morning because things went a little awry; wrote a letter in the evening, and discharged a commission to my *Agent* in Petersburg to transact some business in the Dry-Goods line; took a walk in which I heard the hounds in a chase at the distance of 4 or 5 miles so serene and tranquil was the evening—

Sunday, February 18 Spent the day reading chiefly my Bible; received both political and religious intelligence through the papers as usual; got also a number of the Evangelical Magazine in which Mr Rice's vindication against the Bishop's assertion is warmly and widely pursued;[6] received another number of the National Preacher a periodical publication edited in N.Y[7]—had the company of a friend and relative in the evening, listened to a detailed account of his amusing manouevres and peregrinations; betrayed himself and 'let a *certain cat* out of the bag', made one of the trio which without reserve discoursed *vociferously* in endeavoring to substantiate declared sentiments, much originality in the expression of same; combined they tried to extract from me some *clandestine matters,* but will not trouble my readers with a repetition of such nonsense, into which I yielded a voluntary disclosure for their momentary amusement, after the interchange of much opinion broke up for the night, and am now forced without even a similar pleasure to part with you—

Monday, February 19 Mr[8] took leave of us and his absence revived the solitude and loneliness as before; did nothing all day but worked hard; suffered an unaccountable sort of depression of spirit, indescribable in its nature and hope only temporary in its effects; received three letters, one quite complimentary whether earnest or ironical can not say; got an *untangible* testimonial of regard in the form of a verbal message, such things cost little, of course regarded as little.

Tuesday, February 20 Read in bed by the first glimmerings of light a letter handed me, (quite an epistolary character of late) take me an age to answer them all, made however a commencement by discharging one; I forbear to dwell on the after circumstances of the days unpleasant and painful in the extreme; suffice it to say a detail of them would create little interest, and produce less reciprocity of feeling and sentiment from an unsympathetic reader—you don't understand me, therefore will cease this mysterious and unintelligible jargon; 'tis distressing to reflect on the unavoidableness of past, unpleasant events but trust to tonight's sleep to restore previous feelings, should it prove effectual (which I doubt not, so successful is it generally, as a restorative *panacea* in all my diseases) you may hear from me to-morrow; if not, my temper and mood will be so unconciliating, you'ill be glad to get rid of my company—

Wednesday, February 21 Feel much better to-day after shedding a few relieving tears; Thaddeus of Warsaw[9] put me in quite fine spirits highly interested in it; should have gone off in a 'green and yellow melancholy' but for that fortunate and timely preventive—Mrs[10] has returned home, to my great joy; brought some pleasing intelligence along, doubly welcome of course; attended to the transplanting of some young trees; know they will not prosper because under my unauspicious and unfortunate direction; watch gone wrong, no such thing as regulating it properly; miss it as a *companion;* bought a blank-Book in which I intend to amuse myself making transcriptions and insertions after my own fancy: discharged some money accounts—

Thursday, February 22 Did little else than *devour* poor Thaddeus which was enjoyed to the very last morsel, was truly sorry when he was *consumed,* but would not have his trials prolonged if possible for my exquisite enjoyment; am really quite ashamed of reading so much unprofitable matter; emolument gives place to amusement to my great shame, and temporary entertainment preferred before substantial benefit; I find it not only time thrown away irrevocably but seriously injurious in the end; it incapacitates the mind for the reception and digestion of more indispensible intellectual food; history is rather indigestible after so delicious and palatable a feast; quite sufficient to produce the *dyspepsia;* much delighted to find some imaginary cause for being in the universal fashion; considerably honoured and exalted at being ranked among the *dyspepticks* heard two pieces of intelligence too good I fear to be true, wish they had a little surer foundation, sandy a one as they have am half way inclined to give credence; time is an infallible tell-tale and will divulge secrets undesired by the interested and concerned—

Friday, February 23 Took a long, lonely ride to church, was disappointed in not having M—— to accompany me as was promised; but perfectly excusable on the score of the unlikeliness of the day; was highly gratified, and fully compensated for my ride; the Bishop pretended to nothing like elegance or oratory but the discourse was excellent, plain, intelligible and suited to the comprehension of the lowest capacity, brought forth many simple illustrations to exemplify the subject so perfectly clear and applicable as to exclude all possibility of a misunderstanding; was importunately pressed to dine at —— with M——, declined; not from inclination, but could assign some other cause if I chose; reached home to dinner attended by a *trio* of the *boys;* habits of long acquaintance and intimacy have from me deprived *them* of the rightful *address* of Mr, and am afraid that should they attain to the age of Methuselah, even that degree of antiquity would not command so respectful an *address* from me in common; parted with them in the evening each to their respective homes—was informed to my astonishment Mr C was a Candidate for the next election; wonder what the *wives* think of such things, 'tis well they have not me to deal with, should be sure to *rail* a little, that is, if I'm to be left behind—

Saturday, February 24 Parted with a visitor more profitable and convenient than all in as much as he employed himself making me pens enough to last an age, much obliged to him, for they were truly needed—Copied 300 lines don't give me credit for so much perseverance hand now aches from the cramped, awkward manner of holding my pen—had a considerable hurricane this evening paling blown down, windows to pieces, ladders prostrated, water streaming, will name no more evils; after all saw the sun set unobscured by a cloud and a lonely Rainbow which rendered the scenery quite picturesque and romantic; wrote a letter, saw neither needle or thread, and busily engaged all day doing nothing of the least consequence—

Sunday, February 25 Went to Church; met with —— at the fork of the road, according to appointment; an unusually large audience on the occasion, heard another capital discourse, but might have expected something superior, tho', from a higher order of profession, generally speaking—(not intending to cast any reflection or derogate at all from the ministerial character of the denomination) there is little edification to be received from Methodism, so mistaken is their notion of disapprobation in Theological researches and attainments as being altogether incompatible with clerical duties; 'tis not expected that our own personal feeling, conviction, and conversion should be as powerful an instrument in convincing the reason and enlightening the understanding as a greater degree of Biblical knowledge would be; to be sure, no one rule holds universally; there are some who differ widely in opinion and set themselves to investigate the matter by attention to the Scriptures, accuse me not of prejudice or bigotry; all right to any such accusation I disclaim I am not; only lament the prevalence of such an erroneous opinion and wish it were otherwise for general benefit— returned to dinner bringing along *much folks,* among the number a widower 'tho unknown at the time, I mean the *circumstance* of his *widowerhood,* which piece of ignorance caused us to give him a few hard rubs, made some woful mistakes about the *friskiness* of such characters, and once had recourse to him to decide some case, the privilege granted him on the score of his *present matrimonial state,* which unfortunate reference initiated us into a state of right things and afforded much diversion party broke up and dispersed in the evening—

Monday, February 26 Spent four hours in the cold painting, rather than incommode the rest with my apparatus; that completed made some insertions in my Blank-Book; no reading; little work; some strumming; heard to-day I was certainly engaged to three gentlemen; people are determined to make ample provision for me in that line; feel much indebted to them for their extreme liberality, trying I suppose to *tempt* me to relinquish my notion of *perpetual celibacy,* but such temptations as a catch of either of the three, great as they may seem, shall be resisted, for in the first place two never suffered me to cross their minds, and the other wheel I should like to spoke in it if they will allow me the privilege; they seem to take a peculiar interest in my future welfare, rather they are endeavoring to deter me from all the anticipated horrors of *old-maidenhood*—but I'm not so easily frightened, and know which 'side my bread is buttered' the sweets of independence are greatly preferable to that *charming servitude* under a lord and master; the horrors and disagreeables of anticipation are enough for me; I hope never to *enjoy* the reality; this is a sad predicament to be in don't you think? dread to yield freedom, render obedience, and pay homage to any *one* or the other and only alternative, sad one indeed, bearing and groaning under the curses and stings showered on the *superannuated sisterhood;* no I'll not put up with either, there is still one other refuge to hide in; shall bid you all adieu and take my departure to Georgetown (say not a happy riddance if you please) and spend the residue of my days in that monastery; don't you approve my plan? should you live long enough you'ill see the reality of my intention.

Tuesday, February 27 Much disappointed at not going to Church prevented by unlikely weather; halted some time between inclination and prudence, and as an exception to my general rule yielded to the dictates of the latter;

something unusual indeed; my nature is so unreasonable and obstinate that all powerful inclination ever carrys the point in defiance of all other more rational motives, 'tis not the only time in the course of my life I recollect *one other* at present and 'tho prudential motives forbid my telling; you will nevertheless believe me and give me all the credit I deserve; circumstances in my own opinion entitle me to a double share; but I'ill stop; commenced the last of the Mohicans,[11] do not find it transporting so far, and hope the prosecution of it, will more enlist my interest—

Wednesday, February 28 While reading, was surprised by B——'s [12] stepping in on a pretence of a little business, but in reality only a plea to see us; (see our vanity; woman-like) that urgent matter negotiated, set out again; quite a town-visit only an hour or two; but I forget, the customary mode of visiting, fifteen minutes is excessively ungenteel, and unfashionably long, this was a day in comparison. pursued my novel, found it much more tolerable than yesterday; completed a piece of work, really the employment of not more the three days, but made out to accomplish it in a fortnight; (another specimen of my industry you have;) marked a number of eggs to put under the hens; troublesome things, will not rear their families with my necessary interference; well 'tis better to act in the capacity of setter, than something else—

Thursday, March 1 Been reading an *Essay* on *Old-Maids*·[13] (never heard of the work before quite voluminous too) hoping to glean some little comfort for my present and future destiny, but Oh! the horrors attendant in the description; am almost persuaded to abandon the idea of enlisting myself among the honorable sisterhood; but stay 'tis only the dark side of the picture, that is so appalling, the virtuous shines with a brightness heretofore considered impossible; I mean notwithstanding the many disagreeables that the illiberal, uncharitable world attribute to them, they are nearly balanced by some admirable virtues; feel quite comforted in the reflection that it is *even possible* one single excellence, or good quality can be attached to *Old-Maidism:* I don't like the anonymous author of this publication, he is a complete 'wolf in sheep's clothing' making as many professions of disinterested kindness, and friendly feeling, declares himself a firm supporter, sincere admirer and ready advocate of the whole race, all the while would have the whole set exterminated if he could; in spite of his well-wishing and extreme admiration takes pains to spare them not, (a singular method I think of manifesting our regard for any thing, exposing every foible to the public, if any gross ones do exist and if not, supplying their place with such as our imagination paints to be applicable) and tho' he's obliged sometimes to give them their just due, it goes against his very grain; you will see I have a sympathy in reserve and being myself a noviciate for the state, feel it my duty to defend their cause, and resent their insults in time; that *necessity* when driven to it may not be the only ground of defence, but by this previous *step* secure to me a little virtue in the matter—

Friday, March 2 Finished Last of the Mohicans; can't say much in commendation of it; 'tis of a most ferocious nature as you may suppose, and presents an exact delineation of the Indian character, mode of life, and nature of disposition; I imagine 'tis nothing uncommon for such to exist as the hero was represented to be, (for the author attached no superhuman qualities to him as their usual custom is in the description of so conspicuous ones as the hero and heroine), his virtues and magnanimity would put many a civilized being to the blush, for the last of his acts was the loss of his own life in defending a descendant of the cruel and merciless white man's which source had originally been the cause of all their disgrace and suffering; it ends horridly and the Indian trait of revenge is pictured and evinced to the very last—

Saturday, March 3 Said, done nor thought any thing that will bear a repetition, or undergo an inspection; did some matters in the line of work of little moment and contrived some how or other to get through this day like many previous ones, without the least advantage to myself; 'tis a lamentable truth that my time glides away mispent in fruitless projects, *intended* better purposes, and more profitable and beneficial ends; but so it is; this intention *in reserve* will not answer; we are forever reaching out to the time when these things are to be accomplished, which time is delayed from one more convenient season to another, till we find to our ruin that procrastination has proved fatal indeed, and the close of life finds us no nearer the accomplishment of our designs than when they were originally plan'd; I know 'tis so with me; the hope of anticipated usefulness is all that I can indulge, the charming reality has not been experienced or enjoyed yet—

Sunday, March 4 Went to Church; am uncharitable enough not to feel myself compensated by the sermon, for the cold, comfortless ride; it was truly evangelical and that is saying more for it than many a one I've heard: the Gospel in its most simple attire is most agreeable to me, the spotless purity and merciful nature should ensure it universal admiration and reception, not to mention any of the advantages that accrue to the individual who embraces it; certainly 'tis much more pleasing to the ear when its simplicity is embellished with the (in my opinion) indispensable accompaniments of literature and delivery; human nature requires the gratification of some other organs, to-gether with the means of convincing and determining the judgment and reason; and the superficial appearance of oratory and eloquence tickles our ear, and gains our approbation, oftentimes more than solid argument—

Monday, March 5 Took leave of home for some days, glad I've quitted it for the sake of my already heartily tired reader, hope during my stay to find something to vary the dull monotony of daily and domestic scenes—united in my *undefatigable brother's search* after knowledge (so true is the adage, 'the more we have the more earnest we will be in attaining more', but so good a thing as intellectual improvement, who can complain of superabundance? wish sincerely they would be generous enough to bestow the unnecessary superfluity on some of the deficient ones, myself for instance) by recommencing with him an old and since much neglected study; French; quite delighted with to-days progress and success; anticipate less pleasure in to-morrow's as every step plunges us in new difficulties, and I fear with me insurmountable consider it quite a misfortune that circumstances debar me of the pleasure and profit arising from similar pursuits with him, the advantage of breathing the same atmosphere would be great, for even the most disinclined genius could not help inhaling some little of the spirit by which he is surrounded, and becoming assimilated (in some little degree) with those whom situation compels to associate with; ambition in a moderate measure is necessary to the attainment of exaltation in any and every station; don't mean we are to sacrifice all other motives to ambitious ones, but there's reason in all things, and where this principle (particularly necessary in youth) is excited and encouraged by precept and example, the benefit is obliged to be felt. I hope neither he nor any one else will suppose the least compliment is intended by the expression of these observations; but for fear he should *be exalted above measure* (laying aside all I've said) from a *recent and barefaced compliment* lately appearing in the public paper (indebted too to the *printer* I imagine, a poor source at best) I only tell them all they have seen the *best side* of the *picture,* and the other side when closely examined will be found as replete with blemishes and deficiences as any of ours, and of course measurably disentitles him to much of the commendation apparantly merited by the *exterior*—but I'll tell no more tales on him—

Tuesday, March 6 Did little else than pore over my French exercise all day to but little advantage I fear, can't for my life retain in mind such parts as are indispensible to proceeding, half the time taken up with referring to rules thought were perfectly known and would if necessary be properly applied; but sadly mistaken; so it is wrong and blame lies between bad memory and little knowledge; nothing like practice and ass.duity, wonders have been achieved by them and thus encouraged do not despair—'tis a sad truth that *age*'s unwelcome arrival will make havoc among the original competent abilities of *youth* to which fact I'm a living testimony—willing you see to screen natural deficiences under any cloak—a complete contradiction this: now deny what was just before admitted; that liberal nature had not been sparing in her powers; (such instances are often with me).

Wednesday, March 7 Another forenoon's feast of charming and delicious French Exercise—had the pleasure of Mr H's company in the evening a most entertaining, agreeable, jovial man; a most zealous advocate for matrimony; recommended it to me in the most rapturous and enthusiastic manner as being the only earthly supportable state of existence—my intended celibacy was ridiculed and hooted out of company, found no admittance at all tho' pleaded as warmly for as could a *voluntary, optionary* old-Batchelor, or Maid was represented as being the most despicable, detestable character under the sun—so you see the description was almost terrifying enough to shake the firmest resolution, and escape (if possible) that *indescribably horrible situation,* but I'am not a proselyte to his opinion yet, because tho' he has had a fair opportunity (more than comes to the lot of half) of testifying to the excess of the *bitters* and *sweets* of what is not unfrequently termed 'Connubial felicity' (how justly can't presume to say) yet he undertakes to present the other without ever having tried the *bearableness* of it himself; Oh! no; he can be no judge of the state: his horrors are all imaginary, and had batchelorship been his allotment his railings would have been less justly founded and experience less alarming to others—Let me have a verbal testimony in the person of an ancient, tried, member of the *sisterhood* or *fraternity* against; then may be I'll weigh both matters more equitably—By B's solicitation went to see his newly discovered Marl-banks, and whilst his interested tongue spared not words of commendation, his ears open to every thing like a foretelling future beneficial results, and his very eyes appeared *charmed* and *dazzled* with the *transcendant beauty* and *lustre* of the sight; I for want of science, and experience could form not the least conception of its *invaluable nature,* and saw nothing at all but a mixture of pulverized shell and sand, which would never have attracted notice or attention from me—

Thursday, March 8 Lolled on the bed half the day pretending to study but was quickly overtaken by a nap of sleep (the unavoidable consequence, sure as I indulge) took up accidently Peregrine Pickle [14] you may guess not *intentionally,* since books of that *character* are ever shunned by the *fair sex;* more especially by such *purity of sentiment,* and *refinement of taste* as my own uncommon *degree* (unobjectionable in every respect); as every *one can testify w*ho has seen the contents of the first pages—March winds have set in most furiously; room is now rocking like a cradle; stand in need of no such *lully-by* to create a disposition already more so inclined than is agreeable or desirable—

Friday, March 9 Last night's wind acted as no opiate, but had the very contrary effect; laid awake what appeared to me half the night; a thing heretofore considered almost impossible from any cause, not even a supposed *Love one,* which experimentalists assert to operate so; am rather incredulous towards that assertion, in as much as it may be made without a liability of detecting its truth or falsity—Cupid must be much more powerful in his operations than is ordinarily seen, to usurp the prior claim of Somnus over me who is *generalissimo* over all the minor powers pertaining to me, and mine—Apricots all in full bloom to be killed by the first frost: just like some of my own schemes, in fancy almost accomplished, when the unexpected occurence of one unfavorable circumstance will nip and blast it forever: however my Stoicism is sufficient for these real or imaginary disappointments which leave no legible impression behind and consequently can't have much reality.

Saturday, March 10 Ruffin [15] returned from school, absent all the week; don't know which is the fullest of study in many different forms, he or his father; two gentlemen in the evening all laughed and talked so much, and merrily almost forgot had to come home; started however after delaying and made haste to reach here which did not do till very late had a considerable frolic on the river shore in the form of an *old fashioned fish-fry,* old times revived— I mean because the ladies were permitted to participate in the fun; the occasion was Mr Peter Jones's birthday, he wouldn't invite me and had I have known my volunteers would have come forward dare say should have been of the number myself—had the sole and compensatory satisfaction of seeing the company *tiffled of* in their best bib and tucker streaking across the field; felt quite concerned for fear the wind which was high should disorder their dress; to the agreeable amusement of *picking fish* was added the sailing excursions which makes me quite envious of their pleasure—

Sunday, March 11 Found all at home as usual; missed some company, and two invitations to dine out during my absence: compliments of the kind come so seldom 'tis unfortunate should have been out the way, especially as 'twas a bridal occasion—came across some old Sermons among a parcel of rubbish, written sixty years ago, and are admirably composed; both style and matter vastly superior to some of our modern productions—

Monday, March 12 Fretted and fumed over my French; first attempt without any assistance, can't possibly succeed shall have to abandon all hope of final success as an impossibility—spent the whole undivided attention, and the only profitable or encouraging result was a violent headache—the benefit of which (as a disinterested favor) will freely dispense with to accommodate some more needy friend—Rained incessant—all day—promises this evening a clearing-off from the direction of the wind—blessed or rather cursed most heartily the intolerable garlic with which my milk was so highly flavored and perfumed and of course am obliged to debar myself of a favorite luxury—

> Elizabeth Ruffin—
> Evergreen—
> Prince George—
> Virginia
> These caPitals Rightly cOmbine if You cAn
> tHey'ill exPLain what both Honors and dignifies maN[16]

SECOND JOURNAL

Journal from Prince George to the North cannot say where now—as the route is still undetermined

Sunday, July 29 After much endeavor to appear sorely distressed at leaving home (tho' glad in heart for once, but not more so than they I fancy) arrived at Coggins[17] (not forgetting to ment on a week of preparation which ended in a complete topsy-turvy of every thing) whence we quickly collected our luggage to the point where we had the pleasure of waiting only two hours on the shore for the arrival of the Boat which did come about eleven at the display of our signal not one but both came in, much against our wish (and which by the way was a foolish and unnecessary piece of trouble) but which compliment in a measure compensated for a previous disappointment; after being roughly handled and almost shouldered (rude and uncivil usage indeed for a lady of my consequence) was thrust in but kindly receiv'd by the master who is not at all "backwards in coming forwards"—all strangers; but as usual laying aside all ceremony for the time became 'hail fellows, well met' the trip was pleasant and scenery diversified for a long distance—but Hampton Roads—it will retain a place in my recollection if all things else should give place almost sick unto death; feel perfectly satisfied with pleasantness of rocking; crossed the Bay mostly in the night saw but little of its grandeur tho' a plenty to make a top of my head: passed the N.C. 74 too late to have a fair view of her size or appearance.[18]

Monday, July 30 After a night (may the like never be *enjoyed* by me again) of much vexation found ourselves still almost at sea: land scarcely perceptible, continued on till we reached Dover (Capital of Delaware) 4 o'clock in the evening; took there the fine line of stages, travelled 45 miles at a rapid gait; horses changed every ten, driver also; a most expensive business it is, only 20 drivers and 80 horses employed by the five stages: found it quite a relief for awhile but twelve at night brought very different feelings along; no rest for a nodding, bumping pate, stuck out till 'twas useless to try any longer and by a violent effort roused myself to enjoy and amuse myself at the truly pitible situa—of those around me. Delaware is a remarkably level country scarcely an elevation of six feet the whole distance we went; as to the nature of the soil, sentence was frequently passed by the 'Extrologists' present on its uncommon sterility; crops of Corn (this late hour) knee high only; not all, but a goodly deal of it—Got on board the Franklin went up the river (Delaware) tho' almost taken up bodily and carried off by gallanippers[19] in whose charming company we spent the whole night. so cool in the stage were obliged to collect the cloaks for comfort so different the temperature of the climate—I forgot to mention the most interesting sight yet seen, which was Sunday evening in the Roads the meeting of the four Boats in that expanse of water and the necessary proceeding, the deaf'ning noise, the thorough exchange of passengers, the scene of confusion altogether presented a spectacle so entirely new and awfully grand I was transported beyond measure; all abreast, and apparently touching as they dispersed their bright lights were added to the ships and produced a distant illumination—

Tuesday, July 31 Travelled, since I went to sleep in seven hours, a hundred miles (this is really magic-work) met another Boat (Philadelphia) crowded company, and a display of the City-fashion going to N.Y.—we too landed and are now (hard to realize) in this famous and long heard of place; taken up lodging at the U.S. Hotel, opposite to the superb and costly marble Bank; have not taste enough to admire it myself, being according to my notion a clumsy, disproportion'd and unsightly building—pillars almost all the way of a size, no symmetry or beauty about them: we are as private here as possible, have a chamber and sitting room at our service, go and come as we please but not quite as independent in some respects as the inhabitants (ladies particularly—) after our breakfast eight o'clock, went out shopping carried brother along and entertained him agreeably over the counter no doubt increased his *natural fondness* for the employment by introducing him to the millinary and mantua making department. give him a deal of credit for exercising such strain'd patience, had to stop occasionally to laugh at his piloting, got lost, bewildered and turned about a few times; the morning business all transacted after resumed our excursions for amusement, first visited Peale's Museum [20] and here I would not disparage it by an attempt at description; saw every thing and nothing both nature and art in every form, for we had not time to examine much minutely, but took a slight glimpse at all such a variety always disorders me and incapacitates me for the enjoyment of any unless time amd circumstances would admit of entire satisfaction from examination, tho' highly entertained, my eyes were so unaccommodating as to grow dim and become satiated with seeing for the time: from there we promenaded some beautiful streets (don't know their names, and should not learn their situation in three months) saw some splendid edifices among them the Arcade or new museum built entirely of stone and a quantity of glass, the top being entirely of it looks elegantly and will draw of itself (laying aside the curiosities) no few spectators; the market-house is really worth seeing; it extends a mile in length, right in the middle of the street frequented all times of the day where the women are always ready to receive customers and when not thus engaged, are sewing or knitting by their baskets, never idle I believe they do two-thirds of the business in the whole city, never saw such indefatigable creatures, on the pad all day and walk till eleven at night up and down the long streets, unattended by any gentlemen and seem neither to want. wish nor notice them they have a most peculiar gait (the real ton) strides 'few and far between' indeed and tho' I should have no objection to getting along rapidly yet could not purchase it at the expense of so much ungracefulness, no wonder their feet are so large and spraddling some actually appear as if they had been hammered to incredible dimensions; enter the Stores and the women are only to be seen, manage all matters and almost carry on the whole exclusively, as to the men concerned they are things of nought, negative, unconcerned, insignificant, and seem to have no part or lot in the matter—Cleanliness is really astonishing, the streets every one are regularly swept and the brick part not only swept but nicely washed and brushed and tho' the market-house is never free of eatables from the most delicate to the grossest, still there is not the least unpleasant or offensive smell about it, litter and scraps being instantly removed. I admire this independence much among the females tho' carried rather too far, (driving a cart for instance) and think when I return I shall be induced to venture much farther on old Turtle. Met with Mr Campbell [21] and was delighted to see an acquaintance in these foreign parts and who attended us through this evening's ramble. The town clock is striking two and I still up—

Wednesday, August 1 Rose this morning at 6, so had only 4 hours sleep; would not do at home with so little and tho' not having slept more than 24 hours since we started (something unusual for me) feel no inconvenience at all; so much for excitement and novelty—There were only a dozen visitors to wait on us this morning (deserve none of the compliment myself) but am indebted to the company that kind fortune has thrown in our party—however a visit of five minutes was all we had to bear and can't say with truth, regretted their departure in the least—Strange customs here indeed; tho' we are boarding here in very capital Hotel in all the city and many others also we never see or hear a living creature except one or two servants and they appear not but at meals, or particularly rung for: every thing still as midnight and no sort of intercourse or communication among the boarders; however 'tis very agreeable to me; for when otherwise disposed we can walk where we will both see and be seen; we went this morning in a store, spent about two hours pleasing our eye in a variety of articles; all sorts; toys, jewels, engravings we got nothing but a few caricature paintings; great as was the temptation: saw there a most beautiful Grecian lady a brunette, but the most perfect regularity of feature and the true characteristic profile— went to the Academy of fine Arts and tho' enraptured with the museum it lost much of its beauty and excellency when compared with the other; the most elegant and superior Paintings besides the variety of Statuary, all of which must be seen to be enjoyed, so will leave them to the enjoyment of its visitors: from there continued our walk through many streets viewing their splendor; returned to tea, after which we started again and so formed a part of the fashionable promenaders on Chesnut Street, the place of most general resort for exercise and my feet are now aching from fatigue, not that they are deficient in size at all (being pretty substantial) but are some way unaccommodated for the custom: the streets do indeed look most inviting; the stores are all illuminated but the brightness of the glass-establishments is dazzling almost to blindness—

Thursday, August 2 To-day have been complimented by the particular visit of a young gentleman, but unluckily was not in, all the same tho' to me: but who should we have with us last night but the President of the U.S.[22] dear me! how grand it sounds! occupying the same house with so august a personage: to be sure I had no *kiss* from La Fayette, but will console myself by deeming this a tantamount substitute, but must stop about him for fear of the accidental slip of one *little matter* and so spoil the whole. Had an alarm of fire which called out the Engine and so had a passing glimpse of it, enough tho', to see the contrast between it and ours—went out shopping in the morning and witnessed habits so strange to me; for instance; entered a Shoe-Store, business carried on in a large scale and managed entirely by the females who not merely *sew* them but *sale* them too with their delicate hands not a male to be seen behind many counters and just step to the door and you may see one, single man seated up in a fine carriage (bumping from side to side) riding about for pleasure, a singular reverse of things to me, but every one to their fancy—this evening took a ride about the suburbs of the city and admired much of the scenery on the Schuylkill. Read a lesson with brother in French: parted with Mr C and am closing the day amid a scene of confusion: another fire! bells ringing, people hollowing, engines rattling: all out now and so will go to bed (twelve o'clock) tho' the ladies are still walking up and down the street all alone, and quite unconcerned—

Friday, August 3 Really I am getting right tired of Philadelphia; can't get any waiting on, obliged to do it my self, not so agreeable to me but that not the chief cause of impatience, my eyes have seen till they are saturated and can do their part no longer; my ears satisfied with the sound of bells, rattling of drays and other music a little more melodious and now am ready, willing and anxious to be off: no, not so either, yet, because Sunday is not over from which hope to derive much enjoyment; feel mightily afraid the sermon will not benefit me much because of the splendor and elegance of the interior execution and no doubt would be most awfully alarmed but for the fortunate preparation of having witnessed architecture no less grand—the would-be consequence of so much Prince-George rusticity and ignorance. the first thing done this morning was to see West's painting at the hospital [23] which could not fail to give every one pleasure except brother (that *one by himself* in all things) tho' I will not say a single word against him in any matter whatever, for he has left his *old self* at home and assumed altogether a new character (wonderful metamorphosis surely—) so attentive, so accommodating and even now is groaning under sacrifice and self-denial for my convenience, or in other words wait on some mantua-makers for the completion of my Dresses all too without murmuring or scolding in the least; who will believe me? certainly no soul at home but (incredible as it may seem) 'tis even so, and none shall say for the future he *can't* be gallant before me without a word or two in his favor and for fear my favorable report to others and frequent mention to him of his admirable performance should have a contrary effect will cease my commendations. I think I've digressed a little from the painting—to return; it is in my opinion a most superior and interesting representation, highly gratifying to me— this evening we rode to view the water-works at the Schuylkill; a wonderful specimen of human ingenuity indeed alike beyond my powers of description tonight again we attended a sort of exhibition where were displayed; 'A big tree', a Condor and seventy Rattle-Snakes (interesting things for ladies to wait on) so closes this day—

Saturday, August 4 Have not known what to do with myself the whole day; no society within doors, tho' every room in the house filled (an apparent contradiction) but 'tis a fact; every one keeps within his own limits and manifests no disposition to encourage sociability. Oh! I would not live here for a trifle: I've often heard these Northerners borrowed their frigidity of temperament from the climate, however true it may be in general; certain it is the cause does not exist at this present time, for the heat is almost great enough to do any thing but warm this people, therefore the change should be mutual. I would most cheerfully relinquish their company if walking (in any sort of comfort) was granted me: as perfectly and over satisfied as I am with my delay here, it amuses me to see the ennui and disgust endured by brother for my accommodation altogether tho' he keeps it to himself and bears the cross like a philosopher and only threatens me now and then to make my purse suffer for it; we both parted with our room-mates to-day; a gentleman and his daughter from Carolina who have been of our party all the while and which circumstance has made the blank wider: the most unusual thing I saw to-day was a very decent woman seated up in an old fashioned-carriage in the seat I mean driving it with a very good pair of horses of which she appeared to have perfect command and not at all disconcerted at her conspicuous situation (this is a genuine independence in truth, such as we can not boast of, nor likely to aspire to): we went this evening to another gallery of Paintings and really am so satisfied and tired looking at them that I will see no more tho' they would admit me gratis; my sense of seeing is past the point of admiration or enjoyment in that particular: visited and spent half the time till late, in the American-Sunday-School-Union,[24] an interesting and extensive establishment it is—Miss the crier of 'hot corn' I say he is bawling it out now loudly and will be till we are worried with the sound and amused too 'tis a singular fancy indeed, and the time of selling confin'd altogether to the night; the tune generally lasts till bed-hour and *cold* as it may be 'tis still '*hot corn*' with them—

Sunday, August 5 Well the long wished-for day has at last come and gone and must confess my anticipations of enjoyment have not been realized; we went in the morning to *Brother's church* (the Roman Catholic) the first time I ever witnessed the service; strange does it seem to me and not only strange but nonsensical, ridiculous and unmeaning in the extreme, such a repeating of prayers, crossing themselves, ringing of bells under the tail of the Priest's robe, bowing, kneeling, standing, all done in an instant but to all appear-

ance with most profound solemnity and abstracted devotion; am glad we or
rather I am not obliged to go through the same routine of ceremony there
is such constant motion it must be rather tiresome this warm weather: the
nature of the decorations as well as the Priest's attire is indescribably splendid and must be most grand and elegant when illuminated, the whole of the
exercises lasted not an hour; no sermon only Mass brothers disappointment
tho' I believe has excited some notion of apostacy. We from there went to
the Presbyterian Church but got no admittance (another northern custom I
suppose) no getting in after a certain time, thought it very odd to be turned
away from such a place, when with us the eleventh hour was not too late;
'but when in Rome must do as the Romans do'; succeeded this evening
however by going exactly (unintentionally) the other extreme about half an
hour too early. Dr Wilson [25] gave us a profound discourse wholly historical
and less entertaining to me than if the character had been different, but at
best lost one half (tho' deeply attentive) from his low speaking occasioned
I imagine by the debility of his frame, he is evidently a man of erudition
and fluency of speech but his lowness of voice keeps me constantly on the
stretch to catch a single sentence—as to the music 'tis nothing more than
ordinary, but the Catholics have an Organ and brother (who is a judge)
thinks the music most solemn and grand; for my part am so tasteless as
not to admire it—turned out my own church! did not relish the reflection at all, so took occasion to mention the circumstance to the chamber
maid (with whom I was very gracious)—"Ah! madam says she these *Round-
headed stiff Presbyterians* are entirely too particular for anything of that kind";
which was all I got in favor of my party (for my sociability) that time; am
highly amused often with her conversations which are none of the lightest;
went to night to Mr Skinner's Church [26] who is the opposite of Dr Wilson;
the latter mild, persuasive, conciliating and more temperate (apparently) in
his zeal, and is a Barnabas or "Son of consolation" [27] the former zealous,
ardent, peremptory, and more properly a "Boernerges, or son of thunder"
(to use Scripture language) [28] tho' both worthy of their station and ornament to their profession; his Church is most splendid with the addition of a
superb organ—I would not fail to remark here most particularly Brother's
performance to-day, went to Church *four* times; who will credit me? for
which I give him due credit and note it as a memorable event (as yet) in the
career of his existence, tho' hope sincerely he will be guilty of many more
similar ones (however unimportant deemed by him now) 'ere his existence
terminates—

Monday, August 6 Retired last night at twelve, up this morning at 4. how
industrious truly! no 'tis no inclination, but absolute compulsion for the pur-

pose of proceeding on our trip; took the Boat at Philadelphia (a number of passengers on board) travelled all day including 30 miles of stage-conveyance most insufferably hot and dusty (eleven in our group) enjoyed the view of the most superior scenery in Long Island Sound, and now here we are in N Y; the entrance to which is another thing in point of grandeur to Phila tho' it cannot make such a display of elegant buildings as that city; after our tea (the City Hotel our lodging) we took a promenade in the celebrated Broadway the place of parade, fashion, recreation and every thing else I suppose pertaining to fashionable gentility; 'tis indeed a most beautiful sight, the stores most dazzlingly bright, lighted with gas which presents a most brilliant appearance; 'tis well familiarity has abated my admiration of such magnificence or our drawing-room here would cause me to gaze a little, all things corresponding, such as silver tea equipage from which some danger is to be apprehended for my eyes and for all of which we as usual shall have to pay through our noses—

Tuesday, August 7 Had a most charming serenade last night much too short after the noisy, rattling drays stopped which seemed to me to continue most distressingly loud all night; resumed our strolling after breakfast but saw nothing so delighting as my first debut in the Philadelphia Streets, which enjoyment I suppose was attributable to the novelty of such beauties; the Churches here are many with towering steeples and Carriages or rather public hacks the most gay and finished ready to run over you at every step of crossing: wish I may escape for my part with whole bones out of the constant confusion; this evening went to Castle-Garden to see an exhibition of fire-works and indeed was highly worth seeing. my imagination had never conceived that such transcendant beauty and splendor could be presented by an explosion of Gun-powder; the place represents an ampitheatre surrounded by the most beautiful and diversified views; within the circle of the building was the place of exhibition: there could not have been less than twelve hundred persons present what a pity! out of such a number I could not have found a familiar face, but all strangers—how lonesome the very sound! To-morrow by times we continue our journey—how I dread the thoughts of rising so early: but any thing to get off this Broadway—

Wednesday, August 8 Did succeed this morning in getting up at the appointed hour took my leave of N.Y. probably for ever, can't say my sorrow is great for the time hangs heavily enough in these large cities with me—The Boat in which we came to-day is the most agreeable one yet in every thing but the motion which to me was more than usually felt; quite a moving palace within, and the country up the North River more lovely than any I ever saw or imagined; very thickly settled, many elegant private seats, many towns (at all of which we would drop the passengers) and mountains of rock all covered with low growth in their natural state cragged, steep, barren and of course such parts uncultivated; not altogether either for there were many spots at which the attempt had been made tho' to little success; we touched at many towns—Pougkeepsie, Newburg, Hudson, and West-Point which is built right on the top of one of the mountains; curiosity brought several of the cadets to the wharf, all equipped in their simple uniform—Reached Albany just at the hour we left N.Y. 6 o'clock a hundred and fifty more miles to-day; six hundred from home; Oh! what a distance, don't like to think of it—Albany is about the size of Petersburg but shall have no opportunity of seeing it; it boasts of one good thing many Churches rendered conspicuous by their steeples; but can't say much in favor of the agreeableness or cleanliness of the streets: will take occasion to mention one of their customs, that is a male servant lighting Ladies to their chambers; must confess it seemed rather odd to me, neither relished it so well; surely there can be no females ones here at all—

Thursday, August 9 Well here I am at the famous Saratoga Springs after having come 40 miles to-day (in addition to many others) to reach them in the stage too, smothered with dust tho' more agreeable (bad as it is) than the Steam-Boat to me, I am heartily tired of the dullness and identity of that mode of travelling it will do while a novelty, but one quickly becomes satisfied particularly where every thing like sociability and intercourse among passengers are not encouraged as is the case in these Boats, among these phlegmatic people; whether it proceeds from timidity, want of confidence, pride or any other cause I don't know, but so it is they all stand aloof as though they were afraid to make any advances—But is this Elysium, my ears have so long heard? if so, how unwilling would I be to spend my days among this *happy* and *congenial set;* rather let me be glad my lot is cast among the many and nameless agreeables of the *little-Bed* in the Mama's chamber but I'm too hasty in passing sentence we've just reached here and can only say out of a house full there is not an individual whom we've ever seen or to whom we can converse at all so the means of amusement and entertainment are very limited being confined within our own selves as yet this is pleasant, is it not? but enough to night: hope to report more formally to-morrow. Brother has already fled to the circulating library and has (with me) become a subscriber, making provision in case of a *failure* of *present enjoyment,* which, 'tis to be hoped will not continue.

Friday, August 10 Oh! 'Tis much more sufferable than was anticipated and can get along very well, true they are all strangers still but all ceremony must be waived at such places and indeed I find it the only way; I have made advances, they have met half way (some few) and between us have contrived to be tolerably sociable, but others I dare not approach, they look as chilling as isicles: we went in the morning to the library, lounged about awhile, overhauled the books and from there went to see the American Automaton Chessplayer which every one says is an admirable and successful imitation of the European, 'tis to me a wonderful and unintelligible piece of mechanism and singular to see merely a human figure playing a game which requires the exercise of reasoning principle, genius and application; had I never have seen it most fully persuaded in my own mind should I always have been that there was human artifice at work within but the gentleman is particularly careful to open all places for inspection and the whole box appears filled with the machinery, so, if one is concealed he must be a Lilliputian and withal terribly squeezed[29]—Brother has most fortunately met an acquaintance, but he goes to-morrow; so, he will be as far to seek as ever, should he chance not to stumble on others—

Saturday, August 11 Better and better, I mean as it regards my feeling of ease and independence, but some of these customs I do abominate and shall never be reconciled to, for instance; this dressing regularly twice a day; most distressing in truth, and really 'tis such a general thing among the ladies that it causes you to be much more noticed than if you were to appear in the most costly suit, the gentlemen are not so foolish in that respect except the dandies and fops—We are all rung to our meals, assemble in the sitting room and there eye each other till tea is announced at which signal you are apt to fare rather badly without some one to assist you through the crowd; after tea is over you can stay in the public room with the company or retire which you may do without being missed and which is my choice—as you may suppose, tho' not so this evening for I had the pleasure of having my name asked me, after a day's intercourse with a young lady she ventured thus far which gratified me, and relieved me in the difficulty respecting her's, which of course she told me in return, this led to a formal introduction to her gentlemen acquaintance and among ourselves passed an agreeable evening—I believe I get on much better than brother, not withstanding his fondness for talking which should act as an assistant; he brought his *Virginia pride* along with him which does not so well relish an equal footing with any and every one; his first debut at Saratoga was to be enticed and introduced to the place by a Black-leg[30] which I rather suppose sat heavily on him, that together with the possibility of another equally agreeable deed keeps him aloof and to tell a good joke on him his solidity and venerableness pass him as my father! sad indeed! if he looks old what must I seem? one comfort is, all do not see alike—There is such a fiddling and dancing in my hearing now, my ears are almost deafened with the sound: all my fear is they will suffer from the exercise this hot night besides encroaching on the Sabbath which is not far ahead—(I forgot to say brother was entirely ignorant of the character of his then associate).

Sunday, August 12 This morning went to church, can't say I admired the minister exceedingly not quite as much as brother whose admiration for him it seems consists altogether in the freedom and forwardness which he displays towards his people in lashing them for their coldness and back-slidings—this evening went again lugging brother sorely against his will who says he's determined the sin of my not going shall not be chargeable to him, however give him due credit for doing so directly contrary to incli-nation merely for my pleasure—I'm getting on very smartly and have been frequently accosted to-day by my name which sound my ears hail with glad-ness the widowers tho' I think have manifested more politeness and respect for me than any others; don't know why unless my gravity and matronliness entitle me to it, very old ones particularly, but these grown daughters here are much in his way: in his favor the best policy would be to leave them at home—unfortunately for me just as confidence has come to my assistance a violent cold has made me as hoarse as a raven and so spoils my fun for the present, occasioned by my sleeping with the windows open; 'tis now so cold every body is shawled up, tho' the first of August—

Monday, August 13 This morning turned out quite fashionably and etiqueti-cally, paid a visit to some Richmond ladies; the Virginians are unusually scarce here this season nothing but Yankees scarcely who have almost taught me to speak like them, they are vastly agreeable for all that—for the first time went down to the Spring before breakfast not to drink the water as the rest do, but look about the difference in face, form and manner of its frequenters; all the waters are too unpleasant for my taste, a decoction of salt would be just as palatable, tho' some are more pleasant than others; it has one effect which tends to amuse me—The public houses are all filled and daily applications still making who are forced to put up with accom-modation in the suburbs of the town till vacancies are made; they are going and coming hourly and the passing and repassing of coaches almost as bad as Broadway but the main ambition of the men seems to be in trying the speed of their horses, 'tis a wonder to me they do not break their limbs for 'tis nothing strange to see them galloping in harness—Felt so unwell to-day could receive no enjoyment from company—

Tuesday, August 14 This day has been so cold, rainy, and comfortless I've not been out the house and scarcely out my chamber tho' found abundant amusement from my books: wrote a letter home and have become so excessively genteel that the sewing is laid aside entirely, wish the use of the needle may not be quite forgotten during this trip of fashion: had a fresh importation of people in the place of late vacancies: we have here a variety of face, manner, character, and disposition; some inaccessible by every means as haughty, highminded and proud as Lucifer from such turn away with all possible quickness—others agreeable, affable and advancing even Old-Maidism is not excluded from this scene of enjoyment but reigns in all the 'bloom of antiquated virginity' [31]—The Quakers and clergymen form no inconsiderable part of our company whom I overhear occasionally discussing some theological question; not forgetting to mention disease in a multitude of shapes, such as dropsies, loose jointedness, spiny affections and eruptions which make our establishment quite an infirmary—Some of the oddest and most ill-matched couples; young husbands groaning under the galling rein of an old wife who hen pecks him to the nines: young wives making their old husbands look as suitable and young by brushing up his hair and smarttening him up for dinner, sorely against his will—newly married ones billing and cooing like doves, and old pairs so completely outgrown the novelty of matrimony, they might well pass for some of the venerable sisterhood—

Wednesday, August 15 This morning being an agreeable one a party of us took a walk to the high rock-Spring which is really a curious work of nature; the rock itself is conical, except being flattened just at the top which has an aperture whence the water is procured I can't say what the depth is but the water does not rise within three feet of the top but is in a constant state of agitation and moderate boiling, the taste is pleasant, and the carbonic acid gas powerful and fatal in many experiments they have tried: brother could not let so fine a chance slip without satisfying himself a little as to its effects; he lighted a candle and extinguished it by merely pouring out the invisible gas from a vessel which he had lower'd to receive it, he was unsuccessful in his first attempts in consequence of having no suitable apparatus which occasioned much incredulity on the part of the spectators, who (many of them) never had heard of such a thing, and laughed at his attempting such an impossibility: after having succeeded they walked off quite confounded— We had a considerable diminution in our company to-day, only one and a half of the long tables filled and to crown the whole was asked by a young lady to be good enough to gratify her impertinent curiosity in informing her whether that gentleman who was so very attentive to me was not my husband, not that she would have gone so far for her own gratification about the matter, but she had been frequently asked without being able to give satisfaction; who ever would have supposed that the charge of over politeness should have been laid at his door: they are determined we shall be nearly allied as he stands in the place of both father and husband–

Thursday, August 16 No cessation from rain all day, consequently closely confined, tho' it has had the effect of producing an uncommon degree of sociability among us all both paid and received visits in our little apartments, having thrown away everything like ridiculous etiquette, formality and ceremony and feel independent and domestic and expect the longer I stay the more unwilling shall be to leave it. Our usual number of visitors have again made up yesterday's deficiency and the two long tables filled as before tho' the short space of two days seems to effect almost an entire revolution in the company—We have very good fare and variety but nothing can with me supply the place of hot corn bread which delicious article I never felt the want of before, these careful northerners indulge not in the comfort and luxury of hot living because of its injurious consequence towards the health—My Saratoga appetite is nothing to compare to my Charlottesville one, there it was voracious; now 'tis both reasonable and moderate too much so, and usually make my supper on *whortleberries* (a rare dish and delicacy indeed to come so far to enjoy) which tho' gone long ago with us, I believe will last here all the summer, and like all the rest of the fruit I've tried, have no sort of taste in them—

Friday, August 17 To-day have gone through the same routine of eating, sleeping, reading and walking, went out shopping in the morning and fell in with a masonic funeral—one who twenty five minutes before was perfectly well. In the music line we have an abundance, young ladies proficients in the accomplishment, abounding in songs, duets and catches, the last introduced by brother who (from the interest taken and his natural fondness and consequent nearness to the musicians) was strongly suspected of being deeply smitten with one of the lassies, none supposing for an instant he was married, after they had ascertained the fact of my not being his wife; they assembled in a group and most formally came forward for me to corroborate the report, great was their surprise when rightly informed and occasioned no little diversion among all hands, particularly in their acknowledging their distantness and shyness towards him on that account: people's eyes here must be strangely constructed to see so differently about the same matter some add twenty years, others subtract ten tho' he declares the first is a fabrication of my own, but 'tis not in truth, he certainly does excite a deal of curiosity among them, whether his agreeableness or disagreeableness, youth or age, activity or mopishness, smartness or weakness is the cause, I cannot say, but such is the fact, their many conjectures have amused me highly—Met with a gentleman to-day with whom I became acquainted in Petersburg, was glad to see him.

Saturday, August 18 Every day more and more reconciles me to my situation, this place which at first was insupportable and the time to be spent here anticipated with horror, has become very agreeable to me and is to be attributed solely to the pleasant acquaintance formed: this day had been particularly delightful, do not know why unless the general agreement to go to work has contributed to render it so which did make the hours fly more swiftly, this morning we walked some distance among groves of white pine which is a beautiful growth, and very abundant, the Green Mountains in Vermont are distinctly seen from this, and to the eye of the spectator seem to lose themselves in the clouds; there is nothing pretty or inviting about the place besides that I've seen; the town is not large and what there is of it consists principally of public and boarding houses; there is no lack of Concerts either, we have had two to-day but attended neither, the Chess-player and Ventriloquist (not forgetting numberless Rattle-Snakes) are still waiting the pleasure of the people scarcity of amusement procures them encouragement and popularity—Saratoga has only given me a cold, which is not to be gotten rid of; parted with some of our most intimate company among the number our old widower as we thought but behold he proved to be no one at all; this atmosphere has a most singular effect, that of passing off old married ones for single but does not seem to favor our sex in that respect so well, but I defy all powers to juvenile some of us spinsters, we are past the power of enchantment: a sad state of things truly—

Sunday, August 19 This day we have been a Churching-set (many exceptions to be sure) but cannot answer for their satisfaction, only my own; we heard a young man from N.Y who promises to be an ornament to the ministry, his matter very good, style easy and fluent and whole delivery pleasant and engaging, but Oh! this deliberately setting out to read word after word, it makes me hang my head to get any good, the effect intended is half lost on me, which confession would justify the opinion that the matters held only a secondary place—This *afternoon* (for they have no *evening* here) heard a funeral discourse, which character would not have been known by me but for accidental previous information—to-night, (for I suppose eight o'clock may be termed so) received a letter from Petersburg, tho' not from home but acknowledge much pleasure at the receipt of any communication, while out of the world almost; to-morrow a party of us set out on a temporary excursion to that perfection of scenery and beauty as accounts describe Lake George—I've witnessed one rare sight to-day, and not to-day alone, but last Sunday also and that is, a constant washing and ironing from morn till night just in full view of my chamber—why, I did not suppose such a regular practice was any where kept up in this christianized country, but there is no relief for me I fear from such an eye sore, no riddance but my own removal—

Monday, August 20 Well here we are, and indeed we do deserve most richly to be here, and have our eyes feasted with indescribable beauties for all the disagreeables endured by the way; in the first place the Stage was crowded, the day insufferably hot and roads dusty and rocky beyond description, only 28 miles and from nine to six getting here including of course our dining by the way which detained us a little: I'm sick and tired of stages and boats and do not know which is the least of the two evils; in the last, one is rocked to sleep (tho' not so with me, sleep is changed to sickness) and in the other, you are jostled to a mummy and maybe half mashed by a 300 weight piece of mortality; but now for the sights: Glenn's Falls present the greatest assemblage of natural beauties, most unparalleled in grandeur and sublimity in my opinion, tho' they say 'tis nothing in comparison with Niagara which (dame Nature's masterpiece) we shall not see; this scene represents a rude, misshapen, irregular display of the wildest and largest collection of the Lime stone rock and the water rushing in torrents with immense rapidity and the spray rising like impenetrable smoke—with care we scrambled over the mountains of rock which are all heights in the midst of the apparent vortex, also explored two most awful and rugged caverns, which required no little scuffling, clinging and stumbling to penetrate, but brother who is persevering and curious in such matters, led the way which we quickly followed; the interior is only a narrow pass-way just high enough to let you stand erect, walled each side by the rock and so indented by the water it presents one impressed surface cold and the touch to me resembling the dead, but 'tis not worth my while to presume to do justice to such a place—so a truce to it—We afterwards saw another curiosity no less novel and wonderful to me the Cotton-Factory where the picked cotton is taken, carried through every stage and converted into cloth by magic almost; all the operations going on at once in different stories, the water being the ground-work of the unintelligible performance: connected with this, is a sawing machine worked by the same force and how odd it seems to see the huge logs drawn out the water and changed to nice, smooth plank in a trice, all too without any other manual assistance than the working of the machinery which of course is attended to by persons engaged—The Boat starts at 4 in the morning; bell ring at three our signal to rise; but are all anticipating a disappointment to Ticonderoga the place of our destination, in consequence of the rain which pours fast.

Tuesday, August 21 'Tis even as we expected; trip all knocked in the head; how sad! it is, came so far and then not to enjoy an excursion on the Lake, 'tho can with truth say I was on it; a boast all can't make (our party I mean) as they waited for the morning, while I more fortunate took it in the evening previous; the view we have of the Lake is circumscribed to be sure, but we see enough to form a very good idea of its general character and appearance all the way up superior tho', the higher we go the water is most beautifully clear and the bottom seen I believe at any depth the fish are fine, and always at hand its whole course is through one continued range of mountains which article my eyes have seen till they are tired they are never out of sight and so rocky and steril there is no sort of variety in the growth not even a few tall trees to relieve the tediousness of the undergrowth, our consolation in the disappointment is, we see the water, the mountains and the islands and what more is there to be seen, surely nothing on the Lake itself and what pleasure is there in looking at the ruins of forts none earthly to me, so I contrive to shift the matter off quite philosophically—But this day's ride, return back to home (for it seems like home in a degree) has been the same disagreeable, tedious, jolting business and the only thing that is not bearable and keeps its place in mind and body too, which, has not been the least sufferer from the many jolts—

Wednesday, August 22 Lonesome times these, all my old acquaintance gone and out of the large party we found, only three remaining, true, we've a constant supply on hand; but the fact is, feel no advancing disposition towards them they look rather like the fag-end of gentility and indeed I've toiled and talked till there is nothing more to say and a resting spell is really a treat: the middle of the bed has felt a little of my weight to-day and together with sleeping and reading have whiled away the time pleasantly in my chamber; not pleasantly either but bearably for there is no pleasure or enjoyment here now my only amusement is to watch the manoeuvres of a rich, French, Jew who does slay the food at the table, where he deposits it, I can't imagine; there is not the least obstacle as it regards his mouth which is literally from ear to ear and well accommodated to the necessities of his Anaconda nature; the dandies and clergymen (a most unfortunate coalition) still are the most numerous with us and what the latter come for I'm sure I can't see, for most are as hearty, rosy, fleshy and to all appearance healthy as possible; now the delay of the other important personages can be accounted for 'tis presumable their wardrobe has not been yet wholly exhibited and their desire is to display themselves to the best advantage in every suit— But I'ill not magnify the number; they are few.

Thursday, August 23 A fortnight to-day since we arrived here, time has passed slowly and heavily but not so intolerable as the last few days; we have been expecting Dr Rice[32] some days but has not come yet, should be pleased to see him, 'tis none too late for we start in the morning and rejoiced in spirit am I indeed, neither can my consent be got to 'cast one longing, ling'ring look behind'; we shall go as far as Albany to morrow, the people are resolved our presence and company shall not be missed our places will be more than trebly filled by this evening's arrival a professor from William and Mary is here whose dignified personage appears among our awful catalogue of characters, in close union with dwarfs and clubfeet which objects look most distressing, the maimed and the deformed all I believe resort here—Brother witnessed a curious fact to-day he told me of, he saw a child with its mother and grandmother, the child only *two years* old the grandmother only *twenty eight* a circumstance rather unusual I think; he has also been scratching for earths over which he anticipates a feast of analyzing when he reaches home.

Friday, August 24 This has been a day of no small account and a memorable one among this people, and do hate to mention the facts my eyes have seen and ears heard; but they deserve exposure and I will be one to tell on them: the public execution of a culprit (for the charge of murder) came on and what sport, what fine fun for man, woman and child; don't suppose they would have exchanged the enjoyment derived from and produced by such a cause for any other whatever; we came the most private way from Waterford to Albany, (the distance of eight miles) and in the short distance I counted 530 wagons that we met returning from the show, besides a number too great to calculate standing in heaps on the beach, Oh! the crowd was immense, every steam-Boat on the river was filled to sinking; every stage, post-coach, carriage, wagon and gig packed, even the railing on the top for the purpose of baggage was stowed and the pleasure boats had no end they were in strings trying to ship the passengers across; I can give you no idea of the multitude but this I can say, they were on their return home and in what plight was dreadful to behold, and can be little imagined, they were yelping and howling like bears and dogs and not one single remove above them in any respect and long way past the setting up point it griev'd me to witness so much depravity and insensibility in human nature; neither do I mean to make no mention of the *fair* among this social, convivial and congenial party; they shone conspicuous by their *glowing cheeks* and *audible tongues; suspicion* is very strong on the subject, but I can't tell tales on my own sex since we reached here we have been informed there were 42,000 strangers in the town present at the execution, the particulars of the poor man's death we have not heard: out of the host we met it rejoices me to say there were not half could be termed gentlemen or ladies from their appearance but many there were most certainly: would virginia have disgraced herself thus on a similar occasion? I would fain hope not; at all events this general turning out has given me some idea of the population of N.Y. I also feel quite a desire to know the amount of money collected at the toll-bridge through which they as well as we passed; we asked the man, but he said he did not know, he had not had time, but he should see to morrow to that. thus ends this day's adventure——

Saturday, August 25 This morning we took the stage for our destined place, which we have at last reached, 'tho with some fatigue; after a tantalizing detention we crossed the ferry (almost two hours) and except that we have encountered no difficulty all day; our travelling party was pleasant and affable, consisting of a jovial, facetious Frenchman, a Philadelphia lawyer who used words so smooth, they could not ruffle you, besides a torrent of compliments he poured on the Southerners which is music to my ears and whether 'twas all jest or earnest do not know positively, tho' his earnestness of manner would give no room for the suspicion of insincerity at any rate, I'm willing to believe him true: it pleased for the moment——we had also two Virginians, one from Norfolk who entertained us with an account of the many repulses he had borne and the many chills these *frigid zone* people had given his warmer temperament; our other companion was from Richmond, the express counterpart of a supple-jack [33] but for the sufficiency of stage room his much legs and arms would have fared better twined around his body which a slight effort would have effected——we also had two Delaware Ladies with whom I've staid long, travelled much and who seem more like home folk than any others——We passed the junction of the two canals this evening the Northern and Western 'tis a mighty work and must have cost labor and money on no small scale but Erie and Champlain can now be as communicative and convenient to each other as other places; we saw large boats raised a number of feet merely by the letting in of the water: all new to me——

Sunday, August 26 The place at which we are now is called New Lebanon, one of the most enchanting and delightful situations, incomparably superior to any thing about Saratoga or Ballston either; the country is very high in fine state of cultivation with mountains rising higher and higher till they disappear from view, the place touches nearly Massachusetts we ought to tread on that State's ground to include among our number——Two miles from this is the village of Shaking-Quakers (or as they are called here Shakers) whose worship we have attended to-day the representation and description usually given relative to their mode of worship is unfavorable, ludicrous and non-sensical but just let an individual attend one with any sense at all and I'll vouch he will feel no disposition to turn it to ridicule; their meeting house is a model of simplicity and neatness they in their dress no less so; the females all attired exactly alike not excepting the little girls who are disfigured to death with them by the cut of a cap which I may venture to say will never be sought by any of our moderners; the men's dress is nothing uncommon except the Coat and I am sure Peale's museum can't furnish a greater curiosity, it has no sleeve to it and looks as if all the powers of *old fashion* had combined to antiquate it in the extreme; they are seated apart, the men one side, the women the other, no fear of contamination by touching each other, as to celibacy that vow is inviolable—after a short pause they commenced by all (as it were) instinctively rising up and arranging themselves in well trained militia style, their singing is strong, loud, discordant, without any melody and so sung you cannot distinguish a single word; prayer is also performed by singing tho' in the attitude of kneeling; the elder delivered a sermon which displayed considerable historical knowledge, that being over, they struck up again [. . .] few of them as a chair for the others to dance, as both together would be rather severe exercise—such regularity of motion, such attention to time, such measurement of steps, all which things made the prettiest dance I have seen for an age; so much devotion and sincerity manifested in their countenances; the whole scene made me feel awful and seeing dancing as a exercise of religious adoration could scarcely be realized; every member is in motion the hands keep constant time, and are clapped, raised and lowered and the whole of their minds and bodies engaged in the business; to-morrow we intend visiting them, they are always glad to see strangers and are hospitable to a fault—however that trait is to be tested—

Monday, August 27 We were prevented this morning by a powerful rain from paying our visit to the Shakers, but succeeded this evening never have I seen such consummated nicety, neatness, decency and order; but how can things be otherwise? when they are managed by a set of old-maids and bachelors (who have either all attained unto that venerable state, or are so in expectancy) whose whole study is to excel in this perfection of their various vocations? their kitchens and dairys are models of cleanliness and domestic cheeses arranged just to tempt the visitor, but there is not much more to be said in their favor we tried one which we bought and a piece of white leather is just as pleasant to the taste; we also purchased several little specimens of their ingenuity; they are a kind, industrious, charitable people always willing to receive the destitute and give them an equal share in their common property: but, Oh! how deluded and misguided in their religious principles, they're scarcely a whit behind the Pharisees in my opinion they are setting up and establishing their own righteousness by the sacrifice of every thing that flesh and blood are capable of, they are striving and struggling to secure eternal life (not as other Christians do by faith in Christ) but by self-denial, mortification and forbearance in every imaginable shape; these are all right to be sure when excess or intemperance creep in, but I can not believe a total relinquishment of all innocent enjoyments ever was designed, for all is good when used in moderation—this people tho', after a while become perfectly holy, no further necessity for the practice of their devotional exercises, original self is gotten rid of, human nature is quite thrown aside and of course they are ready to enter into an inheritance earned and justly entitled to—In the description of the manner of their worshipping proceedings 'tis impossible almost to avoid creating in the mind of the hearer, prejudice and unfavorable feeling towards them on account of their apparent ridiculousness and wilful ignorance, but in spite of their singularity there are very few who attend that feel the least desire to indulge in mirth or merriment, on the contrary if their natures are constituted at all like mine, feelings of indescribable solemnity and awe will quickly be substituted, such as I've seldom had—

Tuesday, August 28 All day on the way, first stage then the boat but after much suffering in the flesh we find ourselves on the top of the Catskill Mountains so often sounded in my ears; 'have you been to Catskill'? is the question asked you by every one, 'no'—'no'—till I'm tired, but my little answer shall be changed for the future: there is a house on the summit handsomely finished and furnished and spacious enough to accommodate 200 visitors; the height is nearly 4.000 feet greater than any below you, and the distance so immense above the rest that although what you look down on, you know from experience to be mountainous beyond comfort, yet the whole seems like a perfect level, cultivated fields appear like so many little plant-patches, the beautiful Hudson no larger than a small stream, and whose vessels (but for the sails) hardly discernible. 'Tis a sight most glorious to behold, and tho' I thought myself prepared to see all and more than all we had, heard yet 'the half was not told me'; the whole world is almost deceivingly comprised in the view, and the horizon, the very extent of creation its elevated situation stamps unjust insignificance on every thing below it; what would be the astonishment of an individual (supposing entire ignorance of all concerning it) who after toiling up such a height should find that splendid establishment in a barren, desolate, uninhabited waste where the foot of man it would seem to him had never trod, and whose vast extent would scarcely support life—he surely would believe his every sense was under the influence of enchantment—I should—

Wednesday, August 29 This morning we toiled down the tiresome mountain as we yesterday tugged up and after descending felt as tho' we had come in the world again, notwithstanding its eminence and superiority over all adjacent, did not feel the least wish to continue any longer, much rather be on a footing with less aerial beings; we took the Steam-Boat at the town of Catskill and got to New-York in the morning about 1 slept on board or rather tried to sleep; for between a berth three feet too short for one of my inches squalling children and tho' last not least an evil not unusually met with about beds; I got no rest at all: at six o clock thursday to-day we boarded another boat and after a day of sailing, not forgetting a jolting spell of many miles by the way we find ourselves in Philadelphia where the spending a week when we went on has revived some familiar and home feelings—Oh! how, I dread to rise so early to-morrow morning—We passed through the often heard of town called Princeton the place where our Southern rustics are polished so smoothly; 'tis a pity circumstances could not have favored a little detention on my account, but we had only a glimpse of the building's classic walls which certainly present nothing terrifying or attracting on the exterior; the inside transactions would not be very entertaining to an ignoramus like me; the town is much smaller than I had imagined and but for its Seminaries would be nothing more than many others we've passed through without even enquiring the names—among the rest of to-day's adventures Brother lost his cloak, occasioned by the changing of coaches in great haste; *that of* course with all the rest of bad luck is put on my shoulders well the 'back is fitted to the burden', could he only leave me through mistake what a happy riddance it would be, but I'm likely to continue a thorn in his side for some time to come yet, so he had as well bear with me patiently—

Friday, August 31 Another whole day on the water; how heartily tired of the very sight of the various vehicles; this rising at two in the morning presses most grievously on my sleepy nature to-night we are in Baltimore, if we go on at this rate, we shall quickly run through all the principal cities and towns in the Union; the last three evenings spent in places so widely distant much are we benefitted and gratified by these flying trips, we reach them about dark and leave them long before day arrives, just as ignorant and unsatisfied as ever; we are so much nearer home than we've been since we left it that I'm half inclined to slip in the boat and fly there instead of completing this jaunt another direction to the Bedford-Springs in Pennsylvania the ineffable pleasure still in reserve of a hundred and forty miles land conveyance; how shall I stand it?

Saturday, September 1 Well, I am alive, to be sure but that is most all: 80 miles this day in an uneasy stage, every step up hill on a rugged turnpike, pitched forward every half minute on the back of some segar-smoking codger, or half asleep, bumping your pate against the still harder, unpadded carriage sides; this is what they call 'travelling for pleasure', is it? what a pity my nature is incapable of such exquisite enjoyment, should I only last to attain in our destined place most cheerfully will I resign my seat to one capable of enjoying such bliss; my meat is bruised, my neck bones distorted, and *worst of all my clothes all rubbed* out; these are a few of the experienced ingredients which constitute the cup of pleasure, they are all rather bitter to my taste, but 'tis best to make the best of a bad thing—by way of a digression (for travelling in all ways, with its consequences and attendants, is an abomination to me) there is one curious fact with regard to the Catskill excursion I forgot to mention entirely; that is the very great difference in the temperature of the climate; we quitted an atmosphere too hot for comfort in the morning and on reaching the top of the Mountain all winter clothing was welcome together with a good fire, the next morning there was ice (the 29th—of August) on coming down we doubly felt the effects of a burning sun; they must have but little summer.

Sunday, September 2 How unlike the Sabbath this day has been to me in consequence of my being constrained to spend it in the manner; I have not a moment's respite on the road except at meals and among a set who scarcely knew and cared less about its sanctity, it was extremely unpleasant to hear an oath when there was no such thing as getting out of hearing, but what can not be avoided must be endured—but here we are at our stopping place and that too with whole bones—wonderful indeed—strange to tell the fatigue to-day has been much less than yesterday tho' the road if possible worse, I can't account for it unless that when things reach their height either way, they must take a turn which was my case and the many aches and pains all evaporated most joyfully for me; very unexpectedly we met Mr George Harrison and tho' at home we are almost strangers, he received me here as an old acquaintance and really I should be delighted to see any body or thing that is familiar in these distant parts, where we get no cordial shakes of the hand and scarcely a nod, but comfort myself with the hope of a hearty welcome from all at home—How finely (if not loudly) shall I sleep this night, and shall take care to dispense with the encumbrance of my *clothes, whose agreeable company* I really have not had time to shake off for the last three nights—

Monday, September 3 I suppose here we shall have only a repetition of the Saratoga tune, lounge about and do nothing all day; most luckily for me my long absent appetite has return'd and its indulgence is about my main enjoyment, but who could forbear after so long a privation of such delicacies and treats as *corn meal* in various forms? no one knows how rejoiced my eyes were to behold real Virginia batter cakes show off on the supper-table to-night, should all symptoms both of inclination and face continue, I'ill warrant the land-lord will not make much profit out of me, and Oh! such nice soft peaches and cream too, 'tis glorious times in the eating department; but the bill of fare only makes you discontented and envious of my lot, so will change the theme pleasant as it is—As to the place, 'tis nothing but a small village rather on the decline, but very reputable for its mineral waters and they alone I expect support its existence; the situation is high, mountains abundant, society good and withal something so magnetic about it, visitors can't get away, they are however coaxing themselves off and our party but few in number and sociably and pleasantly disposed (gentlemen more especially) which was the reverse at Saratoga; there; they were nothing but a set of statues and would actually shrink back from the sight of strange young ladies—This evening we rode to the Springs mile and a half from the town which is the chief house for accommodation until the close of the season when little company and lonesomeness drive the people in the village, which last was our alternative; the spot is a very rural and cool one, but almost in its original state of wildness, we took a walk to the top of a near mountain which I accomplished after much puffing and blowing: we had the attendance of an elderly gentleman who did not seem to relish it any more than 'Miss Ruff' as he called me—

Tuesday, September 4 To-day my endeavors have been to ingratiate myself with these fair ladies, succeeded with all but one, who is invulnerable at every point and a most admirable statue, as to a tongue my doubts are very strong whither she possesses one or not, if she has, she will certainly never be got into difficulties by the too much use of it; there is also a young dyspeptic of the very first stamp, more finished in the *art of non-digestion* than any I ever saw, 'tis the theme of her song and through our deal of politeness she gets the *expressed* sympathy of all around; the brown-bread, rye-bread and the whole family of anti-dyspeptics are ushered forth at every meal, besides a formidable host of remedies and prescriptions introduced as a dessert. I shall have the advantage of collecting a catalogue of cures here against the time when I too shall become fashionable in that respect—this morning received an invitation from one of these kind ladies to accompany her in her barouche to the Springs; 'tis true I do not ride in barouches every day but would most willingly have resigned the exalted seat, the hospitable compliment had it not manifested disrespect to the inviter, 'twas a pleasant trip tho', and don't regret the acceptance; we also went up to the house and were introduced to more strangers, the place looks deserted and they had as well close doors for the present season; all are about starting home except us who are likely to remain as long as one is left behind—

Wednesday, September 5 I like this Bedford very much, 'tis a pleasant place as yet or rather the people are so, as to the place itself its charms are still unknown, as dusty walks keep us much in the house, but the pleasure here consists in equality, sociability, unceremoniousness, less gentility and the best of all some cessation from the toilette: a whole family (six in number) added to our party, the young ladies look rather stiff, with heads erect, but for all that shall try them. I wish there were not so many vacant seats in their riding excursions for it is my detestation at all times yet through their politeness and my own awkwardness in rejecting kindnesses I am hauled in sadly against my will—Such droves of cattle we see here daily, sheep, cows and hogs: to-day we passed of cows only eight hundred in the drove, most enormous animals large enough almost to make half a dozen of our puny creatures—This house is the place of Virginia resort, tho' there are no luminaries among the number or any specimens very creditable to her: drawing comparisons between the two States in both civil and political affairs is as much a standing topic of discussion as *bacon* is a standing dish—

Thursday, September 6 Have been in the house all the morning guzzling down soft peaches, more pleasant to me than all the carriage rides or dusty walks— dispatched two letters home to let them see I'm still in existence and almost time to be a burden to them again, (see my mock humility) happy also to say the game of Battle-dore has been introduced into our circle, a most fortunate relief from some of my idle moments—I had some enjoyment after my own mind this evening in a pleasant ride on an agreeably gaited horse; all the politeness of a Va. buck; 'tis an accommodation to me no matter whence the source; there is an old bachelor here whose movements resemble in no small degree those of a setting-turkey in point of slothfulness and particularity, but he has been so kind to me in loaning me books I'll show no more ingratitude by a farther and more minute description—I was no little startled to-day by the accidental entrance of a gentleman in my chamber, poor fellow, how he darted back, overwhelmed with confusion; tho' without any reason I know; besides he was a married man, so it was all affection in him making a 'mountain of a mole-hill'—

Friday, September 7 I really am most seriously tired of doing nothing, this every day sameness and idleness is a great deal more intolerable (even to laziness in grain like me) than work or employment of any kind; books have nearly failed to entertain or in other words my dealings with them have been so frequent I just find myself unworthy of their company and wish some less honest negotiaters, their reproofs and reprimands are too personal and applicable for my conscience's comfort—I have slept till my senses are stupified beyond recovery, scarcely an idea now remaining—I have dressed to the entire display of my whole wardrobe since which exhibition it has had some rest, its limitation now admitting of no more novelty and rejoiced indeed to have attained its close without a just accusation of partiality from any one article—I have eat till ashamed and moderation with reason restrained inclination or rather forbid any further indulgence—the battle-dores have worsted my hands the riding has spared not the flesh and as to needle work, that is not at all accordant with travelling gentility and so scrupulous are my notions on that tender point, I would not forfeit my character how ever strongly inclined—this is really a sad state of things, what is to be done in such a case of desperation? an awful responsibility on *Gentility's* shoulders; there, let the consequence rest rather than on mine—

Saturday, September 8 Poring over the unprofitable novels all day; quite disappointed at not seeing the threatening signs of bad weather fulfill'd. any thing in the world for a change no soft peaches to-day for dinner; that is may be accounting for some of my restlessness, is it possible epicurianism can draw from me such an acknowledgment? 'tis not my usual failing tho', however there is no excuse now, true the waters produce the effect of voraciousness but my dealings with them are but little, amounting to none at all. more addition to our company—a sweet, pretty, but wholly French lady, all I can do is to look and admire with a sealed mouth, so much pleasure lost you see for not being accomplished, think it advisable to direct my next trip across the Atlantic for the purpose, taking along with me a pair of spectacles to aid me through the effects of age—

Sunday, September 9 Six weeks this very day since I left home, every week seems multiplied to a month which is not saying much in favor of a pleasant time; 'There is no place like home'—the simplicity and undoubted truth of the song gains now my three-fold admiration; went to Church this morning but a truce to commenting on sermons, there are more churches here than is common to be seen in a village of this size, which goes a great way to gain my good-will; much do they regard my approbation in any of their matters: streets most abominably filthy, the people generally here are something like tarapins, shelled even to the hiding of their heads all the week till Sunday brings them out as a gentle shower (to continue the *beautiful simile*) operates on them.

Monday, September 10 Oh! how slowly time moves, I'm wearied out with Bedford and any thing around me, how in the world shall I dispose of the rest of the days here? all sources of amusement completely worn thread bare, few enough indeed were their entertaining natures inexhaustible the signs on the opposite stores have been read till they are now eyesores, the *superior display* of dry-goods and hardware (which are the only sort of merchandise seen) have not enticed me to an examination of their quality, besides a formidable file of ploughs, barrels and kettles all of which may possess intrinsic worth but certainly do not external charms; the hotel sign-boards are peering you in the face every other stop but presenting rather an uninviting exterior, to say nothing of a scraping, scratching fiddle incessantly going, doing its office in a dancing-school, poor children—I pity the drums of their ears if very sensitive as much as my own hearing of the sound, these are a few of the dark tints perceptible and glaring on the fair picture of this place, its beauties and charms all swallowed up by familiarity, so is my account of this and would be of every other strange place after a fortnight's visitation, the report after a shorter stay would be more in its favor—so much discontent—

Tuesday, September 11 In a much better humor all day than common; in the first place we were regaled at twelve with a luncheon of poundcake (a very scarce article hitherto) which introduction commenced a smiling countenance and continued by the after-purchase of nice fruit, which temptation employed the interval of idleness; the pleasure too of dividing among my associates was not inconsiderable; took a ride on a prancing black whose beauty and sprightliness got me a little street notice, what a sad mortification—that the *first desire* and *object* of my visit (that of *observation*) should have been effected only through the means of a horse; well, pride must have a fall, but thanks to the animal as also the owner for doing their part towards accomplishing my paramount wishes—This evening we took a foundering walk of two and a half miles, don't mean the distance so much as its nature; the enticement was a view of a beautiful river meandering through lofty mountains, but the most rugged rocky and ascending foot-way you can imagine; true, there was no disappointment after we got over the almost interminable space but not sufficient compensation for the cutting out our shoes and the aching of my individual corns, can't speak for the others on that point, but we passed the time very pleasantly scolding and quarrelling at our guide (brother) for directing us in his chosen ramble, but excused him on the score of its similarity to his own ploughed ground and corn-hills for which he has such sincere attachment even so far as to toil and halt to reach any thing bearing the least resemblance to them—

Wednesday, September 12 No variety, no novelty, no any thing agreeable; saw a funeral procession pass my window, all paired off, a lady and gentleman abreast and all mounted on horseback, the whole appeared handsome and uniform but withal very solemn; played my master-game at battle-dore 450 times which far surpasses my home performance; finished and returned *Mr Batchelor's* books; took another long stroll this evening, wore out my stockings—poor feet will be in a blue way for clothing after a little more indulgence, I need not call it 'indulgence' for 'tis a bitter cross but go I must, in spite of all excuses that can be framed; our leaders are brother and an agreeable, active, elderly lady well matched in that respect and who puts us younger ones much to shame for our inability: but we saw her out and broke her down too this evening—quite a boast—

Thursday, September 13 Morning very cool, huddled around a blazing fire, looking vastly sociable and wintery: we have in our party a *young* Lion in the shape of a *small lawyer* who amuses us by the earnestness, ferocity, and emphatic manner which he uses in conversation, all agree in thinking him most appropriately named, on which account he is admitted as our general *pet;* he would surely burst from his *den* (which is a particular corner in the room) and roar most lustily did he overhear our comparisons, not that they cast any reflection to his disadvantage, but little people are generally more tenacious and 'touch-me-not' than sizeable ones—(all my small readers excepted) The violent exercise of all day has quite disabled my arms no more play for me till after a resting spell and as the amusement (trifling as it is) is the half support of life during this excessive dearth I shall decline into a 'green and yellow melancholy'—This evening took another jaunt on a frisky, skittish, coquettish nag, so full of her air graces and pranks she was as ungovernable and unpleasing in her behavior as some of the *two-legged ones*—what an insult to—

Friday, September 14 If chance or accident should throw *this* into any one's hands who undertakes a perusal, if he does not throw it aside in disgust after a very short time and tired out with an almost unvaried repetition of daily and wearisome occurrences, he has double the patience that the detailer has: indeed my pen from habit can half perform itself its office without any direction and a stupid one it will prove itself to be, if an unaltered and repeated system should not effect its proficiency in the end; it would be a tax on my patience (and a most heavy one too seeing it is so little) to review its contents and nonsense with the least toleration—

In the course of this trip, experience had taught me one all important and positive fact, and that is, there is no life more remote from contentment and happiness, than a life of idleness and what is called pleasure. My choice now would be active and constant employment to inactive and entire laziness; this is my present sentiment and theory, but what six months such practice would say and the evidence then given in—I fear would make me retract my preference; situations different in this natures and felt by us, alone can convince us unbelieving ones of their desirableness or enviableness; perfect contentment may be (though it is not often) bought by trial.

Saturday, September 15 Although I express so much dissatisfaction at and about the whole Bedford appurtenances, 'tis all without just cause and am so pleasantly situated as any one ought to wish; surrounded by many comforts, allowed many privileges, waited on by kind obliging people who anticipate my wants, what more can a 'stranger in a strange land' [34] reasonably require or desire? ingratitude is strongly marked in such murmurings, but I am not so really at heart, it is my nature to idolize my home and no conceivable circumstances I think could entirely reconcile me elsewhere, so long as *that* is within possible reach, just so long will restlessness and anxiousness continue on my part, *there* centre all my hopes, wishes, ends and aims; not that I've got a *house-full* of *husband* and *children* to constitute it such an Elysium, as so many links in the chain of endearment—no indeed—I congratulate myself on the exclusion of all such *agreeables* and (as is commonly deem'd) *indispensables,* tho' in my opinion (beg pardon of the whole sex) they are far, very far from being at all indispensable to happiness, don't speak universally but only individually, that is, as far as appearances will testify in many instances; at any rate, sufficiently to confirm me in the sentiment even if it is wrong; no body believes me I know, that is not expected; vanity says nay—besides admiring in me too the ingenious resource for consolation— the making the best of a bad bargain and recommending it also (fox-like in the fable) to the attention and *disinterested* benefit of others—'Misery loves company'—but no more half-way acknowledgements for the present—

Sunday, September 16 Fortnight to-day since we arrived in Bedford, just the length of time spent at Saratoga and ought to quit here too, but our time is to be given to some place and since decided choice can't have its way, I am perfectly willing to remain here to enjoy the good things, not so willing either for I forget I'm gaining so much flesh, I shall be really *ungenteel* all the movable part of this village has gone to-day to a camp meeting a few miles distant; no preaching in the churches; ministers all absent and of course have had no occasion to go out or hardly see anything without the precincts of my own room, which however overlooks the main street, so there is no obstacle to my seeing all passing there, if disposed so to do.

Monday, September 17 How still every thing has been to-day and except for the cleaning in the house the very mice might be mistaken in the time (speaking comparatively) all the visitors left this morning but us and one of our State gentlemen; we Virginians seem to be most pointedly partial, the partiality however may be accounted for; necessity binds us to the place because we can do no better; inclination (report says) detains our fellow traveller, having met with a much more powerful and resistless cause to ascribe his unusual detention to than either the effects of the waters or the united charms of Bedford, he has dwelt contentedly two months, not the least desire to vary the scene—even by moving from place to place which is almost a stated rule for persons who go in search of health, but is kept here in spite of the daily departure of those who have staid and gone long since he came suspicion may think what it please, I'm sure a man has a right to do as he please in all such matters and very hard it is too that he can't pay a long visit when he pays for it so well without bothering people as to his intentions—No rolling of carriages under my window, company has cleared them out. I shall begin to think the display in that way all came from afar and none really belonging here should the stillness continue much longer— but the *dulcet* notes of that fiddle are still in hearing.

Tuesday, September 18 'Tis most lucky for me I can enjoy solitude and am unacquainted with the feeling of lonesomeness, so unwished for by most people and so impatiently borne by them, society is very pleasant to be sure when we can get the sort we wish but to be obliged to sit up as straight as an arrow, with a rein over your actions and a bridle over your tongue which must be the case some what among the ones met by chance at these places, I say of the 'two evils give the least', that is the pleasure furnished from my own funds; if my disposition were otherwise or my *bump* of *loquacity* were fully developed my unavoidable situation often times would be very insupportable for not a few of the hours now are passed by my own *agreeable self,* sometimes from necessity, frequently from choice so between the two operatives make myself as selfish as a hermit it is the only advantage I believe such persons have over pleasant, affable, social ones that of being satisfied with little mutual intercourse while the other descriptions of disposition are restless and miserable when there is not some one at hand to talk to and when they are permitted a chance what a volley of words (after such an overcharge) tumble from the tongue's tip, no doubt much relieved by the emission such is brother, who at times keeps in for what reasons can't say, may be for want of an antagonist who if he should chance to fall in with will empty on him a torrent of argument but oftener a little something not quite so smooth and civil savoring rather of contention, opposition and disputation which the poor man were he a stranger would consider he had fallen into the hands of the rudest and most uncivilized of overbearing combatants and moreover monopolizing two-thirds of the conversation, he would be thought rather 'bearish' indeed, as a lady's compliment once said of him; but his late knocking-about I think has rubbed off several coats of his *bearishness* and put on a little *polish* which will be *rough* in spite of you—

Wednesday, September 19 This has been a real autumnal day uncomfortably cold and threatening rain—have the addition of two more ladies who came this morning but they like all the rest of us keep close quarters at first till curiosity draws them out and as time has not yet produced that effect on them neither has our own been gratified by a sight. My own share of that article curiosity (woman like) got me in to a little difficulty to-day, I wished to know who a young a man was that had frequently crossed my path and had struck my attention from his remarkable homeliness and altogether uncouth appearance, I was induced to ask; first, tho' undertook to describe him, which description was most true and unflatt'ring and so correct as to be instantly known by the lady to whom the address was made; she replied modestly and blushingly 'he is a near relation of mine', and tho' I was the one to blush and of course look *interesting,* but my confusion was inadequate to the task of penetrating a dark, thick skin and so did not show itself in the form of *pretty rougy tints;* so far she had the advantage of *genteelizing* herself over me; in as much as she possesses that constituent of beauty, of which I can't boast.

Thursday, September 20 Wonderful to tell, I've been busily engaged all day the time has slipped off with half its usual length, after a seven week's fit of laziness took it in my head just as we are about starting home to get into an industrious mood, could not possibly hold out two days longer, but for this purpose, to gratify the notion of the eleventh hour had actually to go out and buy something to sew on; it is an old adage that lazy people idle away all the week and work hard saturday night (metaphorically) its truth has been verified in this instance. there is another, tho' which as a support must be repeated also that is, a regular habit of industry at home will admit of indulgence abroad; if this be true; my course I hope will be thus construed and my character in the way of industry be raised standard-high, to be reached after by all similarly disposed——My whole composition is one indiscriminate jumble of contraries which never act in reason, nor is it expected, so there is much excuse for my disordered and ill-timed doings and influenced to action by the whim of the moment, which impulse always leads me the wrong way——

Friday, September 21 We all took a walk of two and a half miles this morning for the express purpose of robbing a peach orchard, which thing we did do but only in a limited way and the few gotten, a very insufficient reward for such a stroll for it had all the varieties of rocks, gullies, branches, hills and only five fences, the last of which found us very expert climbers, after so much practice; the fruit had been in perfection and abundance (so accounts said) but we were a day after the fare and right it is that all unfair designs should be frustrated; one alone of our party was licensed and on that liberty we all encroached. We have also had a general weighing frolic which was done just across the street in a small pair of scales, the smallness of which produced a little difficulty (and of course merriment) about getting in; we were resolved not to be selfish in the fun (if any was to be had) and so ex-hibited the performance for the like amusement of the public: one meagre, weavel-eaten dyspeptic walked away quietly rather than be balanced with the ladies: mine was the number to make him fear but he would not agree that he was frighten'd off by any such apprehension when I accused him of it. five pounds have I gained here Oh! how awful! well it is lucky we go to morrow, or I should endeavor to expedite our departure by *outright rebellion.*

Monday, September 24 We have reached Washington at last after three days travel and literally going through many ups and downs; breakfasted at Bed-ford Saturday at half after one, the earliest meal I ever eat (and who of you can boast such early hours?) bumped over the worst of roads to Hagar's-Town in Maryland the distance of seventy miles which is entirely too far for one day's ride, at least my feelings find it too much for comfort——tho' I suppose they go on this principle that the quicker a disagreeable job is performed the better and such would be my opinion too if 'paddy's hints' given now and then by the soreness did not remind me that less haste would produce more pleasant results——The village Hagar's-T is very handsome, some superb buildings larger than any of the Pennsylvania ones through which we passed and containing 4.000 inhabitants we were most comfort-ably accommodated, superior fare which was done ample justice to by me, the Stage did not start till three Sunday evening which gave me a chance to attend church the building was inviting, the assembly large, genteel and attentive, which last thing (attention) is not always given either to church or preacher; as for instance *one place* of the same kind I could name. At the appointed time we set off again in a coach that carries twenty persons; what think you of its size? we glided over the best turnpike in the U. S with swiftness, which continued about fifteen miles between Hagars-Town and Frederic-Town you may judge of its excellency as it enabled us to go at the rate of eight miles the hour which is four more than any thing else in the form of a road that I've seen here at all will admit of; the Village itself is very sizeable and country around beautiful and highly cultivated; the next morning (which was this) we continued on having along with us only one fellow passenger who was not one of the most refined or genteel and the vacancies in the Stage could hardly be realized after so much close packing like bales of cotton—The first glimpse we had of this place from an elevation coming in was very commanding, where we had also a view of the Potomac whose beauty added much to the loveliness of the scene and which far surpasses all the pretties and delightfuls about these tiresome watering-places in my partial opinion; but the river has another charm which to me at present is greater than its ornamental ones, that of convenience and rapidity of transportation, the reality of which facilities I'm soon to enjoy; I don't mean there is such enjoyment in the means (no indeed! my appetite is fully satisfied with respect to that luxury) but rather to the tendency of those means As yet we have seen nothing but many buildings scattered over ground enough to occupy twenty reasonable towns nearly, there is not the least uniformity or regularity in the disposition or construction of the houses here but all built it seems to me just any where they happened to fancy a spot; here and there without seeming to have any design towards giving a body to the City—But more tomorrow as it is to be a day off seeing—

Tuesday, September 25 Well we have eyed to-day a portion of the Federal City the houses mostly are nothing uncommon but there some splendid structures the Capitol of course stands preeminent in rank and magnificence which we examined from top to toe from the top (which I did hold out to reach, but at the expence of my whole strength, for the stair-cases— Oh! how many and steep!) we had a most extensive view (not equal tho' to the Catskill-mountain scene) and really George-Town with this appeared to be scattered over all the ground I could see; here a clump of houses, there one superior establishment, this side a decent and respectable group of buildings, that may be as many acres where there is not one at all: as to the centre, I do not believe it has any—But the Capitol, who can do justice to its splendor? I leave it for some more able describer, all I can say is, that the Queen of Sheba's exclamation respecting Solomon's Temple [35] may be by me most justly and truly quoted, but as repetition is not agreeable, will forbear a second quotation of the dear lady's saying, or if you are anxious to know it, you may search and see its applicability and expressiveness; its grandeur exceeds the height of my architectural imaginings, it is at present disrobed of all decoration and much disordered on account of the repairings going on, tho' divested of ornament, enough is left behind to satisfy the visitor; even brother admired the whole (with the exception of the dome) tho' some murmurings and grudgings about the expenditure of so many thousands would slip out—when one visits this, they must look at the public buildings alone and let them make up any deficiency in all other matters; the streets are all divided into avenues which cross and intersect in every direction, forming triangles quite mathematically—Mr C Minge and lady arrived to-day, she is a pleasant and interesting woman but not beautiful in my opinion (don't accuse me of *envy*) as report generally said she was; (but notwithstanding *she has stepped in my place* and ought to be eyed by me rather askance) yet, I am willing to give her all just due; as to him; I never saw him half as agreeable, and no doubt tried himself just to make *me regret—a slight circumstance:* whether the object was effected or not, I will not say but only tell you this, it is not worth while to set down and grieve about a broken pitcher, so must bear the loss with the 'best foot foremost'—Your *conclusions* from the above are anticipated; don't tell my secret, or in other words don't expose my *candid confession*—

Wednesday, September 26 This morning we visited the President's palace even brother's antipathy could not keep him away (as for my own politics they are of too mild and charitable a nature to exert so powerful an influence over me) but was overcome even far beyond the threshold; a disposition to gratify me, is his excuse for going, but 'tis not so, he was no less anxious than myself, tho' he will not acknowledge it; the splendor of the whole, cannot fail to excite admiration in every instance where prejudice and hatred do not produce total blindness which was the case with brother, and would not admit he saw any thing to pay him for his walk and the only compensation was, the *boast* of the *bold, undaunted air* with which he demanded admittance in the house, as for the rest of us all, we were amazed almost to dumbness; we were not however honored with a sight of her Highness or her *billiard playing son* [36]—After finishing looking at the *wonderful sights* we returned with Mr and Mrs M, who were setting off again in the next stage—so we shall see no more of the famous City as our time of departure has past and we now on the way the Boat started at three this evening, stopped at awile at Alexandria; saw the celebrated Mount-Vernon and neither another view of that or any thing else will carry me on deck again this night—

Thursday, September 27 This has been a day of days with us and if one could be unfeeling enough; they might have been highly amused at the really laughable and pitiable scene which our cabin has presented; the Bay was more than usually rough and the rocking so great as to prevent our standing the consequence was, we were all deadly sick—such heaving, grunting, catching for support, demand for beds and basins; besides six children bawling most loudly and refused to be quieted till attended to by the mothers; this is only a part of the interesting farce, the other acts are indescribable and the nature of them I don't choose to intimate. The gentlemen above could be heard pacing the deck with all possible rapidity as a preventive against similar results, which however did not altogether succeed—We passed Old-Point Comfort which was my first sight of it and but for the pleasure of indulging the appetite in the luxury of fine fish I can't imagine what should make it so desirable and popular as a place of summer resort; 'tis a miserably sandy hot spot, not a solitary tree to relieve the eye or refresh the rambler— We reached here (Norfolk) at four and spent all the evening till nine with a friend; fell in there with a gentleman fully accomplished in all the requisites of widowerhood, who attended us to Boat where I am going directly to bed with a chance of getting a little more sleep (as she is standing still) than the last night, if the births were not so much like coffins there would be still more chance of comfort.

Friday, September 28 Almost at home; crossed Hampton-Roads this morning and came off no better than yesterday in the Bay, but had a return of the same scene; got aground at James-Town where we remained till the other Boat exultingly passed on far ahead; at four we landed here (Coggins) where we found all nearly well, to the great relief of us both, but particularly brother, who had suffered inexpressible agony from suspense and anxiety— We found here a house full indeed—all jovial, happy but to-morrow is my day—

Saturday—

The Selma Plantation Journals

1 8 3 5 – 3 7

FIRST JOURNAL

1835

5 o'Clock—I have been very angry this day and I am ashamed of it, it happens so often, that I must watch myself closely, it is very wicked indeed, especially as it is my duty to bear patiently with ignorance, or stupidity, yes I will struggle with this irritable temper of mine and conquer it if possible. We have had refreshing showers all day and it is yet very cloudy. I am quite depressed in spirits, but still not yet unhappy, I believe it is caused by having not any thing to look forward to very shortly, in short the absence of all excitement—I cannot expect any letters for at least three weeks, and have none to dispatch, or at least none that can give me the least satisfaction in that way—I have filed those of Mrs. B———t[1] in a very convenient manner, so that I can read them over as I would a Book or any passage in one, how well she does write, what a very easy natural style—if she would only leave off alluding to a certain *"Shadow"* I am sure she must have found out by this time that it gives me pain, by the strict silence I do observe on that subject, but poor thing she views these matters in a very different light, one thing I am certain of, that her intention is good, and friendly; nevertheless I always feel like suffocating when I come to that part of her letter which contains that most unfortunate apparition; which heaven knows haunts me sufficiently without any prompting.

5 o'Clock — I have been very angry this day and I am ashamed of it, it happens so often, that I must watch myself closely, it is very wicked indeed, especially as it is my duty to bear patiently with ignorance, or stupidity, yes I will struggle with this irritable temper of mine and conquer it if possible. — We have had refreshing showers all day and it is got very cloudy — I am quite depressed in spirits, but still not unhappy, I believe it is caused by having not any thing to look forward too very shortly, in short the absence of all excitement, I cannot expect any letters for at least three weeks, and have none to dispatch, or at least none that can give me the least satisfaction in that way — I have filed those of Mrs B—t in a very convenient manner so that I can read them over as I would a Book or any passage in one how well she does write, what a very easy natural style — if she would only leave off alluding to a certain "Shadow" I am sure she must have found out by this time that it gives me pain, by the strict silence I do observe on that subject, but poor thing she views these matters in a very different light, one thing I am certain of, that her intent is good, and friendly; nevertheless I always feel like suffocating when I come to that part of her letter which contains that most unfortunate apparition; which heaven knows haunts me sufficiently without any prompting. —

June 3d — I neglected letting down my Bar last night, the consequence was that I was stung all night by those villainous

The Selma plantation journals: "I have been very angry this day" (Courtesy of the Louisiana and Lower Mississippi Valley Collections, Louisiana State University Libraries, Baton Rouge)

Wednesday, June 3 I neglected letting down my Bar last night, the consequence was that I was stung all night by those vilainous musquitos—it is still cloudy this morning, and the ground too wet to take a walk. 5 o'Clock— I positively have nothing to say this evening, really it is impossible to lead a more uneventful life than I do at present, I do not believe I have even had a thought, good or bad during this day, always excepting Grammar and Geography and Semibreve's[2] thoughts &c—oh! what was I forgetting? have I not just before Tea followed Mrs S—— into the garden intent upon robbing . . . a nest of mocking Birds? and did I not only find one in it, and too young to be taken away. I am sure that, is a sort of adventure, and not a very innocent one either.

Thursday, June 4 Ever since half past five this morning I have been working with my birds, trying to feed the two young ones, their situation is very difficult indeed, the oldest will not open his mouth, and the little one is in danger of perishing with cold, for all the cotton I can pile upon it seems to have no effect, I am almost sorry for having taken it, but then I wish to raise a mocking bird, and this is the only way—Miss M—— has brought me a tumbler filled with white roses and pomegranate flowers how fresh and sweet they are. five o'Clock—I received this morning another pupil—Miss M—— has looked very ominous ever since, it is very singular that appearing as she does to have a partiality for me, she is so averse to what certainly promotes my interest, had I attended to her prejudices and forebodings I would have a very thin school indeed, and of course a very light pocket in the spring—the fact is that she thinks her cares will be increased by the addition; and like some of the rest of the world thinks of self before all, I do not blame her, but it teaches me the extent of her regard, I am sorry to occasion her any displeasure; but I will be just to myself, especially as Mrs S—— who certainly is the only one who has a right to find fault, has on the contrary the kindness to encourage me to increase my school—so Miss M—— may look as disapproving as she thinks proper—*Je m'en moque*— This is the second time that I have an opportunity of appreciating her real interest for my welfare, and also of judging her disposition. lessons again, oh I am getting wise, and wary I hope.

Friday, June 5 A misty morn, and hot too, slept tolerably at last, until five this morning—what a noise since daylight! I could write the "loves of the black birds" if I had an inclination, I have a fine opportunity of observing their manners and customs here, and their fights too. Miss M—— has smoothed her brow considerably but still the cloud lingers, she spoke to me at breakfast but evidently with some effort. Evening—thanks be to time this is friday again, no body can know how tired I am, neither can any, but those who labour at the pleasant task of "teaching the young idea"[3] &c— feel with me at the prospect of the two days of rest, oh my poor feet how they are aching. the moral Storm is over, not a wrinkle *of passion* remains on the surface of my &c—

Saturday, June 6 I have been very idle to day, that is I have not done any thing useful or important—the whole morning was spent in installing my mocking bird in his new cage, I will be glad when the petted creature will choose to feed itself, I cannot move in the room but he is crying after me with his mouth wide open, I do believe the fellow thinks I am its mother. I finished painting the rose I have had so long on hand, it is a poor daub, the carmine had a yellow tint that ruined it—I practised about half an hour on the Piano, and after dinner lay'd on the bed; we had a fine shower, but the air is not much refreshed—We had some Ochro to day for the first time!! ah me! how things apparently so unconnected will associate together in the mind. I cannot practice "the broken heart"[4] this evening the *chanterelle* of my Guitar broke yesterday evening, and cut a deep gash in my finger—yes yes . . . I will feed you presently—I come.

Monday, June 8 I feel much better this morning than I had expected from the fatigue and head ache of yesterday—I went to spend the day with Mrs S——— at her sister's[5] the ride although of eight miles only, is fatiguing from the roughness of the road—we arrived there at about ten o'Clock found the Dr there several of the negroes being sick—Mrs S——— was extremely kind and hospitable, and Mr S———[6] very polite—a few minutes after we had taken off our bonnets &c strawberies, cake, orange cordial, were brought in and proved very acceptable indeed—I had anticipated a rather tedious day but found it quite otherwise—there was not a great deal of conversation but quite sufficiently for such a hot day, Mr S——— resembles poor Col. R——— very much—and Mrs S——— is like Mrs C———y—we had an excellent dinner after which I rested on the bed for a short time. I learned something there too, Mr S——— remarked that the Ladies of this country invariably rode with the bridle in the right hand, which of course gives them an awkward appearance by bringing the right shoulder on a line with the horse's head. we got home at about sunset, and found there Mr and Mrs D——— and Mrs S——— Mrs D——— much improved in health—she presented me with a pair of delicate gloves of purple silk, in which a beautiful band of gold colour was folded very polite indeed.

Tuesday, June 9 I have been quite indisposed since last Sunday's visit, and particularly so to day, I am feverish nervous, and low spirited, very low indeed for I am not depressed from any momentary circumstance, or any personal disappointment, but from the sad contemplation of the weak petty selfishness of human nature, and of the best specimens of it too, alas! alas! I wish I could weep over it, it would do me good—is it possible that maternal love, the holiest of affections would (and I have proof that it does) generate feelings of hatred, yes of malice towards innocent beings deprived of parents, merely because they have excited the interest of strangers, and because their qualities stand in contrast with the defects of the objects of this all angry engrossing affection—oh yes it is but too true, the indulgent the tender, the self-devoted Mother, will have no sympathy, no humanity, none when her own offspring is not the paramount object of praise and indulgence, she will destroy, she will tear in pieces the lamb whose innocence has been won the protection, of which her more fortunate *young* stand in no need—oh my! how disgusted I am with mankind—I have been thinking very often about Clifton[7] to day—its fate must be decided by this time, and it is a refreshing thought to think upon one who is there, would she too be jealous of an orphan? oh mercy grant that I may never witness it—but no she is too generous, too heavenly, I will write no more this evening, and will try to sleep in that consoling idea.

Wednesday, June 10 I am very little better yet, I feel quite weak and feverish, the weather too is gloomy, it has been raining with very few intermissions for two days, however I should not complain, the rain is very beneficial to every thing at this season, and it accords with my present feelings admirably, nothing gives me pleasure, and almost every thing annoys me, even kind attentions, what an ungrateful being I am, to day again I was out of temper, and behaved very rudely, but I excuse myself somewhat, I felt exhausted after school and I thought on the point of fainting, I sent Cora in haste to get me a glass of water in the next room, but instead of returning with it the child came back telling me that Miss M—— was going to bring it directly, I believe that my impatience recovered me for I replied angrily that I did not want Miss M—— to bring it—Cora went again and brought the water and of course repeated what I had said, and I fear it has wounded the feelings of Miss M—— I am sorry for it but why exposing me to it, why so officious? Why not allow me the satisfaction of a poor glass of water without she be the dispenser of it—it makes me miserable I feel as one who has not even the liberty of its cage—and by the by I begin I think to see through all this kindness and suspect that the love of sway and rule is at the basis of all this apparent affection, I will observe a while longer and if I find my suspicion confirmed, I can soon put an end to these petty vexations for vexations they must be called which rob us of independance, let them be clothed in what garb they may—Mrs S—— is better thanks to a dose of calomel[8]—

Thursday, June 11 I believe myself better to day, indeed I have been too constantly occupied to think of my own precious individuality an instant—my feathered pupils are so numerous and so helpless that every moment I can spare must be devoted to their service, I hope that out of so many, and with the care I take of them I may be able to accomplish one education, to be sure it is expecting somewhat more than is generally attained with the same number of "featherless bipeds", as the wise Plato was pleased to distinguish our Genus[9]—what a stupid affair this Journal of mine is, without the birds, the scholars, the weather, it would be a perfect blank—what would Sabina say if she were to see it? It was her who suggested that I should do something of the sort—bless her heart! I am sure she would not read it to save her from an attack of the rheumatism.

Friday, June 12 Another good dear friday it is always with a new pleasure that I welcome the close of that much slandered day, to me at any rate it is not ill omened, on the contrary, it brings to me repose, and often cheerfulness—another Pupil added to my formidable number, but I find that now a few more or less is of little importance as to the trouble, so let them come I say. I intend going to Natchez to morrow morning early, I will probably hear all the news about the sale of Clifton—oh that I could find some letters! Miss M—— brought me some delicious plums just now, for me to take to E—— to morrow, how kind they all are to me, and how little do I deserve so much attentions—what can I ever do for them to prove how sensibly I feel all their goodness.

Wednesday, July 1 My poor neglected Journal, I had thought that I should never more be permitted to add another line to your uninteresting records, ah me how sick I have been since I last traced the preceeding pages, yes sick, sick, oh health of body and spirit how precious thou art, do return to a poor desolate Exile! oh how I will value thy favours, and prize every moment which thou wilt bless with thy presence, without thee this Life is a chastisement, a forced endurance of misery, with thee all other privations are light, mere summer clouds which can scarcely obscure an instant the brightness of thy joyous influence, bounteous Providence I thank thee for having restored me that choicest of gifts in some degree!—many have been the changes since I have left off this daily task, Clifton has been sold! the family removed to lodgings! Miss H——n[10] has been at the point of death! I have received letters with afflicting communications! and oh what new views I have taken of Life, and of this World! true too true it is that there is no happiness to be obtained here, no indeed, the utmost that can be drawn from the circumstances of it, is a kind of indifference for all its con-

cerns, every occurence is calculated to make us arrive sooner or later to this
melancholy conclusion. I feel it is a luxury to be able to write again, what
singular beings we are, so weak, and yet so filled with an indefinable power
that urges us to action while the poor senses can scarcely perform their very
limited offices, I am conscious of a knowledge of my kind, and yet more
instinctive than calculated for I find myself incapable of expressing what to
me is so evident, every moment adds to this experience, and every individual
affords a new lesson and yet I find it impossible to reduce it to a comprehen-
sible meaning because of the many contradictory positions in which every
character immediately presents itself; of one truth however I am convinced,
and by long and constant observation, by numerous almost universal proofs,
by the very nature of our beings, finally by my own personal experience,
and that is of the general weakness of humanity! let it show itself in words,
in deeds, or in omission, still it is the prevailing infirmity, the very anxiety
all have to conceal or to disguise it, proves the humiliating fact—Heroes!
Warriors! Poets! Monarchs! Legislators! Philosophers! the more I learn of
your actions, and especially of those for which you were most admired the
more do I discover cause for conviction; Courage, Genius, power, wisdom,
learning, weakness, weakness, at the base, and the summit of them all!—
I must go to bed for my eyes partake of this universal frailty—good night
little Journal, you have been the source of more comfort than I should ever
have imagined such an insignificant repository could have afforded.

Thursday, July 2 I commenced this morning by composing an answer to the
note Mrs D—— sent to Cora, she will very soon discover that I am the
author of it and it just what I wish, to make her regret her impertinent
affectation. the weather is surprisingly cool, for two evenings past I have
been very comfortable while seated by a fire in Mrs S—— bed room! the
bitters Mrs S—— has the kindness of administering to me every morning
have I believe been very beneficial, I intend having the receipe for their
preparation, and send it to Mr C—— . I again find some pleasure in practising a little Music, I have played on the Piano, and the Guitar also, to
day, and sung besides, surely I must be better. had a good deal of chit-chat
with Miss M—— this evening, among other remarks she said that she had
often thought it a pity that I had no children, for she believed I was better
calculated to bring them up well, than any other person she ever knew! I
consider this a compliment of the most flattering kind—but I do not know
whether or not I should join in the regret—ah me!—I am very lazy about
sewing I ought to have finished my dress this week, and here it is just as I
have left it last Saturday, this won't do—I am almost tired of feeding my
Birds, what attention they do require. I do not wonder that people who

sell them demand what is considered such a high price, I am sure I would not take such trouble for double the amount. It is almost ten o'Clock, a very late hour for me, I must go to bed, no great loss to my Journal, there has not been any thing at all striking to day—I have thought more than usual (and that is saying a great deal) about lights and *Shadows Shadow* Mrs B—— could say—poor Mrs B—— what business had she to suffer that Shadow (which she so much dislikes) to cross her threshold—oh human nature what inconsistent compound thou art!

Tuesday, July 7 If I merely wrote the history of the day on which I am able to add to this journal, I would pass in silence over the most agreeable portion of my time because when I go to Town or have the pleasure of seeing my friends here I have no leisure for writing. I only returned from Natchez yesterday having been there since last Saturday—E—— had come the day previous to go to visit the indian mounds [11] with us, so on Saturday morning and 4th of July we set out to view these remains of another race— our party consisted of Miss M—— Mr B—— (who by the way is a very interesting youth who has won my very affectionate regard) [12] Mary S—— Louisa B—— [13] E—— and myself—we rode in two carriages E—— and I together in one—Mr B—— on horseback—the ride was delightful, it could scarcely have otherwise with me when in the company of E—— we were in charming spirits having edified ourselves early that morning by the reading of fairy tales, "the invisible Prince", "Cinderella" and the like *new* and *improving* literature and still I think there is a charm in these childish exaggerations, which the moral and religious fictions of the "Lady of the manor" and such modern recreative readings, will ever fail to create—to return to our excursion, one of our Coachmen it appeared had no relish for antiquities, and after driving us up an eminence which commanded a view of the mounds and about one mile from them, he pointed to them, like to another land of promise, and declared that the road to them was too bad, and seemed to be of opinion that this distant sight of them ought to satisfy us the poor man had made a very wrong calculation of our curiosity, for when we beheld the mound to which all others I have before seen can bear no other comparison than that of mole hills, there was no difficulty that we would not have been willing to encounter for the pleasure of reaching the very top of it—with this determination we proceeded, and alighted from our carriages at the foot of them for they are four in number, but the principal one only was the object of attraction, I cannot say what is the height of it, but I know that we were all very tired when we attained the summit, the Sun scorching us all the while, the ascent is difficult owing to the ploughed ground, what a profanation to have destroyed the romantic aspect of these gigantic tombs for a few pounds of Cotton! We searched for remains of indian implements, but found nothing but an *old shoe!* which however we left for some more devoted amateur of *indian curiosities,* E—— picked up some pieces of baked clay of a very dark colour, which possibly may be real, they were striped and similar to some singular pieces in the possession of Mrs S—— —we returned long before dinner time, and found Mrs M'M——[14] Mrs S—— and Mrs M—— eating melons very coolly in the dining room, they had come to spend the 4th with Mrs S—— we partook of the same welcome refreshment, and some cake and wine, and then retired to our room, E—— resumed the fairy tales—and I read some passages in Miss Kemble's Journal,[15] some of them I admire exceedingly, and others I do read with pain because I think I discover in the character of the writer something resembling some of C——'s eccentricities or rather affectation of such. and I don't like it. after dinner rode to Town with E—— and met Sundry *independant* folks, whose company was not altogether desirable so we made way to let them pass, and arrived safely at Mrs P——'s house—we found Mrs P—— seated very composedly, and dressed most sweetly, ready to receive us, after delivering our dispatches—(honey, butter and cakes for the children) we rested ourselves, and in a short time had the pleasure to welcome —— 2 tumblers of ice cream—then went to see Miss H——, who heaven be praised is convalescent—saw Mrs B—— for the first time, she is not attractive, to me at least—received the Courrier!!![16]— Sunday morning E—— handed me a letter from Mrs B——t—to say that I was astonished is not exactly what I felt, at least with regard to her communication, but what struck me as miraculous is that the suspicion which had floated in my mind, and however not admitted by my reason, had positively taken place—what will she think of my last letter? she will think me a magician—returned home Monday morning met H—— S—— and Dr H——[17] on the road, the latter was going to our house, I found him there when I arrived, and Miss M—— introduced him, he is tolerably agreeable, and certainly very handsome, he seemed amused by my talk, and stayed a long time and chatted a good deal—he is evidently a Yankee—nothing of any note occured to day; ah, I was forgetting that Mr and Mrs F—— called this evening and paid balance due—I am most stupidly sleepy and must to bed—thankful to feel so, sleep is a great blessing.

Friday, July 17 Poor neglected Journal I must scribble a few lines to night were it only in token that I have not given you up, it is not for want of matter that I have been so long without journalizing, but pure want of leisure, and even now I must pass in silence over the insurrection, hangings, patroning, and all sorts of frights, because I have neither time or spirits to do them justice, and must be satisfied to record the humble fact that I this day have written to my poor dear Mrs B—— a fact more satisfying to myself than interesting to the public, but as this I am sure will never be in its way I am content to let the newspapers do their duty, and make a flourish with the expulsion of the black-legs &c—to day also I sent dear E—— a fine water melon that grew in my own patch, supported by beautiful pears peaches, and nectarines, I know she will enjoy them this evening, and will share them with Miss H——.

Monday, July 20 I was too much fatigued Saturday evening after returning from Natchez to write a line, besides I had very little to write, I bought some pretty muslin for a wrapper, received four numbers of the "Courrier" put a letter for Mrs B—— in the post office, and to my great surprise and disappointment found nothing from her, something must surely be the matter with her, for she ought to have received two letters from me since she wrote the last, perhaps her father has been worse, and perhaps this rainy weather has delayed the mails, how much I do wish to hear from her,— Yesterday I drew a plan for Mrs P——s green house, I wish it may please her, for I think it would be very pretty—one of my birds died to day, I am afraid I shall lose them all, after all my trouble and boasting. I am convinced that Miss ——'s affections are not deep, though they may be violent, vanity is at their basis what then can be expected; it is wasting one's solicitude to feel any concern for the happiness of such persons, one might as well sympathise with the sorrows of the butterfly. I practised this afternoon the *touching* "il reviendra"—how little did I dream when I sung it last that it should have proved prophetic—now it is ——'s turn to sing it with a slight alteration. I have been this evening in a very contradicting peevish humor for which I am sorry. I must go to bed the musquitoes sing and bite most spitefully to night; the frogs are croaking, the rain of course is pouring, and every one has retired for the night, I must follow their example after looking a few minutes over the "Courrier"—which is the same dear delightful old favorite that it has ever been—

Tuesday, July 21 The first news that I learned this morning were mournful! another of my birds gone poor little creature it had suffered a great deal, how strange!—sent Mrs P—— the plan by Mrs L——'s [18] coachman— received a singular message from Mrs F—— the ignorant are ever ready to dictate—had some very fine peaches. and I have wisely returned to my duty—viz—resumed my dress which I must try to finish this week, I cut out the sleeves, and sewed the band to the body, "dear good little me"—

sung *my song* again this evening, I find it very difficult to master my voice, it will go its own way, and often will stop altogether which is a great disappointment; if the good fairy were to give me three wishes, the first should be to sing as well as "queen Pasta".[19] the second —— &c and of course I would decline a third wish. sat a short time in Mrs S——'s room this evening, and discutee the advantages of being taught to dance, physically speaking—the rain still continues, there was a fire kindled in the school room this evening. R—— brought me a wreath of the loveliest blue flowers imaginable which she had gathered in the woods, I must have some of the seeds and try to make it climb on some of the trees that are to shade my *future Cottage!* heavens! will that airy *Castle* be ever realized? oh if it does how thankful! how grateful! how contented! how humbly proud how everything that is satisfying I hope to be, (if my health is granted always understood) I am afraid to think of it I dread to be disappointed in this favourite scheme, I am naturally very superstitious, and no wonder. I must go to bed, it must be late, the most perfect silence reigns in the house, and my light is burning low, this sounds a little like Mrs Radcliff's style,[2] however I shall not continue in that strain, and only finish using the ink that is in my pen, and then good night Journal, I must not forget to put my white roses out of my room they made my head ache in the night—the ink is nearly out, I did not think it would have lasted so long, I wish there was an invention to supply a pen with ink enough to last a whole page.

Sunday, August 9 Forest[21]—I have been here with Miss H—— since last friday, how much has been changed in this part of the country since I last saw it, every thing is in the most elegant style, table, furniture, attendance, all complete, I can fancy myself in England visiting at some of those beautiful seats we read of. Mrs P—— went to Natchez yesterday evening and will return to morrow and bring dear E—— with her, how I long to see her again, it is astonishing that power she possesses of brightning every object and every place by her presence how dull and faulty every one seems to me compared with her angelic goodness and intelligence Mrs S—— is the only one I have met who can enter in my views respecting her. Miss H—— is now lying on the bed reading Belinda,[22] yesterday we rode on horseback together as far as Mrs H——[23] a delightful ride it was too, fine easy horses, and comfortable english saddles *à la Fanny Kemble*[24]—we ate some delicious fresh bread and butter drank a glass of port and then walked in Mrs H—— lovely garden, flower beds, shady arbors, retired seats dark avenues, every thing in fine I admire in that way are there on a small scale to be sure, which to me renders it more precious, more sweet. just the comparison between a portrait and a miniature—Mrs D—— has just been in our room to propose a rise on horseback before dinner which of course we gladly accepted—what truly lady like manner she has of entertaining her guests.

Monday, November 9 Little did I think when I penned the preceeding page that three months should elapse before I could trace another line on this, but so it is, time glides on steadily and days accummulate into months, months into years, and these into a whole life—3 months then have passed between these two pages so near together in appearance; but how many thoughts, reflexions, emotions, have occupied the mind of the one who has filled them, and what has been the result of this expense of time. I hope not wholly mispent—one thing certain is that I have not wasted it in idleness, no I have laboured faithfully at the task set before me, and not without reward either, I have at last (with the assistance of that good Providence so kind to me unworthy as I am) secured an asylum of my own, and with grateful thanks I acknowledge my happiness at having accomplished this much, humble as it is I vow sincerely that I would not exchange it for a palace—I have this day written to Mrs B—— and the letter will go to morrow, I hope she will be pleased with it—I am thankful also that my health is better and I pray God to continue me this blessing and all those that he pours upon me every day, if so be his holy will to which I desire humbly to submit in all and everything.

Wednesday, November 11 My letter to Mrs B—— has not gone yet, the weather was too stormy to send to Town, it will go to morrow, the weather has turned very cold at once, and my throat is very sore again—I think Salmagundy funny but rather too much of puppyisms; for such juvenile writers however the fault is quite natural[25]—I have done very little to day beside the usual routine, the truth is that I have no time left even for mental exercise; and oh this everlasting thumping on that ill fated Piano, my heart at times bleed for it—while my ears shrink with agony. I was interrupted just now by Miss M—— bringing me a cup of pepper Tea, which certainly is capital cure for the sore throat, but a most severe remedy I am sure much like holding a scald to the fire—however she brought a beautiful bunch of *haws* at the same time, she is the kindest soul inhabiting the "cottage of clay"[26] of a "maiden gentlewoman" I know—I thought poor Mrs S—— had the blues to day, and wondered that so good a person could be attacked by a malady confined to the repining, and the selfish, but indeed I was mistaken in my conjecture, she was ill, physically so, and I am vexed with myself for supposing such absurdity, would that I were as free from such a sinful affection as she is, and indeed altogether like her.

Selma plantation as it is today. (Courtesy of Nancy Williams)

Thursday, November 12 I am writing to help away time while I am anxiously waiting for the return of Perry from Town in hopes that he may bring some letters and some intelligence about M—— L————I wish she may have come, how glad I shall be to see her, and fresh from P——gh[27]—too! my letter gone at last—the weather has moderated considerably—I think I hear the dogs barking—perhaps the waggon is coming—no it is only some negro chopping wood, how long that old fellow takes to go to Natchez; a whole day, he went this morning before sun rise, and it is almost 7 O'Clock, but every body has easy time here, children, negroes, cats, dogs, all do just as they please—I suppose it is as well, and certainly it will make no difference fifty years hence—but still I wish the old man would hurry a little more—I will take care to night not to read a frightful story before going to bed as I did yesterday, how can people write such shameful nonsense— here is the wagon now, for true.

Monday, November 16 I returned from Natchez yesterday, after remaining there three days in expectation of meeting Mrs L—— but only *met* my old acquaintance "Disappointment" and in several ways, the dress which I intended to wear and for the making of which I am charged with such extra extraordinary price was half way up my ancles via knees, and wanted four inches at least to meet in front, had to have another made, of course the loss will not be mine, but it is nevertheless very disagreeable—received no letters—lost one "courrier"—broke my new Casket—and sundry petty disappointments to aggravate the main one—saw Mrs S—— who had the kindness to give me some letters of introduction for Mr R—— who however had gone—saw also Miss H—— dull as ever—Mr W—— ditto—Mr D——[28] queer, quizzical, and complimenting, and upon the whole rather puzzling—he reminds me a very little of —— but I am like the woman whom every person and every possible thing reminded of Joseph in Egypt— Miss M—— came for me and dined with us, we had a tolerably pleasant ride home—received a new pupil to day, Miss W—— she is beautiful, with a most mysterious dark eye—I have been very busy indeed to day packing my seeds but I am not half done—I have also put my guitar in order, and practised a while this evening, I intend studying it this winter—oh I was going to forget the elegant "colored gentleman" who introduced himself to us last friday evening at E——'s for the purpose of displaying his musical talents, and stylish manners,—I must give an account of that entertainment to S—— some day, how she would have enjoyed such a divertimento—

Tuesday, November 17 Surely it is not from a superabundance of facts that this Journal has sprung—but rather from a scarcity of them, but dull as it is it serves to note the time, and to point out that spend it as we will, it goes on, and fast enough too—I have packed some more seeds to day for Mrs C—— and have been very busy besides about many things—played on the guitar this evening until my fingers could bear it no longer—thought a good deal more than usual about "the Shadow" don't know why—thoughts not pleasing though, nor favourable to that "obscurity" either—I think I am not afraid of it now, I hope so at any rate—time will show—marked Pocket handkerchiefs—read "courrier" and a very good article it was—the "english Parliament"—what a sprightly, and graphic way the french have, or at least their writings, I am glad I am french, were it only for the pleasure I derive from reading the language, and from which is better and much rarer, understanding what I read—what nonsense, and what waste of time it is to pretend to learn a language as most (if not all) do, without real study, it serves only to make the people who affect such knowledge ridiculous, and at most enable the possessor to ask for the "loan of a gridiron".

Saturday, November 21 Received a note from dear E—— this evening—and also an invitation to the Ball—but better than all a letter from my poor Mrs

B—— nothing very particular in it, but still delightful, she speaks lightly of serious subjects, and with mock gravity of trifling circumstances—just to amuse me, she is good and kind and reasonable, but alas I see but too well that like me she would cheat herself into the belief that her mind is at ease, and cheerful, but I see a very melancholy philosophy in her advice, and consolation—to enjoy the present forsooth! tell a man in a fit of the gout to enjoy the present! or a woman with the tooth ache to enjoy the present! or any person at hard labour in fact to enjoy the present—oh no my poor friend you were out of it when you gave that counsel—all this and more can be borne, but we must look for enjoyment in the relief from such, not in the suffering—It was cruel to try to show up the future as it will be—and you are placing me again in the dangerous situation of seeking for enjoyment in *shadows* or Poetry as you are pleased to call it—God forbid—

Monday, November 30 I finished my letter to Mrs B—— I hope sincerely that no part of it may give her pain, but I fear it may seem harsh to her to receive such stern advice from me—I have done very little to day besides that letter—I read my Mass—chatted a little with the Ladies, walked in the garden for a few minutes with Mrs S—— and thought a great deal about future plans &c—Mary S—— surprised me very agreeably this evening with a fresh supply of seed for my poor little Billy who had no idea to what extremity he was about to be reduced, the thoughtful little girl had commissioned Hector[29] to bring some from town if he could possibly get to buy them, this being Sunday—the weather is clear and beautiful again but rather cold—how they must be shut up their houses around their red-hot grates in Pittsburgh.

December 5–8 The 5th of December, I bought a lottery ticket in partnership with Eliza—I do not suppose for an instant that we are to get a prize, however she may be one of fortune's favourites, but I rather think my usual fate will preponderate—received a packet containing two letters from Mrs B—— filled with verses! also a Postscript from S—— in downright prose very satisfactory though; how much I do wish she may remain in Alleghany next year, and so near me too—in four months I hope to be on my way to meet old friends once more, will they all be the same towards me? but I, am I the same to all of them? no oh no! there is one who will I hope find me changed!—I have taken to my guitar again, and I play and sing almost every evening, it wiles away the time and it is better than to think and ponder on the past and manufacture the future, and pernicious for the eyes than reading. I wrote the following doggrel last just to try if I had lost my juvenile talents at rhyming; *certes* it has not improved by keeping, and I think I was

younger than the little girl who composed the verses copied by Mrs B——
when I composed the song beginning with

Air "gentil hussard"   Dec 9th 1835

A mon amie——
Je crus longtems que les sons de la Lyre
Ne s'accordaient qu'à des accens d'amour,
Je sens depuis qu'Amitié nous inspire
Chants aussi doux et plus surs de retour.

Réve d'Amour empoisonne la vie
Songe flatteur au reveil sans espoir
Mais le plaisir près d'une bonne Amie
Vient me chercher presque sans le savoir

Serment d'Amour est un souffle, une haleine
Dance ennivrante tel que parfum de fleur
Lien d'Amitié est une aimable chaine
Avec laquelle on fixe le bonheur

Loin d'une Amie la mémoire fidèle
d'heureux momens garde le souvenir
Un son plaintif un air pur la rapèle
Et le bonheur sourit dans l'avenir

Loin d'un Amant, soupçons, pleurs, jalousie
agitent, troublent un trop sensible coeur
Tant semblent dire près d'une autre il t'oublie
Et l'avenir n'offre que la douleur

Ah si l'absence éprouve la tendresse
Quand sont rivaux l'amour et l'amitié
Mon coeur me dit si de près l'amour blesse
l'absence a fait triompher l'amitié

Console toi ma compagne chérie
Bientôt le temps viendra nous réunir
Et dans les bras de ta fidèle Amie
Oublieras tu ce qu'il te fit souffrir?

———————

les couplets qui suivent se composerent d'eux mèmes dans ma tête la nuit
dernière et me tinrent eveillée à la suite des reflexions que je fis dans la

soirée sur la honte qu'il y auroit a ce que la France et l'Amérique devinssent ennemies par l'obstination de Jackson— —.

Air de la "Palisse"

Quel triste avenglement
La sage Amérique
Se choisit un President
Plus entété qu'une Bourique

———

Il passe pour etre vaillant
mais il n'est qu'un opinâtre
ceux qui vont le contrariant
Ils les battroient comme plâtre—quel triste avenglement &c

———

Pour mieux montrer sa valeur
Il cherche noise à la France
Mais il ne nous fait pas peur
Bon chien n'aboie pas d'avance—quel triste avenglement &c

———

et la tête des ingrats
Quand il vent nous faire la guerre
Oublie-t-il que nos soldats
l'affranchirent de l'Angleterre—quel triste avenglement

———

Qu'il apprenne donc une fois
Par cette belle escapade
Qu'on n'effraie point les gaulois
Avec des fanfaronades   quel triste &c

———

Amis chantons désormais
Et que chacun s'écrie
Vive les braves français
Leur gloire et leur Patrie   quel triste &c [30]

———

Friday, December 11 Dec 11th—! This day is the anniversary of my departure from Pittsburgh, this year has glided away like a bark on a smooth stream; and yet it has had its fears its dangers, it is past however, and with thanks to my heavenly Father I look with satisfaction on my labours, I have accomplished more than I had anticipated, and suffered less from disappointments than I feared, and now the time is fast approaching when I shall see whether I really have overcome my weakness!—how sincerely I do hope it will prove so, but time only can show; I thought once before that I had recovered my reason, and oh how mistaken! but I have far other causes now to believe I have. I played and sung this evening, I am getting very fond of my guitar, it is a sweet, a dear thing.

To my Guitar

Compagne de mes courts loisirs,
douce et plaintive mélodie
tes sons se mêlent à mes soupirs,
et font le charme de ma vie.

Que de souvenirs, de soucis
tes tendres accords me rappelent
mais quand tu charmes mes ennuis
le sourire et l'espoir s'éveillent

J'aime à presser près de mon coeur
Ta forme gracieuse et legère.
Je te croirois presqu'une soeur
tant ta voix m'est devenue chère

Ah que ne puis-je t'animer?
te confier toutes ma peine!
t'avertir des malheur d'aimer
de repentir qu'il nous amène
ou que de puis-je comme toi
charmer et rester insensible
N'etant sujette qu'a la loi
dans harmonie tendre et paisible [31]

Saturday, December 12 I have been very busy all day cutting and shaping card boards into all manners of devices for pocket-Books, pin-cushions &c—for the girls, and this evening read some news-papers, this is the amount of this day's occupation, I might well exclaim with the great Titus (I believe it was him who said it) I have lost a day! [32] for really I have done no good whatever, and felt moreover rather peevish, as poor kind M—— no doubt perceived, I am ashamed of myself, nobody in the world will ever be so indulgent to me, how can I treat her so scandalously? who does everything to make me comfortable? I am an ungrateful wretch, God forgive me! and make me better.

Sunday, December 13 Not that I have anything to record worth the trouble, but merely to keep up the habit of scribbling, I don't know whether the habit is good or bad, but I wish to fill up every moment if possible and acquire an active disposition, which I suspect I do not naturally possess, or I would not be so inclined to musings, or so fretted when I have no leisure to indulge in them. I know it is not good for me and I have better blot paper and waste ink than make myself more miserable and disagreeable than I possibly can help—I have literally done nothing this day, I am excusable though, as it happens to be Sunday—and besides not well, I have dawdled about as Miss Kemble would say.[33] the weather is beautiful, the stars are sparkling like diamonds, the simile is not very original to be sure, but it is very appropriate, and besides what is original? I would like to know, has not every thing under and around, and over, and across, and into the Sun been found out, and thought, and said, and done, nothing more is left for us to do but to begin again with all the good sayings and fine ideas of former times, and they sometimes will pass for something new. even fashion has exhausted its genius, and can do no more now than to lenghten the skirts, flatten the sleeves, and enlarge the Bonnet, which is nothing but the renewal of antiquated taste; but I think I could strike upon a bold plan, it is long enough now that the masculine side of the human race has worn the round hat and the *unutterables,* let them now take to the flowing robes, and allow us the use of the boot and spur, the vest, stock &c—there would be advantage to both parties in the exchange, and surely some originality in the execution of the plan.

Tuesday, December 15 My Birth day! oh dear how they do throng upon one another, the Sun I think is running a race (or the Earth I should have said) with some Comet for the last ten years, so I am this day—I won't say how old for fear this document should witness against me—but what are numbers? poor S——a tells me that some people never get old let them live ever so long—I am not one of these I am sure, for I feel very old indeed, quite a grand Mother, especially when I look at Eliza's children,[34] good gracious how foolish it would be to act the youthful when I have the rheumatism in my shoulder, when I can't see across the street, and worse than all have plenty of grey hairs, why I might call myself venerable. I have worked very hard to day—and behaved rudely this evening to poor Miss M—— but she had no business to ask me if I wanted a fire kindled, when she knew very well that I did want one in a room where I was to sit until bed time, and then to come at eight o'Clock when I wanted to be alone, and bringing a handful of chips just for a pretext to sit and talk, and rob me of my precious time, this was too much really so I said that I did not want any fire, that I was warm enough—with this ungracious reception she went off mad enough I know—perhaps I was wrong, I know I was, one should always be polite and never exhibit temper, but the fact is that such conduct is lost on some persons and encourages them to intrude their burdensome company, not that I consider Miss M——'s in that light generally, but at times she is a perfect bore, you cannot make a remark, or ask a question to another person but the answer comes from her, and as soon as any body utters a word she begins a running accompaniment in an upper tone—how opposite to this is Mrs S—— sensible, modest, well bred, the truth is that I think her perfect—*barring* that she spoils her children and that is a very slight blemish—Eliza wrote to me yesterday that our prize was to be drawn that day, and that she would bring it out with her next week when she comes, if it is paid in specie I am afraid the carriage will break down with the load.

I played on my darling guitar this evening, what an infatuation! I am afraid of catching cold, and must hurry to bed.

Wednesday, December 16 This evening received a note from Eliza in which she says that Alfred is very sick with a horrible cold, I am very sorry indeed, and I was afraid it would come to this the last time I saw him. received also a letter from Mr G Co—— accompanying the Books and also an Elegant Juvenile annual for my best Pupil which of course I presented to M S——. how very kind and polite of Mr C—— to send such a gift—My poor little Billy has a sore foot and has not sung for two days; how singular it is that a woman could form an attachment for a little bird. yet so it is, for I positively love that minute being and very fondly too; I am still very busy and very tired, I think the time of Christmass comes on but slowly, I will not attempt again to gratify my scholars by teaching them to make those pretty trifles, it is too laborious for me, and after all I rather suspect that it creates feelings of envy towards those who are more skilful or more praised for their success—I wish I was in the old path again of the regular routine.[35]

theirs. but what does lead me into such bitter vein? ah I know too well—remembrance of the *past!*—yes of the *past* is all the extent of the word and meaning—and of a past never to return either, in any manner whatever. I hope.

Teach me if you can,—Forgetfulness!
I surely shall forget, if you can bid me;
I who have worshipped thee my God on Earth,

I who have bowed me at thy lightest word.
Your last *command*, "forget me," will it not
Sink deeply down within my inmost soul?
Forget thee! ay, forgetfulness will be
A mercy to me. By the many nights
When I have wept for that I dared not sleep,——
A dream had made me live my woes again.
Acting my wretchedness without the hope
My foolish heart still clings to, though that hope
Is like the opiate which may lull a while,
Then wake to double torture; By the days
Passed in long watching and in anxious fears,
When a breath sent the crimson to my cheek,
Like the red gushing of a sudden wound;
By all the careless looks and careless words
Which have to me been like the scorpion's stinging;
My happiness blighted, and by thee, for ever;
By thy eternal work of wretchedness;
By all my withered feelings, ruined health.
Crush'd hopes, and rifled heart, I will forget thee!

——— Alas. my words are vanity. forget thee!
Thy work of wasting is too surely done
The April shower may pass and be forgotten,
The rose fall and one fresh, spring in its place,
And thus it may be with light summer love.
It was not thus with mine:——it did not spring,
Like the bright colour on an evening cloud,
Into a moment's life, brief, beautiful;
Nor amid lighted halls, when flatteries
Steal on the ear like dew upon the rose,
As soft, as soon dispersed, as quickly pass'd;
But you first call'd my woman's feelings forth,
And sought to win, ere I'd scarce heard your name.

——— And yet that name was all
That seemed in language, and to me the world
Was only made for you;——In solitude,
When passions hold their interchange together,
Your image was the *shadow* of my thought,
Never did slave before his eastern Lord,
Tremble as I did when I met your eye,

And yet each look was counted as a prize;
I laid your words up in my heart like pearls
Hid in the Ocean's treasure cave. at last
I learn'd my heart's deep secret: for I hoped,
I dream'd you loved me! wonder, fear, delight,
Swept my heart like a storm; my soul, my life,
Seemed all too little for your happiness;
Had I been mistress of the starry worlds
That light the midnight, they had all been yours,
And I had deem'd such boon but poverty:
As it was I gave all I could—my love!
My deep, my true, my fervent, faithful love;
And now you bid me learn forgetfulness!
It is a lesson that I promise to learn,
A somewhat hard, and cold, and desperate task,
But still I shall learn it.—

　　　What is this tale that I would tell? not one
of strange adventure, but a common tale,
of woman's wretchedness; one to be read,
Daily in many a sad, a blighted heart.
The Lady whom I spake of, rose again
From the red fever's couch, to careless eyes
Perchance the same as she had ever been,
But oh, how altered to herself! she felt
That bird like pining for some gentle home
To which affection might attach itself; she felt
That weariness which hath but outward part
In what the world calls pleasure; and that chill
Which makes life taste the bitterness of Death.

—And *He* she loved so well,—what opiate
Lulled conscience into its selfish sleep?
He said he loved her not; that never vow
Of passionate pleading won her soul for him,
And that he guess'd not her deep tenderness.
Are words then only false? are there no looks
Mute, but most eloquent, no gentle cares
That win so much upon the weak frail things
They seem to guard? and had he not long read
Her heart's hush'd secret in the deep dark eye
Lighted at his approach, and on the cheek

Colouring all crimson at his lightest look?
This is the truth; his spirit wholly turn'd
To stern ambition's dream, that joyless path
Which leads to the world's high places, and car'd not
What plants might perish in his path.

And here at length is somewhat of revenge,
For men's most golden dreams of pride and power,
Are vain as any woman's dream of love;
Both end in weary brow, and withered heart,
And the grave closes over those whose hopes
Have lain there long before.

1836

Sunday, March 20, 1836 This is Sunday and a very gloomy one, it has been raining constantly for three days past, I went to Town last Wednesday in expectation of meeting Mary L—— but of course was disappointed, she had not arrived yet even thursday morning when I left, not being able to stay any longer—we went on wednesday night to see the splendid Mrs Ternan in "Juliet"[1] I must confess that I was disappointed, and yet I cannot tell what in, for she is a beautiful woman, an admirable actress, and grace itself, and yet I have no wish whatever to see her again, indeed quite the contrary, for I secretly wish it may rain to morrow so that I may be freed from a half kind of engagement I have made to go to her benefit. I received a letter from Mrs B——t probably the last as she says herself. she is still rhyming on bless her heart—how queer—I received to day a beautiful indian Basket from Miss M—— as a keep sake, most acceptable, she is as generous as the Sun. what a scribbling I do keep.

Tuesday, March 22 Certainly no one ever presumed to take a pen having (or rather knowing) so little what to say than I do—and yet I feel a restlessness that urges me on to scribble for want of more congenial employment, oh if I had here some one to talk to, openly, without this stiff reserve which positively wears out my very existence—what would I have? why a friend to whom I could open my heart, with whom I could talk, laugh, shout, rattle away any thing, my dear S—— in short—shall this ever be? ah me, heaven grant, I wonder if I could get up a good laugh of old times yet? no, no, I fear that joyous time is gone, I think I have changed very much since that, I know that I have, for I can hardly find any thing now that can give me pleasure even for a moment, I am growing foolish and ungrateful this evening, so I better leave off and go to bed.

SECOND JOURNAL

Part the Second

Continued December 8th 1836—Belfield—Mississippi

by reviewing daily events we keep accounts with experience—

May I never do what I would be ashamed to record—

Thursday, December 8, 1836 If ever there has been a poor female mortal on this terraquous Globe more lonely, more worn out with ennui, more ennuyense, more ready to give up than I am this present minute, which is the fiftieth after eight O'clock P M—I would like to know how she ended, so that I might prepare for the worst—this is no joke, heaven knows! I will not attempt to describe how I feel for I know of no comparison, no expression adequate to the purpose—I can only say that lonely I have been, lonely I am, and lonely I am likely to be for five months to come, that is if I can stand it that long, which I think extremely doubtful, unless some change takes place in me or in the present state of things, for I acknowledge that I am not so amply furnished with intellectual resources of my own as to be able to draw upon them altogether without running the risk of soon exhausting the whole stock—this is an old story to be sure, but it is worth repeating, because it goes point blank to refute and disprove the long believed axiom that every thing changes, well I can maintain that this state of affairs here has not changed, witness the different dates of this book—unless indeed aggravation of a case may be called a changement. this is a promising beginning certainly and a very great encouragement to proceed, I must say—

Friday, December 9 I have been just now turning back the leaves of this Journal to find out what I was about this day last year, and behold it appears that I was writing a song! good gracious but I feel differently this day, heaven only knows! but there is no telling, perhaps next year I may at this very time be dancing a hornpipe, or waltzing a galop who can say? the weather is very warm, and this is friday, two important facts, one at least is of some consequence to me being the day which terminates my *scholastique* week—there has been some jarring of some sort in the machinery of our system to day for I perceived at dinner time that one of the pieces was absent and when I saw it afterwards it appeared somewhat out of order, my departement having no connexion with that branch of the works, I have no means of ascertaining what has occured—this afternoon has been greatly enlivened by the visit of a dutch pedlar! with silks and satins for sale, I was called upon for my opinion, I thought they were all hideous but did not say so before the soi-disant Polonois—and duly assisted Mary in choosing a small shawl this is quite an event, and will be very useful in furnishing us with a subject for conversation for one week at least—we are in the habit here of making the most of these matters.

Monday, December 12 The rain is pouring down in torrents, I am writing this while waiting for the breakfast to be ready, we rarely ever get it now before nine o'Clock, it is past it now—I went to Town last Saturday with Mrs S—— and Mary—had a very unpleasant ride both going and coming— Mrs S—— would not suffer Mary to take the front seat which she always did occupy, and insisted upon taking it herself and was sick all the way, still refusing to change seat with me, it was a very painful kind of politeness to me who felt very much mortified all the time and does yet when I think of it—they were all very well at E——'s—the baby[2] is very pretty—they are anxious to sell their place and Mrs P—— also—she talks now of building at Oakley—and now I ought to congratulate myself for having firmly refused the offer of Mrs P—— what would be the result now if I had spent the little I had in putting up a house for myself on their ground? I would be a hinderance to them—and it would be ruin to me, but fortunately I had foreseen all this. I bought A. Dumas' "impressions de voyage"[3]—and read the first volume yesterday it is very entertaining—we saw Marguerite in Town and would have brought her out with us but she demured—Miss Maria is to go for her next Saturday—for my part I do not intend going to Town before Christmass.

Wednesday, December 14 Finished the delightful "impressions de voyage" to night, I am sorry they are done, how happy Dumas must be to possess so much talent, and yet it is not to be doubted that he has felt and feels yet the cruel pangs of wounded pride, the bitter curse of prejudice rests upon him, and the low, the base, the ignorant, the fool may spit their poison at him! I would glory in rendering my lowly homage to his genius in the presence of the whole world—I wonder what countenance he has? I imagine him thin and rather small, with sharp features and a moderately fashionable look. when I read those books of the modern french litterature I am always seized with violent desire of setting off for France instantly, and then at other times, (this afternoon for instance) I wish for nothing more but to plant flowers in my garden, and have a pleasant book to read occasionnaly. and now for the Journal! I ate two biscuits and drank one cup of coffee for my breakfast—at Dinner had some chicken fricassee and a sweet potatoe—supper—the same as breakfast—cannot remember any thing of greater, or equal importance occurring to me this day—

Friday, December 16 Having no one to whom I may breathe one word about my loneliness and cheerless situation it is still something to be able to come to this book and transfer however feebly and imperfectly some of the feelings that I fear will one day make me commit some act of rashness of which I may repent afterwards. but it is not in human nature to stand forever sighs and uplifted eyes instead of the common intercourse of sociable beings—all day confined to my sufficiently painful task, I have not even the small refreshment of hearing one word spoken at my melancholy meals—what can be the matter? I don't know—Mary is well, and I see no cause for this mournful aspect—perhaps I am the cause of it, if so why not tell me—what can I suppose, or what can I not suppose from this singular state of things—perhaps Mary had made some complaint about her lessons—the truth is that if I had known what I do now I would not by any means have returned here—how I shall go through the time agreed is more than I can tell unless matters alter a great deal but here no change takes place in any thing except an increase of gloominess now and then—Miss Maria is the only human like creature about, for really poor Mrs S—— is only fit for heaven so little is the intercourse she has with earthly creatures except with Mary who is all in all and a great deal more, the Alpha and Omega of her Mother's existence. what business had I to come back. a little more money! and perhaps I shall be disappointed in that, it looks very much like it this far—if this day were the 9th of February 1837—I would most probably resign my post to Margaret and wish her success and fortitude.

Monday, December 19 Monday again—spent most part of yesterday in reading—Margaret W—— sat with me doing the same—Miss M—— had gone to Town on Saturday to bring her home—all here pretty much as usual—received no letters yet—I must try to take things as they come and become more independant of the action of others or else I must look forward to a miserable existence—if letters come, well and good, if not don't fret about them—I had the rheumatism in the head and face yesterday and suffered very much, to day it is well; and so it goes with every thing in life the good and the evil—and so we will arrive at the end of this entertainment of shifting scenes, the instruments still getting tuned, our spirits still getting ready for enjoyment, but the concert will never commence, and the happiness anticipated never be realized! not here at any rate.

Tuesday, December 20 A tremendous storm, the limbs of trees flying in every direction, the weather very warm—had some quizzes yesterday coming to speak about bringing a scholar, I think they will not do it though, this is not the kind of school they were seeking—poor M—— again just came in to tell me not to be alarmed that they were burning the soot in the chymnies, I was practising on the Piano at the time and heard the rumbling and of course had no concern about it—but this would not do. I must not be indifferent to so important a transaction so as I was going on busy with my music, in she came again with a servant and a bunch of straw, still seeing that I was not interrupted she had to come and speak loud in my ear almost that she regretted to interrupt me but that they were going to burn my chimney, there was no withstanding it any longer—so I gave her the satisfaction of turning round and of looking at hector putting the broom up the chimney, and of listening to the rumbling it made—I don't think though that she was perfectly satisfied, for I did not speak sufficiently about the operation and manifested too little interest altogether as to its effect—I would like to know what part of the skull contains the organ of philo-fuss-iveness?— I must absolutely note that this very day one year the same circumstance occured and in the very same manner—viz—"Dec 20th 1835"—

Wednesday, December 21 This day has been excessively cold, the water in my room remained frozen in the pitcher all day—there came a gentleman this evening bringing a letter to Mrs S—— from Mrs H—— all the way from Vermont! guess he found we had a tolerable change of cold weather too!— I have not seen him, but I hear him now making a great racket in his room up above, he is a revd gentleman—Hector has gone to Town this morning and is not back yet he was told to inquire if there were any letters for me, but I do not believe that he will bring me any, so I will not be disappointed, since I expect nothing. I think I hear Hector's voice now speaking to Miss Maria—of course there is nothing for me or she would have brought it in.

1837

Tuesday, January 3, 1837 Another year has commenced it seems (and in fact does) that it brings nearer the period of my return to my little corner of dear A——[1]—I have spent the Christmas holidays with Mrs P—— and

family—on Christmas eve they had an oyster supper at which Dr L——
was invited accidentally—the most complete bore I ever have met with
Catherine S——[2] was also of the party, silent and stiff as any fish—on Sunday it rained and on Monday morning it was excruciatingly cold, however
the dinner party which was to take place at A's—went on and proved very
agreeable Mr D—— with his arm in a sling and his bandaged head was the
lion of the feast of course, he looked so pale and interesting that the ladies
evidently were jealous to show their sympathy, he however played modest
very well and appeared as mild and humble as a lamb—my seat at the table
was next to Mr W—— who entertained me very pleasantly and indeed did
not quite forsake me the rest of the evening—the next day I went to Town
with Amelia[3] and bought a box and materials for transferring, but when we
tried to execute the work it proved a complete failure—on wednesday Mrs
P—— and Sula[4] accompanied me here so that I might get some clothes to
go out to second creek the next day, we met Miss M—— and Mary on the
road to Town about half way—we arrived here long before dinner and to
our surprise Mary and Miss M—— returned in time to dine with us—on
friday we set out for the country, on our way thither called to pay a visit
to Mrs B—— who invited me to spend the next evening—we arrived at
Greenfield[5] at one o'Clock, I with a severe nervous head ache caused by
the children which we had taken along and who kept climbing and kick-
ing and chattering all the way—not finding Mrs D——[6] at home we got
in the carriage again and proceeded to Mr H—— where she was dining,
found them all at the table and took our seats there too—Julia looking very
affectedly sweet, she is not in the least handsome, but she is reported to
be very aimable—we stopped at the Forest on our way back to Greenfield
where we were to sleep—saw Mrs O—— and Mrs F——[7] the former
evidently a lady and very prepossessing, the other looking like a jolly milk
maid and appearing in a very wrong position indeed, but knowing it for
she did try to take as many fine airs as she could manage, but without any
effect but that of disgusting me—we returned to Town Saturday and went
to spend the evening at Capt D——[8] with A—— C—— and D—— and
A—— found quite a numerous company, Mrs W——[9] played and sung
a great deal, and very well—I waltzed with Mr W—— and D—— with
Dr P—— it was rather a pleasant evening, the next day Hector brought
the carriage for me, and I was glad to find myself going home again, the
time had appeared very long while I was away from it and this proves that
its monotony is not without some charm—something awaited me which
I did not expect—a beautiful mocking bird! I received a letter from Mr
C—— while in Town he speaks quite poetically of my little cottage and of
my most unpoetical self—I have a tolerably full school room again and feel

less discontented that I did before the new year commenced, I must try if possible to remain in that temper of mind.

Friday, January 6 Had a very unpleasant transaction to perform to day viz— to refund thirty dollars for part of the time of Misses C—— and M—— they having complained of Miss M——'s treatment and declared their inability to endure it any longer—I could have refused, but wished to avoid any kind of discussion with Mr W—— who is any thing but a gentleman— still I am not satisfied with Miss M—— who had no business to interfere with the girls, and is always some how or other doing me some very unnecessary piece of service. oh how tired I am of this kind of life and must I to the end of my days struggle in this manner against every inclination of my nature, and day after day take up this loathed chain? I fear it must be so, unless indeed—but that would only be changing of bondage—I am sick at heart again—oh the world—oh Life itself—how paltry, how contemptible!

Sunday, January 8 Yesterday I went to Town with Mary, I was not at all inclined to go but Miss C—— had determined that we should be off that day, and go we had—I took my dress to Mrs Dixon who by the by has not much the air of a fashionable mantua maker—went to Myrtle bank found Eliza quite alone, every body gone to the country, dined with her, and looked at "Hardings Tour" [10]—very fine indeed—got home before Tea time—went to bed early—this has been a long long day I am glad that it is nearly over, the rain kept pouring down gloomily, and everything is very dull—I wish I could feel cheerful I do try very hard sometimes, but I cannot, I think I never will be able to get over this discouraged way I am in—and I know it is very wrong, very ungrateful indeed, how many would be happy to be in the same position.

Monday, January 9 The day has been very fine, the same work in school as usual—spent all this evening practising some divine music of the "Sonnambula" [11] every minute the tears coming up in my throat and choking me— I never heard such deeply touching style in my life, I am sure I repeated one page more than twenty and had to tear myself away with a great effort my throat getting so sore that I could not sing another note—what a mysterious thing is music, I know of nothing that can excite my thoughts as it does, if I were mistress of my time it would occupy the principal part of it. as it is my fondness for it is only an addition to my manifold annoyances— I believe every body has gone to bed—so I must go too.

Wednesday, January 11 How the different scents of flowers influence the spirits I have here a hyacinth which I keep smelling to remind me of spring and home, but few of the flowers of this country recall dear and familiar associations—the perpetual rose for instance has no charm for me, on the contrary—I think the homeliest flowers bring the most pleasing feelings—to me the perfume of the Cape Jessamin is singularly associated with the ideas of death and sickness—the double sweet violet with absence, and longing, and false hopes—but the wall flower, the hyacinth, the reseda, that is home indeed home perfumes; and why so? I really cannot tell.

Thursday, January 12 Cold, rainy, lonely night, and no doubt Miss Lyons [12] thinks it quite the reverse for this night she has been getting married, and so it is with all things, and places, and times—just as our own particular circumstances are agreeable or otherwise so we view the surrounding objects—I have been taking a peep "in fancy" at my own little castle and saw nothing but a sheet of snow all around and over it, and the walls and pailings looking dingy and the gallery half filled with snow—I know that is the exact way it does look—in spite of Mr C———'s pretty poetical allusion I find although as busy as any bee I will not bring much honey to the hive after all—money is either very scarce or the people are hoarding up—but no I rather think the gaudy buildings and fantastic improvements are swallowing it as fast as it appears, it is a perfect rage, I am sure that next spring the Town of Natchez will rival Cincinnati, every man is building a villa, or a castle, or a palace, or some such grandioso edifice, I wonder what has set them going. I have been trying to read some of the stories in the "Forget me not" [13] this evening but they are really too foolish, so I gave it up and I believe will go to bed—I would like to have such another pretty dream as I had last night.

Saturday, January 14 I must write if only for the sake of keeping out of bed a few minutes longer, it is not quite half past eight, and I just came out of Mrs S———'s room trying to wear away one hour or so, but I perceived that she was longing to go to bed, so I retired—I have been sewing this day, without doing much either—I painted a little bird this afternoon to please Mary, and practised a song or two. it has cleared up to day but it is cold still—brought my mocking bird into the school room to spend the day with me, he will not sing yet, and he has been here two weeks, I wish I could find a pretty name for him. no letters from Mrs B——— neither from Mrs W——— they have other things to do I have no doubt, but a few lines could not be a great interruption, but perhaps they have not the inclination, and why should I distress myself about it—so I will think no more of it.

time begins to seem heavy again, I think that when we set out on a journey, or commence an undertaking the first part goes swiftly enough, but when about getting towards the middle, it drags along like a snail, until that point is passed and the latter half is encroached upon, and then it moves briskly again, I am now a little over one third of my voyage, and therefore the lagging period has to be gone over, I must hope that a few weeks will bring on the quick pace again, and then both whip and spurs must be used. well I have managed to sit up till nine with my scribbling.

Monday, January 16 The weather is beautiful again, spent yesterday after noon in writing a letter to Mrs Bonnet—I have made a package of the "Impressions" which I will send to her by Mr Lambdin—was bored all the morning by old Harper of Washington [14] he came under pretence of wishing to send his daughter here, but he has no such intention, it is more than he dares do—the methodists would turn him out for his pains—I am not well to night, indeed I have felt badly for several days passed, dear me what singular thing is life, and the world, and man, and more singular than all, woman! morally and physically, yes she is born to suffer, and endure, and not complain, to foresee, to divine almost the results of doings which she has not power to avert or repel! she is made to live upon the breath of another, her very existence is depending on beings upon which she has no control, excepting the mockery submission of the hour when she is marked out by her tyrant for a still deeper slavery—and she knows it all, and still she will go on suffering, and yet smiling, cheering the spirit of the being who dooms her to this bondage, and cherishing the hand that plunges her in the abyss! am I not right to say, that woman is the most singular of all the created things we know of? I do wish I had an amusing book to read, I am so sick of the gilded annuals.

Tuesday, January 17 Very warm evening indeed—this Journal of mine in one respect might prove valuable, as an Almanack of the weather of "the day before" but not of the day after, still as what has been may happen again it might be useful next year—I omitted mentioning yesterday that I was presented with a ring by Ezilda—she was so proud of having a present for me that she could not wait till monday to bring it, she had to come purposely Sunday afternoon, it is a great affair, at least she thinks so. I know few situations more gloomy than to be sitting alone a warm winter night with just enough of fire to remind you of the season, and that fire made out of some sort of wood that does not send any blaze but burns black, and makes such a singing that you keep all the time thinking of passing close to the boilers of a Boat in the act of raising steam, add to this (or rather subtract from the natural comfort of a solitaire,) the wants of books, to be sure here is a case full of them at my back, (for indeed it is my own delectable situation I have been describing) but they are all of the kind the very appearance of which is a sufficient to insure their repose—"Hume" and Locke [15]—and Caesar's commentaries, besides lighter productions such as Matte Brun [16]—and Domestic Encyclopedia [17]—and one odd volume of a french translation of Shakespeare! these and similar works, all strongly bound in leather are at my disposal. Miss M——— has just been with me and chatted a few minutes—and Mrs S——— to see if I could change a hundred dollars note, which I did as may be supposed with pleasure—literally speaking—and now I believe I have no more to say for to day or rather to night for it is ten minutes of nine o'Clock and a moonlight night, which said moon has a large circle around it signifying rain very soon.

Wednesday, January 18 I think I have wound up the day in a most edifying manner by singing three hymns! only three! and no trifling ones either— the truth is that when the duties of the day are over unless I have something to read I can do nothing more recreative than music, it drowns thoughts, and is like a voice that speaks of things beyond this melancholy sphere—I am sitting here without a fire to night, it is like an evening in June, I had my mocking bird out in the yard to day sitting on a table and while I was looking at it from the gallery another mocking bird came and danced upon the table all round the cage as if wishing to get in it, my bird opened his wings and bill and screamed.

Thursday, January 19 The weather still very beautiful and very warm, I am afraid it will not last till Saturday, almost impossible it should—Dr H——— was here this afternoon and stayed to Tea, I came to the table purposely after all the girls were seated so that he could have no opportunity of offering to shake hands with me, he asked if had escaped the bad cold &c— I merely answered, and got up from the table in about five minutes—he perceived that something must have offended me, and remained a long time talking to Mrs Smith—and she told me this evening that he was in great trouble about it, and said that what he had said had been misrepresented &c—and ah his usual palaver—I told Mrs S——— that I did not believe one word of all he might say, and that he might be in trouble all the days of his life if kept telling stories the way he does now—got a note from Eliza this evening Mr L——— has not yet appeared so I may still hope to send my letters by him—no letters for me from Allegheny I suppose I will be back home before they make up their minds to answer my letters—those I am going to send now will be the last that I shall trouble them with unless they do show some inclination to correspond.

Friday, January 20 Just as I had expected, it has turned bitterly cold and cloudy since this morning, I have very little doubts but that to morrow it will snow, or sleet, or blow intolerably, so I must give up all ideas of going to Town to morrow—it cannot be helped; and I would not care about it if I had here what I wanted to bring—Mrs S——n [12]—has spent the day here she had a very pretty fawn colored plush bonnet. I feel very good for nothing to night it is the peculiar feeling of the end of the week, and yet I really cannot go to bed at half past six—it is a sad thing to have no society after all, to be alone in the world in a manner—and yet that is the prospect before me here, or there, but no it must not be so, but who shall I associate to my fate, surely not one who would be a stranger to my tastes my habits, who in fact would only be an incumbrance instead of a companion—Mrs B—— if differently situated would be the very person, but then again she has ways of her own quite incompatible with mine—if it were possible for ——[19] to come and stay with me I would gladly embrace the occasion, but I know there would be many objections on every side, and it cannot be thought of, I must trust to Providence.

Monday, January 23 To my surprise last Saturday morning was a most radiant one, so Miss Maria and I went to Town as we had intended—stopped at Mrs Davis [20] first to get my dress, tried it on and took it away—then went to E——'s—no one at home, but expected shortly—so in the mean time I paid a visit to Mrs T—— [21] found Margaret looking very well and fat, she had no letters from Pittsburg either—met E—— and Sula coming back home—after dinner Miss M—— called for me and we got back home about sun down—yesterday was a fine day too, Mr and Mrs R—— spent the day here—this morning Charlotte H—— [22] brought me a beautiful pair of red birds—I have the rheumatism in the head again and feel but poorly otherwise—I have been sitting up till ten o'Clock to finish reading the "Diary of a Blasé" [23] which I think is any thing but "blasé" for he seems to enjoy himself right well yet, it is not any thing very remarkable either one way or another, any body might have written it, I say so because I had expected something more spirited from Marryat—I like him only on the Sea,[24] that being his element he should not come out of it, I believe there is no such animal as an amphibious Author. for I have seen many a land writer drowned or rather sink for venturing on the tempting waves, I wonder what would be my element? the air I suppose for I make out very well building Castles.

Tuesday, January 24 Turned very cold again the day passed very much as usual, Mr B—— arrived here this evening—played and sung for him, very gentlemanly person—read four chapters of Pickwick,[25] I think it is a poor foolish thing notwithstanding the high encomiums of high authorities, it is the very kind of humor I detest, nothing to be compared to the Irish stories they are what I called genuine wit, this Pickwick is heavy and affected in the extreme—I was very near losing one of my red birds this morning it dashed itself about till it fell down to all appearance dead, the singing of the canaries had frightned it into a fit—I wish this may be the last of the cold weather, I think if spring would but begin the time would not be so tedious in its course, how very slow it moves for me, and yet why wish it to pass away, ah I know well for a change—once that gained and I would wish it to relent and linger oh yes to linger as long as —— how silly I am, better go to bed "perchance to sleep" the chance tolerably certain however.

Thursday, January 26 What a change since yesterday, the sun to day shines beautifully and warms us into cheerfulness, yesterday at this time it was raining, sleeting, snowing and blowing—and so is this world, this day two weeks Mr Lyons[26] was marrying his daughter, to day his friends are taking him to his last earthly home, the house of feasting has soon turned into that of mourning. I have sprained my foot very badly this afternoon, it is very painful—Mr B—— went away this morning before breakfast—Mrs S—— is in bad spirits, she is vexed about what he told her of Dr H—— she thinks his information comes from the S——s—and no doubt but it is the case. finished Pickwick. what a miserable affair. sometimes I really believe that some of these people who write books are trying how far they can go on quizzing the public to their faces, and make them buy the meanest of trash without fear or remorse, what a vile abuse of the liberty of the press and of the noble invention of printing, if I were a Sovereign they might publish their impudent babble, but the bastinado would be their reward, so they would be apt to reflect a little before they would sit about composing to rob the people of their money—that would certainly be a check to the "Diaries" and the "Blasés", and the Ennuyées,[27] and all such affected impudence, and real ignorance—

Friday, January 27 I had been in bed about half an hour last night and could not sleep for the pain of my foot, and I was going to get up and pour cold water upon it as I had heard was sometimes done in such a case, when the loud report of a cannon apparently not far off was heard, I was a little alarmed, but upon reflection I calmed myself by supposing that some of the carpenters at work at Mrs Walton[28] had fired a tree for their amusement, and went on bathing my foot, which relieved me very much, in the course of a few minutes however I heard voices on the gallery and Miss Maria speaking to the servants, so I went to Mrs Smith's room to enquire what was the matter, I found her dressing herself and preparing to go to the quarters, Perry having just had both his hands blown off by the explosion of a flask of gunpowder, which explained the noise we had heard—the doctor was sent for immediately, and Mrs S—— told me this morning that the right hand might possibly be saved—

I have a very bad head ache this evening and will go to bed early to make up for last night's loss of sleep—I have been thinking a great deal to day about last summer, and particularly upon a very particular case which I would like very much to know how to decide on, but probably time will do that for me as it does in every emergency—I wonder if Mrs Malaprop's advice is true?[29] I might ask Mrs E—— she ought to know.

Saturday, January 28 Begin the day by revising my wardrobe, found myself minus nine pocket handkerchiefs! told Miss Maria of it, who went and talked to Adna[30] about it, of course it was of no use, I told also about the scarf— mended several things, then finished a sketch—after dinner went with Mary to see Perry who was much better—it is a long time since I have spent so short a Saturday at home, it probably appeared so on account of the beauty of the weather—planted a slip of apple geranium in a pot. that makes me think of those I left behind me, and my dear beautiful Oleander—and then these lead me to think also of those with whom I have left all that I care for! I fear their care for me is a light weight indeed, three months passed, and not one line—but I do not wish to complain, and still I cannot stifle every feeling at once—it is here, and there, and every where the same, I reproach none, but I learn a painful lesson. heaven knows I am not selfish, perhaps too little so—of course I have that natural desire of having my affection returned, and oh for the certainty of being really dear to one human being I would endure whatever privation, make any sacrifice that could be required: I have and I do not yet love, (not like, not esteem only) but love with all my soul three individuals, and believed for a long time myself loved, if not equally, at least as much so as the circumstance of each could admit of—and now I have learned to doubt, the time may perhaps come when I will do worse than doubt!—I was in a train of thought last night upon this very subject and counting for how many persons I have in my life felt what may be termed love, pure, warm, heart felt affection, which nothing can change, nothing extinguish but death, and not even that—that sort of affection which can be wounded by unkindness; the heart in which it has taken root may be broken but not estranged! well after recapitulating, reflecting, trying by a very certain rule of my own applicable to either sex— viz—whether I would be willing, and consider it a great happiness to be every moment of my life and without the possibility of change, in the company of the person under consideration—this is the rule of trial, besides a peculiar personal fondness, and no motive of interest in any shape. well then I strictly enquired, and after reviewing a number of "highly valued," and of "greatly esteemed," and of very "much liked" and of very "intimate" &c—&c—I found that I have in the whole of my life, truly and from the purest feelings of my nature, loved four individuals! in that number I include friends of both sexes—one of these is no more! of the love of at least one of those four persons I can have no doubt, of that of the others I dare not say so much, but that has nothing to do with my attachment, it is involuntary.

Sunday, January 29 It is raining, and lightening, and thundering, after a sunny day; had Mr and Mrs L—— to dine with us the latter brought me the amount due, all in species! which made quite a heavy purse full, glad to receive it though even if it had been twice as heavy, inelegant as it was to hold—heard bad news about poor Ezilda's parents, what horrid race those F——'s are—it appears that they have parted, poor little woman. Dr D—— married at last he apologized for the long delay by stating the difficulty of meeting with a person of comparatively equal intelligence and talents, and now we may all hope that he has found his match—it is a tremendous storm that is raging now, the lightening is incessant most probably it will terminate by hail—Mrs Smith's new overseer was here too to consult on the management of the people what trouble the wretches do give her. dear me when shall I be home again, in my own little nest, with my things around me? in four months I suppose, four long months! long to look forward to, but short enough when past—well patience must be the watch word, that is all, and in the mean time to keep busy I certainly am not idle, and yet I have a good deal of leisure, now those birds are a great pastime, I spend or indeed waste much time in the green house with them, I hope there is no harm.

Wednesday, February 1 I have felt rather unwell all day, I have commenced dieting for relief, I believe it is better than taking medicine. had a note from Eliza—Mr L—— is in town waiting till he hears that the Ohio is open—oh that I was ready to go with him—I must have patience for three months yet—ninety long days of patience—and yet they will pass away most certainly.

Sunday, February 5 Poor Perry died this morning in consequence of his wounds—a great loss to Mrs Smith—I thought that Mr L—— would have been here to day, but was disappointed. the weather is very warm and very damp very good for planting corn I believe, but not so much so for the health—I have been thinking a great deal about Mrs E—— to day, probably she has thought of me too, I hope with as much kindly feeling as I have—still I get no letters, which is very unaccountable, and sufficiently discouraging. I have been told that the Ohio was opened, this is my last hope—and S—— too how she has neglected me she who knows so well how gratefully I would receive a few lines from her. I have hurt my foot again to day in the very same place I did some time ago, it has kept me quite uneasy all day. poor M—— has been talking right and left since yesterday, how she does enjoy mournful excitement.

Wednesday, February 8 The days succeed one another in gloomy lameness, I cannot find any thing of an interest to add to this already monotonous Journal—Mrs S—— has spent the day here, she looked old and withered, a remark that I may likewise apply to my own appearance, I am certain that the last three months have done the work of years in that way, and I know too that it is not a temporary alteration but the permanent and still increasing change which is generally called "breaking"—I am grieved at it, and the more so because it is without remedy.

Thursday, February 9 I have been quite uneasy last night and this morning about a spider bite on my wrist, they told me so many stories of alarming results from the bite of poisonous insects that I almost imagined myself sick. the weather is charming I was this afternoon assisting Mrs S—— in laying out Mary's garden, saw a great number of blue birds. a sign it is said that the winter is past. certainly the weather here is nothing, we were counting the other day that we had had about one week of very bad weather in all, and upon the whole about two weeks of disagreeable days—and yet it has seemed very long to me in spite of my efforts to make the best of it— "Home sweet home", what a short summer thou hast made me spend— thou art my guiding star still.

Sunday, February 12 Went to Town yesterday and tired myself out looking in vain in the stores for mousseline de laine, was obliged to get a black silk at last—found them all well at Myrtle Bank—Mr L—— was out at Independance painting William's children—got the "gems of Beauty"[31] for Mary—it was sundown when came home, and the air very chilly, found the S——n boys here—this day has been beautiful read the greatest part of it, the "pencillings by the way" I would like Willis[32] better if he were less affected, he writes some things very well, but he is in too great a hurry wants to say too much, that reminds of Miss M—— she is becoming more intolerable every day, it is to that degree that I am afraid of saying the most insignificant thing before her, she lets no one finish a sentence, and all out of a desire to please and entertain, and then she interrupts you without really having any thing to say herself but a kind of incoherent senseless repetitions—Mr S—— dined here to day and took his boys home. what a dull situation is mine I cannot repeat it too often.

Friday, February 17 I began to believe that the difference I once thought existed between persons is not by any means so great as I had supposed, I am inclined to think with Mr Owen[33] that it is almost entirely owing to circumstances and opportunities, and temper makes all the rest, I find that the individual character ought to be judged only after long experience and daily intercourse, and then it is even impossible to pass an unqualified sentence—what singular beings we all are from the best to the worst. It is very cold I am waiting to see what news Hector will bring me from town, I fear I will not be able to go there to morrow, the weather is so unpromising. I am nearly worn out with ennui, and yet I have a long calendar of days before I may allow myself to look towards home.

Wednesday, February 22 I only returned from Town yesterday having only intended to stay until Monday morning, I was detained by the rain, and yesterday by a very disagreeable weather I came back, Amelia and Sula accompanied me here and spent the day, I gave A—— a pretty canary bird, and Mrs S—— placed in her hand as she was going away, four bright Camelia flowers full blown, to carry to the Ball this evening. I have a letter from Mrs B—— at last, it appears that there is a letter from S—— lost— Mrs B—— has another original in tow, how strange it is. saw Mr L—— and gave him my letters and settled the little matter for Mary L—— bought some books; fatigued as I was I sat up till eleven o'Clock to read, and even after getting in bed I could not resist the desire of seeing a little more of it, I read nearly a whole volume—I do not feel very well, my lips and tongue are so sore that I have great difficulty and pain in eating and speaking, but it is an "ill wind that blows nobody good"[34] for it is a sufficient apology for declining going to the Ball. and besides the weather is horrid. Maria is quite cooled towards me I think, or jealous, or coquetting, at any rate there is some change evident, I am not sorry for it quite the contrary.

Sunday, February 26 Hector went to Town this morning purposely to take a letter which I wished to send by Mr L—— and who I was afraid would be gone by to morrow—instead of which E—— writes to me that he is going to remain another week that will make the sixth of his sojourn here. It has been raining all day and I amused myself reading the "Courier"—and counting the days, the balance remaining being yet seventy! that is not a great many—and then the spring is beginning, the charming spring! thank God I have a heart for the enjoyments of nature, and a spirit of hope that is almost happiness at times—and I flatter myself a spice of perseverance not altogether vulgar—so much for my self Eulogium.

Monday, February 27 How in the humour to sing "Haste idle Time" if I had that song—but it is of no use, I am wearing myself out as if I were in the dungeons of Chillon,[35] barring the romantic situation, the position morally is not so very dissimilar as might be imagined—I have to be sure three subjects upon which I may converse, all very interesting no doubt to naturalists, the birds in the green house, the plants in the green house, and the weather outside of the green house; I could affirm upon oath these are the only topics ever touched upon, any thing else is never discussed but from an absolute necessity—never never never I vow shall I place myself willingly in the same situation, any thing and every thing is better than this living death.

Wednesday, March 1 I am writing while waiting for breakfast—Mr F——— came yesterday and spoke about sending E———[36] with me his mind is not quite yet decided on the subject, neither is mine I fear it would be more trouble than profit or satisfaction,—Mrs D——— also has brought an over grown daughter of hers, well worth while to send her to school for two months—Mr B——— has been here since yesterday—he is the youngest and the handsomest of the family I think, played and sung for him last night— I have now the prospect of three scholars for next summer, they would all be very good and profitable.

Friday, March 3 The rain has been incessant for three days and nights, and going to town to morrow cannot be thought of—this is the day of the great race, which will probably be postponed. I hope this weather may change E———'s intention of going up with Mr L——— I have an idea that it would be any thing but an agreeable surprise to her friends unprepared as they would be at this season for visitors, but I think she must have been joking. I had to speechify to my interesting pupils yesterday about the uproar they keep in the evening after school, the poor things have been mute as mice ever since. Mr L——— said that he would positively set off to morrow but I doubt it very much—poor M——— must be very uneasy if as is probable she has not heard from him, it is more than one month since he came.

Tuesday, March 7 It is raining yet—sent my letter for Mr C——— yesterday by Hector, Eliza sent me a note, Mr L——— not gone yet—Mr H———[37] was here last friday to know whether I would take Charlotte with me—said very many flattering things indeed—Miss D—— came back yesterday morning with the *necessary evil*—it was more than I had expected for that family has the name of being negligent of these matters—this day two months will terminate my labours here, I must take up courage and keep very busy for I have a very large class to attend for the conclusion—

Wednesday, March 8 The weather seems to be set for an endless rain, I fear I shall not be able to go to town Saturday if even it should clear up the roads are in such a shocking state—how this gloomy season increases the heaviness of the hours, I thought it was at least three days since I had written in this book, and behold I find that I have written in it yesterday—Miss M—— seems resolved that I shall go to Town this week she is prophesying a change for the better but I have no faith in her oracles because they are always dictated by her wishes. I am in no very good humour to day being nearly tired out and it is only the middle of the week yet—

Thursday, March 9 It has cleared up at last and the new moon promises dry weather, I have nothing more to read so I find the evenings tedious, what a resource books are, I mean novels and the like, for books of science and so forth save me from them, I actually turn sick and faint at the sight of any title of any thing that has the word Philosophy in it, or at any word ending with *logy* or *nomy* or any of the y's in use in this way—give me the book that has no smattering of march of intellect in it, a real old blue light rather than your utilitarian novel that begins with "Mamma are we to attend the chemical lectures this evening" &c—for that is the way the charming works for the entertainment of young Ladies commence now a day or something similar—give me "beauty and the beast" "Cinderella" "the invisible Prince" there is imagination in that—and whoever wishes to know about how the blacksmith shoes a horse, and how the Elephant eats carrots, and about the surprising phenomenon of water turning into steam by boiling &c—may go and see, which will be even more entertaining and much more useful than the written information—

Friday, March 10 I knew it as well as if it had been told me that Maria was determined that I should go to town to morrow she has laid and managed the thing to perfection, now I would rather go to town but it revolts my independance to think that she should always want to control my movements she has been pretending to me all this week that she was going herself, and now that she secured my consent to go she told me this morning that she was not going but that Mary was crazy to go with me, now this is too

officious, she knows now that go I must on Mary's account—I just asked
Mary if she wished to go, she said no.

Sunday, March 12 I did not go to town in spite of all the hints and the astonishment of poor M—— poor Mrs Smith must think me very whimsical as
she does not know how I am wearied of this petty tyranny of officiousness—
she is so kind and unobtrusive herself that she cannot I am sure understand fully that sort of vexations—it has been raining continually to day, I
have read Norman Leslie[38] which Eliza sent to me yesterday—the S——
boys[39] are here detained all night by the weather, I just now come out of
Mrs S——'s room, every attempt I made at a little conversation was always
taken up out of my mouth by Miss M—— and made her own, and the two
opinions which I gave to G—— S—— were flatly contradicted by her—
I would great deal prefer that she would not profess so much affection for
me and leave off her officiousness I would rather be neglected than to be
meddled with in every thing and on every occasion from the lowest trifle to
the most important business she must have to do with all it is really a new
character to me, Mrs S—— must be the superlatively good person that she
is, to be able to stand it, I could not, no not for a kingdom. both Dick and
Jack have been singing together the whole afternoon.

Tuesday, March 14 Raining and cold this morning—I have not yet called in
school though I have been up for two hours, we have breakfast very early
sometimes. I sat up late last night reading ghost stories until I got frightned,
and I thought I heard strange noises after I was in bed. only part of the
scholars have returned since saturday, the rain and storm have carried away
the bridges and made the roads impassable, we are paying up now for our
fine winter. I have discovered or rather it struck me at once like sometimes
a thing that we have seen a hundred times and that we have passed un-
noticed, that —— has one decided fault in a high degree too—well no
one is perfect that is a great source consolation to poor sinners like myself.
I have this day got two most beautiful mocking birds one of them especially
is so tame that it feeds out of my hand already. no I never saw any body so
obstinately tenatious in officiousness as M—— she said to me smirkingly
this evening that if I was going to town next saturday she would stay to
mind the birds—now in the name of obtrusiveness she does want already
to begin again about her everlasting sending me away on saturday—I said
that I did not know that I was going, still that would not do she muttered
and mumbled something (as usual to have the last word) about of course if
the roads, the weather——

Wednesday, March 15 The sun shines at last, but the wind which blows from the north is very cold, there was ice this morning the thickness of dollar— the bird that was hurt is dead, but the fine tame one is still livelier and tamer, we all think it is the one I raised the summer before last—Mrs W—— brought the girls back this morning. I am quite unwell to day, I slept very little last night.

Friday, March 17 Mrs Smith has just gone to Town this morning, I gave her the money to pay Mrs Dixon, it is cold yet and the weather threatens a change for worse so it is very possible that I may have to stay at home to morrow again, it will be four weeks since I was outside of the gate, I felt no inclination to go, and feel none yet, I don't know why, and if I go to morrow it is to avoid appearing singular, to be sure the weather has not been very tempting, and when it is more pleasant I may wish to ride out, however I do not intend at present going to town more than twice before I quit business here.

Saturday, March 18 Rain rain this morning, M—— was so anxious to get me off to town that she should have started me in the face of a threatening storm but I would not be driven, more over she told a most bare faced fib to accomplish her purpose, she did not know that I had heard it all. it may clear off yet for it is early.[40]

wished to go to town, no she said but Mrs M'G—— will go! I immediately replied that I had no notion of it, why not to take a ride? no—well she forced me to this fib by her eternal wish to tyrannize over me in that respect, and I will not go although I wish to do so—I could cry for spite—

Friday, March 31 The last day of March, another month and I am free, I think I will leave this without regret, I have so many petty troubles daily, the girls keep quarrelling and I cannot come at the justice of the matter because Miss M—— is at the bottom of it all, and represents cases according to her prejudices, or her fancy, she is the most officious creature in the world, and will take no hints—It has rained last night which has made the air quite pleasant, the country is full of flowers, but all that does not cheer me up, I am not well, and not happy, I have finished "Henrietta Temple"[41] I do not like it as well as d'Israeli's other works by a great deal, there some pretty things in it, but the story does not please me—in fact I am tired of english novels, how very much better is that novel of fréderic Soulié?[42] there is no comparison in point of feeling imagination style and composition indeed when I compare them "Henrietta T——" seems but poor trash. I wonder what E—— thinks of it—for my part I have done with english novels, since my favorite has failed to interest me—I think English novelists should write one book and quit.

Monday, April 3 It is strange that I should take any pleasure in writing in this book, considering how little I have to record that is agreeable or interesting, but it helps me to pass away the time and to compare the length of it from a period to come from one past—yesterday Mr and Mrs Taylor and Margaret spent the day here, and Miss M—— is going to Town to bring her here to morrow so that she may stay in the school with me to get initiated. the day was delightful and they appeared to enjoy themselves very much—Elizabeth returned here in the evening she is very happy. her mother is going to send her with me. M—— was croaking last night as usual about Steam Boats accidents and how she was going to be uneasy about me, I almost told her that I did not thank her for her trouble, I know how uneasy she is, she is afraid rather that nothing will happen to have an occasion to talk for that is all she does in such cases, I know her now, I am not going to forget very soon how she acted last saturday and how unfeelingly she talked about that young Lady who had been thrown out of her carriage and that we took up in ours, she was positively barbarous, if I had not suggested the making her drink a glass of wine before she was sent on her way alone and in the dark she would have let her start fainting and hurt as she was, oh the abominable selfishness of this world, I am selfish too, but not in that way, I hope—

Tuesday, April 4 Miss M—— did not go to day, there was this morning a delicious April shower that made her give it up—and she insists on my going sometimes when it threatens a tornado—how fearless we are to the dangers of our neighbours—just like our fortitude in supporting their misfortunes. she was saying this morning that the present distress for money was nothing in comparison with what it was going to be when the war in Texas would begin again, like if she knew any thing about war or business or in fact about any thing but driving the little negroes in the yard, and their mothers in the kitchen, I am bitter but I cannot help it, she is getting so unbearable.

Wednesday, April 5 The weather is heavenly, Miss M—— could not go to bring Margaret from Town because the horses are sick—I had a good night's rest at last, there was no blowing of the horn for once. still the time moves very slowly, beautiful as the season is now, I don't enjoy it, I want to be gone or at least going, oh my! one whole month yet—I feel so weak and weary, I know I need to recruit my spirits in some way, but I know very well I cannot hope to do it until I am in my own little parlour, oh that little parlour!—I am tired of birds, I cannot take any interest in them now, indeed I am sick of everything.

Thursday, April 6 We had a tremendous storm this afternoon, Miss Maria and Margaret came home through it all. I have had the head ache all day, and I feel very tired—Miss M—— called at Myrtle bank—Dinah[43] was the only one at home—they were all out in the country, as I supposed they would—Miss M—— just gave me a pair of beautiful gloves. the wind blows hard to night, and from the north too.

Friday, April 7 Nothing of much importance to day, only that I have been very poorly all day, and that Mr G—— came and paid the balance due—I would not let Margaret commence coming into the school on friday for good luck sake, but I have been writing for her a system of regulation for the different studies and exercises of every day, I hope it may be of some service to her. it is cold and clear and much like a northern April day.

Wednesday, April 12 Went last Saturday to dine at Mr H——'s with Miss M—— and Mary, we had a very agreeable visit Mrs W—— was there and Mr H—— determined on accompanying us to Pittsburg—the day was cold and windy and we got back home before sun-set—it is thundering and lightening and raining to day—Margaret stays in the school with me all day, I wonder if she is not both frightened and disgusted at the task before her—I think she is in bad spirits about it—Miss M—— is very kind and atten[44]

are regardless, or rather ignorant of the effect that a few words *written* may produce on the absent, but she knows everything. she knows as well as I do that the kind looks she speaks of had no reference to me (or else why am I here) but she knows the weakness of woman who can even find a charm in what she knows does not exist, or at least does not exist in a manner that is conducive to her happiness—and yet what is happiness? surely not a continued state, I am convinced that it is merely the exaltation of a few moments either of the imagination or of the senses, I don't know whether that is sound philosophy, but it is the only kind of happiness I have ever experienced.

Sunday, April 30 Margaret and I went to Town yesterday morning, the front seat of the carriage entirely occupied with large bunches of roses, pinks, hawthorn, violets—&c—&c—It was an *extatic* ride the beauty of the morning the perfume of the fresh flowers, the excellence of the road, were all combined for enjoyment, we sat in silent contentment. and once in a while said by turns, how sweet, how delightful, but every thing must have an end and on arriving at Myrtle bank, found no one at home and had to walk on to Mrs P————'s *box* as they call it (and it is a real martin box) over the abominable clay thrown out of the rail road, in the burning sun, and when I got there I thought I should go blind, this said box is all windows a complete lantern, without a tree up on a bare, hard, yellow clay hill, no shutters and little bits of rooms, and every thing imaginable that is uncomfortable and painful—well I found her in charming spirits and thinking it the most charming place and very busy moving Eliza's things into the box adjoining to which I went to examine, it is precisely the same kind of an hotel, rather worse than better—they all were at a picknick at Mr H———— since the day before and were expected immediately home, presently D———— came up riding on horse back with Mr M———— and she said that E———— and A———— had also come but that they were too tired and stayed at Myrtle bank's, message after message were sent but no inducement could entrap them, and they were right not to leave that sweet large cool green shaded lovely parlour to come to that tent in the desert of Saharah, and I wished myself with them, however I had to stay until after dinner which took place after three o'Clock, and then I went, and found them both fagged out, they had sent for ice-cream for their dinner—poor E———— is in despair about moving to that caboose, she says that she cannot see what it is for, but her mother will have it so and is doing it for her, I never saw such a tearing up of goods and in the midst of all this turmoil she is expecting to start every hour for the north by land! via Mobile! charleston!—&c—&c—only waiting for her brother A————[45] who is to accompany them—finally Hector brought the carriage and I stopped a short time at Mrs T———— and M———— and I were soon on our way home to the clean cool sweet shady and above all peaceful country, we had a pleasant ride and found our Tea waiting for us—to day Mrs L———— spent the day here, my ears are ringing yet with her chatter, I never heard such a guinea hen in my life.

Tuesday, May 2 Eliza and Amelia with the baby spent the day here yesterday, it was very pleasant indeed we had every thing that was good, and the day appeared quite short although they stayed until half past five—E———— said she expected to find all her things taken out of the house when she would get home, her mother is so anxious to have her moved before she goes to the north, how E———— hates it, she said that A———— could not bear to hear about those wretched boxes, from what she said he must be in great trouble about business—Amelia don't want to go to the north and her mother has consented that she should stay, but who can tell for Mrs P————'s plans are altered oftener than the wind—I hope for my part that this day week shall see me on my way to Pittsburg.

Wednesday, May 3 No sign of rain yet! Mrs S—— and Mrs M—— have been here since yesterday morning, the child of Mrs M—— cried a great deal in the night and kept me awake, I don't know how any body can wish for children—Miss M—— told me this morning that they would have to move out of their fine house and that it was this in part that made Mrs M—— so low spirited besides various other embarrassments of her husband's, this is really a time of trouble for the people of this country, how plainly it shows the truth of reaction in all things, sometimes since and very lately too, the luxury of almost every class was astonishing, and the parade and boast of the rich was insulting to their less fortunate acquaintance, and now it is their turn to envy the insignificant, who have enough for their wants and are free from the persecution of debts and the responsibility of the property and existence of others, never was a change so sudden and so little foreseen— and yet it might have been expected from so much reckless extravagance— I remember I have not long since been looked upon as a poor incredulous spirit not capable of comprehending what an income amounting to millions was, and my friends were nearly angry at my apparently unconvinced understanding—what must they think of it now when the greatest of their pretended nabobs acknowledge that they could not raise a thousand dollars to save their lives. I am truly sorry for all this and wish better times may come for them, this is a very great lesson may they learn it, for I see that some persons here who have always been moderate have a great plenty yet and can afford even to lose by those elegant dashers what was squandered in their follies without suffering any great shock to their wealth or honour!

The Journals of Jane Caroline North

1851–52

FIRST JOURNAL

Journal—Commenced Thursday July 31st 1851. J.C. North
I left Badwell on the 22d of July for Charleston—
Remained here a week & never suffered so much from heat and mus-
quitoes—

Thursday, July 31, 1851 Uncle Henry Aunt Harriette the two children[1] myself & Betsey[2] as attendent left Charleston on board the Wilmington Boat
Vanderbilt at 4 o'clock p.m. Many persons on board among them several
acquaintances—

Friday, August 1 We had a disagreeable night, it rain thundered and light-
ened the whole time. Fortunately for us we were accommodated with a
State room on deck, the weather was very hot and if we had been mewed
into the births below the Saloon, would certainly have been near the end
of our days before morning. As it was we suffered sharply—Smithville is
the most desolate looking spot shabby houses and piles running out into the
river giving an appearance of decay & at the same time reminding me of
what I have read of Old Dutch towns with their defences projecting into
the sea. Wilmington is a considerable place, some what resembling Georgetown except it has a prosperous air. We went from the Boat to the Cars,
on board which we waited an hour or more, finally set off. The country is

a dead level, pine trees, grass and turpentine barrels rolled beside the road ready for export—certainly this portion of N. Carolina does not make the most favorable impression. We passed over beautiful Savannah cover'd with grass and wild flowers, bordering the road for ½ a mile on each side & only bounded by the horizon—one very fine orchard, & one fine field of corn were the only interesting objects I saw in a distance of 166 miles or more! We supped at Weldon where we changed for Petersburg Va—There are opposition houses at Weldon much to the advantage of travellers—we had a nice supper & capital tea at Greshams. From eight until after 12 o'clock at night we were in the cars going from Weldon to Petersburg. There was a shelf sufficiently wide for a person to be comfortable upon extending around the [. . .] above the seat, on this as many men as could get on it were sleeping while those who could accommodated themselves upon the seat. We had every variety of attitude some highly ridiculous. At Petersburg we rested 2 hours then took the Cars for Richmond. I was surprised to find this route so good, having always been told that it was the worst in the Union.

Saturday, August 2 Arrived in Richmond about ½ past six, the morning very cool, a shawl would have been pleasant. The approach to the Town is very pretty, we crossed the James river by a long very high bridge, the houses appear as if built one above another in almost regular lines. The hills are high and with a little fancy one might suppose the buildings, castles perched upon their summits. We stopped first at the American Hotel. Uncle Henry had to return to the Depôt for my poor carpet bag which was reported missing, he was just in time to save the captive from being carried to Washington—it was a great relief to have it back again. The Hotel had been newly painted, it was handsomely furnished but in a state of transition from the "horrors to the decent." The paint was more than Aunt Harrie could bear so after breakfasting (and very nicely too) we changed our quarters and obtained pleasant rooms at the "Powhatan". I feel now as if really in old Virginny the engine that puffed us here was the Pocahantas, & the hotel at which we stay bears the name of the famous old Indian chief! Everything has looked so like home even the barreness of the North Carolina belt, (with the exception of the turpentine barrels) that I did not realize the distance that seperated me from home. After resting a short time Uncle Henry the children & myself walked to the capitol, saw Houdon's statue of Washington[3] & looked at the view from the high portico—we looked in the Representative & Senate chambers also—these are not so comfortable as those in Columbia & the floors were excessively dirty. I was disappointed in the statue the face is quite different from the representations we usually see of Washington it is more full & looks heavy—the dress is admirable the large flapped waistcoat, the hair in cue, the old fashioned coat the whole

in excellent keeping, & representing the dress of the time 1789 I think—
The usual mode of draping statues of public men does not seem to me a
correct one, why should they not be sculptured in the dress of their own
time instead of envelopping them in Greek or Roman robes? Our dinner
today was not so good as our breakfast—the bill of fare was defective in as
much as there were dishes put down in the catalogue not to be found on
the table. Peaches & milk were handed as dessert, the saucer half filled with
sliced peaches covered with lumps of ice to this was added sugar & milk. I
did not approve the arrangement. There were but 2 ladies at the table, men
enough however—Since we left S.C. I have been struck by the difference in
the negroes. Yesterday I thought them the most sturdy saucy looking set, &
since entering Va—every other one is a mulatto. I have never seen so many
as meandered around the tables of the "American" this morning & at dinner
at this house it is really pleasant to see the true ebony & they seem to me
quite distinguished.

    We took a charming drive this afternoon through & about the City. It
is best seen from two views, one from Gamble's Hill where the City seems
chiefly to lie to your left hand the fine Railroad bridge before you & James
River dotted with patches of little green Islands almost at your feet & widen-
ing & stretching away before you—the other view is from the top of a very
high hill just above the port of the old Town, called I think Rockets.[4] the
view from this point is finer than the other from Gamble's Hill, the elevation
is greater than at any other place, one stands higher than the Capitol which
building is conspicuous from every position, crowning a hill on the midst
of the new City. What strikes me with surprise is the number & height of
the hills. New & old Richmond are situated on & between them so that
the effect is very curious & very pretty. Many of the streets are steep &
rough as our backcountry roads. The hill on which we last stood I thought
inaccessible looking up at it from Main St winding at its foot, several turns
& windings brought us to the top—the river was beneath the beyond &
below us. Over the river stretched the richest looking country the corn of
the darkest green & numberless wheat stacks scattered over the fields, the
whole seemed "smiling in the lap of Plenty". We passed a church said to be
very old the hill had been cut down at least 30 feet on one side to make a
street the brick wall was built up against it forming a parapet & overhanging
the edge in one or two places were some old monuments the effect was
very curious. After our delightful drive we took an ice cream, very nice, &
much more than they give in Charleston for the same money.

Sunday, August 3 Attended morning service at St. Paul's, a handsome church,
but too much gilding I thought, the ceiling heavily ornamented.[5] As we
stood in the Porch waiting for the sexton to show us seats, a portly old

gentleman passed with his family, looked at us, paused went on, came back & said to Uncle Henry "you wish seats Sir" "Yes. I have spoken to the sexton, but he seems not to be in the way just now" the old gentleman immediately offered seats with his family at first this politeness was declined as we were so many (4 persons) on being repeated we accepted his kind offer & sat with them. Aunt Harriette had whispered to me that she thought our friend a dry goods merchant & so he proved to be. She is very correct in her conjectures about people generally, amusingly so sometimes. In the afternoon Uncle H. & myself went to the monumental church built on the spot where in 1811 the Richmond theater was burnt down, during a performance and many persons perished all the bodies were buried on the spot, a monument stands within the porch inscribed with the names of those who were destroyed with the building. So great was the shock & distress that the event occasioned that a contribution was made immediately to erect a church on the spot where the theater had stood. It is strangely built & not unlike in the form of the gallery to one in a Theater. We heard a strange young man preach he was very affected and indeed ridiculous in style, not better than some of our back country preachers. I met a curious person in the drawing room this morning. A lady whom I had observed at the table & who was the only one besides ourselves, she had a well dressed little boy with her, for herself, her appearance was very dejected & forlorn smartly dressed however. She talked a great deal to me, & in a most melancholy strain. Her story was a sad one, she was an English woman & must in early youth have been pretty her friends moved to Canada, there she married an officer in the Queen's guards, in a few years her Father failed, & then her husband, who sometime before had left his regiment. She determined to teach & for that purpose to come South as she could not bear to take an inferior position where she had held one among the best. She had been 18 months in Va had been principal of a school somewhere, and now at the end of the term had come to Richmond with the intention of spending a week with some friends who to her distress she found were on the eve of leaving for the Springs, this appeared to complete her troubles, she knew not what to do it was expensive staying at the "Powhatan House", and yet she was not ready to go to the situation where for the next year she was to be governess in a clergyman's family. I felt sorry for the poor woman, she impressed me as being inefficient, complaining, and dissatisfied with every thing—just the person who would weary and distress one to be much thrown with. I hope the poor soul will find her place in the clergyman's family more satisfactory than her situation the last year. I wondered where the husband was all this time, I think they quarreled & seperated, the boy was ill mannered which is not in her favor—

Harriette Petigru Lesesne, miniature by Charles Fraser. (Photograph from Alice R. Huger Smith and D. E. Huger Smith, *Charles Fraser* [New York: Frederick Fairchild Sherman, 1924])

Monday, August 4 We took the Cars for Charlottesville this morning arrived to dinner—the hotel was a most distracted place ill furnished poorly kept— The dinner was scene of confusion & discomfort—the landlord *before* the bell rang requested anxiously that the ladies would seat themselves at table otherwise they would get no seats after that. Soon as the summons rung out (we being established before hand,) such rushing in of rough looking men I never saw. Oh! they were desperate specimens—it was Court week & the town was filled with all sorts of queer, hard visaged people—they ate furiously & everything together. I was amazed at being handed ice-cream after dinner, it was like a gleam of civilization in the midst of barbarism. Uncle Henry engaged an extra with Dr Holmes, & as soon as possible we set off for Brooksville 20 miles distant. We passed the University a mile from the Town, it is a handsome building. Our party consists of Dr Holmes & wife, Mr John Gadsden who is travelling with them,[6] and ourselves. I did not mention that I had met a curious person in Richmond besides the Englishwoman. At the American hotel she spoke to me by asking if "Hal was my son"? saying she supposed not he did not seem very respectful. She had great deal to say, & was a nice looking young lady without being pretty. On the cars we met again. She took a seat beside me & talked incessantly, bantering me on being very sentimental & a great deal equally entertaining I answered in the spirit she talked but wished she would go to her own set & let me alone at last she did, & tho' Betsey informed me afterwards that the lady wanted to sit by me, as Uncle Henry had the place, I remained in place. Just before she left the Cars she came to me & said "dont you want to know who I am? you must think it funny a stranger should be as sociable" "I would be happy to know who you are," I answered "I am Miss Barnwell sister of Mrs Pickney,[7] I knew you were a Miss North, I knew your Grandfather & Uncle" &c I was really glad to find out who she was, for her *talk* was so peculiar that I was certain she was distracted & think so a little still. At Charlottesville we parted she expressed the hope that she would see a great deal of me at the Springs &c—I replyd suitably, but cant say I am very desirous of the pleasure—

Tuesday, August 5 Left Brookville (merely a way side hotel) for Staunton early, we were today fairly among the Blue Ridge, they certainly correspond to the name, tho' I dont know that they looked any more blue than other moun- tains, the country until we entered the mountanous regions was destitute of any beauty, today we have had several pretty scenes, & glimpses of the more distant ranges, looming through their "azure hue". Dined at Staunton, the situation of this town is very striking, among steep hills with the Mountains beyond. On each side of the street entering the Town are handsome public buildings one the asylum for the deaf & dumb the Principals of which are a gentleman & his wife both deaf & dumb—I did not hear what the opposite building was intended for. The hotel was a nice one & the arrangements appeared very comfortable, the dinner well conducted and very good. I saw white waiters for the first time since entering Virginia here at the hotel of this inland Town perched among the high hills bordering the mountain country. This is a flourishing place, & when the rail road is finished connecting it with Charlottesville, it doubtless will be of great importance. We passed today a place where they are tunneling thro' a mountain the work has been in progress three years, and will be finished it is said in one more, the embanking for the railroad is finished in many places, it was a great work to undertake, filling up sufficiently in the valleys tunnelling thro a mountain and overcoming many obstacles they have had to encounter in the route. We changed the stage at Staunton, & left in a rain, the distance to Cloverdale being 30 miles—fortunately it soon cleared, we travelled well but it was ten o'clock at night before we reached our resting place. We were very tired— the children had been asleep two or three hours before we stopped, they have stood the journey very well so far. I was amused at a passage between the stage driver & a man who stopped him on the road to demand his umbrella belonging to him which the driver had picked up the day before on the road. The owner of the umbrella jumped out of his buggy & in the most choleric manner demanded his property, the driver fired up instanter. I thought we would have a scene, but no sooner did our Jehu[8] show the stuff he was made of, than the attackee lowered his tone gave his proofs of ownership among which was a "blister on the handle, got I reckon in the manufacture" after this, all doubts seemed satisfied & the parties separated more amicably than they had met. I had pictured Cloverdale to myself as the prettiest of farms with fine pastures of clover and beautiful grass, surrounding a nice comfortable looking house, no such thing, the mountains are in full view & stand out distinct & bold on every side, but how the place should have received so pretty a name I do not know.—

Wednesday, August 6 We did not leave Cloverdale until nine o'clock having but 20 miles to the Warm Springs. The road is turnpike it is made over the mountains nearly the whole way, & commanding beautiful points of view & in excellent order. From one height I was reminded of the view from Ceasar Head, tho' it was neither so fine or so extensive.[9] After a drive of 15 miles we drove into the "Bath Alum Springs" where the horses were to be watered. These Springs have not been discovered long, this is only the second season. The hotel is of red brick the cottages are pretty little buildings, but must be very hot. The sun was shining his fiercest as we drove up, and the bricks seemed to me really flaming. In a book on the Virginia Springs by Dr Burke,[10] he describes these of Bath Alum as very delightful, & gives the most refreshing account of the trees & ornamental grounds, the shrubbery &c. I looked in vain for any semblance of all this a row of bare poles & a carriage way comprised every beauty to be seen. He drew from that never failing source an Irish imagination. At length at 4 o'clock in the afternoon we arrived at the Warm Springs, I felt a little *scared* I must admit when we got out dusty weary & travel worn and saw several people standing about, on the staircase we met a lady dressed in white bobinet & looking so nice that I thought it would be a desperate undertaking to prepare for dinner, so weary as we were. This trouble was removed to my satisfaction when I found that the hour for dinner had long passed & we were only with our own party. Dressed for the evening, few people here some old gentlemen & ladies chiefly.

Thursday, August 7 This morning I could see the situation of these Springs to more advantage than the last evening—it is beautiful, in the midst of a Valley surrounded with mountains, the hills rise gradually before & at the back of the establishment until they join the Mountains beyond, the richest verdure covers them here & there corn fields, fields that have been harvested and a large garden on the slope of the hill just behind the House—the air is delightful so light & balmy that breathing it is a pleasure, were there nothing else to recommend the place. the water of the Spring is very warm, & slightly sulpherous—the bath is fine the water bubbles up continually breaking in sparkles on the top, the depth is 4 feet & I suppose 10 square. beside the large warm bath is one of icy cold water, many persons go immediately from the warm to the cold. I have not bathed yet. Certainly I must have some physiognomical attraction for queer people—this morning as I was talking to Jamie in the entry beside the drawing room, a fantastically dressed woman spoke to him & so made way to opening communications with me. I was not prepossessed by her appearance she was in a handsome rich silk dark, streaming ribbon round her throat fastened by a large red brooch, lace cap loads of rings, & pink satin bows and streamers in her hair, and cap this climax were two huge imitation pearl pins. She was inclined to be very sociable, but her distracted toilette discouraged any such feeling on my part. After a few remarks I came up stairs not here was it to end however in the drawing after tea she had a vast deal to say I talked too, for evidently I was the only one who had a word to say to her & really felt sorry for her forlornness—she informed me who different people were & made funny remarks told me that I would not find people sociable, she had been here 3 weeks, & found them very unsociable. I agreed as to their reserve but was not so sure that our position would be parallel. I danced to night with a little miss Emma Chapman sister of Miss Ella Chapman the beauty of the Springs. They are the great granddaughters of the proprietors Dr & Mrs Brockenburh, Miss Chapman is beautiful as a statue in the face, perfectly colorless & faultless features—figure indifferent & manners boisterous. The sister is not pretty but very pleasant & talkative. Mr Coles wife & daughter a tall plain girl,[11] Mrs Randolph Aunt by marriage of the Chapmans[12] and a few others are the principal persons, there are but 2 beaus—Mr Gadsen & one other—Little Mrs William Simmons & her sposo from Charleston here, he is sick behaves pleasant enough, she is however the most absurd little self sufficient mortal undertakes to be somewhat patronizing to Aunt Harriette & myself, neither take it in a way to encourage her airs. I suppose she is merely ignorant & knows nothing of good manners.

Friday, August 8 Bathed this morning, found it delightful, the warmth & sulpher as you enter the bath room is very sensible, tho there is a large outlet for the roof—I enjoyed the bath very much. Today my curious acquaintance (Miss Marengo Aunt H. calls her) was friendly to a degree beyond the usual. After dinner I went in the drawing room a little while, Mrs Simmons insisted upon my playing tho' unnecessary for every one around was talking briskly, & I thought it would be only an interruption. I gratified her & then seeing a lady handsomely dressed on the other side of the room talking with another old lady, having heard that it was Mrs Seaton in the morning, I determined to introduce myself which when the old lady to whom she was talking had taken her leave, I did. She received me in the most gracious & cordial manner, having seen her daughter when she visited Charleston with Mr & Mrs Webster. I had a subject immediately, then I mentioned what regard we entertained for Mr Seaton by means of the "National Intelligencer", how we valued the paper, looking for its appearance every week as one expects a pleasant friend, I don't know what I said altogether, but felt I expressed myself to the purpose & well—She seemed very pleased, & said "such words from the lips of a young lady would repay Mr Seaton for all the troubles of the editorial".[13] I spoke of my Uncle Mr Petigru, she said immediately, "I knew in Washington some years ago, a Mr Charles Petigru are you his niece?"[14] She mentioned him as one remembered with pleasure & interest. This is not the first time I have heard of him, spoken of & remembered with great interest by strangers—he seems to have upon every one who ever met him the most charming impression. Mrs S. had inquired my name early in our conversation, this comical dame immediately spoke to me as "Miss Caroline"! I rode with Uncle Henry to the top of Crow's nest mountain this afternoon, the ascent is steep & rugged but nothing dangerous in it, the

Flag staff still stands where it was placed on the rock years ago to mark the spot where a lady rode to. Miss Randolph afterwards Mrs Chapman was the venturous equestrian, as she was the first to perform the feat it made her very celebrated. The view is very fine, I do not like it so much as that from Ceasar's Head, the distance comprised is not more than 20 miles bound in by mountains, & mountains filling the space one after another without much variation in height. I have heard them compared to billows &c, to me they resembled huge graves. The Warm Springs settlement from this point is lovely, nestled in the valley while the Mountains rise like bulwarks on all sides. We will leave for the White Sulpher on Monday. Mr Woodbridge his daughter & sister in law Miss Nicholson will join our party The Holmes & Seatons & W. Simmons were to have gone together tomorrow but can get no stage. By the way Mr Woodbridge made the funniest proposition about his daughter when he heard we were going to Crow's nest, he proposed she should accompany us, appeared a little taken aback when he found we were going on horseback, but immediately answered his daughter's (a girl of 14) objections to riding by saying, "Oh! my daughter I can tie a rope around you & Mr Lesesne can hold the end so you will not fall off"—The young lady was firm tho' & her Aunt equally opposed to such a novel mode of proceeding. She said to me afterwards "Mr Woodbridge has so much simplicity, knows nothing of the world that I am obliged to keep a sharp lookout, or he would something do strange things". It was very amusing notion. Danced this evening as usual. I am making many nice acquaintances, Mrs Seaton is a dear old lady, Miss Coles is pleasant & very conversible. We were astonished to find that Master Hal had been diverting himself by joking Mr Gadsen about me in the most annoying note. Uncle Henry requested Hal to take a walk in the woods and administered an effectual admonition. I was annoyed tho' really amazed at the absurd speeches he made the young man, it will not occur again & it is better it should have been at this early stage—

Saturday, August 9 The Seatons and Holmes cant obtain any description of conveyance every thing being engaged & shoals of people constantly arriving; the President[15] is to be here Monday. when shall we get off! Uncle H. tells me I display great capacity for gaining popularity certainly I "get on" as they say better than I thought possible for me—I have made acquaintance with all the ladies young & old that I cared to cultivate, and am always received in the most cordial manner. Ah! I have nothing strange experience to record. I was seated at after dancing, between Mrs Holmes & Simmons (foolish little woman) this evening when a person whom I had observed before with my fantastic friend came up & patting me under the chin said, "Oh I have had such a compliment paid to me" I drew back so as to avoid the patting & merely bowed & smiled then she laid her hand on my hair & said "Yes, I was taking for you by a gentleman who saw you dancing last night" she looked most benignantly at me, I felt horror struck, the woman is a marvel of ugliness at this moment was perfectly *scary.* I managed to say with composure, "I am glad you were gratified" she gave another smile & left the room—I rushed across the room & exclaimed Aunt H. & Mrs Seaton who were conversing together, "that I had something dreadful to tell them," drew a chair & sank into it as if overcome they entered into the spirit, Mrs Seaton seized a fan Aunt H. something else & pretended to exert themselves for my recovery, with of course ridiculous exaggeration I described what had just occurred to their great diversion—In truth tho' it was not vanity, but the poor woman is so uncommon that I was shocked. She went minutely thro all the man had said on the occasion, "he swore t'was me, that's just { . . . } way of talking"—!! Mrs Seaton gave us the history of Miss Marengo. No 1, she is a Mrs Keep, ten years ago was married & only bride for a day, her husband carried her to Baltimore the morning they were married on a bridal excursion, the next morning went to the bar & asked for a glass of hard cider, was told to help himself, & took by mistake poor creature corrosive sublimate [16] his wife came down stairs to find him a corpse. Since that time she has been in close mourning until the past year. Mrs S. wound up by saying she is a well informed very respectable woman but knows nothing of society, or how to dress & behave to strangers. I never knew her personally in Washington but she instantly spoke to me here— The old mother is a vulgar looking person, very low & unprepossessing in appearance, her daughter is on the register as Mrs K——

Sunday, August 10 Did not attend church this morning service was held by a Methodist travelling preacher. I wish I could receive my letters, there ought to be some from home for me! Mr Woodbridge preached this afternoon, gave an excellent sermon, text—"Come with me all ye that are heavy laden, and I will give you rest" [17]—held service in the Court House. Made the acquaintance of a Miss Dulles from Philadelphia a relative of the Haskells and Cheves! [18] she was introduced to me this morning and is a very curious person.

Monday, August 11 I saw for a short time yesterday a very peculiar person— Miss Dulles of Philadelphia, she is related to the Cheves. Miss Coles intro- duced her to me in the morning she went with us to church in the afternoon & before night was so intimate as to relate me all her tender experiences. Alick Herbemont, [19] my old acquaintance being the hero of the story—she was a good specimen of a foolish, talkative girl, without discretion, or one interesting quality. She left this morning for the White Sulpher, I dont care to see much of her there. The President arrived this morning about 12 o'clock. He is a fine looking sensible perfectly unpretending & unassuming in manner & very gentlemanly. Mr Stuart was the only one of his cabinet with him.[20] Mr. Corcoran the great banker in Washington was of the party.[21] The reception was entirely tame & indifferent. Mr Kennedy a pompous Baltimorean[22] received Mr Filmore & conducted him to the front room a few persons were introduced but no enthusiasm, no demonstration. The dinner was better than usual, the waiters were decorated with cockades & streamers this alone marked the occasion. Aunt H. has been very much indisposed for two days, came down this evening that she might see the President & the evening entertainment, we danced as usual. I the first with Mr Harvey[23] he is a curious person so awkward & uninteresting at first acquaintance & improves so much afterwards I think him almost handsome now—Dr and Mrs Means[24] arrived here yesterday, they sang for us after the grand company had retired, it was very sweet. He has a fine voice & both are very obliging.

Tuesday, August 12 The Means, Uncle Henry & myself took a pleasant walk this morning. Day as usual, danced in the evening, we leave tomorrow for the Hot Springs. Mr Harvey urged me to remain said he would drive me over himself & a vast deal of nonsense. I chanced to remark to a Mr Parker[25] (now at the Hot Springs) a few days ago when he was speaking of Mr Harvey & trying absurdly enough to joke me about him, that I thought him possibly engaged to Miss Brockenburgh, she was a pretty interesting girl and he very attentive, off he goes & tells Mr Harvey who immediately asked me about & since constantly refers & laughs at what he terms my wonderful penetration. It was a stupid thing of Mr Parker, but Mr Harvey & myself are none the worse friends.

—*Hot Springs*—

Wednesday, August 13 This afternoon came over to the Hot Springs, the Du Laneys[26] & ourselves. I was sorry to part with some pleasant acquaintances we made, Mary Coles in particular. Mr Harvey informed me he was coming over to try the waters &c. The drive is a pleasant one, & the country beautiful, fields of the freshest looking green pasture, & high mountains a little distance from the road—As we drove up to the door Capt Du Laney muttered with a half groan, "Oh! Oh! look at the sticks go it ye cripples!" I laughed as did all the party, but it was a sorrowful sight, numbers of unfortunates each with a stick or crutches beside them seated in the piazza, & others limping up from the baths, wretched spectacles! Our accommodations very uncomfortable, Uncle Henry insisted upon taking the room assigned me, I cant bear to turn him out but it is impossible to sleep in the place they gave me. Aunt H. seems better.

Thursday, August 14 I brought a note yesterday from Mary Coles to her cousin who is staying here with her mother a rheumatic.[27] The young lady's name is very peculiar Miss Isaetta Coles her father's name was Isaac & this is the feminine, worse I think than the original. she is an uncommon nice girl tall, fair, & with magnificent auburn hair. withal not pretty, eyebrows too light freckled & teeth dark, but one of the most affable agreeable girls I have ever met. I went to see her mother this morning a pleasant old lady, but who strikes me as inferior to her daughter in refinement. She begged me to go often and see her. We had a wretched Polka tonight, Mrs Parker asked me to dance it with a Miss Wamble, Oh! how she careered, but was nothing, was tame, to a Miss Jackson who asked me to dance with her, as soon could I have held in with my single arm a restive colt the girl capered & cavaulted! I made an excuse & left the dancing room, never again will I form one of such an exhibition, too dreadful!

Friday, August 15 Mr Harvey called this morning and staid to dinner, I thought constantly he was going until the bell rang & he walked in & took his place at the strangers table. He asked me if I was acquainted with a Mr J. A. Calhoun who had just arrived at the warm Springs & gave such a description of him that I said "no, not at all." then remembering what he had said about Mr Gadsden and the impression he had given of intimacy I added that Mr J. A. Calhoun lived I believe in the same district as ourselves, that he was an absurd person & I just gave the slightest sketch of the gentleman. In the afternoon while I was paying a visit at the Coles cabin Betsey brought me a card with W. L. Calhoun, & Samuel Gourdin upon it.[28] In short time I was at the hotel & the Mr J. A. C. proved to be my old friend Willie. he seemed perfectly charmed to see me, repeated frequently, "Oh! Miss Carey. I am so delighted to see you again"—he is a frank nice person, pleasant to me, because he seems so glad to meet and be with me. I told him what had passed with Mr Harvey in the morning, he laughed & said "why, I told him we were great friends, & that I was coming over immediately to see you he asked me about you last night & told me you were here."

Saturday, August 16 I have been misdating my journal since Monday & as I wrote it up after leaving the Warm Springs, even gave the wrong day for the President's visit, he was there on Tuesday instead of Monday. I had a disappointment this afternoon which however I tried to bear with composure. For two afternoons we have endeavored to get either riding horses or a carriage to go over & pay a visit at the Warm Springs. Dr & Mrs Means called yesterday & I wished to return the visit, persuaded Aunt H. to go too, & wished to see Miss Coles, no vehicle could be obtained. Mr Goode (the son of the proprietor of these Springs)[29] a "self-sufficient, insufficient" stupid man, full of pretension and folly offered to get buggies for us, stipulating that he should drive me. I should have mentioned that Isaetta Coles brother arrived here in the stage this morning, & he had been trying to get either a buggy or riding horses for himself & sister. Mr Goode had not the delicacy to perceive that his company was not agreeable & made no offer of his buggy to Mr Coles, because then he would not have had the pleasure of driving Isaetta to the Warm. Finally however it was arranged, Mr Coles drove his sister over, I declined going of course, particularly as it was not offered to me!

Sunday, August 17 Mr Caldwell gave us a most impressive sermon this afternoon from the text "It is finished".[30] Just as the congregation were dismissed (service being held in the Drawing room) in walked Willie Calhoun, S. Gourdin & a Mr Vanderhorst.[31] I introduced them to Miss Coles, they made a long & pleasant visit. Willie begged me "to make a convenance of him at the White Sulpher" where they are all bound tomorrow that he would esteem it an especial favor. Mr Coles had engaged me to take a walk with him but it was so late when they left as to be impracticable, I promised to walk with him at the White Sulpher, and that it should be in the "Lovers walk." He is the most romantic, Byronic, sentimental personage—certainly the reverse in appearance being red haired, burnt red complexion & blue eyes. We have talked lots of nonsense for the time we have been acquainted & I suppose will much more!

Monday, August 18 The Coles left this morning at six o'clock, we go tomorrow. Uncle H. drove me to the Warm Springs after breakfast, we had the warmest welcome. Mary Coles rushed forward to meet & kiss me & all our acquaintances seemed very glad. I saw Mr & Mrs George Calhoun,[32] my first view of George since his marriage. She was as usual insipid & hanging on George. Mary Coles told a great deal about Miss Gist.[33] She is a queer cross eyed girl with the most extraordinary voice. I heard her sing here as she did not go to the Warm Springs for a day after our arrival at the Hot. She trills in the most remarkable manner but the voice otherwise not sweet.

Tuesday, August 19 Left for the White Sulphur, not sorry to take leave of the Goode establishment. Met by the Coles most affectionately

Friday, August 29 White Sulphur—I have allowed ten days to elapse without writing any thing concerning our stay at the White Sulphur, and now must give an abridgement of my usual relations. Our visit was so pleasant that we remained ten days instead of a week as first proposed. The Means & ourselves had travelled in an extra from the Hot Springs Mrs Means is rather a peculiar person, in a state of perpetual excitement about trifles, laughs constantly & says "good morning" or asks you to have any thing at table with the empressement that most others show on rare occasions. Dr Means is the agreeable half, his voice is delightful & he sings most obligingly. Mr Francis Parker was at the White. Uncle Henry and himself have a sincere friendship for each other & we saw a good deal of him. Knowing the Coles was a great advantage to us, they knew everybody, & we consequently were introduced to many pleasant people, among others Miss Emily Rutherford, she is perfectly sweet.[34] I hope we shall see a great deal of her when we go to the Sweet Springs, I like her so much. The Harrisons called, Louisa Harrison is a fine looking woman but rather loud.[35] Mrs Seaton came immediately to see us, she lived in Virginia Row, we in Paradise No. 47. I went to see her several times, & became more & more pleased with her. She introduced me to Mr Corcoran, but rather surprised me tho' I was very much amused by jesting me of him before his face, I laughed it off without any trouble or "confusion of countenance." The President & his party were at the White several days. Never was a man treated with less attention. Mrs Seaton told me that the committee appointed to receive him seemed not to know what to do, they were afraid of being too attentive so fell into the opposite. As usual our S. Carolinians were remarkable for their narrow absurd conduct, it was proposed to give the President a Ball, the Carolina Ladies declared not one of them would attend, and no gentleman from the State would be present at the meeting & *not one* was introduced. Uncle H. paid him a visit one morning a day or two after our arrival & was very much pleased. The President spoke of the condition of affairs with great moderation, alluded to the behavior of the Carolinians he had met & said "of course I could not advance to them". Every evening there is a dance in the Ball Room we frequently went down & I enjoyed it very much. Our three friends Calhoun Vanderhorst & Gourdin were exceedingly attentive to us, they are nice little fellows! I wish they were more striking in appearance, but such insignificant looking little men are seldom seen all together. Isaetta became great friends with them. Willie Calhoun told me that Vanderhorst is desperately in love with her, & intends proposing. Aunt Harrie went as our chaperone very often to the Ball room she looked sweetly pretty, & enjoyed her evenings. Uncle Henry was always most attentive and kind,—how fortunate I am! The Masons we saw frequently. Betty Mason the eldest is such a nice girl![36] She is a member of the church & does not dance but always attracts attention by her pleasant manner. She is an universal favorite with man, woman, & child. They know the N. Carolina Pettigrews very well & spoke in the highest terms of Mary & Johnston, the latter they knew while he was at the Observatory in Washington—Mary they told me was engaged to her *cousin* Frank Bryan.[37]—I was surprised! She cannot share the prejudice I have heard the brothers express on that subject—I wrote to Mr Charles[38] while at the White Mrs Mason was quite complementary in her manner of speaking to me, one day when I was making a visit to them with Mr Stuart. I laughed & said "Oh! must give me kiss after that," she did so very warmly & when I told her goodbye some days afterwards was very affectionate. Fanny Mason the second daughter has a peculiar expression from being without eyelashes upon the upper lid, it seems she was very desirous of having long sweeping lashes, so clipped those she possessed, they stood then like bristles, the only remedy was to pull them out & now she has none, except on the lower lid, the effect is "rather peculiar" The Howells from Columbia are very pleasant people we met at the White. Miss Grace Howell, her brother Malachi[39] & her cousin Tom[40]—the latter is very good looking, & manages a stammering tongue wonderfully well. Mr John Coles with whom I became acquainted is worse that anyone I ever saw except my maid Ellen. He constantly alludes to his misfortune, & instead of being composed & easing the effort to pronounce will knot his face into various twists then jerk out what he wishes to say. He had a delightful open barouche at the Springs, gave me a drive twice. Mr Stuart whom I have mentioned was one of the beaux, had been for years on admirer of Isaetta's. He reminded me of Mr McGowan,[41] is even more blunt, but much handsomer. One speech he made I wont forget. I was engaged to walk to the Ball room with Mr Stuart consequently for the first dance to him. As we went earlier than usual he was not my escort, & I told Uncle Henry that he must dance with me the first set. Mr Stuart coming to claim the dance I told him "no that I was to dance with my Uncle, he had not been at his post" "that was not my fault, he answered, "and as for your Uncle *me* and *him* will walk in the woods tomorrow & settle the matter." That *me and him* had such an ignorant sound. I have been surprised by the twanging tone of even the best of those we had seen of the Virginians. "I reckon so" meets one in every phrase and this from people whom as Stricker Coles elegantly expresses it are "of the right stripe." Stricker and myself agreed extremely well. I laughed at his nonsense, and in truth I never saw a more absurd person in his manner of talking, finally when on one occasion he said, "you know I love you Miss Carey you know your power" I thought it time to stop. In a visit he paid me a few days ago, we talked of various things & I with more *feeling* that usual he told me afterwards that he would always remember me in connection with that visit as being the first time he could say he had ever heard me speak with feeling. I will remember the remark for I took it as a lesson—though in justice to myself I must say I only a little ridiculed his egregious nonsense. The day before we left the White Sulphur he said to me Miss Carey you have had a great deal of experience, I see you know just how to amuse yourself, & yet frustrate me at every turn, you saw my design & determined to prevent it, & I know it, you amused yourself all the time." Mr Mort Singleton[42] was very attentive & kind to me, Mr J. Coles told me that "I had not a better friend than Mr Singleton." Stricker asked me many questions about Minnie,[43] said that Mr Singleton had told him she was very clever & interesting," and other remarks most pleasant for me to hear. I parted with real regret from the Coles. Isa & myself are to correspond. My visit to the White Sulphur altogether will always be remembered with pleasure.

Salt Sulphur—We arrived today just after dinner, first took rooms in the Stone House a large building on the hill, a beautiful mountain slopes up from the back of the House, the valley in front is covered with grass and clover, shade trees & benches or chairs beneath them border the main walk. A small creek runs thro' the grounds if it was clear the effect would be very pretty but it is an unwholesome dirty looking stream. A tolerable bridge crosses it, & the springs are just beyond, one Salt Sulphur the other Iodine. The whole place has the most quiet rural look & gives one an at home feeling. Mr John Vanderhorst came over this morning & attaches himself to our party, I dont know what brought him.

Saturday, August 30 The Howells arrived today. Grace & her brother Malachi. We go to the Ball room in the evenings. Last night there were but a few persons, tonight it was worse, but Mr Washington was introduced to me & I like him very much, he is the Mr W. that Sallie used to tell me about. Mr Howell & Vanderhorst were very attentive, I had a pleasant enough evening however.

Sunday, August 31 Mr More preached this morning, Mr Wagner this afternoon, neither very good. After service walked 3 miles, the Howells, Uncle Henry & myself—

Monday, September 1 Rolled ten pins this morning the Howells Vanderhorst
& ourselves. Uncle H. is not pleased at the devotions of Mr V. It is stupid
but I dont encourage him, & cant help it, both Uncle & Aunt are so particular that I think they attribute more to the foolish man than they. He has
identified himself with our party but I have nothing to do with it. The old
Vanders' arrived today. After dinner I rode with Mr John to the mountain
where an old Mr Calder a scotchman (who spent his winters in Charleston
& his summers among these mountains) built an observatory.[44] The road is
steep & rocky the distance 2 miles & ½. The observatory reminded me of
the pictures I have seen of Chinese Pagodas, large at the base & narrowing
in a peculiar shape to the top. I climbed every round to the last, the steps
were bad here, & did not attempt it. My cavalier had not much appreciation
of the beauties of the view. The high range of the Alleghany bounded the
horizon like a great wall far below lay the town of Union, just at the base
of the mountain the Calders residence, the old man is dead but his wife
keeps the place. I was delighted with the prospect, it would be delightful
to go there with one appreciated it, as it was I enjoyed it in silence, but
shall always be obliged to Mr Vanderhorst, for procuring me the pleasure.
My horse struck lame so that we were rather late returning. The Ballroom
was quite full, the dances very pleasant. I wore my pink flounced barège
with a sprig of a beautiful wild plant in my hair, the effect seemed to meet
with the approval of the company. Mr Washington & myself had a great
deal to say—he is a very nice person but rather too much given to making
pretty speeches. I can well see how Sallie & himself became such friends.
Mr Vanderhorst became quite absurd before the evening was over.

Tuesday, September 2 Uncle Henry, Mr & Miss Howell walked to the observatory this morning—it was a great undertaking, but successfully accomplished. The Rutledges, the statues Uncle Henry calls them, are here now,
the Kennedys Robertsons[45] & other acquaintances. Aunt H. as I walked
from dinner today said very gravely "dont make such a dreadful change in
your manner to Mr Vanderhorst". As she had talked to me in the morning
that my manner was so encouraging, I changed a little. Mr V.'s seat at has
always been with us at table, Hal being between us, today he had ordered
pheasant, mentioned it to me yesterday &c &c. I declined being helped at
first, merely because I did not wish any then, he looked surprised & colored
as he exclaimed "Oh-h! Miss North". He sent the dish to Uncle & Aunt H
helped Hal largely, as well as the Howells. I took some afterwards but was
unlucky in getting a mean slice to which Uncle H. helped me. Mr Vanderhorst never left me the whole evening. I refused to walk with him & sat with
every body else under the trees, I felt sorry for him, for he really looked

distressed but I was resolved to do nothing that could let others talk, his brother planted himself beside us for a long time. I dressed & when to the Ball room first going with Mr Howel. to tell Grace goodbye, they leave for the Sweet Springs early in the morning. I found a number of persons in the drawing room of the Stone House, some playing cards, others talking— after an affectionate leave taking, I went to the Ball room & found Aunt H & Mrs Robertson the only ladies. Uncle Henry, Vanderhorst & Howell the men, our position was ridiculous seated all dressed for a party in the empty room—I insisted on Uncle H. waltzing with me, he did so, & I took a turn with Vanderhorst afterwards. We remained about ½ an hour, as nobody came left. It was altogether a failure, I was provoked to think how nicely I had dressed myself, just to undress again. Mr V talked to me but I only tormented him a little. When we said goodbye, he said something I dont know what. It seems stupid to write all this nonsense, but it is incident of the idle life at the Springs—& there is nothing else to mention,

Wednesday, September 3 The Howells were off this morning, Mr Vanderhorst has departed also, what shall I do without my two attendants! The Porcher party arrived yesterday.[46] We called on them this morning, none of them look to me improved by their excursioning except Charles Lucas.[47] We tried the Ball room once more. Emily Elliott a Miss Taylor[48] Mrs Whittle her sister & myself were the ladies who danced. Mr Elliott was my partner two quadrilles & a waltz.[49] Uncle Henry Mr Whittle, Mr Kennedy were other beaux. Mr Elliott was very pleased to dance and performs very well too.

Thursday, September 4 Aunt Harrie rode this afternoon as far as Union, a wonderful feat for her to accomplish. Wrote a note to Isaetta Coles by Mr Washington, the beginning of our correspondance.

Friday, September 5 Rolled ten pins this morning, found it stupid enough. Emily Elliott asked me to Polk with her, Mrs Vanderhorst played for us & a funny morning we had. Mr Elliott & his daughter Caroline who has been indisposed since their arrival here were at first the only persons present & Mr E. took lessons in the schottisch from me as Mrs V. played rather irregularly. I played the tune that she might get the time. Mrs Van went into extacies, pronounced my touch & time perfect After playing some dances for the Elliotts to practise by I tried at her request some of her music, among others "Sleeping I dreamed Love," she urged me to sing, refusing was of no avail, the old Piano is dreadful, but getting desperate I began (not being much in awe of my judges) what was my consternation when Mrs Van piped up too! Words cannot describe our duett! at the end of the first verse Mr

Elliott snatched up his hat & rushed from the room. I was suffocating with laughter—the Porchers Miss Gaillard & Deveaux the other side of the room were laughing to themselves. I endeavored to escape the 2d verse but Mrs Vanderhorst said "Oh! go on my dear you sing very well, go on, come begin now." I humored her wish and sang the next, she hearing her part with strength. I retained my composure with effort, my voice trembled from the inclination to laugh, but Mrs Vanderhorst was unsuspicious & very pleased with her part. She brought us a nice hot pound cake for lunch & was so kind & obliging in playing schottisch & polkas that I felt sorry I had ever laughed at her—tho' she is very curious person. Mr Elliott & herself took a waltz together which was a sight to behold. She repeated to me three times "what an *acquisition* you must be to your mother" "What a treasure you must be to your mother &cc" "I hope my sons will give me musical daughters-in-law." Before we left the room she invited us all to spend Xmas with her saying she loved young company. She seemed to be the most kind hearted person & very amiable. I never saw any one more neglected by their family neither sons husband or daughter show her the least consideration.

Saturday, September 6 No letters from home—a few old papers from Charleston. I was very disappointed not to hear from Minnie or Lou.[50] Spent the evening in the Stone Parlor pleasantly. The Elliots left this morning for the Sweet Springs. On coming to breakfast I found a note on my plate from Emily Elliott saying goodbye & as usual laughing at some of the visitors. Miss Elisabeth Porcher & Mr C. Lucas gave her great amusement, in the note she takes a thrust at them. Last night she laughed so much at every body that I thought she would have given offence. I was very much amused to hear her attack Miss Susan Rutledge[51] the most perpendicular personnage here & who cannot reply exceptly rudely, or what sounds more the same thing— Uncle H. read prayers this morning the Clarksons,[52] (who arrived yesterday from the Red Sulphur) Mrs Robertson & ourselves the congregation—

Monday, September 8 The Miss Balls sang for us this morning, the eldest Amelia is very handsome & has a delightful voice, her sister is only 13 but sings remarkably well. Mrs Ball[53] is in party with the Rutledges & travelling for her health which seems very bad, she must have been a beautiful woman in youth, of severe temper I have heard. Her daughters are devoted her, & when she is excited & nervous soothe her by their singing. Aunt H. received a letter from Lou it was very old having been a long time at the W. Sulphur. The child writes a very good letter, dear Minnie she says is suffering from her throat the trip to Glenn Springs will benefit them all I hope.

Tuesday, September 9 Played a few duetts with Mrs Vanderhorst, & taught her a schottisch, she was energetic in her thanks. Wrote Emily Elliott a note by the Rutledges who with the Balls left this morning for the Sweet. We were to have gone but could not get a stage.

Wednesday, September 10 Vanderhorsts off this morning, I took a walk with Miss Gardner[54]—Mrs Rose & herself sat sometime with us this morning, talked a great deal We shall go tomorrow—the Robertsons & ourselves have an extra together. I am very glad, for it very dull here, and a change to a more lively place I shall hail with pleasure, as for *this* cheifly we are perigrinating, it is best to enjoy the "gift while we may". Of all the Springs, I have been to this pleases me the most, & had there been more pleasant people would have been charming—

Thursday, September 11 —Red Sweet Springs—After a hot drive we arrived at this place just before dinner Mr and Mrs Robertson with ourselves were the only persons in the stage which rendered it as comfortable as could be in such weather. Thinking it would be pleasanter than at the Old Sweet, & really on my account, Uncle H & Aunt Harrie came here instead of going there first but we made a mistake as more is going on at the Old Sweet, although everywhere persons are leaving & the company dispersing. The Howells are still here but leave on Monday so do the Means—the Elliotts leave tomorrow, & Vanderhorsts, Balls, & several others. I am disappointed for I had anticipated quite a gay time. The place is very pretty the green meadows surrounds the house on all sides, the cottages are situated to the left as you drive up, the bath house is some distance from the main building—the Springs are the prettiest I have seen the three rise from under a large rock, the water as it flows over the sand is of a yellow red colour, the taste very peculiar & strong of the mineral, it is a chalybeate,[55] there is no building over the Springs or enclosure of any sort, the rock half hangs over them, the three uniting flow into the bath house. We had a dance this evening, my first dance was with Mr Langdon Cheves.[56] I did not find the evening very pleasant—[. . .] at all. pleased to meet a Lieut Riall, a poor man, somewhat crackbrained from the effects of a fever in the African coast years ago. He had been introduced to me in Charleston about a year or two since—recognized & was quite disposed to be very attentive. I introduced him to Emily Elliott having previously warned her of my kind intentions— It was to pay her off for some of her pranks. I rid myself of a trouble & had a laugh at her expense She pretended to be very doleful under the infliction, but said "You had the best of it Carey. You turned the laugh on me." Mr Elliott was very much amused at the dance she had with him.

Friday, September 12 I wrote to Minnie a long letter yesterday I received 4 letters on my arrival three from home & one from Isaetta Coles—It was a greater pleasure than I have had for a long time. The Elliotts V's. & several others left today for the Warm Springs. Mrs M'Cord paid us a visit this afternoon.[57] Aunt Harrie did not see her as she was lying down, with a head-ache—She made me quite a long visit—she is a masculine clever person, with the most mannish attitudes & gestures, but interesting & very enter-taining. Mrs Cheves is her step daughter & sister in law [58]—her children are made to call her Aunt, Mrs M'Cord not believing in the relationship of half sister—so I was told at least—The Ball & Rutledge party have gone so that the company is indeed small. Grace Howell is very pleasant but she goes on Monday somehow we have made a mistake as to the time for being here.

Saturday, September 13 After dinner today Mr Howell drove Aunt Harrie Grace & myself to the Old Sweet. We went to see the Holmes particularly, but as we drove up they passed us going out. Aunt H. made us all laugh by exclaiming as we passed each other, "why we hired this hack expressly to come & see you"! It was a curious concern we went in, so much so that Mr Howell was more disposed that we should give up the visit than go in such a caboose. We found the Masons at the Sweet made them a visit—Mrs Seaton I was delighted to meet, not being aware she was there, Mrs Ashley & Cabell were there also. We had the most gracious reception from every one, all expressed wishes that we were staying there. Lieut Riall attached himself to me closely (he paid me a visit this morning). I dread going to the Sweet, because he is such an annoyance, & always devotes himself to the young ladies. Uncle Henry was quite indisposed today, he does not look well—I took my first bath this morning the water chilled me, & I was very pale afterwards. Aunt H was charmed, it exhilerated her, & had altogether an opposite effect to that I experienced. Here is the end of my second book of travels! Really I am a voluminous writer! & much to my own surprise—I dont know how I get over such a deal of paper. If I had an equal opportunity I think I would be a formidable rival to Madame Pfeiffer in the number (*not interest*) of her volumes of travel [59]—

Sunday, September 14 A Mr Farr a Presbyterian preacher this morning he is very inferior to any I have heard & more like the old Baptist preacher at home—

Monday, September 15 Mr Riall put the china to his annoying behaviour by proposing to me after supper. I have done every thing to avoid it, but found by so doing I was only prolonging my own discomfort. The Howells left this morning. I so regret that our plans did not suit for going on together. Grace is a nice girl & Mr Malachia is a nice beau.

Tuesday, September 16 Mrs Seaton called this morning & brought her son. I was amused at her introducing me to him as "Carey"—He has just returned from Europe where he had been five years—he is not handsome, but a manly well bred looking person.

Walked with Uncle H to Beavers Dam Falls. They are very pretty and the scenery above the Falls on the creek, wild & picturesque. We met an old gentleman & his wife (a young woman) at the Falls, he was very talkative and sociable told me I reminded him of a young lady in his town in N. Carolina. "Very much like her indeed" this is only the one thousanth person I have been told this Summer I so much resembled—We crossed the creek on the rock bridge & log—the old gentleman induced his wife to follow our example. He had told Uncle H that there were several caverns higher up the creek, which could be seen very well from the side upon which we were—coming opposite to one he exclaimed "Oh! Sir look there, that's a very *stout* cavern." In all we walked six miles & found it very pleasant—returned just as persons were leaving the supper room—Our friends name was Grist or Rice I dont know which.

Wednesday, September 17 Mr Seaton walked over this morning to know if I would dine with his mother. Uncle Henry & myself returned with him & made a visit but I was not able to remain—which I regretted.

Thursday, September 18 A most melancholy death occurred at the old Sweet last night, a Mrs Warner a gay widow was found dead in her bed this morning. She was perfectly well yesterday played ten pins in the morning walked here in the afternoon made engagements with some ladies for today, played cards until late, then retired after laughing & talking gaily with three or four girls, & was dead this morning. A disease of the heart it is said occasioned her awfully sudden end. I felt inexpressibly shocked when I heard it though I have never seen the poor woman it was fearful to think of her being cut off without one moment's warning—to have closed her eyes in apparent perfect health, & awake in Eternity! Strange, that those who have known this circumstance the sudden death of one in their midst should ever forget it, or live on the same. Mr Calhoun & Gourdin very unexpectedly made their appearance just before supper—they have been all this time with Mr Crawly near the Blue Sulphur. Both look well.

Friday, September 19 We have made the acquaintance of Major Porter his wife & niece Miss Alexander.[60] They are from Savannah & seem very nice people. The Roses & Miss Gardner[61] are here now have been since Tuesday. old Wharley is in their party & I think cultivating Miss Gardner who is smiling.[62] Paid Mrs Seaton a visit—the old Sweet looks cheerless & gloomy, every one there seems depressed. The few persons now at the place have moved into the hotel. A panic spread among them after poor Mrs Warner's death the servants are all possessed with it none of the maids can be induced to remain with the corpse. This morning I had been playing for Miss Gardner & Mr Gourdin sometime when we left the parlor a gentleman advanced to meet me, who proved to be Mr Seaton, his mother was paying Mrs Wickham[63] a visit & he seated in the piazza waiting. I asked him into Aunt Harrie's room which forms generally our parlor. Mrs Seaton came frequently & staid a little while, I am sure they had cold dinner for the last bell rang soon after they left. I walked over with Uncle H and "the Ponies" after dinner the old lady seemed as pleased as though we had not parted a few hours before.

Saturday, September 20 Mr & Mrs Pickens[64] called this morning—in the afternoon Uncle Henry drove Aunt Harrie to the old Sweet—the Miss Pickens sent to say they were coming this afternoon to see me consequently I remained at home—they were very late being detained by the funeral of Mrs Warner which took place this afternoon. Poor thing! her mother & sister are in N. York, she preferred coming to the Springs, but had no friends merely acquaintances with whom she was. I have never heard of a more distressing case. Mrs Bennett, Miss Burgess & Mr Gordon arrived here today.[65] Willie Calhoun calls Mrs Bennett nothing but Mrs Gordon he declares he tries not, but it will come out perversely. Major Porter when introducing her to his wife committed the same mistake, naming her as "Mrs Gorden—ahem Mrs Bennett"—She bowed with her most stately air. I played a great deal tonight. Mr Gordon expressed himself as very much indebted. Mrs Bennett amuses me with her pompous speech it is highly ridiculous sometimes.

Sunday, September 21 No service today as there was no minister at either Spring. The Seatons & Pickens walked over this afternoon, paid a visit.

Monday, September 22 Aunt Harrie & myself proposed bathing at the Old Sweet this morning, she changed her mind and I was near doing the same thing when Mrs Seaton who had come to bid her friend Mrs Wickham goodbye & afterwards called on us, asked me to spend the day with her. Mr Seaton declared himself responsible for my safe return I went on such surety! The bath was not as pleasant to me as the one here, it is so large that I felt as tho' I would be drowned—especially as the water is so bouyant it was impossible for me to keep my feet. The Pickens & Seatons were the only persons except one family who did not approach the parlor. In the immense dining room their numbers looked forlorn. The day passed very pleasantly Mrs Seaton was as pleasant and kind as usual Mr Seaton very agreeable, the Pickens are rather young but nice girls. Mrs Seaton gave me "Hawthornes Twice told Tales"[66] telling me to think of her when I read them. Mr Seaton walked home with me. Passed the evening in the parlor.

Tuesday, September 23 We leave here tomorrow the Forters went today & the Roses are gone also. Every body left the Old Sweet this morning, the Seatons for the Warm Springs, the Pickens home—Mrs Lawrence played for us tonight & I danced the Polka & Schottisch with Willie Calhoun, & waltzed with Uncle Henry, Mr Gordon & Gourdin we had a merry evening the first of that description passed here. Uncle Henry was ready for all that was lively whirled me round the [. . .] the room in double quick time Willie dances rather absurdly I am sorry to say, with a distressing twist in his neck. Mr Gordon sang for us extremely well, Mrs Bennett & Miss Burgess were as amusing (unconsciously) as usual.

Wednesday, September 24 Left the Red Sweet this morning dined at Col. Crow's a worthy who has become very corpulent on his dignity. Stopped at Callahans for the night.

Thursday, September 25 Arrived at the Warm Springs & I felt so pleased to be here again, to me this has been the pleasantest place in the Mountains. I bestowed a groan on the Hot en passant dismal spot that it is! We are lodged in Cabins opposite the Hotel. I had a front & back room just the same as Aunt Harrie, felt like a person of importance with my suite of rooms. For the first time during our travelling went to dinner without preparation, found the reality not so trying as the contemplation of such a step. After supper we went in the parlor. Aunt Harrie & myself having dressed nicely for the evening, I was regreting to Miss Gardner that Mrs Seaton had not arrived as we supposed she would have done when she pointed her out to me across the room. I darted over & there my dear old friend was, but so pale and fatigued from the journey that I was sorry to see it. We met most affectionately—She has the cabin next to mine—I have not mentioned that Lieut Riall was the first person to meet us today. Mr Calhoun & Gourdin who travelled extra with us were resolved to keep him at a distance & kept such guard that he could not be tormenting. I would have laughed today when he said "ladies you are just too late every body has gone" had it not been him who told us. Aunt H. & myself have had amusement in observing how we have arrived after the season at the various Springs. I charged Mr Wickham not to mention that we were coming as I was certain every body would rush from the Warm he seemed highly amused & promised great discretion. I did not think however it would have been so literally fulfilled.

Friday, September 26 Passed a very pleasant day, tho' it began unfavorably. At the breakfast table, I was seated between the two young men with my back to the table opposite, they had been saying a great deal about Mr Seaton, especially Mr Calhoun when I found Mr Seaton at the back of my chair speaking to me, soon after he left I was not aware of being stiff until as we went into the piazza Aunt Harrie said in a low tone "I am quite provoked, what was the matter, you were so stiff to Mr Seaton?" This made me resolve to overcome it—I heard Mrs Seaton was sick in bed, did not at first know which was her cabin & went to her son's instead, a servant directing me, I found her next to my own, tapped at the door, obeyed the summons to walk in & found her in bed much fatigued & feeling badly. I warmly expressed my regret, she put her arm round my neck kissed me & said "Where is Gales? have you seen him?"[67] I was very much amused but answered quietly, I had caught a glimpse of him after breakfast at the back of my chair tho' I had scarcely had an opportunity of speaking—then I left a message asking him to join us in a walk to the top of the Mountain, kissed her & took my leave, she said "I'll tell him I know he would like to go"— Mr Seaton however told Uncle H. who also invited him that he feared he would not be able to join us on his mothers account. Miss Alexander Mr Gourdin, a Mr Johnston from Georgia, Uncle Henry & myself walked to Crow's nest. I was very tired for the path is steep & stoney—we were not much more that two hours going & returning, the others did not seem to mind it but I felt worn out—I gathered a bouquet of wild flowers & carried Mrs Seaton, she had gone to the parlor. I gave them in keeping to Jane the maid who was extremely gracious to me. After dinner as usual we went to the Parlor Mrs Seaton seemed very much gratified by the slight attention, & wore the flowers in her belt Mr Seaton was reading a paper but soon laid it aside to discourse Aunt Harrie. I was seated at a little distance somehow we began talking in a short time & kept the ball rolling for a long while. He is really very pleasant, indeed I believe the most agreeable man we have met in Virginia. Tonight Uncle H. & Mrs Coxe a widow & cousin of Mrs Ashley Mr Gourdin & myself played whist—indeed there was nothing else to do, the room was filled with whist parties. Mrs Wickham came from the Hot Springs this afternoon—Mr Seaton came in before our game was over when we went to the cabin walked down with me, Mrs Seaton parted from us very affectionately hoping to see us in Washington. I thought Mr S. had been taking a glass too much of wine he seemed excited, & when he asked permission to escort me to the cabin was [. . .] a letter with which unintentionally he tapped me in the face. I am very minute certainly, but when persons are pleasant, it is pleasant to record one's recollections or experiences. Heard from Aunt Adèle[68] today—all well—

Saturday, September 27 Left the Warm Springs a little after seven this morning Messrs Calhoun & Gourdin with us. dined at Oaklands & reached Staunton by ½ past six in the evening—a journey of fifty miles—Found the Whittles & Betty Taylor here, saw also an old lady a Mrs Rose who was altogether of an antique pattern, her dress was as plain in cut & material as possible, her cap with out a piece of ribbon except the strings—she is a sister of Mr Seaton (père) looks upon Washington as so dreadful place & the Springs so wicked that she has never visited either, spends her winters in Richmond, & summers in Staunton—she is a strict Methodist—Mrs Seaton had told Aunt H something of her & hoped we would become acquainted.[69]

Sunday, September 28 Attended service at the Episcopal church heard Dr Tyler the principal of the Deaf & Dumb institution preach. Talked to Mrs Rose about two hours this evening, the old lady was very amiable & I think was quite won towards me. We have taken an extra with the Whittles to go on to Winchester tomorrow. Willie Calhoun & Gourdin visited Wear's cave today, were delighted, invited me to accompany them this morning. Tomorrow they leave for Charlottsville.

Monday, September 29 We visited the institution for the Deaf Dumb & Blind this morning. It was extremely interesting, the first class we saw were four blind girls taking a guitar lesson, their teacher perfectly blind also—they sang two or three songs, all having reference in the words to their situation, it was very sad to see & hear them—In the Deaf & Dumb apartment, the mutes were in school divided into various classes according to their proficiency. the first we saw had been instructed about a year their teacher deaf & dumb had been educated in the Institution, they wrote short sentences as he would give them on his fingers, in good hands & correctly spelled. The most advanced class were so intelligent in appearance, so quick performed their parts so admirably that I could hardly realize their great privation. The teacher was an educated gentlemanly person & was not deaf & dumb. One girl was particularly interesting, she was about twelve years old remarkably pretty & intelligent face with beautiful eyes. In a moment she seemed to understand—her teacher wrote with rapidity & perfect correctness her name is Chapell & a lovely looking child. We heard afterwards a little blind girl read, & another examined in Geography, she touched all the places asked without making one mistake. In general they have a sad dejected air very different from their equally unfortunate companions—they for the most part looked cheerful & bright—The visit to the Institution was most interesting & calculated to impress to most careless & indifferent. We visited afterwards the Lunatic Asylum were met in the entry by a man who turned out to be a director tho' I think he is a candidate for a place himself. We saw a few of the superior patients, one the saddest looking woman I ever beheld. We did not remain long but after seeing the chapel & kitchen returned to the Hotel. I wrote Isaetta Coles a note by Mr Calhoun & gave him a letter to Joe Allston[70] as he "Willie" is to be in Columbia Saturday or Sunday next. At three o'clock we left Staunton Mr & Mrs Whittle Miss Whittle, Miss Taylor, little Willie Taylor & maid with ourselves forming a party of twelve—The two gentlemen & Hal rode on the outside there being deck seats—

Tuesday, September 30 Spent last night comfortably in Harrisonburg, left early & drove 65 miles to Winchester—Our route lay thro' the Valley of Va. Miss Taylor & myself rode on the outside for 26 miles in the morning & I for several more miles after dinner which we took at a place called Woodstock. I enjoyed riding on the outside exceedingly—The beautiful undulating country the constant succession of villages, the cultivated broad fields formed a delightful prospect. The Valley deserves the fame it has for being one of the most fertile & beautiful portions of the State. Staid at the Taylor House in Winchester—very nice place, & apparently "blessed" with beds there were four in my room, as many in Aunt H. & the Whittles were equally well provided—

Wednesday, October 1 Baltimore Left Winchester at nine o'clock by eleven arrived at Harpers Ferry—We had scarcely an opportunity of seeing anything of the famed scenery hurrying along in the cars. The Mountain rises in rugged grandeur from the rivers edge, towering several hundred feet above. We remained so short a time at the Ferry that we could not walk about and view the fine scenery or see any thing of the place. After dining at ½ past eleven we took the cars for Baltimore arrived before five, stopped at Barnum's found Mrs Ball & family staying here—the Rutledges & themselves parted at the Red Sweet, I thought Miss Susan was too much for any one to endure peacefully long—I was obliged to make my appearance this evening for a little while in my travelling dress. the lock of my trunk had been injured, & I had to send for a locksmith to open it.

Thursday, October 2 Went out shopping with Uncle Henry, he was admirable in his new capacity, I bought a blue silk at Hamilton & Easter's. On returning to the Hotel I found Mrs Gordon had called she directed me to a Miss Bullen as a dress maker. I met Mrs Torre while out this morning she seemed very glad to see me.

Friday, October 3 Uncle Phil & Aunt Lou arrived from Annapolis en route for New York. Phil has entered the Naval school[71] remarkably well, I was delighted to hear it. The Porters came today. I have bought the prettiest bonnet ever seen—Mr Gourdin made his appearance this evening also. It was the pleasantest surprise to find Aunt Lou here when we came in from walking this afternoon. Mrs Torre & Mrs Norris called today we were out.

Saturday, October 4 Uncle Phil & Aunt Lou left at nine o'clock this morning Charlotte Porcher with them—they are to meet the Corbetts in N. York then go home. The Roses & Miss Gardner arrived today. Aunt Harriette & myself returned the visits made us. Mrs Gordon was out, Mrs Torre in the country, Mrs Norris at home—the cook came to the door at first, Mrs Norris herself afterwards, we had pleasant visit—she was very much confused when she met us at the door I spent this evening at Mrs Gilmer's a sister of Mr Ladson[72] & where the Ladsons are staying. Miss Brien her niece called & invited me to spend the evening I went & found it dull & long there were three young men the five ladies entertained them assiduously, the elderly members of the party sat in the lighted half the drawing room the young people in the other. no intercourse was held between the light & darkness any more than if we had no knowledge of each other. Mr Barney came in about nine o'clock from the moment after speaking he devoted himself to me until I left at ½ past ten—Poor old gentleman! it is painful to hear how foolish he is talking love & nonsense to the young ladies—and really an intelligent agreeable man when conversing sensibly.

Sunday, October 5 Attended service at Christ Church—heard Dr Johns preach.[73] The Music was delightful, the sermon good. The church is handsome the reading desk & pulpit of white marble & beautiful. We sat in Mr James Carrols pew,[74] Aunt H & myself—Mrs Norris had directed us to it— I was sorry we went two or three children were turned out for our convenience, & it was very awkward. Uncle H. & Mr Gourdin sat somewhere else.

In the afternoon Miss Alexander, Mr Gourdin & myself went to the Cathedral.[75] I was astonished having never before heard anything of the Roman service. I was shocked when the priest said "let us contemplate the coronation of the Blessed Virgin in Heaven" Strange that any one who reads the Gospels should ever join *that* Church. We walked thro' the German Catholic Church dedicated to St. Alphonso. The Altar was decorated with vases of artificial flowers, pictures & tapers. There are pictures & statues around the church. In the Cathedral are two large pictures presented by Louis 18th & Charles 10th of France. Mr Harvey escorted me.

Monday, October 6 Left for Washington at nine o'clock arrived at 12 or before Went to Willard's instead of the National as they were painting—Before we dined walked in the grounds in the rear of the Presidents House. At the first view I was disappointed & thought it not sufficiently handsome as the residence of the for the time "Sovereign of the country." The grounds are nicely kept & very pretty. After dinner sent our cards to Mrs Seaton— thought they ought to have gone before then. Walked towards the Capitol, took an omnibus in a little while—we all enjoyed the frolic of the drive. The Capitol is a very handsome building commanding a view & conspicuous from every part of the City—the moon had risen & was pouring a flood of light over the dome & beautiful pillars, the trees threw their shadows on the green sward, the influence of the time the peculiar soft appearance of the whole scene in the moonlight rendered it one not be forgotten. My first view of the Capitol will always dwell fresh in my mind. I thought it must resemble an Italian scene.

Tuesday, October 7 Mrs Seaton called early this morning, said "Gales" would be there immediately. she paid us a delightful visit, while still with us Uncle H. walked in with Mr Reid I would not have recognized him, he is stout, red & pompous in appearance. He said he knew me but I think he was rather doubtful—his imitation of Uncle is disagreeable, he is a strict copyist. After Mrs Seaton left he staid a long time I was sorry to find him so tiresome & ridiculous. He departed after sometime, & not long afterwards Mr Gales Seaton's card was brought in. I was really glad to see him, he proposed to accompany us any where we wished to go. First we went to the Patent Office there saw various curiosities. What I looked upon with most interest was General Washington's uniform, his camp chest, writing desk & tea service & Dr Franklin's walking stick, a very handsome one. It is in vain to attempt an enumeration of the objects of interest days might be spent with pleasure & profit in examining everything, or even a few of the principal collections—From the Patent Office we drove to the Capitol. The pictures in

the rotunda I admired, the statues of Peace & War at the entrance are very
fine. Mr Seaton escorted me about, leaving Aunt Harrie & Uncle H. rather
groping their way, the Hall of Representatives has over the door a clock the
design of which is admirable, a female figure representing History with her
pen & tablet is in a car the wheel of which is formed by the clock. The
Senate Chamber is a fine room, but both this & the Representative Hall was
in great disorder preparing for the approaching session. Mr Seaton pointed
out the gallery to my especial notice saying it was there all the flirtations
of the winter were carried on. It was late before we returned to the Hotel
just as we were getting into the carriage Mr Seaton (père) came up he spoke
in the most friendly manner & seemed as pleased to see us tho' we were
old friends. I do not like the statue of Washington by Greenough,[76] it is too
rude & altogether unsuited to the great subject. After tea Mr Gales joined
us again & we went to the Observatory. This visit I found very ludicrous. a
young man with a lantern went about showing us instrument of which the
name & use were equally unknown Mr Seaton pretended great wisdom on
the occasion—We went to the top of the Observatory where is the large
telescope. We found several persons there, all prepared to stare at the moon.
When Aunt H took her turn, she twisted about a little then exclaimed "this
can't be fixed right, I dont see anything"—every body laughed. Altogether
I thought our visit to the Observatory rather unsatisfactory. Mr Seaton staid
sometime with us on returning to the Hotel—

Wednesday, October 8 We have had a delightful tho' rather fatiguing day—
   Harry arranged to visit Mount Vernon this morning, Mr Seaton was with
us early enough—Uncle H. was opposed to going but it was too late, unless
we would appear fickle and foolish. We waited Oh a long time at the wharf
before the boat came. Uncle H looked grave, Aunt H. rather too. At length
we were safe on board the "Geo. Washington" some few besides ourselves.
We stopped at Alexandria which from the water reminded me of Charleston—next at Fort Washington, finally at Mount Vernon! The tomb is not
far from the landing place a plank walk leading to it—a marble sarcophagus
contains the remains of our Hero. beside it is an other his wife's. A brick
wall surrounds the whole, with a large iron rail door before the spot where
are the sarcophagus. Around are several monuments of different members
of the family—I do not pretend to describe my sensations which looking
at the tomb, I realized his life, his acts, his death. Mr Seaton introduced the
present proprietor of the place to us, Mr Augustine Washington, a grand
nephew of General Washington.[77] He was very polite offered me his arm
leading the way to the house, here he had wine, biscuits, & cakes handed.
We sat in what was the family parlor & never shown to visitors, the peculiar

form, the style of the engravings all brought back long past days—we saw the key of the Bastile sent by La Fayette to Washington & kept in a glass case, there were not many relics, but the house itself was an object of great interest, the piazza is flagged & flat to the ground, the rooms are of old fashioned form, the situation commands a beautiful view of the Potomac or river of Swans—I charmed that one event & shall always feel obliged to Mr Seaton but for whom we should have been treated like all the other strangers—Mr Washington looks like a farmer, he has three daughters, the [*first*] of whom is a beauty, her eyes are magnificent—when grown she will be extremely handsome. The Potomac is a very beautiful stream, broad & clear. We reached Washington at ½ past 3, were engaged at five to dine at the Seatons—how fast we dressed to be punctual! Mr & Mrs Seaton, Miss Scott their niece Capt Burnsides Mr Gales Seaton & ourselves formed the party. The dinner was beautiful, no dish to carve on the table & of six courses. In the middle of the table was a vase containing a beautiful bouquet. Mrs Seaton asked me if "I remembered the flowers I had given her at the Springs & that was for me" Mr Gales presented it as soon as dessert was brought on. The gentlemen left the table with the ladies coffee was handed we remained until ½ past 8 then departed saying goodbye as we expected to leave the next day. Mrs Monroe came in shortly before we left, she is not so pleasing as her mother, too decided in her style. Miss Scott spoke to Aunt H. of Uncle Charles & of having known him very well—she is a pleasant intelligent woman—Mr Gales was quite agreeable today the old gentleman is charming. Mr Barney met us on our return to the Hotel & insisted on our going to see the President—Off we went the President received us most cordially we remained ½ an hour then took our leave. I like him so much, he talked so well, and was so affable—

Thursday October 9 We were packed & ready to start, bonnet & gloves on when Uncle H. determined that it would be better to remain in Washington than rest in Richmond as had been proposed. I wrote a note to Mrs Seaton informing her of the change & received a nice one in reply—not 15 minutes Mr Gales Seaton made his appearance, soon afterwards his mother came. Aunt Harrie & myself accompanied them thro' the President's House & then to Mr Corcorans to see his pictures & the Greek slave.[78] Afterwards to the Smithsonian Institute. The East room at the White House is very handsomely furnished, the sofa & chairs are of a sort of brocade damask, the curtains of crimson satin damask very rich, the carpet rich to correspond—there are 8 mirrors in the room. The pictures at Mr Corcorans are selected with taste & form a beautiful collection the Greek slave is exquisite—refined & perfectly lovely. Mrs Seaton parted at the Hotel saying that she would try & see us again but as she had to dine at 5 o'clock in the country thought it doubtful. We owed a delightful morning to her & Mr Gales. I hope I may meet her again for she is a person to love & remember. Mr Seaton said he had to apologise to Uncle H. for not carrying him to see the pictures, so paid us a visit then carried Uncle H to see them. We bid goodbye again. After tea as I was seated talking to Mr Barney in walked Mr Seaton he took a seat beside me, & there remained till ½ past ten Mr B decamped & nobody else talked to us. He is a nice person & I like him very much. He says he is coming to Charleston in January. I received a beautiful present this afternoon sent without name or message explanatory. I know he was the anonymous friend. he did not deny it when I gave him a message to the person should he ever chance to know who it was. Goodbye to Washington we leave tomorrow—

Friday, October 10 Off for Charleston I—

Saturday, October 11 Reached Wilmington at 12 o'clock went from the Cars to the boat. We left Washington in the Mount Vernon went down the Potomac as far as Aquia Creek took the Cars for Richmond—arrived at 5— left at ½ past 6, supped in Petersburg—travelled to Weldon changed cars breakfasted in Goldsborough, dined on board the Boat at Wilmington

Sunday, October 12 Safe arrived in Charleston.

SECOND JOURNAL

Wednesday, August 4, 1852 It is just a year since I stepped on board the "Vanderbilt" en route for the Virginia Springs, with Uncle Henry & Aunt Harriette. Today at ½ past two with Uncle Tom. Aunt Ann, & Mattie[1] on the same boat we left the Charleston Wharf but not for the same summer's tour—the North & Canada are the places of attraction this time, every where & every thing will be so new that I anticipate great enjoyment. We had a comfortable enough cabin on deck & no thunder storm to try our nerve. Among sixty passengers there were few who looked above the very common, the women were as is always the case in such instances, very coarse in appearance

Thursday, August 5 Arrived at Weldon at three o'clock dined at Whitfields Hotel, not so nice a place as Greshams where we stopped last year, at Weldon, we branched off from the Richmond road taking the Norfolk line—

saw the Roanoke River which brought to my mind "John Randolph of *Roan-oke*"—the river is a muddy stream full of shoals & small islands above & below the railroad bridge. Suffolk is a small town with a church & streets of ample width—At seven we reached Portsmouth on the bank of James river, the appearance of Norfolk on the opposite side is very pretty—the two towns built on the river banks, the ferry boats constantly plying, & the various craft in the river gives an appearance of prosperity and activity pleasant to see. We crossed in one of the Ferry boats being ensconced in a wretched three seat vehicle drawn by one Rosinante of a horse—four of us besides the driver was severe, our appearance was rather of the burlesque order—We were dragged out of the boat & through the streets to Mrs Emersons establishment for entertainment. Our John triumphantly pocketed his money indifferent to our not concealed contempt of his "turn out" & drove off—After supper Uncle Tom introduced us to Mrs Armstead a bright, lively, pretty woman who is very talkative & frank. She said to "Aunt Ann you must not be jealous but I gave the Captain two kisses when he left Norfolk the other day, we all did."[2] Aunt Ann's comment afterwards was "very free I think". Uncle Tom is extremely popular with every one here especially the ladies.

Friday, August 6 Aunt Emily North[3] came to see us this morning she looks very well & was very affectionate, & glad to see me. At eleven o'clock we went to Portsmouth & Gosport visited the Navy Yard, went into the court-martial room for a few minutes, saw a number of captains in uniform all very grave, but struck me as looking "jolly companions every one" The Navy Yard comprises 60 acres, and there are numerous buildings for various purposes—The Pennsylvania which we visited afterwards, is a noble ship of immense size—the decks were clean & white as scrubbing could make them, many of the cannon were mounted giving a most warlike appearance and there are four tier of them. the captains cabin is nicely furnished but I thought rather small in comparison with the great size of the ship—this was my first view of a Man of war, the order neatness & exactness are admirable. I was delighted with the whole—& think it must be a pleasant thing to be ruler of so fine a ship & beautiful arrangements. After dinner drove about the town, saw some pretty residences, & the handsomest Baptist church I have ever seen. Spent the evening with Aunt Emily, (Mattie & myself) Her two sisters & four or five gentlemen were the company—passed a very pleasant evening.

Saturday, August 7 Wrote to Aunt Lou—little Eliza North[4] spent the morning with us she is a bright clever child & will be a very pretty woman.

Returned the visits paid us yesterday found no one at home but Aunt Em. She gave me this morning the prettiest straw basket which Uncle Jim had sent from Madeira,[5] she is as affectionate & attentive as tho' she had known me well. As we returned from walking, Mr Taylor joined us—he is a strange man & wears the most extraordinary old white hat his appearance is described in one word—odd! Uncle Tom says he took a great fancy to me. he talked a great deal & said many comical things—among others, "you'll marry, the ugliest fellow in all South Carolina, ugly enough to stop a mill, I know you will."

Sunday, August 8 Went to church with Aunt Em the rest of the party with the Tazewell Taylors.[6] Heard Mr Cummins one of the most eloquent men, indeed the most eloquent Episcopal minister I have ever listened to.[7] His subject was the confession of Christ nominally & in our lives. In manner I thought him rather studied, but was told it was perfectly natural. Spent the day with Aunt Em. her nice dinner made ample amends for the miserable fare we have had here, we have been almost starved too to make it worse. Miss Susan Klein dined with us, she is a pleasant nice girl not at all pretty. I have thought Mrs Armstead rather too free in manner to be either agreeable or ladylike—today I heard that it is not long since she has been married, she was a shop girl who when she married a master in the Navy could neither read nor write—she regularly goes to school has a natural cleverness & played her cards so well to the President when he made a visit to the Pennsylvania[9] sometime ago. that he promoted her husband—sharp little woman!

Monday, August 9 Returned the Kleins visit this morning—told Aunt Em goodbye she told me she was going to send for a Mahon shawl[10] for me sweet little soul! Had the happiness to leave Norfolk in the "Oceola" at 4 o'clock tiresome place! & most disgusting hotel is Mrs Emersons, a long farewell I hope.

Washington

Tuesday, August 10 We arrived today about one o'clock after a rather tedious passage. stopped at Old Point Comfort to land passengers the breeze was charming, of the place I could not judge from the wharf. None of us were sick, the Chesapeake was in one of its mildest humours. Unfortunately it rained the whole morning coming up the river so that the usually blue waters of the Potomac were dark and muddy—& the beautiful shores concealed almost entirely by the rain & haze. We are staying at the "National Hotel" our room (Mattie's & mine) is very small opening into Aunt Ann's— the latter thought hers too much filled with "show furniture" but we are quite comfortable. Dear me! how different from my last visit—then, Mrs Seaton was our friend whom we looked forward to meeting with pleasure, & who was so pleasant as our cicerone every where—now, I positively dread going to see her, and for sight seeing we must be guided by our own devices. We met Mr Miles here unexpectedly, he lunched with us. walked in the afternoon Ahem! [11]

Wednesday, August 11 This morning we went to the Capitol. the grounds look charmingly green & fresh. several members were seated on the iron sofas under the trees. The new wings are progressing rapidly, but it is said wont be finished in less than ten years. they are now very unsightly and detract from the appearance of the Capitol. On the steps we met Commodore Voorhees & his son,[12] a mere youth who seemed afraid of being seperated an instant from his father's side. After walking about the Rotunda & viewing the pictures we went into the Senate Gallery. Many Senators were absent, the curtains & carpet of the hall were taken down or covered, so that the effect of the whole disappointed me. Few of the Senators looked other than very common men. Mr Soulé & Sumner were absent but I saw Cass & heard him make a few remarks.[13] He is a large, stout, coarse looking man, his face red & very puffed out beneath the eyes, what his remarks were strong & to the point. The senator from California[14] was urging the right of an appropriation being made for the Indians in the justice of which I for one entirely agreed. Judge Butler[15] rather opposed the precedent being established as did some others, but I thought the Californian presented his views best.[16] We left the gallery before the debate was ended. The house of Representatives is distracting, the noise, the roar of sound occasioned by the dome above them so that a whisper is loud, the confusion, the effort of different members & the Speaker to make themselves heard was deafening & dreadful to ears uninitiated. I thought it the most rowdy scene, & left with a headache. The pillars of the two halls are of beautiful marble of different colours quarried on the Potomac. The Senate impresses one most favorably in contrast with the House. the order & gravity appear even greater than in reality, so much have they the advantage of the other House. We visited the Navy Yard & were shown about by one of the officers, name unknown. Capt Powell[17] was not at home—Uncle Tom left his card inviting him to dinner tomorrow— but very curious, said that we were to leave Friday morning so as to avoid any return civility. We do not go until Sunday or Monday in truth. I received two charming letters from home today. I was very much amused at dinner, we had a true son of Erin to wait upon us, Aunt Ann asked for the chicken pie. eh maam? "chicken in pastry" still uncomprehended, "chicken! chicken patties"! off he went & returned with a little paté. "I know what you want but there's none cooked today" without more ado he put down the plate, not entirely discouraged dear Aunt Ann asked him for a slice of ham, he whisked away the plate presently returned it, not a vestige to mark where the chicken had been all clean swept off & a wee piece of ham in solitude possessing the plate. Aunt Ann's look of dismay upon seeing the destitution of her plate & losing half her dinner so entirely without her own consent, was so ludicrous that I almost "screamed" with laughter—to complete the performance Paddy inquired in his broadest brogue, "if she was satisfied & had all she wanted"? Uncle Tom introduced a Mr Pemble to us this afternoon, he had employed him on some business when he was in Washington the other day—he is a lawyer I believe. We walked to the Capitol to hear the music, which is played by the Marine Band twice a week, Mr Pemble accompanied us, he is very affected, rather handsome, & talks well enough. We were just too late to hear more than Yankee Doodle which is the finale of the entertainment. Mr Shields joined us there walked with Mattie he is an improvement on his old Father [8] whom we saw frequently in Norfolk. It has rained off & on the whole day—

Thursday, August 12 Rose very early & wrote a letter on foolscap to Mamma giving an account of everything but found the paper too small for all I had to say. Went to the Capitol & heard Mr Soulé on the fishery question.[19] He is too inflamable in matter, but an energetic interesting speaker, full of animation & lively gesture—his enunciation is slow & deliberate, the French accent very strong. Mr Cass who replied for a few minutes, appeared tame & tiresome then rose dear old Senator Butler, without preparation, without pretension to oratorical effect, his words were straight to the point, far from insisting on War as the only settlement of the question, he strongly deprecated what he termed "conjectural causes," and was clear concise and direct, in all he said opposing Mr Soulé's views. He declared himself then unprepared but that he would take an opportunity soon to present his opinions to the consideration of the Senate. How powerful is the sentiment which connects us with those who possess the same common interests, the same country or spot as home with ourselves! not the less "potent spell" for being often unknown, now certainly I never suspected myself of any *attachment* or especial interest towards Judge Butler, but no sooner did he rise today shake those distracted locks of his at the President of the Senate as a preparatory motion, rub one eye as if to wake up, than I felt roused to unusual attention, once or twice when he stammered, & had great difficulty in untwisting his tongue I turned cold from a sort of apprehension of failure & was delighted when he concluded in the most satisfactory & I thought convincing manner. As we came down from the Gallery we met him at the foot of the steps, "Why Petigru you here" evidently showed his knowledge for the first time of our being in the City. He grasped my arm with no light hand saying "where are my constituents to be found?" "at the National" I answered, "coming to see you" he was trembling still I observed from excitement. Capt Powell dined with Uncle Tom today he is a stiff wooden sort of person looks as though he never smiled but by rule. In Virginia last Summer we met his wife she is a contrast very affable & agreeable. I did not remember him at all tho' he was pleased to say where he had seen me. I assented without showing my forgetfulness of him. I called on Mrs Seaton this morning, & against mon oncle's opinion wrote on the card I left the name of our Hotel. On inquiring of Capt Powell I was sorry to hear that the old lady's health is so bad she had gone a week ago to the Capon Springs "with some member of her family," which "member" is the interesting Gales I suppose. Poor Mrs Seaton! I feel very sorry for her, she is a nice person it is a shame her son is not more satisfactory—if all "they say" be true—

Friday, August 13 Went to the Patent Office for two hours this morning—a dreadfully tiresome place in my opinion—but doubtless very useful! There *were* not many additions to their collection I saw last Fall with Uncle & Aunt Henry. some things from the World's Fair but nothing extraordinary. I saw specimens of the Peruvian mummies today at the Office which I had not looked at before, they are the most hideous objects imaginable & very disgusting. Mattie & myself paid Mrs Thom a visit after leaving the Office, found her at home & very pleased to see us she seems comfortably situated in rooms over a store—nicely furnished cool parlor. Several persons called while we were out. the Aikens [20] among others—Uncle Allston Aunt Adèle & Adèle arrived unexpectedly today—they are staying at Gadsbys leave before we do probably, for West Point—I was very glad to find them all looking well. Uncle Allston much better than I had expected. Drove to Georgetown after dinner very pleasant drive but could not obtain admission at the Convent which we wished to visit. The Cemetery Mr Corcoran presented to the City of Georgetown, is a beautiful spot, carefully laid out and kept. Mr Pember [21] called this evening and remained until after eleven o'clock—I thought he was never going! one ridiculous thing occurred, I was speaking of Mr Henry Washington [22] as an agreeable interesting person with large handsome blue eyes—now Mr Pember possesses just such, I made my remarks very unawares until attracted by a peculiar smile on his countenance & his looking full at me & opening his eyes quite large for a second—Mattie was highly diverted & I was too. She thinks this young gentleman very handsome, I think him very affected & too well aware of his advantages of white teeth blue eyes, dark hair & mustache to be handsome. Mr Shields told us goodbye this evening, he returns to Norfolk tomorrow. Uncle Tom must have given him some hint I think which prevented his paying us much attention while here.

Saturday, August 14 Received a note from Mrs Aiken inviting us to tea with her after going to hear the music in the President's grounds I wrote an answer accepting. Mr Pember called after dinner and accompanied us to the grounds Adèle Mattie & myself. Uncle & Aunt Tom Uncle & Aunt Allston joined us there. We met Mr & Mrs Aiken who were very friendly & Mr & Mrs Thom, by the way he called this morning. I was not favorably impressed by him he looks like a Jew & fidgets continually—The scene at the Presidents was gay and interesting, groups of persons moving in all directions over the luxuriant green plats & through the winding walks, the band of musicians in the center of the principal circle dressed in bright red uniforms & playing their best tunes, children & their nurses, pretty women (very few of these however) & mustached beaux, navy men & civilians, the buzz of voices, & the variety of dress, "gay & grave" all contributed to render it an animated entertaining new scene to us. There were two or three Indians in their own costume & a solitary Turk in a calico shirt to heighten the novelty. I fancied the turbaned individual was no true son of Mahomet, but rather a poor imitation from his appearance—the Indians were genuine, but wore hats instead of two or three feathers, or bare heads as I would have preferred & have seen in pictures. Mr Fillmore his wife & daughter[23] were standing on the Portico bowing & smiling to their friends & ready to be introduced to whoever desired the honor. Mattie & myself spent the evening with the Aikens. we found it entirely pleasant, three or four gentlemen, Miss Tayloe & Mr & Mrs Thom were the company, it was really what we were invited to, a sociable tea. Mr Clingman of N.C.[24] was introduced to me & talked in the most tiresome style paying me such compliments that I felt provoked—he called me Miss Petigru & said he hoped I did not resemble in one particular the family in North Carolina, that of never changing their name &c &c the amount of nonsense he talked was amazing & not worth relating.

Sunday, August 15 Church at the Capitol heard a sermon (Uncle Tom says, "a Chapter of Isaiah acted") by the Methodist chaplin of the House.[25] It was very little like church, & nothing but the Novelty carried us, we sat in the seats of the hall of Representatives—it was full, but rather common looking people Afternoon we staid at home there being no service at Trinity where otherwise we should have gone.

Monday, August 16 This morning we returned the visits paid us, Mrs Powell, Ballard[26] &c &c no body at home which I very much regretted, really wishing to see Mrs Powell. As we passed Colonel Henderson's of the Marines,[27] Uncle Tom remembering he owed a visit there, stopped to pay it, while we remained in the carriage. In a few moments he came out accompanied by an old white haired gentleman whom he introduced as Colonel Henderson who invited us in the house with the utmost cordiality. Uncle Tom saying that our cousin Mary Pettigrew was there, whom we had hoped to meet before in Washington. We required no pressing, a moment & I was introduced to the lady cousin, I have so long desired to know—there was a slight hesitation, some murmuring of cousin, & then a cordial embrace. She resembles neither Mr Charles nor Johnston, perhaps the latter a very little her eyes are blue & very expressive, her mouth pretty, hair dark & glossy, pale white complexion altogether a "right" pretty woman as they say in Virginia. She talks well & there is that in the expression of her mouth, & tone of voice showing a steadfast will of her own. I was, we were all very much pleased with the visit & with our cousin—How queer my own name sounded at first to my ears pronounced by a stranger voice! "Carey" "Mary" "Mattie" was said immediately. She has been near two weeks in Washington, heard that some of the family were staying at Georgetown but knew nothing positive, or where to find us. I wish we had known of her being in the City, the opportunity would not have been lost of becoming better acquainted.

I received a letter from Johnston last night he is on the eve of returning to America—has given up his secretaryship at the Court of Spain. It must be a severe disappointment to him. I dont think he wishes to come home at all at all, & am really sorry for what ever cause has induced him to decide upon returning. After leaving the Hendersons, we went to the Senate but were too late to hear Judge Butler's speech the only thing which carried us. A young Mr Henderson "Dick" I think his papa called him, joined us at the Capitol, he is a nice boy with quite sufficiently a good opinion of his own merits & will be very handsome in a few years. The evening we spent with the Thoms, it was not altogether agreeable. Mary Lucia is rather querulous in her manner to Mr Thom, & he is too much of a fidget—Mr Sargent of the "Republic"[28] talked to me a long time! So slow & self sufficient was he that I progressively opposed every thing he said, until he roused up into a more interesting style & was far more agreeable. Mr Pember was at the

Hotel door waiting for us, he is tiresomely attentive. I feel it is ungrateful to say so, but somehow——

Tuesday, August 17 A misty musty morning when cloudy was the weather, we left Washington (for how long?) nothing discouraged by the lowering aspect of all without doors. Mr Pember the indefatigable was at the Depôt waiting our appearance, & presented Mattie & myself each with a pretty bouquet. the young gentleman disturbed me by one of his performances. the cover of my basket requiring a fastener, I asked him to get me a scrap of cane I saw, that would answer, instead, he seized his luckless pocket handkerchief between his teeth & tore off a strip unheeding my earnest remonstrance. It had all the effect required but I was sorry he should spoil so unnecessarily his handkerchief. We left Washington at nine, reached Baltimore at eleven o'clock. Here ended my experience gathered by last Summer's journeyings. Baltimore being as far North as we had come. From this City to Philadelphia the country is charming from the cultivation, the fertility, the beautiful meadows & pastures with the finest Cattle grazing, & large flocks of sheep—— The activity of Wilmington tho' we passed through only a small portion of the town, was striking in comparison with the more southern cities—the Farms in Delaware bordering in succession the Rail road are most fertile, abundant, & well cultivated in appearance, they reminded me of descriptions I have read of the country in England—the houses were generally in sight of the road some very pretty, others were style of Gothic buildings. In the villages thro' which we passed the people all seemed to have some occupation, & there were no idle dirty negroes to cumber the land, and pain the eyes. We crossed the Susquehannah & had glimpses of the Delaware—— the different grain crops bordering the banks—it looked to me like a silver twist in enameled setting. About ½ past four we arrived in Philadelphia. I was not impressed by the approaches to the City, & the streets as narrow to inconvenience. We came to the Girard House, *the* establishment of the place. Uncle Allston who had arrived at one o'clock, kindly had taken rooms for us or we should have had some difficulty in getting accommodation. "Rest & food" we certainly required, I have seldom been as weary [*and*] hungry.

Philadelphia

Wednesday, August 18 Opened most unwillingly my sleep laden eyes, for the first time in "the City of brotherly love" and Quakerdom—Both which characteristics I dare say belong now, principally "to the olden time" or the "*good* old days" pretty much synonomous terms—"The Girard" is conducted on the handsomest plan & so great the popularity it has at present, that the rooms are entirely filled, we enjoying undesirable altitude perched up in the fifth story—the turns & stairs to go thro' & up & down, before one can descend to the common level of the other inhabitants are exhausting to my limited capabilities for such undertakings. Mattie & myself walked with Uncle Tom some distance up Chesnut St.[29] the people nearly knocked us down, one little miserable of a boy, rushed against me, & before I recovered the shock, he had torn the lace of my defenceless mantilla bearing off the fragments fluttering like a pennon to the breeze on his peach basket— The Allstons left this afternoon for New York. We go in a few days—Saw Lewis Robinson at the table today, he was very friendly—I dont like him. Uncle Tom treated us to an Ice cream this afternoon it well supported the reputation of the place.

Thursday, August 19 Visited the Navy Yard this morning it is not so handsome as either the Norfolk or Washington Yards we saw the War steamer Saranac,[30] and the sectional dry Dock. I did not understand much about the Dock, the Steamship was very dirty, and the sun beaming hot, without the cooling shade trees to protect us. So that we were thankful to leave. Afterwards walked with Mattie up Chesnut St, went to Baileys the great jewellers, it is a beautiful display of the most costly things, there was the handsomest diamond set that I ever saw—went to Solomons for an ice cream, they are made in Philadelphia better than any I have ever tasted— there were a number of ladies taking lunch—some, tea & coffee altogether a breakfast array. In the afternoon drove to Laurel Hill the dust was excessive, so as to destroy the pleasure of the drive—the cemetery is beautifully laid out, the most interesting object, the group of "Old Mortality & Sir Walter Scott"[31]—the expression of the old man's face is admirable, one almost expects to see the lips part & hear him speak. So much have I heard however of this cemetery that I was rather disappointed, the group of statuary alone satisfied my expectations Many of the monuments evince very ostentatious grief I think, & show more the pretension of the living than sorrow for the dead. I was forcibly reminded by some of the monuments of Dr Johnstons remark, tho' I do not remember the words, but to the effect that one doubts the depth of grief that consoles itself by conceits & ostentatious display— We visited the Institution for the Deaf & Dumb[32] being vacation we were disappointed in seeing any of the exercises. Dr Cohen wife & daughter were our companions, the tickets having been obtained by him, he is the best looking Jew I ever chanced to meet. Went to the circus as a finale—there were no horses introduced but just stupid people, talking stupid. I felt the want of quadruped performers, as they are generally the most interesting of the company. Was Oh! so weary before going to bed.

Friday, August 20 Walked up Chesnut St with Aunt Ann & Mattie, bought some gloves &c &c. The streets no longer retain their former reputation of cleanliness—they seem to me not nicer kept, than those of Baltimore or even Washington. Some of the stores are very handsome with rich display of goods at the windows, the little stalls of fruit & candies or coffee & breads for sale about the streets look queer to a stranger. Mrs Sinkler called today. Mr Sinkler & Mr Wharton his brotherinlaw had called yesterday but she was then indisposed.[33] Aunt Harriette gave me a letter to her—she is very pretty, was most friendly talks a great deal, & seems charmed to see you. while talking she glances about in a manner that shows nothing escapes her observation. She wished us to spend tomorrow evening with her but we leave at eight in the morning for New York—With our indefatigable friend Dr Cohen visited the House of Refuge for girls & boys, Girard's College and the Fairmount Water works. To the House of Refuge boys & girls are sent for improper conduct, petty larceny &c parents who do not or cannot manage them at home send them here for punishment, little vagrants are also taken care of. They are strictly kept as tho' in prison, locked into their cells every night which they are required to keep with the utmost neatness—the girls department showed the ruling passion strong, every little cell so narrow as to contain the straightest beds, it is furnished with a strip of carpet & the smallest description of toilet, in which was arranged any picture, or print, or bright piece of calico they might possess—on the beds were patch rock quilts of their own make—We saw the boys of who number a 150 at work, making wicker seat chairs and razor strap & boxes the girls were no where visible. From here we went to Girard's College—the magnificent pillars are of solid marble the pillars within the building & the stairs of the same material. a statue of Stephen Girard is in the vestibule as you enter just in front of his tomb of bluish marble perfectly plain. the poor old man left a strange clause in his will prohibiting the admission of any clergyman within the building & forbidding religious instruction. One of the Directors or the President however reads prayers every morning & on Sunday a chapter of the Bible which he explains but this is all. I went out on the roof of the College, this is also of solid marble in large squares, lapping each other with barrels of marble or bars if I may say so, fastening them down—the view of the City is fine & commands a portion of the adjacent country—we went to the dining room where were two women one with a machine very like a straw cutter cutting huge slices of bread while the other spread on the butter, they use seven barrels of bread alone a day—the pupils number 312. if fatherless, they are admitted as orphans, none are received under six, or over ten, at least they are supposed between or about those ages— the grounds are extensive and nicely kept—the professors houses we did not visit but in the building containing the sleeping & dining rooms the staircases & pillars were all of marble tho' not so handsome as the principal College. From here we went to the Fairmount waterworks which supply the City with water and which are deservedly celebrated The wire suspension bridge here crosses the Schuylkill, it is a wonderful work thrown without support except the wire fastened securely at either end, with immense ropes formed of a multitude of small wires extending from the heavy stone pillars to the ground—to understand it one must either see the bridge or a good picture of it. The Fairmount works repaid us amply for the fatigue & trouble of going through the dreadful dust & after walking over Girard's College beforehand—the hill on the top of which eight large resvoirs are built is very high, on one side it has been cut down and terraced, on the side next the river it is a rugged steep rock covered in many places by luxuriant vines, beautiful trees grow at the foot & a grassy plat stretches to the river—in the midst of this there is a large fountain surrounded by four willow trees, the green of the long drooping branches mingling with & seen thro' the spray of the fountain is charming to the eye. there is a bust, in a small temple, (it might be called) of white marble of the man who built the works, his name I could not learn[34]—100 steps lead to the top of the hill, but we did not go up. the wheels which force the water up are immense & the whole machinery worked by steam. there is a very pretty jet from the side of the rock overhanging the basin, a nymph with a swan in her hand & water spouting from the rock on which she stands—the entire arrangement excites ones admiration and wonder by the beautiful union of nature and art.

New York

Saturday, August 21 Really in New York! I scarcely believe it, and yet I am impatient to go on—et Voila! at eight this morning we left Philadelphia in the cars, or to be *very* accurate in the boat to the cars across the river— From Amboy we again took the Boat for New York intending to proceed straight up the river to West Point—the Boat left the City at 4 o'clock due at the Point at eight. Uncle Tom disliked traveling after night especially as we must cross the river to reach the Point, so here we are stationary until Monday, no Cars or Boat running tomorrow. We came to the Girard House! (a very different one from that we left this morning!) because it is most

convenient the North River line, & here unluckily we are to stay—I do not
think the people are in the habit of entertaining above rather common passengers, but they are obliging & "solicitous to please ever"—We walked to
Broadway which is near the Hotel the rush & throng have given me a headache it was confusing, but really not as much so as I have heard & imagined
of Broadway would doubtless be realized. this afternoon I can only say it
was disagreeable, and did not impress me as either handsome or astonishing
in any manner—the omnibus' to be sure literally lined both sides of the
streets going & coming down. near this boarding house is the North River
dêpot the constant activity and noise, the numbers of people passing to &
fro afford an evenings occupation to observe. We saw numerous Emigrants
near the wharf where we landed, Germans I suppose, there were standing
before a boarding house with a sign inscribed in the crookedest letters, all
the capitals like flying dragons, which they seemed carefully reading. Poor
creatures they had a truly forlorn look, I felt very sorry for them. Dear
Uncle Tom! he is kindness itself—yesterday he gave Mattie and myself each
a very handsome tortoise shell comb which he had had made in Philadelphia
from shell he brought from the Feejee Island, it is a beautiful & valuable
present—this afternoon he carried us to Stewarts the candy manufactory,
merely because we expressed a wish carelessly to go—we have a supply of
candy that will last sometime—

Sunday, August 22 Passed the day in the house, to unpack & dress would
have been too troublesome, we are far from the churches, and nobody do
we see in the hotel, merely taking our meals at a private table, & staying
in our rooms which is the most agreeable for many reasons. I was amused
by the proprietor telling Uncle Tom that his house was kept according to
the European plan—there are no regular hours, but one orders what they
wish from the bill of fare after waiting sometime it is brought—things are
not nice though—Mattie & myself passed a miserable night the musquitoes
were dreadfully attackive & severe—the bed of tolerable size for one person
the room *very* small. I am thankful we leave at six in the morning for West
Point. I have been entertained observing the hundreds of people passing
about today—a sort of omnibus car runs to some station from before the
door of the hotel it has constantly been crammed, & crowds waiting the
return every time. There is not much appearance of Sunday, except that
every one seems in their holyday suit. Wrote to Mary Pettigrew & also to
Minnie today—My first impressions of N.Y. are a long day & great ennuie.

West Point

Monday, August 23 We left New York this morning at six o'clock, arrived at West Point between ten & eleven. The scenery on the Hudson realized my expectations, it is not often one can say as much. the rugged hills, sometimes rising abruptly from the water's edge, then again sloping up from a stretch of plain upon almost all of which were small villages, or pretty country seats dotting either bank of the river, the smooth waters of which flow in continous windings among their highland bordering & form a perpetual and beautiful contrast. As we approached West Point the mountains appeared more steep & inaccessible, the sides were huge masses of rock with their rugged fronts towering high above us—I feel that I do not express by any means a full description, but there are places on the river and just about the Point itself of which words do not convey an adequate impression & to be properly felt must be seen. Mountain scenery, especially such as I saw here, the combination of plain, hill & water, strongly affects me, but when I wish to express it, I feel oppressed as it were, and an utter impossibility to put in language the impressions my mind I may almost my heart receives. Our accommodations are worse than limited, they are literally none at all. At first Aunt Ann & Uncle Tom were given a room comfortable enough not far from the one assigned Mattie & myself. We were dressing when Aunt Ann with a most perturbed countenance walked in several things in her hand, saying they had been turned out of their room which had been before hand engaged by persons then waiting for it, that she had had scarcely time to change her dress when they were routed out & she would be obliged to occupy the room with us, & Uncle Tom a cot in some corner some where else. This apartment of ours scarcely accommodated ourselves & luggage. at night the trunks were piled one upon the other until there was room for a small mattress which was Aunt Anns bed, as she would not hear of Mattie or myself taking it instead. It was difficult to dress or look nicely after arranging in such small quarters but we managed—Uncle Allston, Aunt Adèle & Adèle we saw just before dinner which important meal takes place at one o'clock, military hours they say. No one dressed much for dinner, principally wore morning dresses for so early an hour. Ben[35] came in after dinner, he has changed but little except that he resembles more and more his father not only in appearance but manner. He was delighted to see us, it was three years last June since I had seen him, he looks well, & has a very military air, it was a sincere pleasure to meet the dear fellow again. We did not go to the afternoon drill, as we were fatigued from travelling & discomfort, & besides intended going to the Cadets hop, we rested until 6 then dressed & went to tea & afterwards with Uncle A. Aunt Adèle, Ben

& Adèle to the "hop" which was given in the Academic building. Uncle Tom did not care to go & Aunt Ann preferred staying & looking after her preparations for the night—my horror Mr Riell presented himself today as soon as we arrived, he gave his card to Uncle Tom saying he knew us, poor unfortunate man I perfectly dread him, he is so crazy & disagreeable. Ben danced the first quadrille with me, Mattie with a young Livingston a Cadet & a nice little fellow[36]—there were but two quadrilles, the other dances Polkas schottisch & Redowas. I would not know my partners again for to me they all looked alike. We had a very pleasant evening. Ben was as attentive as possible introducing several persons. Uncle Allston introduced Mr Donaldson, a goodlooking young officer who graduated three or four years ago & has since been stationed in Oregon, he talks pleasantly & is altogether a nice person.[37] Poor Riell! came up to me & asked permission to introduce an officer whom I saw at a little distance regarding the proceedings, first inquiring his name & hearing it was Bryan, I consented knowing him to be a near relation of the N.C. Pettigrews—Mr Riell paused inquired if I "was *participating* in the dancing" of which I should have thought he had sufficient demonstration. then went to Mattie, requested permission for the introduction & then went off, nothing more did we see or hear of him until some time afterwards he brought up Mr Bryan[38] & introduced him—this distracted proceeding we could not understand & Mr Bryan told me he had requested him after keeping him waiting a long time to promenade then suddenly brought him right up to us. Mr Bryan of whom I had heard in Virginia as engaged to Mary Pettigrew—the Masons had spoken of him as such a captivating person that I thought of course he must be very handsome & charming—he is just a frank, manly, neither handsome nor ugly man, & quite pleasant—We had a subject of interest in our mutual relatives, there is one thing I am struck by, no one I have ever spoken to about the family seem to know much of James, invariably they say less of him than any other member of the family. I dont think Mr Bryan was ever engaged to his *cousin*, I will talk to him of her when we are better "acquaint"—

Tuesday, August 24 We determined to remain today in hope of getting rooms and so being able to stay a week—but all in vain, & the inconvenience and discomfort is such that we must leave tomorrow. We are all very sorry, everything else promises to be so pleasant, the Streets from Hartford whom we known on a visit they made Charleston once & called upon there are now at the Point and very agreeable & sociable. Mr General Scott[39] was introduced to us last evening by Aunt Adèle, Mr Bryan & Donaldson are two nice beaux & there are other persons whom we would find pleasant to know Nothing but that essential accommodation is requisite to our enjoyment—

We walked about the grounds with the Allstons after attending artillery parade. When we came in Mr Bryan joined us, we sat in the side piazza commanding the most beautiful view of the Hudson, the town of Newburg in the bend of the river opposite, Crow's Nest with the bare rocks looking so rugged & scarped towering above on the one side two or three hundred feet—on a peak near are the ruins of Fort Putman, below between the two mountains I believe, Washingtons Valley, & on the opposite side is Constitution Island & "shaggy hill" beyond—the river appears narrower here & was always smooth as glass while numerous fishing boats & small craft were slowly sailing over the bright surface of its waters—occasionally a steamboat would come puffing round the sharp point of the Island (thought the most dangerous portion of the Navigation) but these I dislike to see, with their ugly boilers & black smoke they were not in harmony with the beauties of the scene. After dinner Mr Bryan accompanied us to drill, it began to rain so we went to the drawing room, & Painting gallery, there were some very good pictures, all are the work of different graduates, which annually are selected & kept here. We saw the model of a Mexican silver mine sent home by some of the officers after the War, also the model of a beseiged City. Mr Bryan was altogether at home here & gave us an explanation of every thing. I shall always for the future in reading understand about bastions & scarps & counter scarps. we visited afterwards the Library where all the examinations are held—the flags & standards captured in Mexico are preserved here—Rosciusko's Monument is handsome & stands on an elevated position and can be seen from the river. there are two or three other monuments on the grounds erected to officers from that institution who have distinguished themselves—In the afternoon there was a small hop in the house—the Cadets remained until ½ past nine, then tattoo, & away they go to camp. Only Polkas &c &c were danced, some of them perform very well. I told Mr Bryan tonight while we were speaking of Mary, "that I had wished to see him before I had—a bow—because I wished to know that person who it was said was to be my cousin" he laughed & said that was a report of ten years standing & untrue. The Streets & ourselves had a good deal to say to each other, they seem really to regret our leaving tomorrow—indeed the acquaintances we have made are very kind in expressing their wishes that we could remain. Ben hoped to see us in the morning so we did say goodbye. Joe is expected here tomorrow—we have received no letters from home, of course they will arrive upon our departure—As Mattie & myself were going to bed Mr Donaldson whom we had not seen during the day, & Mr Bryan whom we had seen meet us in the entry, we stopped & talked for almost ten minutes—packed almost entirely before eleven o'clock so as to have time in the morning—Mr Riell was in the room this evening, but not intrusive. he remembers Virginia I dare say—and certainly in none of the party has he found the slightest encouragement to be attentive—I am so sorry we are obliged to go tomorrow but another night would make dear Aunt Ann ill—

Saratoga

Wednesday, August 25 We left West Point this morning in the steamer Francis Skiddy the same in which we had come from New York, & the largest & best boat I have ever seen. We did not see Ben as he had to go to work after morning parade. Aunt & Uncle A being on the grounds we also missed. Our two friends Donaldson & Bryan were there to say goodbye. Mr B. stood beside me as I was putting on bonnet gloves, veil, &c &c holding my shawl & basket, "thank heaven! he exclaimed that I was not born a lady, it would never have answered, what do you do with all these things" At the carriage door Uncle Tom asked me two or three times if I had left nothing. I would take it literally & reply "nothing" "have you left nothing" said Mr Donaldson with the most smiling countenance. "I am sorry you have not left your heart"—Our day on the river was pretty much as the former had been, except the scenery is not as fine. we stopped at several small towns coming up, until about three oclock we arrived at Albany in a drizzling rain. Finding that the cars did not leave until ½ past 6, we went to the Delavan House and dined as we had not done so on the Boat. Dinner very good—we saw nothing of the town the rain keeping us in doors. At last we were off, & travelled with the Western train to Schenectady, where we changed engines and came on to Saratoga arriving between eight and nine. At Schenectady Uncle Tom bought some of the largest plums I have ever seen anywhere, they were the size of moderately small apples, & nice to the taste. The town appears a flourishing one from the short glimpse we had of some the streets—We are staying at the United States the best Hotel of Saratoga— the crowd is great—the Wards & Sparkmans still here.[40] The waiters are all black, except the chamber maids who are white—the airs of the blacks are truly disagreeable, the first sight I saw on arriving was, a "Nig" on a sofa lounging at his ease in the entry and gentlemen moving about without noticing him—to me how very strange it appeared!

Thursday, August 26 Saw the Wards & Sparkmans after breakfast, they were very cordial. Poor Mr Ward is a wreck of his former self, I felt sincerely sorry to see him so sadly changed, he speaks with difficulty & his mind seems to me very much injured. When I last saw him he was in robust health, and good spirits, now a hopeless paryletic! Dr Sparkman thinks him not improved, he is restless and looks sad & uninterested in what goes on around him—Poor gentleman his life of toil the years spent in amassing his large fortune has come to this melancholy end. Not one of his children who will take his place in the country, is in any manner equal to him. "t'is a sad sentence of an ancient date" may be applied in a different sense from what the poet meant, to him. I talked sometime with Mrs Ward & found her a pleasant person. Aunt Jane Chisolm arrived today with Emily Thurston & the Bees with whom they are travelling.[41] I was delighted to see them— they are just from Sharon where they have all improved & enjoyed themselves. This afternoon walked to the Indian camp, a short distance from the Hotel on the edge of the woods—the tents were poor concerns of cloth & a few of leather, the women most of them frightful ugly were employed in making baskets or bead work I felt great interest in seeing the poor creatures, & pictured to myself their past condition when Lords of the soil they roamed the forest free contrasted with their present degraded situation an almost extinct people. There were two rather goodlooking young girls, to one of whom a young man was making pretty speeches, & she seemed too rather to understand the rôle of coquette. They are a remnant of the Oneida tribe, & very inferior. I saw a little papoose strapped to its board & crying strongly. This evening walking in the piazza I was very glad to see Mary McDuffie.[42] She had arrived but an hour or two before with her Aunt Mrs John Singleton.[43] We passed the rest of the evening pretty much together very pleasantly—we had not met for near two years & of course had a great deal to talk about. Mrs James Chesnut[44] is here, she is friendly & agreeable, mais je ne l'aime pas!

Friday, August 27 Mattie & myself rose early, walked to the Spring before breakfast drank three tumblers walked round the hill & returned I saw promenading in the piazza Mrs Rush of Philadelphia,[45] she is a large coarse woman rouged beyond all semblance to nature, & wears her dress so very décoltée as to be disgusting—she wears black just for fancy, with colored ribbons, says the ladies here dress too much & she brought but two dresses to give them a lesson in good taste. Her bust under the thin black covering looks very like an india rubber pillow when half filled with air—no one seems to admire her but the men, who declare she walks them to death, but as she is clever of immense wealth they consent to be martyrised, her balls & suppers make the amends—Mrs Joseph Allston is very polite & cordial— the old Joe is an awful object.[46] Mary McDuffie & myself had a funny talk after dinner walking in the piazza while the band played as usual. We have made none or a few acquaintances.

Saturday, August 28 The Singleton party left today at twelve o'clock. Hal Fraser seems to be traveling with them, poor young man! he is throwing away his pains I think—Mary is a quiet flirt in her way. Bought some trifles for Minnie & Lou, straw earrings &c &c. I find Saratoga very tiresome—"the season" was over before we came, not only have most of the pleasantest people gone but those that remain have formed their acquaintances, or about leaving do not care to make others. Mrs Chesnut was very right when she said we had come at a bad time, either for entertainment or acquaintances. Went to the ballroom this evening for a little while saw some pretty polking &c &c

Sunday, August 29 It rained all day until near night. I put on my india rubbers as soon as it was practicable to go out & went to Putnam Spring with Emily Thurston. Received a letter from ma chère mère today and one from Aunt Lou. Wrote to Aunt Harriette. I do not feel well—

Monday, August 30 Feeling very badly I spent the morning entirely in my room. Of all the places we have visited this famous Saratoga pleases me least—to be sure we are after the season, tho' when we arrived there was still a great number of persons the most agreeable we were told had generally gone, & I can readily believe so. Mrs Joseph Allston is the only one of the habitués of the Springs that we knew, she is a nice person—otherwise, and judging from appearances we have no reason to be particularly pleased—the women are with scarcely an exception ugly, the men not handsome, saunter about, their hands in their pockets staring around them, with the most vainglorious air imaginable. the description of one would answer for all, their good looks consisting of a fondly cared for mustache which in many instances seems reluctant to make its appearance and only acknowledging the much coaxing by a slight & visible return—black eyes, and hair, of pomatum smoothness. I chanced to hear one giving a lady his reasons for not marrying which really must have been discouraging to the belles. The waiters amuse me at the table, the chief of the corporation is a negro of a true ebon hue as tho' a descendant of the well known "Rose" of "coal black" description & poetic memory—*Mr* Maurice as the domestics style him is the most important person here by far, his men wait by military rule, and march in & out at a clap of his hands in excellent order. they are all afraid of him, a threat of complaining to Maurice it is said makes them behave instantly. The man of authority dresses three times a day very handsomely & fashionably. I saw him yesterday with a card & large gold pencil taking notes of the vacant seats. near a hundred persons have left in the course of the day. No white waiter is permitted here, the blacks are supreme, we

Tuesday 31st The last day of the month & the last day of our stay here. I regret going but for one reason, the waters are benefiting me & I would like to give them a longer trial, for no other could I desire to remain a moment longer — the place is dull and tiresome, Mrs Chesnut seems to find it "dreadful" they go on Friday to Philadelphia. She is certainly clever, & sometimes very amusing, but she impresses me as a person who having gained a reputation rather beyond her merit makes a constant effort not to fall short. I like her better however than I did last winter — yesterday we were walking for sometime together talking very pleasantly. After an (à la speaking of some one else having lead to it) she said — "I always prefer shining in conversation to attracting attention by dress, or paying much attention to anything of that sort." It was not said at all in a manner that was either vain or unpleasant, but it finished off completely the opinion I had formed of her. Mr Chesnut is a cleverer person, & less pretension.

The Jane Caroline North journals: "She is certainly clever, & sometimes very amusing" (Courtesy of the Southern Historical Collection, Wilson Library of the University of North Carolina at Chapel Hill) have found them very civil, but it is easy to see the least provocation would make them otherwise. The Sparkmans left for Niagara this morning—paid the Wards a visit this afternoon, they are comfortably situated in a cottage.

Tuesday, August 31 The last day of the month & the last day of our stay here. I regret going but for one reason, the waters are benefiting me. I would like to give them a longer trial, for no other could I desire to remain a moment longer—the place is dull and tiresome, Mrs Chesnut seems to find it "dreadful!" they go on Friday to Philadelphia. She is certainly clever, & sometimes very amusing, but she impresses me as a person who having gained a reputation rather beyond her merit, makes a constant effort not to fall short. I like her better however than I did last winter—yesterday we were walking for sometime together talking very pleasantly, after a while (speaking of some one else having lead to it) she said, "I always prefered shining in conversation to attracting by dress, or paying much attention to any thing of that sort." It was not said at all in a manner that was either vain or unpleasant—but it finished off completely the opinion I had formed of her. Mr Chesnut is a cleverer person, & less pretension.

Niagara! September

Wednesday, September 1 To our surprise yesterday just before dinner Uncle Tom told us that if we could be ready by six he would prefer leaving Saratoga, & spending the night in Schenectady when we might take the eight o'clock train this morning & reach the Falls by ½ past eight at night—I have never packed so briskly in my life & wonderful to say left nothing—by the hour appointed we were all ready, said goodbye & departed. Aunt Jane regretted our leaving & the Chesnuts also seemed very sorry. I was nothing loth to turn my back on Saratoga for to me it has been very tiresome. Aunt Ann too has scarcely been well since we came which was another reason for going, but how I regretted the waters! they were decidedly beneficial to me & could I have come earlier, & remained longer I am convinced would have entirely restored me—it could not be, and there's an end on it—I am very glad to have had this rest by which some day I may benefit. We spent last night at Givens' Hotel Schenectady—a tolerable house, better than its reputation. Mr Howard the clergyman from Georgetown was at the same place he has become too stout I think to suit his calling. I dont like to see a minister fat, there is too much of earth in the appearance—At eight we left in the express train and scoured thro' the country at a rapid rate. We changed cars at Utica taking from there the Rochester express. Of the town we saw nothing the train passing on the outskirt as it were. At Syracuse the famous place for asserting women's rights the cars stopped ½ an hour for the passengers to dine, we preferred not getting out, & Uncle Tom brought us something. Passing thro' Auburn we saw the state prison, a large building of stone surrounded by a high wall, few would ever make their escape from such a "lock up place" At Rochester we changed cars again. This seems a large flourishing town. Occasionally we had glimpses of the small lakes Skaneateles and Cayuga, the waters were so blue, the trees edging the bank so green, & the meadow land sloping to the water covered with luxuriant grass, were beautiful & refreshing to weary travellers. At Albion we paused, then on we rushed thro' numerous villages putting out, & taking in passengers until at length near ten o'clock arrived in the Village of Niagara— having since eight in the morning traversed nearly, the entire state of New York from East to West, from Schenectady to Niagara being 326 miles— the distance, & the numerous towns, and Villages at which we stop along the route render it very fatiguing. We are at the International Hotel—there is more style about the arrangements than I had expected—the Sparkmans seem very glad to meet us again. But to think I am really at Niagara!! I can scarcely believe it true tho' the hoarse sound of the cataract is distinctly heard. I shall sleep sound tonight with that rushing of the mighty waters filling my ears like a great lullaby.

Thursday, September 2 After breakfast we drove to the Canada shore, preferred walking to driving over the suspension bridge, the better to enjoy the view of the Falls which are some distance above. The Bridge is an immense work the wires which support it are twisted together to the size of cable rope, it is capable of supporting more than 3000 weight, but yet trembles at every step one takes causing a sensasion of giddiness by no means agreeable—the water of the river just above the bridge flows in a slow steady current, below it breaks in a thousand waves of whitest foam over the sunken rocks—the color of the water before reaching these is the clearest richest green, as I looked, I thought it the color of a stream of melted Emeralds would be. Nothing can be more beautiful! The first view of the Falls disappointed me, I had imagined them of greater height & terrific grandeur—the civilization around both shores purveys the latter impression, at first, the position from which we saw them being on a level the height is not realized. The longer I looked the stronger became the effect. On the American side the water falls in one mass of foam & spray over the precipice a smaller fall is seperated from the large one by a jutting point of land & rock part I think of Goat Island—it was from this spot that terrible accident happened 3 years ago, when a Mr Addington in trying to save a child who had fallen over the precipice lost his own life both perished in the abyss beneath. Next Goat Island the British Falls, are broken into spouts of water & foam by huge rocks that seemed piled up from the depths below, then, for a little space over the height in a clear stream of green pours the bright water streaked with foam, again as it approaches the shore down it plunges & leaps like a mad thing of life the great sheet of foam while the white mist rises, & circles & eddies constantly beaten back by the rushing waters into the depths below from which it seems struggling to escape. In this I give but a faint description of the mighty cataract. Nothing has ever impressed me so much, nothing can ever impress me more with a sense of the Deity—with the power of the Creator "who holds the waters in the hollow of his hand". We stopped at the Clifton House and were so much pleased with the appearance of every thing & the situation commanding the best view of the Falls, that Uncle Tom engaged rooms immediately. We returned to the American side walked to & over Goat Island which might be rendered a beautiful spot, returned to the "International," dined & in the afternoon moved over to the Canada shore. We crossed the river in a row boat just below the American Falls, the descent from the top of the cliffs would have been too steep to be practicable, some enterprising person cut a way slanting to the waters edge, we were seated in a curious little car like a succession of steps rising one above another,—& by means of pulleys safely descended to the boat. I was delighted with this mode of crossing—then one realizes the height of the Fall & the stupendous force with which the water rushes over the precipice—the mist drifts so thickly down the river that it is like a fine rain, and until ½ across umbrellas are necessary. We drank some of the water which is very good & said to be 250 feet deep— the color the rich emerald green which is so beautiful! As I was writing to Mamma Uncle Tom called us to see Niagara under a different aspect—the Moon was obscured in great measure by heavy clouds that spread like a dark curtain over half the heaven, it had been raining, & occasionally flashes of lightening illuminated all around. Of the Falls the appearance was that of a great white wall, while distant thunder mingled with the full, deep, rushing sound of the swift waters. On the British side the beautiful green Fall could not be seen, but slowly rose as tho' from its profoundest depths a huge body of mist, that seemed to me like a giant spectre wreathing in fantastic shapes its vapoury form along the front of the waters, or hanging over the cataract seeming beckoning in triumph to the struggling mass below. I shuddered as I looked, so mysterious, so awful was the appearance. The Indians called these Falls, "the Might of the Spirit of the Waters" and the name conveys the impression made on the mind the more one sees them. I remember once among the Mountains standing on Ceasar's Head in a dense mist that like a great white sheet seemed let down from heaven covering the whole world except the spot on which we stood—the feeling I then experienced was as tho' suddenly seperated forever from the rest of creation, but there was not the thrill, the feeling of the supernatural, with which I watched the great Phantom of the Waters rise from its bed, and slowly ascend until it mingled with the clouds above, while yet resting on the white masses of those below!

Friday, September 3 We drove after breakfast to a house built a very short distance from the Falls, from the top the view is fine the great basin is immediately below you the river can be seen some distance above increasing in swiftness as it approaches the brink & then with tremendous velocity sweep in one eternal rush over the height. The mist rises & falls continually, but forms dense body at the foot of the cataract which it forever conceals within its impenetrable veil of white. We bought a few specimens of Indian work then went to the Museum as it is termed the most interesting thing I saw were two live Buffalo, a bull & cow—the bull was a monstrous creature, huge shoulders & head, which last looks like an immense bullet, the fore part of the body is larger & taller than the hind part which gives it a misshapen ugly appearance. He was very fierce & butt furiously several times against the fence—the last plunge was so severe we left him to his hay & retreated. The cow was a mild ugly creature who composedly turned her back & took no notice of us. After seeing the Falls by Camera Obscura we returned to Clifton House, lunched & left at near two in the horse car for Queenston— this is a curious but pleasant mode of traveling—there is a regular railroad, one car divided into compartments and drawn by horses driven tandem— the distance was 4 miles—at Queenston we took an omnibus, crossed the Niagara by a grand Suspension Bridge said to be the longest in the World & reached Lewiston a small town on the American side in time for the Steamer "Bay State"—On the heights of Queenston is a tower monument erected to General Brock who fell in their defense[47]—there, our gallant General Pike also perished[48]—but he I believe has no monument. While I write we are on the broad bosom of Lake Ontario—It is so smooth that there is scarcely any motion—the Sun has just set crimson in the water.

Saturday, September 4 When we woke this morning we had already entered the St Lawrence the "River of a thousand Isles," and it well deserves the latter name—in every direction there were small green Islands seem only just resting on the water which flowed in numerous curves & winding among them. Some were cultivated to the river's edge others thickly wooded were of smaller size. the trees of beautiful foliage grew close to the water sweeping their branches over the bank as tho' to have them in the clear stream below. At Ogdensburg we changed Steamers, & took the "Jenny Lind" for Montreal—it is an American boat but smaller than the "Bay State," & built to go down the rapids. These were not so dreadful to encounter as I had expected—They are caused by a fall in the bed of the river of 50 feet, no boat can ascend them so that a canal has been cut up which we saw two or three boats slowly returning—they are twice the time returning from that they are coming to Montreal. We took on board an Indian Pilot just before reaching the last rapid, said to be the worst of the five in the navigation— The boat did pitch & scrap severely. Aunt Ann was convinced we were on a rock every time we soughed down in the rapid. In stormy weather the route must be a dangerous one. At five o'clock we came in sight of Montreal—the spires of the churches were glittering in the sunlight, and a confused mass of buildings stretched along the shore. There was no noise, no discordant cries of furious hackmen pulling one to pieces—the Omnibus & curious looking cabs were arranged at a certain distance while three or four police men kept the drivers in order. We came to the "St Lawrence Hall" & are tolerably comfortable. Uncle Tom received a telegraph despatched from Charles Pettigrew saying himself & sister were at Niagara & would be here Tuesday evening—We shall be very glad to see them, I thought it improbable their doing so, & acquit Mr Charles of only making pretty speeches.

Montreal

Sunday, September 5 It was only when I saw from the window this morning the British arms on a building opposite, that I felt really in a *foreign country* and I have seen quite enough today to convince me had there been any lingering doubts—We went to the Cathedral at ½ past nine this morning. It is a very handsome building of stone, capable we were told of containing 20,000 persons. This was the first time I had seen the full service of the Roman church, & wonder how one born & educated a Protestant could ever change. The ceremonies & numerous genuflexions were displeasing to every feeling but one's curiosity—We heard a sermon in French & contributed to the "aumônes". At one o'clock after luncheon (very necessary in this establishment!) we attended service at the Military church, heard an excellent sermon & saw for the first time the redoubtable red coats—they are a fine looking set of men & paid strict attention to the services. How curious to our ears to hear our queen Victoria & all the Royal family prayed for! The Sparkmans joined us after church & walked to the "St Lawrence" with us, paid a pleasant visit. One thing in the English service was very different from ours, the Psalms were sung instead of being said alternately by the clergyman & congregation. I do not like it so well, one would not be as apt to follow while others sang—I forgot to mention that we met Mrs Monk at the Cathedral this morning. She looks remarkably well, was friendly nothing more in manner. She has joined the Gadsdens[49] finding the move to join Uncle and Aunt Tom not encouraged. I saw the order of "Grey Nuns" & of "Black Nuns" filing out of the Cathedral & a troop of children dressed in the most peculiar caps with them these were orphans whom they educate. There are several large pictures around the walls, & our saviour hanging on the cross. One of these was of silver with tall wax candles burning beside it. What can be the influence that induces people to abandon a simpler faith!

Monday, September 6 Walked about and went to some of the principal stores—the worsted goods are much cheaper than with us. We spent the morning shopping and seeing pretty things Aunt Ann bought two worsted dresses. I bought Minnie & Lou each a pretty cashmere shawl.

Tuesday, September 7 Mr Charles Pettigrew & his sister Mary arrived today about five o'clock. He looks just as I saw him in Charleston near 3 years ago. I am sure Mary & myself will be good friends. This morning we drove round the Mountain. it was too hazy to see much of the surrounding country but the residences along the road are pretty & the drive a pleasant one. Mr Rogers of the British army introduced himself to Uncle Tom this evening who presented him afterwards to us.[50] He seems a curious person not particularly pleasing.

Wednesday, September 8 The morning was very warm. we walked about a good deal to our discomfort. Dined at one o'clock, packed, & ready to leave for Quebec at seven. The Steamer "John Innes" is the Boat—very small all accomodations nearly destroyed by fleas!

Quebec

Thursday, September 9 What a curious foreign looking City this is—the lower town built down upon the river edge—the upper surrounded by a high wall & containing the Citadel built upon a very high hill. The Citadel deserves the name of the "Gibraltar of America"—situated on almost a mountain its stone walls mounted with cannon commanding all approaches by the river it indeed appears impregnable. the streets of the city are narrow & mostly planked, many of the side walks being also of wood instead of brick of flagged and I like them better. We stopped first at "Russel Brothers" but not getting accomodation went to Swords—here they were so full that Mary, Mattie & myself had to occupy one room, a parlor metamorphosed for the occasion. As soon as we made ourselves seeable we sallied out to look about the Town. Went first to the Parliament House a gentleman Mr Charles made some inquiry of at the door proved to be the President of the Council Mons Carron—He called a very respectable looking person to show us the rooms, and we were carried every where. The House of Lords as they call the upper house is very handsomely furnished tho' not yet finished—the Chair of the Governor General is of carved rose wood the seat & back of scarlet cloth, surmounted the carved work is the crown and the arms of England embroidered in gold thread & colored silk on the scarlet ground— a canopy is over head reaching nearly to the ceiling the crown on the top & the Lions couchant on either side. Circular steps covered with scarlet lead to the Chair of State—On a curious stand very like a long cradle the large mace representing the scepter is kept, when the house is in session this is laid on crimson velvet cushions on the handsome table before the Governors seat. A velvet carpet covers the floor, the seats of the members large comfortable arm chairs of crimson morocco. At the end of the room is a brass railing dividing off a small part here the members of the lower house, or the Commons, stand with their speaker at their head when the Governor prorogues Parliament, or on any other important occasion. Two pictures the size of life hang at the upper part of the room, one the Queen, the other George the Fourth. Extending round the room is a place for spectators, and above a gallery for the same purpose. The order of every thing was conspicuous & there were no frightful spitoons to be seen as among us. From the Parliament House we visited the Horticultural exhibition, the flowers were miserable with the exception of the Dahlias they were very fine. There was nothing of much interest, the sun was very hot, & we determined to return to the Parliament House & stay in the Library until ½ past 3 when the house would be in session. Uncle Tom & Aunt Ann returned to the Hotel, but we had a nice time seated in the different alcoves of the Library I read the greater part of De Lavigne's play "Don Juan d'Autriche".[51] Mary amused herself with Carlyle & Mattie had something equally interesting. A few members were scattered about, & I saw an usher in full black suit, knee britches, pumps & buckles, hair in a ribbon & silver sword occasionally circulating through the room. The Library is a handsome one, but has many empty shelves—At ½ half past 3 we went to the Lower House, the Upper not meeting for want of a quorum, much to my disappointment. We heard Mr Papineau[52] & two or three others—there was an animated debate in which a Col Christy[53] held a conspicuous part, once when called to order (as was frequently necessary) by the Speaker he retort that "the Speaker himself was out of order"—he seemed a fiery old fellow. All the speakers hesitated, some of them stammered considerably, there was not one fluent man among those we heard. Dined at six. Mr Webb[54] to whom we brought a letter from Mr Rogers has called twice today.

Friday, September 10 Mr Webb who yesterday was so unsuccessful in finding us at home called this morning & offered his services to show us every thing in his way—of the Convents he knew nothing, but the Citadel & Falls &c he would be our guide—The wind was blowing a gale as we walked to the Citadel & winding up the road the high walls were no protection. When we stood beside the parapet it was furious & our silk dresses flounshed in the air against our utmost exertions to keep them in proper order—crossing the yard we were driven before the gale in the most ridiculous manner mantles & shawls careering wildly around after the example of our fly away skirts. "rather blowy here" said Commissary General Webb. I thought it a mild description for the tornado. The impression the Citadel made upon me only seeing it from the river was increased as I walked about it, saw the strong defences in all directions, the walls being in many places built into the hill side, while above would rise another of the same strength. The views from different points were beautiful & somehow reminded me of pictures of Italian cities. I thought Quebec from one or two points must resemble Naples—I was charmed with them, plain river, hills & mountains forming the background spread out below & before me & as far as the sight could reach a succession of villages on either bank of the St Lawrence. It is beautiful!—A very nice Capt Fane[55] was introduced to us, he carried us into his quarters, pictures were hung round the walls of his sitting room a nice piano on one side, & small organ or Seraphina at the other, books, music, &c, on the table & every thing in orderly confusion. A half finished sketch of Quebec was lying on the window. The Capt himself is the handsomest specimen of an Englishman I have seen, & very pleasant. walking with me I chanced to say some thing about Canadian ponies, he immediately offered to show me some horses & off we went. All in the Stables were exhibited to us the Canadiens of glossy black I liked the best I must say the first stable we visited shocked me not little by its want of cleanliness. I thought Englishmen kept the places for their darling animals nearly as nice as their own houses—After this last specimen in the way of sight seeing we made our thanks & adieus to the handsome Captain, & returned to the Hotel for Lunch. Then with Mr Webb as guide our party in two open carriages we drove to the falls of Montmorenci. Mary went with Uncle & Aunt Tom in the first carriage, as she had had the entertaining of our friend in the morning was resolved she said to make us do our share—Mr Charles mounted beside the driver Mr Webb on the front seat discoursed Mattie and myself. When introduced to him first this morning he struck me as stiff, conscious, & rather a drawling dandy. Before we accomplished the nine miles to the Falls, I changed my mind—hearing that he had spent 14 years in Australia I asked him some questions about the country—he became really interesting in describing what he had seen, & some of his escapes & dangers by land & sea—told me he was the first white man who had taught an Australian to read & write & in a word christianized him—since which time there had been schools established for the purpose—he had written a book about the country & natives & seemed to feel a warm interest in them. A little above the Falls we left the carriages, having a short distance to walk. He inquired if I was a good climber & then lead the way down a broken scrambling path I following—Mary Pettigrew came next. We hesitated as the others remained on the hill above, but calling to cousin Charles to follow on we kept—a very steep place we went down by a ladder but the distance was short, & had we fallen would have been caught on a platform at the foot of the ladder—a little more clambering & we were safely standing on a rock just opposite & much lower than the falls. Mr Charles would not come near the edge, neither would Mr Webb. I told Charles "he wished us to peep out from behind the trees" I believed but nothing would induce him to approach. It was really not foolhardiness but never becoming giddy there is really no venturing on my part. When we scrambled to the top of the hill or what ever it might be called I was concerned to see Aunt Ann pale from terror, & inwardly resolved never again to give her such discomfort merely in pursuit of my own gratification. We had time on returning to Quebec to attend a race which was to take place in the plains of Abraham at 3 o'clock—when we arrived at the spot there was a great crowd, but no ladies except ourselves, we obtained a place in one of the stands, but saw nothing of the race the horses having started just before we reached there, & running but one heat—Capt Fane was driving his blacks 4 in hand, & offered to take two of us in his barouche, first to the Governor Generals merely to leave a friend & then take us to the Hotel. I would very much have liked to go especially when he came & repeated the offer to me—but Uncle Tom looked disapproving, & I did not like the idea of Mattie who seemed disinclined, returning to Town without us—it would not have been agreeable so I was very sorry to decline. Mr Webb dined with us, wore an undress uniform being a jacket & scarlet vest, trimmed with gold cord.

Saturday, September 11 It was decided much to the regret of Mary & myself that we leave this afternoon for Montreal so that Monday we may take the cars for Boston by the way of Lakes Champlain & George We would prefer staying longer here, there is still a great deal to see, the Indian village Lorette,[56] the plains of Abraham & the column marking the spot where Wolf fell, the Governor Generals &c &c but we must give it up—Mr Webb did me a great service today, by some means of which I have no recollection. I put Mattie's keys in her trunk (which we have together mine being left in Montreal with some of the luggage) & shut down the top, as it is a spring lock of course they were secure out of reach. I knew nothing of this misfortune until I wished to get my dress out, when the keys could not be found, & Mattie said I had locked them up. Uncle Tom Aunt Ann & Mattie having some shopping to do went out, Mary & Mr Charles waited for me, the locksmith could not open it when he came. Mr Webb hearing of the difficulty most kind & politely went to the ordnance office & sent the best armourer in their regiment who by filing my key succeeded. I felt really greatly obliged by the services—Among his other qualifications Mr Webb plays and sings on the Piano, he sang for us last night very pleasantly some of Moores melodies & some old Irish songs—He gave the words of one of his own compositions to Uncle Tom at his request & said he would send the Music that I might play it. Just before we left he called again & brought his sleigh bells & some of the other ornaments to show us—he had given me a description yesterday at dinner & told me I should see them. Another thing he mentioned I must not forget it is so curious a custom. The Officers of the Garrison & only the officers have the privilege of choosing a lady at the beginning of the season to be their "Muffin" it is termed. She is their belle for the winter, drives with him, he carries her to balls, always dances with her & on every occasion is her devoted—his sleigh, his horses, himself, are at her service. As soon as the season closes, the "Muffinage" terminates & nothing more is thought of it. I asked him if very different consequences did not sometimes follow the Muffinage "Oh! frequently he answered, most of the officers marriages & they constantly marry here are brought about by this system". Civilians are not allowed the same privilege. It is very curious. Mr Webb came to the boat to see us off. We have reason to be obliged not only to him, but are indebted to Mr Rogers for introducing us to so nice & attentive a person. The "Montreal" Royal mail line is our steamer. I am sorry to say adieu to Quebec, we might have passed two or three days more very pleasantly & had that drive with Capt Fane!

—*Montreal*—

Sunday, September 12 Arrived at seven this morning in a rain—found the "St Lawrence Hall" very full. We three are mounted up many flights into the top of the house but have better rooms than before. Mary went to church in the morning it rained so much that I would not go by reason of my cold, or I strained myself clambering at the Falls on Friday. I have had a stiffness ever since & pain in all the muscles of my poor "limbs"——At dinner today Mr Rogers sat beside me, I have not liked him from the first, but of course was very civil, he amused me as I have not often been. by his absurd remarks upon the party. began by inquiring if "the old lady had not been sick this morning", then, "nice looking old lady is'nt she?" told me he could not talk to Mary, "that she didnt like him he knew it from the first minute, he felt afraid to sit by her & talk, tho' she looked so quiet" &c &c——I said my other cousin was the most quiet of the two, "oh! I cant make head or tail of the one over yonder." this was so unexpected, so ridiculous, I nearly screamed!

Monday, September 13 Repacked my trunk &c &c walked a little, dined on Muligatawny soup, & at 3 o'clock bid adieu to Montreal & "St Larence Hall" as the Irish waiters say. We crossed in a small crowded steamer to La Prairie, there took the cars. At Rouse's Point on Lake Champlain changed cars for Burlington where we spent the night. The difference is very perceptible as soon as one crosses the border between the Canadians & our people—there is so much more activity & "go ahead" every where with us, the children look as tho' they too know how to take care of themselves.

Tuesday, September 14 Walked thro' the town pretty much before the arrival of the Boat. The situation is pretty & the [. . .] a rising place. The green hills of Vermont looked more blue than corresponded with their name in the misty morning. On board the "R. W. Sherman" we arrived about three at Ticonderoga—where we determined to spend the night instead of proceeding to Caldwell. The hotel is curiously built in sight of the Lake the Old Fort some distance back on the hill. We passed the afternoon walking over the hills, examining the Ruins, & enjoying the pretty prospects all around. I was charmed with the "voyage" today, the views on either side of the Lake, the rugged Mountains, the trees just beginning to change their foliage, bright yellow mingling with the soberer shades of green, the smooth water winding in & out among numerous little Islands. was to me. a continued pleasure! The walk this afternoon I enjoyed nearly as much the grass was so soft & pleasant to the feet after tramping over hard pavements as we have lately done, & seated on a stone of the Old Fort I thought of the days gone by, of the Indians, the French, the English, & lastly ourselves The outer walls alone remain of a part of the Fortress, heaps of stones in every direction, many having been taken away to make stone fences, others scattered over the hill side. Walking among the ruins made one solemn, the martial deeds of the Past embodied in the crumbling Wall! the masses of broken stone while the

Peace of the Present was betoken by the grass covered battlements whose "every trip may" have been a "soldiers sepulchre," and the cultivated fields extending around. The evening was delightful, the air just cool enough, & the rich green carpet of Nature's handiwork softer than any velvet it is a walk & afternoon to be remembered!

Wednesday, September 15 I was quite surprised to see Joe Allston today, he was on his way to Niagara & stopped only a few minutes, looks well & in excellent spirits—At 3 o'clock took the stage to Lake George 5 miles distant. Here the Boat again—it was crowded with children who had been enjoying the delights of an excursion up the Lake. We stopped at different places along the shore putting out parties of the youthful revellers with their guardians. They reminded me of a Buffalo congregation in Abbeville, & cheifly very common looking. Arrived at Caldwell near dark after a pleasant trip—

Thursday, September 16 We are nicely situated at the Lake House, a very comfortable hotel—After breakfast walked some distance on the shores of the Lake, the scenery is generally prefered to that of Lake Champlain—it is wilder, the Mountains with little interruption rising from the water & towering like protecting bulwarks the whole length of the Lake—I admired the scenery greatly & sat on the deck until the sun had set in billowing clouds of gold & crimson behind the dark western ridge while the opposite heights were still tinged by the last touches of yellow light. Cousin Charles Mary, Mattie & myself climbed one of the Mountains fronting the hotel, we had from different points beautiful views of the Lake, the Mountains, & country for a short distance but the trees were too thick to have a very extended view. Left the Lake House at ½ past 3, & drove to Glenns Falls, from there to Monroe's Station for the night. The Hudson River is here a narrow insignificant stream.

Boston

Friday, September 17 After a day's journey in the Cars we arrived in Boston—about six o'clock. Went to the "Revere House"—said to be the best Uncle Tom displeased with the accommodations, all rooms too small.

Saturday, September 18 Moved from the Revere House to the "Winthrop House" opposite Boston Common so famous in Peter Parley. As we dine at ½ past 2 o'clock we had no time for any thing this morning. Walked in the Common the afternoon, it is a very pretty spot, many of the trees are elms, the largest I have ever seen, & carefully kept. where they have been bruised pieces of coarse cloth tacked over the wound. In the midst of the common is an old grave yard. I am anxious to go in, & read some of the tombstones which I dare say belong many of them to the Puritan Fathers— Being enclosed by an Iron railing & the gate locked I doubt if I can be gratified.

Sunday, September 19 Went to Church morning & afternoon, heard good sermons.

Monday, September 20 Mr Charles, Mary, & myself (Mattie declined going) had a charming drive this morning round the city—We visited Cambridge, the Library of Harvard we walked through, nothing more for bars were placed before the alcoves so that there was no entering them, & we were forbidden to touch the books by notices at every turn. The grounds around the colleges are pretty being a nicely kept lawn with fine trees—none of the buildings are handsome but the library. From Cambridge we drove some miles to Mr Cushings garden.⁵⁷ the country thro' which we passed is highly cultivated. handsome houses & pretty grounds succeed one another the whole distance. But the garden that was the crown of the whole the Hot houses, the flowers the fruit, the shrubbery, the management of the whole rendered it exquisite. I was charmed. Have some nectarine stones for Badwell &—

Tuesday, September 21 Surprise of surprises! mais commencer en commencement! Having driven (morning & afternoon included) yesterday about 40 miles thro' & around Boston we were quiet disposed today only going to walk in the afternoon & visiting the Museum, (which is not so attractive as I had imagined.) Uncle Tom had some engagement & did not go with us, Aunt Ann staid at home also—when we returned at dusk I heard voices in their room tapped at the door. Aunt Ann opened & we saw Uncle Tom discoursing a gentleman but with rather a puzzled air—he introduced him as Mr Smith of Richmond, we bowed in due form, were amazed at Aunt Ann's laughing in rather an hysterical manner, but still more when Mr Charles stepped forward with "Johnston". Never was surprise more complete— even now I do not feel as if he were really here. He arrived a week ago, & hearing of our whereabouts pushed on & joined us.

Wednesday, September 22 Johnston has changed entirely I would not have known him at all. his fierce yellow mustache makes the greatest difference in his appearance and his hair cut short I do not like as much. He is dreadfully accomplished, I am really half afraid to talk to him—Mr Charles, Mary, James & myself drove to Mount Auburn It is a beautiful cemetary more solemn I think than Laurel Hill—I saw Judge Storeys monument a plain shaft & white marble inscribed with his name, birth, & death, his memory required no long epitaph his name was sufficient memorial. Visited Bunker Hill Monument, the view from the top of the City is fine. In the evening went to the theatre to see Lola Montez [58]—she appeared in a play called Lola Montez & pretending to exhibit some incidents in her life. I did not like it, or her acting, she is very extravagant—her coquettish ways are pretty & attractive. She is not handsome except her eyes which are fine.

Thursday, September 23 Joe Allston arrived this morning—I was shocked to see his arm in a sling & hear that he had dislocated his right shoulder at Niagara slipping down a rock—he was suffering when he walked but turned off inquiries by saying, "Oh! it's nothing" otherwise he looks well & in good spirits. Uncle Allston called today, he arrived last night & walking in State Street met the Revd Mr Potter formerly of Pendleton. I have not seen him for a long time he recognized me immediately & was very glad to see me. Uncle Allston left Aunt Adèle & Adèle at West Point, he returns himself in a day or two, as soon as they can proceed to the Beach. The accounts of yellow fever from Charleston are alarming & now I do not know when we shall reach home. Had an oyster supper tonight at Vintons a confectioner in Washington St. Have had a pleasant day—

Friday, September 24 Did not go out this morning except for a short walk on the common not pleasant—Uncle Allston called this evening & we all went to see Anderson the Professor of Natural Magic. James had chill & instead went to bed—

Saturday, September 25 Mr Charles had intended leaving for New York today, but James not being well, he changed his mind & remained Uncle Tom, Mary, Mattie, cousin Charles, Joe, & myself went to Lowel. Aunt Ann declined going not being altogether well. The distance is but 26 miles, & by the Cars is scarcely an hour including stoppages. Lieut Humphreys of the Navy is the superintendent of the cloth factory. He received us very politely having known Uncle Tom before. We went thro' a large building several stories high in every one of which some different operation is carried on. Weaving, spinning, dyeing, pressing—&c the two first were very interesting, I wish we had machines of the sort at home! What an amount of time and labor they save. The Carpet Factory is very curious & pretty, the numerous looms with the various colors of the warp & the bright patterns forming under your eye rendered this factory much the most interesting. The patterns are formed by means of strips of punctured paper, which regulates the warp & is over the head of the weaver—It is impossible to say how it is managed— The Hamilton works are for cottons & homespun just the same as those at Graniteville—All the factories are worked by Water power from the Merrimac River—the Canal by which they have drawn off the water for some distance is an ornament to the town with its stone walk and rows of trees on either bank, forming a pretty promenade—We returned to Boston at three o'clock, found the two half invalids both better. The accounts from Charleston of yellow fever are very alarming I feel anxious for Aunt Lou.

Sunday, September 26 Attended service this morning at a church near the Hotel, did not hear the minister Dr Vinton[59] but a stranger. In the afternoon went to Trinity Church. I dont like the music of this church at all, am ashamed to say I laughed during one of the Chants. Mr Charles as I sat down put on the most distressed countenance saying "did you ever hear the like"! As the whole party were similarly affected I was not peculiar—A good sermon—

Monday, September 27 Mary & cousin Charles left this morning for New York where I hope we will join them. James has a dinner given him by some of the professors his friends at Cambridge so waits for that.—We visited the Glass Works today—they are very curious. One man was making lamp shades, it was strange to see the glass thrust into the fiery furnace drawn out glowing & shaped as he wish by an instrument like a compass. We leave for New Haven tomorrow.

New Haven

Tuesday, September 28 Left Boston at eight o'clock the cars crowded. I should like some day to visit the "Athens of America" again there is a great deal to interest one. I forgot to mention that Mrs Willington[60] & her sister Mrs Whitney called on me Saturday—I returned the visit yesterday, saw Mr & Mrs Young who had just come from New York—she was very friendly & pleasant—Mrs Whitney was not at home—I was sorry to decline an invitation they gave me to spend the evening. We arrived today at one o'clock. Driving to the New Haven Hotel (to which we had been recommended by the Streets[61] at West Point) I was struck with the rural appearance of the town the rows of large trees on each side of the Street giving particularly that effect—After dinner walked about a good deal Uncle, Aunt, & cousin paid a visit to Miss Baldwin an old lady with whom they had boarded 13 years ago. I went too of course. She was delighted to see them again & asked lots of questions.

Wednesday, September 29 At the corner nearly opposite our hotel is Yale College, the famous old university—On the Square directly in front is the State House & three churches—one of a very pretty dark stone building—with a beautiful creeping plant covering the walls between the pointed windows thick with its rich clustering leaves. I admire it greatly, there is another like it in the town & I think they are its chief ornaments. Paid with Aunt Ann & Mattie a visit to Mrs Flagg[62]—she is dreadfully deaf & used a trumpet, long tube, with a large cup shaped concern at the end into which she seemed to catch ones words as they spoke. As we dine at one, there was not time after a pretty extended visit for more than the walk home. Mrs Street & her son in law called after dinner—Mattie & myself paid Miss Street (who was too indisposed to come) a visit afterwards. Poor girl! I dont think she is long for this world. She was most cordial—in her reception—Mr Foote carried us after tea to the Horticultural exhibition—well worth seeing. the flowers were arranged with great taste—the fruit & vegetable the finest we have seen. Quebec & Boston were entirely outshone. Mr Foote is very anxious we should not go tomorrow says he would give us a drive around New Haven &c, &c, but Uncle Tom prefers leaving in the morning for New York, having some business there. The Streets have been very polite, they are nice people. Mr, or rather Lieut Foote[63] is a Navy man, not so prepossessing, though equally civil—He presented me with a Dahlia tonight which on some provocation I pulled to pieces before his face—he was quite diverted, taking some of the leaves declared he would keep them &c—I forgot to mention that yesterday we stopped for a few minutes in the afternoon at a Whig meeting in the square opposite. I was amused very much by some of the remarks I heard, one man said to another "look here, what are you splitting your throat shouting so for? "I dont know, for Scott & Graham I suppose, but let's go home to tea that's better" Off the two patriots rushed instanter—[64]

The Journals of Ann Lewis Hardeman

1850–67

N'er to the chambers where the mighty rest
Since their foundation came a nobler guest
Nor e'er was to the towers of bliss conveyed
A fairer spirit or welcome shade——[1]

1850

Monday, June 24, 1850 Monday morning. All in usual health—Colo Stuart[2] left in the 20th inst. for Meadville—from thence to Greenville Mi. My dear bror received a letter from Tenn yesterday morning from Mr Marshall—

Tuesday, June 25 At the same work to day as yesterday, 25th (to-day) have had some uneasiness about the boys.—have been deeply wounded but have been able to keep "my tongue from evil" & trust in God—

Thursday, June 27 Rain—Spent the day at Mrs Sessions[3] yesterday—sister C.[4] still there—all well the children doing tolerably well.

Thursday, July 4 James & Oscar[5] went to a Review of SS. schools & heard an address by Colo C. S. Tarpley,[6] was highly delighted—went in the after-noon to the District school house or got part of the way & heard that the company had left—met an old school mate (Archibald Forbes) & turned back—

Monday, July 8 They were invited to take a birth night supper or tea at 4 oclock—did not go until 6 were very much pleased with the entertainment Mr & Mrs Petre[7] were very kind to them.

Tuesday, July 9 Ann Sessions spent the day here and Ma[8] & sister Mary[9] went to town.—Our dear little Jane has been quite ill of Diarhea for a fort night. looks badly—the balance are tolerably well—Adelaide improving—Betty can spell—Thursday early in the morning—had some little difficulty with Oscar—& Adelaide this morning.

Thursday, July 11 Oscar for an untruth & Adelaide for tearing her book.

Friday, July 19 Oscar at home two days from an eruption caused by touching poison oak vine—A. G. Sessions here since day before yesterday with *Joseph*—James goes home with him to-night to go fishing with some of their friends tomorrow—children all doing very well the dear little babe[10] quite sick this morning—On the 17th & 18th Had some difficulty in subduing her will—my dear bror took her in another room & conquered her—I must confess it was a very hard struggle with me. & nothing but conscientious scruples can have induced me to persevere.

Tuesday, July 23 A.M. A. G. Sessions went home this morning accompanied by my sister C. after spending several days with us & going to Church on Sunday & visiting on Monday & shopping—Jane & Nannie[11] convalescent. The session will close to-morrow—We had on Saturday last an illustration of the fidelity of the Dog. James' dog arrived from Meadville by Steam B. & R. R. after having been seperated over two years he recognized James & Oscar all three being in an ecstacy of joy—The children all doing tolerably well—

Wednesday, July 24 James & Oscar's school closed yesterday early in the afternoon—their teacher (Mr H. W. Holman)[12] gave them a treat of ice cream & distributed the rewards. James got "Mc auleys History of England" 1st & 2nd Vol. in pamphlet form—[13]

This morning he has commenced teaching the little ones in due form —Oscar—Adelaide & Betty—Edward[14] occasionally. Hope they will do well they have so far commenced well—9 oclock is the hour—for the morning—

Saturday, August 3 Have just taken leave of my dear bror & my dear James also—he expects to accompany his uncle William to Tenn.—will be gone

5 weeks—sister Mary went as far as Canton after taking leave of my dear James & bror Wm—who left Canton on Monday Augst 5 in company with Mr Lester [15] for Tenn. Lord I have by faith committed them into thy hands— O preserve them from the "Pestilence that walketh at Noon Day & from the Arrow that flieth by night." [16] O how long will the weeks, days & hours, be until I see them again—

Sunday, August 11 Did not attend Church.

Monday, August 19 Sister Mary received a letter from bror Wm at Holly Springs all well—going on very well—Mrs Bowman [17] came down on Teusday last to spend some time with us during my bros absence—Received a letter last week from my dear Niece Ann Sessions from Natchez whither she had gone to have the benefit of Dr Davis's advice—one this week from Mr Sessions informs us that she is no better—has no appetite &c.

Children all doing well the dear little baby I am thankful to say is well again—Oscar started to S.S. yesterday to the Episcopal Church brought none but a "Library book" "The Two Friends" [18]—Have not succeeded in my work as well as I wished.

Tuesday, August 20 Have commenced teaching the children since yesterday morning succeeded quite well—

Wednesday, August 21 Did not commence in time this morning

Friday, August 23 Have succeeded tolerably well with the children during the past week they are much happier than when they do not say lessons. Adelaide commenced Geography this morning—Cousin Wm P. Perkins [19] left this morning for his residence on the River—his family being absent in Tenn. Colo Stuart here yet & well. Sister Mary received a letter from Mr S. informing us of dear little Nannies convalescence—hope she will be well soon & at home—

Sunday, August 25 Sister M. Colo Stuart with Oscar & Adelaide went to Church got a large jug of Well water to-day from "Coopers Well." [20] No news of James yet or my dear bror for some time—

Tuesday, August 27 The children said lessons very well for about 10 days— ·
Received to-day a very handsomely bound copy of the "Vicar of Wakefield" [21] from my sister Mary M. M. Hardeman & heard with gratitude that my bror had reached his place of distination (viz) Franklin.

Wednesday, August 28 Sister Mary received last night a letter from my dear bror from which we learned that he was well—& dear James done very well—was glad he took him with him &c. Have been hearing the childrens lessons they have not done so well to-day (patience much tried).

Thursday, August 29 Did not get along so well to-day Colo Bowman went home—did not begin the lessons until a little after 11 oclock—Rain to-day—wind from the West.

Friday, August 30 Rain again to-day.

Tuesday, September 3 Colo Stuart left this morning for Meadville (via) Natchez in good health—Heard of one case of cholera in town yesterday. Sister Mary confined to her room with the glands of her throat cousin Betty not well—received a kind invitation to dine at Mrs Tarpleys [22] to-day but sister M. wrote an excuse—children all well Adelaide taking more interest in her studies than Oscar—hope they will have good lessons to-day—

Wednesday, September 4 They did have a few good lessons but we were interrupted—commenced to-day at 11 oclock. Last night at twilight Mr. White [23] & Miss Hetty Chilton [24] came Mr W. left this morning Miss C. will remain some weeks—

Friday, September 13 Have had very little pleasure in hearing the childrens lessons this week—have heard from Colo Stuart of the loss & recovery of his trunk though do not know whether it was robbed or not hope to hear soon—have heard from James and my bror several times both well & will be at home we hope next week—

Sunday, September 15 The anniversary of my lamented bros death 14 years ago [25] he was taken from us—since then we have been called to resign two sisters (viz) Mary N. Perkins (widow) [26] who died on the 1st Oct 1846—after many years of suffering—Sarah Jane Eleanor Stuart was taken on the 25th April 1849. After lingering 3 months under unparalled sufferings, leaving six small children to my care—how utterly unfit do I feel myself for the discharge of so high & important a trust—May God help me by his grace to discharge my duty towards them with an eye single to his glory—

Monday, September 23 My dear bror & James returned on the 20th inst. in good health for which I feel truly thankful—James will commence with his school again this morning—hope he may succeed.

Tuesday, October 1 Received some dry goods from Natchez sent by Colo Stuart. The children have not been doing so well—Dr Barbee[27] has not commenced school yet expects to do so next Monday

Thursday, October 3 Had the pleasure of a visit from cousin Glenn O. Hardeman a son of uncle John Hardeman[28]—who was on his way to California— could not take leave of him—he is a Physician & prescribed for our dear little Jane who had the first symptom of Croup last night—

Sunday, October 6 Did not go to Church to-day the boys went to S. School— & church—The baby convalescent. The Misses Skipwith Sally and Cornelia[29] spent a day or two here last week Miss Chilton expects to leave in the morning with my bror for Vicks.

Wednesday, October 9 Miss Chilton left this morning under my bros care for Vicksburg—started 10 hands up to cousin Wm P's to pick out cotton— fine weather—wrote to aunt Betsey[30] on the 7th inst.

Tuesday, October 15 All well sister Caroline at Mr Sessions he being about of Yazoo got my Wardrobe & Basket in order the boys started to school to Dr Barbee 30th Sepr on Monday—doing tolerably well Adelaide still recites her lessons to me had to punish her just now, an exceedingly disagreeable task—

Thursday, October 17 The 3 children Adelaide Betty & the babe Sarah Jane are all gone on to Mr Sessions to spend the day—sister Mary gone out visiting—the boys have not done so well at school seemed to be ashamed of it when I lectured about it—Mr Sessions is expected to-day—has been gone a week—

Sunday, October 20 Mr S. Arrived last night. He & sister C. went to Church to-day to hear Rev. J. B. Walker[31] preach—my bror his wife the 4 eldest children are gone to the Episcopal Church—the two boys go to S. School there—On the 18th inst James had the misfortune to get his cheek cut with a lathe at school—one of the school boys (viz) (William Morgan) threw it at him & came very near putting his eye out I hope however that it will not leave a scar—

Friday, October 25 Adelaide is 7 years old to-day—the first cold weather we have had—My bror & wife went up on the River to see cousin Wm P. Perkins—who is very ill accompanied by Dr Pugh his wife & two children Joseph & youngest Sally Jane[32]—Received a letter yesterday from my niece

Bethenia [33] informing us of the death of dear little Harry who died on the 3rd of September—had commenced writing to Bethenia a day or two before—

Saturday, October 26 At 4 oclock I took all the children in the carriage to Mr Session's to a party given in honour of Master Charles Dubuisson [34] the children enjoyed their visit very much all behaved very well except Bettie

Sunday, October 27 Ann Sessions & Mrs Dubuisson [35] came to take leave of us as she will leave in the morning for her home in Natchez—

I found her to be a very pleasant & agreeable lady—was very much pleased with her—& felt very much gratified to have made her acquaintance—

Sunday, November 3 The boys went to S. School this morning my bror & wife not returned yet—Mr Sessions & Ann spent a part of two days & one night during their absence—Went to a party at Mr Daniel Adams' [36] on Thursday 31st Octr. enjoyed themselves had a very pleasant party Colo Bowman came on the same evening & spent the night—Mrs Bowman was kind enough to send me the patterns of a sack & pants for Edward which will save me a great deal of trouble—I wrote her a note of thanks the Colo returned last night & left this morning 3rd inst for home.—A. G. Sessions came over this evening spent an hour or two—

Monday, November 4 No news of my bror & sister Mary yet the boys staid in at school—have not succeeded in my business & work to-day as I could wish—

Sunday, November 10 My bror & wife returned on Teusday evening late— sister Mary had severe attack of Dangue [37] an epidemic which prevailed in Vicksburg as they passed up the River left cousin Wm P. Perkins very low— heard from him last night it is probable he died on Thursday—though we have not heard certainly—Colo Stuart sent by my bror 40$ to pay Mr Holman for tuition of boys last session

Thursday, November 14 Thursday Night Mr Sessions & Ann came over to-day—about ½ an hour after they came sister Mary was taken very ill with pains in her head & throat—is better to-night—to-day also we received intelligence of the death of Cousin Wm P. Perkins (who had been very ill for some time past—) which occurred on Saturday 9th inst. at his Residence on the River—between 9 & 10 oclock—he was a very dear friend of both my dear bros to-night have had to drink some of the *bitter* portions of my cup—children not doing well—too idle—

Sunday, November 24 Did not go to Church to-day though very pleasant Mr White spent the night here—reports all well at his house & also at Mrs Fausts his sisters—Dr & Mrs Pugh called on their return home from Chocktaw Bend the residence of her late Father they expect to move up there the first of Jan. received a letter from Colo Stuart describing the Minister (Rev: Mr Campbell of the Vicksburg District) who attended cousin Wm P. Perkins in his last illness—preached his funeral cn Wednesday & was buried on Friday—Children not doing well—Adelaide has given up her regular lessons—Bettie says one occasionally. the boys take very little interest in their school—my heart is pained to see them shew so little interest in their education

Ages of my dear sisters children—
James Hardeman Stuart was born Octr 8th A.D. 1838
Oscar Ewing Stuart was born August 21st A.D. 1841
Adelaide Stuart was born October 25th A.D. 1843
Annie Elizabeth Stuart was born May 9th A.D. 1845
Edward Stuart was born February 17th A.D. 1847
Sarah Jane Stuart was born January 15th A.D. 1849 on Monday morning 4 oclock

Her mother survived her birth 3 months & 10 days—After (I humbly trust) being made perfect through suffering expired about ½ past 11 oclock on Wednesday night 25th of April 1849.

Wednesday, December 4 Have not heard the childrens lessons for some time several weeks—not doing so well at school take no interest in their studies —Went to town shopping for the children on the 27th Nov: Wrote to my bror D yesterday—Mrs Faust came on Teusday Ann came on Monday—left this morning her little girl quite ill with diarhea—Mrs F here now on her way to S.C. Mr White left this morning for Tokeba—his place of residence in Yazoo Cty.

Thursday, December 5 James has promised to be more particular in the choice of his books Oscar & Adelaide have been very idle—have to chastise them both . . . .—after talking to them hope they will now do better

Sunday, December 8 Did not go to Church to-day—the boys went to S.S.— sister Caroline at Mr S's yet expect to send for her this evening—have succeeded tolerably with my work— & childrens lessons the past week received a letter on business from Franklin this morning—

Thursday, December 19 My cousin Locke Hardeman arrived yesterday from Arrow Rock Mo.[38] left this evening—for Yalabusha to visit his sister[39]—to return in about 10 days—A. G. Sessions has been here for several days—Mr. S gone to Yazoo—Teusday Mrs Faust left with Maj Maney & Mr Murfree[40]—the latter bound for Tenn. Mrs F. for her residence in Yazoo bror Wm left on Sunday last—on business in Holmes Yazoo &c. About dawn on Saturday we were awakened by the servant Jenny who makes the fires with the alarm of fire—my bros Gin with a mill attached & Dr Youngs[41] cotton (several bales) was entirely consumed—.

Sunday, December 22 A bleak day—none of the family attended Church—a good deal of rain & wind—received a letter from Aunt Betsey to-day—

Sunday, December 29 No person went to church to-day but James—Oscar & James have been a little indisposed but are now convalescent—Ma received a letter from Colo Stuart to-day was on his way to Meadville to remove the remains of my dear sister to Jackson Public burying ground—contemplates going to N Orleans to live & read Civil Law—

1851

Wednesday, January 1, 1851 All the children sick with colds very bad day—confined to the home

Thursday, January 2 James & Oscar went to school this morning though neither of them well—the 3 youngest took Turpentine combined with molasses not well myself sister C. got nearly through with the childrens Winter clothes

Sunday, January 5 Sister Mary went home with Colo Bowman—this morning to see Mrs B & Mrs Pugh also—boys went to Church James (I regret to say) very reluctantly—children convalescing Adelaide & Bettie a little naughty this morning—had to correct them both & hope it was done in a proper spirit—

Tuesday, January 7 About two oclock my bror D from Texas arrived—to our great joy as we had been expecting him—but had ceased to do so as the gentleman with whom he had business had gone to N. O. to meet him has determined to send his daughter to Ashwood school in Tenn. expects to send his daughter Bethenia here & from this proceed with her uncle

(T. Nicholson)[1] to Carolina. Ann Sessions staid here from Teusday until Saturday morning—bror Wm went Canton Saturday morning—bror D remained with us but two nights: left with Mr Sessions as far as Jackson to join him in the evening to go as far as Natchez—he to N.O.—children all tolerably well—

Thursday, January 16 Bror Wm Received a latter from cousin J. Locke Hardeman informing us of bror Ds movements left for Tenn. to be gone 12 or 13 days to join J. L. H. in N. O. from thence to Texas from whence cousin Locke will return with my dear Bethenia who will accompany her uncle Thomas Nicholson to N. C. to spend a year—children all well except colds learning tolerably well Bettie is learning to read & Adelaide to write—15th My dear little (treasure) Sarah Jane's birthday—was very playful until she went to bed—her aunt Caroline & I gave her a box apiece & her aunt Mary a little book very small & beautiful, a description of the "Holy Land." O that we may be able to train her up in the nurture & admonition of the Lord—

Saturday, January 18 Adelaide commenced a hexigon bed quilt for herself— under the superintendance of her aunt Caroline made three circles—

Sunday, January 19 Mr bror received a telegraphic dispatch to-day from Colo Stuart saying that he was at Vicksburg with the remains of my dear sister— to be brought here to-night & buried to-morrow in the Public Burying Ground in the vicinity of Jackson—my own health has been very bad for some time & I expect ere long to rest by her side—sister Caroline, Oscar & James went over to the grave yard this evening to select a place if permitted by the civil authorities—my bror made the request & it was granted—On Sunday about night fall the remains of my dear sister arrived here was taken to the Public Graveyard about 10 oclock—on Monday 20th no one being present but the family & Mr & Mrs Boddie[2] who lived near—Rev J. B. Walker of the M. E. Church—read the Burial service—we remained until the grave was filled up & returned home—It was a solemn & impressive occasion—O that it may be sanctified. her husband who remained here quite ill—& the dear—dear children who were all present & seemed to feel their loss—Lord help us to discharge our duty towards them in an acceptable manner—

Saturday, January 25 Have been looking over my accounts—find myself deficient in keeping them—& feel that I have been too extravagant—& hope to repair the loss by a rigid economy in future.

Sunday, February 2 Raining no one went to Church—Cousin Locke Hardeman returned from N.O. on Thursday Jan 30th in good health—dined at Mr Sessions on Saturday gone to Canton to-day to see some friends will return soon—Dr Barbee gave up his school on Tuesday 2oth ult—Mr Holman their former teacher will take the school again—their Father still here.

Tuesday, February 4 Rain yesterday & to-day 5th Colo Stuart left without any definite destination this morning on the cars—either for Greenville Natchez or N.O. Children all doing very well—my dear brother quite ill of Diarhea have felt greatly depressed—sad, & melancholy—hope to be in better spirits soon—Lord I look to Thee & thee alone—James & Oscar commenced school to-day under Mr Holmans tuition—8 scholars present.

Monday, February 24 Our dear little Bettie has been quite ill—is now convalescent—Adelaide went to Church yesterday said all her lessons last week—Sister Mary made a visit to Colo Bowman's last week all well—Mrs Bowman has added a son to her family of boys she has 3 now.

Wednesday, February 26 Feel *very* very sad have had a bad spell of a weeks duration.

Friday, February 28 Bettie convalescent eats at the "big table." Mr Sessions returned from N. Orleans (Tuesday 25th night) whither he had gone to hear Jenny Lind [3] sing—brought us all presents Colo Stuart (whom he saw there) sent Betty & Adelaide a beautiful Sunday bonnet a piece—

Sunday, March 2 Received a letter from my dear Aunt Betsey who is now at cousin Thomas Hardemans & will visit us as soon as the roads & weather will permit—bror Wm received a letter also from Colo Stuart who was at Natchez on his way home from N. O. whither he had gone to hear the "Sweedish Nightingale" sing & having other business also—had the misfortune to lose his watch chain & a fine gold pen which had been presented to him by Dr J. J. Pugh—I regret the loss of both very much—

Thursday, March 6 My birth day very wet cold & disagreeable weather—sister Caroline over at Mrs Sessions since Monday last somewhat indisposed—we are lonely without her. Adelaide commenced "Parley's first Book of History" [4] this morning did very well—Edward took Colomel last night as a Vermifuge [5]—has been taking Vermifuge for three mornings past.

Sunday, March 9 Did not go to Church—Sally Terrill came out on Saturday—the boys did not go to S.S. but to Church. The children doing very well Adelaide has said her lessons without giving me any trouble during the past week—think she will succeed very well with her History—Sister C. returned from Mrs Sessions yesterday evening—

Monday, March 10 Went to town to-day with sister M. to take dear little Sally Terril in to school & to see Mrs Dr Hall who is very low not expected to live & to shop a little—

Tuesday, March 11 A pleasant day but none of the family went to Church—James was indisposed this morning—am not well myself—took cold bath this morning.

Thursday, March 20 My bror Wm wife Mr Sessions wife & James Oscar & Adelaide all gone to the Theatre—performance by two little girls one 5 the other 7 years old—are said to be prodigies—as they perform with ease *Shakspeares plays* without being able to read them.

Sunday, March 23 Went to the M. E. Church & heard a most excellent sermon—by a stranger Communion day Quarterly Meeting—went in the P.M. to see the two little Batemans Kate & Ellen who with their father were spending the day at Mr Sessions—Children doing tolerably well.

Monday, March 24 Adelaide recommenced writing to-day—lessons all to be recited by 12 oclock.

Tuesday, March 25 Did not retire until ½ past 1 oclock last night was excited—servant woman did not do well—feel badly this morning nervous & excitable yet making an effort to retain my balance—Lord help me for of myself I am nothing nothing. Sister M. bror Wm & Ann Sessions gone to Dr Allstons[6] to spend the day some miles off.

Sunday, March 30 My dear Aunt Betsey & my dear cousin Lucretia arrived—which brought balm to my poor heart Ann Sessions & my dear bror gone this morning the former to Vicksburg the latter to join her husband at Yazoo [. . .]

Thursday, April 10 Aunt Betsey sister Mary & myself went to town shopping—was very much fatigued—am not well yet.

Friday, April 11 Aunt B. sister M. & Ma dined at Gen. Clark's[7]—my Mother with James, Oscar, & Adelaide went with my aunt to the Christian Church bror Walker came out yesterday evening & brought some S.S. Books—Mr Johnstons[8] sent in his resignation as I understand bror Wm received a letter from Colo Stuart.

Sunday, April 20 (Good Friday) no one went to Church save Sister Mary & Aunt Betsey my bror gone to Canton since Friday Mrs Johnston wife of the Episcopal Minister died on Friday night—Children all doing tolerably well.[9]

Friday, April 25 The second anniversary of my dear sisters death—children all well & doing very well—my dear Aunt is still with us—Mrs Bowman also since Sunday P.M. Ann Sessions & family with sister Mary will leave for Tenn. to-morrow morning 26th April. Heard by a letter from Teny[10] that she is to be married to a Dr Vizer[11] about the last of this month or first of next—Feel desolate—heart stricken & sorrowful no confidence in myself—

O that I may be sustained by Grace divine—in the discharge of the various duties which devolve upon me—Sister Mary left this morning with my bror who will perhaps accompany her as far as her bros & return it was painful to give her up but hope to be resigned—sister M. received a letter from cousin J. L. Hardeman a few days ago—

Sunday, April 27 The boys have been going to the M. E..C. to S. School for 3 successive sabbaths. Aunt Betsey went to Church this morning 27th taking little Bettie with her & Albert to drive.

Sunday, May 4 No person went to Church none well enough—My bror D's birthday to-day he is 45 to-day—have not heard from him for some time—heard by a letter from Bethenia to sister Mary on the eve at her departure for Tenn. that she was to be married to a Dr Vizer about the last of April or the 1st of May. May God bless their union.

Friday, May 9 My Dear little Betties birth-day 7 years of her afflicted life has passed away—am thankful to record however that her health has improved for some time past though not very well just now—All the dear children are very well—the colporteur staid here last night I purchased (or my bror did for me) 2 vols of the "Women of Israel" & "Mammas Birth Day"[12]—

Bettie had a little party was crowned Queen—& when seated on a throne after tea was presented with gifts books & kisses all of which she received gracefully.

8th My bror Williams birth-day—49 years old—was at home for supper.

Friday, May 16 Not well—went with my aunt & bror on the Wednesday 14th to Coopers Well enjoyed the visit—Children all in training yesterday morning—about 10 oclock Adelaide still distresses herself about her lessons—but says she will try to correct the fault herself—

Monday, May 19 My dear bror left for Bolivar Court this morning wrote to Colo S. sent James to town twice to-day—Children too idle done very little to-day—none of the family went to Church except the boys—who went to S S. only—

Sunday, May 25 Aunt Betsey & sister Caroline went to Church latter to the M. E. C. the former to the Christian Church my bror not yet returned— received a letter on Friday 23rd of May—wrote to sister Mary this morning 26th—

Friday, May 30 A M. Went shopping with A. G. S. Aunt Betsey was very much fatigued & a little dissatisfied with myself as usual—children all doing well.

Sunday, June 1 No one except my Aunt & Mother went to Church to-day received a letter from my bror yesterday informing us of his detention & going over to Yazoo City—James Lester[13] came over this morning & took breakfast—to inform us of his Fathers going over to Yazoo City he went to S.S. with the boys.

Monday, June 2 Received a letter from my bror D from N.O. all well—a News paper containing the marriage notice of my dear Bethenia which was celebrated on the 29th of April 1851 to Dr Napolean B. Viser—they seem to be highly pleased—hope they will do well—he writes despondingly about his pecuniary affairs—My dear nieces Sally & Bethenia are now married. May God bless them & prosper them in all things.—& make them good wives & a blessing to their husbands—Sally has a little girl Ellen Lewis Hardeman not—not quite a year old a very interesting child.

Thursday, June 12 Heard this day of the death of my dear cousin Lucretia Nash Hardeman which took place on 11th inst at 5 oclock A M. received a Telegraphic Despatch informing us of the melancholy event & that her funeral would be preached at 3 on the 12th but a violent storm came up about that time which must have prevented—
I regret her loss as it deprived me of a sincere friend & relative for whom I had formed a strong attachment—& I have reason to beleive it was mutual—she left 3 children 1 daughter & two sons [4]—who will be well provided for—my dear Aunt Betsey who had brought up my cousin from

infancy (having lost her mother at a very early age when quite an infant) she will leave here on the 16th (Monday) to take charge of her children—May they be protected guided & governed by the wisdom & Grace of Almighty God—& may this bereavement be sanctified to us all—

Friday, June 13 Just received an unfinished letter from my dearest cousin dated 6th inst—finished by her husband to my bror Wm before her death—giving an account of her situation—&c.

Peace to thy manes my well beloved friend & cousin! Farewell! until the Resurrection Morn when I hope to hail thee with my dear sister!! who preceded thee to the grace 2 years 1 month & 19 days—And one sister 5 years & a bror 15 years ago—

Sunday, June 15 Maria's child died this morning about 5 oclock of teething & summer complaint—Lucys little child George quite ill of typhoid fever—Fannys child Donaldson also sick of summer complaint—no other cases that I know of—

Aunt Betsey expects to leave in the morning for Myrtle Hill—she & my mother go to Church to-day—

Monday, June 16 My Dear Aunt Betsey left for Myrtle Hill—she was not very well & was unwilling to take so long a journey with no person but her servants—I commended her to Our common Father knowing that He will in his own time fulfil all his promises—

Sunday, June 22 No one went to Church except the boys—bror Wm received a letter from cousin Thomas Hardeman M. giving an account of my dear cousins death—which was inflamation of the brain—expressed some apprehensions for his daughters health—hope to hear soon what disposition they will make of the dear children.

Wednesday, June 25 Wrote to Cousin Dolly Alsobrook & to Colo Stuart at length this week. Received a letter from sister Mary in answer to mine must try & and answer it to-day—(Thursday). all well again Adelaide has been quite sick took Vermifuge—Cut out two shirts for bror Wm yesterday & a pr pants & sack for Edward—

Thursday, June 26 Heard from my dear Aunt & the particulars of my lamented cousins death—in a letter to my Mother—Cut out to-day 3 pr pants of cottonade for Edward—& sack for Adelaide—2 brown pr linnen pants for Edward—am going to write to sister Mary to-night.

Friday, June 27 All well wrote to sister M. to-day & to Aunt Betsey—by the same mail.

Saturday, June 28 Righting up & mending & patching arranging Betties & Adelaides drawers.

Monday, June 30 A G S. came here this morning spent the day—am making or going to make a shirt & a sack for each of the boys a pr pants. my dear Ann has kindly offered to have the pants made.

Friday, July 4 Friday succeeded in finishing the boys. sister Caroline made the shirt & part of the sacks—Ann had 1 pr pants made & part of another—while I trimmed her bonnet—bror Wm went to the Wells this morning very early—boys went to S S. celebration James received a prize of a red morocco bound Bible—with a strap—which did my heart good. Oscar was a little mortified at not having any mark of distinction—says he will try next time—

Sunday, July 6 My brother Thomas' birth day had he lived would have been 52 years old to-day—the 15th of next Septr he will have been dead 15 years—But thou art not yet forgotten my bror—thy memory is still cherished by thy devoted brors & sisters.

   None of the family except the boys went to Church to-day—Received a note from Colo Stuart yesterday will not be here for 20 or 30 days to come—perhaps sometime in August—Wrote to Sister Mary & Mrs Cameron Colo S.

Friday, July 11 Received a letter from Mrs Cameron who was in Meadville—Made Brandy Peaches & preserves for this year—No news of dear sister Mary yet—All are uneasy her bror. Went to town this morning—to put a letter in the office & to Telegraph them if possible—

Sunday, July 13 None but the boys went to Church to-day—heard from sister M. this morning.

Wednesday, July 16 (My sister Janes birth day had she lived would have been 35 yrs old—has been dead 2 yrs 3 mo. She *rests in heaven* but thy memory is still fondly cherished by thy *family*.) Bishop Green[15] at Jackson expects to settle here—& institute a college—Mrs Tarpley came out A.M.

Thursday, July 17 Mr Nichol[16] Colo & Mrs Napier[17] with their children were here this morning just after I had endured a severe trial of heart trouble of a domestic nature (sister).

Sunday, July 20 Bror Wm sister Caroline James & Sarah Jane went to church in the buggy all well—have commenced writing to Mrs Cameron—Mr Lewin the Episcopal Minister [18] officiated to-day.

Monday, July 21 Wrote to my friend Mrs Cameron—James went to the P.O. last night & lost 50 cts of his uncles money the children did not get to their lessons this morning in time—were idle—James commenced reading the life of "John Randolph of Roanoake" [19]—Saturday 18th July.

Wednesday, July 23 A. G. Sessions come over spent the day & night little Nannie ill of hooping cough we suppose—symptoms are very like it—but hope it may be cold—all our children well—

Saturday, July 26 Mrs Bullis Mrs Cage & Mrs Scott [20]—came late Saturday evening after spending the day with Mrs Petre—Mrs Sessions bror Phillip is on a visit to their house—we expected them over to-day—but received a note from Mr S. saying they could not come—all complaining—Nannie not well.

Sunday, July 27 The boys went to S. S. this morning—sister C. preparing to go—all well except Edward who had Diarrhea—from eating corn & water melon—

Sunday, August 3 Heard from sister Mary this morning—well & will be here on Teusday next—the 4 younger children been very ill with influenza— all better now—for which I feel truly grateful—No one went to Church to-day had rain this morning Mr Sessions & Ann left this evening.

Monday, August 4 Dear Sister Mary arrived from Tenn. in good health—Received a letter for Aunt Betsey from Arrow Rock Mo. She & cousin Thos did not agree in the management of the children—& of course were no more friends—answered her on the 17th inst—Colo Stuart here yet moody.

Monday, September 1 Mr Bigelow the Colporteur [21] left here this morning after spending the Saturday & Sunday night with us had the misfortune to have the end of his middle finger torn off by the rein of his buggy harness he & my bror returned & I tied up his finger—for which he did not have the civility to say "good morning" as he left—Colo Stuart not up yet, now 10 oclock—went to Church yesterday P.M. to hear Mr Lewin—

James not well—has some fever he & Oscar with Edward have been picking out Cotton—for about a week have done very little as yet—too much rain.

Thursday, September 4 Colo Stuart left yesterday morning for Meadville in my bros buggy & Mr Sessions horse—my dear little Edward was taken with fever on the 3rd is not well yet—James is I beleive quite well again—Oscar came in about 4 oclock said he had picked out 64 lb cotton staid in as he complained of headache

⟨remainder of the page⟩

Monday was taken with fever, my bror gone to Canton—

On the 14th Sunday my dear little Nannie was baptised for whom I stood with her uncle William & Aunt Mary God mother & Father—she behaved very well indeed—Mr Lewin preached a very good sermon—

⟨remainder of the page⟩

for we were *bereft indeed*—my dear cousin Lucretia was married on the 15 Septr 1835 & died 9th June 1851—She was married in the same room which my bror died in—

Monday, September 22 Went to town visiting & shopping to-day with A. G. S. & sister M.

Saturday, September 27 About nightfall I was taken with a violent chill—(the first I ever had) from which I am just recovering—I never suffered with my head as on this occasion—

Wednesday, October 8 My dear James' birth-day he is 13 yrs old to-day—May God protect & guard him from the snares & follies to which his volatile disposition may expose him—Thy grace alone O God can sustain him wilt thou in mercy grant it to him—

no news from my dear bros family or my dear aunt

Monday, October 13 My dear bror has been quite ill for some days is now I am thankful to say convalescent—James, Bettie & Edward all also a little sick—all better now—James staid at home to-day—Oscar went to school alone—he grieved me yesterday & last night—but promises amendment.

Friday, October 17 My sister Carolines birth day—she is 47 yrs old to-day— she has lived through much affliction. May God sustain her through her remaining days & grant her the comforts & consolations of His Holy Spirit—

I have been to Mr Sessions for several days—took Adelaide with me— had a very pleasant visit—

Monday, October 27 Saturday 25th was my little Adelaides birth-day—her kind aunt gave her a very pretty supper—& they amused themselves by dancing & their brothers delivered their speeches & they retired wearied with their own amusements—with the exception of little Edward who wished to sit up longer & cried to do so—but was prevailed upon to retire. None of the family attended Church yesterday—

Monday, November 3, and Tuesday, November 4 Election day Mr Sessions returned but have seen nothing of him since—James received a letter from his Pa a few days ago all well—Sister Caroline is making Betties linnen blue checked apron she has 5—

⟨*third of a page*⟩

Monday, November 10 ⟨*third of a page*⟩ heard of the arrival of Maj & Mrs Maney on Teusday last—from Tenn. My bror & sister Mary will leave home tomorrow to be gone a week—

Tuesday, November 11 Ma accompanied them this morning Teusday all alone just finished my letter to my bror D—now 10 oclock am going to make Adelaides sack or ⟨. . . .⟩ finished it

⟨*third of a page*⟩

hither they

⟨*third of a page*⟩

magnificent present of a Crape Shawl—very handsomely embroidered with deep pritting & fringe—presented by her sister-in-law Mrs Isaac Hilliard [22]—

Tuesday, November 25 Yesterday sister M. received a

⟨*third of a page*⟩

Sunday, December 7 Have not written for some time nothing has occurred however of much consequence all the children have coughs—fear it is hooping cough—sister Caroline has had a severe attack of Influenza now convalescing—Ma has also been ill with it. I have a cough myself—received a letter from my dear Sallie [23] the 6th inst from which I learn that she has been in bad health for two years but after a Summer residence on the Coast is quite restored—not however until cold weather set in.

Sunday, December 14 Sister Mary went to church accompanied by Mr T. Nicholson who came yesterday

⟨*third of a page*⟩

Wednesday, December 24 Our neighbour Mr Petrie[24] who has been ill for about 12 or 15 days—died on the 24th—in his proper senses & perfectly resigned—the little boys Charles & Henry[25] came over & spent a few days here—& went home with the expectation of seeing their Father improved in health but alas! he was a corpse!!—this has cast a gloom over the neighbourhood as he was a very estimable man—I never saw him myself but respected him for his kindness to James & Oscar—was buried to-day at 10 o clock Ma went over with Ann Sessions—sister M Having to go early— by request—My bror left on Monday evening for Yazoo to be gone an indefinite time—regret his absence very much—

1852

Sunday, February 8, 1852 Have not written for some time many things have occurred which I would like to have noted—but have been so much engaged I have not thought of it—My niece Sallie E. Hardeman arrived from Tenn. after spending some time in Memphis—with her uncle Washington Perkins[1] whom I shall ever respect for his kindness to her—Colo Polk[2] has made a visit of a few days & sister M's two brothers[3] have been here also sister M. accompanied the former to Grand Lake remained a fortnight my bror quite ill on his return from Grand Lake—at Vicksburg—My cousin Thomas Hardeman has also made us a visit of a few days—had our pork packed the day after he left about 8 or ten days of extremely cold weather— then came Colo Stuart in good health & agreeable all the time wore his clothes right all the time on the 2nd inst My dear niece Eudora[4] came from Texas in company with a Mr Powell & family—we were truly delighted to see her on the 7th inst Mr Sessions his wife & Sallie left for N.O. Colo Stuart made one of the party they expected to remain in Natchez a few days & return in a fortnight left little Narnie here until their return—all doing very well Sister M. Donna[5] my bror & the two boys went to Church—a Mr Ingraham was ordained to-day.[6]

Monday. February 9 Noon—The 3 younger children Adelaide Bettie & Edward have recommenced their lessons at home during an interval of 2 ½ months they have recited no lessons (i e) Adelaide has not Bettie has been more attentive Edward has not said regularly his lesson is now on the 23rd page of "Websters Elementary" Speller beginning with the 22 lesson—

Betties & Adelaides at the 109 p. the former spelling & reading only, the latter spelling reading—writing—Parleys 1st book of History & Defining

Sunday, February 15 My bror sister M. & Eudora gone to Church—James & Oscar to S.S. I fear too late—The dear children have done well during the past week—am truly thankful that I am spared the trial of recording any unpleasnt occurrence—

Monday, March 1 1 oclock Have commenced with the children on Rev: Mr Lewins plan—have heard their lessons for to-day—have been wounded by my niece Eudora—

Thursday, March 4 Spent yesterday at Mr Sessions Eudora remained—all well—& doing well. Wrote to Sally in Texas to-day.

Sunday, March 7 Yesterday was the anniversary of my 49th birth-day am now in my 50th year—O that the future may be more profitably spent than the past—& whether my days are many or few—Lord let them *all* be spent in thy service.

Monday, March 15 Colo Stuart returned last night. Oscar remained at home —not well enough to go to school—

Wednesday, March 24 Colo Stuart left for St Louis this morning on the Carrs—heard from him at Vicksburg going on well sent Randall out here his negro man—

Friday, March 26 All well. the children have had a long seige of hooping cough—the dear little one S.J.S. had the chicken pox very bad—I believe they are all taking it now.

Friday, April 9 Sister Mary went to Church no school until Teusday— Church today.

Sunday, April 11 To-morrow Easter Monday. Ma received a letter from A. G. S. to-day all well—

Thursday, April 15 Heard from Colo Stuart on the 25th March was forty years old that day heard again from Memphis on the 30th March had gone thence to get within the range of St Louis Boats we have all been made uneasy about him in consequence of the explosion of the S.B. "Glencoe" which took place on the 4th inst at the St Louis wharf & we have heard nothing from him since—12 days since the explosion—of which we have heard but few particulars—very few names given among those who were lost the Boat took fire & burned to the waters edge—very few of those found could be recognised—so horribly mutilated & mangled were they—

Received a letter from Aunt Corzine a few days ago (11th inst) was in tolerable health must answer it soon—

My bror received a letter from Colo Stuart which informed us of his safe arrival at St Louis on the 1st inst in good health—much pleased with his situation—

Thursday, April 22 Received a letter from Colo Stuart to-day—was anxious to hear from us—

Sunday, April 25 The second anniversary of my lamented sisters death—this day three years ago we were in the deepest trouble & affliction the weather brought vividly to my remembrance the death scene from the 15th to the 25th—am now writing to Colo Stuart at St Louis Mo.—

Monday, May 17 My bror in Yazoo sister Mary will leave for that place to-day—A.G.S. & Sallie were here yesterday did not go to church yesterday—am now tolerably well only several of the negroes sick Edward sick last night

Thursday, June 10 My dear A.G.S. & Sallie took leave of us last night will leave for Tenn. this morning not to return until Autumn it was sad to part—Sister M. gone to the Wells with a lady friend to return this evening—Mr G. W. H.[7] highly intoxicated correcting the servants &c. James spent the night before last with Mr Lewin—was not well enough to come home—I suffered great uneasiness on his account—fear he will not be able to stand the walk to school—

(May 27th Was the 35th anniversary of my lamented Fathers death—many & varied have been the scenes through which I have passed since

⟨third of a page⟩

been suffering immensely with biles for the last fort-night—one on my left foot is exceedingly painful—

On the 14th inst. we received the painful intelligence of Dr Visers death the husband of my dear niece Bethenia—who is well nigh heart broken— He died on the 24th the same day of the month on which my father died— I had thought of dear Bethenia a good deal on that day & prayed for her— as I had heard that she was not in good health but little did I think that the final blow was struck to her earthly happiness—dear child I humbly trust that her bereavements may be sanctified to her & that she may be sustained under all her trials by the Grace of God

⟨*third of a page*⟩

Sunday, July 4 Had some little difficulty with my niece Eudora on account of Adelaide which was however soon dropped—

O that God may help me for I feel as if I needed his assistance—The childrens lessons have been suspended for about ten days in consequence of having a house full of company—& the marriage of a relation (Mr Daniel Marr) to Miss Salina J. Eubank[8] which took place on Thursday the 24th June—Mrs Pugh the Dr & two of their children Mr & Mrs Curry (her sister) from N.O. spent a week here—Eudora Received a letter from Texas yesterday informing us of dear Tenies continued bad health. How sincerely do I sympathize with her. Shall make an effort to write to my dear Aunt to-day.

Sunday, July 18 Went to (Episcopal) Church with all the children except Edward to see My niece E.C.H. baptized. Heard an excellent sermon from Mr Lewin. Except your righteousness of the scribes &c.[9]

Monday, July 26 Cousin Thomas M. arrived here this evening with his two boys Lent & Nash his daughter Cornelia has been here some weeks she is very amiable—he speaks of taking her to Salem—the Convention closed last night—with Missionary sermon from Mr Lewin said to be an interesting occasion.

Wednesday, July 28 Cousin Thomas left to-day with our dear Cornelia for whom we had all formed a sincere attachment—& regretted the necessity for her leaving to enter school undetermined what one she would join—or enter for a term—perhaps 4 years—they are interesting children—O that they may be preserved from the snares and temptations incident to their youth & orphanage—into the care of Him who has promised to protect them would I commend them—

Thursday, July 29 My bror & sister M his wife went to Coopers Well—remained until Sunday my bror returned to the Wells from thence to Raymond on Monday—difficulty with the negroes told my bror about it last night Aug 4th.

Thursday, August 5 Came to the school room—to hear the childrens lessons—noon have heard none yet.

2 oclock All recited good lessons in a good humour & wrote work for the evening & walk.

Saturday, August 7 Saturday have written but two letters last week—took medicine last night Jenny the nurse & Eliza both sick—children all well except Sarah Jane & she is up—

Sunday, August 8 Sister M. did not go to Church Eudora Florence Pugh & Adelaide went with their Uncle Wm—servants not much better the children all up—have not felt well myself.

Thursday, August 12 No school yesterday all well except the servants Jenny, Green, Angeline & Hester. sister M. & Donna gone visiting to-day. James wrote a disagreeable letter to his father yesterday but has not sent it yet—no letters yet from our friends—

Sunday, August 15 No one went to Church except the two boys James & Oscar James brought home a sermon from Bhp Green—text "The sin which doth so easily beset us"[10] I read it with great pleasure

Maj Bowman & family came on Wednesday 11th to spend a month—My Bror went to the "Wells" this morning 15th to take Florence Pugh the Dr & family have been very kind to offer me a room in their cottage. I feel greatly obliged to them—but could not accept.

"Remarks by which persons in all ranks of life may be benefited.

GOOD TEMPER, or a constant willingness to serve & please those with whom we are connected; to bear with failings, & pass over injuries; to receive reproof with meekness and submit to circumstances with serenity and cheerfulness.

INDUSTRY—an idle person is a contemptible being wherever he may be found.

REGULARITY—for without this, a vast deal of activity may be spent to no good purpose: things might almost as well be left undone, as not to be done at the right time.

FORECAST or GOOD MANAGEMENT: for without this a constant habit of looking forward, to consider *what* will be wanted—& *when*—we shall be liable to a continual return of wants; which we are not prepared to meet." S.S. book called the "Premium"[11]

⟨*nine pages*⟩

When thus reviled or persecuted we are to be meek, patient, humble; not angry; not reviling again; but endeavouring to do good to our persecutors & slanderers (2nd Tim. II 24 25):[12] . . . . Long since, it became a proverb that the "blood of the martyrs is the seed of the Church"[13]

1853

⟨*nine pages*⟩

Tuesday, July 26, 1853 A M.

I will endeavour to note down from memory some of the most trying scenes through which we have passed for the last few months

On the 30th of April 1853 James took sick with Diarhea on Friday night— on Saturday—he went in the field some distance from the house to plant his water melons—had fever that night—continued to grow worse—& after using every domestic remedy—sent on Teusday for Dr Green[1] (Dr Langley[2] being absent at his plantation on the River) his case was then a critical one—The balance of the children never were in better health—Our dear little Sarah Jane particularly—was in excellent health. But alas!!! the destroyer was making ready & on Saturday May 7th evening about 7 oclock— she was attacked with the same horrid disease—but we apprehended no danger—until Wednesday—when alarming symptoms—appeared on the evening of this day about night fall my dear niece Sallie E. Hardeman with Mr Sessions arrived from Yazoo—leaving my dear nieces Ann & Nannie there—Sallie nursed with untiring care & sat up every night the dear little darling was so "glad to see her cousin Sallie"—whose kind & unremitting attentions I *never never* can forget—she was the dearest idol of my heart—& though I must say "Thy will be done" what agonies it has cost my dear sister & self to do so—indeed all the household—being tenderly attached to her Uncle Wm whom she called "Pa" & also her Aunt Mary—she would say "I love you Aunt Mary"—she grew worse on Wed. night—On Fri. late in the evening she grew worse but her countenance became radiant with smiles & looked heavenly—she said "O how bright—what looks so bright"—I

never saw a child bear pain with more patience—she observed to her bror
James who was present "brother James I know what God made me sick for
to learn me patience"—Some months previous to her illness she awoke in
the night & asked me if I would let her call me Ma saying "my own Ma is
in Heaven—will you let me call you Ma?" I told her yes—she never called
me by any other name—after that. O never while memory retains a place
in my poor heart can my sister & I forget the incidents of that *Night* of
Sorrow! May God have mercy upon me & sanctify his great bereavement to
the good of my soul—On one occasion I was talking to her about visiting
her mothers grave—& told her if she was a good girl God would let the
Angels watch over her—immediately on awaking she called me & said "now
brother James will get the buggy & we will go & see Ma's grave—she died
& gave me to you." I proposed to her to say her prayers—she would not
let me repeat them for her as usual but said "let me say them myself" she
then repeated them correctly & with an Angelic expression of countenance
added "Now God will let the Angels watch over me." During her illness
was asked by her cousin Sallie who she wanted to have her watch—(her
mothers which was intended for her)—she replied with emphasis—"My
Ma"—she called for "Pa Stuart" & her "Pa Hardeman"—said they should
have Ice.

I visited with my dear Niece & her family my native state of Tennessee
the ensuing Autumn to witness the nuptials of my dear Sallie to Mr Charles
De France[3]—but my health was so much impaired that I could not enjoy
the visit—[4]

My little darling lingered from 7 oclock on Sat 7th until Sat 14th just as
the Sun left the horizon she "entered through the gates into the city"—
having been a sojourner here 4 years 4 months & 14 days. God in mercy
no doubt took her from the evil to come & I have tried to acquiesce—I
feel that I shall not be detained here long—O that she may be the *first* to
welcome me—if I shall ever reach that abode of rest.

Monday, August 1 James & Oscars vacation commenced this morning, Mrs
Bowman sister Caroline & I have concluded to employ James as a teacher
during his vacation—He will have Oscar, Adelaide, Bettie, Edward, Willie,
& Josey Bowman—Oscar & Adelaice at the rate of 1.50 pr month the
balance at 1$ he has been teaching about 10 days & has succeeded so far
very well—

Sunday, August 7 Communion day. A.G.S. came over & went to church to-
day Eudora has been staying there for several days returned this morning.
She received letters from home last night the 6th & I received one from

dear Bethenia & one to sister C. & myself from little *Ellen*—Eudora's was from her sisters Eveline[5] & Sally—all were well & we were rejoiced to hear from them they were the first letters received since the death of my little Jane—& comforted me a great deal—

Monday, August 8 James commenced school & did tolerably well—all got along very well.

Tuesday, August 9 The children did not attend school on account of having some little friends visit them—(viz) Charlie & Henry Petrie. they spent the day in mirth & Jollity.

Wednesday, August 10 Eudoras birth-day—17 yrs old to-day—at home— some little difficulty with Edward & Bettie. O that their little hearts may be inclined to that which is right—have progressed with my work tolerably well—

Thursday, August 11 Children all recited good lessons except Edward who had to stay in—sister C still over at Mr Sessions since Sunday evening— all well—

Friday, August 12 All did tolerably well at school—dress not done yet—am still working on it. Sister C not come home yet—sister Mary mentioned for the first time my going to Tenn: wishes me to go.

Saturday, August 13 Children—(viz) James—Willie—Edward—& Josey— spent the day at Mr Sessions—Adelaide & Bettie did only tolerably well— Adelaide gave a journal at night—Oscar spent the day at Mrs Petries behaved well I hope as he came home with his clothes properly adjusted—& clean.

Sunday, August 14 All gone to church to-day except myself & sister who is over at Mr Sessions'—This day three months ago my little darling was taken from us—the severest blow I have felt since my dear brors death & my dear Nicholas'—Had some little difficulty with Eudora about the children—spoke to my bror about it—all passed off however without any serious effects—I hope—Ann S. came over & I may go over home with her to return with sister C.

Monday, August 15 James & Oscar went up to Tivoli to bring Mr Bowmans carriage horses down of course no school to-day—the children are delighted—Adelaide & Bettie have worked some—expect to go to town in the morning.

Tuesday, August 16 Went to town but as the horse took sick had to send to Mr Sessions & borrow Anns horses & driver & took sister M's old carriage—

Wednesday, August 17 James & Oscar returned about 12 oclock—after perpetrating a piece of mischief—tying the horses tails together but did not tell of it until there were enquired of about it—I was called into sister Marys room & told of it—but it was 11 oclock before I said any thing to them about it—I talked to them about it & they both promised to try & be more independant & fill their responsibilites.

Thursday, August 18 Sister Mary Ma Eudora & Willie & Josey went over to Mr Sessions to spend the day—the A M. in visiting—along the road—the last place to Colo Napiers—I received a letter from My dear Sallie 17th. Which I sent to A.G.S. to read—have not seen it yet—

Wednesday was a day of severe trial to me the children did not do well Adelaide & Bettie behaved *very badly*.

Friday, August 19 They had school this morning & did very well—all quiet now—

James & Oscar saw Mrs Bowman & told her about it last night she excused it had some words with sister Mary about it she said that she thought James ought to have been put in the Penitentiary one week for it & I told her I did not think so—whereupon we had a general reckoning & all so far as I am concerned is right again—My dear bror & sister are two excellent people—may God reward them for all their kindness to us—Adelaide received a letter from her father last night—

Sunday, August 21 All well the family gone to church—

Sunday, August 28 Sunday. No one went to church last Sunday went home with My dear niece A.G.S. & remained until Wednesday late in the evening she sent me home. on Thursday we went to town & I went with her to see Mr Kausler & Mrs L. Hommedue[6] went to Mrs Pomroys[7]—& shopping purchased a travelling dress in anticipation of a journey to Tenn. I suppose it will be for the best—& I have determined to go if my health will admit of it—though it will be a very hard trial.

On 26 August we received intelligence of the death of Mrs Isaac Hilliard

—which took place on the 21st. she was an admirable woman combining in her character the most rare & valuable characteristics of her sex—We were very much attached to her—& most sincerely lament her death (which we hope was peaceful)—& sympathize with her bereaved husband—

Have been engaged during the week in making preparations for a trip to Tenn.—expect to leave on the 6th inst though I feel a great reluctance to go on account of dear sister Caroline who

⟨*most of a page*⟩

Saturday, November 26 Left on the 8th Sepr for Tenn. & arrived without serious accident—found all well well except Mr Figuers who is very low with consumption—had no health most of the time—was confined to the bed at my aunts nearly 3 weeks—My dear Sallie was married on the 25th Oct 1853 at 9 oclock in the morning—we left for home in ½ half an hour after & arrived on the 8th Nov: found all well—& glad to see us—& we were equally so to see them—was thankful to see them all looking so well—

Eudora & the two little girls sister Caroline over at Mr Sessions to stay during Mr S. absence to Yazoo—sister Mary indisposed but better than

⟨*most of a page*⟩

Sunday, December 18 The 9th Anniversary of my dear Nicholas' death—have been in Mi. 5 years & have never seen his grave but he is *not forgotten*—

The family went to Church this morning

Monday, December 26 Sister Mary bror William & Mrs Bowman left us for Tenn. cold damp weather all well except little Sue Fannys little girl who is ill from Pneumonia—Dr Cabiness[8] has been out twice—

Mr Sessions & family came over & are here yet—children all well but—are crazy with excitement—James is teaching this week for 1$.

Saturday, December 31 Received a Dispatch last night from Memphis all well—bror not returned little Sue improving Mr S. left yesterday for Yazoo—Anna is quite sick with sun pain

⟨*three quarters of a page*⟩

1854

Sunday, January 1, 1854 My dear bror returned last night—had a cold—Eudora & Adelaide went to Church—killed the pork

Tuesday, January 3 All the family well—Mr Bass[1] a very clever gentleman has staid here several nights—left this morning on the carrs—made out very well—

Wednesday, January 11, or Thursday, January 12 All well except William who has symptoms of Pneumonia—some difficulty with Jinnys carelessness about the childrens clothes—On Monday cousin G. W. Ferkins—his daughter Miss Mary Ford—& Mr Crawford were announced from Memphis—Mr P. came out early Mon & A.S. & I went in & the ladies came out—the gentlemen dined here on Teus. Mr S. & family here things going on tolerable only—bad weather (Teus 11th) unfortunately Nelson killed 6 wild hogs was almost compelled to do so—hope it will be saved—They could

⟨*three quarters of a page*⟩

Sunday, January 15 The 5th Anniversary of my little Janes birth she wanted one day to complete her four & half years—when she took her flight to Heaven—& left me *a mourner the balance of my life.*

My dear bror returned from Deer Creek whither he had gone to undertake the business of settling up Mr Hills Estate—or the Agency of it &c.[2] On Saturday evening in good health Monday he settled up a/c all day—his own, Colo Stuarts, & ours—

Tuesday, January 17 Mr Sessions & family left for Natchez this morning—very bad weather yesterday was very warm—to-day it is cool again—

Received a letter from Mr De France—all well except Mr F. it was very gratifying to hear from him & the more so as it informed me of the slight prospect of our dear Willies coming down. Received a letter from my dear Sallie last week.

Wednesday, February 1–Monday, February 6 1st week in Feb. Mr Figuers[3] & Willie had gone to Florida via Savannah Ga. They have settled in Lake Providence will board with Mr De France's brother.

Mr Sessions & family returned on Thursday 2nd Feb. bringing with them Judge Dubuissons little boy 2 yrs old an interesting little creature spent the day here on Friday—Mr John Hilliard[4] came here on Monday Jan 28th was quite sick during his stay with us—left on Teusday Feb 6th—Received a box of drugs from Dr C. A Cutler same day—am using it now—Oscar is studying his lessons more industriously than formerly—Edward said one lesson to-day.

Wednesday, February 22 Morning my dear bror left for N.O. having received a dispatch the evening before from Mr I. Hilliard does not know how long he will be gone. We (A.G.S. & I) went the same day at 4 oclock to bring Mrs Judge Lambkin[5] out—she & her little daughter came out & spent the night—she returned next morning & left Fanny—A.G.S. Eudora & I went in with Mrs L. & left her at the tavern—& went shopping—I got a silk & calico dress for myself—Eudora gave me the calico one—

Friday, February 24 All well—rain.

Wednesdcy, March 1 Received a letter from Colo Stuart & one from sister Mary from Franklin—Edward went in sight seeing—was highly pleased—commenced school & am pleased to say I have had no trouble so far—The children seem to be very much pleased—

Friday, March 3 Had some trouble to-day James & Oscar would not go to school (rain).

Sunday, March 5 My dear bro returned last night from N.O. whither he had gone to meet Mr I. H. Hilliard & Colo G. W. Polk & some other gentlemen on business—was quite well during his absence no one here—Eudora Adelaide & Edward went to Church—Communion day.

Monday, March 6 My birth day am writing to Colo Stuart—send the boys reports by this morning mail—I am 51 yrs old to-day. O that I may improve the few remaining days I may have allotted me on earth—have heard of the death of Uncle Tom Jones Hardeman[6] which took place on the 11th Jan. I regret his loss very much—but am gratified to hear that he died in hope of a glorious immortality—An organ grinder came to the door this morning—took 15 cts of market money—10 cts to Eudora—25 for eggs at the quarter.

Wednesdcy, March 8 Had school to-day—very agreeable—except Adelaide who did not get her Geography lesson—had to stay in—

Monday, March 13 No one went to Church yesterday. no school to-day—had to cut out—Julia sick shall have trouble with the keys—Isbel brought 8$ home on Saturday night 11th inst.

Tuesday, March 14 Heard the childrens lessons—all good—

Wednesday, March 15 Mr Sessions & family came over & spent the night & left on the carrs this morning for Yazoo to spend two months—we shall miss them a great deal particularly dear little Nannie who clasped me round the neck so fondly—

Thursday, March 16 Eudora went to town to the Dentist Dr Lemman[7]—went to the book store & the tinner shop—bought a slop tub & water bucket—for this room took 2$ for sister Caroline (to get a chair for her) & bror Wm gave me another which I wish to put with the two my little darling left—as a contribution to the purchase of a tombstone—

Monday, March 27 The scarlet fever has made its appearance in the College. Oscar has come home with fever this evening—heard to-night that dear sister Mary was on her way home—my dear bror who is really joyful went on the carrs to Vicksburg this morning to meet her & they will probably be here this evening—at 5 oclock—gave Porter 50 cts for seed & Arch 60 cts for butter—Porter returned 20 cts Fanny has two dresses round for the women apiece except Sabra Rose & Margaret & they have one.

Wednesday, March 29 My dear bror & sister returned this evening about 5 oclock—after an absence of three months & 3 days—we were all truly delighted to see her once more—was quite well during her absence & left all friends well—Oscar has had quite a serious attack of scarlet Fever—hope he is now better & will soon be well again—

Saturday, April 1 Edward was taken with Fever—Adelaide & Bettie are also unwell with cold—will soon have fever—the Dr has seen Edward to-day for the first time—

Sunday, April 9 I am happy to record the recovery of the 4 youngest children from scarlet fever Edward was very ill—for 3 days—Oscars was also a very bad case—also Adelaides. Bettie had it lighter than any of the others—James has been very prudent & has in consequence escaped—Eudora has been with us 2 years—will leave us soon for Texas—

Friday, April 14 Good Friday—Mr Nicholson & our dear Donna left us this morning for Texas. I wrote to her Father by Mail. Sister Mary has just received a letter from her sister informing her of the re-interment of her sister-in-law Mrs Miriam B. Hilliard & her two children[8] in the burying ground attached to St Johns Church Ashwood Maury Cty. Tenn. her Father Mr Brannin her husband & Colo G. W. Polk superintended it March 29th (I believe).

Sister Mary who is still really ill with sore throat—got out of bed & wrote to her sister—but received one from her before hers was sent to the P.O.—Poor Donna we miss her so much.

Sunday, April 16 Easter Sunday Mr Lewins last day—expects to go to Florida—The children are expecting to have some Easter Eggs to-morrow morning hope they will succeed—

Monday, April 17 Sister C & myself made a good many experiments—succeeded tolerably—the dear children were pleased & amused—Sister Mary still quite ill—with inflamed tonsil—which suppurated & was lanced—several sick at the quarter—children improving—do not feel well myself—sister Caroline keeps up astonishingly—waits on all the sick—

Wednesday, April 19 Took to my bed—am sure I never felt so exhausted & fatigued before—

Saturday, April 22 Am somewhat improved—on Thursday last cousin Thos M. came with his son Nash—remained until to-day reproved the dear boy for his mothers sake he used his Makers name in vain told his Father—hope he will not do so any more.

Wednesday, April 26 Yesterday all the children & myself & bror wrote to Colo Stuart it being the fifth anniversary of my dear sister Janes death—her dear children have had scarlet fever not yet recovered—they with ourselves feel her loss *deeply* very *deeply*—this time last year our little Darling was with us a bright beautiful child *altogether lovely*—But she is now in the society of her Angelic mother—& the heavenly host—O that we may have resignation.

Sunday, May 7 This day one year ago our little darling was taken sick unto death—We apprehended no danger until Thursday 12th she grew worse until Saturday when she breathed her last as the sun disappeared from the horizon but I am comforted in the reflection that "*God took her*" her remains now rest beside those of her beloved mother in the public burying ground near the City of Jackson Mss. Peace to thy precious remains my little Angel—O that thy Spirit may be permitted to watch over the helpless ones thou hast left in a world of care—

Received last night a paper from my dear Sallie De France—

Monday, May 8 My dear brors birthday he is 53 yrs old to-day—his head silvered over & is in the sear & yellow leaf[9]—May God give him a new heart—he has already the most admirable traits of character that ever was enshrined—My daily prayer is that he may be the subject of converting grace—

I should have noted first in order the birthday of my dear bror D which was the 4 of May—he is 48 yrs old & very stout—but I fear without the knowledge of God in the pardon of his sins—My daily prayer is for him also—O that he be induced to think of his condition—& the relation he sustains to his Maker—& be made a recipient of his grace—

O how vividly are the scenes of the last May brought to my poor heart & fear that I am not yet resigned—that I am not yet sufficiently chastened—May God sanctify this sore dispensation of his providence to me.

Sunday, May 14 A beautiful day—just such an one as we had at this time last year—but at this hour 4 oclock—what agonies!! what throes were not mine! Our darling Sarah Jane was suffering the agonies of death! & closed her eyes upon this sinful world just as the sun left the Horizon—she often admired the appearance of the Horizon at sun set & would call our attention to it—Rest—Rest—my little darling until the resurrection morn when I hope to hail thee with thy angel Mother.

Monday, May 15 Monday morning At this hour one year ago the remains of my precious little Sarah Jane were here & I could see her Angelic face lovely even in death—What a struggle to give her up—she died as the sun went down & was consigned to the tomb just as that glorious orb (in all the brilliancy & beauty of a May day) disappeared from the horizon—

The tear has not ceased to flow—the heart to ache—for thy loss my little darling one but God gave thee & he can take thee to himself—I know that in wisdom he has done it all—O that I could feel more resigned—

Wednesday, May 17 Dear sister Caroline quite ill with dropsical affection—Dr Green came out to see her yesterday put a blister on the back of her neck to-day Julias children worse—poor little Phillis neither better or worse—Adelaide Bettie & Edward all have colds—

Sunday, May 21–June Sister Caroline improved but still quite ill—Julias children a little better—Phillis not improving—All went to church to-day except James & Oscar—James received a letter from his Pa last night which he did not shew me—

My dear sister continued ill & grew worse—did not rest well at night & suffered a great deal with an affection of the heart—though we did not apprehend any immediate danger as she went to the table & would not make herself an invalid. Sunday night was the last time she ever sat at the table—My bror took the stage for Canton—she followed him to take an affectionate leave of him seemed quite ill—but never did I witness such an example of patience in my life—she was indeed an *uncomplaining sufferer*— she complained mostly of her right ear—& her left side—on Wednesday night she grew worse—& about 3 oclock was taken with congestion of the heart & lungs—& about 5 oclock on Thursday June 1st she breathed her last as calmly as an infant—& was taken by "Angels to the bosom of Abraham." [10]

My precious sister thou wert all of earth to me—the world seems sad without thee—My poor heart is stricken indeed—it is a trial for which I invoke the aid of my heavenly Father to bear—At the Resurrection morn I hope to hail thee my precious darling sister—with our little darling who rests by thy side & that of her precious mother—

Wednesday, June 28 Sister M. went to town purchased 1 calico 2 white spreads 1 pr long mits for Bettie & a tooth brush for Bettie & Edward—Colo Stuart presented me with a basket—at 2.$ a present I prize very highly—

Friday, June 29 This day 4 weeks ago My dear sister Caroline was suffering from congestion of heart & lungs—but I could not think she would die! she seemed to have so few of the usual symptoms of death about her— she suffered a great deal—& bore it with *unexampled patience* & christian fortitude & breathed her last as quietly as an infants slumber about 5 oclock on Thursday June 1st 1854—I cannot realize that she is gone—& often find myself almost talking to her—I depended so much upon her for every thing.

Sunday, July 9 A beautiful day—none of the children went to Church except Oscar—cousin Mary Helen Marr (daughter of John Marr—) [11] who has been at the "Wells" for some time & came out to make us a visit—a very agreeable young lady—has been staying at Gen McMackins [12] in town— remained there to-day—Colo Stuart came here on Monday morning 12th June—bringing Ned with him—from Port Gibson. made quite an agreeable visit of 10 days left on Thursday 22 for Holmesville his present place of residence—taking Ned with him to hire out there, we have heard nothing of him since but hope to receive letters soon—

My dear niece A.G.S. did not arrive here from Yazoo until the day after my dear sister was buried—she & Mr S. were very much affected—

Dear Sallie did not get here until the 10th the following Saturday she & Mr De F were also much affected—poor Sallie is now sick & will not be well soon I fear. This day six weeks ago my ever lamented sister sat at table with us—& every day I feel her loss more keenly—I have been trying to arrange our papers—letters etc—& put my house in order for I know not what a day may bring forth.

Sunday, July 16 The anniversary of my sister Sarah Janes birth—she would have been 38 yrs old if she had lived but alas—she rests in peace by the side of her little Sarah Jane (nearly 4 yrs old) & my dear sister Caroline— On Friday 14th My dear Oscar had the misfortune to break his leg. about 4 oclock Drs Green & Craft[13] were called in & succeeded in setting it—both bones were broken just above the ankle—he bore it very well indeed did not complain until after it was bandaged—had a very bad night indeed—& did not rest well until the night of the 16th the Drs came out & dressed it this morning said it was doing very well—he is very cheerful whistles sings & plays on the Jews harp—my dear Sallie & Ann came over on Saturday morning—with Nannie. Mr S. spoke of going to Yazoo this morning—but do not know whether he did or not—as I have not heard from them—my dear bror has nursed Oscar himself & staid with him three or four nights he got along very well indeed—suffering very little pain—except at intervals—it has been 12 days since it occurred—to-day 25 he hurt it in some way or other & it bled profusely—about 11 oclock A.M. the Drs came out & dressed it thought the bleeding unfavourable he is more restless than usual to-night—Mr Sessions & family went to Yazoo on Teusday morning—have not heard from them since they left—Received a letter from Colo Stuart to-night seems greatly distressed at Oscars misfortune—Sallie is improving under the care of Dr Cabiness—

Sunday, July 30 My dear Ann & family returned accompanied by Mrs White —who came over next day & the day following went to the Wells with Mr Sessions who left her quite indisposed—Sallie went home (to Mr Sessions) on Teusday 2nd August & she & her sister better—

Wednesday, August 2 Oscars leg was put in a new box which Dr Craft had made for it & packed in wheat bran—which has answered an excellent purpose—so far they came out & dressed it again this evening the ulcer is doing very well seems to be healing—received a letter from Colo Stuart on Monday night 31st July on Sunday 30th Dr Manday dressed Oscars leg—James commenced school on Tuesday 1st Augst. has succeeded very well so far they occupy Oscars room—

Friday, August 4 James cut his ankle with a hatchet—had been trimming trees—spent the day at Mrs Sessions with bror Wm cousins Eliza McKissack & Mary Marr [14]—

Saturday, August 5 To-day 5th Sat. am laid up again with swelling of the hip & leg. Oscar doing very well.

Sunday, August 6 Monday July 31st Julias babe was born named Nelson—doing very well—Celias Sunday 6th Augst.

Monday, August 7 Am still confined & no better, Dr Cabiness was called in yesterday—am using tepid baths only—as yet—Oscar has been very careless with his leg—though it is doing very well—

James has bought with his own money without my knowledge several lbs of ice for which I feel deeply grateful to the dear boy.

Tuesday, August 29 Oscars leg sufficiently improved to have crutches this morning—he was perfectly delighted & came in to see me we took a kiss—he is going to write to his Pa. James has taken one lesson in dancing—commenced on Saturday 26th.

Sunday, September 3, or Monday, September 4 Cousin C Perkins & his wife came here last night—came to my room to see me. to-morrow will be 4 weeks since I have been confined to my bed—I am truly thankfull to my Heavenly Father that I have been able to dress & sit up to-day—a part of the day.

Friday, September 15 (Anniversary of my bror T's death) Went to Mr Sessions with the little girls in Mr Whites carriage to see Mrs Maury & Sallie. had another attack—I have had 5 weeks of severe suffering & am still suffering a good deal—

Thursday, October 5 James went to College this morning—A severe trial to me May Angels guard him & I have engaged Oscars services as teacher at 50 cts pr week—for Edward & Bettie Adelaide not well enough—she has been quite indisposed for some time—Dr Craft & Dr Cabiness consulted I suppose—on her case—

Sunday, October 15 My dear Adelaide still indisposed—I fear very much she has an absess formed internally—Bishop Green preached at the Asylum this afternoon at 4 oclock—no one went but sister Mary & James—Yellow Fever abating in Jackson—Mr Sessions & family going to Yazoo in the morning 16th Sallie too ill to be brought over—am better to-day than I have been for some time—& have commenced *answering* letters & writing to my bror D who never writes to any of us. have not spent the day as I wished.

Sunday, October 22 Fever increasing in town—no church to-day—had trouble with the children this morning—while reading & hearing their S.S. lesson Was engaged all last week about the counterpanes & sheets—&c. my bror received sewing machine on the 18th (I beleive) but does not know from whence it came.

Wednesday, October 25 A bright beautiful day just such an one as we had one year ago—this is the Ninth anniversary of my dear Adelaides birth & of my dear Sallies wedding both are invalids now—God grant them a speedy restoration to health & a long & happy life—

Sunday, October 29 No service at the Asylum my bror gone from home—rather a cloudy day children behaved well to-day for which I feel thankful—A visit from cousins Martha & Nannie Lewis.[15]

Sunday, November 5 No service at the Asylum cousin Martha made a visit to a friend up in Madison returned on Saturday evening—did not spend the day profitably—children said no S.S. lesson—made 2 dresses for the little girls sewed all the seams on the machine—

Monday, November 6 Have done nothing to-day—received a letter from Colo Stuart 5th Inst & one from Lent Hardeman who is now at Spring Hill Tenn.—

Monday, November 13 A fortnight since we had a visit from cousins Martha & Nannie Lewis from La. & Mr Sage their cousin[16]—remained with us about a week—left on Teusday last for their home in Opelousa La. their visit was a great gratification to me—have been able to make a dress for myself with the aid of the machine & 3 for the girls—A & B.

Monday, November 20 My dear Adelaide has had another attack—was taken violently on Thursday night—but is now able to get out of the bed & is dressing—Mr Sessions & family Mr De France & Sallie Dr Cabiness dined with us yesterday—*sister Mary received a letter from Colo Stuart Sat night.* Have just got my work arranged & have 60 garments to make besides some little extra sewing—am going to cut out the boys pants to-day. succeeded in cutting the patterns of pants & also the pants—feel very much fatigued.

November 1854–January 1855 On Thursday 24th (I beleive) P.M. We were blessed with a visit from our dear Tenie & Eudora came in unexpectedly— What a balm to my poor heart to embrace my darling Tenie after an absence of nearly 7 yrs—we have both drank deeply of the cup of sorrow & afflic- tion—the same evening my dear Aunt Betsey came & the next morning my dear Sister Sally with her bror & my dear bror D. Aunt B. brought with two nephews James Sneed[17] & James Dotson[18]—the latter has had a violent attack of Pneumonia & is still very ill—My bror his wife & Eudora left for Texas on the 6 Dec 1854—Our dear Tenie remained with us until Spring— Our dearest Willie D[19] came on the same day with Sister Sally—it was too much joy—all at once—

1855

January 1855 Jan 1st 1855 My dear bror went away from home—the children commenced their lessons to-day all did very well—

15th of January was the Anniversary of my little Darlings birth—she would have been 6 yrs old—but she was taken to a brighter world on the 14th of May 1853. She rests beside her dear mother & her devoted aunt Caroline—who was every thing to me—life is a blank without her.

14th Jan. was my dear Mothers birth-day she was 79 yrs old 1855—being born 14th Jan. 1776. My dear Niece Sallie De France introduced a beautiful little daughter on Sat the 13th Jan. 1855. whom they gave me the honour & privilege of naming. accordingly I named her "Annie Howard" for Mr De F's mother & Mrs Sessions her sister—Blessings on the little precious treasure—May God watch over her for good & shield her from the snares incident to youth & childhood—May her Mother be enabled to train her up in the "nurture & admonition of the Lord" I expect to stand Sponser with her Aunt Sessions—at the request of her parents.

Sunday, February 11 Last evening Mrs Polk & family *entire*[1]—arrived late yesterday evening—also Messrs Isaac & George Hilliard—Mrs Lineau with dear Lavenia[2]—Mr I. H's two little boy servants for each family etc etc— Mrs Polks children all doing well & looking finely regret Colo Polks slight indisposition.

dear Mrs Lineau seems near the borders of the grave—

February–March On Thursday 15th[3] The children got into a difficulty Edward & Georgy Polk James & Rufus came in contact—Sister Mary took offence—did not enquire into the matter—but threw the entire blame upon James—who did exactly right as I thought at the time, found afterwards that he was somewhat to blame. Colo Polk did not enquire about it but took Rufus & James with him to N.O. James will have to be boarded out as a natural consequence—I regret the circumstance exceedingly—Monday 12th March.

Sister Mary wrote to Colo Stuart about it that night—& moreover requested him to "take James & Oscar away & place them were they *would* be *managed*—as *I* could not do it & my bror hadn't time." James remained until Friday March 2nd—when he was sent to the College to stay—Oscar having been sent there on account of his leg. on the 12 Feb. Sister M. insisting for James to stay with us at her house—until the difficulty with her nephew—I did not mention it in my letter to their Father & did not know until the answer to Sister Marys letter came—that it was made a serious matter of—otherwise James should not have remained so long—I knew it was disagreeable to sister Mary for him to remain but I could not have a conversation with my bror—I have thought too that it would give rise to a good deal of idle gossip—I look a little ill-natured in me—my bror however gave his consent for James to go on the 2nd—On Friday 10th March Colo Polk & family with sister Mary left for Grand Lake—Mr Hilliard Mrs Leineau with Lavenia his daughter & his two little boys Isaac Henry—& Edwin Somers—having left the preceding Wednesday 28 Feb: Colo Polk & family intending to remain some time at Grand Lake from thence to Tennessee—My dear bror returned from N.O. Sat 10th inst—& left in the Stage for Canton Sunday P.M. returned on Monday 12th. all well James came over remained all day Oscar could not come—having hurt his knee a little though he went to church—Oscars reports for the 3 last months are better than James'.

Thursday, March 15 My dear bror not well—went to Vicksburg this morning or expected to go when he left—laid off the childrens gardens yesterday—A & B. Edward had his seed planted in beds. Our dear Willie D has remained with us during the absence of my brother—who left for Grand Lake on Teusday 20th heard from him at Vickbg—They may be at home some time this week—perhaps to-morrow a beautiful day but no one went to church—all well—children doing tolerably well—

Monday, March 26 Commenced school—did very well—Mr & Mrs Thomas Jones[4] came down after my dear Tenie—but as sister M. is not at home she did not go.

Monday, April 2 All well—wrote to sister Bethenia[5] yesterday & to-day will finish & send to the office soon. James & Oscar came home Friday evening & remained until this morning.

Willie D (left for Tenn) went to Vicksburg this morning

Tuesday, April 10 Adelaide took sick last night about 2 oclock—was in great pain with her old complaint.

Thursday, April 12 Adelaide improving—Mrs Murfree & family[6] came last night from Mr Galloways on the M. River—On the 31st March my cousin Nash Hardeman was caught in a mill & dredfully injured—is not expected to live—dear little fellow he will miss his dear mother how much he will!

Sunday, April 15 Sister M. & Tenie went to Church—Adelaide is going about & Bettie had a cold—Oscar went to Church James did not—had to settle a difficulty between Edward & his sisters.

James & Oscar came home Friday P.M. had to chide Oscar & James on Edwards account.

Friday, April 20 My dear boys came home again. have been confined to my bed for 3 days since Teusday 17th last—Mr Sessions & family returned from Yazoo last night came over to-day—all well babie grown a good deal— heard the particulars of Mr Cages death.

Teusday 19 April 1855. had an attack of Dysentary & my old complaint Boils—

Saturday, April 21 My bror got his foot hurt.

Thursday, May 3 Our dear Tenie left us with aching hearts for her home in Texas—May God reward her for all the kindness she has shewn to me & mine—feel greatly depressed in spirits—

Sunday, May 6 The children went to Church with the exception of Edward— My bror stood God Father to Mr Wirt Adams little daughter "Annie Wissacher"[7]—

Monday, May 7–Thursday, May 10 Sat up all day cut out Edwards clothes— Mon & Teus. righted up bureau drawers.

Wed. was our dear little Betties birth day she was 10 yrs old her Aunt Mary gave her a pr of buses—& her uncle Wm a pr of ear rings—Was quite sick all day yesterday—am better to day 10th.

Sunday, May 13 No one went to Church to-day rained a little still cloudy.

Monday, May 14 Took Breakfast with the family this morning—to-morrow will be the 2nd anniversary of my little darlings death—Mistaken in the day of the month—Monday was the 14th—wrote to Colo Stuart—O how vividly were the incidents of that sad week set in array before me—her expressions—her sufferings & patience—O *how much*—*how much* of bitterness was crowded in that *one week*—I fear that I am not resigned even yet—Truly am I now shorn of every idol.

Saturday, May 19 Mr Bass came—Mrs Skipwith & her daughters[8] & niece spent the day here—

Sunday, May 20 No one went to church except Oscar. Mr Bass—Mr Lester & Maj. Work[9] (I beleive) are here—

Monday, May 21 Sallie De France her dear little Annie Howard & Polly her nurse (pro tem) came this evening—The boys were at home since Fri. P.M. are here now.

Sunday, May 27 The 37th of my dear fathers death—& the third of Dr N. B. Visers my dear Tenies husband—left us in a world of care—but God has provided the kindest of friends & brothers—May He reward them for the tender care they have shewn to us—My bror & sister M. Oscar & the little girls went to Church—

Friday, June 1 The 1st Anniversary of my ever lamented sisters death. I had thought to have been with her before this—but God knows best—I know that He will do all things well—O that my last end may be like hers, for she said "I have tried to make the preperation"—

Monday, June 4 Sister Mary & Sallie gone to Town visiting & shopping—Bettie improved—

Monday, June 11 Went in again to-day—This is the 3rd Anniversary of my dear cousin Lucretia's death—her youngest son Nash is now suffering from a severe wound received from his imprudence in trying to walk on some part of the machinery of the mill while it was going—he (almost miraculously) escaped with his life—hope he will soon be well & have the perfect use of his limbs—poor little fellow he has had a time of suffering & hope he will be more cautious in future—his lamented mother is spared the intense anxiety she would have suffered on his account—I feel that the separation will not be much longer—

Friday, June 15 My dear Sallie Thomasella[10] & Mr De France came over last night to take leave of us they expect to take the Carrs this morning for Tenn—to return in Oct. Am now confined to my bed again—

Monday, June 25 Colo Stuart came in the twilight of Thursday 21st inst— The dear children ran in clapping their hands for joy—My dear niece A. G. Sessions came to spent the time of her husbands absence in Yazoo with us she & sister Mary went to the Wells—on Friday—have not yet returned— 25th. Heard of the death of Mrs Sue Hintons Baby—she is now about on a visit to the Virginia Springs—Mr Sessions & family spent the day with us—Children took their Vermifuge this morning—25th Mon.

Sunday rain at 11 oclock sister Mary Adelaide & Bettie went to Church.

James & Oscar here James did not come on Friday—Children all well Col. Stuart still here—

Monday, July 2 Colo Stuart left for Hot Springs in Arkansas—

Friday, July 6 James & Oscar came home—their Session will soon be out James will probably go to Oxford[11] this Autumn—

Tuesday, July 10 Mr Hilliard came to spend the Summer yesterday evening— 9th. My dear bror stays at home a little—to transact some business of Mr Hills Estate. My bror having returned from town between 12 & 1 oclock Adelaide got on the horse & rode down in the lot some distance when Edward cut the horse with a switch which made him gallop & she fell off—& bruised herself considerably—her head particularly—is not so well to-day her stomach is a little out of order—

Saturday, July 14 This day one year ago our dear Oscar had his leg broken— I am now thankful to record the goodness of God in his entire restoration without injury to his limb—Is gone to-day with his two bros James & Edward (in his Pa's buggy) to a Know-Nothing dinner given by the party in Jackson—Miss Dubuisson Mrs S. & Mrs H. also attended & Mr. G.H.[12]

Sunday, July 15 The three boys went in the Buggy Sister M & the girls went to Church Miss Dubuisson is expected here to spend a few days—

Sunday, July 22 Sister Mary my bror & the little girls to church Bish. Green preached—have been able to keep up all the past week—finished Adelaides muslin dress—she made the greater part of it & wore it to-day—No news from Colo Stuart yet—James received a letter from Texas from D which informed us of our dear Tenies slow convalescence—is yet in Brazorice & will not be able to get home from thence under a month. his letter bearing date 18th June & this is the 22 July. hope she is at home now.

Sunday, July 29 Sister M. and the 4 eldest children gone to church—heard from Colo Stuart who is doing very well—will be gone a month—Fanny finished all my dresses except the white one & that will soon be done—

Sunday, August 5 My dear niece A G S. is here while Mr S. is gone to Yazoo—went to hear Gen. Wm R. Miles[13] deliver a speech or Oration last night & to church to-day—All well—No intelligence from my dear Tenie for some time—heard from Colo Stuart to-day through Gen J D. Freeman[14]—who had received a letter from him.

Sunday, August 12 Received a letter from my dear Tenie yesterday & a P.S. from my dear Sally—all well again for which I feel truly thankful—My dear Ann & Nannie stayed with us while Mr S. went to Yazoo—returned last night 11th—all well—My bror left on Teusday 9th to look at the lands on the River not yet returned—all went to church to-day & I wrote to Tenie & Ellen to-day but heard no S.S. lessons.

Monday, August 13 Colo Stuart arrived from Hot Springs Ark. renewed in health—cured of Neuralgia—Sister M. was kind enough to let Fanny assist in making 6 pr drawers for him the little girls & myself made two barred muslin shirts for him also. My bror who had been absent nearly a week—arrived the same evening in good health delighted with the country & purchased a plantation in Louisiana on Tensas River in the neighbourhood of Miss Sharkey & Colo Withers—Will send two hands Albert & Joe over to-morrow to deaden the timber preparatory to the planting of a crop next year—there is but very little cleared land on it—

Sunday, August 19 No one went to Church to-day but sister M. & Adele.

Tuesday, August 21 My dear Oscars birth day little Nannie Sessions was here & they were all very busy this morning in distributing the presents to Oscar—his Father left this morning for Holmesville after a stay of a week—Am now very much engaged in preparing James for College—I expect he will leave for Oxford about the 2nd week in Septr.

Thursday, August 23 Trouble with all the children James in a freak of idle humour. hung Betties Doll (in dishabille) up to the bed post & called the attention of Mr H to it which outraged her feelings very much—& he did not show the least sympathy for her but laughed at her calamity or her trouble—They determined to be avenged & hung James in Effigy next morning & sewed up Edwards clothes—as a trick upon them—they however made a mistake & put Oscars hat on the effigy—& he got exceedingly angry & I had to correct him & Edward all got too much excited—Oscar Edward & Eliza had a difficulty which resulted in the use of all the strength I had on board.

Friday, August 24 Have continued a rigid discipline—

Wednesday, August 29 Heard of the severe illness of Dr J.J. Pugh—my bror sent out for a few clothes & went out to see him taking Drs Cabiness & Skipwith with him—on seeing him Dr Cabiness pronounced it Yellow Fever!!— he died at 10 oclock next morning—& was buried at 6 the following A.M. my bror met a messenger coming after him—Mrs Curry Mrs Ps sister was quite ill also—It is a terrible reflection they did not know I suppose until Dr Cabiness told them—that it was *Yellow Fever!!* But so it was—

He was greatly beloved—& deservedly so he was the best of sons—the kindest & most affectionate of husbands—conscientious in the discharge of his Domestic and Professional duties—the warmest most devoted & disinterested of *friends* of whom he could number a very *large circle*—is it any wonder that his bereaved wife should *feel in all its bearings* the meaning of that sad word "Widow"! is it any wonder that his devoted children should feel *keenly* feel their orphanage? no! truly does my own sad heart weep drop for drop with you, my beloved bereaved one—God help thee and sanctify this (to us all) terrible calamity—& enable us to say from our hearts "Thy will O Lord be done"!

The family moved to the neighbourhood of Miss. Springs & escaped the dreadful Pestilence—which broke with the force of a thunderbolt the strongest link which bound them to earth—Dr Brickell went out from Vicksburg—& kindly offered his services—& pronounced the disease Bilious *Fever*—After his arrival—there he addressed a note to my bror— offering his Proffessional services—A kindness I shall *never* forget!! My dear brother ran the risk of his life in remaining there—Mr & Mrs Sessions my niece & Nephew with a heroism worthy of them went to see dear

Mrs Pugh—& are now with my dear bror (who was quarantined) remain *unscathed* through the mercy of that God who watches over us for good.

On the 9th of September 1855 at 8 oclock P.M. my dear James took leave of us in the stage for a term of 4 yrs at Oxford—it was a trial to part with him—I very carelessly retained his trunk keys but sent them by the next stage—The Yellow Fever was raging with some violence in Canton—the Stage stopped there to change horses—how earnestly did I pray that he might escape the Pestilence that walketh in darkness O that God may watch over him for good—& restore him to us again. My dear bror furnished James with the money 140$ to defray his expenses & dear sister Mary with her characteristic kindness—assisted in fitting him out—though complaining of indisposition all the while.

James Stuart Septr 9th 1855

$120 In sack

  20 Portmonie

———

$140

My dear bror with our niece A.G.S. arrived from the Wells on Saturday & by permission went to town on Monday & returned bringing with him Mrs McMackin & little Anna Hilzheim [15] who were also quarantined—their time will be out to-morrow—

Thursday, September 13 All said good lessons to-day—The Fever has made its appearance in Jackson—Canton—& Livingston—my dear bror will go to Tiger Bayou to-morrow—with Mr Wirt Adams—Washing Machine came to-day.

Saturday, September 15 The Ninteenth Anniversary of my dear bror Thomas' death—Though so long a time has elapsed—thou art not forgotten my precious brother!! but with our dear sister Mary N. P. our dear Father our Grand father Grand mother & dear little Algernon (bror Ds son) rest not far from thee—with two sisters Jane & Caroline with our precious little Jane who are resting in the grave yard near us—O that we might *all* rise together at the resurrection of the *just*—

Sunday, September 16 Fever not yet prevailing in Jackson—though no one went to Church to-day—raging most fearfully in Canton—Have read some to the children—"Wesleys Sermon on the resurrection" [16] aloud—Have been teaching one week—from 9 oclock A.M. until 11.

Wednesday, September 19 Little Nannie Sessions has been quite sick for some days—have not been able to go to see her Mr Hilzheim & his bride [17] came out to-day—& took a family dinner with us—Dear little Anna his daughter with Mrs McMackin—have been staying some time with us—

no fever in Jackson—but raging in Canton most fearfully has increased within the last few days.

Friday, September 21 Still increasing cases now amount to 108—increasing in Vicksburg also Gen. McMackin has a case in his family spent yesterday at Mr Sessions am suffering a good deal to-day (21st). Received a letter from my dear James to-day—have had little pleasure in teaching to-day—They promise amendment—& I have consented to continue.

Monday, September 24 All doing very well—

Tuesday, September 25 All well—Fever on the increase in Vicksburg Mrs Mc received a letter from her husband last night—Mr C. A. Jackson died yesterday A.M. Made its appearance at Pass Christian. 180 cases in Canton—What an awful visitation from the Almighty—O that thy people may be more diligent as Christians—"And while thy judgements are abroad in the land grant that the inhabitants thereof may learn righteousness."[18]

Wednesday, October 3 The Anniversary of my dear sister Janes marriage—which took place in 1837—Have not had much pleasure in teaching this week—this morning got out of temper or rather got in one.

Thursday, October 4 Heard to-day of the death of dear Mrs Dr Green—who died yesterday at 5 oclock—she was a very amiable woman and left 2 dear little boys—very interesting children—May God take care of them. Mrs Tift died on the 2nd & her sister[19] on the 10th inst. Rev Mr Corbyn[20] on the 19th—I was attacked with Bilious Fever on the 5th (Friday) & have had no school since—expect to begin in the morning—if possible—Fever abating in Jackson.

Wednesday, October 24–Saturday, November 3 My bror started a waggon some cattle a few mules with 16 negroes—

Oscar went with them & will camp out—poor fellow! he had the misfortune to have his gun burst in his hand while in the act of shooting it off—injuring the finger of his left hand very much—but am truly thankful that he escaped with his life—it happened on (Teusday) the 16th & on Wednesday the 24th started over to La. on Tensas—we have heard nothing from them since they left—my bror left on the following Friday 26th to join them at Vicksburg cross & go all the way by land—

I have been greatly troubled for the last 10 or 12 days on dear James account poor boy! he is in trouble—but will not confide the cause of it to us—he has moved his boarding on account of some difficulty with the stewards—I have written to him & hope for a speedy answer—

Mrs McMackin (who has been staying with us during the Epidemic) left on the 27th—received a letter from Eudora last night 2nd Nov: informing me of her marriage with Mr Wm F. Davis.

Wednesday, November 7 My dear A.G.S. & our dear Nannie spent the day with us—received a letter from Colo Stuart to Oscar & I one from James did not explain or give the least satisfaction in regard to his difficulty &c.

Thursday, November 8 Spent the day with all the family (who were at home)— at Mr Sessions. We intended going to town to-day but Mr Sessions invited some gentlemen to dine with him & of course we are disappointed—expect to go tomorrow—received a letter from my dear Aunt E.O.C. on Wed 7th to my bror & wife.

Saturday, November 10 Went to town to-day shopping together with Sister M. & A.G.S. returned late—& a short time after my dear bror returned from Tensas Oscar coming by land from Vicksbg arrived between 10 & 11 oclock—all well & doing well—

Sunday, November 11 Fever still in Jackson—but not many cases—cloudy to-day—

Thursday, November 15 Received a letter from dear James in trouble—wrote him 8 pages that night he enclosed one of his Fathers letters—The teacher Mrs Petrie has engaged arrived to-day I do not know whether the children will go or not.

Friday, November 16, or Saturday, November 17 Have proposed for Jenny to be sent over to Tensas.

Tuesday, November 20 Jenny Washington Laura & Ellie—were sent over to Tensas—Jinnys child Daniel has been quite ill of Yellow Fever—for about a week—

Mr Thos Nicholson with his wife & sister-in-law—Miss Tempe Thorn [21] —came yesterday—before dinner—

The children Oscar, Adelaide, & Bettie went to school—started on the morning of the 20th (Teusday)—Oscar & Adelaide are studying Latin Gram. Arithmetic

Friday, November 23 Jacob came heard from Mr De France & Sallie all well.

Monday, November 26 Daniel recovering—My bror dined in town on Sat. went in on Sun. returned early—

Sunday, December 2 Went in town on the 30th Nov. had two likenesses taken—but neither would answer—
    Dec. 1st—Quite ill—am now in bed.

Monday, December 3 Very little better—wrote to James yesterday—Mrs Lenoir & Mrs Galloway [22] came last night. came down to room to see me & sat some time bror came while they were here—

Monday, December 10 Am up to-day for the first time in 8 days.

Sunday, December 9 or 16 Sun. evening. Mrs Lenoir & Mrs Galloway staid here all night from Mr Murfrees—I was very much pleased with both!

Monday, December 17 Mrs T. Nicholson & her sister came this evening my dear bror did not come till late—

Friday, December 21 Mr & Mrs Nicholson with Miss Thorne left this morning at 7 oclock for N.O. Mr & Mrs Galloway & Mrs Lenoir with the dear little boys for Glencoe their home on the River. A lovely family.
    Maj Maney & son Thomas arrived yesterday—20th—

Saturday, December 29 My dear little Nannies Birth-day she is 8 yrs old to-day—May she be the blessing & joy of her Fathers house & a comfort & treasure to her dear mother—I would be happy to greet thee my little darling! May God grant thee many, many, returns of thy Natal Day.

1857

Monday, April 27, 1857 On Wednesday 22nd our dear little Nannie was taken with scarlet Fever—The morning of the 23rd it made its appearance on the skin after the usual symptom of head ache & fever the previous night—The disease has progressed so far 27th without any alarming symptoms—except her extreme nervousness—of which she is now almost relieved—she has been a good child, patient & uncomplaining—has submitted to the treatment prescribed by her Physicians—I thank God that she is now in a

fair way to recover as the fever is subsiding—& she rests well at night—
her uncle Wm & Aunt Mary staid all night with her—while Ma & all the
children staid at home—I felt all the *points* of my condition most *acutely* but
from my heart I trusted them to the care our Heavenly Father & I hope they
were watched over. The 25th inst was the anniversary of my dear sisters
death—I have felt more than I have ever done on previous occasions—the
trials of bereavement—O that I may be able to discharge my duty to the
dear children—I feel but too truly that it is the *only* tie I have to earth—
save my old mother—who is now 81 years old— & has very good health except Rheumatism—On Monday the 20th Adelaide & Bettie went to school
accompanied by their Aunt Mary who visited Mrs Czanne[1] who told her
that Adelaide had said she was going to remain at home during her Pappa's
visit—there was some little misunderstanding about it which Adelaide first
explained to her Aunt Mary & uncle Wm—& then to me in a note—I have
been staying here with my dear Niece who came home or to La Vega ill
from Yazoo on the 27th March & came to Rose Cottage her home on the
30th—has been confined to her bed since the 27 or 28th of March—

Wednesday, April 29 Our dear Nannie much improved—her mother not so
well to-day—We my bror received 2 letters yesterday one from Texas informing us of the illness of dear D at Montgomery Alabama on his return
to N.C. whither he had gone to attend school—but was compelled to return home (in Texas) with his bror Dickinson—who had been very ill at
his uncles D brought his bror to N.O. & I suppose returned to N.C. from
thence. Our dear Sallie had also lost her babie at 8 days old—she was doing
very well—My dear bror & sister Mary staid here all night with our dear
Nannie her aunt Mary is a great favourite with her—

Thursday, April 30 Nannie still improving—though her dear mother is quite
indisposed to-day is perfectly exhausted from her excitement about Nannie
—heard to-day that my dear bror & sister Mary were both indisposed—
both had colds.

Friday, May 1 Rain yesterday—cloudy to-day A.G.S. grew worse yesterday
the excitement about Nannie having subsided she sank from exhaustion—
seems very feeble & weak—took chloroform last night—

Monday, May 4 This is the Anniversary my dear bror D's birth-day—he is
51 years old to-day—I will write to him if I can—May our Heavenly Father
watch over him for good—& provide some way for him to extricate himself
from his present embarrassments—Many Many returns to thee my dear

bror—May 2nd. Spent the day at home all the family dined together—
the children being at home from school—poor little Violet was taken with
Scarlet fever on Friday night—was very ill on Sat. have not seen her since—
but hear she is very ill—Drs Cabiness & Buck [2] think her case very doubtful.
I expect to go home to-morrow.

⟨*two pages*⟩

Friday, May 8 My dear bror Wms 56th birth-day—Many Many returns to
thee my dear bror—May Angels guide thee & watch over thee for good—&
conduct thee at last to a home in Heaven—May the eye that never slumbers
be ever on thee—

Monday, May 11 10th Sun. late P.M. came home—
    Have made a shade for James this morning which I hope he will get very
soon—Dr Buck thinks me dear Niece may have a protracted case illness—
but hope for the best—Dr Buck visited her for the first time on Friday 8th
May '57 & again on Sat. A M & I suppose on Mon. to-day.

Thursday, May 14 A sad day the anniversary of my little Darlings death—she
had been gone from among us (& I hope has watched over us) four yrs to-
day. I have had a weary pilgrimage so far—but hope & pray that I may be
more resigned—Our dear Ann is somewhat improved—

Tuesday, May 19 The Dr came out this morning—also Judge Dubuisson made
a short visit—Mr Sessions went with them to town 9 oclock to-night not
returned yet—fear something is the matter. On last Sat. Edward & Oscar
came over and I returned with them—My bror left for Tensas & Millikens
Bend—on Sat. morning 16th May will be gone sometime—

Wednesday, May 20 Bright beautiful morning Mr S returned last night nothing the matter. My dear A. improving slowly—she keeps good spirits for
an invalid—O how earnestly do I desire her recovery—if it be Gods
will—Received a letter from Bettie yesterday morning—which gratified
me very much—

Friday, May 22 Sister M. & my Mother came over & spent the day—& in
the evening Mr S. sent his own carriage for the little girls—they came late
& both were sick Bettie with Diarhea & Adelaide with headaches—she remained at home to-day or at her cousin A's. I was a little impatient with my
dear Bettie this morning she however went off cheerfully saying she would

try & do right & be neat &c. My dear A. not so well to-day—but cheerful sister M. came over again on Sunday evening & I went over home—to spend only a few hours.

Tuesday, May 26 June 1st 57 [3] My dear sister Caroline has been 3 years from us today—"she is not for God has taken her"—this being the 3rd Anniversary of her death—O how dreary is my life with out thee my dear lamented sister—thy life was one of trial & sacrifice—would that mine were more so—I pray however for submission to the will of God in all things—but particularly in this afflictive bereavement—(May 26th A Mistake).

Wednesday, May 27 The anniversary of my dear Fathers death—39 yrs have passed since I have heard thy parental voice. My dear Father—But thy counsels & advices are still in my memory—O that I may ever be guided by them—& I know that I shall be safe—I pray for aid to do so. This is also the anniversary of Dr Visers death—my dear Teries husband who was a very amiable man—

Dear Adelaide has just left for school—expect her to remain at home next week—(I did not have my Almarac—convenient & made some mistake as to the time of the anni. of my sisters death—)

Sunday, June 14 It is now 14th June & he has never seen her but once—& she has taken one bottle of Iron mixture—she took the last dose on the 12th inst—

Received another bottle of Med from the drug store—she makes no effort herself as yet to restore her health—takes very little exercise is perfectly *inert* in every respect. it grieves my heart to record it. Returned home this week to stay have been assisting sister M. in the making of trimming for sleeves &c. as she expects to go to Yazoo soon on a visit to Mrs White & family.

⟨ . . . . ⟩

Mr Sessions was kind enough to go for him but he came on the Carrs & dined with us at Mr Sessions on Friday—& on this evening Bettie & Mary Bailey came out—some trouble on Sun. morning with Eliza & Mary—

Monday, June 15, or Tuesday, June 16 Colo Perkins came home with my bror was not well myself sister M. received a letter from Eudora all well.

Thursday, June 18 Mrs Petrie & Mrs Helm [4] were here but did not see them—

Friday, June 19 My dear Bettie gave way to her temper. O how my poor heart ached for her—the 3 youngest did not go to Church to-day 20th

⟨ . . . . ⟩

inertness—it is a source of trouble to me—O how earnestly & fervently are my prayers for her restoration to health again.

On Thurs. 25th June Mr Joe Nicholson & family left here for the North & to spend the summer taking Carolina in their route.

Friday, July 3 Mr & Mrs Higgins will be here to dine (from Natchez)—Mr Fore came in the evening—Mr Wygan (an Italian—Artist)[5] came on Sat. to dinner—left on Sun. evening for Canton. My bror went up on Mon. & returned on Wed.

Thursday, July 9 My dear niece A.G.S. was brought over on a litter late this evening—the Anniversary of her. . . .[6]

Henry[7]—Willie Lewis George Scott Fearn Watkins & Eddie Scott—acquitted themselves very handsomely. little Herbert repeated a pretty speech at last—

Saturday, July 11 This morning sister Mary & Mr Sessions left for Yazoo— to make a visit to Mrs White & other friends.

Tuesday, July 14 My dear bror left this morning for Yazoo on business & to make a few visits.

Wednesday, July 15 Edward has a very bad rising in his left ear—waded in a pond after some minies small fish which he ate for breakfast—&c.

Saturday, July 18 Went to town to have Nannies Daguerreotype taken Bettie went also & they both insisted that I should have mine taken I sat for it— but it was an utter failure—a miserable picture. had to correct Edward.

Tuesday, August 18[8] My heart was *pained* for dear Bettie. May God protect her always [. . .] to Church—To-night [. . .] time of trial for me—on account of my dear little girls (O what gall & wormwood have been mixt in my cup for some weeks). (God help me I pray for I have no other aid). God help me to discharge my duties to them as I ought dear little Bettie is greatly distressed (she acted properly throughout).

Monday, July 20 My dear James arrived to-day from Oxford came in & surprised us all. O how thankful I felt that I could see him once more—his Pa came the next day.

Sunday, July 26 James & Oscar went to Church to-day. James saw Archie Forbes—I have had a close & *confidential* conversation with James. he is a noble boy—in regard to his little brors & sisters—May God enable him to sustain them. My dear Adelaide has been sick better than a week with chills & fever—I fear very much that she will have a long fit of illness of typhoid character—Dr Buck has visited her & she is nearly well—

Monday, July 27 Mr Ozannes Examination. dear Bettie dressed at home & went in (she & Nannie with her dear Papa James & Oscar staid until the close)—except that James brought Eddie out drenched with rain & dressed & returned again—leaving E. at home. Staid all night at Judge Yergers[9] & visited some ladies & returned home. A was very attentive to Miss Bettie Wharton.[10] They did not attend to their sister Bettie as they ought to have done—if their Father had not there she would have been left in the Hall through some mistake—this pained me much—I fear that the boys do not feel such an identity with their sisters as they ought—Our dear Bettie stood a very good Examination in the City Hall her Father was pleased.

Wednesday, July 29 My dear bror left for Memphis—to be absent 10 or 15 days—

Monday, August 3 Colo Stuart left for Holmesville by S.B. reproached me severely for making any accounts in town—&c—We must exercise more economy in future—& have no accounts in town—the die is cast & *it must be so*—{. . . .} gone until Thurs. my dear bror not yet returned.

Wednesday, August 12 Received a sad letter from Colo Stuart dated from N.O. 3 oclock at night—I am now going to answer it—had a severe trial with Adelaide yesterday morning—God help me & sustain me—& enable me to discharge my duty to the dear children conscientiously & as in his sight—
   Servants had some little difficulty about Porters dog.

Thursday, August 13–Sunday, August 16 Cut Betties hair to-day. About 4 oclock. My dear bror arrived in good health after being in the swamp (of Sunflower) two days & enduring fatigue & hardship—Went to Canton Sat. 15th expects to leave for Tensas on Teus—
   Adelaide has had a chill & Fever today 16th {. . . .} very affectionate since

she spoke ha{. . .} dear bror—but craved his pardon {. . .} very willing to grant it—Oscar has been cutt . . . weeds for a few days—Adelaide answered her Pa's letter to-day in which I put a P.S.—have not spent the day as I wished—I pray for the strength which comes from above—

Monday, August 24 Went to Mr Sessions & to the grave yard thence home—James drove me in Mr S. buggy—Found the square overrun with weeds—hope to have the tombstone over my dear & ever lamented sister my own little darling Jane—soon—sister Mary went to Mrs Christmas'[11] on Sun. evening returned on Teus.

Late August My bror returned from Tensas (on Teus 25 Augst)

⟨*three lines*⟩

My dear Niece Mr De France & their dear little Annie Howard arrived on Sat. evening came over on Sun. evening to see us—& to-day they came over—also Mrs Maury & spent the day—Adelaide looked badly all day. {. . .} towards me—May she ever {. . .}ected by that God who has prom{. . .} to watch over the helpless—May He subdue her strong will—& grant her grace to become patient & humble before Him—

Thursday, September 3 Mr De France & Sallie with dear little Annie Howard came over & staid until Sat. evening late—

Sunday, September 6 My bror went over to Mr Sessions' to-day—we are alone our dear James will leave to-morrow for Oxford—It is a painful task to give him up—May Our Heavenly Father watch over him for good—& ever guide him aright. no one went to Church to-day.

Monday, September 7 Monday morning Septr 7th 1857. Our dear James took leave of us this morning for Oxford—for his third course (Junior). May God watch over him always & "be as the shadow of a great rock in a weary land"[12] to him also his Counsellor & guide {. . .} all occasions—preserve him, & sustain him ⟨. . . .⟩

Wednesday, September 9 Adelaide & Bettie went with Oscar who will go tomorrow as a scholar—they seem to take great pleasure in it—& progress very well—

Thursday, September 10 Sallie De. & Mrs Maury[13] came over this morning—dear Sallie releived me a great deal by giving me some instructions about the dear childrens clothes—

Saturday, September 12 Oscar went to dancing school yesterday evening at 3 oclock—Mr Clissey the teacher[14] will make up the time he has lost—went to his room this morning for that purpose & took one lesson.

Sunday, September 13 Had some little trouble with Edward the past week—but on Sat. he did a good deal better—merely talked to him—all went to Church to-day (viz) Sister Mary Adelaide Bettie Oscar & Edward. hope they may have a good sermon—

⟨. . . .⟩ & ever guide us by his counsel & grace.

Tuesday, September 15 This is the 21st Anniversary of my dear brors death—there are now but three of us remaining my bror Wm with whom we reside & my bror D in Texas—Our eldest & our counsellor & guide was taken first it seemed at first to be our one sorrow. O what a blight to our poor hearts—most fondly is thy memory still cherished my precious bror—& though thou wert stricken down in the strength & flower of thy manhood—& left a family—we have most religiously endeavoured to discharge our duty to them & especially bror Wm who attended to the settlement of the estate—he has undergone many trials but has proven himself as firm as the Oak of centuries in the discharge of every duty—relative to the interests of the family—May God sustain thee my dear bror—& bring thee to Himself at last—
Mr De France & Sallie were here this evening.

Wednesday, September 16 Oscar A. & B. went to dancing school to-day—& enjoyed themselves very much.

Friday, September 18 All went in together—on Friday instead of Wed. Sat. Sister Mary went to Mr Sessions to spend the day—Nannie is not well has a cough—dear little things—wish they were well & I could see them.

Saturday, September 19 We were alone.

Sunday, September 20 Sallie & Mr De France came over—in the evening.

Monday, September 21 Sister Mary went to town—it was Sallie De Frances birthday—the children went to dancing school—& again yesterday evening—Sallie went with them—

Saturday, September 26 Went to Jackson to-day & dined with my dear Nieces Ann & Sallie—my bror went over & returned with us—left all the children at home—

Monday, September 28 Went to town to-day with Sallie to look at Machines [. . . .] at Kauslers & Newcomers [15]—saw several friends. Mrs Johnston Clark Miss Mary Clark—& several others Mrs Lester [16]—returned home while they were at dinner—girls ready for the dancing school—sister Mary went with them—& in returning some one told her that they had come out with Mrs Nichol—she returned home without them & appeared to send the carriage back for them if she knew where to send—& offered to send William the servant to enquire about them—to which I objected—They fortunately however went to Crafts stable [17] & the old man was very kind & sent them home &c. Oscar took them to the Church door until the carriage was ready. I was in the *deepest* trouble when they arrived.

Adelaide took cold but Bettie did not—they went in once more as pupils & the last day to a party—on the 30 Septr—sister M went with them.

Monday, October 5 Went in with the girls—to school myself & had a very pleasant satisfactory visit had an introduction to Mrs Newell & the Teachers neither of the girls were well—To the guardian care & protection of our Heavenly Father do I commend them—

Wednesday, October 7 Have not progressed with my work as I wished—wrote to the girls to-night—Sister M. left her room to-day—

Thursday, October 8 This is my James Natal day!! numbers 19th years—May God watch over him for good—guide & direct him & give him a proper balance of character & prepare him the duties which lie before him—he is the first born of six children—one of whom now forms a part of the Heavenly Host—At present he promises all we could reasonably expect or wish—with the exception of being a christian—O that he may become one.

Monday, October 12 Went this morning with the little girls to school to see Mrs Ozanne about putting Helen Ingersol in their room—she did not like it—but said she would remove her.

came by "Home schools" to give Adelaide a box of pills which Dr Buck had prepared for her—sent it in from the gate by a boy—came home took dinner & went over to Mr Sessions & took another as they had not dined returned in the evening. Mr S. & Will e D went in their carriage to town after Mr Hilliard who had arrived from N. Orleans. Mr Sessions was kind enough to get the "Mothers Recompense" for me according to my request—

Saturday, October 17 The Anniversary of my dear sisters birth—my darling sister Carolines. O what a blight has her death cast upon my poor heart— & in all my domestic arrangements in managing the children—I felt as a blank while she was living & still more so now.

Spent the day at A Sessions—who has improved a good deal—

Monday, October 19 Spent yesterday with my dear Ann Mr Albert Sessions[18] & wife were there on a visit had tooth ache which gave me infinite pain just as we were leaving Mrs Judge Yerger[19] & Mrs Bramlett[20] came—Mr Hilliard who has been here on a visit for some days left on Friday my bror left at the same time for Sonora—heard from there last night several sick—& only 25 bales cotton picked out.

Friday, October 23 The dear little girls came home—do not like Mrs Ozannes manner towards them.

Saturday, October 24 Adelaide assisted me with my dress which I had been making all the

⟨*two pages*⟩

free man—& the reward of 50$ which had been offered for him—induced some one to put him in jail so that they could get it—remained in jail one week & was taken out to be sold for jail fees—some one recognizing him wrote to my bror—concerning the matter—who went up & secured him—in jail until he is sold. Mr Barnes proposed that Oscar should hear the girls lessons—& offered to instruct him in any branch which he was unacquainted with—

Wednesday, November 25 Mrs Lester & family[21] are expected to dine here to-day.

On Wed. 18th Nov. Mr. Bodie[22] Music Teacher came out to give the girls music lessons—Adelaide is taking "Hazel Dell"—Bettie will take a piece to-morrow—he merely examined them the first time & will come again on the 23rd Mon. & give them lessons—regularly—he will be here on 30th.

Thursday, November 26 Thurs. Sister M. went out visiting—about 9 oclock. Mr & Mrs Jones came to make a visit—on Fri. they returned while we were at dinner—my bror came with Colo Perkins & son—Colo Gaines & Mr Edward Yellowly—Colo Gaines a very old gentleman from Mobile remained all night. Sat 27 [23] Bob brought over a note of invitation to spend the day at Mr Sessions ("the entire family") of course we went—& spent a very pleasant day dear little Nannie—was gratified—& enjoyed the visit.

D 25th [24] Wed Mr & Mrs Lester & their two daughters spent a very pleasant day with us.

Tuesday, December 1 Sister Mary Ma A. & B. my bror & Mr Byron Hilliard [25]— dined at Mr Lesters—I remained at home—& had my carpet taken up my room cleaned—&c. Mr Byron Hilliard returned with them.

Wednesday, December 2 Dr Maney received Despatches of the illness & death of his little grand-daughter Lavenia who died on 1st Dec. 1857—daughter of Mr Lewis & Adeline Maney—Received a letter from Eva Hardeman—& Oscar one from James—

Friday, December 4 Mr Bode gave the girls another lesson but they find great difficulty in practising.

Saturday, December 5 Mrs Skipwith her two daughters Virginia & Kate—& her son Green [26]—just as they left Mr Byron Hilliard came—

My Brother received a letter from Mr Sibley his Overseer—informing us of the birth of Jinnys daughter on the 25th Nov 1857 Adelaide & Bettie are very busy making up a wardrobe for it. Had rain yesterday & ⟨. . . .⟩

Sunday, December 6 The weather still warm & rained occasionally—heard from dear Ann yesterday—she took a relapse which will I fear retard her recovery for some time. Adelaide is not well this morning—did not go to church.

Tuesday, December 15 Went over to Mr Sessions to stay with my dear niece until his return—on Sat. the little girls had a party—Nannie had spent Fri. night with Fannie Buck (daughter of her Mothers attending Physician) [27] they seemed to enjoy themselves very much—Fannie returned home on Sun. morning & we on Mon. evening when they sent the carriage for Mr S. I went in with Nannie went in on Fri evening I went with her & bought 1 yd blk merino to finish my dress—& 12 yds cambric for Polly—1 long comb for Nannie—I was grieved at not getting something for the children—but was under the necessity (under consideration of the hard times) to deny myself that pleasure—I returned by home to see Colo Polk—who was here on a visit—about Mr I. H. Hilliard—they made a very pleasant visit of a few days—& left on Teus 22nd Maj & Dr Maney arrived just before I left for Rose Cottage Have been very much engaged since my return in arranging the girls dresses to send to Mrs Hurd[28]—was wearied last night Sat. with the effort—but did not succeed—hope I shall be able to get through to-morrow—if I am able to be up.

Sunday, December 27 Sister Mary went to church to-day—also Oscar Bettie & Edward—had trouble nearly all day.

Monday, December 28 The children all wrote to their Father & bror James—& I completed my cutting out & got things ready to send off—two dresses for Bettie & one calico for Adelaide—have commenced James' coat & cravats—

Tuesday, December 29 Dear little Nannies birth-day—many long & happy days to thee my darling! May guardian Angels watch over thee! & make thee the joy of thy mothers heart.

Thursday, December 31 12 P.M. The old year with its joys & sorrows is just making its exit—& the New Year of 1858 is ushering in—with resolutions for amendments & improvements in the lives & actions of thousands with whom I would like to number my poor weak erring self—the clock is now striking the hour of 12—Farewell old year it is not without a tear of regret that I bid thee Adieu.

1858

Sunday, January 3, 1858 No one went to Church a bad day Mr Nicholson & son Edward[1] came to breakfast this morning *I* only had an unpleasant day—

Monday, January 4 Have been writing all day—&c. We are expecting a visit from my dear bror D who went to Ala. to see a Mr Sorsby who owned some land near him which he wished to purchase. as he had sold out his entire plantation with the exception of 200 acres having his house on it—he sold one half of his farm to a Mr Wiggins & the balance to Sam Hardeman & Wm Davis—his sons in-law—we were very much disappointed in not seeing our dear bror D.

Tuesday, January 5 I went to town with sister M. from thence to Rose Cottage spent two nights & one day & she returned with me & stood the ride very well—she is with us now & with the exception of a little drawback from loss of sleep & sitting up too late she is doing very well & improving a good deal—Mr S. returned last night—My dear bror went to Canton on the 9th (Sat.). no one went to Church but Oscar I have been wanting Oscar to get a new coat but it seems that it cannot be done—

Thursday, January 14 My dear mothers birth day she has numbered 82 years— & is blessed with good health except Rheumatism—this evening about 4 oclock dear sister Bethenia & Thomasella & cousin Washington Perkins arrived from Tenn. we were very glad to see them—Cousin Thos Hardeman M. came on Mon 11th is here to-night expects to leave in the morning— or to-morrow—

Friday, January 15 Cousin Thos left for home though the roads were almost impassable—Dined with all the family at Mr Sessions.

Saturday, January 16 Phil. Sessions (son of Mr A. Sessions) came home with us—staid all night & Oscar returned with him this morning no one went from here to church—Phil went to town—Sun. morning.

Wednesday, January 20, and Thursday, January 21 Bishop Green & wife[2] made a morning call—in ½ an hour Mr Hilliard Christmas came—& on Thurs. 21st Maj & Dr Maney came to breakfast—are here now—Maj & sister Mary went over to Rose Cottage.

Friday, January 22 Maj Maney left for Tenn. Dr M. for his plantation on Trio. Tommie came over on Nannie's Poney yesterday evening with Oscar. Sister Bethenia came over this evening in the buggy with Mr Sessions. Adelaide took the "Cotton Field Polka" yesterday 22nd—My bror bought a Poney— out of a drove from Illinois.

Sunday, January 24 Cloudy day. My dear sister Bethenia & Tommie came & staid until Sat evening—went to church to-day—Oscar went to church & saw them—I have not been well—had bleeding at the nose—on Fri. night.

Thursday, January 28 Bleeding at the nose again—it may terminate in sudden death—& since I can no longer fulfill the duties assigned to me—"It is well"—may my Heavenly father prepare me for a safe entrance into His heavenly Kingdom—into his hands would I commend myself & all that I have & am.

Children not doing well—fear I have provoked them to do many things which they would not otherwise have done—God forgive the sin—I would live to make them happy & promote their happiness—but it seems that cannot be—this consideration lessens my desire to live.

Saturday, January 30 Sister Bethenia & Tommie rode over—& spent the day—Oscar & Edward returned with them—they anticipate a visit to N. Orleans. On Fri 29th My dear bror Wm left for N O. on the carrs—may God watch over him for good—& restore him to us soon. dear sister Mary is waiting for her bror to go down with her.

Monday, February 1 Cold weather—O. & E. better.

Tuesday, February 2 Went with sister to town (very unexpectedly) to call on our Ministers family—Rev Mr Forsythe.[3] was very much pleased—from thence to Mrs Shacklefords saw her two daughters Sally & Mildred[4]—stopped at Mrs Petries at first—who did not seem to be very cordial—until we left—(towards me)—but very much so towards sister M. went from thence to Mr Sessions where we heard of Mr De Frances arrival—great difficulty about getting off &c. with sister Bethenia & Tommie—as they were not ready—in consequence Mr Hilliard was Telegraphed to the effect & they will now go on Friday morning—Rain—Rain—I shall feel uneasy about them—until their return.

Thursday, February 4 Mr DeFrance came over for Adelaide & I went also—staid until nearly sundown. Bob returned with us—we brought over a collar & pair of sleeves to finish for our dear Tommie—& succeeded in finishing them—at 1 & ½ oclock—but did not retire until 3 oclock—& could not sleep then but got a little nap before {. . .} Mary got off for New Orleans {. . .} very hurriedly—May God watch {. . .} restore them all to us again {. . .} have a pleasant trip down—& enjoy the amusements & pleasures of the city—so far as they are compatible with good taste & a sense of right. & the love & fear of God—

Tuesday, February 9 Had my dear sister Mary have lived she would have numbered 60 years—she was 45 in Feb. 1843 & died 1st Oct. of the same year—she was truly a child of afflictions from her youth up she was married March 12th March (I beleive) & became a widow in 22 I think (I write altogether from memory)[5] she was educated in Salem N.C. Her brothers & sisters rise up & call her blessed—& remember with sadness & true reflection her many virtues & noble qualities of heart & head—in all the relations of life she sustained herself a christian lady—she had many—many sorrows but she showed true christian fortitude in the endurance of them.

{. . .} we have had good weather since Fri. & all are getting on well

Sunday, February 14 All are well except Porter & Julia—Children doing tolerably well—I find it difficult to get them up in the morning—received a letter to-day from Mr De France—all well except dear sister Mary—My dear bror D in N.O. but we do not expect to see him as he will return to Texas as soon as he can—

Sunday, February 21 My dear bror & sister Mary arrived last night from N.O. whither they had gone to enjoy & participate in the pleasures of the Season—which they did with much zest. sister Bethenia & Tommie will go to Yazoo. I regretted that we should see them no more. Mrs Richard Sessions[6] & her two children Mary & Howard arrived on Mon. we made them a visit on Fri. morn. bror Wm sister Mary Adelaide & Bettie went there from Church. Saw Dr Williamson to-day for the first time.

1859

Rules for 1859

1st Mon. Repair clothing of every kind & put them in place—annex a penalty to the omission of this duty.
2nd Teus. If a garment is commenced work diligently with a view to completion within the week.
3rd Wed. If we should be dress making, use every exertion to complete it in as short a time as possible. be patient diligent & industrious.
4th Thurs. Attend to the *wash particularly* & have every article noted & required to be returned in due time.
5th Fri. Be diligent in gaining time for a little rest on Sat. A.M.
6th Sat. Prepare work for the ensuing week—Save time enough to get the mind off the world a little on this evening.
Add one rule viz Write two hours every day—March 5th 1860[1]

Saturday, May 7, 1859 A day of sadness & sorrow to me as this is the 6th Anniversary of my little Janes illness—she was taken on the evening of the

7th—& this year it has occurred on the same day of the week—Colo Stuart is here expects to leave to-morrow—went only to Vicksburg returned in a few days—18th. Sister M. & Oscar gone to Gen. Clarkes to Miss M. C's wedding. She will change her name for Vaughn—My dear A.G.S. came over on Sun. & again to-day went to town & to Bishop Greenes—returned home this evening—Bettie wrote to her bror James to-day—

Monday, July 4 My dear bror & his wife dear sister Mary who went on to Tenn left for Oxford yesterday P.M.—Our dear James will graduate with the first Honour—but it is uncertain when we shall see him. I feel truly thankful that his College term has not been stained with anything which will bring regret in old age or early manhood. I pray for Heavens blessing on his future.

Sunday, July 10 Our dear James arrived with his uncle Wm from Oxford where he had spent the last 4 yrs to complete his term at College—having left Septr 8th 1855—I do not hesitate to say that he has in every respect fulfilled the expectations of his *entire* family—May he be watched over by the eye that never slumbers & in whose hands the balances of life will be properly adjusted—may he ever watch with a vigilent eye over the conduct of life of his *dear sisters* & supply the place of *Mother* & *Father* to them. our dear Oscar we expect to part with in a few weeks for Oxford. On Sat 16th Dear A.G.S. & family spent the day with us—Mr Purnell[2] came out to breakfast—& went fishing with the boys & returned home to Brandon—in the evening 19th Teus. My dear bror returned from Sonora in health though much fatigued—brought Henry over—& left a fine growing crop & all well—& satisfied & contented.

Wednesday, July 20 I wrote to Cornelia this morning 20th & to Mrs Cox about the Machines—have got along but poorly with my work. done nothing this week—except to assist Adelaide in fitting & making an underbody—&c. since Eliza has been sick (16th July '59) I have had a good deal more to do than usual—

Monday, July 25 Wrote to sister Mary yesterday 24th—Mon 25th. A cool pleasant morning all well—except Fanny complains of her back—Mr Sage is expected to dinner he & Miss Kate Lewis drove out here on Sat. late made a short call—I stitched 2 pr linnen pillow cases for my dear niece A.G.S. the first work I have done on the Machine which she was kind enough to give me—this is my day of repairs of clothes—of every kind—must not forget my rules—I have passed a long interim. My dear Niece took me home with her & cured me—I have taken no note of any thing for a long time—but hope I shall be able to keep up—my usual routine—of duties—however complicated they may be—must go now to repairing Edwards clothes first

Tuesday, July 26 Mrs Skipwith spent the day with us after calling on Ann Sessions—went to Brandon in the evening—will return on Fri. evening Mr S expects to go to Yazoo on Thurs. & we shall then see our dear A. & N. we had quite a pleasant day sad & melancholy but pleasant too—Mr Barnes took leave of us this evening the last day of his school.

Wednesday, July 27 Mrs Tarpley & Mrs Buckley[3] came out this evening—it has become cool—as an Autumn evening & is quite pleasant the boys went to the River—

Thursday, July 28 Our dear A.G.S. came over to remain during Mr S's absence to Yazoo has set up too late for two nights—

Friday, July 29 Mrs Skipwith & her 3 daughters came out & spent the night & returned the next morning—Mrs Charles Scott died on the 27 inst— her remains were brought up to the Jackson cemetery on the 30th & were interred my bror was one of the pall bearers.

Monday, August 1 My bror left this morning for Tenn. in good health & spirits—will not return before the 20th—hope when he joins his Mollie he will be happier still—to-night after supper we were all sitting in the hall when a carriage drove up & rather an elderly gentleman came in who proved to be Mr McLane who married Miss Sue Marr—have done some work to-day though not much—have read nothing.

Tuesday, August 2 Have had rather a disagreeable day—the children have not been quiet my dear Bettie particularly—James is a dear friend & Oscar is an excellent boy or child to me—the dear girls it seems have gone too far with their plays they have been doing better since—

Thursday, August 4 Yesterday Mrs Green her two daughters & Berkley her son[4]—came over—& spent the day—what a charming woman she is! I like her very much they went to church at 5 oclock—this morning our dear A.G.S. & our pet Nannie left us—as Mr S. I suppose has returned— I do miss them so much sent a letter to Sallie in Tex. this morning past 10 oclock have cut out some this evening for Adelaide—6 chimese—

Saturday, August 6 Cut out 6 petticoats—finished Jackonet underbody—sewed some on the Machine—tried to use hemmer but failed—Adelaide worked with it some time & set it to sewing properly—

Sunday, August 7 James rode to church—Bettie & Oscar went to the Episcopal Church—I suppose—Servants not doing their duty—at least a part of them. On Fri. 5th inst at night—Oscar made some very severe charges against me—& was very disrespectful—I was angry & mortified & may have said something to him—if any thing could be done to distress me more—I would pray for a fresh supply of strength to bear it—May my Heavenly Father aid & sustain me in this trying position—

Monday, August 8 Mr Sessions brought a letter from my dear bror (sent by private hand) who was at Memphis & doing well &c. Wrote to my little nieces in Texas yesterday—Ellen, Fannie, Johnnie, Sallys children Eudora's little Sally—also to Billy P Hardeman[5] but expect to write to Tenie & Nicholson—Oscar gone to town James is gone fishing. wrote to Tenie & all the children finished—Mon. P.M. cut out for Adelaide & Bettie—cut out 2 shirts for James 3 pr pants for Edward—4 linnen chimeses for Adelaide 6 domestic—6 petticoats 4 pr drawers she had 2 new pr which she had never been worn—making 6 pr new ones—On Wed. evening began to make James shirts succeeded with the hemmer—On James N.Shirts—Thurs 6 oclock—am ready to go to sewing—but have to wait for cleaning up—sent Mrs Green a large fish yesterday but did not write as I intended—have heard but once from my bror—

Thursday, August 11 Sent or the boys did some "Oregon Trout" over to A.G.S. she wrote a note informing me of a visit from Mrs Judge Yerger & her daughters[6]—& that little Blanche Clifton[7] had scarlet Fever—Mrs Y. & her two eldest daughters came out this evening—had rather a pleasant day—James & Oscar keep the table supplied with fish—they have been going to the River every morning early & late in the evening—have lines out &c.

Friday, August 12 Have heard nothing from my bror & sister M. yet but heard last night that there were letters in the P.O. hope we shall get them this morning. Adelaide did receive one from sister M. All were well—but did not know when they would be at home—

Saturday, August 13 Had a copious rain—in the evening late. James went to the River & got very wet—

Sunday, August 14 James Adelaide & Bettie went to the M.E.C. servants did not behave properly—this is the 5th anniversary of dear Oscars misfortune of breaking his leg or ancle from the fall of a horse.

Sunday, October 23, to Wednesday, November 9 Two months & a half have elapsed since I have made any entry in my journal—since then my bror & sister have returned the last of Augst from Tenn. in good health & spirits & made us all happy again—My dear James took an office in the yard after being well fitted up by his Aunt Mary—& commenced reading Law on Thurs 29th Sepr 59. Under the supervision of Judge Wm Yerger he has studied very well indeed—I beleive he will commence Blackstone on Mon 24th Octr '59.

On Wed. Octr 19th '59. My dear niece Evyline arrived from Madison—she came out with Mr Thos Jones & his family—from Carolina a fort-night before—we had not seen her since she was 3 yrs old—she is all we could expect or wish—my heart is full of gratitude to the giver of all good—for guarding her through a term of 3 yrs at two different schools—Salem N.C. & Patapsco M.d. she left under very favourable auspices—I pray that she may ever be the object of Our Fathers peculiar care—On Thursday 29th Septr 1859. My dear Oscar left for Oxford University of Miss.—A painful Adieu. My dear bror wrote just before his arrival that our dear Adelaide & Bettie would be sent on to the North to school—perhaps to Patapsco—but upon inquiry he found that Burlington was a better school & concluded to send or take them thither accordingly they left on the 25th Octr 1859 on Teus. 8 oclock A.M. to be absent 2 yrs for Adelaide—3 for Bettie—I need not record the pain it gave me to give them up—the seperation was truly so I have however commended them in faith & confidence to the care & guidance of our Heavenly Father—Received letters frcm Bettie & Adelaide from Memphis. All well & doing well—heard no more from them until this morning Sun Nov: 6th (59) When my dear bror returned—we hailed him with joy & gratitude—was in good health & spirits made some stay at W. City & saw all the curiosities of the place—said dear Bettie had lost her satchel & new Bible—besides various other articles—lost her Uncles hat—I feel truly thankful that it was no worse—

On Wed. 9th. I received a letter from my dear Bettie & Ma one from dear Oscar both were well & well pleased with their school—

Thursday, November 10 Commenced my window curtains but did not finish them as I expected but hope to get them put up by to-morrow night.

Saturday, November 12 Received a letter from my dear Nephew D Hardeman of Texas who is now at Chapel Hill N. Carolina.

Sunday, November 13 James & Edward went to Church together rode the two ponies—last Sun. Mr Ben. Green came out & dined with us—was much improved in health & appearance—

Monday, November 14 Our State Fair commenced—the family attended—bror Wm gave my dear James a very fine overcoat which he had purchased for himself & 3 dollars—for the Fair—my dear Eva gave me a dollar to give to Edward as she had heard me say I was out of money—I however borrowed some from sister Mary—she was exceedingly kind—offered me more than I wanted. I took seven dollars for J. & E. during the Fair—They only exhibited the various things which had been entered—Eva put her picture of Washington—there were landscapes wrought in cruels & a very pretty saddle riding dress & cap with a plume &c.

Tuesday, November 15 To-day 15th I am trying to make Ma dress (it was to-day that I borrowed the money) the ladies left James—but he rode the poney.

Wednesday, November 16 James was dispirited did not seem to have enjoyed himself—all were fatigued had a good deal of company—(viz) Mr Frazier from Tenn.—Mr Eastin—Mr Robert Hilliard[8] & Mr Fore—the Tournament took place to-day Mr J. Ravenscroft Greene[9] took several premiums—a pitcher waiter & cup—was pronounced a graceful rider &c.

Thursday, November 17 Tournament continued—exhibited horses—again—for 3 days in succession. My heart was cheered last night by the reception of a letter from my dear Adelaide also one from my dear Cornelia which I must answer soon—

Friday, November 18 Last day of the Fair young Wm Yerger[10] rode his sisters horse & got a premium—a silver goblet—gave it to his sister (as I understand) nothing but racing—on Friday—Sat we spent the day with cousin Mary Smith[11] & Mary Brickell[12]—at Mr Sessions' my dear niece indisposed from over fatigue the day before at the Fair—being a cold disagreeable day.

Sunday, November 20 Sister M. Eva—& James are going to church—hope Edward will too—am now writing to Cornelia—expect to write to Bettie & Oscar then to Adelaide—wrote Mrs Skipwith to-day.

Monday, November 21 Cousin Mary Smith & Mary Brickell her grand daughter a very amiable girl came early to go to the inauguration of Gov. Pettus[13]—heard of the severe illness of Mr Albert Sessions—has sent or written for his bror James to go up—who expects to leave this evening on the carrs—Our dear A. will be over here this morning to stay with us—until his return—most sincerely do I sympathise with dear Mrs Sessions & the family—I love them very much—may God sustain her in this trying hour.

Tuesday, November 22 All dined here to-day left late in the evening—a letter was brought me from my dear Oscar was by my bror—directed "Colo A.L. Hardeman" thinking that was the name of my bror which was read at the table—Mr S left for Holmes Cty. Brougham—to see his bror who is no better.

Wednesday, November 23 Spent the day with my dear niece—cousin Mary Smith & Mary Brickell—Eva has been some days afflicted with a cold—had her feet bathed & got a stew of horse radish—My dear bror left this morning for Wash. & Bolivar Ctys—& the Carpenter Estate—for an indefinite time we miss him so much—I lost control of my temper to-night Eliza provoked me very much—was insolent—& behaved very badly. I will try & regain my balance—anger is majestic—but makes slaves of weak minds. Miss Bettie Wharton is 16 yrs old to-day as I understand—she bids fair to make a woman of the first order—

Thursday, November 24 Thanks giving day—Sister Mary—gone to Church—our dear A.G.S. coming over as Mr S. is gone to Holmes to see his bror—want to write to Oscar to-day—

Monday, November 28 Sent my letter to the Office—am now writing to my dear Adelaide—Our dear A & Nannie with Mr S. left us yesterday evening my dear bror not yet returned—O that he could be more at home—We are very anxious about him—as there was Typhoid Fever—on Carpenter Estate—I regret his engagement to manage it as receivership—&c. am not getting on well with my work—have a good deal of writing to do—Sister M. received a letter from her sister Mrs Polk yesterday which informed her that she would be here soon—I must make my dresses up—if possible though I have no patterns—

Tuesday, November 29 A cloudy day—Eliza is sewing on the old G. B. Machine—on Julia's clothes who is not well. I am going to repair James' coat—25 minutes after 10 sat up last night till 12—must try to retire earlier—

Wednesday, November 30 My dear bror returned from the River!—

Thursday, December 1 Dr Maney Mr & Mrs Keeble with their two children a son 13 yrs old & a little daughter 4 (I suppose)—Miss Sallie Bell—& Miss Sue Thompson arrived they had determined to go to N.O. on Sat 2nd but on Fri Morning Dr Maj. Maney came with a Dispatch from Tenn. to inform them of the death of Mrs D. Maneys child—Miss S. Bells nephew she was greatly distressed & they determined to return home immediately—& left that evening in the carrs. Miss Bell was deeply bereaved. I was very favourably impressed by her—& could but feel the deepest sympathy for her—May Our heavenly Father sanctify her bereavement to herself & sister & sustain her through life.

Tuesday, December 6 On Mon 5th. Mrs Agathy Inge my 4th cousin came out—on the carrs from N.O. intending to go to Tuscaloosa by R.R. but we had a hard rain last night & to-day—but to-night 6th we have severe sleet & cold—which induced her to return to N.O. & take a steamer for Mobile. I have done nothing this week but look over & arrange old letters & papers have sewed a little to-night. James received a letter from Adelaide yesterday & my dear Ann one from my dear Bettie—What would I not give to know that they were comfortable this bleak inclement night—O that they may be watched over—& provided for & cared for—

Saturday, December 10 Sat 10th (I beleive) Wrote to my dear Bettie last night & my bror kindly offered to wait till I finished just sent it in—Eva went over to Mr S.' on Thurs. evening may—may perhaps return this evening—
   I am thankful to see another bright beautiful day Miss Bettie Lester was married on Thurs 8th. None of the family went but James—who enjoyed himself very well indeed—heard good news on the same night I beleive viz that Mrs Skipwith had a relation to die suddenly in Baton Rouge who was wealthy—& left his Estate with a Spanish claim in Litigation to her children! I look upon it as a special Providence as it proved to her that she was not forgotten by Him who counts the hairs of our head,[14] & that He had not forgotten *her*. May she like Job ever have a just appreciation of His mercies to her—may he sustain her even in her prosperity—

Sunday, December 11 Heard of the death of Dr Dewees of Madison (formerly of Philadelphia) who died of cancer in the stomach—he had an Infirmary & was an eminent Physician[15]—he was here once—Mr Thos Nicholson came on Sun. night 4th inst on his way to Texas—had a very painful foot—had only hurt him the night before—went on however on Mon. morning—but was detained in the City of N.O. 10 days on account of it he is now at his plantation in Mad. Mr Edward Yellowley came out with my bror & spent the night—my bror brought letters from Adelaide & Colo Stuart & Adelaides & Betties Report—for Nov. Medium 8 in conduct the balance was very well—hope it will be better & that they may feel the importance of making 9 in all their studies—O that they may be watched over & cared for properly—may they ever on all occasions be conscientious & act in reference to the future—No one went to church except James—Mr Yellowly is gone. I had been writing to my dear Sally when the tea bell rang—we had not all left the table when we heard some one at the front door—& my bror Wm in passing to the Parlour saw & announced the name & arrival of my dear bror D from Texas—also Mr T W Nicholson who had gone over a few weeks before to look at lands—I regret that Eva his last daughter [16] will leave us so soon—she is anxious to return home & I wish her to do so— to see her family whom she has not seen for 3½ yrs—O that I could visit my dear Sally who is I fear a confirmed invalid—but perhaps it is best— I pray for submission. my bror went up on the Carrs last night to see Mr T.W. Nicholson his bror in law—James staid all ngt with his cousin A.G.S. sister M. & Eva have gone to return her calls—My dear bror returned on 13th & left for N.O. that evening—we felt reluctant to give up our dear Eva—our gentle Dove like Eva—they expected to leave N.O. for Galveston this morning Sat. 17th the wind is blowing briskly—but hope they may have had a safe voyage. Our dear A.G.S. came over on 13th—is here now— on the 15th our dear W.D. came—was quite sick with chills—look badly.

Saturday, December 17 W.D. much improved—Colo Stuart came on the 13th left this morning—

Sunday, December 18 We had just returned from breakfast when Colo Polk & family arrived all in good health—all the children much grown—
   no one except James went to church—Eddie is in my room writing to his sister Adelaide.

Friday, December 23 We went to town & purchased Christmas presents for children but was sorry I could not get any thing scarcely for the servants—

Monday, December 26 Our dear A.G.S. came over on yesterday 25th & dined with us—had a pleasant day—my dear bror went home—Only wrote to the dear absent children—26th Mon. My dear bror left this morning for Sonora taking with him Belinda—a stout overgrown girl of 10 yrs old— Betsey & Madison—4 & 5 yrs old—& Tenie a woman who has been at Dr Dewees for some time—will be gone I expect about 10 days—Our dear

A.G.S. came over we have had very warm weather for several days during this week—

Friday, December 30 Yesterday Mr John Hilliard came from Texas—we were very glad to see him—Mrs Polks baby seems to be quite sick—but not dangerous—I received a letter from my dear Bettie couched in rather an excited state of feeling—I answered it last night 29th—To-day 30th I have been sewing on the Machine succeeded very poorly—though I think it will sew better now—received a letter also from dear cousin Agatha Inge.[17]

1860

Sunday, January 1, 1860 10 oclock P.M. Sat up to see the old year go out & the New year come in—Have not felt well to-day—have not spent the day as I wished—Our dear A.G.S. went home this evening & I neglected a duty to my dear Nannie that I feel uncomfortable about—

Friday, January 6 Spent the day at Mrs A.G.S. had a sumptuous dinner all well our dear Ann sat at the table—it rained in the afternoon & Ma remained—went to James' room last night—Maj Maney came last night— also Colo Polk James[1] & George—Thurs 5th. My dear bror returned not well but seems better now—

Saturday, January 7 A bright day—after several of rain & clouds—wrote to Adelaide to-day.

Sunday, January 8 No one went to church except James—all well but Maj Maney—who was not well when he came.

Tuesday, January 10 Colo Polk & his son James left this morning 4 oclock— the former for Tenn. the latter for Chapel Hill—N.C. James Polk was 18 yrs old on the 8th—a handsome promising young gentleman may he be all that his fond parents could wish him—Had written to Bettie to-day received letters from them yesterday—our dear Bettie was sick with inflammatory sore throat—My dear bror has not been well for some time has dysentary. dear James took B. Mass yesterday—is better to-day—Mrs Tarpley came out this morning—through the rain—Wed April 7th 1859.[2] Adelaide & Oscar commenced reading Scotts Novels—began with the "Antiquary"[3] finished it Teus 13th (copied this from an old journal)—

Sunday, January 15 Sister M. & little Susan went to church—Mr Bell & family are expected here to-night—heard that Colo Polk had arrived at home on Fri 13th inst. received letters from the girls Oscar & Cornelia & one from Eva yesterday—all well—

Monday, January 16 A bright beautiful day. Mr Dick Bell & family with Miss Thompson arrived last night. will be here during the week—James still away—tomorrow hope he will be at home—Georgie & Edward started to school to-day—have been sewing on the Machine last week a little—On Sun. A.M. Met Mrs Polk in the Parlour had a long conversation with her— she talks well & feels the necessity of having her spirits rallied & of a reaction taking place—but how is it to be effected? my heart aches when I think of the once happy face of her girlhood—& cannot realize that it is the same though an uninterrupted scene of prosperity has been extended to her— during her unmarried life & her married life has been remarkably happy— her house having "*no skeleton*" (allusion to a good story)

Wednesday, January 18 James came home from Mr S. yesterday evening— Mr Bell & family left this morning Miss Thompson goes in the morning I understand—Mr Hilliard left for Texas Teus 17th Jan '60—Miss Thompson left about one oclock—sister M. went in with her—& remained until night—my bror came home before night & we were at supper when sister M & James came—

Saturday, January 21 I went to town & met our dear Ann—she did some shopping—called to see Mrs Skipwith & met Mrs Foute[4] who seems to be in great affliction from the death of her two children did a good deal of shopping—& regret a part of it very much—but hope I shall not go in again until late in the Spring if I do then—it is a very disagreeable task—as I know so little about it—& no doubt trespass on the kindness & indulgence of my dear bror when I neither wish or intend it.—God help me to act uprightly in all things & ever to act in referance to the future.

Sunday, January 22 Our Quarterly meeting is in progress—& I did expect to go—but could not as I felt too much fatigued to do so—

Tuesday, January 24 Spent the day at Mr Sessions all the family went & Ma remained had quite a pleasant day—children walked home Edward went to town—I have not succeeded with my work this week—have felt very badly my head feels very uncomfortable—from indulging too much in luxuries—

Monday, January 30 Have had some trouble this morning—Mrs P. not well—little Mary highly offended because I sprinkled her face &c—

Sometime in the early part of the month of Jan. My bror came to dinner & told us he had engaged to be the "Receiver" of several plantations for Mr Wm F. Smith—went with Mr S. to N.O. returned on Wed. 25th left on Thurs. 26—to visit the plantations he will have the care of—he has not yet returned from his tour on the River—O that he may be watched over & cared for by our heavenly Father—

Wednesday, February 1 Have been very busy finishing some articles of clothing to send the girls—hope to finish them—to send by Mr Daniels[5]—who leaves on Wed 9th—

Friday, February 3 Heard from my dear bror Wm to-day the 3rd was well—will not be at home for some time—Our dear Willie D Sallie & Tommie arrived this evening—Mrs Polk improving sister M. not well.

Saturday, February 4 Mr De France—Sally dear little Annie Howard—Willie D & Tommie came over to see us & brought my Mother home—dear Willie was taken sick—last night—is quite sick yet—

Sunday, February 5 This morning 5th Mr De France brought the buggy over & I returned with him—as he was kind enough to come after me—we had a good deal of rain—& I came home in the carriage heard from my dear bror to-day through Mr Hilliard—he will perhaps go to Tensas before he returns—after visiting the Carpenter Estate have not succeeded with my work during the past week—neither have I written to my dear girls—or Oscar—hope to be able to do so next week & also to dear Eva—

Monday, February 13 Wrote last night Feb 12 to Eva—From the time of my last entry my bror returned from a long tour which fatigued him very much—Colo Polk also returned from his plantation—& remained a few days during which we had a very severe snow storm—on Teus morning Colo P. left for N.O. on Fri 10 Colo Stuart came—is here yet—received letters from the dear girls on that day—sent a bundle in to Mr Daniels to deliver to the girls—had some trouble about it—wrote to both the girls & directed to Bettie—succeeded with my work better than I expected. the Machine skipped a little—stitched a little—Mon 13th. I have this morning resumed my old plan of trying to do every thing by rule—expect to[6] Mend & repair clothing to-day—My dear James has been in trouble for the last few days—O how hard it is to begin life with utter poverty & have every dime counted down—but perhaps it is best—it may give an impetus to exertion—though to a proud spirit *it is humiliating*—I humbly hope however that the "ways of God may be justified to *him*" thereby—

13th Mon. I have all my life wished to have a certain sum allotted me— but it has never been convenient to do so—I could not make a proper or correct estimate myself & consequently it was neglected or not spoken of any more—but to-night I had occasion to borrow a little money & the subject was again agitated—I mentioned five dollars per month—sister Mary generously sd she thought one hundred dollars for Ma & myself would do for the balance of the yr. I wished to borrow $5.00 & she brought me 15 I wld not accept it as a gift but took it as an allowance.

Wednesday, February 15 Colo Polk arrived from N.O. yesterday morning Mr Hilliard this evening 15th yesterday 14th was the day for exchange of Valentines—James sent only one—& received only one—on the comic order. My dear bror did not look well to-night. Went with sister M. Colo & Mrs Polk—over to Rose Cottage—staid only a few minutes perhaps an hour— James sent Adelaide a check for $25.00 to-day to pay for calisthenics & dancing.

Thursday, February 16–Friday, February 24 Mr Hilliard & Albert Vaught a boy of 12 or 14 (I suppose) who was going up to fish & hunt on the plantation came. Mr H. left the next morning—which was Wed. 15th Thurs. morning 16th left for N.O. & my bror left for Tensas. Colo Polk went to Anemeka on Fri. 17th—Mon 20th A bright day of sunshine but cold—began to dress Susies[7] doll on Sat. but did not get through. James received a letter from Mr Purnell—last week—I will if possible make my entries more regularly—as I forget the dates very often. My dear Sallie & Thomasella came over with little Annie Howard & staid until Wed. when I returned in company with my Mother to Rose Cottage with them—& remained until Fri. 24th when our dear Nannie returned with us—to stay until to-morrow—just as I was about to sit down to my work Mrs Harry Christmas her daughter Mary & Mr Thos C. her son were announced—Mr S. brought a letter out from dear Adelaide—yesterday some *expressions* in it which were rather *objectionable*—but very good letters—have been trying to cut Edward pants out— must do so now—my dear bror is absent so much that I forgot to mention his arrival last night—saw him to-day at dinner—heard from dear Cousin Ann Pugh—she is improving—also dear W.D. who has lost a very valuable woman—who was brought down in Jan.

Saturday, February 25 Passed rather a vexatious day—Machine did not do well & my work was not arranged—but at night it seemed well though I only tried a small cloth—

Sunday, February 26 A beautiful & delightful day just cold enough to make it pleasant—My dear bror left—this morning between 7 & 8 oclock with Susannah (servant) for G.L. Ark.[3] & many other places to be gone three weeks—Mr De France (who was expected last night) did not come Sallie received a letter from him informing her of his intention to be here on Teus. AM. James went in as he says to visit some ladies hope he will—

Monday, February 27 A bright day—¼ of 10 oclock—wrote a long letter to my dear Bettie yesterday & last night—complied also with my 1st rule—

Tuesday, February 28 Could do no work—

Wednesday, February 29 Have cut out eight pr drawers 6 for Edward & 2 pr for Colo Stuart—mended my calico dress Sister Mary received a letter from Oscar & bror Wm to-day my dear Oscar sent me a scissors grinder but I have not seen it—little Willie[9] seems quite sick—is cutting teeth.

Thursday, March 1 Sister Mary went to town to-day a bright balmy one—& took the little children—Susie, Junius, & Hilliard, went by Mr S's—furnished James Office—gave him an arm chair—and furnished many other comforts. Mrs Polk has been quite sick for some days late in the evening Mr De France Mr Harper Sallie, Tommie, & Annie Howard—came—sister Mary returned during their stay—they came to take leave of us as they were going off—Mr De France & Family going to Floyd their home in La. taking Tommie with them to return last of May or 1st of June—When they will all return to Tenn. Mr Harper is the gentleman with whose fate Tommie expects to unite her own on the 21st June—Blessings on the dear girl—she is peculiarly dear to me—Mr H. seems to be a very clever gentleman but I have no acquaintance with him as yet—though the accounts of him are very flattering—I know his family—he is a widower with a little daughter 4 yrs old—his 1st wife was a Miss Valentine of La.

Friday, March 2 In the evening Mrs Skipwith & Mr Ben. Green came out—a little later & Colo Polk Georgie his son & Susannah Nune came.

Saturday, March 3 Dr Cabiness sent for to see Mrs Polk—though she is up now—

Sunday, March 4 No one went to church. Mrs Polk improved—wrote hastily to my dear Adelaide to-day—from a letter received from her I learn that she & her sister were Baptised on Ash Wednesday. May they realise the responsibilities of that rite—they had been baptised in infancy but the Minister & Bishop thought it was not valid—I can only hope that they may make sincere & *honest christians*—may they honour their profession & be useful through life—is my humble prayer.

Monday, March 5 Am mending as this is the day appropriated for that purpose—

Tuesday, March 6 This day I have numbered fifty seven years—& regret that my life has not been a more *profitable* one—I would be an humble self denying christian—O that I may spend the little time which remains— in making due preparation for my final hour—nothing has occurred to-day except that dear James went *visiting* the ladies—is gone to a debating society—

Wednesday, March 7 Heard from my dear bror Wm by a letter to sister Mary—is well but—but will not be at home for some time this is the 15th day of his absence hope to see him soon—

Thursday, March 8 Commenced apr pants for Edward on Teus—finished them late to-night but he did not like them & behaved unkindly to me— though he did not mean to do so—

Friday, March 9 Sister Mary Colo & Mrs Polk went to town brought letters from my dears Adelaide & Bettie.

Saturday, March 10 The Reports from St Marys Hall were received—very good—Adelaides 9 throughout & Bettie had only 8s for French & History—As we were sitting at dinner the door opened & my dear brother D entered—from Texas—was well staid only a few hours went in at 11 oclock—at night—but was compelled to go on account of business— speaks of purchasing lands on the San Antonio river near Goliad—but hope he will remain at his own home—dear dear brothers how full of business that both are—I regret that my dear bror Wm was not at home—They have just returned from Church at 2 oclock—On the 4th of March 1860 My dearest Bettie was confirmed in the chapel at Burlington N. Jersey—I pray that her vows may be as a mentor to guide her in the right way—O that she may ever be subject to the guardian care & guidance of Our Heavenly

Father my poor heart is full of gratitude for their early return to Him—Adelde is still indecided—but hope she may soon become a member of the Church of Christ also—my dear James is a Member of the M.E.C. A & B. of the Episcopal—I humbly hope it may make no difference between them.

Monday, March 12 Pleasant weather—Colo Polk left this morning at 5 oclock for Anameka on the River—taking Georgie with him—had a good deal of trouble to find the Receipts of Patton & Barfield for Music—but succeeded at last—have now to attend to my 1st rule—at 11 oclock.

Tuesday, March 13 Succeeded in finishing James' coat this evening time enough for him to wear it lined throughout—my eyes were weakened by the labour. Heard this evening of the death of Mrs Frank Hamer who died on 10th inst. leaving an infant son—she possessed many admirable traits of character—a kind & generous heart—with the "Charity which never faileth" & which is portrayed in the 13th Chap. Cor.[9] in many respects she "being dead yet speaketh"[11]—her memory will live in the hearts of those who have been taken from the desolate hearthstone & shared her maternal care—her record is on high—

Wednesday, March 14 Did not succeed with my work to-day—have been unusually depressed—Mrs Tarpley came out this evening—Mrs Buckley also—they are both very interesting ladies—Mrs Polk is much better Mary is not so wel—has a cold & sore throat my dear Edward accidently stuck his knife in his thigh this evening—which gave him much pain—

⟨. . . .⟩ Edward went to school—James went to

⟨. . . .⟩

This evening I had the pleasure of seeing the two Mr Porters whom I have not seen since they were children Wm had been in California 10 yrs—Daniel Price[12] is a practising Lawyer in Jackson—Mr Wm Porter gave us some information of our relatives in Cal. who had emigrated to Oregon from thence to Cal. where they have accumulated fortunes & are doing very well—he spoke in flattering terms of Mary Smith the daughter of my friend & cousin Constantia Burnett—who married a Mr Miller of Ky. who was struck by lightning afterwards married Mr Smith—of Va.[13] James went in to prayer meeting last night & conducted it. was—was but 3 out—Batey & Allen & himself—

Saturday, March 17 My dear Niece A.G.S. returned last night on the Carrs—will be here this morning—wrote to Oscar—& sent him 3 cravats & 5$

⟨. . . .⟩

knows that I try to do what is right—& act conscientiously under all circumstances & feel a willingness to abide the issue—I was rejoiced to see my dear dear bror whom I had not seen for 3 weeks—my dear Mother was over come—he is looking well. I am glad he can travel about to relieve the confinement of his office—

Tuesday, March 20 Received a letter from dear Bettie on the 17th which informed me of Adelaides & her confirmation—for which I feel thankful & humbly trust they may be humble & holy that they may each live the life of a christian—It has been a very long time I beleive a year since I have felt as I now do—I feel as one groping in the dark—desolate & forsaken without

⟨. . . .⟩

about—it is a great privation to be without her but hope she will enjoy herself—

Wednesday, March 21 About nightfall Mr & Mrs White with their daughter Mary came from Yazoo City. We have been expecting them for some time—Mrs W. is looking very well—I have not seen Mr White—

Thursday, March 22 All were very kind indeed—particularly dear Mrs Polk—left my bed to-day at about 10 clock it is past 10 now—my bror saw Mr W.F. Smith in town to-day—Mrs White is talking with him now in the parlour on business—sewed some on Edwards drawers Mary White has grown a good deal—looks extremely delicate—Mrs Polk up to-day & seems well—

Friday, March 23 Cloudy with a little wind sat up late last night—but was up & dressed by the time breakfast was ready—though very far from being at all well one enough to go about—feel very badly every way—I cannot tell how this attack will terminate—I often feel that my errand on earth was accomplished—though I still feel anxious to see how my dear children will do—but they will I trust be the objects of our heavenly Fathers care they have kind friends now—but they may have none when most needed—About nightfall—an Omnibus was seen to drive up & the little ones shouted for joy at the arrival of their Father as they thought—but it proved to be my dear Cornelia—& her bror Lent—from N.O.—whither she had gone some weeks previously on a visit to her Grandmother Dunica—I was so glad to see them.

Saturday, March 24 The ladies all except Mrs Polk & Cornelia went in sight seeing Mrs W. sister M. & Mary Murfree & Mary White before they left however Mrs White came down & said rather jestingly—that Mr White had proposed to put herself Mrs H. & all the children in the carriage & he would take the box—at which she demurred very properly—if she had done it with a due regard to the feeling of dear Cornelia—but she took as I thought a very singular way to tell her that there was no room for her sister M. came in & asked C. if she would go—she very properly refused— they went & staid until late in the evening no it was near 2 oclock Sun 25th.

Sunday, March 25 All went to church—Cornelia sister M. & the two little boys went in her carriage—Mrs White Mrs Polk—Lent—Mary Murfree Susie Spratt also Mr I. H. Hilliard all rode in Mrs Whites carriage—but met Col. Polk & *turned back.*

Monday, March 26 Mr & Mrs White with their daughter Mary took their leave—went to Mrs Treadwells—from thence to Mrs Cages thence home—

Tuesday, March 27 My dear Nieces birth Day—she is now absent on Yazoo— her health improving blessings on her—may she long live to bless us with her cheerful happy disposition May God watch over her & bring her to "the knowledge of the truth as it is in Jesus." & finally may she enjoy the rest which remains for the righteous.—

Wednesday, March 28 Mr Isaac Hilliard (who is in bad health from too free a use of tobacco) left for N.O. sister Mary Mrs Polk & Colo Polk accompanied him to the Depot.

Thursday, March 29 Colo Polk & family left for Tenn after spending three months & eleven days—We have passed a very pleasant time—the dear little children endeared themselves to us so much—that we regretted the necessity they felt for leaving. I miss the dear little ones so much—& dear Sally since the death of a dear little baby boy (of 2 yrs old) has lost her elasticity & seems to have given way to her sorrow & bereavement & the 18th inst. being the anniversary of his first attack—her spirits were very low— May God help her to rally—she is certainly a very superiour woman—

O that she could for the sake of her family *be herself again*—I hope I shall not soon forget the warm clasp of the neck which the dear little baby gave me— On Fri. 23rd My dear Cornelia came with her bror Lent—from N.O.— they are with us yet has been nursing James & myself since she has been here—what a dear dear child she is to me. On Sun. evening Col. Stuart came—went to Canton. staid several days returned on Fri. took leave of us this morning for Summit where he now resides—yesterday about 7 oclock our dear Cornelia & Lent left us for their home in Carroll Cty. I regretted the necessity for their departure—left at 5 oclock Sunday morning—

Sunday, April 1 Sister Mary went to church alone—Communion day heard of the effects of the storm at Trio—

Tuesday, April 3 My bror going to Vicksbg this evening April 3rd—

Wednesday, April 4 Sister Mary went in to church this evening My dear bror returned from Vicksbg & went on to Trio—will return the day after tomorrow—James not so well to-day—Edward also better. I have worked a little to-day on James shirts but did not finish—James cut his thumb badly this evening—have heard nothing from the dear girls yet—sister M. heard to-day through Henry Christmas who made some stay at Oxford on his return from Tenn. that our dear Oscar was not well.

Friday, April 6 (Good Friday) Service at the Episcopal Church to-day Sister Mary just gone—James just went in to-day for the first time—also Edward went to school though he still has a sore toe from having stuck a splinter in it which caused it to fester. I have been very uneasy about our dear absent children for some time at night fall James returned from the office & brought letters from Adelaide & Oscar said Bettie was well I felt truly & sincerely thankful—O that the Almighty may make them the objects of his care & "give them His fear before their eyes" always.

Saturday, April 7 Wrote a very long letter to Adelaide—my head is very painful—sister M. went in to-day my bror returned about 4 oclock—James did not go in today is reading one of Coopers Novels.

Sunday, April 8 No one went to Church but Sister Mary had communion & a large congregation.

Monday, April 9 My dear bror left for N.O. at 7 oclock this evening— This morning dear sister Mary went in to assist in making Mr Crane (the

Rector)[14] comfortable for house keeping—a Parsonage has been bought—
the house fitted up & the ladies have been very liberal in their donations—&
the entire house was well furnished—handsomely furnished—& the ladies
with their husbands & many others had a Levee to welcome the family[15]
to their "Home sweet Home"!! (What untold pleasures & real comforts
dwell in that short sentence)—they have hearts to appreciate the blessings
& luxuries bestowed upon them—Mr Crane from what I can learn has the
love of God in his heart—& his works do praise him & give him favour in
the eyes of the people to whom he ministers—May they ever be under his
guidance & direction & May he be guided by a "Pillar of cloud by day & of
fire by night"[16]—Mr & Mrs George Yerger[17] were the principal actors.

Wednesday, April 11 Went to town to select some dresses for my self—

Saturday, April 14 My dear bror came about 3 oclock at night from N.O.
bringing with him a treat of Bananas & Strawberries.

Sunday, April 15 No one went to church except Edward—it has been rather
a long day to me—James not well came home indisposed yesterday evening—looks pale & weak.

Monday, April 16 Attended to my first rule to-day finished James & Edwards
clothes their last summer clothes Eliza sewed some—Ma hemmed some
towels have been sick all day feel very badly to-night.

Tuesday, April 17 Mr White came this morning about 6 oclock—remained
until 4 went to Vicksbg sent him to the Depot in the carriage—through
the rain—

Wednesday, April 18 Went to town & regretted it very much—as I indulged
in the purchase of a linnen dress at six dollars—with several other articles
some of which I could have done without I shall not go again soon—cut out
Ma's dress but only covered the cord—&c. From the 1st to the 25th of this
month in 1849 was a trying season with all of us—as we were deprived of
a very dear sister by death on the 25th—it was indeed a night of sorrow to
us—six lovely children composed our family band but "one is not" for God
took her on the 14th of May 1853—a bright beautiful little girl—whom we
had nursed ourselves—& who was indeed the light of our eyes & the joy
of our hearts—but our most valued gifts are due to Him who gives us all
things—I pray for resignation & humble submission to his holy will in all
things—

Friday, April 20 When my dear bror returned from town to-day about 3 oclock—he brought us the sad & painful news of Mr George Yergers death [18]—he was on his plantation & we have heard nothing *definite* as yet—expect that he died of Appoplexy in the night—his remains have not yet arrived—are expected tomorrow evening—He was the main pillar of the Episcopal Church here—was liberal—charitable—& kind to the poor—he was ever ready with his purse & personal efforts in the line of a christian gentlemans duty—he has doubtless been called to the fruition of those joys—which he sought with so much diligence here—I feel the deepest sympathy for his devoted but truly bereaved wife & family—may they be comforted by the reflection that he has only preceded them a short time to that "rest which remains for the people of God"—

My dear bror went to Canton at 4 this evening expecting to return at 4 in the morning—dear sister Mary was sick last night & to-day though I think her much improved to-night.

Saturday, April 21 My bror accompanied Judge Yerger & Mr Kausler to Yazoo City to remove the remains of Mr G.S. Yerger to his residence in Jackson—had a copious shower of rain yesterday at 3½ oclock—There is to be confirmation held at Yazoo City to-morrow—the daughter of my bros friends Mr & Mrs J.J.B. White is to be confirmed.

Sunday, April 22 Sister Mary has just left for church—dined at Mr Cranes—rained soon after her return—

my dear bror returned this evening through the rain—seemed well—but much fatigued—the remains of Mr G.S. Yerger were deposited in the basement story of the church whither Mrs Y. went to see them—his burial & the funeral took place to-day at 11 oclock—the largest concourse that ever was in Jackson—Mr Crane said a great deal in illustration of the character of Mr Yerger. he was his friend—his guide—his counsellor & always gave liberally to the church—& in aid of the suffering poor & destitute his loss will be mourned by every class of people.

On the 30th April 1860 Colo C.S. Tarpley died! about 3 oclock—He was the pillar of the Methodist Church & a zealous christian—ever ready to releive the wants of suffering humanity devoted to his family & they to him—My warmest sympathies for his bereaved wife & family—whom I love very much—O that she could find comfort in Christ—& his holy religion—may she be resigned & submit to his will—that she may join her husband in the heaven of eternal rest—May his spirit be permitted to watch over their footsteps thither—their stay—& their prop is gone he is not "for

God took him"—Colo Tarpley was buried with the honours of Masonry—
the Fire Company—& the Military also—every respect was shewn to his
memory—Rev. C.K. Marshall[19] preached his Funeral Sermon—which was
very good & appropriate—said also a good deal about Mr G.S. Yerger—

On April 28th I took to my bed—got up a while on Sun. evening—
but retired again to my bed of suffering—from whence I have not yet recovered—was greatly afflicted with vomiting on Mon. & part of Teus. Dr
Cabiness came out Teus morn. My dear niece A.G.S. returned from G. Gulph
the same evening. I am truly thankful for kind attentions & they were doubly
dear because extended by my own dear Mother—my dear brother—& dear
sister Mary. May God reward them for the kindness & luxuries provided for
me during this night of suffering—of which I feel altogether unworthy—

I have not mentioned in its proper place the departure of my dear James
& Edward for Sonora on Mar 10th ult. I parted with great reluctance &
dear James took an affectionate farewell twice & expressed his reluctance
to leave—& I would not express my fears of a severe attack—& tried to
part with as much fortitude as possible—

Monday, May 7 About this time 6 years ago my darling little Janie was taken
sick of the dreadful disease which admitted her into Heaven—"Far from a
world of grief & sin. With God eternally shut in." I see I have neglected to
mention in its proper place the anniversary of my sisters death my much
beloved & lamented sister though each day passed off with a vivid recollection of the scenes which occurred at the time—thou wert not forgotten my
dear—dear—sister—I find but too much to remind me of thee—would
that I could feel—that thy spirit watched over thy children & thy sorrowing sister & Mother with brothers who loved thee & a sister who nursed
& watched over thy last moments—May we never forget the scenes of the
last 3 months of thy life.

Tuesday, May 8 My dear bror Wms Natal Day. I scarcely know how to express
a blessing upon thee my darling precious brother—May God watch over
thee—sustain & guide thee through all the vicissitudes which you may yet
have to pass—But my most fervent prayer is that the "goodness & mercy of
God may lead thee to repentance"[20]—Mayest thou be brought as a lamb to
the fold—(59 yrs old). Last Friday 4th Was my dear brother D's anniversary
I would ask the same for him that I would for my dear brother William.

Wednesday, May 9 My darling Betties 15th Anniversary—must write to her
to-day—have been quite sick to-day cannot tell how this indisposition will

terminate. I pray for resignation & submission to His will with a due preparation for my final hour I often feel that my errand on earth is accomplished—
In God alone do I put my trust.

Thursday, May 10 Spent the day with my dear Niece A.G.S. whom we found
in bed—Mr S. not well or Nannie dear child—she was reluctant to take
leave felt depressed in the morning but it passed off & my spirits were better
in the evening.

Friday, May 11 Wrote a little note to my dear niece who is not so well—
Mr S. sick—Wrote to my dear Cornelia hope to be able to fill up my time
next week more profitably than the past—James & Edward will surely be
at home to-morrow—

Sunday, May 13 Did not feel as well yesterday as the day before—& this
morning while I was making my toilette a sudden but severe pain struck me
at the edge of my right shoulder—could not draw a long breath &c. had it
rubbed with camphor but it is not releived—a cold cloudy day & my dear
James & Edward have not returned yet—How vividly do the scenes & little
incidents of my little darlings illness occur to me—At this time 7 yrs ago
the cup of sorrow was filling to the brim for my dear sister & J—the light
of our eyes & the joy of our hearts was taken in the shape of our dear

⟨ . . . . ⟩

would I say Thy Will Be Done—

Monday, May 14 This is the 7th anniversary of her death—I trust she is an
inmate of that home whose inhabitants shall never say "I am sick" [21]—while
I am still a pilgrim here—may the spirits of our loved ones watch over our
journeying until we join them—& Praise God together ⟨ . . . . ⟩ at 6 oclock
for Greenville to attend court & visit 4 Plantations—I miss him a great
deal—no one at home but sister Mary—Ma & myself—

Tuesday, May 15 My dear James & Edward came home this morning had
enjoyed their visit

⟨ . . . . ⟩

yesterday morning had rain last night. to-day Mr Fayette McConnico dined
here with the Messrs Maney—also Mr Sessions—have felt very weak &

lanquid all day—it is now past 11 oclock—P.M. dear sister Mary was kind enough to read a paper to-night—

⟨. . . .⟩

Friday, May 18 Our Minister Rev. Mr Harrington[22] came out to see us this morning—& this evening Mrs came out with her children the baby & Eva—

Saturday, May 19 Spent a very pleasant day at Rose Cottage—

⟨. . . .⟩

when I do go—

Sunday, May 20 Sister Mary & Edward only went to Church—James is not well—cousin Washington Perkins & Mr Cheatham[23] came over this evening—

Thursday, May 24 Mon. 21st Sister M. & A. went to town & returned by 2 oclock—Teus. Maj Maney came—My dear James has been quite sick since Sat. 19th—is improving—Teus. 22nd was Mrs Wm Maneys birth-day—59 yrs has she numbered—Wed. 23rd Spent the day at Rose Cottage with Maj Maney—that night after our return my dear mother was taken sick of Diarhea she was not well all day & this morning 24th—she is con-siderably worse—is suffering a great deal. James is well he says—received a letter from my dear Bettie on the 23rd Wed. also one from my Aunt Corzine & an "Advocate"—

Friday, May 25 My dear Mother improving—sister M. received letters from her husband & brother—the former will perhaps be at home Teus. or Wed. O we miss him so much—what a treasure he is to his family.

Saturday, May 26 Received a letter from my dear Willie—I was much grati-fied at receiving it as it gave me information of his improved health—&c. have been at work since Mon P.M.

Sunday, May 27 The 42nd anniversary of my dear Fathers death—Thy coun-sels & advice are still remembered—my lamented father but I do not feel that I have answered thy expectations or those of my dear family—but I have tried my utmost to be what thou wouldst have had me—Edward joined P.E. S.School to-day—Mr James Yerger[24] is his teacher—

Monday, May 28 My dear brother returned to-day—we were very glad to see him looking so well—

Tuesday, May 29 Sister Mary & James went to Edward's Depot—will return tomorrow Ma not well to-day—fatigues herself too much—

My bror rec. a letter from Oscar to-day was well & wld. be at home about the 1st June I am truly thankful [25]

Thursday, May 31 Mrs Wheat—the two Miss Hays [26] my dear Niece A.G.S. spent the day here found Mrs W. a very agreeable lady the Miss Hays' also— I did not see them when they left—& fear I did wrong in noticing the ommission—most humbly would I ask for the grace & strength which is requisite for these little trials & mortifications.

Friday, June 1 The 6th Anniversary of my lamented sister Carolines death— 6 weary years have I survived thee my dear sister but thou hast never been forgotten. I miss thee in every department my dear dear sister. Our fraternal affection was more than ordinary & the true excellencies of thy character are daily brought to my remembrance—

Saturday, June 2 Expected Dr Carter & Profr Richardson [27] here but they did not come—they are still in Jackson—

Sunday, June 3 Dr C. preached in town to-day—or rather on Sun 3rd June— Mr Purnell came last night spent the night here—My bror sister M. J.H.S. & Mr P. went in to church the former to hear Mr Wheat the latter to hear Dr Carter—our Minister is quite sick with Measles—

Monday, June 4 Wrote to our dear Adelaide to-day & of course neglected my rules partially—This morning my dear bror was quite indisposed has been confined to his bed—

Tuesday, June 5 My dear bror is improving it is now nearly 12 oclock & he is up writing—

James has just come—I feel fatigued.

Wednesday, June 6 Did not feel well all day—

Thursday, June 7 Spent the day at Rose Cottage met My dear Nieces Sallie & Tommie & dear little Annie Howard—Mr D in Vickbg—

Friday, June 8 10 oclock have not had my thimble on yet—but must make up the time in the evening Mr De France came having left dear Annie Howard Sallie, Tommie, & Annie H. Sessions in town—they came late remained all night & left about 10 oclock this morning for Rose Cottage & at 4½ oclock this evening took the carrs for Tenn.—

Sunday, June 10 Rain last night slightly & this morning for the first time in some weeks—none of the family went to church except Edward my bror & sister M. Both indisposed & James did not feel like riding any horse except Poney & he has a very sore foot.

Monday, June 11 Have not progressed with my work to-day—have not been equal to any exertion but did make an effort to sew a little—had a little rain last night—My bror very busily engaged in making out his Bank a/c—&c. sits up too late—

Wednesday, June 13 My dear bror left early this morning (Wed 13th) for Sonora in La—to be gone a week—arose early & saw him before he left & thought of course the breakfast very late at 8 oclock—My dear niece went to town sister Mary met her there to assist her in shopping—remained all day & in the evening late my dear bror returned home exhausted—wrote till late & was up in time to take the carrs this morning—Our dearest niece is with us for the last night—as she intends leaving soon for Tenn to be gone three months—it a trial to give her up for she is a great comfort to us all—& dear Nannie—we shall miss her so much—

Thursday, June 14 Went up to look at the place beyond the quarter—as my niece wished to select a place to build—she then returned home & met her husband—

Friday, June 15 Heard from all of our dear absent ones to-day—Sat was very busy sister Mary & A.G.S. met in town—sister M. was kind enough to get me two calico dresses instead of one. one of them is a very wide stripe though pretty—

Sunday, June 17 Sister Mary went to church & our dear A. & N. came over to spend an hour or two before leaving on the carrs for Tenn.—

the family dined with us & left for the Depot & passed at 4 oclock—they will be gone 3 mos. it is sad to be separated so long but it gives me pleasure to think that their enjoyment will be enhanced thereby. our dear Tommie will be married on the 20th inst—yesterday was the 36th anniversary of my dear bros & dear sister Marys wedding—A long & happy life to each of them hope they may live out the "sear & yellow leaf" & arrive at a happy old age—& reach the "golden wedding"—

Monday, June 18 P.M. James is gone in to see if Mr Purnell came on the Carrs as we were looking for him my heart ached to-day—19 Teus. Had a storm of wind—& some rain but not enough for the parched ground—My dear bror Wm was in the storm—I felt confident that he was—at the time— heard to-day of the death of a dear—dear—little one whom I loved very much & I thought she loved me also—Little Lilly Skipwith Burwell [28]— 6 yrs old—"He who gives us richly all things to enjoy" [29] is certainly entitled to our best gifts—He gave her to fond parents on earth—then took her to embellish his kingdom in Heaven—"Blessed be his holy Name"

⟨. . . .⟩

Tuesday, July 3 Just at night fall Mrs Joseph Nicholson with her three chil-dren came—next morning the glorious *Fourth* was ushered in—sister Mary accompanied Mrs N. to the celebration at the Fair Grounds—Our dear James and J. R. Yerger were the chosen Orators of the day—but James S. had been absent & had no time to prepare a speech & of course declined— J.Y. had his speech prepared but alas! the night before he was to deliver it—he heard of the death of his uncle Mr Arthur Rucks—he therefore declined—

Thursday, July 5 Rec. a letter from my dear Adelaide to-day—also one from my dear Nannie—Mrs N. left this morning—sister M. rec. one from dear Evie—says they have gone to Crescent Village—to spend the summer— will soon move to Goliad Cty 12 m. of the town of Goliad—hope it will be his permanent home—our dear Sally has another son named Bailey for his grand-father [30]—All were well Dickey was at home—D well—&c.

Friday, July 6 My dear lamented bror Thos' Natal Day!! Though he has been resting in his grave since 15th Septr 1836—he is not forgotten by his bros & sisters—Did a good deal yesterday—such as righting up chests— wardrobes &c. am greatly fatigued took my bureau into the account also—

Saturday, July 7 Always a busy day—with those who do not manage rightly —& unfortunately I am of that class—but I try "to struggle & to wait"— I am too much inclined to look into the past—

Sunday, July 8 Sister M. & my bror went to Church so did Oscar, James, & Edward, in the evening—Colo Stuart came—& remained until this morning Mr De France S. & dear little Annie Howard came on Thurs. morning.

Friday, July 13 About 2 oclock my dear bror came home bringing my dear Adelaides painting with him in the buggy—my very heart yearned to see them—& I felt truly thankful that she had succeeded so well—the picture is beautiful—It would do justice to more experience—the shading is exquisite. Fri the Picture came!! We were truly glad to see it—it is hanging in the Parlour!

Sunday, July 15 No one went to church except Mr De F bror Wm & sister Mary—My dear Sally remained with her Gr ma & me & also dear little Annie Howard.

Monday, July 16 Mr De France & family left this morning I parted with them reluctantly—very—their visit was *particularly* pleasant & agreeable—We arose very early that they might not be too late for the Carrs—I was not able to sit up all day—in the afternoon did a little work—

Tuesday, July 17 Sewed for O. on the Machine succeeded tolerably well—

Wednesday, July 18 Nearly 9 oclock—Sister Mary gone out to-day visiting Mrs Bishop Green—Sharkey—Adams—&c &c.

Thursday, July 19 Sister M. went again to-day saw dear Mrs Tarpley—Mrs Yerger etc. etc.—have sewed none on my dresses this week—Fri. & Sat at various sewings.

Sunday, July 22 Sister M. went to church—The weather has been very oppressive this Summer—within the last few weeks unusually so—it is said to be the hottest Sum. since '28. We have been greatly blessed with the products of the soil—& every other comfort—

Tuesday, July 24 My bror did—dear Willie D has gone to Tenn. Our young cousin Hinton Marr[31] came out yesterday—left this morning—have been engaged making James' under shirts the Machine did very well—at supper I did not do right.

Thursday, July 26 Sewed yesterday but was writing all day to-day.

Friday, July 27 My dear bror left for Sonora this morning but I did not see him although I was up but did not get ready to go out as I forgot—he intended leaving—May he be watched over by the All seeing eye—& restored to us again. What a treasure he is to us all. he *toils* for *us*—but no one *toils* for *him*. Yesterday 26th was a day to be remembered by me on my dear Edwards account—he came home from school without reciting his lessons & had some difficulty with his Teacher—A gentleman whom we all respect—& esteem—he has taken a great deal of pains with Edward—my heart is sore pained within me—God help me to bear these things as I ought—I fear very much that my duty has not been discharged as it should have been. O that the occasion may result in good to himself.

Sunday, July 29 Last night about 3 oclock I found sister Mary on awaking sitting by my bed—Eliza had come down to let her know that Tenie (a sick servant woman) was very ill—sent for the Dr early this morning—he thinks her case doubtful—

Monday, July 30 Sister M. went to town to see Mrs Tarpley & to call on several ladies—heard of the severe illness of dear Mrs Green—who has a family—I regret it very much—but trust that she may have the influences of the Holy Spirit to sustain her in this trying affliction—she seems to be a real christian one who feareth God alway—& discharges her duty to a large family conscientiously. my dear bror expected to-morrow—we miss him so much—so much—though I see so little of him when he is at home yet the thought that he is here is a great pleasure—

Sunday, October 7 9 oclock P.M. I have been suffering for some time with my head & ear—the last two months seem to have been entirely lost to me.

Tuesday, October 16 My head & ear still on the sick list—but seem to be improving—not so painful except occasionally the most acute pains run through my neck, head, & ears, fear I shall lose the use of my left ear—but I am truly thankful that I am able to sit up & work a little—& have no *constant pain*—my appetite is good—but my entire system seems paralysed—slightly—My dear bror Wm left 15th (Mon.) for the River to be gone a few days—dear sister Mary left this morn. 16th to make a visit to Mrs Hintons & Mrs Christmas'—expects to return to-morrow—

Wednesday, October 17 We did very well last night James staid with his cousin A. & Nannie as they were alone—my poor head is improving slowly—but do not know how it will terminate—I pray God to prepare me for living or dieing—I sometimes feel that my errand on earth is done—I would like to see the dear absent ones if it were his will—but if not I wld pray for submission & a due preparation for my final change.

Friday, October 19 Sister Mary went over to Mr Sessions to-day spent a few hours—James stays there every night during Mr S. absence.

Saturday, October 20 A bright beautiful day—feel very nervous to-day—my head & neck not much improved—but I am thankful that I am able to be up.

Sunday, October 21 Another bright beautiful day—arose earlier than usual this morning to take leave of my *dear* bror Wm who expects to be absent about a Fortnight or three weeks on the River—O that these long absences were done with—& we could see more of our only earthly prop & stay upon earth—for the present—as we are living with him—he & his dear wife are exceedingly kind & attentive to our wants of every kind—not only to us but to the children who were left to their care and have had a home with them since May 1849. May their reward here after shew with what fidelity they have discharged their duties to them. May the choicest blessings of Heaven rest upon them—it so rarely happens that we see a wife sustain & assist her husband in the discharge of such responsible duties their dear Mother requested that they with myself should have the controul & management of her dear children accordingly they were brought to my brors house in a few weeks after the death of their Mother & have remained here ever since except when they were at school. Our darling little Pet of the Household was transplanted in a more congenial clime after remaining with us four & a half years. her death made a blank in our poor hearts. May those who remain make a due preparation to meet her in the "Land of pure delight" [32]—"The Land of the Hereafter." [33]

Thursday, October 25 My dear Adelaides Natal Day! will try & write her a short letter on the completion of her 17th!! Birth day—May Our Heavenly Father ever watch with unceasing care over thee my precious one—& guide thee safely to the habitation of thy dear Mother & sister—where the "Inhabitants shall never say I am sick."

Colo Stuart came last night—had been sick with Dangue—but has recovered. I am trying to write to Adelaide & Bettie but fear I shall not succeed—

Friday, October 26 Did not send any letter—

Sunday, October 28 Am still an invalid—my head very little better—have not been able to write to the dear children yet—(but once to A.& B.) no one went to church to-day—weather cloudy but did not rain much sun shone out this evening—

Tuesday, October 30 Teus. 29th (mistake 30th) A beautiful day of sunshine feel some better to-day though I fear I indulge too much in luxuries &c.

Wednesday, October 31 (12 oclock) A cloudy day—but no rain as yet—have not written to Oscar yet—

Monday, November 5 My dear bror returned last evening Sun. had a slight attack of Flux—looks badly—May he soon be restored health—again— Had a visit from Colo Stuart last week had been confined with Dangue— remained a week & left on Sat. Nov. 3rd Mr I H. Hilliard came on Fri. 2nd—& left with Colo Stuart to return to G. Lake—Col Stuart to Summit.

Thursday, November 8 Mr James Rucks Yerger was married in the Episcopal Church—to Miss Rebecca Stith[34]—a young lady of great merit—May Heavenly blessings be dispensed to them—in rich profusion—& may they ever "live as becometh the Gospel of Christ."[35] Received a letter from my dear Cornelia last Sun. 4th inst.—it gratified me to know that I was not forgotten by one whom I have cherished so fondly—& love so dearly. My neck—Ear & Head—are sick with—with Carbuncle—or Tumour of some kind which makes me very nervous indeed—May God help me to be patient & enduring & may these Afflictions which are but for a moment work out for me a far more exceeding & Eternal weight of Glory.[36]

Sunday, November 11 My head very little better. we have had a bright beautiful day have suffered more than usual to-day.

Monday, November 19 Have been able to make a visit to my dear Niece A.G.S. to spend a few days—came home on Sat. improving *very slowly.*

Tuesday, November 20[37] My poor head has troubled me to-day & I fear I do not contemplate the result as seriously as I ought. I humbly pray that I may have grace to sustain me under every trial—& especially through the last conflict—which may be very near. Monday 19th Nov. 1860. James made a pleasant visit to Judge Yergers—I have done little to-day—do not feel as well as I did yesterday.

Thursday, November 22 A rainy day gloomy—going to make or commence a quilt for James if I can—on Mon. next—My neck & eye improving slowly feel greatly depressed in spirits—&c.

Friday, November 23 A dark rainy day—have not sent my letters to the P.O. not finished yet—sent in on 23rd—

Sunday, November 25 Sister Mary & James & Edward went to S. School & church My dear bror came to-day from the River &c.

Monday, November 26 Mr Wm F. Davis (Eudora's husband) came up to see us from N.O. I was much gratified at his visit—as he seemed friendly & kind—May God bless him & his dear family & prosper them in all things—

Saturday, December 1 Colo Polk came with Maj Lewis Maney—staid only a few hours—(have done very little work). I went in the Parlour to see them—Colo Polk is looking better that I have seen him for a very long time—left all well at home.

Sunday, December 2 All went to Church on Sun 2nd—.

Monday, December 3 Have done but little to-day—Mr T. W. Nicholson came this morning—looks very well also *left* all well was glad to hear D was doing well at College hope he will stay long enough to graduate—have done nothing to-day—scarcely there is no work that I fancy as much as patch work but I cannot indulge it much longer—as I have a good deal to do for winter—I feel the want of energy—my poor ear & jaw & neck are improving *very slowly*—my mouth all to one side—if I should recover I shall not I fear have a human appearance—but I do hope to be resigned to the will of my Heavenly Father—May He ever guide me in the right way—& receive my soul at last.

Wednesday, December 5 Edward wrote to his Father to-day—I received one from Cornelia yesterday on the 4th—Our dear niece A.G.S. spent the day with us yesterday—Mr S. on the Jury & could not come—to-night my dear James went in to call at Judge Yergers—& rode an unsafe horse—which makes me very unhappy—but I would commend him to the care of our Heavenly Father—
 Edward rec. a letter from his bror Oscar to-day—was well—& wished to hear from me. dear Oscar it would be a great pleasure to see him—but I

will try to write to him soon—O that he may ever be watched over by the eye that never slumbers & guided by His wisdom—

Thursday, December 6 Have been making an effort to get my patch work properly arranged did not succeed very well—but could not finish any one of them for want of proper materials filled up the intervals with knitting &c.

Sunday, December 9 Sister Mary went into church but there was no service as Mr Crane the Rector had gone to Holly Springs to see Rev: Mr Ingraham who had accidently shot off one of his arms. he with his family have our deepest sympathy—we formed a slight acquaintance cn board the Boat in '47 & '48—Mrs Ingraham [38] made a very favourable impression on us in our downward trip—Sister M. very properly called to see Mrs Tarpley—who is still in afflictive bereavement—

Monday, December 17 None of the family went to Church except Edward— gloomy day. Our dear A G S & Nannie came & spent a few hours—this morn. I have spent in cleaning my desk & expect to finish Amelia Marrs Doll—it is now half past 11 oclock—so good bye journal—

Tuesday, December 18 ½ past 12 oclock Teus. This is the Anniversary of my dear Nicholas' death!—He was *very very dear to me*, though I was not so intimately associated with him after the death of his Father as before— yesterday was a day of some trial to my poor weak heart—I made some little expression to my dear James to which he took exceptions—I was greived— & am still so—May God help me I pray to be watchful—silent & *careful* in regard to others my memory is improving slowly—I do not wish to say any thing which may wound the feelings of any one—My dear Mother was siezed with a violent pain in her breast while reading in the "Advocate" to me is much better this morning.

Wednesday, December 19 My dear Nephew D came from N.C. left College to return home at his fathers request scarcely knows what to do—hope he will do well he is so amiable & clever—

Sunday, December 23 Our dear D left last night to take the night train to N.O. from thence to Texas by way of Berwicks Bay—he went with the expectation of returning again—but I think it uncertair hope he will prosecute the study of Medicine as he intended had not his Father called or required his presence at home—have felt rather gloomy to-day but try not to indulge it—

Tuesday, December 25 Christmas Day. I should have esteemed it a privilege to have assembled with those who "fear God & walk in his ways"—but am too much afflicted with my neck & head. we breakfasted alone I do not know whether any one will dine with us or not—This Christmas is lonely to me having only two of my dear ones with us—& three at school—our dear Oscar at Oxford—Adelaide & Bettie at Burlington N.J. May God bless you all my precious ones watch over yr pathway & guide you through lifes vicissitudes into the Haven of eternal rest—My dear James & Edward are at home do not know whether he will attend service at the E.C. or not—hope he did.

Monday, December 31 The last day of the old year with all its vicissitudes—trials & deep afflictions—have passed away—I would record with a grateful heart the goodness & mercy of my God they have been manifold—though I am now but a wreck—I find my faculties returning & I may have some little interest in life if I may live to see my dear absent ones Adelaide Bettie & Oscar again—my dear James is a Jewel—but I fear he does not understand me—sometimes—though I know I must do many things to try his patience nothing could be further from my mind & heart than to do so *wilfully*—May every Blessing both temporal & spiritual rest upon you my precious Nephew—& May Guardian Angels watch over yr pathway—with care & guidance—Dear Edward has not been well—there seems to be some difficulty in curing a sore throat & cold which has affected him for some time—I feel very uneasy about him—kept awake last night in spite of my efforts to sleep—I do hope he will have a character which may in all respects be well balanced not right yet 1860—My blessings & prayers are for you my darling Nephew—How earnestly do I hope & pray that you may in all respects be "guided by His Wisdom & directed by His unerring counsel" [39]—

I have not recd letters from either of my dear girls for some time—My heart aches to think of them in the land of Yankees & often fear they may need the ordinary comforts of life—May you & you dear bror ever be sustained & guided by the *spirit* of our Heavenly Father—may it ever "guide you into *all truth*." [40]

My dear bror & sister Mary with my dear Mother are suffering with cold at least my bror & Mother have cold—dear sister Mary is well—she watched over my sick couch during my long night of affliction with a vigilance that no other could bestow. Earth is too poor to estimate the value of such care or to repay it except in the same way—& I hope that may never be—I can therefore only have a grateful heart—& pray for her prosperity & happiness—May she & her dear Wm (her beloved spouse) pass through the scenes & vicissitudes of life in such a way as to secure a rich inheritance *above*—Blessings upon them—

1861

Wednesday, January 2, 1861 Sat up but did not think of it at the time & did not improve it in the usual way—Our Watch Nights are very interesting occasions—Yesterday was the beginning of a New Year!! O that I may be able by Divine assistance to make the present a commentary on the past—which will be favourable in its results to my poor soul. I must now live in the constant expectation of a change—May I ever be on the *watch*—in as much as I do not "know the day or the hour wherein the Son of Man cometh." [1] May our Heavenly Father watch with vigilance over my dear children—is the prayer of my *HEART.*

Saturday, January 5 Took a violent cold on Wed. 2nd inst—this is the 4th day & I feel worse than I have done yet—May God help me I pray—I do not feel as if I had much more to do with earth—Others will I hope do better by the dear children than I have done—O help me I pray as I enter the dark Valley of the Shadow of death—& sustain me until I reach it. There seems to be great excitement throughout the entire Country—Companies are organizing & wearing badges—&c. besides many other demonstrations of Antagonism—War! War!! War!! is the cry through North & South! O that God may allay the impending Storm. Mr J. B. B. White & his son Blake just from Charleston S.C. (aged 17 yrs) Mr W. came I suppose to attend the Convention to be held in Jackson to-morrow or 7th Mon.

Sunday, January 6 No one went to Church but Edward went in to S.S. returned about 1 oclock—James did not go in—Had his Daguerotype taken for a very *dear Friend*—on the 5th Jan. 1861—

Monday, January 7 My bror with Mr White & Blake—James remained at home—

Wednesday, January 9 Sister Mary went to town, yesterday was New Years day—Mr White & his son Blake left for town this morning had a good deal of trouble with Florence—

Thursday, January 10 They returned in high spirits last evening 9th with news that Miss—Had seceeded!! My heart is like lead—but I will put my trust in the God of battles. O that *He* may be as "the shadow of a great Rock in a weary land" to us—as a people—

Saturday, January 12 My cold no better—am making an effort to get things ready for next week—it is now 2 oclock—have done but little as yet—am going to try the Machine & see if it will sew—succeeded tolerably well—though I have not sewed any to-day—this morning I was much gratified at the reception of a letter from my dear Bettie—for which I was truly thankful.

Friday, January 18 This morning Colo Stuart came very early—Our dear James has had a headache to-day from too close application to his books hope he will be more prudent in future—they went to town—I took supper at the table my cold better my mouth most wretchedly out of order—

Tuesday, January 22 Sat up late last night to finish letters to my dear A. & B. sent them this morning by James our dear James who was well—
   Mr Brittain (from Madison) came last night Sunday night Mr John Hardeman (a relation of ours) came out after supper & returned in ½ an hour—A bright day of sunshine—nearly 12 oclock.

Wednesday, January 23 10½ oclock. About 2 oclock yesterday Mr Thos Christmas with his bride her cousin—with his two sisters—Mary—& Mildred—the two latter have been down to see me—they will I suppose spend a few days with sister Mary—The company left this evening on the Carrs to visit Mrs Montgomery a relative of theirs near Canton—We expect to visit Rose Cottage in the morning—we have not been there for some time.

Thursday, January 24 Went over to-day 24th. Our dear Willie D came soon after we arrived there—spent quite a pleasant day—our dear A.G.S. going about & looking so well.

Friday, January 25 Dr Maney & his grandson Edwin Keeble came yesterday are here to-day—our dear Willie D & Mr Sessions dined here also W.D. remained all night—Colo Stuart here to-night—talked a little about Jane and the dear children—a theme in which I could take much pleasure for some time.

Tuesday, January 29 Colo Stuart here yet—at dinner yesterday I heard that Oscar was expected the last of this week—my dear bror wrote him to come & sent the money—O that I may see him once more—

Wednesday, January 30 A beautiful day though rather smokey—sat up until nearly 11 oclock last night to finish my letter to Adelaide.

Thursday, January 31 I expect dear Oscar will be home to-day—O. did come just before dinner my heart rejoiced in anticipation of his coming—I feel thankful that I am permitted to have that pleasure before I die Mrs Dr Bailey & Mrs Galloway are expected here to-day (to spend the day)—I went in & sat with them a short time—both have babies—

Sunday, February 3 My dear mother presented me with her old family Bible this morning though it is plain & worn—I prize it very highly—as I have read it through at the age of 19—& wish to read it through again if I should be spared so long—expect to commence it to-night—On Friday 1st inst we spent a night at Rose Cottage—had a great rain—had to stay all night—returned Sat. evening—the family expected to go to Yazoo—but were disappointed by the rain.

Monday, February 4 Our dear A.G.S. & family spent the day with us—very pleasantly—they will leave for their Plantation on Yazoo as soon as the road is mended—I sat in the Parlour to-day & also at the table—by request—Edward—eat meat at the breakfast table—reluctantly—I felt pained at heart though it was right may he take more heed to his ways & ever be guided by the dictates of his conscience. O that he may ever be watched over & guided by Our Heavenly Father—

Thursday, February 7 The Rector of the P.E. Church has been called to endure a great trial in the loss of his wife who died at 5 oclock on Teus P.M. of Typhoid Pneumonia—On account of ill health I had not the pleasure of an intimate acquaintance with her—though she had lived here some time—her health (as I have understood) was much impaired & having a family she visited but little in the country she leaves a daughter nearly grown—a son who has been to school or Col. in Md. but had returned home a short time previous to her death—the youngest a girl 3 or 4 yrs old—a boy perhaps 5 or 6. they have my best sympathies—May God sustain them in this their hour of trial—& be as the "shadow of a great rock in a weary land"—may He be a guide & guardian to the dear children—may He put it into the hearts of His people to sustain them as a family—& be kind & good to the dear—little ones—Mr Sessions & family left this morning for Yazoo heard from them at Vicksburg through my dear nephew W L H rained Fri. & Sat—also Sun.

Saturday, February 9 Was my dear sister Mary N. Perkins' anniversary though she has been taken from us she is not forgotten—My dear Nephew J.H.S. came home to-day with the sad news that War with all its horrors was *inevitable!!* I cannot describe my feelings—Lord have mercy upon me—& sustain me in time of sore trial & danger—"thou O God art my only refuge"[2]—

Saturday, February 16 My humble prayer is that we may be spared this threatened War—my poor heart aches with anxiety about the dear children four of whom are now grown—& dear Edward was 14 last Sun—being the 14 anniversary of his birth—no notice was taken of it—May God watch thee my precious child & may you ever keep his fear before your eyes—may His counsels be as a "lantern to thy feet & a light unto thy path."[3] May the *fear of God ever* be before your eyes—& His grace dwell "richly in thy heart"

Did very little last week—righted up & repaired clothes last week—but did not finish & of course must keep on from day to day until all be finished—am now repairing Oscars clothes—get on slowly with them as my eyes & head are still *very very weak*—I have been a good deal depressed in spirit to-day—my efforts seem almost unavailing—but I pray for aid to do all my duty—am still repairing clothes for J.O.E.—would that I could be more efficient—I have no energy—have not written to my dear Cornelia yet—

Thursday, February 21 Have been very anxious about my dear Adelaide & Bettie—to-day my dear bror—rec'd a letter from B. & sister Mary one from Adelaide—my heart is truly gratified for the privilege of *hearing* from them—How earnestly do I pray that they may be guided by proper motives—& a good conscience—with the fear of God ever before their eyes. May you ever be watched over & guided—by our Heavenly Father—

Sister Mary with Oscar & my dear bror went in to hear a little negro boy who was blind 10 yrs old—he is a wonderful prodigy—blind—but can perform with great accuracy—the most difficult pieces.[4]

Friday, February 22 The great Washingtons Natal Day!! it was celebrated in Jackson—a Ball to-night as I understand—succeeded with my work tolerably well—but really suffer with depression of spirits—have thoughts of the dear absent ones—

Monday, February 25 Have succeeded with my work to-day tolerably well—have been repairing J.O. & E's clothes of every description—received a letter from dear Nannie to-day—sister Mary wrote to her—in answer to a letter she rec. last week—I feel very very sad on account of my dear bror leaving in the morning for the River—came late this evening or to-night—was engaged &c. am repairing Oscars shirts—but must write some letters this week—to Cornelia Sally in Tex. Adelde.

Wednesday, February 27 Have written no letters have been very much engaged for several days past in repairing clothes—feel ashamed to think of my neglect—every article of clothing being out of order—Eliza did not mend them—& I was somewhat to blame for neglecting to *superintend* it *in person* when I recovered sufficiently—"but woe is me" I have very little energy as yet—hope to improve.

My dear bror left for the River yesterday morning (26th Teus.) I had not seen him since the morning before—I regretted not seeing him—but he merely said good morning & passed on making no stay at the door for I went to it directly to get a glympse of him as he passed off—but did not see him—but my prayers have ascended for him—O that he may be watched over guided & guarded with vigilance—& restored to his devoted family again—27th Have been repairing today—but have not finished—must write to Cornelia—& Adelaide this week—if possible sister Mary rec'd letters from her sister—& also from cousin Bettie Bowman—all well—James & Oscar set out trees this eve.

Thursday, February 28 Wrote to Adelaide & Cornelia—& sent the letters by dear James—should not have done so had it not been for dear Oscar who was kind enough to overtake James as he had started to town—wrote to Nannie—to-day—have done no work—of any kind—

Friday, March 1 Have been employed at the same work of repairing—have buttons to put on overcoat & several vests—do not despair of getting through (Eliza came down this morning).

Monday, March 4 This day the President elect is to be inaugurated—at Washington! no one knows what a day may bring forth—O that God may make our cause His own—for we are "His people & the sheep of His pasture." [5]— Am going to try the Machine this week—if it will work at all I will make Edwards drawers.

Tuesday, March 5 Succeeded very well with the Machine had Florence & Eliza to sew yesterday must finish a pair to-day if possible—Sat up too late last night but did not know it—as I made a mistake instead of what 11 as I *thought* it was 12 oclock—

10 P.M. Succeeded tolerably well with my work to-day sewed some on the Machine—which did very well until late this evening—J & O sat here awhile—E got his lesson here sister M. was kind enough to write a very interesting letter to A.G.S. my dear Niece—(who is absent—on their plantation in Yazoo—) in answer to one she wrote to her Grandma—

Thursday, March 7 Yesterday 6th March I completed my 58th year—the last of which was one of great affliction—I can but hope it was in part sanctified to the good of my soul—I still hope that the future may be more pleasant than the past—I would commend my self & all in which & in whom I feel an interest to His guardian care and guidance—knowing that He will do "better by me than I can ask or think." [6]

Friday, March 8 9½ oclock—Have done very little to-day but feel much wearied—had a copious rain to-day—Oscar went to town to one of his College friends—Edward rec'd a letter from his sister Adelaide on the 7th inst. they were well—I was truly thankful for the privilege of hearing from them. James & Mr Wm Johns called on some ladies yesterday Mrs Tarpley & Mrs Buckley were out yesterday. I was glad to see them though dear Mrs B. looked very thin—I feel weary & sad—my dear bror is away—heard from him by a letter to sister Mary—shall look for him Teus. or Wed. O that he may be able to return in safety to us again—these long absences are painful to us all. God Bless Thee my dear & much loved bror. few if any have discharged the duties of life with more alacrity & fidelity than you—& your devoted wife dear sister M. how nearly art thou allied to each other in sentiment & feeling—May you long enjoy the society of each other & at last be inseparable—in Heaven. This is the Anniversary of dear Mrs Hilliard's death—I looked at her speaking Portrait this morning & could recall vividly many scenes of "Lang Syne"—Thou wert loved in life & not forgotten in the "Land of the hereafter"—Young Mr McLemore came out & spent the night with Oscar he came down from Oxford on business for the Society of which he is a member—Oscar went in to see him at the Bowman House—

Sunday, March 10 All gone to Church except Edward & Ma & myself—

Monday, March 11 P.M. Have done very little to-day my dear bror came to-day—about 4 oclock P.M. had stood & walked while on the River until his ankle & foot are swollen & slightly ulcerated—from fever—I was much gratified to see him—Must write to dear Adelaide this week—sent Betties letter in by J. this morning.

Tuesday, March 12 A most delightful day—James received a letter from his cousin Mrs Chevelier[7] in Texas. I have received none yet from the dear absent ones A. & B. my heart's desire is to see them but must try to be resigned—& prepare for my final change—I pray that I may be be ready for the summons—if I should never see my dear girls in this world—they will know that so far as I have been able they have been borne in humble prayer to that God who has promised to sustain them & me—may "He ever be as a light to their paths & a lantern to their feet"—my darling children.

Wednesday, March 13 Was hurried to get ready for breakfast—was a little too late—have been very busy all day—but can see very little that I have done—looked in Ma's bureau for some cap trimming but could find none—put a cap together for Ma—have read very *little* to-day wonder what my darlings A. & B. are doing at this hour—I have received no letters from them for three weeks. my heart aches with apprehension—but to thy guardian care God do I commend them in faith & verity—fulfil thy promise in regard to them—& give me resignation & fortitude to meet the dispensations of thy Providence as I ought—

Thursday, March 14 Mrs Skipwith Mrs Robinson & Miss Virginia Skipwith[8] spent the day here. Mrs S. came down to my room & sat a little while it brought back old memories—spoke of Mr Green—in the most affectionate manner—had quite a pleasant day.

Friday, March 15 Was late going to breakfast—arose with the resolution to write to dear Adelaide—but have not been able to do so. should have written but sister Mary said she had written—& so had James—must write to-morrow I am owing Adelaide a letter—but as they have both written to her beleive I will write to Bettie—We were much gratified at dinner to hear that Mr Sessions & family would be at home in the morning.

March 11th 1861. Our dear A.G.S. Nannie Lelia & Miss Wilson arrived from Yazoo (Mr S. remained in Vicksburg) the former dined here we delighted to see them—to-night had the pleasure of having my trio in my room until they retired for the night my dear bror also—may every blessing descend upon them—dear James finished reviewing "Blackstone"[9] to-day—fear he is studying too much—

Monday, March 18 Spent a very pleasant day at Rose Cottage—bror Wm staid at home—I regretted it very much—Our dear A.G.S. thinks of going to N.O. in about 10 days—

Tuesday, March 19 All have been busy to-day—*I* have however done but little—though I have made the effort—commenced Colo S's garments to-day—drawers 1st—& last—as I shall make some (if able) for James—& Edward—& Oscar—then continue my own wardrobe.

Wednesday, March 20 About 2 oclock to-day Mrs Wm Hinton[10] her sister Miss Mary Christmas & her bror Henry—came spent a very pleasant evening—James Oscar Henry & Mary Christmas went out to see the sheep—have sewed a little on the Machine this evening am making Colo Stuart drawers which were cut out some time ago—

Saturday, March 23 This morning Mr Sessions came by in his buggy bringing Mr J.J.B. White with him—did not see him as I did not go in the Parlour. cannot go in to see any one—sister Mary spent the day at Rose Cottage Mrs White returned with her. I have just returned from sister M's room—while sitting at the hearthstone Mrs Kate Scales[11] death was spoken of—I had not heard from her for some time—How sincerely do I sympathise with her—bereaved mother who has now but one son & a daughter left—*they will* no doubt their post in this trying & afflictive dispensation of Divine Providence—O that it may be sanctified to her bereaved husband & her mother—bror—& sister. Have felt unusually depressed to-day—cannot tell why—I wld in all things be resigned to the will of our Heavenly Father—my stay upon earth cannot be long—I would therefore devote my time to a due preparation for my final hour—

Monday, March 25 All gone to town to-day—sight seeing—Mr & Mrs White have made us a very pleasant visit—spent two nights with us.

Tuesday, March 26 Sister Mary Mr & Mrs White with my Mother went to Hatches garden[12] & to the grave yard—to see Mrs George Yergers adornment of her lamented husbands grave—she is indefatigable in her exertions to complete it—I should like to see ours neatly enclosed a plain fence of some kind.

Mr & Mrs White took leave of us this evening for Yazoo City—or for Rose Cottage—from thence to Yazoo City sister Mary went as far as Rose Cottage to spend the night &c.

Wednesday, March 27 My dear nieces (A.G.S.') birth-day! No notice of it I regret it very much—as we have hitherto noticed it in some way or other—but she is one of the brightest jewels of my heart. May the richest of Heavens gifts be granted to her & may she ever be a consciencious christian! is the prayer of her Aunt she loves her as her own soul.

Thursday, March 28 Sister Mary received a letter from my dear bror who is now in N.O. written in the haste—his ankle was nearly well—expects to stop at Port Gibson to attend Court could not tell when he wld be at home—we miss him so much. May guardian Angels watch over thee my best of bros & restore thee in safety to us again—I have been wishing to write to my darling Bettie this week—hope to do so—may Our Father in Heaven watch over thy pathway & restore both you & dear Adelaide to our waiting hearts.

Friday, March 29 Mr & Mrs Sessions left on the Carrs for N.O. to be absent a week or ten days—stormy to-night at 12 oclock—Oscar gone over to Rose Cottage to stay with Miss Wilson & Nannie—James & Edward occupy his room—sister Mary went to Church to-day—as it is Good Friday—hope our dear absent A. & B. are enjoying the benefits of "Natures sweet restorer balmy sleep" [13]—(12 oclock). I have righted up the book case to-day but have done no work—feel very much fatigued.

Monday, April 1 Have just written to my dear Cornelia—Am going to write dear Bettie as I have not written to her during all of March could not help it—Oscar has just finished one department of his studies (viz) "Muscles" whch sd to be the most difficult—am writing to Bettie by candle light—

Tuesday, April 2 Finished my letter & it is now ready for the first errand to town—have done no work to-day—but looked over my work & arranged some of my dresses—which my dear Sallie had cut & arranged for me before she left—my poor "heart issued bills which are never protested" in looking through my drawers & seeing what had been done for me—by my dear Sally—May she & her family with her sister Fannie & family all of them—ever be the care of Our Heavenly Father—dear Willie with his Mother & her little ones included.

Wednesday, April 3 Sun not bright took my letter to Bettie to the table this morning to give to James—I felt sad—& sympathised with him, he looked melancholy—hope he will hear good news to-day—O he is a treasure—my prayer is that the God whom he serves will sustain him.

Friday, April 5 Still cloudy with an occasional gleam of sunshine—James remains at home—dear B.Y. no better as I learned at breakfast—O that this severe chastisment may be sanctified to all but particularly to her dear family—my heart is full of sympathy for her dear Mother (& L.)—may she feel that she is sustained by *Grace Divine*. she is not forgotten in my humble petitions to that God who "counts the hairs of our head" & who too

> "Looks down & *watches all our dust*
> Till *He* shall *bid it rise* "

My Dear bror with Mr Wm L. Murfree have just arrived—We were much gratified to see Mr Murfree & to hear particularly from his dear family he told me that Fannie was nearly grown & that dear little Mary had improved a good deal. Willie had grown—but not as tall as we thought he would be—though he will no doubt be very tall—Mrs Murfree well enough to go out & superintend her improvements—

Saturday, April 6 Mr M. & My dear bror went in to-day & staid late it was 3 oclock when we dined—I have felt rather sad to-day—all day though I had the pleasure of hearing from my dear Adelaide & Bettie—through sister Mary which gave me much pleasure she read the letters aloud—have had a swelling on my left hand which is troublesome—O how much do I miss my dear girls my hearts richest treasures! for whom I would live & for whom I would die—O when I think of having the grave to close over me without seeing them—it startles me—But I would acknowledge the goodness & mercy of God in granting my prayer which was to see them grown & afloat on the broad ocean of earthly & human effort—& become *actors* in the strange scenes & *realities* of life—But all I can now do is to *pray* for their *success* and happiness—

Sunday, April 7 Sister Mary & O. went to Church—heard this evening that Bettie Yerger was better for which I feel truly thankful—May her dear mother be sustained during this dark night of affliction. have spent the day in a desultory way—as I could do no more—

Monday, April 8 Mrs Langley (the Drs Mother)[14] spent the day here found her very pleasant & agreeable—she completed her 75th year to-day—she has passed through "Jordan" & the "Caanan" of life "trustingly" & "faith-fully"—her face is the index of a well balanced character—she has no doubt been true to *herself* during her long & eventful life—I felt that it was a privilege to talk to her & hear a fund of interesting incidents of the past—

she saw Gen Washington at the age of six yrs—had retained a distinct recollection of him—Did no work to-day

Tuesday, April 9 Did not feel well this morning when leaving my bed—had a head ache—to-night at 10 oclock feel no better—would be good to be able to finish dear Adelaides letter but cannot. dear Bettie Yerger I am thankful to say is still improving—

Wednesday, April 10 Have had a very great rain. talked of our dear A.G.S. & she walked in! got her feet wet a little—but was not sick. I was made happy to-day by the reception of a letter from my dear Adelaide—I felt truly thankful for it—O that they may be watched over & guarded by the watchful eye of our Heavenly Father—My humble prayer is that they may succeed in their efforts to acquire an Education—& answer the expectations of their friends—To thy guardian came protection & direction do I commend them O God—with the prayer that the very "hairs of their heads will *all* be numbered *by Thee.*"

Sunday, April 14 A most delightful day. sister Mary & James went to Church. J. to the M.E.C. my bror went also—Mr Crane preached an excellent sermon—& appropriate to the times & congregation—Never do I expect to mingle again with worshippers—but must bide my time—& make the effort to live so that I may worship around the throne of God—spent a pleasant day at Rose Cottage Sat. 13. Our dear A.G.S. looking better than usual Mr S. much improved also—they went on a visit to his sister-in-law Mrs R.S. & his Niece Mrs Higgins—enjoyed their visit very much—

Monday, April 15 Cloudy day A.M. but no rain—Phillis (servt) came to my room to tell me that Miss Mollie Daniels[15] wished to see us—Ma & I went in to see her as she is the young lady who went on with my dear nieces A. & B. she is very pretty but too modest & retiring to tell me much about my dear—dear—girls O how my poor heart aches with solicitude for their future—dear Eddie is quite sick to-night—with a cold—& a sore on his heel made by a stiff shoe—I trust he may be better by morning—put a slippery elm poultice to his heel & gave him sage tea &c.

Tuesday, April 16 Edward—the same—his heel very little better—have felt badly myself to-day in spirits—sister Mary went out visiting—my dear bror returned to dinner & left for Tensas or Sonora—to be absent several days— hope he will hear something of our dear nieces Sally & Tommie May he be watched over & restored to us again.

Wednesday, April 17 A bright beautiful day—expect the two Mr & Mrs Sessions over to dine—just dressed Edwards foot—a little improved—I feel weary & sad.

Thursday, April 18 Last night we were sitting round our fire-side—the door was opened & Colo Stuart entered came he sd. to go after the girls at Burlington seems greatly excited—wishes to go on *immediately*—I expect to write to Bettie to-day—if able—sister Mary took sick with sneezes & cold—is confined to her bed to-day—went in to see her.

Friday, April 19 Sister Mary up at breakfast—much improved but looking thin—& pale—did very little work yesterday—feel now the *depths* of my position. My dear James & Oscar are so anxious to go to the wars—& will I suppose join the army—my poor heart sickens at the thought but to the care & guidance of our Heavenly Father do I commend them all—God help those who remain.

Monday, April 22 Colo Stuart left yesterday—on the morning train for Summit—expects to return this evening or in the morning—my dear bror not returned yet—expect him to-day or to-morrow—great Military excitement every where what is in the future for us we cannot tell Our dear girls are still at St. Marys Burlington N. Jersey so far from us—it is needless to say that my poor heart is pained—from day to day but I have tried to commend them in humble confidence to the care of our Heavenly Father.

Wednesday, April 24 This morning my dear James took leave of us & took the carrs for Burlington N.J. May God speed him on his way & watch over him & his dear sisters & restore them to us again—God only can know the agonies I have passed through within the last fort-night—on account of the dear girls & the difficulties attending their return—& a few nights ago— our dear Oscar joined a company of Volunteers Dr Burt's (I beleive) [16] I seem really to have undergone a *petrifying process* within the last few weeks— O that I could realize that command of the Almighty "Be *still* & *know* that *I* am God" [17] but I am filled with so many tumultuous emotions which can only be allayed by the grace of God—which alone can sustain the stricken heart—O that He would grant me a *double portion* of it—for Christ's sake wrote a short letter to my dear A. & B. last night 7 oclock P.M. Just returned from Rose Cottage where we spent the day very pleasantly—if my poor heart had not ached for the safety of those who are far dearer than life— I must make the effort to prepare myself for every & any emergency—& trial which may be in reserve for me.

Thursday, April 25 Morning cloudy—A day of sad remembrances to us—for on this day 12 years ago our dear children were deprived of one of the best of mothers—their early years promised a bright future—but alas! the War cloud has been gathering & it has burst with all its fury upon the South. Our dear Oscar has volunteered to defend the South—James has been prudent—& is very diligent at the Law. expects to get his License next Spring but there are so many demonstrations of War that is thought necessary to go to for his dear sisters who have been at Burlington since Octr 1859 my heart aches with apprehension for dear J. & when I did not hear his accustomed step at my door with the balmy salutation "good evening Aunt Ann"—my heart sunk—& I took a cry—may God protect my precious trio—& restore them to us for Christs sake.

Friday, April 26 My heart has pained me all day—have felt nervous—on Edwards account & the thought of my dear Oscar—have been trying to sew but did very little—I seem to have entered on a new mode of existence—I would hope that my dear family may have patience with me until I go hence—James our dear James is by this time in the North—& may perhaps reach Burlington to-morrow—O that they may return in safety to us again—may God in His infinite mercy "set a watch before the mouth" of dear James—& "keep the door of his lips"[18]—while in the North—& among strangers. O that the "Everlasting arms may be underneath." may he have the fear of God continually before his eyes & His grace in his Heart.

Saturday, April 27 Dear Edward had a difficulty—adjusted amicably—this is the fourth day since dear James left—hope he reached Burlington in safety this morning—& that they will leave on the return train—O that they may be cared for by Our Heavenly Father—& have a prosperous journey. the whole country N. & S. is in one blaze of excitement—& I am in continual apprehensions about our dear James Adelaide—& Bettie—I feel to-day that I could weep my life away—but strive against it. Our dear—dear—Oscar left early this morning to go on the carrs with the company to Monroe Cty to partake of a dinner tendered the Captain & his company—I am in distress on account of the rain which has fallen since their departure—May they have a pleasant time & return in safety to us again—at least our Oscar.

Sunday, April 28 No one went to Church except Edward. A beautiful day—would be gratified to have our dear ones together once more—before I die if it be Gods will—(this morning spit clotted blood) Colo Stuart here & doing very well—I hear nothing of any concessions on either side N. or S. War of course is *inevitable*—The North may come in myriads—but she will find foemen worthy of her steel[19] for what she lacks in numbers she will make up in Valour—

Monday, April 29 Cloudy dear Oscar sitting at my fire-side playing on his Guitar—"home sweet home." I can but feel the deepest anxiety about the dear absent ones James Adelaide & Bettie. O that God may watch over them all along & bring them in safety to us again. I feel as if petrified—cannot realize the events which are transpiring—do not feel well.

Tuesday, April 30 Heard nothing of my dear James yet but trust to Our Heavenly Father for his safety & that of his dear sisters—may He who "watches all our dust" conduct them in safety to us again & we will together render thanks unto Thee our gracious God—Dear Oscar went in last night to drill—a rain fell during his absence which made it very muddy (it is a subject cannot touch God help me). 30th Teus. 9½ oclock P.M. The Despatches to the Whig distressed me a good deal—reports that Troops are being transported to Cairo Illinois & at several places through which dear James will have to pass—my poor *heart aches* with apprehension—but I have tried in humble faith & confidence to entrust him to the care & guidance of Our Heavenly Father—with the hope that "He will do better by them (his sisters) than they can ask or think"—"May the Everlasting arms be underneath"—O that they may be protected & watched over by Him who "never slumbers or sleeps"[20]—It is but little I can do now for my precious dear dear children—but they have my constant prayers—for their welfare & success in life—but when I think of their future now my heart is sick— War is no doubt—*inevitable*—I can but look upon our new President as an instrument in the hands of God—to execute his designs & chastisements toward us as His people—O that He may forgive our sins & transgressions & return us to His favour again.

Wednesday, May 1 The 5th day since our dear James left for Burlington—to bring his sisters home—the day is balmy & beautiful dear Oscar left us this morning for the Fair Grounds with a basket of flowers—spent yesterday there with the young people who seemed (from his account) to have enjoyed themselves very much. no doubt they had a very pleasant time—O that we could hear from our dear absent ones—the tide of transportation of troops is so great that I fear it will detain them & bring them into trouble—May they keep a watch before their mouths & have the door of their life kept by Almighty Wisdom as the Psalmist sd. "Set a *watch* O Lord before my *mouth*—and keep *Thou* the door of my lips." All the gentlemen gone to town Colo Stuart is almost like a crazy man about the dear ones away but *my trust* is in *God alone*—knowing that He has watched as by "a pillar of cloud by day & of fire by night" our precedents & I would in humility thank and adore Him for the mercy & goodness which has followed us up to this time.

Bror Wm received a Despatch to-day from Grand Junction Tenn. from which we learned that our dear absent ones would be at home to-night—it is now 1 oclock but the Carrs have not come—Hope deferred maketh the heart sick—my poor heart ached with gratitude to Our Heavenly Father for this instance of His watchful care—How thankful I feel for the safe (as I hope) return of my dear dear girls Adelaide & Bettie who have been gone since Octr 25th 1859—I trust they have come! the carrs have just passed what a tumult is in my heart—May 1st Wed.

Sunday, May 5 This morning our dear Oscar—left us to go into camp near Jackson—I feel that it is the mercy of God alone which upholds me—poor fellow I fear so much that he will take cold—dear James is quite sick from fatigue—took medicine to-night—May guardian Angels watch over thee my dear—dear—absent one—my dear Oscar—O that you may ever have the fear of God before your eyes—& His grace in your heart—

Our dear girls Adelaide & bettie have arrived & spread a halo of joy & pleasure throughout our family circle—they are in good health & much improved for which we feel truly thankful—Our dear Oscar remained only one day with them & was ordered into camp near Jackson. we have not seen him since 3rd inst Fri—his Pa visited him yesterday—returned last night Henry Christmas staid here Sat. night & went to Church on Sun.

Monday, May 6 Commenced Oscars shirts of checked linnen—have felt badly today in spirits—Mrs White her two daughters Lazinka [21] & Mary— came—several companies are here from various adjacent counties.

Tuesday, May 7 This morning Sister Mary Mrs White her daughter Lazinka & Adelaide—went to the Camp near Jackson enjoyed their visit very much— this evening Mrs Allston [22] Mrs Dr Knapp [23] & Miss Sallie Hay came & to-night Our dear Oscar came to see us—he looks very well indeed. Camp life agrees with him. May he ever be the object of Our Heavenly Fathers care & guidance—Mary White & Bettie will go to see them to-morrow. Blake White (Son of Mrs White) is just grown up—& "off to the Wars"—O that God may take our cause into His own hands & guide our Armies as he did Israel of old "by a pillar of cloud by day & of Fire by night"—

Wednesday, May 8 My dear Brother Wms Birth-Day—he has numbered 60 years—is in usual health—O that I might add that he has chosen God for his portion—Blessings on thee my dear dear bror you & your idolized better half have discharged the duties resigned to each of you most faithfully—& the children with an aged Mother & sister can all rise up & call you both blessed—Our dear Oscar dined with us to-day—also Mr Blake White—my heart was pained at parting. May guardian Angels watch over thee my dear Oscar & restore you in safety to yr friends again.

Thursday, May 9 Dear Bettie completes her Sixteenth Birth-day! All except dear Oscar at home (& he is in Camp—heard the Cannon just now which was fired no doubt at hearing of the secession of another State—).

May you dear child be guided—& watched over—& ever sustained—by Him who hath said "I will never leave thee nor *forsake thee*"[24]—A. has just come in to see if I was not sitting up How my poor heart overflows with gratitude—for the safe return of our dear A. & B. but dear—dear—Oscar—how can I give him up—God help me I pray—& sustain me in this severest of trials for I know full well I shall never see him again in this world—O that he may be "brought to the knowledge of the truth as it is in Jesus"—

Friday, May 10 Sister Mary & Mrs White went over to Rose Cottage after dinner—during their absence the girls rec. tickets to a party at Dr Russells[25]—Lazinka—A. & B. went—Mr Blake White was their escort—James went to town & returned early—I have been unusually depressed in spirits yesterday & to-day.

Saturday, May 11 Our dear Cornelia & her husband Dr Armistead—came late this evening—I was much gratified to see her—she is the same as of years gone by—the Dr seems to be a very nice gentleman & one who can sustain himself in the position he has taken—success to them—May the blessings of the new & everlasting covenant be dispensed to them—I knew nothing of it before hand—he is a member of the Presbyterian Church—most humbly do I hope that dear Cornelia may soon unite with him at the same Communion—& be a faithful follower of Christ—"May she ever be guided by His counsels & directed by His unerring Wisdom" & thereby receive the consolations which she will so much need—in her new phase of life—may she ever be sustained by that arm of strength which on occasions may serve as "the shadow of a *great rock* in a *weary* land"—May she with her husband brors & Father so live that they may gain an inheritance with their dear mother—who left us (sorrowing)—1st June 1852.—[26]

⟨two pages⟩

The die is cast!—early this morning we resigned our "household gods"—James & Oscar Stuart they are offered upon the Alter of Patriotism by prayerful—but aching hearts—I need not write what *I can only feel with all the intensity of maternal devotion*—

May their paths be directed by unerring Wisdom may they be sustained & comforted by the influences of His Holy Spirit—& restored to us again in health & happiness—

Our cause is a just & Holy one—& God will protect the right—O that they may ever be the objects of *His Peculiar care*—& while our aching hearts are sending up prayers for them & the success of the cause they have chosen to defend—may they be sustained by that grace which will enable them to be true to themselves—Between 7 & 8 oclock on Thursday morning 23rd May 1861 I bade them Farewell! on the Nursery Hearthstone. God help me for Christs sake.

Friday, May 24 The trains passed but I did not (by accident see the one which contained my hearts treasures—). Mrs White & daughters left this morning for her home in Yazoo City—We enjoyed their visit very much—Lazinka is a girl of noble characteristics & is destined to make her *mark*—Mary the younger is more sedate literary in her taste a beautiful contrast to her sister—whose dawning genius for Authorship—&c. promise laurels of fame for her brow—

Saturday, May 25 With an aching heart I tried to work—did a little sewing—

Sunday, May 26 Sister M.A. & B. went to Church—sd Mr Crane preached an excellent sermon—have heard nothing from Corinth—Mon.

Monday, May 27 Rec'd a letter from my dear dear James! he & dear Oscar were well—for which I feel truly & deeply thankful—wrote a few lines to dear James—by Gen. Griffith [27]—May they perform their duty & keep the fear of God ever before their eyes & His grace in their hearts—27th Mr White arrived to-night from Pensacola in good health—Gen. Griffith left this evening with a large company of soldiers—we do not know as yet what regiment—our dear James & Oscar will be placed in—Capt Burt is going to offer himself for Colos place—& Mr J. Fearn [28] may be their Capt—how difficult & trying it is to give up those who constitute mainly our happiness—"O that the everlasting arms may be underneath them" & as the shadow of a great rock in a weary land." my poor "heart is lifted up in prayer" for them—

Tuesday, May 28 Wrote to dear Oscar to-day—but in conclusion to *both*—heard that several of the "Burt Rifles" had resigned & returned he is elected Colo—& they did not like it—My dear James & Oscar will be true Patriots I know—May God watch over & take care of them—& make them the objects of His *peculiar care*—watch over them & sustain them & keep them in the hour of temptation trial & danger—O that I might see them again.

Thursday, May 30 Our troops at Corinth yet. hope to hear from dear James & Oscar soon—must write to them to-morrow—dear sister Mary sent them a box containing various kinds of provisions—& refreshments which they will get tonight—wld have written before but did not know that the letter could go. Our Postal arrangements will go into operation 1st June—the day after to-morrow.

Sunday, June 2 All went to church except E. Ma & I read—prayed & am writing to our three Soldiers W.D.—James—& Oscar—Stuart.

Thursday, June 6 Have heard nothing from our dear absent ones—1st inst was vivid in reminiscence my dear sister Caroline died in '59—a sad day to me feel badly this morning.

Friday, June 7 Fri. 7th (I beleive). Have been sad to-day but not for any particular cause—except that I have been remiss in watching myself & of course the girls seemed annoyed by me—hope I shall improve or *isolate myself.* I feel as inanimate as iron—God help me & sustain me too on account of my *need* & for the sake of my dear family may He "Be our refuge until these calamities be overpast" [29]—O how much I miss dear James & Oscar—how my poor heart clings to them—"May the everlasting arms be underneath" them and may they ever keep his fear before their eyes & His grace in their hearts"—To His guardian care do we commend them in all humility & faith—trusting that "His mercy & goodness may be over all His works concerning them."

Saturday, June 8 Sister M. took A.L.S. in to have her dress lining cut—sister Mary rec'd a letter from dear James to-day acknowledging the recpt of the box sent last week—have not felt so well to-day in spirits—Mr Crane—Rector of St Andrews Church came out to-day.

Sunday, June 9 No one went to Church—Sat A.M. Cousin Jane Marr & her three children & nurse came—did not spent the Sabbath in a proper way—did not read or write properly (Judge Smith[30] who has a son in the same Company with our dear James & Oscar & in their mess)—came from the camp at Corinth Sat 9th—brought letters from each of our Soldier Nephews—who expected to leave for Richmond Va. on Sat. 8th P.M. It was a struggle to give them up—but to the guardian care & guidance of Our Heavenly Father do I commend them—knowing that "He will do better by them than I can ask or think"—May He ever keep them under the shadow of His protecting wings.

Tuesday, June 11 Mrs R.K. Marr left for N.O. with her three children (a beautiful day) Mrs I.H. Hilliard came about 12 or 1 oclock. heard through Mr Hilliard of dear W.D. who was in fine spirits & doing well—&c. for which I felt truly thankful—have heard nothing from dear Sallie De France or from Tenn. Our dear J. & O. have no doubt left for Richmond Va. & per-haps have arrived there by this time—O that they may sustain themselves as Christians, as Soldiers, & as Gentlemen—When I think of never seeing them again—my life becomes a perfect blank—Rev. Mr Fontaine (Episco-pal Minister Had charge of a church) commands the Company[31] of which our dear James & Oscar form a part—Colo Burt commands the Regiment (18th)—my poor heart is filled with gratitude as I resign my earthly inter-est in them more willingly—when I have some assurance of their being in a Regiment & company—whose Officers are christians—& most of the men—are *Friends* & Fellow Soldiers—May our Heavenly Father direct all their movements & be as a "Pillar of cloud by day—& of fire by night"—To His guardian care & guidance do I now commend you my hearts precious treasures—May He also watch over the three who are left with us—Past 12 oclock "Gude night"—

Thursday, June 13 This day has been set apart as a day of humiliation—Fast-ing—& Prayer—by the Episcopal (& perhaps all the Churches). I took a cup of coffee & some butter cakes & roll—did not intend to take any thing but dear Adelaide insisted & I yielded. 10 minutes of 2 oclock sister M. & the girls returned ½ an hour ago—from Church the text was in Psalms—3rd ch. & 8v. "Salvation *belongeth* unto the Lord: thy blessing *is* upon thy people" Selah. Mr. I.H. Hilliard left today—after breakfast went by way of Mr Sessions & thence to Jackson where he takes the Carrs at 1. oclock for N.O. We enjoyed his visit more than any previous one for some time—as it was more quiet—blessings attend him. & give success to his anticipated trip to Richmond Va. for the political purposes.

Friday, June 14 This day (& one month) 7 years ago were bereft of our of our treasures! our little Sarah Jane was transplanted to heaven—& to-night & last night I have been drinking the "waters of Marah"[32] or tasting it—God help me—for I am in trouble my dear Edward is not here & my very heart is sick—O that he may be "brought to the knowledge of the truth as it is in Jesus". May he "*choose God* for his portion" O that the dear dear boy may be watched over & restored to us again—What wld I not give to know where he is on my dear bros account—& to relieve the intense feeling of distress which afflicts me now—May our heavenly Father make us resigned to His Holy will in all things—

Saturday, June 15 To-day about 11 oclock dear Edward had staid out all night on the lawn—seems to have correct views of his conduct—his sister Adelaide talked to—& so did his uncle Wm—who had laid awake all night—dear boy he looks troubled.

Sunday, June 16 Edward seems to feel that he has done wrong—but he will not make any concessions to his uncle Wm & he has concluded to send him down to Summit to his Father to go to school—O how my heart aches—God help me I pray for no other help have I. This is the Sabbath—but it has not been properly spent by me—hope to pay more attention to this duty in future—where now is my dear J. & O.—comfortable I trust—May they ever be under the special care & guidance of our Heavenly Father. May our dear James ever enjoy that "peace which shall flow as a river".[33] may dear Oscar "acknowledge God in all *His* ways"—

Monday, June 17 Have heard nothing as yet from my dear James & Oscar—but trust I shall soon hear—as the Regiment to which he was attached reached Lynchburg Va. having been ordered to that point—Went on a visit to Rose Cottage yesterday—spent a very pleasant day—Mr Crane called in & took dinner—Miss Wilson & her sister (both teachers) Miss Jennie Wilson the elder is N. & D. Sessions Governess—wld like to know her better—

Wednesday, June 19 Have done but little to-day have read the N. Papers sister M. & the girls went in to Church—heard to-night—of the death of Mrs Thos Jones. She was amiable & affectionate in her domestic relations & an exemplary christian—rest in peace till "God shall bid thee rise"—May He watch with vigilence over the dear little ones she has left—she was quite resigned to death—I feel the deepest sympathy for her bereaved husband—& trust that he may find comfort & consolation in religion.

Thursday, June 20 Have done but little to-day—read the N. Papers too much—hope to rise earlier & be more efficient in future—Miss Wilson her sister—Nannie—& Delia—called this evening.

Sunday, June 23 Sister Mary & the girls went in to Church—Edward remained—had a trial this morning—my heart was & is still sick. O that I could be more watchful over every *word* & *action*—I have indeed great need of watchfulness over myself—"The praying spirit breathe The Watching power impart From all entanglements beneath—Call off my peaceful heart"³⁴—A letter from our dear James to-day—for which I feel truly & deeply thankful—were well I suppose & sent for sword & money—pants, socks, & mockasins, or slippers—dear bror Wm did not go to Church—but made the effort to get every thing ready to send them by Mr Ledbetter & young Mr Ellis³⁵—who will go on Teus.

Monday, June 24 Fine day. sister Mary, Adelaide, & Bettie, went in to pay some calls—&c. I sent James & Oscar an old sheet for gun rags—& wrote a few lines—I hope to observe careful watch over my *words* & acts this day—expect to write to my dear bror D & to little Ellen—as soon as I can—we cannot hear from them.

Tuesday, June 25 Rec'd a letter to-day from dear Cornelia—this has been a day of idle listlessness with me. our cousin Hinton Marr came from N.O. Sister Mary went with the girls to return some calls—pd. only 4 visits—I have felt a sadness & apprehension about our dear James—& Oscar—they are on the eve of battle though I cannot realize it & feel that my petitions do not reach the throne of grace—do not feel right—May he in whom I have trusted—sustain me in the hour of dark trial—though it is wisely hid from me—

Thursday, June 27 With an aching heart & much apprehension I have just taken leave of dear sister Mary who will take the Carrs for Tenn. this evening at 6 oclock—a great trial to us all—but hope it may be for the best—May Our Heavenly Father sustain her & watch over her & restore her in safety to us again for Christs sake—have been unusually sad to-day—how my poor heart aches to think of our dear James, & Oscar. May God protect them I fear the result of the battle at Manassus Gap. in God alone would I trust in this hour—May the God of battles direct their aims & grant us the victory without loss. for Christs sake.

Saturday, June 29 Adelaide & Bettie wrote the bros J & O. to-day. I am going write if possible—though I feel very sad—but must try for the sake of others to be more courageous & self sustaining—& humbly hope to receive aid from above—I need it much—am threatened again with tumours—I pray God to avert it.

Sunday, June 30 No one went to Church this morning but Adelaide & Bettie—Edward remains at home though I have not seen him to-day—I feel deeply grieved at the course he had pursued since the departure of his brothers—has been reading "The Romance of the Forest" [36] a very improper Novel for him to read—&c. I humbly trust a reaction will soon take place & that he will make himself more agreeable—I have & still intend to pray for him—Young Mr Wm Nicholson [37] came to-day just before dinner—son of Mr T.W. Nicholson of N.C.—Graduate of Chapel Hill—We have not been in the parlour—the girls or myself—Mr N left for N.O. early Mon. morning.

Monday, July 1 Have done very little work this week except to read the N.P. did however sew a little on A's bonnet—this evening—heard to-day of the conduct of Ned (a slave of Colo Stuarts) aiding his wife in some conspiracy against her mistress &c. he may be dealt with according to Law—ought at least—My bror rec. a letter from Colo Polk informing him of another daughter being added to his household—on the 27th ult.

Thursday, July 4 The 85th Anniversary of American Independence but we are now going through a Revolution—in which our treasures James & Oscar Stuart are participating in Va. at Manassus Gap—Burs command—besides two nephews Wm D Hardeman & Thos Wm D Hardeman of Texas as one of the elder Wm D 1st named the son of my eldest bror Thos Hardeman (who died in '36) called for my younger bror D father of Thos Wm D of Texas named after my three bros Thos. Wm D the latter of whom is his Father & a resident of Texas—D is in Gen. Van Dorn's Command [38] somewhere on the coast of Texas—I fear I never shall be able to do justice to the position which I now occupy—& have found that my own poor wicked heart is the cause. I pray from henceforth to be removed & feel that my mission on earth is fully accomplished. whether well or ill—with good or bad intentions—remains *yet* to be *determined*—I trust to the *mercy* of *God* alone. about ½ past 10 oclock this morning my poor heart was pained to hear that I had not attended to the duty of *Silence* as I ought to have done—thereby endangering or rather marring the happiness of those—who are far dearer to me than life & for whom I have tried to *live*—but if I have failed in this main object—I have no motive so far as *I* am concerned for human existence but I would in all humility be resigned to the will of God—it is my desire to trust Him for time & for Eternity—Life is a load when the head is grey with age & one feels that they are of no further *use*—I would not use a complaining expression though I am troubled now—but I need trouble sometimes—to discipline me as a christian—to enable me to perform promptly the duties of one—if I know any thing of my heart it is my first desire to be one after the pattern of *the Sermon on the Mount*—

Friday, July 5 This day I rec. a letter from my dear Aunt Betsey Corzine who lives in Texas—I was much gratified at hearing from her again—must answer it very soon—& write to dear sister Mary too—Ma received a letter from her yesterday all well—

Saturday, July 6 11 oclock P.M. Colo Stuart rec. a letter from dear Oscar today from Manassas Junction—he had a cold—I was grieved to hear it and fear very much it will affect his lungs—he is promoted to Seargant Maj & wants money to get his uniform &c. he & dear James were doing well— O that "the everlasting arms may be around them—& may he be as the shadow of a great rock in a weary land"—our dear Nannie & Delia came over this morning to see us. I was very glad to have them with us. This is the 25th Anniversary of my lamented bror Thos' death—which occurred on the 15th Septr 1836—Peace to thy manes my dear & honoured bror—The World has not looked as bright in some respects as when thou wert with us—our band was complete my dear bros Wm & D have discharged their duties devolving upon them with the utmost care & vigilence—for which they have our gratitude & prayers—my dear & honoured bror Wm (with whom we live) in conjunction with his best of helpmates—have discharged the duties of both Father & bror to his helpless old Mother—(who is stout for 85 last Jan) but I mean in regard to herself & affairs is inefficient though possessing great energy for her age—

Tuesday, July 9 The Anniversary of our dear A.G.S.'s Wedding day—she has been in bad health for some years but I am truly thankful to record some improvement in that respect. what a treasure she has been & still is to all of us. May she be restored to health again—& devote her life to the service of Our Heavenly Father shall be my constant prayer & also that her husband may "be brought to the knowledge of the truth as it is in Jesus."

Visited Rose Cottage this evening found nearly all the family indisposed. Our dear A. & some of the servants Miss Wilson also—who has recently heard of the death of her Father who resided in Wheeling Va.

Wednesday, July 10 A. & B. went in this morning to return some calls—expected to go to Rose Cottage on their return—had a heavy shower of rain. my carpet shared it through the W. window also the curtains—while I was in the front part of the house—no harm done however have felt unusually depressed on account our dear James & Oscar for some days have dreamed—of James twice—the first time I thought he was in the act of lying down on his pallet & was not well—2nd time which was last night—thought he came in & looked so pleased to see us—shook hands with all & we were so *much rejoiced* to see him—I awoke from sleep—being so much excited—but I have felt very *sad* to-day—May the Eye of God be ever upon them & help them to keep His fear before their eyes & His grace in their hearts—How my poor heart aches—I *need the compassion of my God!* but do not feel that I have done my duty as a christian.

Friday, July 12 Did not write any last night was reading. was up for breakfast this morning—now ½ past 10 oclock—have done nothing to-day—but have been making an effort &c. Wrote to my dear James & Oscar a day or two ago—sent it this morning (have done very little work this week). I wrote to both at the same time on account of the difficulty of sending it hope however our Postal affairs will soon be arranged—my dear Edward pained me this morning but made voluntary & honourable concessions & we are all right again—though my physical energies are sadly out of order—Truly do I *need the forbearance & mercy of my God*—

Saturday, July 13 My dear bror left this morning for the River do not know whether he will go to Tensas or not—we miss him so much—heard from dear sister Mary yesterday from a letter to Adelaide—all well—A note came this morning addressed to sister Mary from Mrs Barksdale[39] who is on a Committee—to solicit aid for the sick soldiers at Union City. This morning Colo Stuart went in returned at tea time with a letter from dear James had orders to be ready at a moments warning to march—Great God—have mercy upon my dear James & Oscar—& direct the movements of our Army & grant that all thing may be done in thy fear—my dear Bettie has unwittingly caused me pain—hope they will have patience with me—until it is the good pleasure of Our Heavenly Father to call me hence—O that I could be more amiable—I am continually being chided by some one—

Sunday, July 14 The Holy Sabbath—yesterday my very heart yearned to hear from dear James & Oscar—& sure enough at supper Colo Stuart who had been to town said he received one from James—they were both well &c. I felt truly & deeply thankful—May they be guided & guarded at all times—

by the unseen arm of Omnipotence. May He ever give me a heart to pray for them in a right spirit—save them, save them, for Christs sake & sustain them in the hour of conflict & of trial—may the trials which I am now enduring drive me nearer to thee O my God—& enable me to bear them as becometh one—who has counted the cost "of giving up all for Thee—

Monday, July 15 A letter came from dear sister Mary to-night to my dear bror—all well expects to return about 8th August—we are rejoiced to hear it—Colo Stuart spent the day at Mr Sessions' dear A. sat up a little—Adelaide will go over in the morning.

Tuesday, July 16 Night 16 July. My dear Sisters Anniversary of her 52nd year had she lived—her dear children are all doing well—The two eldest have joined the Confederate Army—18th Regiment Mi. V. Col. E.R. Burt—the eldest a private (from choice) the younger is being promoted—are now at Manassas Junction Va. & pleased with their location—how my poor heart yearns over them—& what a struggle to give them up May *sustaining* grace be granted to unworthy me—may they be watched over & guided by His unerring Hand—& at last be ready for the summons—I pray that I may go first—if it be His will—O sustain me in this my hour of trial—

Dear Adelaide went over to Rose Cottage—spent a very pleasant day of course we always do—Our dear invalid is improving—may the blessing of health be granted to her—for she is indeed a treasure to us all—

Wednesday, July 17 Am going now to finish a letter which I commenced a few days ago—to our dear James & Oscar—for around them cluster the treasured memories of the past & our hopes for the future—O that peace could with justice to each party be *fully established*—but that can never be until the best blood of the South has flown—

Thursday, July 18 Heard from our Jewels to-day by Mr E.P. Russel[40]—from two letters to my dear bror—which was very satisfactory—except that dear Oscar had the Measles—but was doing well—& dear James had a cough—but was selected by his Col. & Adjutant (Nicholson) as an *intelligent* Private to give signals—an *important duty*—I feel deeply grateful for the goodness of God in giving us intelligence of them—may He guide & guard them—& sustain them & restore them to health for Christs sake—May he guide our Armies direct every movement—& give them success. Wrote to-day by Mr James Clark[41]—who goes to the seat of War as an independant—he has kindly offered to take *letters* to them.

Friday, July 19 A beautiful day—saw a Despatch from Manassas to-day have had a battle—which lasted an hour at a time—Federalists tried to cross a creek but did not succeed—do not recollect the particulars—any further—the day has passed pleasantly my spirits have been depressed on account of dear Oscar—O that he may be watched over—& cared for—dear James has a cough—so I have some cause for uneasiness about each of my dear absent ones—my heart is sick—I cannot indulge in thinking & talking about them—though I must say it would give me great pleasure to speak of them often—even if it causes a sigh—to think they really are not present—my prayers are for you—my dear James & Oscar—that you may escape the evils of the campaign & return to your friends & family again—how many waiting hearts are ready to greet you.

Sunday, July 21, and Monday, July 22 My dear bror brought a Despatch with him at dinner time which brought the news of a long & sanguinary battle between the two forces—which has resulted in a glorious victory on our behalf—for which my very heart went up in gratitude to our heavenly Father. "*who gave us the victory*"!!!! Our attack was in the form of a V. Gen Beauregard[42] on the right. Gen. Johnston[43] on the left & our President & Chief in Command[44] took the centre Column—& routed the enemy with great slaughter—Our enemies Column was led by Generals Scott Patterson & McDowel[45]—Washingtonians panic struck (if the Despatch can be relied on) hurried the sending of Cannor & Mortars to renew the attack (I suppose) the Southerners having taken several field pieces—in the engagement at "Bulls Runn"—four miles from "Manassas Junction"—We have heard that dear Oscar had been sick with measles—& that dear James was sent out to learn the code of signals—my patriotism dies when I think of them & how much I owe to them—& how much they have contributed to my happiness & how watchful they were over me during my attack of Typhoid Fever—even when I was unconscious—though not my constant watchers they performed their part well & cheerfully—dear sister Mary & my darling bror Wm were all kindness to me. they felt responsible for my being well nursed—& it was done most kindly & cheerfully—for which I feel deeply thankful & pray that they may never need such attention in return—& now that my darling Oscar is sick he is many hundreds of miles from me—I have been distressed all day & have prayed that I might be prepared for whatever might befall me—(May my gracious God sustain me in this hour of trial & grant us some intelligence of them for Christs sake amen). May the everlasting arms be about thee to sustain thee my hearts treasures—O that you may be ever watched over by the eye of Omnipotence & sustained under every trial & conflict—& May He give you the victory—O heavenly Father into thy guardian care would I commend them—with an aching heart—laden with humble prayers for them—And be with them for Christs sake—

Tuesday, July 23 Heard nothing definitely from our dear dear James & Oscar. O grant us some intelligence of them in mercy—President Davis—Despatched to-day—Mr Farish & a Mr Anderson were killed in battle—Lord have mercy upon me & all of us—with unfeigned gratitude would I thank thee O Lord for the victory thou hast granted us as a people—but O how my poor heart aches with dread & apprehension—Lord prepare me for the worst & sustain us under every trial.

Wednesday, July 24 A Despatch from our dear James saying "All Well." O what a load it removed from our poor hearts—I felt truly & deeply grateful. May I seek & enjoy those comforts & pleasures which come from God alone & which is sanctioned by His Word *alone*—I would be an humble consciencious christian—drank of the waters of "Marah" to-night—talked to dear Eddie & intruded on dear Bettie hope she will excuse me I forget that she is *not* a *child*—Hope for a better spirit.

Sunday, July 28 Have not written for 4 days—have done nothing—this morning had some conversation with dear Adelaide—in regard to our relative positions &c. & no harm done on my part except that I talk too much & it seems to annoy every one as my memory is not sufficiently restored to make myself agreeable—I pray that my Heavenly Father may aid me in becoming taciturn & keep myself out of the way as much as possible—& God I trust will enable me so to act that I may be acquitted at the day of account—

Monday, July 29 My memory is improving some little—but do not see that I ever can be reinstated—O that my Heavenly Father may enable me to persevere in the exercise of every christian grace & virtue. I would humbly pray for the aid of His Holy Spirit—to sustain & comfort me under the trials through which I may have to pass—for I have "Lightning without & fears within"[46]—all are kind & forbearing toward me—for which I feel thankful—I would pray for a heart to appreciate these mercies—& to watch over & sustain the dear fine children—two are far from us—perhaps in the battle field—gracious God wilt thou be their shield & buckler—& their sure defence—wilt thou nerve the arm that strikes for liberty & Independence for it is indeed a *priceless boon*—have had my carpet taken up today room white-washed—&c.

Tuesday, July 30 Am going to make an effort to write to James & Oscar—have done so but have to copy it—but must write to sister Mary first—have done so—Have done but little to-day. Adelaide rec. a letter from dear Mrs Tarpley in which she expressed her intention of sending a barrel of dried fruit to Captn Fontaine. hope she will—dear A. & B. had some little amusement—Col. S. not well—brought a letter from our dear Willie D to bror Wm from "Fort Smith" Ark which rejoiced my poor heart—all were delighted to hear from him—I had felt so anxious about him for some time—heard also through our friend Joseph Sessions from our dear James & Oscar. it was also a great relief to my aching heart—for we had not heard for some time. I felt truly gratified to our Heavenly Father for intelligence from them—

Thursday, August 1 Had a very severe thunder storm but very little rain. My dear brother arrived just in time to escape it—(Colo Stuart was walking—sent the horse after him between Mrs Hunters & home)—all well at Sonora & cousin Ann Pughs—could not go to see Mr De France & Mr Hunter.

Friday, August 2 Spent a pleasant day at Mr Sessions—dear A.G.S. walking about—the gentlemen did not come out to dinner I gave way to temper before leaving—am not as watchful as I should be—I pray for the strength which comes from above. I am under apprehensions about dear James & Oscar—& our friends & acquaintances—May they be protected & watched over by the watchful eye of our Heavenly Father—my soul is sorrowful—

Saturday, August 3 Have felt greatly depressed all day—& this evening read in the Delta that they were fighting at Pigs Point—&c. Have read several accounts of the battles at Bulls Run Manassus—&c. places not yet officially designated. I suppose the *18th Regiment are engaged some where*—O that our Heavenly Father may be as a wall of defence to our dear James & Oscar Willie D & D in Texas—may our Army "be directed by unerring wisdom" & guided by the counsel of Jehovah!—

Sunday, August 4 Adelaide & Bettie went into Church bror Wm rode on horse back—Edward did not go—bror Wm saw Mr George Long—whom we knew in Tenn. & invited him out came out & is spending the night here—he is very agreeable—is a member of the Legislature here—

I intended copying an account of Battles &c. but declined it—did not feel equal to the task.

Monday, August 5 Have felt great solicitude about the battles—but have heard nothing from any of my dear nephews for some time or the battles fought since the great Victory on "Manassas Plains"—an attack on Springfield (Missouri) is expected—O that my dear Willie D may be safe—& watched over by the vigilent eye of our Heavenly Father—I feel unhappy about my own dear James & Oscar Stuart why can I not hear from you my hearts treasures—thick clouds of darkness envelope me this morning. God help me for Christs sake—& May He ever be a wall of defence to my dear James & Oscar—may He ever give them his fear before their eyes & His grace in their hearts—pour in the oil & wine of consolation into the heart of my dear James & grant to sanctify some means by which my dear Oscar may be brought to the "knowledge of the truth as it in Jesus"—may their fraternal affection be like that of David & Jonathan—dear dear Oscar how my poor heart yearns over you—O that you may "seek the Lord while He may be found & call upon Him while He is near." May He ever watch over you & guard you both on every hand—& provide friends & comforts for you—& you ever have His grace in your hearts & His fear ever before your eyes—prays yr truly devoted sorrowing Aunt Ann. God be with you & guide you always—10 oclock P.M. Colo Stuart went in—but—heard no news either from Va or Mo. my bror informed me tonight that Mr James Rucks [47] would leave for Va. on Wed. 7th inst. I was truly gratified to hear it as *he* will no doubt see our dear J & O. hope I shall have a chance of writing to them—may guardian Angels watch over thee my treasures "in earthen vessels" [48] & grant you a safe return to us again. Heard from our dear soldiers James & Oscar to-day! for which I am deeply grateful—dear Oscar has joined the Regiment again & James dear James is I suppose giving signals—I would like to hear the particular position which the 18th Reg. occupied in the sanguinary conflict of the 18th & 20th ult. I have seen some little complimentary notice of the part they took—but cannot tell—we send to-morrow 4 pairs drawers to our dear James & Oscar—May they be the objects of Our heavenly Fathers care guidance & sustaining grace—

Thursday, August 8 Have felt sad very sad to-day. could send my dear James & Oscar nothing. dear bror Wm got the cloth & Adelaide superintended the making of 4 prs. of drawers—some papers & old letters written during our excitement when the great Battle was being fought—I regret the sending of it very much—but cannot help it now if I should live—it may cost me many a tear & heart ache. O that I could be more taciturn & secluded— for I *feel* but too truly that I intrude & there is nothing further from my wish or intention than to do so—my mission on earth is no doubt well nigh accomplished—& I humbly trust I may be prepared for the issue—come when it may—& in whatever shape—

Friday, August 9 Heard from our dear James & Oscar—for which I feel the deepest emotions of gratitude he wrote to his Pa—& directed it to this place (Jackson).

Saturday, August 10 We can hear nothing of dear Sister Mary yet—the wires did not operate yesterday—hope they will to-day—Mr Rucks left yesterday 9th in company with Mr McAfee (Candidate for Gov.).[49] sent 4 prs drawers to dear James & Oscar besides letters—O that you may ask & receive the care & guidance of Our Heavenly Father—May you ever find friends & comforts wherever you may be. My dear bror brought at dinner time—the painful intelligence of Henry Petries death! how sincerely do I sympathise with his mother & sisters—may her afflictive bereavement be sanctified to her souls good—her Father Dr Farrar[50] went on to the seat of War some time previous to his death—Our dear Oscar was sick also but he had recovered & joined the Regiment they had the Measles—& I heard that Oscar & James each had a cough—O how my poor heart aches to think of them—Gracious God be a Father to them, & sustain them under every phase in which thy Providence may place them & have mercy on me—for Christs sake & grant me thy sustaining grace—

Monday, August 12 12½ oclock—Have been reading N.P. to-day—read yesterday Adelaide & Bettie went to Church. bror Wm remained at home—but I did not see him—at least I had no conversation—I scarcely know what to do to-day I seem really to have no motive for existence I pray for energy & industry—but am still deficient—Wilt thou deign to aid me O Lord for no other help have I. My dear bror said that he had requested Mr Rucks to prevail on Oscar our dear Oscar to return with him!!! but it would be a great trial for them to separate I should feel great sympathy for dear—dear James—how sincerely do I trust that he is in the enjoyment of that "peace which the world knows nothing of"—My dear bror received on 10th inst a Despatch requiring his presence at Grand Junction on 15th inst which will be *Thurs.* next—to meet dear Sister Mary!! We were all rejoiced to hear it—for we are anxious to see her—

Tuesday, August 13 My dear bror left to-day for the Junction at 6 P.M. went out twice to see the Carrs pass but they were freight trains & missed seeing them pass as I expected—I pray that he may be watched over by Almighty power & goodness—& return in safety to us again dear sister Mary will be received with joy by our waiting hearts. Our dear Anna Nannie & Delia came over & Mrs Clark came out at the same time—

Wednesday, August 14 A pleasant morning Colo Stuart gone to town Adelaide cutting Citron—Bettie sewing on her Pa's clothes—&c. do not know where Edward is I believe he is gone after grapes A. said so at dinner— With the deepest gratitude I received a letter from my dear James!! what a balm it was to my poor suffering heart—but he is not well—& Oscar returned out too soon after having Measles—I feel great uneasiness on his account—dear dear Oscar would that I could see you & contribute to your comfort in some way or other—but I can only pray that you may be cared for & be provided with comforts by those for whose safety you have left home & friends to defend—& protect—I should dislike for him to leave dear James—but I humbly trust & pray that God may watch over him & guide & direct him in all things though if it were His Holy will I would be so thankful to have him come home—

Thursday, August 15 Dear Sister Mary arrived to-day!! no to-night—at 11½ oclock—she & my dear bror much fatigued—my dear bror Wm went to Memphis staid only a short time—but was at the Junction in time to join sister & made no delay—saw dear Cornelia & Lent who were returning home or to their Fathers from Union City—We were rejoiced to see dear sister Mary after an absence of seven weeks—Adelaide has filled her position with much credit to herself—Has given satisfaction to *all* so far as I know—

Saturday, August 17–Monday, August 19 Sat. Night. Heard of another battle today—but Mon. 19th it is contradicted—have passed the day pleasantly— though have done no work. Colo Stuart speaks of leaving in the morning— this morning a prayer from my heart went up & at dinner time a letter came from dear James to Bettie—not that it was an answer to *my prayer* but at the goodness of God—I feel deeply grateful for any news from the dear ones who are so *near & dear to us*—

Wednesday, August 21 This day one month ago the Plains of Manassas were drenched in blood!! The conflict continued from 9 A.M. to 7 P.M. The results of the conflict of the 18th & 21st July 1861 will stigmatise the *Northern Army* with imbecility & entire inefficiency—they came like Sennacherib against Judah & met with a similar fate [51]—impartial Historians will I hope give it a prominant place on their pages—which are to be handed down to other generations—The day has not been passed as pleasantly as I could have wished—but nothing out of the way—but my own inertness—received a letter from Mr De France my dear Nephew—must answer it soon sister Mary speaks of going to Rose Cottage to-morrow—Wrote to dear James—a few days ago—hope he will excuse my crazy letters—but I feel as though they must know that they are ever in my thoughts—May the everlasting arms be about you my dear James & Oscar & Willie D. & may He grant us some intelligence of you my own ones also D V Dickinson of Texas—may they ever keep the fear of God before their eyes & His grace in their hearts.

Thursday, August 22 Spent the day at Rose Cottage—very pleasantly—my dear A. not well enough to go about—Adelaide & Edward remained at home—we returned late—my dear bror Wm dined there—Mr Rucks has not yet returned—I feel deeply & anxiously the face of dear Oscar—but trust him & dear James to the Guardian care of Our Heavenly Father—with the prayer that "His fear may ever be before their eyes & His grace in their hearts."

Sunday, August 25 Sister Mary & the girls went to Church—our cousin H. Marr has been spending a few days with us—Miss Wilson was here last evening to take leave of us as she is going to see some friend & relatives—to Placquemines Parrish La. This day has not been spent as could have desired—feel restless & unhappy—cannot hear from dear James or Oscar. Mr Rucks has not yet returned—at least I have not heard of it—heard of Capt Estelle [52] going sometime soon—on business I beleive—

Monday, August 26 Am unusually depressed this morning—my heart has a leaden weight—my dear James & Oscar are not well—O. has had Measles J. a touch of Rheumatism—from sitting on the ground & I fear very much for want of warm clothing blankets &c. though Gen McAfee has taken a good many articles of clothing but do not know whether his supply included the 18th Reg. or not—

Tuesday, August 27 Heard no news from the Va. Army to-day—or from Missouri—feel great anxiety about my dear Nephew W.D. Hardeman & my two Nephews in Texas—O that we could have some compromise—some treaty by which we could with *safety* be recognised as a *free & Independent People*—we have been subject to Northern rule not *rule* exactly but—we have made ourselves so dependant upon them—by our inertness as a people—that we needed a little chastisement & we have had it with a *witness*—I do hope this *attempt* to "subjugate" *the South* will be a *closer* to our *baby* dependence upon them—& when we want a spool of cotton or a pair of knitting needles, get a Foreign Machinist to come *Here* & make them for us—hope we shall have as a people *direct* trade with England & France—or some Foreign Power—To thee do we look Almighty Father for the guidance of our movements in the battles which are still to be fought before the close of this unholy War—mayest thou set every outpost & lead our Army to certain Victory—for our trust is in *thee* O God—

Wednesday, August 28 Sister Mary & Adelaide went in visiting to-day & went to see Mrs Anderson [53] about taking our dear Bettie as a boarder in her family—she will attend Miss Ingrahams school—a short distance from her home & she has a niece who will also attend with her—as she did not complete her course of studies at "Burlington N.J." I feel much gratified at the prospect of her being sent to school again—my dear bror & sister Mary have been undecided about the selection of a school but fortunately the daughter of Professor Ingraham—expects to commence a school—on Mon 1st Septr—I humbly trust that dear Bettie may sustain herself & family with credit—O that she may be guided by unerring wisdom & the counsel of Our Heavenly Father. may she ever keep His *fear* before her eyes & His grace in her *heart*.

Thursday, August 29 This morning our dear A came over with dear Nannie & Mr S. came out to dinner—will spend the day here & night also—& to-morrow—we are so much gratified to have them with us—Our dear A is still an invalid—how much do we desire her restoration to health—

From the N.P. we learn that another Battle is in anticipation the Confederate Pickets are inching to Washington they may however enter Maryland & attack it in the rear—O God! be Thou their strength be thou their stay sustain our dear ones James & Oscar in the hour of conflict—may He nerve the arm that strikes for the priceless boon of *Liberty & Independence*—& be a shield & buckler to our dear ones Willie D in Mo. D in Texas & Dickinson—with many other friends & relatives—

Friday, August 30 No news to-day—the wires are stopped—no one knows any thing about the movements of the Army. May Our Heavenly Father be with our Army & direct every movement—I am troubled to-day on account of our dear James & Oscar—& Willie D. & D & D in Mo & Texas—O that we may have some intelligence of our dear James & Oscar to-morrow—"Be thou their stay & support in this hour of conflict"—sustain us O Heavenly Father by thy grace—we humbly pray thee for Christs sake—Our dear A.G.S. went home this morning left Nannie Mrs Young & Sallie Dunning her daughter [54] spent the day here—

Saturday, August 31 We have every indication of a battle some where Most gracious God—our Heavenly Father—will Thou give it importance by thy signal blessing upon our efforts to establish the Freedom & Independence of our Confederacy guide the movements of our Army give our soldiers "Thy fear ever before their eyes—& thy grace in their hearts" & wilt Thou deign to so order events that our *victory* may be *full* & complete & thine shall be glory & honour—enable me O Lord to be prepared for coming events—into thy hands O God do I commend my cause—& I would as in the dust entreat thy guardian care for my dear James & Oscar & dear Willie D—will thou watch over them & sustain them in every conflict & spare them O Lord if it be thy holy will to their families—if not prepare them for their fate & grant that they may leave the assurance of their acceptance with thee—for Christs sake—

Have been depressed all day—may thy grace be sufficient for me & our dear family—& for all whom thou hast made it our duty to pray for—my nose bled today.

Sunday, September 1 My bror sister M. & the girls went to Church—I have not been able to enjoy that privilege for some time—My dear Bettie leaves in the morning—to board with Mrs Anderson & to go to school to Miss Ingraham—(daughter of Professor Ingraham dec'd). O that she may be sustained & guided & guarded by the wisdom which comes from above—& may thy grace O heavenly Father dwell in her heart richly—I do not know what will be done with dear Edward he is losing time—but there is no Teacher except in town—& I do object to his going there but sister M. says she will see that he goes to Mr Brown & Mothershead [55] (the same who taught in Mr Ozannes school)—

Monday, September 2 Sister Mary took Bettie in—& she will for some weeks board at Mr Cranes until Mrs Ingram can take her—as a boarder—the school commenced to-day. I earnestly desired this morning & petitioned for intelligence of our dear James & Oscar—at dinner bror Wm brought a letter to Adelaide from dear James (but did not say a word about me)—but he did not know where our dear Oscar was—I have been & still am very anxious about him as he had not sufficiently recovered from measles to be on duty—but I humbly trust he will be watched over by Our Heavenly Father—may *He* preside at *our* battles & gain the Victory!!—And to Him we will ascribe the glory which is due to *Him*—O that Peace may reign—throughout our borders—& may we yet be a united & happy people! Wilt thou O Lord watch with vigilent care over my dear *Oscar* as I fear he is in more *imminent* danger than dear James who is I suppose at the "Signal Station" at Centreville Va.—where I humbly trust he will be watched over by Our Heavenly Father & sustained by His grace—May he & dear Oscar be one in heart & spirit.

Wednesday, September 4 A.M. Mrs [. . .] Daniels (can't make a dee)[56] & her two daughters Mary & Bell[57] were here this morning Ma did not go but I did as they asked for me & Ma also but she could [*not*] leave her bureau drawers—am going now to work on dear Betties clothes—

Friday, September 6 Came over yesterday morning to Rose Cottage—my dear niece quite indisposed. would that I could be more like her to the mercy of my God do I look—I have not been as unhappy for a long time as the last 10 or 12 days & worse than all I have not sufficient strength to meet the troubles which have come upon me & feel wholly unprepared—perhaps I have let Satan get the advantage—by thinking too much about my dear absent ones & the Army—I pray for mercy & forgiveness at His hands—& hope to receive it—O that thou wouldst grant me some intelligence of my dear James & Oscar dear Oscar I fear is making his way with the Army to Washington the thought of it makes me nervous—O most merciful Father watch over them & keep them by thine Almighty power—& if Oscar is where I suspect be a wall of defence to him—& shield & protect him in the hour of danger I would humbly pray for Christs sake.

Sunday, September 8 Nannie went to Church—dear Bettie came over last night & staid until this morning when she went over time enough to go to Church. She left us last Monday to attend Miss Ingrahams school & will board at Rev. Mr Cranes—Rector at St Andrews Church Jackson—both he & his daughter will assist in the school—Bettie is staying with them for a few weeks when Mrs Ingraham will take her as a boarder. I came over to Rose Cottage on Fri. morning Sept 6th 1861. expect to stay sometime with my dear Niece—she is not well enough to keep up but can walk about— very little—O that I could see her restored to health again she is very dear to us all—May our Heavenly Father watch over & guide you through every trial & difficulty which may yet lie in your way—I commenced a letter to dear Oscar to-day a letter from him to his Aunt Mary informed us of his being at Leesburg—where they are throwing up entrenchments—& some important movement is contemplated—the Confederates are concentrating at "Stone Bridge & Shuters Hill" they may attack Arlington heights & then take Washington—God be with you my dear James & Oscar. O that He may ever be a shelter from the "*storm wind & tempest*"[53]—& ever keep you in safety & near Him in peace—May He be as a wall of defence to you—

Monday, September 9 Have done very little to-day—sister Mary came over this evening all well—spent a pleasant evening—sister M. purchased some flannel for the dear soldiers James & Oscar—dear Bettie received a letter from Oscar to-day they were both well—he wished some hoarhound candy to be sent—but said he was jesting—I will send him some if possible my heart is sad & weary without apparent cause—to an observer—but I find there is "Many a *word* at random spoken

May heal or wound a heart that's broken"

I am too sensitive however & will try to make the best of every thing & bide my time I pray that I may not have a disposition to take things in my own hands—but trust all to God believing & knowing that He will do better by me than I can ask or think—Our dear Nannie left her dear Mamma to go to school to Miss Ingraham & will board for the present at Rev Mr Cranes until Mrs Ingraham can take them—

Tuesday, September 10 Heard from dear Bettie & our dear Nannie to-day—they were well & sent a kiss to each of us—hope they will do well & be kind to each other & live by the golden rule have had a pleasant day—dear A as usual.

Wednesday, September 11 A letter from dear dear James has made me almost buoyant—I feel grateful as I can possibly feel and acknowledge the goodness of God in all—His works toward me—May I ever have a heart to appreciate the blessing which I receive at his hands. We heard in fact from all our dear Soldiers—our dear—dear—Willie D. in Mo. wrote a long letter to his uncle Wm and enclosed also a draft of the Battle Ground—which was very satisfactory indeed—May you ever be under the care of Our Heavenly Father & May He ever be as a wall of defence to you my dear Willie & sustain you in every conflict & sustain you throughout—

Thursday, September 12 Have not worked well to-day spent a pleasant day—may God help me to be more acceptable to Himself & to those about me.

Friday, September 13 Have had quite a pleasant day dear little Nannie came out with her Father after having been absent four days & a half, she was welcomed by her dear mother—& was delighted with her school—& prefers it to a home school—have not written to any of our dear Soldiers yet but must write very soon—as I have rec. a letter from my dear James it was a balm to my wounded heart—dear Oscar wrote to his uncle Wm recd to-day—was well—O that you may be under the guidance & protection of

Our Heavenly Father O that our Army may be directed by his wisdom—& guided by his counsel—may dear James ever be sustained by His grace—& dear Willie D May he ever have the fear of God before his eyes & His grace in his heart—may He ever bless you my dear absent ones shall be my prayer.

Saturday, September 14 This evening had a visit from the family (ie) sister Mary Adelaide Bettie & Ma—my dear old Mother who wept at parting—not ready to return yet—I do not know what to do with myself—I suppose they will have company on Mon. & Mrs Young is coming to stay some time a few days—dear Edward I hear is at work—To thy guardian care O God do I commend him & his dear sisters—with our dear James & Oscar—O watch over them & give them all Thy Fear ever before their eyes & Thy grace in their hearts—Wilt Thou O God deign to guide me through the breakers Thou alone canst help me save me from the wreck which threatens *more* than life—for it is indeed no more than a vapour. Septr 15th 1836. We were called to bear a great trial—in the death of my dear brother Thomas it was a severe blow to us all—he left five children—the eldest of whom—has been in ill health for some time—her daughter goes to school in town—for the first time. she has had a Teacher in the house for the last ten months having been previously taught by her invalid mother the Primary branches—

Monday, September 16 Mrs Young came out this morning—my dear bror came out with Mrs Sessions sister Mary & Adelaide came after they staid late—my dear old Mother came over yesterday morning but returned this evening—went off cheerfully—dear Eddie I hope will be more watchful over himself—I have felt the scathing justice of the Almighty in my present *crisis*—in thy mercy do I trust O Heavenly Father—"bring thou me out of all my troubles . . ." [59] for I feel that they are more than I can bear—without a due portion of thy grace—

Tuesday, September 17 Mrs Young is on a visit here—a very pleasant lady a former neighbour of ours. Mr Sessions brought me at dinner time a Letter from dear James!! It was with unfeighned gratitude I received it—my poor heart which has been undergoing as seried process for some days or weeks was greatly releived for I have suffered from depression of spirits & heart trouble—I find that from weakness—bad temper & irritibility—I say & do many things which seems to try their patience—I humbly trust that the end for which I have been continued on earth may be fully answered—I must with the assistance of Divine grace try & amend my life—& set my house in order by prayer & watchfulness—O that I may have the aid of Almighty Wisdom—for Christs sake.

Wednesday, September 18 Dear Nannie came out with her Pa to-day—reported dear Bettie with a headache Mrs Tarpley brought her out home as I have heard—O how my poor heart aches for her—as I fear she may have an attack of Fever—O that I may be spared if it may be thy Holy Will—& grant to prepare me for every event of Thy Providence Had a conversation with my dear Niece to-day may she be rewarded even in this life for all her kindness to me & those who are dearer to me than life—far dearer—for *I do value their happiness* but do not think my life valuable *(to any one now)* but God knows best & into His hands do I in humble confidence commend myself & all those in whom I have an interest by right—& whether that right is recognised by them or not—though it is due to them to say that they have performed their part well—perhaps better than *I* have—may I be more resigned to His righteous Providence toward me & submit to them all without *murmuring* or *complaint*. I would have a Faith which will at all times *illustrate* the *principle* of *action* by which I am governed—May I ever have His assisting grace—to aid & direct me in the path of *duty*—have written to dear James & Oscar—& my dear bror D—also to several others—some of my dear little neices in Texas. I have written to my bror but no one else—must write soon—to my dear Nephew—Willie D in Mo. to Sallie Hardeman Tenie Viser Eudora & Eva also to the dear boys as soon as I find out where they are.

Saturday, September 21 Sat. night all asleep—have had a day of trouble in some respects—thought a good deal about my own troubles in reference to the War—I am apprehensive of a battle O God Wilt thou deign to be as a wall of defence to my dear ones James & Oscar—may they ever keep thy fear before their eyes & thy grace in their hearts—O prepare them for every event which may be in reserve for them—I pray for Christs sake Amen.

Monday, October 7 Tomorrow is the 24th Anniversary of our dear James birth—& my bror received a letter from him to-day which informed us of an anticipated Battle. May the God of battles defend & sustain thee my hearts treasures my dear James & Oscar O that the faith of each may not fail—may thy grace O Heavenly Father sustain them & comfort them—& administer to their wants of every kind. Our dear Neices Sallie De France & Thomasella Harper with their dear little girls & a Babie each all doing well—& looking very well. Sallie's named "Wm D. Hardeman De France" & Tommie's "Robert Harper"—We were very glad to see them—they came over from Rose Cottage Sat. to spend a few days at La Vega. I received a letter from dear Oscar a few days ago—but do not know when I shall be able to answer it—God help me I pray—for truly do I need thy assisting grace—the day has not been spent as pleasantly as I could wish—I cannot realize the depreciation of my family—if it be from physical causes it should call forth their *sympathies*—if *mental*—their *sympathy* & *kindness*—& forbearance but it is difficult to bear with persons who are cut off from society by ill health—& have of course become splenetic & disagreeable generally. I pray for strength to combat & meet with crosses of every kind—& grace to sustain me in every conflict—with the adversary of my soul.

Tuesday, October 8 This day our dear James Numbers 24 years! I find it difficult to realize it he is far away from us—from last accounts at "Fairfax Station Va" a member of the "Signal Corps Army of the Potomac"—I fear he has not fared so well for the last few weeks—had moved from Centreville to F.S. had a view of the Dome of the Capitol & various other points & places of interest—I suppose they are on the eve of battle—O God protect them & watch over them for Christ's sake Amen—May every blessing which is couched in the new & everlasting covenant be extended to you my dear dear James—& I pray that your future (should you be spared) may be fraught with a long a prosperous & christian life—may you ever be the object of Our Heavenly Fathers peculiar care—shall ever be the prayer of yr devoted Aunt Ann—how my poor heart yearns to see you my dear James—& Oscar—the latter I fear—is near Washington & of course in much danger—my poor heart yearns over you my dear dear Oscar— O that you may be watched over & protected—on every hand—may you ever have the fear of God before your eyes & His grace in your heart—for Christs sake—

Wednesday, October 16 This has been a day of morbid feeling with me—the "troubles of my heart are enlarged"[60]—O God help me to be resigned to Thy Holy Will in the dispensations of thy Providence toward me—I feel that I am a burden to every body—do not think I improve in many things—

Wednesday, October 23 Returned from Rose Cottage our dear A.G.S. brought Ma & myself (the latter had gone over on Mon. with sister Mary)—Tomorrow Mr S & A will leave for Yazoo—to be absent some weeks—I shall be very uneasy about them as she is not well enough I fear to take the trip— I would be truly thankful to see her health improve—Heard to-night of a Battle being fought near Leesburg in which the 18th Reg. was engaged— my poor heart aches to hear from my dear dear Oscar—O that he may be cared for & protected & watched over by His vigilent Eye—& sustained by His power—into thy hands O God have I committed in humility & confidence—wilt Thou deign to watch over them for good—& grant us some intelligence of them—Lord into thy care would I commend them this night—watch over them for Christs sake.

Thursday, October 24 News from Manassus! had a great Battle at Leesburg Va. the 21st inst. Our dear Oscar safe!! a Despatch from dear James came to-night saying—"Oscar is safe" after the Battle of Leesburg—the Colo E.R. Burt commanding the 18th Reg. Miss. Vol. to which he was attached was wounded & died at Manassus & his remains were brought to Jackson for interment—what a load it removed from my poor heart—My gratitude was intense. O How thankful do I still feel & hope I shall ever continue to acknowledge God in all my ways & in all that concerns me—Heard with the deepest regard that Colo Burt was wounded severely—Mr John Fearn—young Mr Pettus son of the Gov.[61] about 30 reported on one side—1200 Yankees with many valuable spoils—in Arms amunitons &c.—

Friday, October 25 This day completes my darling Adelaides 18th year—tomorrow she will enter her 19th—dear child she will unawares be nearing up to womanhood!! May God watch over thee for good my precious child & sustain thee through every phase of thy life. O that it may be devoted to *Him*—that it may result in good for thee—My Blessing & prayers are for you my precious one.

Tuesday, October 29 To night I have felt some little bitterness in my soul—tears flowed more freely than usual & I felt thankful for the releif which this afforded—heard to-day of Colo Burts death! I mourn & sympathise with his large family—& I know dear Oscar has lost a personal friend in him—May He who has promised to be a "husband to the widow & a father to the Fatherless" be their stay & support

Thursday, October 31 A very wet day—com. raining last night—The remains of Colo Burt are expected to-day—A meeting of the citizens took place yesterday—to decide upon some mode of testifying their respect for him as a gentleman & soldier—I was induced to say a few bitter bitter words to dear A. last night—in reference to myself &c.—though I wish now that I had not done so—& that I had not been so weak as to give way—but to let my troubles—cares—& distresses be enshrined in my own heart alone—I must & will here after look to God alone for aid from Him—for vain is the help of man. My dear dear Oscar! I need not say how much it would releive my poor heart—to hear from you this morning—hope the weather will not be unfavourably to yr wounds—dear, dear James I humbly trust is with him—God help each of them—& sustain them in *every* trial through which they may have to pass—& grant a portion of thy grace to strengthen their hearts—O that they may be had in remembrance before Thee—

Sunday, November 3 Heard at night of the particulars of our dear Oscars escape between two fires which were pouring in upon him—but as Adjutant Nicholson will be here to-morrow I will wait & see him.

Monday, November 4 10 oclock have had the pleasure of seeing Mr Tim. Nicholson (of the 18th Reg. Miss. Vol) but have only heard the same statement (viz) that the 13 Reg. (Cols Barksdale)[62] hailed him but they did not recognize him—& the Fed. & Confederates Pickets were so mingled that he could make no distinction—hence his immediate escape became necessary—he succeeded in making it—with little injury to life or limb except a shot wound between the wrist & elbow—& having Mr Bs horse wounded also—

Tuesday, November 5 I have spent a part of this day in much anguish of spirit—my head still feels very bad. Dr Cabiness brought out the Electrical Machine Dr Maney & his son Maj Lewis Maney left for their plantations & Mr Nugent a son of my cousin Ann Nugent[63] came out—to spend the night. I am pleased with him seems to be a natural character—is a Lawyer & a member of the M.E.C.S. gave some information of my dear cousins whom I have not seen for years & never expect to see again—Heard from dear James & Oscar to-day at dinner—my bror & Adelaide rec. letters—Oscar to his Uncle & James to Adelaide—dated 20 & 25th.

Wednesday, November 6 Have been more quiet to-day than usual—for which I feel truly thankful—

Thursday, November 7 A bright beautiful morning—enough to drive away care & trouble—if *externals* could be a Panacea for a sick heart—though they are often enjoyed by those possessed of a melancholy temperament with good effect—I regret that I cannot avail myself of such an agreeable antidote—but my doom seems to have been written so far—& trust in the mercy & compassion of my God alone humbly intreating His sustaining grace to the end—

Saturday, November 9 Had some trouble to-day. dear Adelaide & I talked about her name. I took my evening walk as usual *alone*—returned by the quarter—Bettie & Nannie brought home their reports which were perfect (written by fire light).

Sunday, November 10 All well went to church except Edward & Nannie— have not spent the day as I could desire—I fear I do often infringe upon the Sabbath—hope to improve in this respect—have received no letters from dear James & Oscar for a very long time—do not know when I shall be able to write to them perhaps never again as my letters are no doubt insignificant I have written to no one for some time & fear I never shall be able to indulge in that pleasure again—there seems also to be so much difficulty in our Postal arrangements—but enough.

Monday, November 11 Bettie & Nannie went in this morning sister Mary went in with them & on her return presented me with a nice workbasket with pockets—have had a pleasant day—dear Edward wrote his composition in the Nursery tonight—his sister heard his lesson & corrected his com. bade us a kind good night with a kiss which was a balm to my heart—

Tuesday, November 12 Edward did not behave well this morning at breakfast— took A's letter to Oscar to the P.O. I wrote a short one to Oscar—& put it in her envelope she found by accident—the envelopes which I thought she & Bettie had used—they are five cent ones. have had a pleasant day so far— except my dear old mother who is 86 & very childish—Mrs Wharton & her daughter Bettie were out this morning but they did not ask for me or my Mother—& we did not go in.

Wednesday, November 13 Yesterday evening while taking my usual walk—I felt the deepest anxiety about dear James & Oscar—I sat up & sewed or basted the hem of my dark calico dress candle went out just after I got in bed & I did not get to sleep when I heard a tap at my window! the moon was shining "silver bright"—but thinking that it might be some of the servants coming in for medicine—for some of their children &c. arose & went leisurely to the window & putting the curtain aside saw from the moon light—My dear—dear—Oscar! standing looking up & saying "let Oscar come in!!" but the minutes which intervened between seeing him & getting the key (which had been taken out of the door) seemed so many hours but I was permitted to meet him *first* as I was up. I sent immediately to his sisters room—she dressed & came out to see him we sat up some time & all retired—about 1. oclock—but I could not sleep until very late. I would acknowledge the goodness of God in restoring our dear Oscar to us even for 60 days commencing from 30th Octr—but dear—dear—James is not with him—but I will not ask more than thou O God art willing to bestow at present—my heart is full of gratitude for the mercies I receive at thy hand.

Friday, November 15 Was appointed by the President as a day of fasting & prayer—all went in to Church. Rev. Mr Crane preached Rev. Mr Fontaine assisting—a great many in attendence—I had some desire to hear the sermon but could not go it is though a great privation—& one which I have always participated in with pleasure.

Saturday, November 16 Sister Mary went with Oscar to see Mrs Burt—he remained in town till late & to-night Colo Stuart came—I have had a pain in my left shoulder since yesterday evening—my dear bror returned with the ladies—to dinner leaving his horse for dear Oscar—who has grown a good deal & had become more robust than when he left home—my dear bror & Oscar rec. letter from dear James to-day—he was well. O that he was here to-night—but it cannot be—he is in Va. & all here except him—May he ever be the object of Our heavenly Fathers care & guidance—May He ever as a wall of defence to you my dear dear James.

Sunday, November 17 Have not spent the day as I could have wished—though I have not—though I have not been able to read—my head ached—took a long walk this evening—have had some heart aches but rather a pleasant day—dear O. went in this evening & brought the N.P. my bror read at the table News from the Army of the N.W. Confederates took *Ten* Vessels of the Federal fleet—at Port Royal—on the Coast of S.C.

Monday, November 18 Have felt sad to-day—but have improved a little very little—my nose has bled for two nights—& my poor head is very much affected—May I ever feel that I am sustained by grace divine.

Tuesday, November 19 Have had a pleasant day—walked this morning—my dear bror returned to dinner—but Colo Stuart remained in town tonight—dear Oscar sat in my room to-night & when Edward dear boy! finished his lesson Oscar talked to him very kindly—& I hope he will appreciate it—I know there are very few indeed who approve the manner in which they have been trained or treated in childhood—& do not consider that it is an ordeal through which all have to pass & their future must show the result of good or bad training—I can see innumerable defects in my mode of training—& have often thought that the trust reposed in me was unfortunate—so far as I am concerned—for I feel that no effort to discharge the arduous duties of my position—has been neglected—though I can see many very many defects in the retrospect of 12 years—May I receive the forgiveness of it my heavenly Father for all the errors I have committed during my Noviciate my heart is sad when I think of the past the *varied* past! but I feel that this tabernacle is dissolving—my hold on the earth is abating—& I must now look to the tomb for refuge—May He in whom I have trusted—look upon me with that charity which He requires of all who His children—To *Thee* O God do I look & to no other—

Wednesday, November 20 Have passed a day of agreeable intercourse—with some slight exceptions—I find that I am rather a bore to the entire family— never knowing when it suits their pleasure or convenience to have any inter- course with me—& I have at last come to the conclusion to be *more* exclu- sive—had thought myself sufficiently so before—Mrs Foute from Memphis & Mrs McLaurin called this morning—sister Mary & Adelaide went in to church service this evening A. remained—& spent the night with Miss Bodie at Mrs Clarks—will not return before Fri. heard to-day too that Mrs Ingraham had moved to town to live with Mr Crane her bror-in-law— & our girls Bettie & Nannie will have to board else where—dear A. not returned yet from Yazoo—hope she will soon—

Sunday, November 24 All the family went to Church except Edward—have been taking long walks for 8 or 10 days—& feel better from it—how thank- ful I would feel to be reinstated—but fear that I never shall—the ordeal through which I have to pass—is a most trying one—may strength be given for every trial—O that I could be silent & self sustaining—I feel ashamed of my weakness—May God help me to do His will on earth as it is done in heaven—

Monday, November 25 Passed the day pleasantly—took a long walk towards the quarter ⟨*four and a half lines*⟩

Tuesday, November 26 A. & her Aunt Mary went to town & to Mrs Andersons to procure a more suitable place for Bettie to board at—To Thy care & guidance would I commend her O God—this day has been varied some what—said too much this morning—about rooms &c. "set a watch O Lord before my mouth & keep the door of my lips" Bettie & Nannie are at Rev. Mr Cranes—for the present—Mrs Anderson is to give an answer this week about her board—dear Oscar & his sister A. went with their Aunt Mary to town—& made or returned some calls—his arm not so well this evening—

Wednesday, November 27 Mr Sessions & family did not come this evening— This afternoon has been fraught w th much distress of mind to me—it has been a very long time since I have felt the *bitterness* of my ⟨. . .⟩ position in the family ⟨*four and a half lines*⟩ as deeply as I have this evening—& what is worse than all *I* am the *sole cause*—no improvement in me yet & I fear never will be—I utterly despair of regaining in the least degree my faculties of mental or physical energy—I would commend myself & all that I am to the care & protection of Our Heavenly Father—May He guide dear Bettie & Nannie—& Edward in all things—dear Oscar & Adelaide are at home in health & do in all respects answer the expectations of their family & friends—dear James is in Va. may God watch over him & be with him always—& bless our Army with his care & guidance—

Thursday, November 28 Have passed through vexations & little troubles—I pray to be more silent and charitable—& kind—O that I could be releived of these nervous tumults—(if it be a correct expression—) I would be consistent in all things & consciencious—as one who is amenable to God for all things—may I be more watchful for the future—& especially in my intercourse with others.

Thursday, December 5 Have passed the day without any particular excitement—more quiet than yesterday—am making the effort to become more *silent & unobtrusive*—On yesterday Sister Mary & Adelaide went into a concert & Tableaux at the City Hall—went by Mrs Lynches [64]—where Bettie & Nannie have been boarding since last Mon. took them also—came late about 11 oclock—I sat a little while with my dear bror by invitation & read the papers—Mr G.W. Hilliard was there also—heard very little about the entertainment—I felt more interest in it on account of the distribution of the proceeds for some com. in the Virginia Army—hope they realized a good sum—& that the appropriation may be duly appreciated—

Friday, December 6 A pleasant day our dear A.G. Sessions returned from Yazoo last night & came over to-day we were so delighted to see her—sent for dear Bettie who came home quite sick from a barn with fever—but the day was spent pleasantly with some little exceptions—but this evening & to-night my poor heart has bled at every pore—I have felt in all its bitterness the position which I have occupied for some years—but have been by affliction released from it—the fact of having some one to rest my starved affections upon has hitherto filled a vacuum in my life—but I am now set aside—and those whom I have fondly cherished—& loved are consigned to another—& I am trying to bear the alienation of the dear ones who were consigned to me by their dear Mother on her death bed—the task has been difficult—& it may cost much pain at heart—but still I live on—if I could be as they are it would be better for me—but I trust in the mercy of my God—& humbly ask the grace which will be sufficient for me—under every trial—May He ever watch over with vigilance & care—the dear ones whom I still love with the truest devotion—my prayers are for them—& hope they may in all respects be "guided by unerring wisdom."

Sunday, December 8 A day of sun shine—but my heart has never been more depressed that it has been this day when I awoke this morning I had what is called a crick in the neck but—it affected my arm also—my very *soul* has felt *dark* & troubled to-day much more so than usual intended to have written to dear James—but it is now bed time & too late of course must defer it until to-morrow—My dear Niece AGS & Nannie came over this evening to see us—perhaps they will all go to town in the morning—

Monday, December 9 All went to town except dear Bettie who is indisposed & A. went to the exhibition of Tableux at "concert hall"—the day has passed off more pleasantly than yesterday though not without some heart aches—I will try & "forget—the things which are behind" & look to the future as an incentive to diligence in making my calling & election sure—

Tuesday, December 10 Rather a sad day & a sadder night—the dear children were all sitting around the table when I came in—& I thought I might cast a gloom over them by remaining—I went to James' room—while there two letters from James to Oscar (my mother came down for me—it made me *sad to see her*) were read—I inquired if he was well which gave rise to a little misunderstanding between Oscar & myself—troubles which under former circumstances would have been insignificant—now appear mountainous to me. O that God would help me out of my troubles & aid me in my efforts to discharge every duty to those about me & to myself also— O that I could look more to the present & the future & prepare for my final end—which I hope is not far distant—as I am evidently a *dreg* to my family—but I will make an effort to be resigned to His will in all things— dear B. convalescing—

Thursday, December 19 I scarcely know how to record the incidents of the last few weeks—let it suffice that a variety of them have transpired which are of the same character of those which have preceded them—Edward dear boy talked to me last night—in a way that I did not like but he seemed to be reconciled after a little conversation—& we are as usual—I pray God to sustain him & guide & protect him always may He ever be "guided by *His* counsel & directed by His unerring wisdom." hope dear Bettie will sustain herself as a christian who acknowledges *Him* in *all* her ways—may He ever bless & protect her—may He also watch over darling Adelaide & be her guide & counsellor under all circumstances—dear dear James & Oscar—may He be as a Wall of defence to them on every hand & ever give them "His fear before their eyes & His grace in their hearts"—& restore them to their family again—

Spent the day at Rose Cottage all well saw Mr Mitchell who married a daughter of Rev Lewis Garrett—my dear bror Wm dined there also. spent the day pleasantly—was enabled to be *silent*—& unobtrusive—Oscar & Adelaide—go to town every day—to assist in dressing the Church remained there to-night to go to the exhibition of some negroe Minstrelsy & other amusements—by the consent of citizens &c.—

Wednesday, December 25 Dear Oscar did not dine with us to-day had no one but Mr S & family.

Thursday, December 26 Our dear—dear—Oscar left us this evening in good health. O what a trial to give him up—May he ever be under the peculiar care & guidance of Our Heavenly Father—May James also be the object of His peculiar care & guidance—I have been sick at heart—to-day—& last night.

Friday, December 27 Our dear A.G.S. is here to-night—with Nannie our pet—Mr S gone to Yazoo. what a relief it would be to know where our dear Oscar is tonight—heard to-night that dear James was in some Telegraph Office—why can we not hear from him. May each of you be watched over by the eye of Omnipotence—& sustained by His grace—

Saturday, December 28 Colo Stuart left this morning rather hastily—& excitedly—does not know what he is going to do—can get no business & may perhaps go to Ky. dear Adelaide is quite sick with a cold—& has not been out to-day. has been taking Lobelia & Parygoric after a foot bath last night—May she soon be restored to our fireside & in health—O that God may direct us in all things—& guide our hearts treasures dear James & Oscar—& grant us some news from them soon—May he ever Bless them & watch over them & be "a wall of defence to them" for Christs sake—my heart was some what pained in A's room I opened an Album—& read a name after hearing to whom it belonged but committed an *unpardonable offence*—I said too much—in extenuation & otherwise also—but I cannot help it—but will try by the assistance of Our Heavenly Father to watch against such intrusions again. O that God would help me to adapt myself to every phase of my new life—I need His guiding hand in this trying exigency—& trust that it may be afforded in due time & on all occasions.

Sunday, December 29 Sister Mary & Bettie went to Church Adelaide was not well enough to go—took B.M. to-night—I have been in trouble to-day— & have been depressed in spirits—I have nothing to cheer me—my dear A.G.S. is here it is so pleasant to have her with us—it is to me dear Nannie is 13 years old to-day! I would wish thee many returns my darling may God grant that you may be made a blessing to your house hold—

Monday, December 30 The day passed off pleasantly until my dear bro's re- turn—when he went out & set the grass on fire & burnt his hand—but fortunately not *very* badly—I was present at the dressing of it this morn- ing—dear Adelaide is up & was at breakfast this morning before I was— I was however rather unfortunate in expressing myself to her in regard to her bror . . . asked or expressed the wish that I would not repeat it.

my dear A.G.S. & Nannie left us this morning for Rose Cottage—to return this evening—My poor heart aches to think of dear James—& Oscar—& the dangers to which they are exposed—O that God may pro- tect then & bless them & grant them a safe return to their family & friends again—dear Edward got angry this morning about his bucket—& said more than became his years.

1862

Wednesday, January 1, 1862 January 1st 1862! Wednesday—Cloudy day— Our dear A. has spent several nights with us & the day at home—Mr S. on Yazoo. I would humbly trust that the ensuing year may be fraught with more quiet than the one which has preceded it—O that Peace may reign within our borders & may we once more be an independant People—Jan 1st Am unusually distressed this morning.

Sunday, January 5 No one went to Church to-day except sister Mary—dear Adelaide has had Measles three days & dear Bettie has had a violent cold—& Edward also—but he is nearly well—my dear mother has a cough.

Tuesday, January 7 Have done very little work—dear A. convalescent has not yet left her room may do so to-morrow—the eruption has disappeared have done *tolerably* well though I say too many ill-natured things & fear some times that my heart is not right—O that it may be made so.

Wednesday, January 8 My dear Mother has been quite sick with something like Pneumonia for several days—& grows worse—this evening she had a paroxysm of coughing—Edward on his return from school was anxious to send for a Dr—but it was not done—as she seemed relieved—I have had my *heart full* of trouble all day—God help me I pray for Christs sake. Ma was speaking of James & Oscar this morning—seemed rather excited about James as she had seen Oscar last—said she "would give every thing she had to see Jimmie"—she often speaks of them both—she was much gratified at Edwards desire to send for a Dr—mentioned it several times— may the grace of God sustain thee my dear Mother & prepare thee for living or dying—it will be a trial to give you up—but I cannot expect to stay long after you—& I trust the seperation will be short if it be Gods will— as I have so little to live for now—but God knows best & I will endeavour to submit to it.

Tuesday, January 14 My dear Mothers Natal day—she has suffered a great deal—I had a desire that she should live to see it & Our Heavenly Father has granted it—about 10 oclock at night Teus. through much pain & suffering of which she did not complain—I humbly trust she "entered through the gates into the City of our God"—my heart is now desolate—for she is not in her accustomed place—O I shall *miss* her so *much*—I feel my errand on *earth* is *done*—& as she said "it will *not* be *long*" I *humbly trust it will not*— unless I can be useful to those about me—but that can *never be*—May I be sustained by that grace which has been promised & which alone will be sufficient for me—*my spirit is wounded*—O be thou my strength be thou my *stay* my gracious God—

Wednesday, January 29 I have been alternately at Rose Cottage & at home— Our dear Willie & Capt Richards came yesterday 27th from Richmond. I felt truly thankful to see him once more—he is in Gen. McColloughs Command in Mo. Bettie & Nannie came home to-day to see them—I have sat in the parlour last night but not to-day—except a little while this morning— Our dear A.G.S. is here—

Saturday, February 1 Have done but little of any thing—I am now (since Fri 31st Jany) domiciled in the old Nursery—where I hope if it be the will of God to make the effort to live to *purpose* by discharging the duties which may devolve upon me with a grateful & cheerful heart—

Sunday, February 2 Have not spent the day as I wished. read no sermons or any thing else to profit. dear A. at home—the weather gloomy—& the rain continues—

Monday, February 3 The rain continues. my dear bror came home about 3 oclock—had some conversation to-night of a business character—very

Ann Neely Hardeman. (Courtesy of Ada Mae Hardeman)

satisfactory—there could not be a kinder or more indulgent brother than he has ever been to me—& dear sister Mary has acted and has ever been true to herself & acted the part of a help mate to her dear husband in his munificent provision for us—by aiding him in his arrangements for the completion of the education of the dear children entrusted to their care. May they ever appreciate the kind care & paternal interest they have ever shewn in them—their reward must come from a higher source than this earth—my prayers are for them—"that they may blessed in their basket & in their store" [1]—& that they may ever be the objects of Our Heavenly Fathers care shall be my unceasing prayer—I was sitting by my fire ruminating on the past—present, & future—when this verse of a hymn occurred to me—"Peace troubled soul thou need'st not fear

> Thy great provider still is near
> Who fed the last will feed thee still
> Be calm & sink into His will." [2]

I will try & comply with the last line O that I could be more confident & trust God for *all all*.

Tuesday, February 4 Have spent the day without any break in my own course—but I feel an utter desolation which I cannot account for except that I have not strength to meet the varied petty trials which usually occur—did not hear from our dear James & Oscar to-day had hoped to do so—dear James is in a dangerous position—how my heart aches when I think of him—to His (Our heavenly Fathers) guardian care & protection do I commend him & dear Oscar—

Friday, February 7 A letter came from Joseph Sessions giving some news of dear Oscar—had very unfavorable accounts of the burning of a bridge across Tenn. River.

Thursday, February 13 My dear bror left this morning for the River to go to the Peru place I beleive—may God watch over him & restore him to us again—A. staid with her Aunt Mary during his absence—spent the day at Rose Cottage no one at home except dear A.G.S. & Nannie—& they will leave on Sat. for Yazoo or rather Rokeby their plantation to be absent until last June or first July—may they be watched over & restored to us again—we shall miss them so much—I shall—but I must now learn a lesson of exclusiveness to which I shall address myself with unwonted energy as I have been rather social in my disposition. I trust in the mercy of my God alone—for my success in the effort—I would like to be taciturn if possible—since

I find it necessary for the *happiness* of *others* that I should—for it seems that I cannot speak without giving offence to some one.

Friday, February 14–Wednesday, April 2 Had some conversation with dear Edward to-night—& last night also—he wrote to his bror James—I wrote a note to my dear niece—who leaves in the morning. just one month since I parted with my dear Mother—O that my Heavenly Father may guide me & assist me in the effort to make sure my claims to an inheritance above—At night finished my letter to dear Tenie—& got some paper from sister Mary to-night—6 sheets of large blue paper & three of very fine small square sheets—& two envelopes have felt sad today—heard from dear James & Oscar by letters to bror Wm & sister Mary—this 2nd April '62. Commenced joining dear Adelaides Quilt the hexigons were made by her own hands at the age of 10—commenced when she was very young—before she ever went to school—at about 8 yrs old.

Thursday, April 3 Mr I H Hilliard came to-night—looking well & says his little boys are well & pleased with their school—the Yankees took Mr Shute[3] prisoner for about 24 hours & released him—they also dined & staid all night at her house.

Saturday, April 19 Clouds & a gloomy day—feel sad very sad to-day—heard from our dear A.G.S. last night through a letter to her Aunt Mary—had declined (partially) her visit home—health not much improved—it would give me infinite pleasure to see her but I must learn submission as a lesson.

Sunday, April 20 No one went to Church—very cold & damp—rained a little to-day have felt the bitterness of my position to-day ⟨. . . .⟩—only record it as an act of injustice both to himself & to the children & myself it will I hope be the last he will have it in his power to *inflict* upon *me* I feel great anxiety about my dear bror Wm who is absent on Tensas—expected him to-day—but he did not come to the guardian ⟨. . . .⟩ Our Heavenly Father do I commend ⟨. . . .⟩ dear bror. This is Easter Sunday ⟨. . .⟩

Thursday, April 24 On 23rd inst—Mr Keeble & his family or his wife & two daughters & two servants came on the carrs from Trio dear Mrs Keeble is in very low health she will see some Physician soon but has seen none as yet. Dr Cabiness was to have been out to-day but has not come yet—Mrs K. suffers very much in the same way that dear Sally Green did—may she soon recover & be once more the life & comfort of her agreeable family— It is now 11 oclock at night Thurs. the day has passed off without any thing having occurred of a disagreeable nature. I will make the effort to be more *silent* & *unobtrusive*—I hope to be able to live more as a christian—to keep the fear of God before my eyes & His grace in my heart—O that He would "Direct controul suggest this day. All I design or do or say"[4]—& "set a watch before my mouth & keep the *door* of *my lips*"—I have great *need* of *watchfulness*—for I give offence to so many that I feel discouraged—I am alone a great deal—I suppose in consequence of it—yesterday was the 13th Anniversary of my dear sisters death—it was a sad day to me—I wrote to dear James—but could not write to dear Oscar—the letter has not been sent & I will try to write so that they may be sent together—Feel sad yet & desolate—O nothing but the balm of *religion* can comfort me now—may I feel its influence in every action of my life—& live in reference to eternity.

Monday, April 28 Mrs Keeble better to-day—I have commenced writing to dear Anna but did not finish—This closes my fifth book of journallising—dear James desired to have them but I think the best disposition I can make of them would be to burn them—but I must comply with the requisitions of the 15th Psalm—"Though I promise to my loss I must make my promise good"[5]—they are perfect nondescripts & may serve to while away a rainy evening when alone—if sufficiently legible—I trust dear James—they may remind you of your Aunt Ann—who loves you.

Friday, June 20–Friday, August 1 Our 3rd and last treasure was resigned at 3 oclock P.M.—It was a struggle to give him up—on account of his age & inexperience—he took an *affectionate leave* of *me*—& it has been as a balm to my heart ever since—may I be sustained by that grace which comes from *God alone* dear—dear—boy—he will I hope live to return to us again—& be a blessing to us—His Capt. Joseph Sessions wrote me a very satisfactory letter—about him—a favour—which I prize very highly—he is an old *friend* & I esteem him *as such*—is also a friend of dear James, & Oscar, & Edward, he is wounded in six places—but is convalescing—Augst 1st returned to his fathers house—hope to see him before he returns.

Late August Letter rec. Aug. 12 1862. Edwards letter dated 6 Sep. Sat 30 Aug. Battle on the Plains of Manassus in which the eldest of our jewels fell while charging a battery. God help me. "would to God I had died for thee" my James my dear James.[6]

I suppose in consequence of it. Yesterday was
the 13th anniversary of my dear sisters death—it was
a sad day to me—I wrote to dear James—but could
not write to dear Oscar—the letter has not been
sent & I will to write so that they may be
sent together—feel sad yet & desolate—O
nothing but the balm of religion can comfort me now—may I feel its influence in en
action of my life—& live in reference to eternity
28th Mon— Mrs Keeble better to-day—I have
commenced writing to dear Anna but did
not finish—This closes my fifth book of jou-
-rnalising—dear James desires to have them
but I think the best disposition I can make
of them would be to burn them—but I
must comply with the requisitions of the
15th Psalm. Though I promise to my loss I
must make my promise good—they are perfect
sun descripts—& may serve to while away a rainy
evening when alone—& sufficiently legible—
trust dear James this may remind you of
Yr Aunt Ann who has

The Ann Lewis Hardeman journals: "a rainy evening when alone." (Courtesy of the
Mississippi Department of Archives and History, Jackson)

1863

Saturday, February 14, 1863 On 25th Jan 1863 our dear Edward arrived—Sun morning & took breakfast with the family—To-day Feb. 14th Mr Ben Green made us a visit—will leave for Va. on Mon. 15th next—

Tuesday, February 17 Our dear Edward attains his 17th Birth-day with the dawn of this morning—he is not well is at home on Furlough (my heart aches at the thought of his leaving—again God help me I pray)—& that he may also watch over him & his dear bror Oscar—"may he ever be guarded by His counsel & directed by His wisdom"—"may he be brought to the knowledge of the truth as it is in Jesus"—& may he & dear—dear—Oscar "choose God for their portion" I pray for Christs sake—

Friday, March 6 This day completes my 59th year—regret to record the wreck of my health—but still feel disposed to acknowledge the goodness & mercy of God in bringing me to see this day—"though my heart & my strength faileth"[7] yet God is my portion of strength. "Forsake me not when I am old & grey headed"[8] March 6 1863.

Sunday, March 15 We were all seated around the Nursery hearthstone—enjoying the pleasure of family intercourse—when I heard Bettie make an exclamation & on looking up who should I behold but my darling Oscar!!! he came home on furlough—my heart was full of gratitude.

Friday, April 17 Oscar came on the 15th March & left with Edward on Fri. P.M. 17th April—1863.

1864

May 1864 We have heard nothing from dear Edward since 17th April I have written to him also his sisters & his last letter was in answer to his Fathers letter to him—I wrote 28th to him & hope he will receive it—We have heard with much regret of the death of Gen J.E.B. Stuart—In him the Confederacy has lost one of her noblest champions—he was the bravest of the brave—we shall long mourn thee our noble chieftain I trust thy spirit has ascended to the bosom of thy God—

Wednesday, June 1 This evening our darling Adelaide took leave of us for Columbia S.C. I need not say that it was the hardest trial of my life of 62 years—God help me I pray—& sustain me under it—My dear Bettie & I are left alone—I trust we shall have sustaining grace—she & her sister were all that was left to remain with me of the six that were once "a family band"—dear dear Adelaide I would commend thee my precious child to the care of Him who has promised "never to leave thee or forsake thee"—may you be true to yourself—& live in the discharge of every christian & relative duty—"may the everlasting arms be beneath"—I would pray that those about you may be kindly disposed towards you Heavenly Father to thy care direction & protection would I commend you—may the vigilant eye that never slumbers watch over you—& sustain you under every difficulty trial & danger—and I would humbly pray that you may return in safety to us again—

Tuesday, June 7 We received a note from dear A. to-day from Atlanta going on well—O I feel so thankful to hear from them—she is now no doubt at Columbia—may her paths be directed in wisdom—

cut out two shirts for dear Edward to-day—but have not put one stitch in them.

1865

Friday, July 28, or Sunday, July 30, 1865 Dear Adelaide has been in Jackson more than a month & we have not seen her yet. her Father has been gone 10 days after her—I need scarcely add that dear Annie & I are now & have been in the most painful suspense—We have heard nothing definite from dear Edward yet—May our heavenly Father watch over him & grant him a safe return to us again—

Sunday, August 6, or Monday, August 7 Dear Edward left this morning with his father & Judge Cassedy[9] to make a visit of some weeks—to Mrs John Newman[10] about seven miles off.

Monday, August 14 3 oclock {. . . .} dear Adelaide left us this morning accompanied by Mrs Proby for M{. . .} Browns about four & a half miles distant where she expects to take charge of five Pupils four of them will take music lessons. I need not say it was a great trial to give her up & my prayers have been & still are that she may be guided & sustained by Almighty goodness & wisdom. We miss her from our circle *very much*—hope she & dear Edward will meet as often as it may suit their convenience to do so for [. . .] during the week to [. . .] to Friday evening as day [. . .]—Dear Annie resumed her labours as teacher yesterday after suspending her school one week in consequence of her sisters arrival from Virginia—

Wednesday, August 16 The weather excessively warm—dear Annie nor I could sleep last night—I am not well this morning—she is teaching—

Friday, August 18 Went to Mrs Weathersbys school to hear some displays of eloquence—

Sunday, September 24, or Monday, September 25 Have felt very, very anxious about dear Edward to-day—as he did not come down this week—he is I fear very sick as his friend Mr Rodolph Newman is quite ill—& no doubt he has been nursing him—he sd when he was down last that he "felt as weak as a woman" but he went off in apparent good spirits. We have heard nothing of him since he left. May God watch over you & help you precious one.

Thursday, September 21 [11] Have heard nothing of dear Edward yet—feel very solicitous about him. Have heard nothing from dear Adelaide since she left us on Sunday evening—O that she may be watched over & sustained by him who has promised never to leave us or forsake us. I pray that she may have "strength equal to her day"—I feel deeply grateful for the strength afforded her in the hour of trial—during the week—God help & bless you my precious child & keep thee as under the shadow of his wings—I pray for Christs sake—

Good temper or a constant willingness to please those with whom we are connected—to bear with failings & pass over injuries—to receive reproof with meekness & to submit to circumstances with serenity & cheerfulness. Industry—An idle person is a contemptible being where ever he may be found—therefore "Whatsoever thy hand findeth to do—*do it* with *thy might*" [12]—Regularity. For without this a vast deal of activity may be spent to no good purpose things might almost as well be left undone as—not to be done at the right time.
Forecast or Good Management—For without this constant habit of looking forward, to consider what will be wanted & when—we shall be liable to a continual return of wants—which we are not prepared to meet.
Extract from Premium S.S. Book

Wednesday, October 25 The 22nd Anniversary of my darling Adelaide's birth— She has been a great blessing to us all and I pray God she may continue so to be—blessings on you my precious child. may each one descend like the "dew of Hermon" and as the dew that descended upon the mountains of Zion: as it was there that the "Lord commanded the blessing *even life forever more*" [13] may you ever be made by *good works* a blessing to your dear Father—Sister & darling brother & even me also and feel for them the care & maternal affection of an elder daughter & sister,—O that he may ever watch over & comfort you—& direct your paths. I will ever pray for Christs sake—My darling Annie has not been well for some time we made a visit to Mr Brown [14] last week it was pleasant to see so large a family—returned on Monday morning saw dear Edward on Sat. & Sun. God bless him—& sustain him in every phase of his life & make him a blessing to us—dearest Annie is better to-day I trust she will improve she taught the children this morning She has one rather difficult to manage—

Thursday, November 2 Commenced raining yesterday continues to-day— Bettie & I are greatly disappointed at not being able to see dear Adelaide to-morrow—dear Annie is better to-day took dinner with us—& did not take the pills of Blue Mass—that I had prepared for her last night—I trust she may be restored to her wonted health—if it be his holy will—The day has been gloomy—Annie is teaching in our room while the weaning goes on in the next room—

Sunday, November 5 Our dear Adelaide came last night quite late just before dark she stays up—I am too much fatigued &c.

Sunday, November 12 We were much to gratified to receive a visit from A. on Wed 8th E. came on Fri evening & remained until Sat. left about four oclock P.M.—Adelaide is emphatically "The Head of the family"—We have excused our dear Bettie from practical duties—as she seems to be more devoted to literary pursuits that any other—though Adelaide is still an indefatigable student or reader—after having finished (or very nearly so) her course at St Marys Burlington N.J each of them have succeeded beyond, *far beyond* our anticipations—O how much do I desire that they may be releived from teaching as I fear it does not suit them—but I must submit to the will of our Heavenly Father—

Sunday, November 19 Had the pleasure of seeing dear Edward yesterday—I succeeded (with Mrs Probys & dear Betties assistance) in finishing his black jeans pants—he expected to go to Natchez with Mr Rodolph Newman who will leave for France where he expects to finish his education. Edward will return in the carriage from Natchez he is a dear boy—or young man—will be 19 the 17th of Feb. next—he seems anxious to improve his mind but

I fear he does not fear God. how much do I desire that he may become a christian—Darling Bettie read one of Rev. H. B. Bascom's sermons[15] to me this morning—we liked it very much. the subject was "Heaven" Text was Rev 7th—9—17. I feel as I have often done after having been to church.

The day has closed—& I fear I have wearied dear Betties patience with my garrulity—as I am *old enough* to be *garrulous*—Our dear Adelaide did not come over this week & we are *disappointed* of *course*—for it affords us so much pleasure to meet occasionally—but we must submit to circumstances & trust to God for guidance & protection—dear A has thirty five days to teach now—

Sunday, November 26 Another week has passed but dear Adelaide has not come—it is a great privation to us to be deprived of her society—dear Bettie has been sewing & altered a dress for herself which fits very well indeed. Mrs Proby went to Natchez last Wednesday 22nd—in company with her sister-in-law Mrs Cassedy[16]—returned on yesterday 25th made quite a pleasant trip & shopped a good deal—have had delightful weather for some time. Have commenced reading "Trial of the Witnesses of the resurrection of Jesus Christ"[17] have not read much—have been troubled with drowsiness for some time—

Sunday, December 3 Yesterday 2nd December 1865 Capt Crawford left for Port Hudson his home—did not take leave of us—This morning Colo Stuart came from Summit. We have not seen our dear Adelaide or Edward for two weeks—& know not when we shall see them again—I pray that they may be directed by Almighty wisdom & goodness—

Friday, December 8 We were ready to go over to Mr Browns to see dear Adelaide when she came up & entered the room—we were truly delighted to see her she remained with us until Sunday evening when Mr Brown & his little son Floyd came after her—She cut out on Sat 9th a pair of pants for dear Edward & two garments for herself I am going to do the plain work of hers also.

Sunday, December 10 The circuit preacher I suppose preached at Meadville to-day—no one went from Mrs Probys—Judge Cassedy was quite sick of bilious cholic & Mrs Proby went over to see him—dear A. left before her return—I find I am mistaken it was soon after her return—I am able to be up all day I pray that I may continue so—mercies & blessings are bestowed upon me & the dear dear children most humbly do I pray that they may ever be the objects of our Fathers care. dear Annie read one of Mr Wesleys sermons to me this evening—she is not well & I fear she did wrong in reading it aloud—O that thou wouldst make all her bed in her sickness may God bless & watch over you precious one—

Sunday, December 17 Have had no word from dear Adelaide or Edward—though we are looking for them next Friday—as her first school term closes on that day—I pray that a blessing may attend her efforts at teaching—she & dear Annie are conscientious—& I am thankful to record the faithful discharge of every incumbent duty—O that they with dear Edward may be directed by Almighty wisdom—in every phase of their lives—if it were Gods will I wld be thankful to see them settled in life before I die—but if not—he will I trust fulfil his promise in taking care of them—Judge Cassedy has been sitting up & is convalescent—he has been very polite & kind to us since we have been here—I can but feel great apprehension about the dear girls lest they should be separated from me—it would be a great trial but if it be thy will I must acquiesce knowing that thou doest all things well.

Monday, December 25 Christmas day!! at Mrs Proby's in Franklin Cty Miss. We are all here to-night no one dined here except Messers McGee—Rhodes—Mr Strait & Colo Stuart, Edward, Adelaide & Annie—& myself—besides the family—Mrs Proby had a very good dinner indeed—but I was not well enough to enjoy it had some excellent rolls for dinner—& good coffee which I enjoyed—as an exile should—O that our paths may be directed by him who watches over us for good.

Tuesday, December 26 Dark & gloomy—with strong wind—Adelaide has headache—& Annie is in bed reading—I have done nothing but look over some old letters to find one which Edward wished to see—but did not succeed in finding it—

Sunday, December 31 The old year with all its gloomy forebodings—our subjugation & all the consequences incident to a down trodden people has closed and though I still believe that God will sustain the right we are in sack cloth & ashes. our hearts are bereaved of those who were far dearer to us than life—our beloved James & Oscar were martyrs to the cause they defended with their last breath—I trust & beleve they are at rest "where the wicked cease from troubling & the weary are at rest" [18]—none but God knoweth the depth of our hearts great trial & bereavement—O that it may be sanctified to us—while we journey through the eventful scenes of the future—until we meet again *in heaven!* We are still at Mrs Proby's. dear

Edward was down to-day—he expects to go to Summit to learn the carpenters trade under a Mr Stuart—I pray that he may succeed—my heart yearns over him—he is *inexpressibly* dear to me I pray the coming year may be spent as pleasantly as the past—& that we may trace the goodness & guidance of our heavenly father in our pathway through life. dear Adelaide has been with us about 10 days her school closed about the same time that her sisters did. dear Bettie has finished her second term of teaching. 1st at Mr McLaurins in Simpson county & the 2nd at Mrs Prooy's in Franklin Cty. it is now uncertain where they or I will go—I pray God to direct our paths & that we may be with those who fear him—

1866

Sunday, January 7, 1866 Mrs Cassidy came over this morning & spent the day—tonight our dear Adelaide talked about old Richmond—read one of Mr Wesleys sermons—aloud. we spent the day in reading & conversation—I have written a little—O that my affections could be set more permanently upon things above & not on things on the earth for I feel the importance of laying up treasure in heaven—

Sunday, February 25 At the house of my dear Niece Mrs Sessions—since Thurs. 22nd A.M. am not yet recovered from the fatigue consequent upon our journey up on the Carrs—

Wednesday, February 28 11 P.M. Have not been well since I came up & have been anxious about dear Annie—I am grateful for the priviledge of seeing dear sister Mary again & my dear niece & family—Mr S. has been confined to his room since we came sat up to-day—

Thursday, March 1 A.M. Have not heard from dear Adelaide for several days. hope to hear from her soon—must write to dear Edward soon. the weather has been very good for gardening—

Sunday, March 4 The day has not been spent as I wished—have not been able to read as usual on account of my poor eyes dear Annie read part of a sermon to me—on the great sin of assimilating with the world &c—feel anxious to hear from dear Adelaide & Edward—O that our paths may be directed by infinite wisdom & goodness—Mr S. can go about my dear niece fatigues herself too much—though dear sister Mary assists her a good deal—

Tuesday, March 6 The sixty third return of my natal day!! am still endeavouring to live as I shall "wish I had done when I come to die"——I humbly trust I shall be sustained under every trial & at last find an entrance "through the gates into the city"——Dear sister Mary presented me with a large concordance——just such an one as I have been wanting dear sister M. is a sacred trust to us now, & I pray that we may be able to comfort her bereaved heart——& make her feel that she is *one of us still.*

Wednesday, March 7 A bright day with wind——Annie rec'd a letter from dear Adelaide yesterday——

Wednesday, March 14 Dear Annie went to town yesterday accompanied by her aunt Mary & Nannie the girls remained to spend the balance of the week at Judge Yergers——& Dr Poindexters [19]——rec'd a very kind letter from dear Adelaide——referring to the past &c. how it comforts the heart to receive any testimonial of the gratitude of a child——& Bettie one from dear Edward my poor heart yearns over them——I pray God to watch over them & direct their paths & "make them of one heart and one soul." cloudy to-day Sun. No one went to church to-day——on account of bad road & broken bridges &c. Annie & I have been domiciled in the house of my dear niece A. G. Sessions who has been indisposed for some days——dear sister Mary is able to keep up——wrote to Colo Stuart to-day as it was his birthday——had two of our old servants to see us to-day Jinny & Eliza & Eliza's little girl Belle—— who is very precocious there is one here——who is a prodigy——the child of a hired woman poor Isbel (our former cook) is a great sufferer——with fits as they call it——she has been very badly burned several times by falling in the fire——poor creature what a relief death would be to her she is very religious——must go now & see my dear niece & the family.

Tuesday, March 27 My dear nieces natal day! May the richest blessings of heaven descend upon her & her dear family——

My dear Annie will not return until Sun. she will spend this week at Mrs Poindexters in Jackson——hope she may have a pleasant visit have felt sad to-day——to-morrow will be the third Anniversary of my dear brother Wms death——O that *I could* have *gone in his stead*——for the world is dreary without thee my precious bror——I would acknowledge the goodness of God in providing for me since I have been thrown upon the cold charities of the world——which has been the case with thousands of persons during this terrible War which has raged for the last four years——We have been robbed of nearly all we possessed——what will become of us? we "must live each *short revolving day as if it were our last"* [20] or endeavour so to do.

Sunday, April 8 A.M. We have had incessant rain for some days—but this morning our eyes opened on a resplendent Sun—which was hailed with joy. I have been wishing to write to dear Adelaide for some time, but have not done so yet—hope to do so to-day.

Sunday, April 15 Wrote to her & received an answer to-day. April 15th Sun. morning—she sent a package by Express. in consequence of the rain it could not be brought out—We were delighted to hear from them again particularly dear Edward—who has had a good deal of trouble with his ⟨. . . .⟩

Sunday, May 6 We have not heard from dear Adelaide for some time—her father came to-night & informed us that she had chill & fever—which must account for her silence—I regret it very much indeed—it has been some months since I saw her—dear Bettie is not well—

Tuesday, May 8 The anniversary of my dear bror Williams natal day—but he sleeps in the church-yard until the morning of the resurrection—may God help me I *pray* to him in due preparation for that day that I may meet thee my darling brother—O how dreary {. . .} his world without thee—

Wednesday, May 9 My dear Bettie has numbered her 21st natal day!! We are now sojourning for the present with my dear niece Mrs Sessions who wrote a letter of invitation—during our stay in Franklin Cty. Mr Sessions has been very kind—Bettie my dear Bettie will soon leave me I suppose to go to town & board—the Convention is now in session at Jackson—We heard of a sad accident a few days ago—a dear {. . .} girl of Mrs Kauslers was shot by accident—her Physician thinks she will not lose her sight. young Harrold a boy—who was looking at his gun when the contents were lodged in dear little Fannies neck head & shoulders—It is hoped & her physician thinks her eyes can be restored—I trust they will be—Darling Annie left us on Teus. last for Jackson where she expects to board the ensuing summer with the intention of completing her French & Mathematics—under the Rev. Mr Crane & his daughter Mary [21] &c. I pray {. . .} may be under the guidance {. . .} him who sd "I will {. . .} leave thee or forsake thee" Sister Mary went in to spent the balance of the week—Teus is day on which dear Nannie goes in to take her music lesson.

Sunday, May 27 How many sad memories does the date above recall to mind—58 yrs ago I was deprived of one of the best fathers—though still green in my impaired memory—never can I forget thy counsels advice &

lectures while young—may they be the guide of *my old age* On this day also my dear Bethenia was bereft of a kind husband D⁻ Vizer they had been married nearly one year. heard from dear Be{. . .} she has not written y{. . .} I have written to her—This {. . .} has not been spent profitably & hope I shall not repeat it. dear sister Mary returned from town to-day—she was hailed with great joy—How much do I miss *my dear Bettie,* I cannot realize that she is *really gone.*

Sunday, June 3 Heard that dear Annie was not well had a headache—& did not come down to see her Aunt Mary & Nannie who went in to Church— dear child I trust she may meet with kind friends where ever she may be she is a *dear dear child* to me. she *would stay with me* though she was persuaded by all the family not to do it—they thought it wld be wrong for her to do so—We have not heard from dear Adelaide & E. for some time—O how much do I wish to see them they will I hope be up during this month—A sd she would—I long to see her {. . .}ec'd a long letter from {. . .} Edward this evening—for {. . .} I felt grateful—sd he had been reading "Gibbons Rome."²² he is a dear dear child to me—& I pray that he may be watched over & cared for—O "that his paths may be directed by Almighty wis- dom"—I hope dear Adelaide & Annie are well—dear Sister Mary has been kind enough to read to me—she has read "Household of Bouverie"²³— & The Ravensdale or fatal duel²⁴—I did not like the last—We have had three stormy nights this is the fourth—rec'd a letter from my dear Ade- laide to-day still at Mrs Hoovers—had taken her first swimming lesson got strangled—but recovered & held on to Mrs Hoover—it makes me nervous when I think of it. hope she will not venture too far in future—

Friday, June 15, or Saturday, June 16 A.M. Had a visit from dear Mrs Clarke this morning she is a dear woman—I feel very much attached to her— she is going up {. . .} country somewhere to see some friends {. . .} Mon. our dear {. . .} yesterday or to-day {. . .}ing—the *family* are {. . .} is going about—Wrote to Edward & Bettie yesterday & last night sent them this morning by Mr Sessions did not read much yesterday—

Tuesday, June 26 Dear sister Mary & I looked over some old Texas letters at least she read them to me—& we wept over them—My dear A. does not improve as rapidly as I could wish—O that she may be restored to us soon again. I pray that her affliction may be sanctified to the good of her soul.

Wednesday, July 4 About 3 oclock dear sister Mary took leave of us to return to Tenn. with the intention of returning here in Nov I humbly trust she

may make {. . .} safe journey have a pleasant {. . .}mmer & return to us
(if we {. . .}) soon again—{. . .} that she may be watched over {. . .} 66.
I received one hundred {. . .}ars in gold from my nieces in Texas—Mrs
Sarah A. Hardeman—& Mrs Bethenia T. Viser—and my grand niece Miss
Ellen Lewis Hardeman 16 yrs [. . .] all urging me to go to to them as they
could administer to my wants more conveniently if I could be with them—
it would be a source of great pleasure to see them my sister-in-law & the
dear dear children—whom I have desired to see so much—but I could not
leave Adelaide [. . .] now though they are not [. . .] have not seen dear
Edward since Feb. I feel [. . .]

Wednesday, October 17 My natal day! but she [25]

Saturday, November 3 Dear sister Caroline is I trust in the enjoyment of that
rest which remains for the righteous—I need not write that I miss thee my
precious sister in every relation of life as thou wert a guide & counsellor
in whom I could & did trust even my very hearts best thoughts—but God
shewed me that he had a pryor claim to thee—& took thee for thou art
not but it is a comfort to think that thou dost watch over thy sorrowing sister—while she is travelling in "sorrowing—path below" & she feels
sometimes that her mission on earth is done—& that every one is tired
of her except the dear children for whom I have cared in childhood—but
all all have left me & saving the one with whom I am now domiciled I am
desolate & alone—I pray God to watch over them & sustain them by his
grace—under every trial, & if it be his will grant us a meeting in that land
where the inhabitants shall not say "*I am sick*"—I feel the loss of my dear
sisters children more severely than any other on account their dear mothers
bequest of them to me—they could not be *more identified with me than they
are*—they are indeed as a part & parcel of *myself*—

Sunday, November 4 ½ hour of 12 oclock Nov 4th Sun. have not heard from
any of the children for some days. dear Bettie wrote that she was well. I
suppose she was not at Mr Whites—yet I will try & write to her to morrow
if possible also to Adelaide & Edward—as I feel so *anxicus* to hear from *them*
I pray God to watch over them & direct the paths of such of them. my
brother-in-law their father had his office with contents which consisted of a
library—& office furniture &c with all his clothing & every momento of his
family destroyed by the fire I trust that good may come out of this seeming
evil—dear Adelaide wrote that his friends were very kind indeed—& hope
he will soon be reinstated—I regretted that I could not assist him—I have
not spent this sabbath as I wished—have read very little—must write to

dear D in Texas—if I were able to undertake such a journey I feel willing to go as I am separated from the children—dear Adelaide is near Summit—Edward at Osyka—& dear Bettie r. Yazoo City.

Have not written to my dear Edward since his removal to Osyka whither he has gone to work I suppose as his father wishes him to learn some trade as a resource & perhaps it may be very well at this time—

Tuesday, November 13 Have done little to-day. have been knitting Mary (former servant) a pr of stockings—one done. The rain has been almost incessant all day—so much so that I could not go down to dinner have breakfasted & dined in my room. Rained Wed. & Thurs. Fri. At night fall our dear friends Mrs White & Miss Fortescue came to visit & [. . .] we enjoyed their visit very much. Left this Sun. early in the morning [. . .] dear Bettie had nothing to send her but love. Mr & Mrs White have taken dear Bettie to their house & would not consent to [. . .] her going out to board. He is an old & familiar freind of my dear brothers Wm & D. The attachment that existed between them was natural & very very strong & uninterrupted

I was much gratified & feel deeply grateful to them for their kind care of her—& from what they told me of dear Bettie she has been fortunate in making a favourable impression, My prayers are for you my precious child

Sunday, December 9 Rec'd last night a letter from my dear Bettie—& one from dear Adelaide a few days before. have not rec'd any from dear Edward for some months. We were expecting dear sister Mary on this mornings Train—but instead rec'd a letter from her to dear Ann saying she would be here on Thurs. 12th. she expects to come with Mrs Yeatman & her bror George whose destination is N.O.—& will of course take Jackson in their route—

Dec. 5th [26] Dear sister Mary came to-day is not well—but not confined to her room—I am truly thankful that she has arrived—I wished so much to see her. she is indeed a comfort & blessing to us al. & I pray God to give us hearts to appreciate her in every respect. may our paths be directed by divine wisdom & goodness.

Monday, December 31 Mr Hilliard not arrived yet—Mr Sessions very sick complains of his head—has been confined to his bed to-day. This is the last of the old year—it is perhaps bidding us farewell! Yes with all its joys & sorrows it has passed away—more of the latter than the former has fallen to my lot but God gave them to me as a correction & I hope it will not have been administered in vain—I pray that whatever may be my portion for the ensuing year I may be able to improve upon the past—the bitter past. O that God may enable me to be watchful in all things—& perform the duties which devolve upon me both christian & relative with an eye single to his glory, Amen. Farewell thou dying year Farewell! A.L.H last of 1866.

1867

Thursday, March 28, 1867 As this is the anniversary of the day on which our hearthstone was made desolate & our hearts bereaved I thought I would notice it. we hear not now the well known foot fall which announced the approach of him whose happiness consisted in the diffusion of it to those who constituted his household. his tasks were energetically disposed of— & the domestic enjoyments of a pleasant delightful home were entered into with a zest—How cheerfully & delightfully passed the time while he was in our midst—& we could have his assistance & advice—for he was our counsellor & guide in all things—never shrinking from any responsibility— or duty—energetic unwearied & diligent in the discharge of every incumbent duty. his labours for others were incessant—& many of those who had no claims upon him, availed themselves of them without stint—truly his life was spent in doing good to others—always exercising the most rigid economy in his personal expenditures—but generous & liberal to a fault in regard to others—O how idly are we fitted for the balance of our journey without thee my precious brother. the "thorns & briers" which are strewn in our path we do not regard—but O how dreary is the world without thee my precious brother—I often feel that my heart is rebellious at providence which bereft us of him—but God knows best & I trust in him for the dark future—May he protect guide & sustain thou whom he cared for while living—

GENEALOGICAL CHARTS

NOTES

INDEX

The Ruffin Family

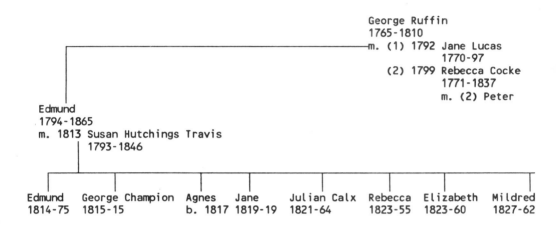

George Ruffin
1765-1810
m. (1) 1792 Jane Lucas
1770-97
(2) 1799 Rebecca Cocke
1771-1837
m. (2) Peter

Edmund
1794-1865
m. 1813 Susan Hutchings Travis
1793-1846

Edmund	George Champion	Agnes	Jane	Julian Calx	Rebecca	Elizabeth	Mildred
1814-75	1815-15	b. 1817	1819-19	1821-64	1823-55	1823-60	1827-62

Jane Skipwith
1800-1870
m. 1817 William Jones Dupuy

George
1801-2

Rebecca
1803-3

Juliana
1806-76
m. (1) Carter Coupland
d. 1833
(2) Mr. Dorsey

Horatio

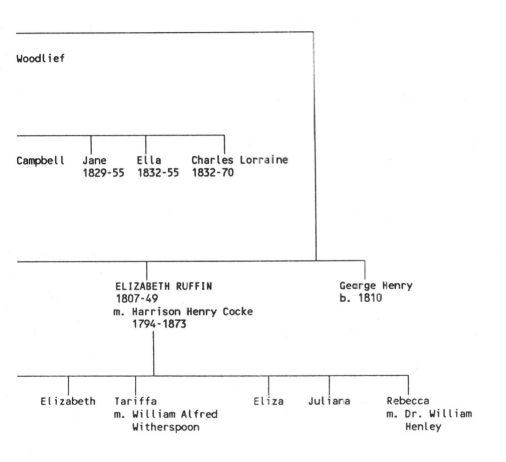

Woodlief

Campbell Jane   Ella   Charles Lorraine
          1829-55   1832-55   1832-70

ELIZABETH RUFFIN   George Henry
1807-49   b. 1810
m. Harrison Henry Cocke
1794-1873

Elizabeth   Tariffa   Eliza   Juliana   Rebecca
            m. William Alfred   m. Dr. William
            Witherspoon   Henley

The Brandon Family

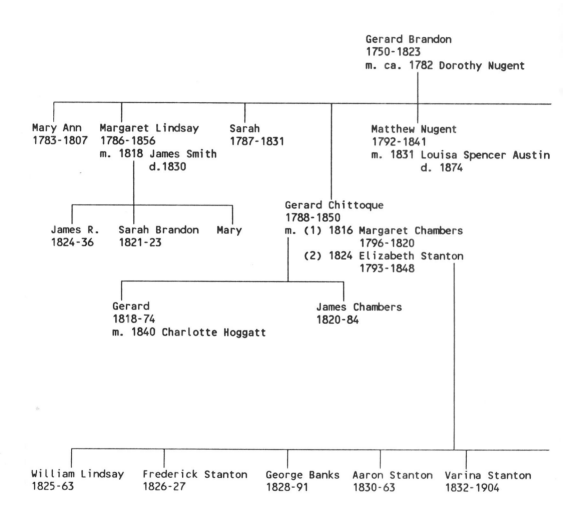

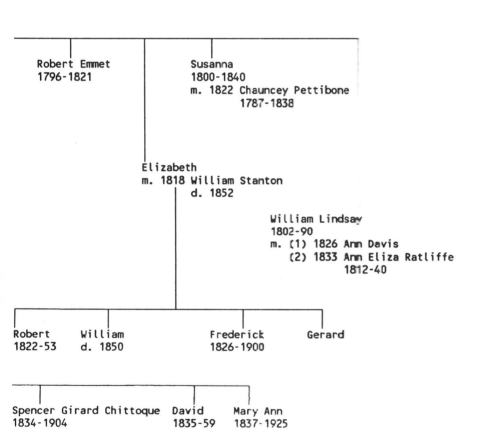

Robert Emmet
1796-1821

Susanna
1800-1840
m. 1822 Chauncey Pettibone
1787-1838

Elizabeth
m. 1818 William Stanton
d. 1852

William Lindsay
1802-90
m. (1) 1826 Ann Davis
(2) 1833 Ann Eliza Ratliffe
1812-40

Robert   William   Frederick   Gerard
1822-53   d. 1850   1826-1900

Spencer Girard Chittoque   David   Mary Ann
1834-1904   1835-59   1837-1925

The North Family

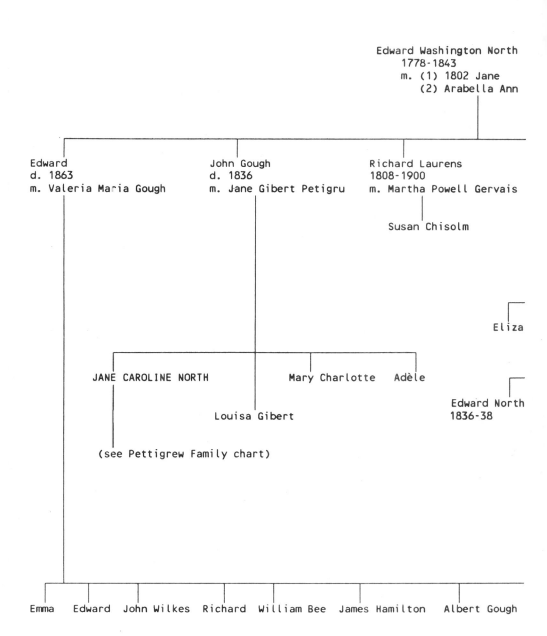

Edward Washington North
1778-1843
m. (1) 1802 Jane
      (2) Arabella Ann

Edward
d. 1863
m. Valeria Maria Gough

John Gough
d. 1836
m. Jane Gibert Petigru

Richard Laurens
1808-1900
m. Martha Powell Gervais

Susan Chisolm

Eliza

JANE CAROLINE NORTH   Mary Charlotte   Adèle

Louisa Gibert

Edward North
1836-38

(see Pettigrew Family chart)

Emma   Edward   John Wilkes   Richard   William Bee   James Hamilton   Albert Gough

Caroline Gough Parker
Baron Burt

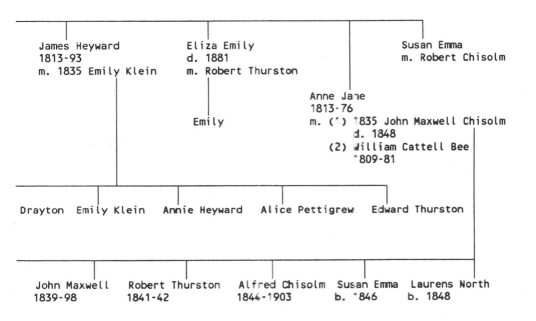

James Heyward
1813-93
m. 1835 Emily Klein

Eliza Emily
d. 1881
m. Robert Thurston

Emily

Susan Emma
m. Robert Chisolm

Anne Jane
1813-76
m. (1) 1835 John Maxwell Chisolm
        d. 1848
    (2) William Cattell Bee
        1809-81

Drayton   Emily Klein   Annie Heyward   Alice Pettigrew   Edward Thurston

John Maxwell
1839-98

Robert Thurston
1841-42

Alfred Chisolm
1844-1903

Susan Emma
b. 1846

Laurens North
b. 1848

Robert Thurston   Henry Perroneau   Charles   Rebecca Bee

The Petigru Family of South Carolina

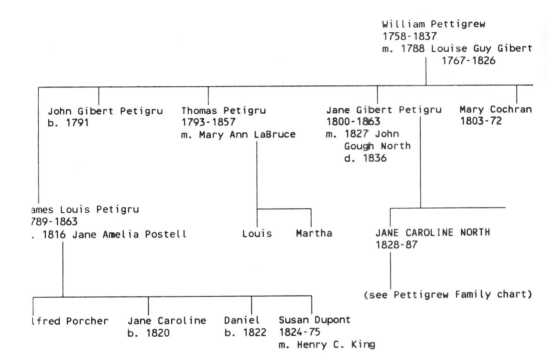

William Pettigrew
1758-1837
m. 1788 Louise Guy Gibert
1767-1826

John Gibert Petigru
b. 1791

Thomas Petigru
1793-1857
m. Mary Ann LaBruce

Jane Gibert Petigru
1800-1863
m. 1827 John
Gough North
d. 1836

Mary Cochran
1803-72

ames Louis Petigru
789-1863
. 1816 Jane Amelia Postell

Louis   Martha

JANE CAROLINE NORTH
1828-87

lfred Porcher
Jane Caroline
b. 1820
Daniel
b. 1822
Susan Dupont
1824-75
m. Henry C. King

(see Pettigrew Family chart)

Henry Russell
1842-65

Louise
1845-ca. 1850

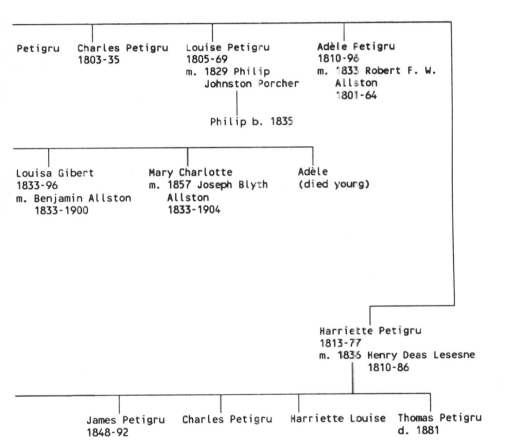

Petigru   Charles Petigru   Louise Petigru   Adèle Petigru
          1803-35   1805-69   1810-96
                         m. 1829 Philip   m. 1833 Robert F. W.
                           Johnston Porcher   Allston
                                        1801-64

Philip b. 1835

Louisa Gibert   Mary Charlotte   Adèle
1833-96   m. 1857 Joseph Blyth   (died young)
m. Benjamin Allston   Allston
1833-1900   1833-1904

Harriette Petigru
1813-77
m. 1836 Henry Deas Lesesne
               1810-86

James Petigru   Charles Petigru   Harriette Louise   Thomas Petigru
1848-92   d. 1881

The Pettigrew Family of North Carolina

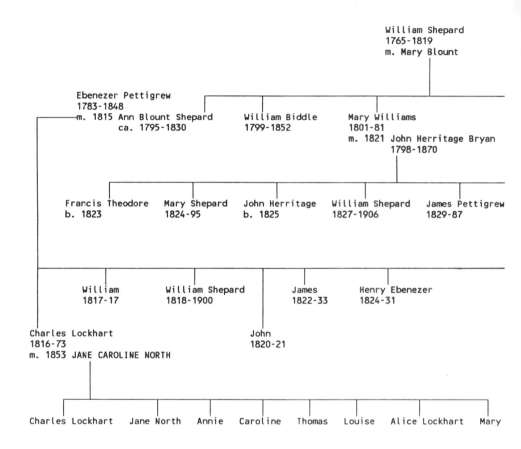

William Shepard
1765-1819
m. Mary Blount

Ebenezer Pettigrew
1783-1848
m. 1815 Ann Blount Shepard
ca. 1795-1830

William Biddle
1799-1852

Mary Williams
1801-81
m. 1821 John Herritage Bryan
1798-1870

Francis Theodore
b. 1823

Mary Shepard
1824-95

John Herritage
b. 1825

William Shepard
1827-1906

James Pettigrew
1829-87

William
1817-17

William Shepard
1818-1900

James
1822-33

Henry Ebenezer
1824-31

Charles Lockhart
1816-73
m. 1853 JANE CAROLINE NORTH

John
1820-21

Charles Lockhart   Jane North   Annie   Caroline   Thomas   Louise   Alice Lockhart   Mary

```
│                           │
Hannah Biddle        5 other children
d. 1818


│            │                │              │
Elizabeth Herritage    Charles Shepard   Octavia    Henry Ravenscroft
·b. 1831               1832-76          b. ˉ834    1836-1919


│            │                        │              │
Mary Blount                     James Johnston   Ann Blount Shepard
1826-87                          1828-63         1830-64
m. 1868 P. Fielding Browne                       m. 1863 Rev. Neill
                                                      McKay
```

The Hardeman Family (1)

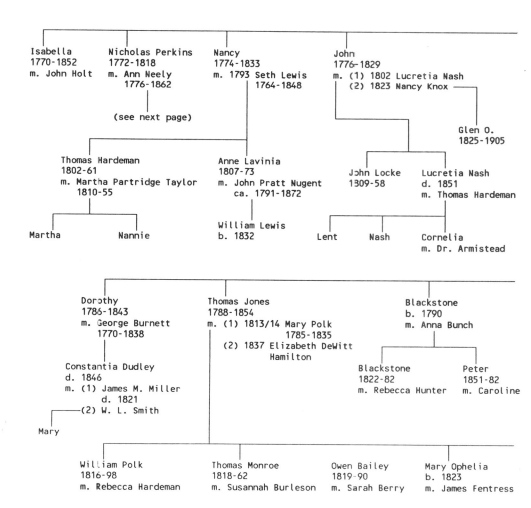

Isabella
1770-1852
m. John Holt

Nicholas Perkins
1772-1818
m. Ann Neely
1776-1862

(see next page)

Nancy
1774-1833
m. 1793 Seth Lewis
1764-1848

John
1776-1829
m. (1) 1802 Lucretia Nash
   (2) 1823 Nancy Knox

Glen O.
1825-1905

Thomas Hardeman
1802-61
m. Martha Partridge Taylor
1810-55

Anne Lavinia
1807-73
m. John Pratt Nugent
ca. 1791-1872

John Locke
1809-58

Lucretia Nash
d. 1851
m. Thomas Hardeman

Martha   Nannie

William Lewis
b. 1832

Lent   Nash

Cornelia
m. Dr. Armistead

Dorothy
1786-1843
m. George Burnett
1770-1838

Thomas Jones
1788-1854
m. (1) 1813/14 Mary Polk
        1785-1835
   (2) 1837 Elizabeth DeWitt
        Hamilton

Blackstone
b. 1790
m. Anna Bunch

Constantia Dudley
d. 1846
m. (1) James M. Miller
       d. 1821
   (2) W. L. Smith

Blackstone
1822-82
m. Rebecca Hunter

Peter
1851-82
m. Caroline

Mary

William Polk
1816-98
m. Rebecca Hardeman

Thomas Monroe
1818-62
m. Susannah Burleson

Owen Bailey
1819-90
m. Sarah Berry

Mary Ophelia
b. 1823
m. James Fentress

Thomas Hardeman
1750-1833
m. (1) 1770 Mary Perkins
            1754-98
    (2) 1799 Susan Perkins Marr
            b. 1750

Constantine   Julia Ann   Peter
1778-1850   1782-1860   1784-1820
m. (1) 1799 Sarah Marr   m. (1) Mr. Davis   m. Susan Stone
    (2) 1824 Mary Little   (2) Thomas Bacon

Susannah Perkins   John Marr
1802-59   1804-91
m. Constantine Perkins Sneed   m. Mary Hardeman
    1790-1864

James H.
1828-1904

Elizabeth   Pitt   Bailey   Franklin
1791-1870   1793-93   1795-1836   1796-96
m. (1) 1809 Glen Owen   m. 1820 Rebecca Amanda
    (2) Reese Corzine   F. Wilson

                            Samuel Wilson   John
Keese

Leonidas Polk
1825-92
m. Tullius Hamilton
    1834-1904

The Hardeman Family (2)

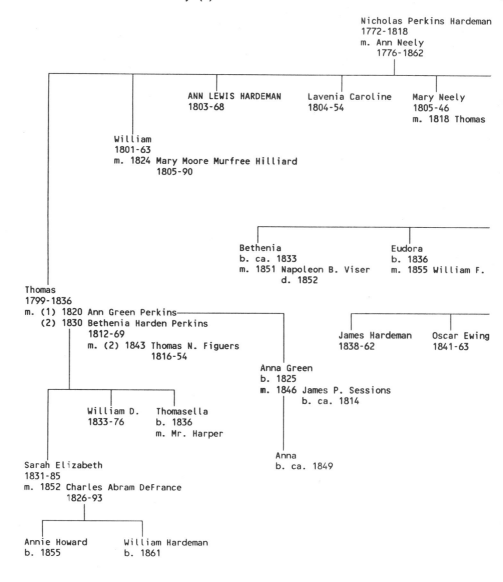

Nicholas Perkins Hardeman
1772-1818
m. Ann Neely
1776-1862

ANN LEWIS HARDEMAN
1803-68

Lavenia Caroline
1804-54

Mary Neely
1805-46
m. 1818 Thomas

William
1801-63
m. 1824 Mary Moore Murfree Hilliard
1805-90

Bethenia
b. ca. 1833
m. 1851 Napoleon B. Viser
d. 1852

Eudora
b. 1836
m. 1855 William F.

Thomas
1799-1836
m. (1) 1820 Ann Green Perkins
   (2) 1830 Bethenia Harden Perkins
        1812-69
        m. (2) 1843 Thomas N. Figuers
             1816-54

James Hardeman
1838-62

Oscar Ewing
1841-63

Anna Green
b. 1825
m. 1846 James P. Sessions
          b. ca. 1814

William D.
1833-76

Thomasella
b. 1836
m. Mr. Harper

Anna
b. ca. 1849

Sarah Elizabeth
1831-85
m. 1852 Charles Abram DeFrance
          1826-93

Annie Howard
b. 1855

William Hardeman
b. 1861

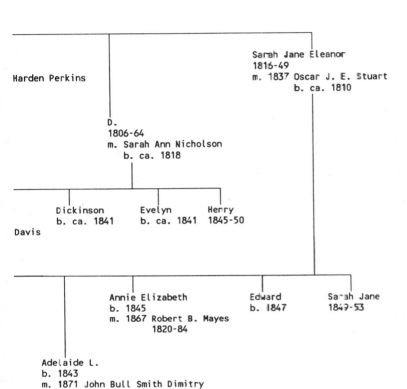

Harden Perkins

Sarah Jane Eleanor
1816-49
m. 1837 Oscar J. E. Stuart
b. ca. 1810

D.
1806-64
m. Sarah Ann Nicholson
b. ca. 1818

Dickinson   Evelyn   Henry
b. ca. 1841   b. ca. 1841   1845-50

Davis

Annie Elizabeth   Edward   Sarah Jane
b. 1845   b. 1847   1849-53
m. 1867 Robert B. Mayes
        1820-84

Adelaide L.
b. 1843
m. 1871 John Bull Smith Dimitry

The Hilliard Family

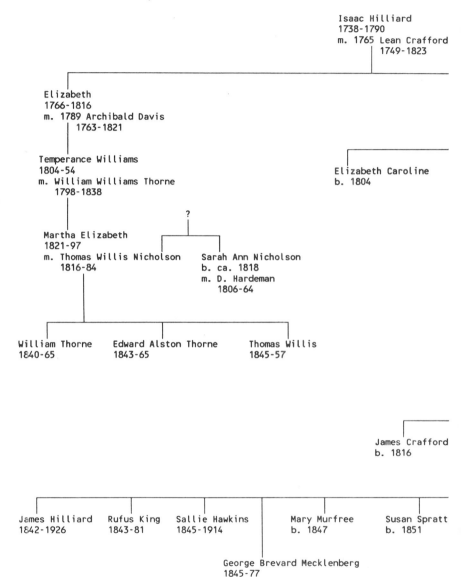

Isaac Hilliard
1738-1790
m. 1765 Lean Crafford
1749-1823

Elizabeth
1766-1816
m. 1789 Archibald Davis
1763-1821

Elizabeth Caroline
b. 1804

Temperance Williams
1804-54
m. William Williams Thorne
1798-1838

Martha Elizabeth
1821-97
m. Thomas Willis Nicholson
1816-84

?

Sarah Ann Nicholson
b. ca. 1818
m. D. Hardeman
1806-64

William Thorne
1840-65

Edward Alston Thorne
1843-65

Thomas Willis
1845-57

James Crafford
b. 1816

James Hilliard
1842-1926

Rufus King
1843-81

Sallie Hawkins
1845-1914

Mary Murfree
b. 1847

Susan Spratt
b. 1851

George Brevard Mecklenberg
1845-77

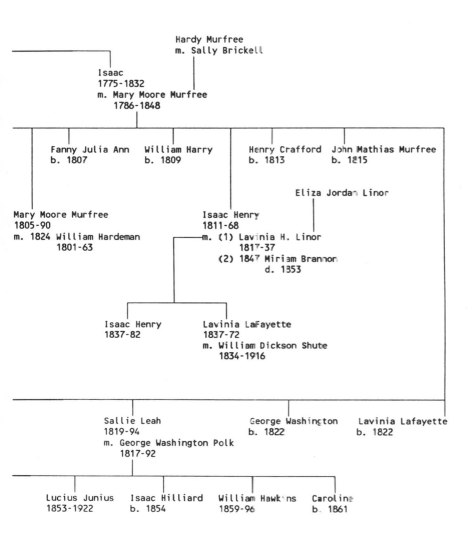

Hardy Murfree
m. Sally Brickell

Isaac
1775-1832
m. Mary Moore Murfree
1786-1848

Fanny Julia Ann
b. 1807

William Harry
b. 1809

Henry Crafford
b. 1813

John Mathias Murfree
b. 1815

Eliza Jordan Linor

Mary Moore Murfree
1805-90
m. 1824 William Hardeman
1801-63

Isaac Henry
1811-68
m. (1) Lavinia H. Linor
1817-37
(2) 1847 Miriam Brannon
d. 1853

Isaac Henry
1837-82

Lavinia LaFayette
1837-72
m. William Dickson Shute
1834-1916

Sallie Leah
1819-94
m. George Washington Polk
1817-92

George Washington
b. 1822

Lavinia Lafayette
b. 1822

Lucius Junius
1853-1922

Isaac Hilliard
b. 1854

William Hawkins
1859-96

Caroline
b. 1861

Notes

INTRODUCTION

1. The literature is growing rapidly, but its range can be sampled in the following works: Jan Lewis, *The Pursuit of Happiness: Family and Values in Jefferson's Virginia* (Cambridge, 1983); Catherine Clinton, *The Plantation Mistress: Woman's World in the Old South* (New York, 1982); Suzanne Lebsock, *The Free Women of Petersburg: Status and Culture in a Southern Town, 1784–1860* (New York, 1984); Jean E. Friedman, *The Enclosed Garden: Women and Community in the Evangelical South, 1830–1900* (Chapel Hill, N.C., 1985); Deborah Gray White, *Ar'n't I a Woman? Female Slaves in the Plantation South* (New York, 1985); Elizabeth Fox-Genovese, *Within the Plantation Household: Black and White Women in the Old South* (Chapel Hill, 1988); Carol Bleser, ed., *In Joy and in Sorrow: Women, Family, and Marriage in the Victorian South* (New York, 1991). Lee Virginia Chambers-Schiller, *Liberty, a Better Husband: Single Women in America, the Generations of 1780–1840* (New Haven, 1984) concentrates on Northern women of the upper middle class but is suggestive. It is doubtful, however, that spinsters in the antebellum South had developed as encouraging a view of their condition as those studied by Chambers-Schiler.

2. Jane H. Pease and William H. Pease, *Ladies, Women, and Wenches: Choice and Constraint in Antebellum Charleston and Boston* (Chapel Hill, N.C., 1990), 1.

3. Since marriage was illegal for slaves though not for the class of free blacks, the question of single black women in the South would have to be differently, less formally, framed.

4. All four women preferred the term journal to diary. This conforms to early nineteenth-century usage, though not to the modern tendency to use the words interchangeably. Throughout I refer to the texts themselves as journals, but to their composers as diarists, since the older and more accurate word journalist has now a quite other meaning.

5. The genre of the travel journal began among men, who of course have never abandoned it. See, for example, "Of Travaile," in Sir Francis Bacon, *The Essayes or Counsels, Civill and Morall,* ed. Michael Kiernan (Cambridge, Mass., 1985), 56: "It is a strange Thing, that in Sea voyages, where there is nothing to be seene, but Sky and Sea, Men should make Diaries; But in Land-Travaile, wherein so much is to be observed, for the most part, they omit it; As if Chance were fitter to be registred, then Observation. Let Diaries, therefore, be brought in use." Bacon goes on to list exhaustively the fit objects for observation.

6. Jane Austen, *Northanger Abbey and Persuasion,* ed. John Davie (Oxford, 1971), 23; Béatrice Didier, *Le journal intime* (Paris, 1976), 116–37.

7. The fact of this transmutation modifies the usefulness of earlier diaries as evidence for women's private worlds and emotions, a use to which they are widely put in feminist scholarship. See, for example, Mary Jane Moffatt and Charlotte Painter, eds., *Revelations: Diaries of Women* (New York, 1974), 5. On the relative absence of a "self" from eighteenth-century women's journals, see Felicity A. Nussbaum, "Eighteenth-Century Women's Autobiographical Commonplaces," in Shari Benstock, ed., *The Private Self: Theory and Practice of Women's Autobiographical Writings* (Chapel Hill, N.C., 1988), 147–76.

8. Elizabeth Fox-Genovese suggests that journals were written by antebellum Southern women to be read by their daughters. I can find only modest evidence for this, though the nature of this volume influences my understanding. For naturally the childless seldom write for children, unless they are the children of others. Yet journals were very often written by those not yet married, as a rite of passage. Such people were too uncertain about the prospect of marriage to set themselves up as dispensers of advice and experience to as-yet imaginary offspring. See Fox-Genovese, "Between Individualism and Community: Autobiographies of Southern Women," in *Located Lives: Place and Idea in Southern Autobiography,* ed. J. Bill Berry (Athens, Ga., 1990), 20–38.

9. See, for example, Steven M. Stowe, "City, Country, and the Feminine Voice," in Michael O'Brien and David Moltke-Hansen, eds., *Intellectual Life in Antebellum Charleston* (Knoxville, Tenn., 1986), 315–16; and C. Vann Woodward, "Mary Chesnut in Search of Her Genre," *The Future of the Past* (New York, 1989), 250–62.

10. Oscar Wilde, *Complete Works* (London, 1981), 357.

11. The literature on Edmund Ruffin is large but see especially: Avery O. Craven, *Edmund Ruffin, Southerner: A Study in Secession* (New York, 1932); Betty L. Mitchell, *Edmund Ruffin: a Biography* (Bloomington, 1981); Drew Gilpin Faust, *A Sacred Circle: The Dilemma of the Intellectual in the Old South, 1840–1860* (Baltimore, 1977); William M. Mathew, *Edmund Ruffin and the Crisis of Slavery in the Old South: The Failure of Agricultural Reform* (Athens, Ga., 1988); and David F. Allmendinger, *Ruffin: Family and Reform in the Old South* (New York, 1990). Of these, only Allmendinger has paid any significant attention to Elizabeth Ruffin, and then mainly as part of the demography of the Ruffin family. The only book of which I am aware that has used her journals is Fox-Genovese, *Within the Plantation Household.*

12. David F. Allmendinger, ed., *Incidents of My Life: Edmund Ruffin's Autobiographical Essays* (Charlottesville, Va., 1990), 222, 233–34; Allmendinger, *Ruffin: Family and Reform in the Old South,* 13–21.

13. Elizabeth Ruffin to Edmund Ruffin, Feb. 18, 1828, and undated letter beginning "The contents of this letter will no doubt make you pause," Edmund Ruffin Papers, Southern Historical Collection, Library of the University of North Carolina at Chapel Hill (a microfilm of original manuscripts now housed at the Virginia Historical Society, Richmond).

14. Ibid., undated letter beginning "The truth of your reasons."

15. Elizabeth Ruffin to Edmund Ruffin, undated letter beginning "The contents of this letter will no doubt make you pause"; and Elizabeth Ruffin Cocke to Edmund Ruffin, April 12, [1849], ibid.

16. Elizabeth Ruffin Cocke to Tariffa Cocke, May 9, 1848, Harrison Henry Cocke Papers, Southern Historical Collection.

17. Elizabeth Ruffin Cocke to Mary C. Ruffin, July 25 [no year given], ibid. The symptoms may indicate some form of poisoning, perhaps from the rat poison that was often placed in the hold of ships. But some sort of fever cannot be ruled out.

18. Ibid.

19. Her husband had purchased Evergreen in 1831; see Indenture of Jan. 1, 1831, Cocke Family (of Dinwiddie County) Papers, Virginia Historical Society.

20. Juliana Ruffin Coupland Dorsey to Edmund Ruffin, March 15, May 13, April 12, 1849; Elizabeth Ruffin Cocke to Edmund Ruffin, March 30, 1849, April 12 [1849], Ruffin Papers.

21. In fact, this failure of communication first led me to think that the original had been lost. The copyediting of this book had been completed when a chance reading of Bertram Wyatt-Brown, *Southern Honor: Ethics and Behavior in the Old South* (New York, 1982) alerted me to the existence of the original journal in Baton Rouge. I am under a great obligation to Professor Wyatt-Brown for saving me from so marked an error.

22. B. L. C. Wailes, *Memoir of Leonard Covington*, ed. Nellie Wailes Brandon and W. M. Drake (Natchez, Miss., 1928).

23. Deed, Sept. 25, 1850, in Deed Book HH, pp. 275–76, Adams County Courthouse, Natchez, Mississippi (viewed on microfilm at the Family History Library, Genealogical Society of Utah, Salt Lake City). Nellie Wailes Brandon, in a manuscript now in the possession of Mrs. Wilton R. Dale of Vidalia. elaborated on the Wilson Academy, though without annotated evidence: "After this institution [the Elizabeth Female College] no longer carried on, a smaller girl's school arose, owned and conducted by the sisters, Mary and Margaret Wilson of Pennsylvania. It was called the Wilson Academy. The land on which this school was located was bought by Margaret Wilson in 1849. Whether it already contained the building which afterwards housed the school, or whether Miss Wilson built it, is not known. It carried on from 1849 until after the civil war, and at one time and another had in its student list, not only every girl in the community, but many from other states." She went on to mention that Wilson had been governess to the Smith family and added, "The Wilson Academy, in the last stages of delapidation, has recently been wiped from the landscape by the so called hand of progress in the shape of good roads."

24. The 1853 Mississippi State Census lists "M. B. Wilson" as the head of a household of three females, among those counted in Adams County outside of Natchez (originals in Jackson; viewed on microfilm at the Family History Library). This would seem to indicate that Mary B. Wilson was the elder sister.

25. Just to confuse matters further, two sisters called Wilson who are schoolteachers and governesses occur in the diary of Ann Hardeman. The elder is called Jennie, however, and their father seems to have resided in Wheeling, Virginia. See the entries for March 15, March 29, June 17, June 20, July 9, Aug. 25, 1851.

26. William R. Hogan and Edwin A. Davis, eds., *William Johnson's Natchez: The Ante-Bellum Diary of a Free Negro* (Baton Rouge, La., 1951), 373–74; William T. Blain, *Education in the Old Southwest: A History of Jefferson College, Washington, Mississippi* (Washington, Miss., 1976); see also Robert W. Weathersby II, *J. H. Ingraham* (Boston, 1980); Charles S. Sydnor, *A Gentleman of the Old Natchez Region: Benjamin L. C. Wailes* (Durham, N.C., 1938); Susanna Smith, "Washington, Mississippi: Antebellum Elysium," *Journal of Mississippi History* 40 (May 1978): 143–65.

27. *Biographical and Historical Memoirs of Mississippi*, 2 vols. (Chicago, 1891), 1:419.

28. "Inventory and appraisement of the property of Mrs Margaret Smith deceased," March 31, 1856, Adams County Courthouse (copy in the possession of Mrs. Dale).

29. A further doubt about Nellie Wailes Brandon's gloss is her observation that Margaret Wilson remained governess until 1848, when the children had grown up. In

fact, after the death of the younger James Smith in 1836, the only child in the household was Mary Smith, and she married Richard Phillips in 1843. On the other hand, the diarist's school served more than the Smith household; children of local planters came. It is just possible, though unlikely, that Margaret Smith permitted such a school in her home past the moment of her own need for it.

It is worth noting that the son James does not appear in the journal, which is odd. However, the diarist falls silent between Dec. 16, 1835, and March 20, 1836. This could be explained by the son's death on Jan. 9, 1836.

30. File 1, p. 5, Cemetery Records, Adams County, in Genealogical File, Mississippi Department of Archives and History, Jackson.

31. As the diarist was not a "Southerner," I gave some thought to excluding the journal from this volume. I retained it for several reasons: in a region that saw much migration, many residents of Southern states were not native-born and to exclude such people from our studies would be to impoverish our scope; whatever her provenance, the diarist was an observer of things Southern; and the diary is unlikely to be sponsored by scholars of Pennsylvania.

32. Charles L. Pettigrew to Jane Caroline North (hereinafter JCN), Jan. 11, 1849, Pettigrew Family Papers, Southern Historical Collection.

33. James Petigru Carson, *Life, Letters, and Speeches of James Louis Petigru* (Washington, D.C., 1920), 182; Sarah McCulloch Lemmon, ed., *The Pettigrew Papers,* vol. 2, *1819–1843* (Raleigh, N.C., 1988), 86; William J. Grayson, *James Louis Petigru, a Biographical Sketch* (New York, 1866), 30. The plantation originally belonged to the Giberts, the family of Jane North's mother.

34. Carson, *Petigru,* 17–27; Grayson, *Petigru,* 163–64.

35. JCN to Jane G. North, February 5, 1849, Pettigrew Papers.

36. JCN to Mary Petigru, Feb. 19, 1849, ibid.

37. Ibid.

38. JCN to Mary Petigru, March 26, 1849, to James Johnston Pettigrew, June 29, 1849, March 1850, to Charles L. Pettigrew, July 11, 1851, to Jane G. North, May 22, 1850, ibid

39. Adèle Petigru Allston to Robert F. W. Allston, June 4, 1850, in J. H. Easterby, ed., *The South Carolina Rice Plantation as Revealed in the Papers of Robert F. W. Allston* (Chicago, 1945), 100; JCN to Charles L. Pettigrew, July 11, 1851, Pettigrew Papers.

40. See also JCN to Mary Charlotte North, Sept. 11 and 12, 1851, Pettigrew Papers.

41. Ibid.

42. Jane G. North to JCN, Jan. 16, 1849, ibid.

43. Wayne K. Durrill, *War of Another Kind: A Southern Community in the Great Rebellion* (New York, 1990), 7; List of births and deaths in the Pettigrew family [probably by William Shepard Pettigrew], undated MS in folder 647, Pettigrew Papers.

44. Durrill, *War of Another Kind,* 221–22, claims that Carey agreed to marry William and then broke her promise. But his notes offer no evidence, and in its absence I am inclined to doubt.

45. Mary B. Pettigrew to James Johnston Pettigrew, March 25, 1849, JCN to James Johnston Pettigrew, Nov. 9, 1849, Pettigrew Papers.

46. Mary B. Pettigrew to James Johnston Pettigrew, March 25, 1849, JCN to Charles L. Pettigrew, Nov. 11, 1850, February 24, 1851, William S. Pettigrew to James Johnston Pettigrew, March 8, 1849, ibid.

47. In 1848 Johnston Pettigrew had a capital of $15,000 and had inherited a single

slave: see Clyde N. Wilson, *Carolina Cavalier: The Life and Mind of James Johnston Pettigrew* (Athens, Ga., 1990), 28–29.

48. JCN to Jane G. North, Nov. 10, 1851, Pettigrew Papers.

49. Charles Lockhart, Jane North, Annie, Caroline, Thomas, Louise, Alice Lockhart, and Mary.

50. This story is ably told in Durrill, *War of Another Kind*.

51. Jane Caroline Pettigrew to Charles L. Pettigrew, Jan 14, Jan. 21, Feb. 17, 1866, Pettigrew Papers.

52. I draw this account from the introduction to the very full inventory of the Pettigrew Papers, written by Roslyn Holdzkom and Lisa Tolbert, with the assistance of Mark Beasley, in 1989.

53. Nicholas Perkins Hardeman, *Wilderness Calling: The Hardeman Family in the American Westward Movement, 1750–1900* (Knoxville, Tenn., 1977), 3.

54. Indenture, Jan. 7, 1835, in vol. 6, p. 235, Deed Records of the Chancery Clerk, Hinds County, Miss., Hinds County Courthouse (microfilm at Family History Library).

55. Oscar J. E. Stuart to Capt James Eads, undated letter beginning "Sir, In the summer of 1852," Mayes-Dimitry-Stuart Papers, Mississippi Department of Archives and History, Jackson, observes that during the Civil War, "I lost all my slaves as did my children, who had a seperate property from myself."

56. William Hardeman to Ann L. Hardeman (hereinafter ALH), November 23, 1848, Oscar J. E. Stuart Papers, Mississippi Department of Archives and History, Jackson; Mary Hardeman to James H. Stuart, August 26, 1858, to ALH, November 15, 1865, John Bull Smith Dimitry Papers, William R. Perkins Library, Duke University.

57. William Hardeman to ALH, Nov. 23, 1848, Stuart Papers.

58. For example, he paid for the education of Adelaide and Bettie Stuart in New Jersey: see William Hardeman to Adelaide Stuart, July 26, 1860, ibid.

59. James Stuart to Annie Elizabeth Hardeman, Jan. 15, 1859, Edward Stuart to Mary Hardeman, Nov. 18, 1863, ibid.

60. ALH to Adelaide Stuart, April 1, 1867, to Annie Elizabeth Stuart, June 2, 1867, Dimitry Papers. A fragment in the Stuart Papers, perhaps written by Annie Elizabeth Mayes, notes: "Aunt Ann was in wretched health, her trouble being of the kind that predisposes to melancholy. Yet she was a cheerful pleasant companion. She *did* receive unkindness from some, but never from Grandpa & his children, who loved her with all the ardent love that was her *due.*"

61. Edward Stuart to Mary Hardeman, Nov. 18, 1863, Stuart Papers.

62. Alexander H. H. Stuart to Oscar J. E. Stuart, Nov. 10, 1866, Dimitry Papers.

63. Oscar J. E. Stuart to Capt James Eads, undated letter beginning "Sir, In the summer of 1852," Mayes-Dimitry-Stuart Papers.

64. Oscar J. E. Stuart, undated manuscript beginning ' and wept God only knows," Stuart Papers. The 1860 federal census for Pike County Mississippi, locates him in Holmesville and credits him with $100 of real estate and $10,000 in personalty. In his household were a J. C. Dick, twenty-six, a carpenter, and two male slaves aged twenty-six and thirty-four.

65. ALH to Adelaide Stuart, Feb. 25, 1866, Mayes-Dimitry-Stuart Papers.

66. Notation on typescript copy of Edward Stuart to William Hardeman, Oct. 28, 1862, Dimitry Papers.

67. William and Mary Hardeman sold, for $800, a right of way over their plantation to the Canton & Jackson Rail Road Company on April 15, 1859: see vol. 27, p. 115,

Deed Records of the Chancery Clerk, Hinds County Courthouse (microfilm at Family History Library).

68. William D. McCain, *The Story of Jackson: a History of the Capital of Mississippi, 1821–1951*, 2 vols. (Jackson, Miss, 1953), 1:52. Oddly, William Hardeman is referred to as "Dr. W. Hardeman" here, but there is no other evidence of his having had medical training.

69. Ibid., 207. In this paragraph I have relied on this book for my understanding of Jackson.

70. ALH to Adelaide Stuart, Dec. 19, 1866, to Annie Elizabeth Stuart, Feb. 14, April 26, May 9, 1867, Mayes-Dimitry-Stuart Papers.

71. On April 28, 1862, she refers to ending her "fifth book of journallising," though only four volumes up to 1862 survive.

72. R. B. Mayes to Dunbar Rowland, Dec. 19, 1911, James Hardeman Stuart Papers, Mississippi Department of Archives and History, Jackson. Much of the Dimitry Papers collection at Duke University consists of typescripts, evidently made to serve this project. There is just a single page of ALH's journal among them.

73. Charles B. Clayman, ed., *The American Medical Association Encyclopedia of Medicine* (New York, 1989), 667. I am grateful to Dr. Clint Joiner of the University of Cincinnati for suggesting this diagnosis.

74. G. Berkeley [illegible surname] to Oscar E. Stuart, September 1862, Stuart Papers.

75. John A. Barksdale to Oscar J. E. Stuart, June 29, 1863, ibid.

76. Edward Stuart to Adelaide Stuart, Nov. 20, 1864, ibid.

77. Annie Elizabeth Stuart to ALH, Sept. 22, 1866, Mayes-Dimitry-Stuart Papers.

78. ALH to Adelaide Stuart, Sept. 30, Dec. 23, 1866, Dimitry Papers; ALH to Annie Elizabeth Stuart, April 26, 1867, Mayes-Dimitry-Stuart Papers.

79. ALH to Adelaide Stuart, Nov. 21, Dec. 9, 1867, Mayes-Dimitry-Stuart Papers.

EDITORIAL NOTE

1. ALH to Edward Stuart, Nov. 4, 1862, Stuart Papers.

2. In fact, I went through several other counties, since the finding aid for the Stuart Papers incorrectly identifies Ann Hardeman as living in Summit, Mississippi, which is in Pike County. For a while, I did not know where the Hardemans lived and had to find them through the internal evidence of the journal and the census.

RUFFIN JOURNALS

1. Somnus, the Roman god of sleep, was the son of Night and the twin brother of Death.

2. Love conquers all. This phrase is from Vergil, *Eclogues* 10.69 and is best known for decorating the brooch worn by the Prioress in Chaucer's *Canterbury Tales*. See "Prologue," lines 158–62, in *The Complete Works of Geoffrey Chaucer*, ed. W. W. Skeat, 6 vols. (Oxford, 1894), 4:5–6:

> Of small coral aboute hir arm she bar
> A peire of bedes, gauded al with grene;
> And ther-on heng a broche of gold ful shene,

On which ther was first write a crowned A,
And after, *Amor vincit omnia.*

3. *The New Monthly and Literary Journal* lasted from 1814 to 1884, under various names; in 1827 it was edited by T. Campbell.

4. Henry Fielding, *The History of Tom Jones, a Foundling* (1749).

5. "Advice from a Father to His Only Daughter," *American Farmer* 45 (Jan. 26, 1827): 357–58. An editorial preface notes, "The following letter is said to be from the pen of one of the best and greatest men that Virginia has produced."

6. A review of Rt. Rev. John Stark Ravenscroft's *The Doctrines of the Church Vindicated from the Misrepresentations of Dr. John Rice; and the Integrity of Revealed Religion Defended against the "No Comment Principle" of Promiscucus Bible Societies* (Raleigh, N.C.: J. Gales & Son, 1826) ran in the *Literary and Evangelical Magazine* of Richmond every month from July 1826 until June 1827. Ravenscroft (1772–1830) had been Episcopal bishop of North Carolina since 1823.

7. *National Preacher* 1 (Jan. 1827) contains a sermon by Baxter Dickinson of Massachusetts on "The Day of Pentecost"; the issue for February has one by John Matthews of Shepherdstown, Va., on "The Benefit of Afflictions." The periodical was dedicated to printing "original monthly sermons by living ministers."

8. Possibly Peter Woodlief, Elizabeth Ruffin's stepfather.

9. Jane Porter, *Thaddeus of Warsaw* (London: T. N. Longman & O. Rees, 1803).

10. Presumably Elizabeth Ruffin's mother, Rebecca Cocke Ruffin Woodlief (1771–1837).

11. James Fenimore Cooper, *The Last of the Mohicans: A Narrative of 1757* (Philadelphia: Carey & Lea, 1826).

12. Presumably "B" for Brother, i.e., Edmund Ruffin (1794–1865). See the entry for March 5 below.

13. Probably *A Philosophical, Historical, and Moral Essay on Old Maids by a Friend to the Sisterhood*, 3 vols. (London: T. Cadell, 1793). The author was William Hayley (1745–1820), a poet and the biographer of William Blake.

14. Tobias George Smollett, *The Adventures of Peregrine Pickle, In Which Are Included, Memoirs of a Lady of Quality* (1751).

15. Presumably Edmund Ruffin, Jr. (1814–1875).

16. Philanthropy.

17. Edmund Ruffin's farm, Coggin's Point.

18. The U.S. naval ship North Carolina, built in 1813, had seventy-four guns.

19. Large mosquitoes.

20. The Museum founded by Charles Willson Peale in 1784 at first contained portraits of American Revolutionary heroes but expanded to include assorted natural curiosities. It was most famous for the skeleton of a mammoth, found (fittingly for an exhibit to be viewed by the Ruffins) in a marlpit in New York in 1799. The museum had various homes in Philadelphia but was then on the second story of the State House.

21. Possibly a member of the Campbell family of Petersburg, Va. James W. Campbell, a bookseller, was married to Mildred Campbell, both of whom Edmund Ruffin knew well. Their son, Charles, became a historian of Virginia.

22. John Quincy Adams.

23. In 1817 Benjamin West donated a copy of his Christ Healing the Sick to the Philadelphia Museum; it was housed in a special building on Spruce Street, for which one paid 25 cents admission.

24. Founded in 1824, the American Sunday School Union was located at 1122 Chestnut Street.

25. James Patriot Wilson had been pastor of the First Presbyterian Church on Market Street from 1806 to 1820.

26. Thomas H. Skinner was pastor of the Fifth Presbyterian Church on Arch Street; a "New School" Presbyterian, he had led a schism from Wilson's First Presbyterian Church in 1816.

27. "And Joses, who by the apostles was surnamed Barnabas, (which is, being interpreted, The son of consolation,) a Levite, and of the country of Cyprus" (Acts 4:36).

28. Boanerges was the name given by Christ to James and John, the sons of Zebedee: "he surnamed them Boanerges, which is, The sons of thunder," (Mark 3:17).

29. Baron Kempelen constructed a machine, in Hungary in 1769, that he claimed could play chess without the aid of human agency. It was exhibited throughout Europe during the next decades until Kempelen died in 1804 and it passed into the hands of Johann Nepomuk Maelzel. The Automaton is said to have played chess with Napoleon at Schönbrunn Palace after the battle of Wagram in 1809. Maelzel brought the machine to the United States in 1826 and toured American cities. In August 1827 it was on hiatus from a long engagement in Baltimore. In May of the same year, an American named Walker built an imitation and exhibited it in New York before going on tour to Saratoga, Ballston, and elsewhere. Both machines were controlled by a man concealed within the cabinet, who shifted his position as various doors that exposed the interior mechanism were opened. See Edgar Allan Poe's skeptical essay, "Maelzel's Chess-Player," *Southern Literary Messenger* 2 (April 1836): 318–26. The best account is "The History of the Automaton Chess-Player in America," in *The Book of the First American Chess Congress,* ed. Daniel Willard Fiske (New York, 1859), 420–84.

30. Not, as in present usage, a strikebreaker, but a swindler who specialized in horseracing.

31. Possibly a misquotation from Samuel Johnson, "Unhappiness of Women (39)," in *The Rambler* (1750–52: rept., London, 1953), 91. The full sentence reads: "Marriage, though a certain security from the reproach and solitude of antiquated virginity, has yet, as it is usually conducted, many disadvantages that take away much from the pleasure which society promises and might afford if pleasures and pains were honestly shared and mutual confidence inviolably preserved."

32. John Holt Rice (1777–1831), professor of theology in the Presbyterian Seminary of Hampden-Sydney College and probably Virginia's leading Presbyterian.

33. Originally the name of a tough climbing and twining shrub found in tropical and subtropical climates, but also applied to a cane made of its bark and, in American usage, to a puppet manipulated by a string.

34. When Moses was in exile in the land of Midian, he married Zipporah: "And she bare him a son, and he called his name Gershom: for he said, I have been a stranger in a strange land," (Exodus 2:22).

35. "It was a true report that I heard in mine own land of thy acts and of thy wisdom. Howbeit I believed not the words, until I came, and mine eyes had seen it: and, behold, the half was not told me: thy wisdom and prosperity exceedeth the fame which I heard" (1 Kings 10:6–7).

36. John Quincy Adams and Louisa Catherine Johnson Adams had three sons: George Washington, Charles Francis, and John. The installation of a billiards table in the White House, at public expense, had occasioned a furore in 1825.

SELMA PLANTATION JOURNALS: 1835

1. As a number of names frequently occur in the journal but are identified only by initials, it will be useful to identify them

Mrs. B——— or B———t: Mrs. Bonnet of Pittsburgh.

Mr. D———: Dr. William Dunbar (1793–1847), the son of William Dunbar I.

Mrs. D———: Mary Field Dunbar (d. 1875).

E———: Eliza Dunbar Cochran (1812–1886), the daughter of Samuel and Anne Dunbar Postlethwaite, granddaughter of William Dunbar I, and wife of Alfred Cochran (d. 1837) of Pittsburgh.

Mr. L———: James Reid Lambdin (1807–1889) of Pittsburgh, a portrait painter who had studied under Thomas Sully.

Miss M———: Maria Chambers, the sister of Margaret Chambers Brandon (1796–1820), the first wife of Governor Gerard Chittoque Brandon (1788–1850).

Mary: Mary Smith, the daughter of Margaret and James Smith.

Mrs. P———: Anne Dunbar Postlethwaite (1786–1864), the widow of Samuel Postlethwaite and daughter of William Dunbar I.

Mrs. S———: Margaret Lindsay Brandon Smith (1786–1856), the daughter of Gerard Brandon I and widow of James Smith; she was the owner of Selma plantation.

S———: Sabina, a friend or relative in Pittsburgh.

2. That is, music.

3. "Delightful task! to rear the tender thought, / To teach the young idea how to shoot" (James Thomson, *The Seasons. Spring,* ll. 1152–53).

4. Perhaps the traditional song, "The Bonnie Banks o' Loch Lomon'," which has the line, "But the broken heart it kens nae second spring again."

5. Elizabeth Brandon Stanton.

6. William Stanton (d. 1852).

7. A villa sold by the Postlethwaite family to Anna Linton.

8. Calomel, or mercurous chloride, was widely used as a medicine.

9. Plato, in the *Definitions:* "Man is a wingless animal with two feet and flat nails."

10. Probably Helen Dunlop, the only child of Margaret Dunbar Dunlop (1788–1851), the daughter of William Dunbar I and widow of James Dunlop. A "Miss H———" frequently appears later in the journal, usually in the vicinity of a Dunbar or Postlethwaite.

11. E. G. Squier and E. H. Davis, *Ancient Monuments of the Mississippi Valley* (Washington, D.C., 1847), 117–18, observe that this "great mound at Selzertown" near Washington, Miss., was "a truncated pyramid" 600 feet long, 400 feet broad, and 40 feet high, covering six acres at its base, four acres at its summit. In it "vast quantities of human skeletons were found; also numerous specimens of pottery, including vases filled with pigments, ashes, ornaments, etc." Around it were a number of smaller mounds.

12. Later described as "the youngest and the handsomest of the family," this may be James Chambers Brandon (1820–1884), the eldest son of Gerard Chittoque Brandon by Margaret Chambers; he is the only Brandon young enough to be so described and old enough to be interesting.

13. Perhaps Louisa Spencer Austin Brandon (d. 1874), the wife of Matthew Nugent Brandon (1792–1841), the son of Gerard Brandon I.

14. Perhaps the wife of John T. McMurran, a leading Natchez Whig and law partner of John A. Quitman.

15. Frances Anne Butler, *Journal* (London, 1835).

16. The *Courrier Français,* a Parisian periodical.

17. Possibly Dr. Samuel Hogg, a physician in Natchez: he had an office on Main Street and lived in the Mansion House Hotel. Or perhaps Dr. John M. Hubbard, with an office in Natchez at the corner of Franklin and Pearl streets.

18. Possibly Aurora Cox Lyons, the wife of Joseph B. Lyons.

19. Giuditta Pasta (1798–1865), the Italian soprano, for whom Bellini wrote *La Sonnambula,* which the diarist praises later. She was a singer much admired by Fanny Kemble; see Butler, *Journal* 2:43.

20. Ann Radcliffe (1764–1823), the Gothic novelist, best known for *The Mysteries of Udolpho* (1794).

21. The Forest, the plantation created by William Dunbar I. Its mansion was built by his widow in about 1817 and inherited by Dr. William Dunbar, by lot, in the partition of his father's estate in 1826.

22. Maria Edgeworth, *Belinda* (1801).

23. Possibly Charlotte Hoggatt (ca. 1788–1836), the wife of Nathaniel Hoggatt (1777–1853), who bought in 1833 the plantation later called Brandon Hall; she died on Dec. 24, 1836, and the last mention of a Mrs. H—in the journal is on Dec. 21, 1836. Or possibly Helen Dunbar Huntington, the daughter of William and Dinah Dunbar, whose house was on land adjacent to the Forest plantation.

24. Perhaps Butler, *Journal* 2:87: "When he was gone, rode for an hour without any pommel, and found I managed it famously."

25. *Salmagundi; or, the Whim-Whams and Opinions of Launcelot Langstaff, Esq. and Others,* satirical essays and poems by Washington Irving, J. K. Paulding, and others, originally published as periodical pamphlets and as a book in 1808. It was modeled on the *Spectator.*

26. The *Oxford English Dictionary* cites Bishop Joseph Hall, *A Recollection of Such Treatises As Have Been Heretofore Severally Published and Are Now Revised* (1614), 166: "Kings use not to dwell in cottages of clay." This seems unlikely as a direct source, so presumably the phrase passed into more accessible hands.

27. Pittsburgh.

28. Mr. W—— and Mr. D—— (who occur in proximity in the journal) may be Robert J. Walker (1801–1869), the Jacksonian senator, and Stephen Duncan (1787–67), the Mississippi planter and banker: they were cousins, both being born in Pennsylvania, Walker near Harrisburg and Duncan in Carlisle.

29. In the inventory of the estate of Margaret Smith, dated March 31, 1856, Adams County Courthouse, a slave named Hector, aged fifty, is listed and valued at $1,000. He would have been about thirty in 1835.

30. Translation:

To My Friend

I long thought that the notes of the lyre
Were fitted only for the strains of love.
I now feel that friendship inspires in us
Songs as sweet and as sure of a response.

The dream of Love poisons one's life,
Is a deceitful dream with no hope of awakening.
But the pleasure found in a true friend
Comes to find me, almost without my knowing it.

An avowal of love is a breath, a whisper,
A drunken dance like the scent of a flower.

A bond of friendship is a pleasant chain
With which to bind happiness.

When far from a friend, faithful memory
Recalls those moments of happiness.
A plaintive note, a pure song reminds one
And the prospect of happiness smiles.

When far from a lover, suspicion, tears, jealousy
Vex and trouble the too-feeling heart
While seeming to say that he forgets you with another
And the future offers only pain.

Ah, absence tests the tenderness
Of both love and friendship
My heart tells me that, if love wounds when close,
Absence favors friendship.

Be comforted, my dear friend,
Soon time will reunite us,
And in the arms of your dear friend
You will soon forget what has made you suffer.

The couplets that follow formed themselves in my head last night and kept me awake as, during the evening, I pondered how shameful it would be if France and America became enemies, because of Jackson's stubbornness.

Air of "La Palisse"

What sad blindness
That wise America
Should choose a President
As stubborn as an ass.

He is considered courageous
But he is only stubborn.
Those who contradicted him
Were broken like plaster—what sad blindness etc.

To better show his bravery,
He tries to pick a quarrel with France.
But he does not frighten us.
A good dog does not bark first—what sad blindness etc.

And, in the vanguard of the ungrateful,
He comes to make war on us,
Does he forget that our soldiers
Liberated him from England?—what sad blindness etc.

He should therefore learn now.
From this fine escapade,
That one cannot frighten Gauls
With bluster.—what sad etc.

Friends, let us henceforth sing,

> And let each cry out,
> Long live the gallant French,
> Their glory and their country—what sad etc.

31. Translation:

To My Guitar

> Companion of my fleeting leisure,
> Your soft and plaintive melody,
> Your notes mingle with my sighs,
> And bewitch my life.
> How many memories, how many cares,
> Your sweet chords bring back to me.
> But when you beguile my troubles
> Smiling hope awakens.
> I love to press near to my heart
> Your light and graceful form.
> I think of you almost as a sister,
> So dear to me has your voice become.
> Oh why cannot I bring you to life?
> And confess to you all my woes!
> Warn you of the unhappiness of love
> And of the remorse it brings us.
> Oh that I could be like you
> To be able to enchant and be indifferent,
> Subject only to the law
> Of tender and peaceful harmony.

32. "Amici, diem perdidi." In Robert Graves's translation: "One evening at dinner, realizing that he [Titus] had done nobody any favour since the previous night, he spoke these memorable words: 'My friends, I have wasted a day' " (Suetonius, *The Twelve Caesars* 8:8).

33. Butler, *Journal* 2:8.

34. Then numbering two, Ursula Rose Cochran (1832–1870) and Alfred Dunbar Cochran (1833–1857). She had a third, George Cochran, on Nov. 11, 1836.

35. A number of pages are missing here; the binding is loose and they evidently dropped out.

SELMA PLANTATION JOURNALS: 1836

1. Fanny Jarman Ternan (b. 1805), an English actress who was on tour in the United States, made her debut in Philadelphia in November 1834 as Juliet and ended up in Boston as Jeannie Deans in December 1836. She appeared at the Saint Charles Theatre, New Orleans, from December 1835 to February 1836 and presumably was working her way up the Mississippi River.

2. George Cochran, just a month old.

3. Alexandre Dumas, *Impressions de voyage,* 5 vols. (Paris, 1833–37).

SELMA PLANTATION JOURNALS: 1837

1. Allegheny?

2. Perhaps Catharine Surget (1817–1838), the daughter of Francis and Eliza Dunbar Surget.

3. Possibly Amelia Coulter Postlethwaite (1818–1876), Eliza Cochran's sister.

4. Ursula Cochran, Eliza's daughter.

5. A plantation adjacent to the Forest, earlier known as Foster Fields. On the Foster family history, see Wyatt-Brown, *Southern Honor*, 462–95.

6. Perhaps Margaret Dunlop.

7. Mary Foster, according to Wyatt-Brown, *Southern Honor*, 474.

8. Perhaps the Captain Dawson mentioned by William Johnson on July 22, 1837: "To night a Black Girl of Capt Dawsons Sends him word to Come after awhile and get his hankerchiefs—the fact is he has Got a few Lace or fringed hanks and the infernal fool has given [them] to wash to Every Negro wench that he can possibly have any talk with Oh the Rascal" (William R. Hogan and Edwin A. Davis, eds., *William Johnson's Natchez: The Ante-Bellum Diary of a Free Negro* [Baton Rouge, La., 1951], 185).

9. If Mr W—— is Robert J. Walker, this might be Mary Bache Walker, his wife.

10. Probably Benjamin Harding, *A Tour through the Western Country, A.D. 1818 and 1819* (New London, Conn., 1819).

11. Vincenzo Bellini's opera, *La Sonnambula*, first performed in Milan in 1831.

12. A daughter of Joseph B. Lyons, she married Thomas Winn.

13. *Forget-me-not: a Christmas, New Year's, and Birthday Present*, an annual published in London and Philadelphia from 1825 to 1847, edited in 1837 by F. Shober.

14. The 1830 federal census for Adams County lists only one head of household with the surname of Harper living outside Natchez. Miles Harper is given as being between fifty and sixty years and having in his household three males under thirty, two females under five, and one female between thirty and forty (presumably his wife).

15. In the early nineteenth century the most commonly read texts of Hume and Locke were, for the former, *The History of England* and, less frequently, the *Essays* and, for the latter, the *Essay on Human Understanding*, far more usual than the *Second Treatise on Government*, which is a modern taste.

16. Conrad Malte-Brun (1775–1826) was the author of various geographical works, of which the most important was probably *La géographie mathématique, physique et politique de toutes les parties du monde*, 16 vols. (Paris, 1803–7). His works were popularly translated into English and abridged, as in *A System of Universal Geography, or, A Description of All Parts of the World* (Boston, 1834).

17. Anthony F. M. Willich, *The Domestic Encyclopedia: or, A Dictionary of Facts and Useful Knowledge, Comprehending a Concise View of the Latest Discoveries, Inventions, and Improvements, Chiefly Applicable to Rural and Domestic Economy* (London, 1802).

18. Presumably Stanton, but there were several Mrs. Stantons.

19. A letter that looks like "F" has been very firmly scratched out here.

20. Possibly Elizabeth Davis, listed in Natchez as a head of household in the 1830 federal census for Adams County.

21. Mrs. Taylor.

22. Probably Charlotte Hoggatt, the daughter of Nathaniel and Charlotte Hoggatt, who was to marry Gerard Brandon III (1818–1874), son of the governor, in 1840.

23. Frederick Marryat, *Diary of a Blasé* (Philadelphia, 1836).

24. Probably Marryat's most famous novel was *Mr. Midshipman Easy* (1836).

25. Charles Dickens, *The Posthumous Papers of the Pickwick Club* (1837).

26. Joseph B. Lyons, according to William Johnson, "was Taken with an appoplectic Fit and Died in a few moments" (Hogan and Davis, eds., *William Johnson's Natchez*, 160).

27. Anna Brownell Murphy Jameson, *The Diary of an Ennuyée* (London, 1826), a travel journal of Italy. Cf. Butler, *Journal* 2:207: "I have begun the Diary of an Ennuyée again: that book is most enchanting to me,—merely to read the names of the places in which one's imagination goes sunning itself for ever, is delightful."

28. The Walton family had an adjoining plantation, Walton Wood.

29. Mrs. Malaprop is not niggardly of advice, but this is probably her remarks to Lydia Languish: "What preference have you, Miss, with *preference* and *aversion*? They don't become a young woman; and you ought to know, that as both always wear off, 'tis safest in matrimony to begin with a little *aversion*. I am sure I hated your poor dear uncle before marriage as if he'd been a black-a-moor—and yet, Miss, you are sensible what a wife I made!—and when it pleas'd Heav'n to release me from him, 'tis unknown what tears I shed!" (Richard Brinsley Sheridan, *The Rivals* 1.2.7–13).

30. The 1856 inventory of the Margaret Smith estate lists a slave named Edna, aged fifty and valued at $700.

31. Probably Edmund Thomas Parris, *Gems of Beauty Displayed in a Series of Twelve . . . Engravings from Designs by E. T. Parris . . . with Fanciful Illustrations, in Verse, by the Countess Blessington* (New York, 1836).

32. Nathaniel Parker Willis (1806–1867), the American author. His travel book *Pencillings by the Way* was published in London in 1835 and in Philadelphia in 1836.

33. Robert Owen (1771–1858) was the British founder of the utopian community of New Harmony in Indiana and author of *A New View of Society* (1813).

34. A proverbial saying, of course, but originally from the sixteenth-century poet Thomas Tusser, in his "Description of the Properties of Winds": "Yet true it is, as cow chaws cud, / And trees at spring do yield forth bud, / Except wind stands as never it stood, / It is an ill wind turns none to good."

35. An allusion to Byron's poem *The Prisoner of Chillon* (1816), which deals with the incarceration of François de Bonnivard in the Castle of Chillon on Lake Geneva from 1530 to 1536.

36. Ezilda, a pupil.

37. Probably Nathaniel Hoggatt.

38. Theodore S. Fay, *Norman Leslie: A Tale of the Present Time* (New York, 1835).

39. Perhaps the sons of Elizabeth Brandon Stanton, who were Robert (1822–1853), William (d. 1850), Frederick (1826–1900), and Gerard.

40. Pages appear to be missing here.

41. Benjamin Disraeli, *Henrietta Temple* (1837).

42. Frédéric Soulié (1800–1847), the French author of "gloomily sensational" novels, notably *Les deux cadavres* (1832).

43. Probably Dinah Clark Postlethwaite (1815–1885), Eliza's sister.

44. Pages appear to be missing here.

45. Anne Dunbar Postlethwaite seems to have had only one brother, Dr. William Dunbar.

NORTH JOURNALS: 1851

1. Harriette Petigru (1813–1877) married Henry Deas Lesesne (1810–1886) in 1836: she was the sister of Jane Gibert Petigru North (1800–1863). They eventually had six children: Henry Russell (1842–1865), Louise (who died young at the age of six), James Petigru (1848–1892), Charles Petigru, Harriette Louise, and Thomas Petigru (d. 1881). The two children mentioned in the journal are Henry Russell, known as "Hal," and James Petigru Lesesne. The latter is named only once in the journal, but a contemporary letter makes clear that he is the second child on the expedition: see JCN to Mary Charlotte North, Aug. 19, 1851, Petigrew Papers.

2. A slave, who seems to have belonged to Henry Lesesne: see JCN to Jane G. North, March 27, 1851, ibid.

3. Jean Antoine Houdon's statue of Washington was placed in the Capitol in 1796.

4. Rocketts Landing.

5. St. Paul's Episcopal Church, built in 1845, was situated at the corner of 9th Street and Grace Street.

6. Possibly Francis Simmons Holmes (1815–1882), then professor of geology and palaeontology at the College of Charleston; his wife was Elizabeth S. Toomer Holmes. If so, this is probably John Gadsder (b. 1833), the son of Rev. Philip Gadsden and Susan Branford Hamilton Gadsden, who went to the College of Charleston in 1849 but transferred to college in Maryland in 1851 and graduated there in 1853. After the war he became professor of history and economics at the College of Charleston.

7. Rev. Charles Cotesworth Pinckney married in 1847 Esther H. Barnwell, who had eight siblings; the most likely candidates as "Miss Barnwell" are her two unmarried sisters, Martha A. Barnwell (1818–1895) and Margaret Harriet Barnwell (1822–1900).

8. "And Jehu followed after him, and said, Smite him also in the chariot" (2 Kings 9:27).

9. Caesars Head is in the extreme northwest corner of South Carolina, near the North Carolina line. JCN had visited it in October 1849: see JCN to Lucy, Oct. 12, 1849, Pettigrew Papers.

10. William Burke, *The Mineral Springs of Western Virginia* (New York, 1842). Burke had purchased the Red Sulphur Springs in 1832.

11. Perhaps James Coles, thirty-six, of Greenbrier County, Virginia, and his wife Sarah, thirty-one. The federal census gives their daughter, Mary, as nine in 1850, but this may be an error.

12. Lucinda Anne Patterson Randolph was the second wife of Thomas Mann Randolph, Jr. (1791–1851). By his first wife, Harriot Wilson Randolph, he had had six children; one of them, Mary Gabriella Randolph (b. 1814) married Dr. John Biddle Chapman. This last couple had two children: Mary Gabriella Chapman (b. 1834), who later married Bernard Luis ce Potestad, the marquis of Potestad-Fornari, and Emily Louise Chapman (b. 1835), who married Prince Joseph Pignatelli.

13. William Winston Seaton (1785–1866) of Virginia was an editor, with Joseph Gales, of the *National Intelligencer* in Washington. The two are best known for their reports, *The Debates and Proceedings in the Congress of the United States* (42 vols., 1834–56), and the *American State Papers* (38 vols., 1832–61). Seaton married Gales's sister, Sarah Weston Gales (d. 1863), in 1812. She was an accomplished linguist, who translated documents from the Spanish for her husband's use. W. W. Seaton was a close friend of Daniel Webster, who visited the South in 1847 and was accompanied by the Seatons' daughter Josephine.

14. Charles Petigru (1805–1835) was a brother of James Louis Petigru (1789–1863). He was a soldier, who died in Florida during the Seminole War

15. Millard Fillmore (1880–1874).

16. A poison, usually mercuric chloride.

17. Matthew 11:28.

18. The Cheves family was related to the Dulles family by the marriage of Langdon Cheves (1776–1857) to Mary Elizabeth Dulles (1789–1836). Their child, Sophia Lovell Cheves (1809–1881), married Charles Thomson Haskell (1802–1873) of Orangeburg, S.C., in 1830. This is Mary Cheves Dulles (1830–1905), a niece of Mary Elizabeth Cheves.

19. Alexander Herbemont, a lawyer of Columbia, S.C., later U.S. consul to Genoa, was married to Martha Davis Bay Herbemont.

20. Alexander H. H. Stuart of Virginia, secretary of the interior.

21. William W. Corcoran, of the Washington, D.C., bank of Corcoran and Riggs.

22. John Pendleton Kennedy (1795–1870), the novelist. For Kennedy's own account of these events, see John Pendleton Kennedy, Journal, vol. 7 (July 14, 1851, to June 1, 1852), John Pendleton Kennedy Papers, Peabody Institute, Baltimore. The entry for Aug. 1, 1851, reads: "The place is full of South Carolinians, who are all in hostility to the General Government. It is curious to observe the position of these men. The present generation of South Carolinians are educated in the most settled hatred of the United States."

23. JCN to Mary Charlotte North, Aug. 19, 1851, Pettigrew Papers, describes Harvey as a Virginian and a grandson of John Marshall. Hence he was William Wallace Harvie (d. 1868), the only surviving son of Mary Marshall Harvie (a daughter of John Marshall) and General Jacquelin B. Harvie.

24. Perhaps Alexander Means (1801–1883) and his wife, Sarah Ann Eliza Winston Means. He was a physician, scientist, Methodist minister, and, in 1851, professor of natural science at Emory College in Georgia.

25. If this "Mr Parker" is the Francis Parker mentioned later, this may be Dr. Francis Simons Parker (1814–1865) of Charleston, who was married to Mary Taylor Lance Parker (1818–1885).

26. The Dulaneys were a prominent Maryland family.

27. Juliana Coles, fifty-one, of Charlottesville, Virginia, had two children: Isaetta, twenty, and John Stricker, nineteen.

28. William Lowndes Calhoun (1829–1858) was the youngest son of John C. Calhoun. The Gourdins were a prominent South Carolina merchant family, in which the name Samuel was common.

29. Thomas Goode had purchased the Hot Springs in 1832.

30. In John's account, these were Christ's last words on the Cross: 'When Jesus therefore had received the vinegar, he said, It is finished: and he bowed his head, and gave up the ghost" (John 19:30).

31. The VanderHorsts were a prominent South Carolina family. Adèle Alston (1842–1915), JCN's cousin, was later to marry Arnoldus VanderHorst.

32. George McDuffie Calhoun (1828–1916), the son of William and Catherine Jenna de Graffenreid Calhoun and nephew of John C. Calhoun, married Julia Goodwyn in 1850. The Goodwyns were a prominent Columbia, S.C., family.

33. Perhaps one of the eleven children of William Henry Gist (1807–1874) of South Carolina, whose second wife was Mary Elizabeth Rice Gist (1813–1889).

34. Emily Ann Rutherfoord (1830–1880) was the daughter of John Rutherfoord

(1792–1866), who was governor of Virginia, 1841–42, and Emily Ann Coles Rutherfoord (1795–1871).

35. Louisa McKinley Collins Harrison was the daughter of Joseph and Rebecca Collins of Edenton, N.C.: her first husband was Dr. Thomas Harrison.

36. Probably Elizabeth Mason, the daughter of Richard Sharpe Mason (1795–1874), Episcopal minister and rector of Christ Church, Raleigh.

37. Mary Blount Pettigrew (1826–1887) and James Johnston Pettigrew (1828–1863) were brother and sister. After the death of their mother, Ann Blount Shepard Pettigrew (ca. 1795–1830), Mary had lived with the family of John Herritage Bryan (1798–1870) of New Bern, N.C., whose wife Mary Williams Shepard Bryan (1801–1881) was sister to the deceased Mrs. Pettigrew. Francis Theodore Bryan (b. 1823) was their eldest child; after serving in the Mexican War, he lived in St. Louis.

38. Charles Lockhart Pettigrew (1816–1873) was the eldest brother of Mary and James Johnston Pettigrew. JCN married him in 1853.

39. The Howells were one of the founding families of Columbia, S.C.; Malachi and Grace were traditional family names. They were extensively intermarried with the Taylors, also of Columbia. Jesse Malachi Howell (d. 1882) later married Martha Taylor.

40. Probably Thomas Taylor (1824–1905), the son of Benjamin Franklin Taylor (1791–1852) and Sally Webb Coles Taylor (1800–1887); he married Sally Elmore in 1856.

41. Perhaps Samuel McGowan (1819–1897) of Abbeville, S.C., lawyer, state legislator, later brigadier general, C.S.A.

42. Probably a relation of Richard Singleton (1776–1852), who kept a cottage at White Sulphur Springs, was a man of the turf, and a South Carolina planter. The genealogists identify no Mort Singleton, although Richard Singleton did have a son named Matthew Richard (1817–1854), who may have been known as Mort.

43. Mary Charlotte North, the sister of JCN.

44. Probably Alexander Calder of Edinburgh (1773–1849), a cabinetmaker in Charleston from 1796 to 1807 and afterwards a hotelier; he had owned the Planters Hotel and the same-named hotel on Sullivans Island.

45. The Kennedys might be Richard Evans Kennedy (1811–1855) and Sarah deGraffenried Kennedy (1818–1860) of Chesterville, S.C. JCN to Mary Charlotte North, Sept. 17, 1851, Pettigrew Papers, observes that Mr. and Mrs. Robertson were "nice pleasant people from Charlottesville." The 1850 federal census for Albemarle County lists two probable Robertson families: William Robertson, a lawyer, and Hannah Robertson, both thirty-three; and Archibald Robertson, sixty-six, and Mary Robertson, sixty-four. Since the second of these couples is listed as "insane," this is probably the former.

46. JCN to Jane G. North, Sept. 5, 1851, Pettigrew Papers, explains that "the party consists of two Miss Porchers (one of them the young Lady whose charms were so fatal to Dr Sinkler) Miss Lydia Gaillard (familiarly called 'Lyd') Miss Deveaux not the one engaged to Mr Octave—the protectors of this body of ladies are Mr Charles Lucas and Tom Porcher. Mary Anne Porcher is very lively & ready for amusement, the others consider themselves 'on the bench' as one of them told me, so behave accordingly."

47. Dr. Charles Baring Lucas (1829–1874), a physician and planter at Wappahoola plantation in South Carolina, who in 1852 married Elizabeth Lydia Porcher (1825–1872). She is mentioned below.

48. Perhaps the "Betty Taylor" mentioned below, probably a daughter of Benjamin Franklin and Sally Webb Coles Taylor, who had a long friendship with Richard Singleton. Mrs. Taylor was a relative of the Coles of Charlottesville, Virginia, mentioned above.

49. William Elliott (1788–1863) of Edisto River, S.C., was a planter, sportsman, and author. He is best known for his *Carolina Sports by Land and Water* (Charleston, S.C., 1846). His daughters included Caroline Phoebe (b. 1827) and Emily (b. 1829). Their visit to the Virginia springs is documented in Beverley Scafidel, ed., "The Letters of William Elliott" (Ph.D. diss., University of South Carolina, 1978), 643–57.

50. Louisa Gibert North (1833–1896), the sister of JCN.

51. Susan Rose Rutledge of Charleston.

52. Possibly Colonel Thomas Boston Clarkson (1809–1879) and his wife Sarah Caroline Heriot Clarkson (1807–1877); they had homes near Brevard, N.C., and in Columbia, S.C. Or perhaps William Clarkson (1807–1858) and his wife Amelia Garden Pringle Clarkson (1812–93) of Columbia, S.C.

53. Amelia B. Waring Ball (1812–1870), the widow of Elias Octavius Ball (1809–1843). Her daughters were Amelia Waring Ball (b. 1832), who was to marry Hugh Rose Rutledge in 1853, and Sophia Malbone Ball (1837–1891).

54. Probably a descendant of James and Deborah Taylor Gardner of Pasquotank, S.C.; the latter was the aunt of Benjamin F. Taylor.

55. That is, impregnated or flavored with iron.

56. Langdon Cheves, Jr. (1814–1863) was a planter near Savannah; he was the son of Langdon Cheves.

57. Louisa Susanna Cheves McCord (1810–1879) was the author of *Caius Gracchus: A Tragedy* (New York, 1851) and numerous essays on political economy, slavery, and feminism in Southern periodicals. She was the daughter of Langdon Cheves and the wife of David James McCord (1797–1855).

58. Charlotte Lorain McCord Cheves (1818–1879) was the daughter of David James McCord (by his first marriage to Emmeline Wagener) and the wife of Langdon Cheves, Jr. Hence, she was both the stepdaughter and sister-in-law of Louisa McCord.

59. Ida Reyer Pfeiffer was a German traveler and, by 1851, author of *Reise einer Wienerin in das heilege Land* (Vienna, 1846) and *Eine Frauenfart um die Welt: Reise von Wien nach Brasilien, Chili, Otahaiti, China, Ost-Indien, Persien, und Kleinasien* (Vienna, 1850). These were translated as *Journey to Iceland* (London, 1852) and *A Lady's Travels round the World* (London, 1852).

60. Anthony Porter (1788–1869), a former governor of Georgia, was then president of the Bank of Georgia: he married Louisa Alexander (1807–1888) in 1824. Her brother, Adam Leopold Alexander (1803–1882), had six daughters: Louisa Frederika (1824–1895), Sarah Gilbert (1826–1897), Harriet Virginia (1828–1910), Mary Clifford (1830–1914), Marion Brackett (1842–1901), and Alice Vanyeverine (1848–1902). As the first was married in 1850 and the second in 1845, it seems likely that this Miss Alexander is either Harriet Virginia or Mary Clifford.

61. JCN to Jane G. North, Sept. 5, 1851, Pettigrew Papers, mentions the presence of "the Arthur Roses & Miss Gardner, & the John Rutledges." The second husband of Elizabeth Wigg Barnwell (b. 1798) was Arthur Rose, the cashier of the Bank of Charleston. The Rose and Rutledge families were connected by the marriages of James Rose to Julia Rutledge and of Maria Rose (1801–1881), James's sister, to John Rutledge (1792–1864). A daughter of the latter union was Susan Rose Rutledge, mentioned above, whose brother Hugh Rose Rutledge would marry Amelia Waring Ball, also mentioned above, in 1853.

62. Probably Major James Warley (1797–1877) of Walterboro, S.C., who was not to marry until 1858, but not to Miss Gardner.

63. James L. Petigru to Susan Petigru King, Sept. 4, 1845, written from Sweet Springs,

in Carson, *Petigru,* 246–47, has: "Mrs. Wickham, a dowager with a good jointure, many years a belle and long at the head of Richmond society, was one of the convives."

64. Perhaps Francis W. Pickens (1805–1869), the South Carolina politician. He was married three times: in 1828 to Eliza Simkins (1808–1842), in 1843 to Marion Antoinette Dearing (1824–1853), and in 1858 to Lucy Petway Holcombe (1832–1899). This would be the second wife. He had five daughters by his first wife: Eliza and Rebecca (twins born in 1833), Susan, Maria, and Anna. The twins are probably the Pickens "girls" mentioned below.

65. The second wife of Thomas Bennett (1781–1865), a former governor of South Carolina, was Mrs. Jane Burgess Gordon Bennett; they were married in 1840. She was the widow of John Gordon, a Charleston architect who had died in 1835. "Miss Burgess & Mr Gordon" are evidently her relatives.

66. Nathaniel Hawthorne's *Twice-Told Tales* was first published in 1837, enlarged in 1842, and reissued in 1851.

67. Gales Seaton (1817–1857), the son of William and Sarah Seaton, had been secretary to the American Legation in Berlin.

68. Adèle Petigru Allston (1810–1896), the sister of Jane Gibert Petigru North, was married in 1833 to Robert Francis Withers Allston (1801–1864), the South Carolina rice planter and politician.

69. Lucy Seaton (b. 1778), W. W. Seaton's sister, had married Thomas Rose of Richmond.

70. Joseph Blyth Allston (1833–1904), who would marry JCN's sister Mary Charlotte and acquire Badwell plantation after the Civil War; he was the son of Joseph Waties Allston (1798–1834) and the nephew of R. F. W. Allston.

71. Louise Petigru (1805–1869), the daughter of William Pettigrew (1758–1837) and Louise Gibert Pettigrew (1767–1826), married Philip Johnston Porcher at Badwell in 1829. Their son Philip (b. 1835) graduated first in his class from the U.S. Naval Academy in 1855; he drowned when the blockade runner *Juno* sank between Charleston and Nassau in 1863.

72. Sarah Reeve Ladson Gilmor, the widow of Robert Gilmor, Jr. (1774–1848).

73. John Johns (1796–1876) had been minister of Christ Church, Baltimore, from 1828 to 1842. In 1851 he was professor of moral and intellectual philosophy at the College of William and Mary.

74. James Carroll (1791–1873), a former U.S. congressman and member of the notable Maryland family.

75. Designed by Benjamin Latrobe and consecrated in 1821.

76. Horatio Greenough (1805–1852) completed his statue of Washington in 1843.

77. John Augustine Washington (1821–1861), who was to sell the plantation and mansion to the Mount Vernon Ladies' Association of the Union in 1858, partly because he could not afford the scale of hospitality he offered to the likes of JCN and numerous other visitors.

78. The sculpture by Hiram Powers.

NORTH JOURNALS: 1852

1. Thomas Petigru (1793–1857), who was a commander in the U.S. Navy; his wife, Mary Ann LaBruce Petigru and their daughter Martha.

2. Thomas Petigru had been court-martialed in June 1852 in Norfolk. He had served as captain of the USS *Falmouth* on the Californian coast in 1829: it was his first command, which, considering that he had enlisted as a midshipman during the War of 1812, denoted an unmeteoric career. It was alleged that he was often drunk on duty and, worse, that he had used the ship to capture in Mexico a wanted murderer and collect a $3,000 reward. He was acquitted. His experience doubtless explains the family's visit to the court-martial room described in the next entry. (I am grateful to Jane and William Pease for letting me see the manuscript of their forthcoming biography of James Louis Petigru, where this incident is documented: their main source is John DeCamp, *Reply of Com[mander] John Decamp, to Aspersions Upon His Character Contained in an Article Published in the* Charleston Mercury, *of November 6, 1855, Entitled "Commander Thomas Petigru and the Naval Board"* [n.p., 1856]).

3. Emily Klein had married James Heyward North (1813–1893) in 1835; he was JCN's uncle.

4. Eliza Drayton North, the daughter of James Heyward North (1813–1893) and Emily Klein North.

5. James Heyward North was a lieutenant in the U.S. Navy.

6. The Taylors were a prominent Norfolk family. Tazewell Taylor was later on the Board of Visitors of the College of William and Mary.

7. George David Cummins (1822–1876) had been rector of Christ Church in Norfolk since 1847; he was assistant bishop of Kentucky (1866–73).

8. Millard Fillmore.

9. The USS *Pennsylvania,* a 120-gun ship, was launched in 1837.

10. The original text would make more sense if it read "Manton shawl," i.e., *manton de Manilla,* a Spanish shawl of heavy silk crepe covered with embroidered flowers and birds, but the adjective is clearly "Mahon." It is possible that the word refers to Mahón, the capital of Minorca, one of the Balearic Islands.

11. The Mileses were an extensive South Carolina family. The member most likely to provoke an "Ahem!" in a young lady was William Porcher Miles (1822–1899); in 1852 he was professor of mathematics at the College of Charleston.

12. Philip Falkerson Voorhees (1792–1862), who had been court-martialed by the U.S. Navy in 1845 for disobedience in actions against the Argentine squadron, dismissed from the service, reinstated by President Polk, and suspended until 1847. He had two children.

13. Pierre Soulé (1801–1870), Democratic senator from Louisiana; Charles Sumner (1811–1874), senator from Massachusetts and a Free-Soiler; Lewis Cass (1782–1866), Democratic senator from Michigan.

14. John B. Weller (1812–1875), a Democrat from California, was in the Senate from 1852 to 1857.

15. Andrew Pickens Butler (1776–1857) had been senator from South Carolina since 1846; he had been a circuit and appeal court judge.

16. Weller was attempting to raise an appropriation for the relief of Californian Indians from $3,000 to $100,000, in order to prevent their starvation on reservations or their being driven, by desperation, into war.

17. Probably Levin Minn Powell (1803–1885) of Virginia, then a commander in the U.S. Navy.

18. William C. Shields was editor of the Norfolk *Daily Courier.*

19. At issue was Great Britain's denial of access for American fishermen to certain

waters off the northeastern United States and Canada, notably the Bay of Fundy, a subject on which Soulé was passionate. Senator Butler was concerned to prevent such antagonisms from drifting into war and was inclined to think that the Bay of Fundy might indeed be regarded as a British bay.

20. Probably William Aiken (1806–1887), U.S. congressman from Charleston, and his wife Harriet Lowndes Aiken (1812–1892).

21. If Mr. Pember is the same person referred to above as Pemble, this may be Thomas Pember (d. 1861), a Boston lawyer who married Phoebe Yates Levy (1823–1913) of Charleston, the daughter of Jacob and Fanny Yates Levy and the author of *A Southern Woman's Story* (1879). If so, the reference below to a Mr. and Mrs. Cohen may be to Phoebe Levy's sister Henrietta and her husband Octavus Cohen.

22. Perhaps Henry Augustine Washington (1820–1858), professor of history at the College of William and Mary and second editor of Thomas Jefferson's papers.

23. Abigail Powers Fillmore (1798–1853) and Mary Abigail Fillmore (1832–1854).

24. Thomas Lanier Clingman (1812–1897) was U.S. congressman from Buncombe County, N.C.; he was a Whig, in the process of becoming a Democrat.

25. Clement Moore Butler (1810–1890) was rector of Trinity Church in Washington, D.C., from 1849 to 1861.

26. Perhaps Henry E. Ballard, a captain in the U.S. Navy.

27. Archibald Henderson (1785–1859), a Virginian, had been a colonel in the U.S. Marine Corps since 1834.

28. Nathan Sargent (1794–1875), a journalist.

29. JCN spells "Chestnut" Street as though it were the Chesnut family of South Carolina.

30. A paddle steamer built in 1848.

31. A sculpture by James Thom (1802–1850) of Ayrshire in Scotland, later a resident of New Jersey.

32. The Pennsylvania Asylum for the Deaf and Dumb, located on Market Street, had been founded by David G. Seixas in 1841.

33. Charles Sinkler (1818–1894) of South Carolina, who served from 1836 to 1847 in the U.S. Navy, had married Emily Wharton (1823–1875) in 1842. She was the daughter of Judge Thomas Isaac Wharton (1791–1856) of Philadelphia, whose children included Francis Wharton (1820–1889) and Henry Wharton (1827–1880), both of whom were lawyers.

34. Frederick Graff, the designer of the Fairmount Water Works. The bust had been there since about 1848.

35. Benjamin Allston (1833–1900), the son of R. F. W. and Adèle Allston, was in 1882 to marry, as his second wife, JCN's sister Louisa.

36. La Rhett L. Livingston of New York, who was a cadet from 1849 to 1853.

37. Andrew Jackson Donelson, Jr. (1826–1859) was then attached to the Company of Sappers, Miners, and Pontoniers at West Point; he was the great-nephew of Andrew Jackson and the son of Andrew Jackson Donelson (1799–1871) of Tennessee, who was then a U.S. senator.

38. This is probably Francis Theodore Bryan, mentioned above, who was a West Point graduate and Mexican War veteran.

39. Maria Mayo Scott (1739–1862) of Richmond had married Winfield Scott (1786–1866) in 1817; she was buried at West Point.

40. Joshua John Ward (1800–1853) had married Joanna Douglass Hasell (1805–1878)

in 1825; James Ritchie Sparkman, M.D. (1815–1897) had married Mary Elizabeth Heriot (1827–1912) in 1845. Both couples lived near Georgetown, S.C., and the Allstons.

41. Anne Jane North (1813–1876), JCN's aunt, was twice married, first to John Maxwell Chisolm (d. 1848), by whom she had six children, and then in 1858 to William Cattell Bee (1809–1881) of Beaufort District, S.C. Emily Thurston was the daughter of Robert Thurston and Eliza Emily North (d. 1881), another of JCN's aunts. The Bees were an extensive South Carolina family.

42. Mary McDuffie (1830–1874) was the daughter of George McDuffie (1790–1851), the nullifier. She later became the second wife of Wade Hampton (1818–1902).

43. The Singletons and McDuffies were related by the marriage of Mary Rebecca Singleton (d. 1830) to George McDuffie. Her brother John Coles Singleton (1813–1852), who would die on September 20, had married Mary Lewis Carter (1817–1887) in 1836.

44. Mary Boykin Miller Chesnut (1823–1886), the diarist, was married to James Chesnut, Jr. (1815–1885), then in the South Carolina state legislature and later a U.S. senator.

45. Perhaps Catherine E. Murray Rush, the wife of Richard Rush (1780–1859), the Philadelphia lawyer and diplomat; they had married in 1809.

46. This is probably Joseph Alston (d. 1861), who had married Helen Mason of New York; he was the son of William Algernon Alston (1782–1860), and Mary Allston Young (d. 1841).

47. Major General Sir Isaac Brock (1769–1812) was killed on Oct. 13 while defending Queenston against the Americans under Major General Stephen Van Rensselaer.

48. Brigadier General Zebulon Montgomery Pike (1779–1813).

49. Perhaps James Gadsden (1788–1858), a South Carolinian and the former U.S. minister to Mexico; his wife was Susanna Gibbes Hort Gadsden.

50. Probably Robert Naylor Rogers, a staff officer of pensioners; he had served at the battle of Waterloo.

51. *Don Juan d'Autriche, ou, La vocation,* a comedy by Jean François Casimir Delavigne (1793–1843), first performed in Paris in 1835.

52. Louis Jean Papineau (1786–1871) was a leader of the French Canadians and then represented Deux-Montagnes in the Legislative Assembly of Canada.

53. Robert Christie (1788–1856), who represented Gaspé; he was also a historian, best known for his multivolume *History of the Late Province of Lower Canada* (1848–1855).

54. George Joseph Webb, a deputy assistant commissary-general.

55. Francis Fane had been a captain in the Fifty-fourth (The West Norfolk) Regiment of Foot since January 10, 1851.

56. A Huron village.

57. The conservatory in Watertown, Mass., of John Perkins Cushing (1787–1862) was open to the public when the flowers were in bloom; Cushing had a great estate, built upon a fortune made during thirty years in China.

58. Lola Montez was the stage name of Marie Dolores Eliza Rosanna Gilbert (1818–1861), who passed herself off as a Spanish dancer but was, in fact, Irish. She was known as a bad dancer but an interesting lover, especially with Ludwig I of Bavaria.

59. Alexander Hamilton Vinton (1807–1881) was rector of St. Paul's Episcopal Church, Boston, from 1842 to 1858.

60. Presumably Mrs. S. T. Willington, the wife of Aaron Smith Willington (1781–1862), one of the founders of the New England Society of Charleston.

61. Probably Augustus Russell Street (1791–1866) of New Haven; he was a philan-

thropist who especially encouraged the fine arts and theology at Yale. He had married Caroline Leffingwell in 1815; they had seven children.

62. Probably Martha Whiting Flagg (1792–1875), the wife of Henry Collins Flagg (1790–1863); she was a native of New Haven, he of Charleston; he edited the *Connecticut Herald*.

63. Andrew H. Foote had been a lieutenant in the U.S. Navy since 1830; he became a commander later in 1852.

64. Pasted on the next page is a poem, in a different hand:

Ever Thine

To Cary

Fate has decreed we must sever,
But Oh! how bitter is the pang
To part with thee, for weeks, for months
Nay perhaps—For ever.

———

How many changes old time will bring
Who, Oh! who may tell
Not that I would use dark forebodings sting
Or on sorrows dwell.

———

No when thou art gone, my thoughts shall rest on thee
And when in sorrows vale,
Or joys bright transitory hour
Thou'll ever feel a friend in me.

———

HARDEMAN JOURNALS: 1850

1. Thomas Tickell, "To the Earl of Warwick, on the Death of Mr. Addison," ll. 44–47. More correctly, the poem reads: "Ne'er to these chambers, where the mighty rest, / Since their foundation, came a nobler guest / Nor e'er was to the bowers of bliss convey'd / A fairer spirit or more welcome shade."

2. Oscar J. E. Stuart, forty, a lawyer.

3. Anna Green Perkins Hardeman Sessions, twenty-five, was the daughter of Thomas Hardeman (1799–1836), ALH's brother, and his first wife, Ann Green Perkins Hardeman. Anna Hardeman was married in 1846 to James P. Sessions: he was thirty-six in 1850 and would be mayor of Jackson, Miss., in 1868–69.

4. Lavenia Caroline Hardeman (1804–1854), ALH's sister.

5. James Hardeman Stuart (1838–1862) and Oscar Ewing Stuart (1841–1863), the eldest sons of Sarah Jane Eleanor Hardeman Stuart (1816–1849) and Oscar J. E. Stuart.

6. Colin S. Tarpley (1802–1860) was a lawyer, promoter of the New Orleans and Jackson Railroad, and agricultural reformer.

7. Samuel W. Petrie, thirty-six, a planter, originally from Maine, and Rosa M. Petrie (1824–1905), from Virginia, had several children, of whom two occur later in the diary, Charles W., seven in 1850, and Henry, ten in 1860. The father died in 1851, and Mrs. Petrie married Rev. John Hunter (1824–1899) in 1858.

8. Ann Neely Hardeman (1776–1862), ALH's mother and the widow of Nicholas Perkins Hardeman (1772–1818).

9. Mary Moore Murfree Hilliard Hardeman (1805–1890), the wife of William Hardeman (1801–1863), ALH's brother.

10. Sarah Jane Stuart (1849–1853), the youngest daughter of Sarah and Oscar Stuart.

11. Anna H. Sessions, one, the daughter of Anna and James Sessions.

12. Probably Hollis Holman, who had directed the Richland Male and Female Academy in Holmes County, Miss., with his sister, Mary B. Holman.

13. Thomas Babington Macaulay, *The History of England from the Accession of James II*, 5 vols. (London, 1848–61, and many later editions). The first two volumes were published together in 1848.

14. Adelaide L. Stuart (b. 1843), who married John Bull Smith Dimitry in 1871; Annie Elizabeth Stuart (b. 1845), who married Robert B. Mayes (1820–1884) in 1867; Edward Stuart (b. 1847). They were the third, fourth, and fifth children of Sarah and Oscar Stuart.

15. Probably Sterling H. Lester (1798–1876), a Hinds County farmer.

16. "Thou shall not be afraid for the terror by night; Nor for the arrow that flieth by day; Nor for the pestilence that walketh in darkness; Nor for the destruction that wasteth at noonday" (Psalms 91:5–6).

17. Possibly Eliza Reeves Bowman (1816–1893), the wife of Willis Bowman (1822–1893).

18. *The Two Friends; or Religion the Best Guide for Youth* (Philadelphia, 1827).

19. William P. Perkins (d. 1850) came to Mississippi in 1820, married Jane Stewart in the same year, and owned Mound plantation in Bolivar County; he was the son of Daniel Perkins (1768–1834) and Bethenia Perkins Perkins. The Hardemans were connected to the Perkins family by the marriage in 1770 of Thomas Hardeman I (1750–1833), ALH's grandfather, to Mary Perkins (1754–1798), and then in 1799 to her sister, the widowed Susan Perkins Marr (b. 1750).

20. A spa near Jackson.

21. Oliver Goldsmith, *The Vicar of Wakefield* (1766).

22. Eliza Tarpley, thirty-one, originally from Alabama.

23. Possibly James J. B. White.

24. Hetty Chilton was later to marry a Mr. Stewart and live near Lake Village, Ark., where Isaac Henry Hilliard (1811–1868), a brother of Mary Hardeman, and Richard Sessions, a brother of James Sessions, lived; see William Hardeman to Annie E. Stuart, Feb. 3, 1861, Dimitry Papers.

25. Thomas Hardeman, ALH's brother, who married in 1820 Ann Green Perkins and in 1830 Bethenia Harden Perkins (1812–1869).

26. Mary Neely Hardeman Perkins (1805–1846), ALH's sister, had married Dr. Thomas Harden Perkins of Nashville in 1818.

27. Perhaps Dr. William J. Barbee, pastor of the Christian Church in Jackson until 1853.

28. John Hardeman (1776–1829), ALH's paternal uncle, was married in 1802 to Lucretia Nash, then in 1823 to Nancy Knox. Glen O. Hardeman (1825–1905) was a son of the second marriage. In 1850 he was on his way, via Panama, to California and the Gold Rush.

29. Sarah A. Skipwith (1834–1859), who later married Benjamin J. Henry Greene,

and Cornelia, her sister, twenty, both originally from Tennessee, were the daughters of George Greene Skipwith (1806–1850) and Mary Ann Skipwith (1809–1890).

30. Elizabeth Hardeman Owen Corzine (1791–1870), the daughter of Thomas and Mary Perkins Hardeman and ALH's aunt, was twice married: in 1809 to Glen Owen, who was killed by Indians in Missouri in the mid-1820s, then (back in Tennessee) to Dr. Reese Corzine.

31. Joseph B. Walker, thirty-three, preached Methodism in Jackson in 1847 and again from 1850 to 1851.

32. Dr. Joseph J. Pugh was a physician, with a practice in Cooper's Wells. His wife was Ann Green Perkins Pugh, the daughter of William F. and Jane Stewart Perkins; they had two children, Florence and Sallie Pugh.

33. Bethenia Hardeman, seventeen, the daughter of ALH's brother D. Hardeman (1806–1864) of Matagorda County, Tex. Harry apparently was her brother Henry Hardeman (1845–50).

34. Probably Charles J. Dubuisson, eight, the son of Charles L. Dubuisson, who became president of Jefferson College in Washington, Miss., in 1835 and was later a lawyer. The family lived in Natchez in 1850.

35. Mrs. D. S. Dubuisson, thirty-three, the wife of Charles J. Dubuisson.

36. Daniel W. Adams, twenty-nine, a Jackson attorney.

37. ALH described this, in a later letter, as "Dangue (or break bone fever)" (ALH to Adelaide Stuart, Oct. 8, 1867, Dimitry Papers). Dengue fever, also called dandy or break-bone fever, was an infectious eruptive disease that occasioned sharp pains in the joints; it was seldom fatal. It was endemic in East Africa and had spread to the West Indies and the southern United States by the 1820s.

38. John Locke Hardeman (1809–1858) was the son of ALH's uncle John and Lucretia Nash Hardeman. The son was named for the philosopher, his father being a deist and believer in Locke's theories of human understanding, and had a plantation near Arrow Rock, Mo.

39. Lucretia Nash Hardeman (d. 1850), the daughter of John and Lucretia Nash Hardeman, was married to Thomas M. Hardeman, her cousin (not to be confused with Thomas Hardeman, ALH's brother).

40. William Law Murfree was related to the Hardemans through Mary Hilliard Hardeman's mother, Mary Moore Murfree (1785–1848), who married Isaac Hilliard (1775–1832) in 1803.

41. William H. Young, thirty-nine, a physician, originally from Ireland.

HARDEMAN JOURNALS: 1851

1. Thomas Willis Nicholson (1816–1884) of Halifax County, N.C., was the brother of Sarah Ann Nicholson Hardeman (b. ca. 1818), the wife of D. Hardeman.

2. Possibly William B. Boddie, thirty-seven, a planter, and his wife Eliza, who was the same age. Or perhaps George W. Boddie, who married Mrs. Louisa A. Forbes in 1844.

3. The Swedish singer.

4. [Samuel Griswold Goodrich], *The First Book of History, for Children and Youth, by the Author of* Peter Parley's Tales (Boston, 183[?], and many subsequent editions).

5. Any medicine designed to expel worms from the intestines.

6. Possibly Dr. Kemp P. Alston (1820–1857).

7. Possibly General William Clark, the father of Louisa Forbes Boddie.

8. William P. C. Johnson, forty-four, an Episcopal preacher, was born in Pennsylvania.

9. Mrs. Anna E. Johnson, forty-three, had three children: Bushrod, eighteen, William J., eight, and George C. W., three.

10. I.e., Bethenia Hardeman, the daughter of D. Hardeman.

11. Napoleon B. Viser (d. 1852).

12. *Mamma's Birthday, or, The Surpise; A Comedietta, Adapted from the French* (London, 1851).

13. James Lester, twelve, the son of Sterling H. Lester.

14. Lent, Nash, and Cornelia Hardeman.

15. William Mercer Green (1798–1887), Episcopal bishop of Mississippi.

16. Perhaps William Nichols, an architect, who had designed the Mississippi Capitol.

17. Perhaps Thomas J. Napier, who in 1853 had a general agency and collecting office with H. V. Barr.

18. Rev. Meyer Lewin, rector of St. Andrew's Episcopal Church, Jackson.

19. Hugh A. Garland, *The Life of John Randolph of Roanoke,* 2 vols. (New York, 1850).

20. These women were from interconnected families. Sarah G. Cage, fifty-one, the widow of Jesse Cage, lived in the household of Daniel W. Adams; she had first been married to a Bullus and in 1843 had married Jesse Cage at the home of Charles Scott (1811–1861), chancellor of the state of Mississippi from 1853 to 1857 and husband of Elizabeth M. Bullus Scott (1822–1859). Mrs. Anne M. Bullus Adams (1825–1890) had been Daniel Adams's wife since 1844.

21. The 1850 federal census for Adams County, Miss., lists D. J. Bigelow, thirty, a book agent born in New York, as living in the boardinghouse of Elijah Mount in Vicksburg.

22. Miriam Brannon Hilliard (d. 1853) was the second wife (in 1847) of Isaac Henry Hilliard, the brother of Mary Hardeman. Her name is sometimes spelled Mirream.

23. Sarah Elizabeth Hardeman (1831–1885), the daughter of Thomas and Bethenia Harden Perkins Hardeman, and hence the half sister of Anna Sessions.

24. Lemuel W. Petrie (1794–1851).

25. Henry Frederick Petrie (d. 1861).

HARDEMAN JOURNALS: 1852

1. George Washington Perkins, the son of Nicholas Perkins (d. 1829) and Elizabeth Stowers Perkins (1784–1815) and the brother of Bethenia Harden Perkins Hardeman, ALH's sister-in-law.

2. George Washington Polk (1817–1892) of Maury County, Tenn., was married to Mary Hardeman's younger sister Sallie Leah Hilliard Polk (1819–1894).

3. Mary Hardeman had six brothers: William Harry Hilliard (b. 1809), Isaac Henry (mentioned above), Henry Crafford (b. 1813), John Mathias Murfree (b. 1815), James Crafford (b. 1816), and George Washington (b. 1822). These would seem to be Isaac and George.

4. Eudora Hardeman (b. 1836), a daughter of D. Hardeman, married William F. Davis in 1855.

5. Donna seems to be a familiar name for Eudora Hardeman.

6. Joseph H. Ingraham (1809–1861) was an Episcopal minister who later ran St. Thomas's Hall, a boys school in Holly Springs, Miss. He came from Maine, had seen revolutionary action in South America, had taught languages at Jefferson College, and had written travel books and "romances of wild adventure."

7. I.e., George W. Hilliard.

8. Selina Eubank, twenty-four, the daughter of Richard N. Eubank, a Hinds County planter, was marrying Daniel Perkins Marr, the son of William Miller Marr (1782–1807) and Nancy Green Perkins Marr (b. 1789) of Tuscaloosa. The Marrs were related to the Hardemans by the marriage of Thomas Hardeman (ALH's grandfather) to Susan Perkins Marr shortly after the death of his first wife in 1798; she was a widow with seven children. William and Mary Hardeman were to sell Richard Eubank forty acres in Hinds County on April 2, 1860 (vol. 27, p. 592, Deed Records of the Chancery Clerk, Hinds County Courthouse [microfilm at Family History Library]).

9. From the Sermon on the Mount: "For I say unto you, That except your righteousness shall exceed the righteousness of the scribes and Pharisees, ye shall in no case enter into the kingdom of heaven" (Matthew 5:20).

10. Hebrews 12:1.

11. Perhaps *The Premium: A Present for All Seasons; Consisting of Elegant Selections from British and American Writers of the Nineteenth Century* (Philadelphia, 1833).

12. "And the servant of the Lord must not strive; but be gentle unto all men, apt to teach, patient, in meekness instructing those that oppose themselves" (2 Timothy 2:24–25).

13. The traditional rendering of Tertullian in the *Apologeticus:* "Plures efficimur quoties metimur a vobis, semen est sanguis Christianorum."

HARDEMAN JOURNALS: 1853

1. Dr. Joshua S. Green (1811–1887) began his medical practice in Jackson in 1852.

2. Dr. William S. Langley, forty-four, a physician, was one of the first commissioners of the Mississippi State Lunatic Asylum in Jackson.

3. Charles Abram DeFrance (1826–1893), originally from Port Gibson, Miss.

4. This paragraph, interpolated in the account of Sarah Jane Stuart's death, refers to a visit that happens later in 1853. This suggests the death scene was written later in the year.

5. Evelyn Hardeman, nine.

6. Jacob A. Kausler, thirty-four, a dry goods merchant in Jackson, was then in partnership with F. A. Whiting. In the federal census for Hinds County in 1850, there is listed a Catharine Hommedun, forty-two, the landlady of a boardinghouse. By 1860 she appears as C. A. L. Homedeen in the household of Jacob Kausler. Her name appears in many guises, of which the most plausible is L'Hommedieu.

7. Probably the wife of Rev. A. Pomroy, a Baptist who ran the Jackson Male Academy from 1851 to 1855 and in 1856 became principal of the Deaf and Dumb Institute, of which Mrs. Pomroy was the matron.

8. Alfred B. Cabaniss (1808–1871), one of Jackson's leading physicians, later became superintendent of the State Insane Asylum.

HARDEMAN JOURNALS: 1854

1. Perhaps H. V. Bass, twenty-five, a lawyer.

2. On March 1, 1854, James Dick Hill of the state of Louisiana sold to William Hardeman 1,020 acres in Hinds County for $6,500. On May 16, 1854, John M. Bass and J. D. Hill, executors, granted to William Hardeman the power of attorney to settle the estate of H. R. W. Hill, the father of J. D. Hill (vol. 23, pp. 239–40, 309, Deed Records of the Chancery Clerk, Hinds County Courthouse [microfilm at Family History Library]).

3. Thomas Norfleet Figuers (1816–1854) married Bethenia Harden Perkins Hardeman, the widow of ALH's brother Thomas, in 1843.

4. Presumably John Mathias Murfree Hilliard, Mary Hardeman's brother.

5. Probably Thurza Ann Kilgore Lamkin, the wife of the lawyer John Tillman Lamkin (1811–1870) of Holmesville, Miss.

6. Thomas Jones Hardeman (1788–1854), the brother of ALH's father, was a pioneer of Hardeman County, Tenn., which was named for him. He went with his brother, Bailey Hardeman (1795–1836), to Texas in the 1830s, there to help found the Republic of Texas.

7. Two brothers, D. R. and D. S. Lemman, practiced dentistry in Jackson from 1853. The former married Kate Skipwith (1844–1916), who may be the daughter of George and Mary Skipwith listed in the 1850 federal census for Hinds County as Catharine, eight.

8. Edwin Summers Hilliard and Mary Hardeman Hilliard, who both died in infancy.

9. "I have lived long enough: my way of life / Is fall'n into the sear, the yellow leaf" (Shakespeare, *Macbeth* 4.3.22–23).

10. In the story of Lazarus: "And it came to pass, that the beggar died, and was carried by the angels into Abraham's bosom" (Luke 16:22).

11. Mary Helen Marr is probably the granddaughter and John Marr the son of Susannah Perkins and John Miller Marr.

12. General Thomas C. McMackin, founder of the town of Pontotoc, Miss., was a tavern keeper and hotelier. Mary Helen Marr may have been staying at a hotel he was running, though it is certain only that he operated the Union Hall in Jackson from 1844 to 1847 and had a restaurant on State Street from December 1853.

13. Mijaman Sidney Craft (1827–1888) was a physician; his office was above the store of Whiting and Kausler on State Street.

14. Perhaps Mary Jane Marr, the daughter of William Miller and Nancy Green Perkins Marr.

15. The Hardemans were connected to the Lewis family of Opelousas, La., by the marriage of Nancy Hardeman (1774–1833), the sister of ALH's father, to Seth Lewis (1764–1848), judge of the fifth judicial circuit in Louisiana from 1812 to 1839. Their son, Thomas Hardeman Lewis (1802–1861), married Martha Partridge Taylor (1810–1855) and had many children, among them Nannie and Martha.

16. Bernard Sage, a grandson of Mary Lewis Sage, the sister of Seth Lewis.

17. James H. Sneed (1828–1904) was the son of Susannah Perkins Hardeman Sneed (1802–1859) and Constantine Perkins Sneed (1790–1864) of Brentwood, Tenn. His mother

was a daughter of Constantine Hardeman (1778–1850), the brother of Elizabeth Corzine, and his first wife, Sarah Marr Hardeman.

18. Probably James D. Dotson, who would begin practice as a Jackson lawyer in 1858.

19. William D. Hardeman (1833–1876), the son of Thomas and Bethenia Harden Perkins Hardeman.

HARDEMAN JOURNALS: 1855

1. Sallie Leah Hilliard Polk, the sister of Mary Hardeman, eventually had twelve children, but only eight had been born by 1855: James Hilliard (1842–1926), Rufus King (1843–1881), Sallie Hawkins (1845–1914), George Brevard Mecklenberg (1848–1877), Mary Murfree (b. 1847), Susan Spratt (b. 1851), Lucius Junius (1853–1922), and Isaac Hilliard (b. 1854).

2. Mrs. Eliza Jordon Linor was the mother of Lavinia H. Linor Hilliard (1817–1837), Isaac Henry Hilliard's first wife. "Lavenia" is probably Lavinia LaFayette Hilliard (1837–1872), their daughter.

3. I.e., on Feb. 15.

4. Thomas M. Jones of Williamson County, Tenn., married Marietta Perkins in 1838; she was the daughter of Charles Perkins (1790–1827) and Harriet Field Perkins, as well as the niece of Ann Green Perkins Hardeman, the first wife of Thomas Hardeman, ALH's brother.

5. I.e., Bethenia Harden Perkins Hardeman, ALH's sister-in-law.

6. Fanny Priscilla Dickinson Murfree, the wife of William Law Murfree, had three surviving children: Fanny Noailles Dickinson (b. 1846), Mary Noailles (1850–1922), and William Law, Jr. (b. March 26, 1854). Mary N. Murfree later wrote "local color" novels under the pseudonym of Charles Egbert Craddock

7. William Wirt Adams (1819–1888), a banker, planter, and politician, was offered the post of postmaster general of the Confederacy in 1861 but preferred to command a cavalry regiment. He married Sallie Huger Mayrart in 1850.

8. In the 1850 federal census for Hinds County, Mary Ann Skipwith is credited with six daughters, of whom Cornelia and Sarah have been mentioned above. The others were Lelia, Mary, Virginia, and Catharine. A seventh daughter, Jenny Cary Skipwith (1826–1909), had married and left the household.

9. Possibly George Work, commissioner of public buildings in Mississippi from 1836 to 1841, a lawyer and prominent Baptist.

10. Thomasella Hardeman (b. 1836), the daughter of Thomas and Bethenia Harden Perkins Hardeman.

11. The University of Mississippi, which had opened in 1848.

12. George W. Hilliard.

13. William R. Miles, thirty-eight, an attorney.

14. John D. Freeman was attorney general of Mississippi for ten years from 1841 and a Unionist member of Congress from 1851 to 1853.

15. Probably the wife of General T. C. McMackin, the hotelier. Their daughter, Martha Margaret Hilzheim (1825–1850), had been married to Heyman Hilzheim, the proprietor of the leading Jackson hotel, the Bowman House; Anna Hilzheim was their daughter.

16. Albert C. Outler, ed., *The Works of John Wesley,* 4 vols. (Nashville, 1987), 4:528–30, notes that the sermon "On the Resurrection of the Dead" was written by Benjamin Calamy in 1687 and abridged by Wesley in 1732. It was published as though by Wesley in the seventh volume of Thomas Jackson, ed., *The Works of the Rev. John Wesley,* 3d ed., 14 vols. (London, 1829–31).

17. Heyman Hilzheim and, presumably, his second wife; Martha Hilzheim, the mother of Anna, had died in 1850.

18. "With my soul have I desired thee in the night; yea, with my spirit within me will I seek thee early; for when thy judgments are in the earth, the inhabitants of the world will learn righteousness" (Isaiah 26:9).

19. Before her marriage to Solomon Tifft in 1852, Martha Hale had run the Select Ladies School in Jackson with her sister Mary. The sisters are buried together in the Jackson City Cemetery.

20. Rev. A. D. Corbyn was rector of the College of St. Andrew, the Episcopal college founded by Bishop William Mercer Green in 1851 and closed in 1856.

21. Thomas Willis Nicholson's wife, Martha Elizabeth Thorne Nicholson (1821–1897), was the sister of Temperance Davis Thorne (1836–1927). The Thornes, like the Nicholsons, came from Halifax County, N.C.

22. The *Weekly Mississippian,* April 10, 1860, has an obituary for Mrs. Sarah Lenoir, who died at the residence of her son-in-law, Colonel Galloway, near Memphis.

HARDEMAN JOURNALS: 1857

1. Rev. Thomas D. Ozanne and his wife ran the Jackson High School for Young Ladies.

2. Robert Luther Buck (1816–1866) had a medical practice with Alfred Cabaniss in Jackson.

3. ALH seems to have begun this entry under the impression that it was June 1, 1857, and hence the anniversary of her sister's death. Eventually she realized it was May 26.

4. Possibly Mary Helm (1820–1875), the wife of Thomas Erskine Helm (1813–1893).

5. Probably Charles F. Weigandt, an artist with a studio in Jackson: he was to marry Emma L'Hommedieu, the daughter of Catharine L'Hommedieu, in 1860.

6. This ellipsis is ALH's.

7. This word begins a new page of the manuscript. Since there are no excisions of the text, this abrupt change of subject is puzzling.

8. This entry is oddly interpolated in that for July 18.

9. William Yerger (1816–1872), judge on the Mississippi High Court of Errors and Appeals.

10. Louisa E. Wharton was the daughter of Judge Thomas Jesse Wharton, then attorney general of Mississippi. She was later engaged to Oscar E. Stuart but died on Aug. 30, 1862, the same day that James H. Stuart was killed at Second Manassas.

11. Ann Dixon Christmas, forty-four, was the widow of Harry Christmas, who was killed in a steamboat explosion in 1850.

12. "And a man shall be as an hiding place from the wind, and a covert from the tempest; as rivers of water in a dry place, as the shadow of a great rock in a weary land" (Isaiah 32:2).

13. Possibly Caroline L. Sessions Maury, who married John M. Maury of Adams County, Miss., in 1829.

14. P. Clissey had a dancing school by 1857; in 1860 it was located at the "Ladies Ice Cream Saloon."

15. A dry goods store in Jackson.

16. Mary R. Lester, fifty-five, the wife of Sterling H. Lester. William and Mary Hardeman had sold her $2,666.23 worth of land in Hinds County on Aug. 3, 1850 (vol. 22, p. 414, Deed Records of the Chancery Clerk. Hinds County Courthouse [microfilm at Family History Library]).

17. Craft's Livery Stable, owned by a Major Craft, was located on Amite Street west of the Bowman House.

18. The brother of James P. Sessions.

19. M. Yerger, thirty-seven, the wife of William Yerger.

20. Possibly M. C. Bramlitt, the wife of J. M. Bramlitt, a Jackson merchant.

21. Sterling H. and Mary R. Lester are credited with eight children in 1860: Lucy, James, Mary, H. D., B. W., Ida W., B. Y., and J. W.

22. Perhaps Philip L. Bode, who was professor of music at the Seneca Institute for Girls in Brandon, Miss., in 1845.

23. Nov. 27, 1857, was a Friday.

24. This is no explanation of why this entry—evidently for Christmas Day—is interpolated here.

25. Possibly John James Byron Hilliard (1832–190.), a lawyer in Halifax and Nash counties, N.C.

26. Nathaniel Green Skipwith, ten, the son of George and Mary Skipwith.

27. Fanny Buck, ten, the daughter of Robert L. Buck.

28. Perhaps E. Hurd, thirty-two, a milliner.

HARDEMAN JOURNALS: 1858

1. Edward Alston Thorne Nicholson (1843–1865), the son of Thomas Willis and Martha Elizabeth Thorne Nicholson.

2. Charlotte Isabella Fleming Green (b. 1810) was the bishop's second wife; they were married in 1835.

3. Rev. J. L. Forsyth, pastor of the Methodist church at the corner of Yazoo and Congress streets in Jackson.

4. Elizabeth A. Shackleford, forty-eight, the proprietor of a boardinghouse opposite the Vicksburg Railroad Depot in Jackson was the widow of Henry D. Shackleford who, from 1848 to 1856, owned the Eagle Hotel, which was demolished to make way for the Bowman House. She was the daughter of Harden Perkins (d. 1821) and Mildred Moore Perkins, and hence a relative of ALH.

5. As mentioned in the entry for Sept. 15, 1850, ALH's sister Mary Neely Hardeman Perkins had died in 1846, at the age of about forty-one, so this entry is puzzling.

6. Mary Gibson Sessions, the wife of Richard R. Sessions (the brother of James P. Sessions) of Lake Village, Chicot County, Ark.

HARDEMAN JOURNALS: 1859

1. Evidently this final rule was added in 1860.

2. Perhaps H. W. Purnell of Schula, Miss., a classmate of James Hardeman Stuart at the University of Mississippi.

3. Possibly M. F. Buckley, the wife of F. S. Buckley; they had a daughter, Eliza Tarpley Buckley, whose name indicates a connection with the Tarpley family.

4. Sallie S. Green, eleven, E. W. Green, twelve, and Berkley Green, eighteen.

5. William Polk Hardeman (1816–1898), the son of ALH's uncle Thomas Jones Hardeman, was among the founders of the Republic of Texas, served in the Civil War, and afterwards briefly exiled himself to Mexico.

6. One of these daughters, Louise Yerger, was later to be engaged to James H. Stuart; after his death, she is said to have entered a convent.

7. Perhaps the B. Clifton, aged eight, listed in the household of E. M. Clifton in the 1860 federal census for Hinds County.

8. Probably Robert Carter Hilliard (1824–1883) of The Meadows, Nash County, N.C., who was a nephew of Mary Hardeman's father.

9. John Ravenscroft Green, twenty-nine, the bishop's son.

10. William Yerger, seventeen, the son of Judge William Yerger.

11. Mary Smith was the daughter of W. L. Smith and Constantia Dudley Burnett Smith (d. 1846), who was, in turn, the daughter of Dorothy Hardeman Burnett (1786–1843), ALH's aunt, and George Burnett (1770–1838), who migrated to Missouri.

12. The Brickell family was connected to the Hilliards (and hence the Hardemans) by the marriage of Sally Brickell of Murfreesboro, Tenn., to Colonel Hardy Murfree; their daughter, Mary Moore Murfree Hilliard, was Mary Hardeman's mother.

13. John Jones Pettus (1813–1867) was governor of Mississippi from 1859 to 1863.

14. "But the very hairs of your head are all numbered" (Matthew 10:30).

15. Charles D. Dewees, forty-five.

16. That is, of D. Hardeman.

17. Agatha Susannah Marr Inge was the daughter of William Miller and Nancy Green Perkins Marr and the wife of Robert Inge of Tuscaloosa.

HARDEMAN JOURNALS: 1860

1. James Hilliard Polk, the son of George Washington Polk.

2. Again, oddly, this entry is interpolated.

3. Walter Scott, *The Antiquary* (1816).

4. Jenny Cary Skipwith Foute, the daughter of George and Mary Skipwith and the wife of Green P. Foute, an attorney.

5. Possibly Henry C. Daniels, forty-eight, of Hinds County.

6. There is a fragmentary piece of paper, stuck in at this point in the diary, numbered 18, in ALH's hand: "Mrs G. W. Polk arrived here on the 16th inst. Teus. to-day Wed. she left about 4 oclock."

7. Susan Spratt Polk, the daughter of Sallie and George Polk.

8. Grand Lake, Ark.

9. William Hawkins Polk (1859–1896), the youngest son of Sallie and George Polk.

10. The chapter that begins, "Though I speak with the tongues of men and of

angels, and have not charity, I am become as sounding brass, or a tinkling cymbal" (1 Corinthians 1:1).

11. "By faith Abel offered unto God a more excellent sacrifice than Cain, by which he obtained witness that he was righteous, God testifying of his gifts: and by it he being dead yet speaketh" (Hebrews 11:4).

12. Daniel Price Porter (1835–1899).

13. Constantia Dudley Burnett was married first to James M. Miller, who died in 1821, then to W. L. Smith, a merchant in Liberty, Mo.

14. Rev. William Cross Crane (ca. 1315–1877) was rector of St. Andrew's Church, at the corner of Amite and President streets in Jackson; he had succeeded Meyer Lewin.

15. The rector had a wife, C. M. Crane (1817–1861), and four children.

16. Exodus 13:21–22.

17. George Shall Yerger (1802–1860), lawyer and Whig, and his wife, Sarah Scott Yerger (1809–1870), the sister of Charles Scott, Yerger's former law partner.

18. Yerger died "from over exertion while hunting in Bolivar County," according to the *Encyclopedia of Mississippi History,* ed. Dunbar Rowland, 2 vols. (Madison, Wis., 1907), 2:1021.

19. Charles Kimball Marshall (1811–1891), a Methodist minister in Vicksburg.

20. "Or despisest thou the riches of his goodness and forbearance and longsuffering; not knowing that the goodness of God leadeth thee to repentance?" (Romans 2:4).

21. In a passage describing Zion: "And the inhabitant shall not say, I am sick: the people that dwell therein shall be forgiven their iniquity" (Isaiah 33:24).

22. Whitfield Harrington was pastor of the Methodist church at the corner of Yazoo and Congress streets in Jackson, 1860–61.

23. Probably Major C. Cheatnam (Major was his Christian name) of Yazoo City; he was married to Bethenia Smith Cheatham (d. 1879), the daughter of Mary O'Neal Perkins and Nicholas Perkins Smith of Williamson County, Tenn.

24. James Rucks Yerger (1840–1891), the son of Judge William Yerger.

25. Between this page and the next is a pressed white rose, wrapped in a blue paper, marked: "White Rose / From Mrs J. G. Brown / June 22 1863 / Wednesday."

26. The 1860 federal census for Hinds County has M. Hay, eighteen, and Sallie Hay, sixteen, living in the household of Ellen Lynch. Sallie Hay (1843–1873) later married Rev. Duncan Green.

27. Probably George Carter, D.D., professor of mental and moral philosophy, and William Gaines Richardson, professor of Latin and modern languages, at the University of Mississippi.

28. Perhaps the daughter of Armistead Burwell, who shared with William Hardeman the trusteeship of the estate of Erastus R. Strickland (indenture, March 14, 1855, in vol. 24, pp. 45–46, Deed Records of the Chancery Clerk, Hinds County Courthouse [microfilm at Family History Library]).

29. "Charge them that are rich in this world, that they be not highminded, nor trust in uncertain riches, but in the living God, who giveth us richly all things to enjoy" (1 Timothy 6:17).

30. Bailey Hardeman, ALH's uncle.

31. Probably a son of Peter Nicholas Marr (1792–1865) and his first wife, Anna Goodloe Hinton Marr; they lived in Missouri.

32. "There is a land of pure delight, / Where saints immortal reign; / Infinite day

excludes the night, / And pleasures banish pain" (Isaac Watts's hymn, "There is a Land of Pure Delight").

33. "For he sang of peace and freedom, / Sang of beauty, love and longing; / Sang of death, and life undying / In the Islands of the Blessed, / In the kingdom of Ponemah, / In the Land of the Hereafter" (Henry Wadsworth Longfellow, *The Song of Hiawatha* 6.65–70).

34. Rebecca Stith Yerger (1841–1917).

35. "Only let your conversation be as it becometh the gospel of Christ" (Philippians 1:27).

36. "For our light affliction, which is but for a moment, worketh for us a far more exceeding and eternal weight of glory" (2 Corinthians 4:17).

37. Next to the date for this entry, in the margin, is a drawing of two hands shaking, with the initials "J.H.S." and "L.Y." next to it. "Monday" is indented as though to leave room for it, so it may be by ALH. The initials stand for James Hardeman Stuart and Louise Yerger, his fiancée.

38. Mrs. Mary Brooks Ingraham (1816–1862), the daughter of a Natchez planter.

39. Perhaps from Phillip Doddridge's hymn "Great God, We Sing That Mighty Hand," whose fourth stanza has: "By day, by night, at home abroad / Still are we guarded by our God: / By his incessant bounty fed, / By his unerring counsel led."

40. "Howbeit when he, the Spirit of truth, is come, he will guide you into all truth" (John 16:13).

HARDEMAN JOURNALS: 1861

1. "Watch therefore, for ye know neither the day nor the hour wherein the Son of man cometh" (Matthew 25:13).

2. "The eternal God is thy refuge, and underneath are the everlasting arms" (Deuteronomy 23:27).

3. "Thy word is a lantern unto my feet: and a light unto my paths" (Book of Common Prayer, Psalms 118:105).

4. See Mary M. Hardeman to Annie E. Stuart, Feb. 27, 1861, Dimitry Papers: "*Tom the blind negro boy Pianist,* 11 years of age—'the marvel of the age' played for us. . . . Who that sits under the sound & looks at his brilliant and tastefully executed performance of La Fille du Regiment, Norma, Linda, Lucrezia Borgia &c &c And hears his inimitable Imitations can doubt the existence of a *God!* I looked, and wondered and wept, at the humble means chosen to perform *his wonders!*"

5. "So we thy people and sheep of thy pasture / Will give thee thanks forever" (Psalms 79:13).

6. "Him that is able to do exceeding abundantly above all that we ask or think" (Ephesians 2:20).

7. Bethenia Pannill Stuart Chevalier (1819-ca. 1910) was the sister of J. E. B. Stuart; she married Rev. Nicholas Chevalier (d. 1866) and lived in Texas.

8. Virginia G. Skipwith, twenty, the daughter of George and Mary Skipwith.

9. William Blackstone, *Commentaries on the Laws of England* (1765–69).

10. Probably Mary Ann Hinton (1843–1916), the wife of William Henry Hinton (1832–1912); they are buried in the Brownsville Community Cemetery in Hinds County.

11. Kate Lewis Scales, twenty-two, was the daughter of William Lewis (1815–1847) and Ann E. Briggs Lewis; she was a relative of ALH.

12. A. L. Hatch & Co., a nursery in Jackson.

13. "Tir'd nature's sweet restorer, balmy sleep!" (Edward Young, *Night Thoughts* [1742], Night I, l. 1).

14. Hannah M. Langley, a widow, the mother of William S. Langley.

15. Perhaps M. Daniels, fourteen, the daughter of Henry C. and Mary Daniels, who attended school in Burlington, N.J., with Adelaide and Bettie Stuart.

16. Erasmus R. Burt, the Mississippi state auditor, organized the Burt Rifles, of which he was captain. At Corinth it became part of the Eighteenth Mississippi Regiment, of which he was elected colonel. He was killed at Leesburg on Oct. 21, 1861.

17. Psalms 46:10.

18. "Set a watch, O Lord, before my mouth: and keep the door of my lips." (Book of Common Prayer, Psalms 141:2).

19. "Respect was mingled with surprise, / And the stern joy which warriors feel / In foemen worthy of their steel" (Walter Scott, *The Lady of the Lake* 5.10.10–12).

20. "Behold, he that keepeth Israel / shall neither slumber nor sleep" (Psalms 121:4).

21. In fact, her name was spelled Lezinka.

22. Possibly Adaline Alston, forty-one, the wife of P. M. Alston, a Hinds County farmer.

23. Belle McLaurin Knapp (1823–1916) and Dr. C. S. Knapp, a dentist; he was a Jackson alderman in 1861.

24. "As I was with Moses, so I will be with thee: I will not fail thee, nor forsake thee" (Joshua 1:5).

25. M. C. Russell, thirty-seven, a physician with an office on State Street in Jackson.

26. In fact, according to the journal, on June 11, 1851.

27. Probably General Richard Griffith.

28. J. B. Fearn (1833–1883), the son of George Fearn, a Jackson merchant and some-time secretary of the Jackson and Brandon Railroad and Bridge Company.

29. "Yea, in the shadow of thy wings will I make my refuge, / Until these calamities be overpast" (Psalms 57:1).

30. Probably C. P. Smith, chief justice of the Mississippi High Court of Errors and Appeals.

31. Rev. Edward Fontaine (1814–1887), who lived on Belvidere plantation near Jackson, was captain of the Burt Rifles, Company K, Eighteenth Regiment, and later chief of ordnance for Mississippi.

32. "And when they came to Marah, they could not drink of the waters of Marah, for they were bitter" (Exodus 15:23).

33. Probably "O that thou hadst hearkened to my commandments! then had thy peace been as a river, and thy righteousness as the waves of the sea" (Isaiah 48:18).

34. A hymn by John Wesley.

35. Probably Richard R. Ledbetter (d. 1890), the son of Joseph H. Ledbetter (1811–1873) who with Turner M. Ellis had the leading mercantile house in Jackson, Ellis & Ledbetter. "Young Mr Ellis" is presumably his cousin, for Turner Ellis's sister Susan (1815–1885) married J. H. Ledbetter.

36. Ann Radcliffe, *The Romance of the Forest* (1791).

37. William Thorne Nicholson (1840–1862), killed at Petersburg.

38. Earl Van Dorn (1820–1863), originally from Port Gibson.

39. Perhaps Mary S. Scruggs Barksdale (1796–1886), the widow of Alexander Barksdale.

40. E. P. Russell, forty-one, a former merchant on State Street in Jackson, a former city collector in 1859, and a leading Mason. He had the distinction of being the first druggist in Jackson to have a soda fountain.

41. Possibly J. B. Clarke, listed as a lawyer in the Jackson *Business Directory* of 1860 (p. 12).

42. Pierre Gustave Toutant Beauregard (1818–1893).

43. Joseph Eggleston Johnston (1807–1891), later in command of the Army of Tennessee.

44. Jefferson Davis.

45. Winfield Scott, Robert Patterson, and Irvin McDowell.

46. Perhaps "For, when we were come into Macedonia, our flesh had no rest, but we were troubled on every side; without were fightings, within were fears" (2 Corinthians 7:5).

47. James T. Rucks, thirty-eight, a lawyer and former commissioner of the State Lunatic Asylum.

48. "But we have this treasure in earthen vessels, that the excellency of the power may be of God, and not of us" (2 Corinthians 4:7).

49. Madison McAfee received only 234 votes to the 30,169 for John J. Pettus.

50. Dr. S. C. Farrar (1796–1867), Rosa Petrie Hunter's father.

51. "Now in the fourteenth year of king Hezekiah did Sennacherib king of Assyria come up against all the fenced cities of Judah, and took them" (2 Kings 18:13). After protracted discussion with Hezekiah, God smote the army of Sennacherib, who was later killed by his own sons.

52. William M. Estell, thirty-six, a lawyer, then captain of the Thirty-eighth Cavalry.

53. Possibly Martha Anderson, the wife of Warren P. Anderson, a Jackson lawyer.

54. Probably Louisa Young, forty-four, the wife of Dr. William H. Young, and their daughter Sarah L., twenty-six.

55. T. P. Mothershead, principal of the School for Boys in Jackson, and James F. M. Brown, his assistant.

56. Evidently a commentary by ALH on the awkwardness with which she had formed the "D" of Daniels.

57. Mary I. Daniels, eighteen, and Arabella Daniels, sixteen, the daughters of Henry C. and Mary Daniels.

58. "I would hasten my escape / From the windy storm and tempest" (Psalms 55:8).

59. Perhaps "The righteous cry, and the Lord heareth, / And delivereth them out of all their troubles" (Psalms 34:17).

60. "The troubles of my heart are enlarged; / O bring thou me out of my distresses" (Psalms 25:17).

61. John A. Pettus.

62. William Barksdale (1821–1863), Democratic congressman when Mississippi seceded, was elected colonel of the Thirteenth Mississippi Regiment in 1861. He was killed at Gettysburg.

63. Anne Lavinia Lewis Nugent (1807–1873) was the daughter of Seth and Nancy Hardeman Lewis. She married John Pratt Nugent (ca. 1791–1872) and had six children. This son is probably William Lewis Nugent (b. 1832), who was a Jackson lawyer. The

other sons were Perry (b. 1831), Richard James (b. 1834), John Pratt, Jr. (b. 1836), Thomas Lewis (b. 1841), and Clarence Jewell (b. 1843).

64. Perhaps Ellen Lynch, thirty-one.

HARDEMAN JOURNALS: 1862–67

1. "Blessed shall be thy basket and thy store" (Deuteronomy 28:5).

2. The unattributed hymn, "Peace, troubled spirit," which first appeared in the *Pocket Hymn Book* (York, Eng., 1786) and was reprinted in many American collections.

3. Probably William Dickson Shute (1834–1916), who married Mary Hardeman's niece Lavinia LaFayette Hilliard in 1856; she was the daughter of Isaac Henry Hilliard.

4. Thomas Ken's hymn (usually with music by Thomas Tallis), "Awake, My Soul and with the Sun." Stanza 3 reads: "Direct, control, suggest this day. / All I design or do or say, / That all my powers, with thought and will, / And with thyself my spirit fill."

5. Not, in fact, the biblical version, but Psalm 15 in Nahum Tate and Nicholas Brady, *New Versions of the Psalms of David* (1696 and popularly reprinted).

6. The lamentation of King David on the death of his son: "O my son Absalom, my son, my son Absalom! would God I had died for thee, O Absalom, my son, my son!" (2 Samuel 18:33).

7. "My heart panteth, my strength faileth me" (Psalms 38:10).

8. "Now also when I am old and greyheaded, / O God, forsake me not" (Psalms 71:18).

9. Judge Hiram Cassedy (1820–1881) of Franklin County, once Speaker of the Mississippi House of Representatives.

10. Possibly Mrs. P. A. Newman, twenty-nine, the wife of John Newman, thirty-one, a Warren County farmer.

11. This, oddly, follows the preceding entry in the original text.

12. Ecclesiastes 9:10.

13. These are all quotations from Psalms 133.

14. Possibly William Jasper Brown (1815–1901), the husband of Sarah W. C. Lincoln Brown (1824–1907); at least six of their children are buried in the City Cemetery of Jackson.

15. Henry Bidleman Bascom, *Sermons from the Pulpit* (Louisville, Ky., 1850).

16. Mary Proby, the daughter of the Hon. William Proby, a probate judge in Franklin, married Hiram Cassedy in 1844.

17. Thomas Sherlock, *The Trial of the Witnesses of the Resurrection of Christ: in Answer to the Objections of Mr. Woolston and Others* (1729; New York, 1849 and many other editions). Sherlock (1678–1761) was bishop of London and this book was a refutation of deism and a defense of miracles.

18. "There the wicked cease from troubling; and there the weary be at rest" (Job 3:17).

19. Dr. William Quarles Poindexter, who married Ellen Lester in 1862.

20. John Wesley's hymn "We Lift Our Hearts to Thee," in the fourth stanza.

21. Mary C. Crane, twenty-eight.

22. Edward Gibbon, *The History of the Decline and Fall of the Roman Empire*, 6 vols. (London, 1776–88).

23. Catharine Ann Ware Warfield, *The Household of Bouverie; or, The Elixir of Gold. A Romance, by a Southern Lady* (New York, 1860).

24. Possibly *Ravensdale: A Tale, by a Lady* (Dublin, 1845).

25. This is written on the fly leaf of the journal, puzzlingly so, as ALH's birthday was March 6.

26. This presumably is a misdating by ALH, as the preceding paragraph, written on Dec. 9, indicates that Mary Hardeman had yet to arrive.

Index

THE PUBLICATIONS OF THE
SOUTHERN TEXTS SOCIETY

An Evening When Alone:
Four Journals of Single Women in the South, 1827–67
Edited by Michael O'Brien

Louisa S. McCord:
Political and Social Essays
Edited by Richard C. Lounsbury

Civilization and Black Progress.
Selected Writings of Alexander Crummell on the South
Edited by J. R. Oldfield

Louisa S. McCord: Poems, Drama, Biography, Letters
Edited by Richard C. Lounsbury